PRINCIPLES OF
COMPUTER SCIENCE

An Invigorating, Hands-on Approach

Joshua Crotts

J.ROSS
PUBLISHING

To my Viola.

Acknowledgments

Many were skeptical of my desire to not only write but finish a textbook. Some tried to dissuade me from the idea altogether, claiming it was too much of a time sink. Indeed, while it took over much of my life, I am proud to present the finished product.

Special thanks to the many students and UIs from C211/H211 (Introduction to Computer Science) and C212 (Introduction to Software Systems) at Indiana University for their encouragements and willingness to read the book upon release. Moreover, my friends at IU and UNC Greensboro have constantly provided extensive motivation to continue when times were tough.

I very much appreciate William Orrell, Peter Stratta, and Cliff Mansfield for taking the time to read through partial drafts of the book.

The help and work invested by Gabriel Costa de Oliveira into the first chapter is extremely acknowledged and appreciated.

I thank those who answered the many questions that I posted to the TeX StackExchange regarding LaTeX formatting issues; I hope they are as invaluable to others as they were for myself.

Andrew (Matsurf) Matzureff is always a joy to talk with, and his comments on parts of the book and discussions on continuations were hilariously informative.

In writing *Principles of Computer Science*, I drew inspiration from many authors of other textbooks: including Jeremy Siek, Dan Friedman, Daniel Holden, Robert (Bob) Nystrom, Matthias Felleisen, and others as cited in the bibliography.

Andy Huber's comments, suggestions, and corrections turned this from a textbook into a work of art.

Thanks also to those professors and teachers who taught me everything I know and love about both logic and computer science: Steve Tate, Insa Lawler, Nancy Green, Dan Friedman, Gary Ebbs, Chung-chieh (Ken) Shan, and Sam Tobin-Hochstadt (as well as those not listed). Moreover, Mary Beth Ferrell instilled many lessons on grammar and writing from her AP Literature and Composition course that I utilize to this day (alongside the ever present nightmares of having to complete in-class essays or forgetting to finish an assignment).

I am also sincerely grateful for the inspirational comments from my parents and my wife.

Lastly, I am absolutely and deeply indebted to Tony Smith: my former Advanced Placement Computer Science teacher. Thanks for everything.

Table of Contents

List of Figures

Preface

In July 2021, I had the privilege of meeting Dan Friedman, an esteemed figure in the realms of theoretical computer science and programming languages. Our encounter opened the door for me to delve into the realm of functional programming, particularly in the context of Scheme. I concluded that the best approach to learning Scheme was by implementing it myself. Thus, I embarked on the journey of crafting a simple Scheme interpreter using Java, which, although functional, remained rudimentary. Nevertheless, my affection for the language continued to blossom. Despite being content with the initial version of the interpreter, I made the daring decision to rewrite the entire project in C, an undertaking brimming with both excitement and peril. Drawing inspiration from Dan Holden's remarkable work, *Build Your Own Lisp*, and his exceptional parser combinator library, I undertook the task of reconstructing a Scheme in the C language.

Why should you, as the reader, care about all of this? It led me to a profound realization that certain subjects within theoretical computer science, such as language design and implementation, are often inaccessible to beginners without significant programming experience. I found myself pondering, "How can I make these concepts approachable for those new to this field?" and "What steps can I take to showcase the awe-inspiring nature of computer science to readers?" Undoubtedly, computer science can be intimidating and requires time to master. Some individuals may have the curiosity and drive to embark on this journey, while others may initially fail to recognize or comprehend its allure. This book endeavors to enlighten both these curious audiences and many more, introducing them to a world of design, creativity, and boundless expression.

Prerequisite Knowledge

The primary target audience for this book is individuals who do not have a background in computer science. We assume that readers possess only high-school level knowledge of algebra, and for the majority of the text, we relax the requirement for trigonometry. While an interest in computing is preferred, it is not strictly necessary, as we aim to cultivate that interest through each successive chapter. The book is structured linearly, intending that readers progress from the beginning to the end in most cases. Those with a background in discrete math or some aspects of computer science, however, have the option to skip the first five chapters should they so choose. Similarly, programmers proficient in C may skip Chapter 5.2. By this point, our goal is that all readers are at least familiar with the topics presented, thereby leveling the playing field, so to speak.

Exercises

Practice makes perfect in computer science, which is why we supplement our text with code listings and exercises, the latter of which range in difficulty using the following scale:

- Exercises marked with one star (⋆) are "finger exercises", meaning they can be completed in either a few seconds or, at most, a couple of minutes. They often involve writing one or two lines of code or a sentence derivation.

- Exercises marked with two stars (⋆⋆) are slightly more complex, as they may entail defining a function or something that requires a bit more thinking, taking around 5 to 15 minutes to complete.

- Exercises marked with three stars (⋆⋆⋆) are moderately difficult and may take some time to understand and finish. Depending on the reader, this time may be between 15 minutes and an hour. Large function definitions, or complicated code, are common in this type of exercise.

- Exercises marked with four stars (⋆⋆⋆⋆) are the most challenging problems. Significant thought must be invested into these exercises, but once complete, demonstrate extremely high proficiency. Very large programs, multiple function definitions, and more are what lie ahead, taking multiple hours or even (broken up) days to finish.

- Exercises marked with five gold stars (⋆⋆⋆⋆⋆) often introduce new concepts to coincide with the presented task. While we present all the relevant material to complete the problem, some outside references or resources may be necessary to fully understand everything. Gold star problems are even harder than four star problems, but they do not necessarily entail writing *more* code than the latter.

Every exercise in this book is designed to be achievable for any reader and are presented to stimulate creativity. We firmly believe in not writing exercises that are overly (and perhaps unnecessarily) challenging and may demotivate learners. If you find an exercise to be too difficult after making a genuine effort, feel free to skip it and return to it later at your own pace.

Programming Environment

The majority of the code presented in this text is written in C (do not worry if you are not familiar with C yet). As a result, all C listings are tailored to function on MacOS and Linux operating systems, which regrettably excludes Windows users, who form a significant portion of the audience. One possible workaround for Windows users could be to utilize an online compiler, e.g., https://replit.com. In the event that any readers have trouble setting up their coding environment, we provide a setup on replit containing all necessary files and packages. Appendix 11.3 describes how to get started with programming in C on MacOS, Linux, and the replit sandbox.

Reading Tips and Tricks

In order to make the most of reading this book, it is important to approach it with care and a deliberate pace. Remember, the words will always be there on the page, and there is no rush to reach the non-existent finish line. It can be beneficial to have a pencil or pen at hand to take notes in the margins. For digital readers, using markup software to annotate the text can serve the same purpose. It is not mandatory to code alongside the text, as doing so may potentially disrupt the reading experience. At the end of each section, however, it is advisable to practice with the code that has been provided, as it offers an opportunity for hands-on learning.

The diction and punctuation throughout this book have been carefully chosen and scrutinized. We introduce commas to break a sentence up into chunks, which aid in conveying either a message or serve as to make the dialog more conversational. Semi-colons, on the other hand, relate concepts together whose central idea would be weakened if separated by a full-stop period. Colons are often accompanied by an explanation, code listing, or exercise; they denote the significance of what immediately follows the colon. Footnotes often provide further information about a topic, reference a popular citation/author, or break up the text monotony. These footnotes should not be ignored, and ought to be read as soon as you arrive at their linking footnote index.

One Last Remark

Being a PhD student, I acknowledge that my teaching qualifications may be deemed modest and subject to scrutiny. I sincerely hope that the absence of a formal background, for now at least, does not diminish my aspirations for both the audience and myself. In the process of imparting knowledge to my students, I am constantly learning alongside them. Teaching is a deep-rooted passion of mine, yet I firmly believe that learning is a perpetual skill that we can never truly master.

Have a blast!
Joshua Crotts

 Web
Added
Value™

At J. Ross Publishing we are committed to providing today's professional with practical, hands-on tools that enhance the learning experience and give read-ers an opportunity to apply what they have learned. That is why we offer free ancillary materials available for download on this book and all participating Web Added Value™ publications. These online resources may include interac-tive versions of the material that appears in the book or supplemental templates, worksheets, models, plans, case studies, proposals, spreadsheets and assessment tools, among other things. Whenever you see the WAV™ symbol in any of our publications, it means bonus materials accompany the book and are available from the Web Added Value Download Resource Center at www.jrosspub.com.

Downloads for *Principles of Computer Science* include the Library of Congress Cataloging-in-Publication data and information on a GitHub repository featuring instructional material for classroom use (lecture slides, exercise solutions, etc.).

1   A Computing Mindset

Any sufficiently advanced technology is indistinguishable from magic.

—Arthur C. Clarke

1.1   Computer Heuristics

And magic, it is! Or... is it? Instead of going straight to ones and zeros, let us take several steps back in an attempt to look at these fantastic machines with the critical eyes of a careful spectator in a magic show. As we watch the wondrous tricks and disappearing elephants,[1] we will examine how we got there and how much of that magic can be mastered through many different methods. To this end, we will use a descriptive approach to explore the nature of a computer, its functions, and the manner in which it operates.

A Filing System

Remember those big-old filing cabinets? Perhaps you are too young for that. You might have seen them in movies at some point. Regardless, imagine for a second you are in the 1950's equipped with no digital computers.[2] Every aspect of your day-to-day life, both significant and otherwise, involves laborious manual accounting for your self-established retail business.

Your company has various employees: sales people, front-desk assistants, general managers, and so on. Every single employee has a file in your main filing system. Each file has information on it such as the employee's name, their address, their general salary, commission rate, etc. We will call that information *data*.

---

[1] Perhaps "elephant" is an ill-phrased metaphor for some magical phenomena.

[2] The term *computer* was first used in "The Yong Mans Gleanings", where it referred to an individual who performed monotonous mathematical calculations [Braithwaite, 1613]. In the early 20th century, to support the effort towards the United States' involvement in World War II, women were hired as computers for this very task, often overshadowed by their male counterparts [Smith, 2013].

Every month, you must *compute* your general expenses. You gather your accounting team to meticulously examine each file, adding up the general salaries of all employees. For sales personnel, they locate an additional file containing monthly sales information, including the salesperson's name and the amount sold. Accounting then applies the commission rate from their records, multiplying it by the sales figure. Voila! They record each employee's total in a substantial accounting book, calculate the sum, and that becomes your general expenses. The same process is more or less followed for revenue, but you can imagine that part. This repetitive task is carried out month after month.

Now, just picture for a moment that you are presented with a new employee. This individual possesses extraordinary speed—five times faster than your entire accounting team. It seems magical! There is one predicament, however: this employee lacks intelligence. To enable them to adequately perform the job, you must meticulously document every single task they need to carry out.

An Algorithm

On its first day at work, your faster-than-human employee sits at a desk and finds this on a notecard:

1. Go to the second floor.

2. Open the cabinet that reads: "Employees"

3. For all cards in the "Employees" cabinet, write down, in the accounting book, their name in the first column and their salary in the second column.

4. If the employee is a salesperson, find the monthly sales book.

5. Look up the total sales for that employee and multiply that number by the employees commission rate on their card.

6. Sum the result with their base salary and write down the total value next to their name in the accounting book.

7. When you are done with all the employees in the cabinet, sum all of the payments and write down that number as the last entry in the accounting book.

This, as simplified as it can be, is an *algorithm*: A set of well-established instructions that can be performed potentially repeatedly by your employee. Once written down, it can be interpreted in a way that, in the end, produces a desirable result, assuming it is clearly written.[1]

---

[1] A "clearly written" algorithm is one that is unambiguous. The unplugged "peanut butter and jelly sandwich" (wherein students write a meticulous algorithm that a computer might use to construct a peanut butter and jelly sandwich) project is an excellent introduction to this idea.

Now, is this not delightful? We not only save precious time, but our employee becomes more cost-effective. But why stop there? Picture this: your staffing agency presents you with an even faster employee. This individual is absolutely astonishing, approximately ten times swifter than your previous superhuman staff member. Quite appealing, right? There is just one small snag: this new addition lacks knowledge of division and multiplication. Their speed, however, is unparalleled–truly remarkable. This employee can retrieve information so rapidly that you are contemplating breaking down your algorithm even further! All you need to do is create lookup tables for multiplication. Even better, you can define multiplication as the consecutive addition of a number to itself. For example, 3 times 5 is simply $5 + 5 + 5$. So, now you proceed to devise a methodology for explaining how multiplication works to your new employee. Perhaps something like what follows:

To multiply two numbers a and b together, do the following:

1. Look up the multiplication table for a.

2. Find the value where it crosses b in the table.

3. Get result.

This would be pretty easy for the new employee. After all, they are really fast at looking things up. An alternative would be:

To multiply two numbers a and b together, do the following:

1. Get the larger number and add to itself as many times as the smaller number.

This is a solution that involves just adding the number, your new employee knows how to add, and does it fast![1] Now, we have simplified this as an example, but the ideal trajectory should be clear.

Our next call from the staffing agent promises the impossible. There is a new guy; one with, dare we say, unrivaled potential. Nearly as fast as the speed of light, things for this magical creature happen basically instantaneously. So you are asking yourself: "What is the catch?" Well, the new employee does not know how to read. In fact, it cannot derive meaning out of anything. All your previous algorithms are no longer useful, but you must, somehow, tap into this employee's power!

A Computer Language

The staffing agency informs you that this new individual excels at information retrieval and basic operations, given the right set of instructions. Moreover, they have no need for rest or sustenance, nor do they require a salary. Allow us to explain how this particular employee functions.

---

[1]We will ignore the complexities of determining the "largest" of two numbers for the time being and assume the new employee understands this concept.

Firstly, they possess the ability to look up information. Secondly, they can store a limited amount of data in their memory. Thirdly, they are capable of performing basic arithmetic. It is important to note, though, that their knowledge is restricted to only eight digits.

At this point, you might express concern regarding the limitations of such a narrow numerical range. How could they possibly accomplish anything with only two eight digits?

Rest assured, the staffing agency states, with utmost confidence, that they have a solution. All you need to do is *codify* your filing system in a way that enables the employee to navigate and identify the desired information. For instance, you can devise a system where the first two digits indicate the floor of a file, the following two digits indicate the room, and the last four digits indicate the cabinet. Admittedly, this system, even for the most astute among us, is not the most optimal 8-bit system. Nevertheless, it allows you to encode your files accordingly. The first two numbers can represent the department to which the file belongs, and so on. You can easily envision where this is leading.

At this point you may starting to convince yourself that maybe this poor fool of a machine can actually be useful. You think, to yourself: "if all I need to do is codify my file system and algorithm, then this can work!"

So you start codifying your file system; that was easy. You then start writing instructions.

---

1. Go to 00010100

2. Go to 00000101

3. Put value of 00100010 in Memory 0

4. Go to 01001000

5. Go to 00010000

6. Put value of 00100011 in Memory 1

7. Add value in Memory 0 to value in Memory 1.

8. Write result in 00000100

You look at it with a puzzled gaze. You do not remember what any of these 1's and 0's mean. You tell yourself: "this will not work; how can any one keep track of any of this? It is impossible!"

Along comes Alice, who is your smartest employee. She's been working at the company for many years and she is on track to be its newest CEO next year. She informs you that this can work; all you need to do is to make this thing readable and devise a way where the readable bit can be turned into this primitive set of instructions for your new machine.

Alright, fasten your seat-belts because the adventure is about to begin! What you've read so far was just a prelude to the exciting journey that lies ahead. It is not simply about employees racing through a company's building or the basic functions of computers; it is a thrilling exploration of the intricate world of computers and how they shape our lives. Let us make one thing clear: computer science goes beyond the physical machines; we dive deep into programming language design, unraveling its mysteries alongside the underlying mathematics. We embrace the challenges, unearthing the secrets of computation and pushing the boundaries of what is possible. So, get ready to embark on this epic adventure where the foundations of computer science and its theoretical concepts blend harmoniously with practical applications. Brace yourself for a wild ride, as we delve deeper into uncharted territories and satisfy your thirst for knowledge with each turn of the page.

2   A Logic Primer

Science is not a substitute for common sense, but an extension of it.

—Willard Van Orman Quine

2.1   Zeroth-Order Logic

What is logic? A general definition is the use of reasoning to determine the truthfulness of some claim. For instance, it is logical to close the refrigerator door after opening it and retrieving your desired items because if we did not, the cold temperature is no longer encapsulated, leading to some foods or ingredients going bad. We can simply say something to the effect of, "If I do not close the refrigerator door, my food will go bad." This is known as an argument involving deductive reasoning. In other words, we used a form of reasoning which involves premises that lead to, or imply, a conclusion. For this small example, it is easy to understand the reasoning behind the argument. What happens, though, if we create a larger and more complicated argument? Suppose that, in the following example, each itemized bullet point is a proposition to an argument (note that we will examine the argument in greater detail later in the chapter—we introduce it here as motivation).

- Janet goes to university.

- If someone is a mathematician, then they have a lot of experience with using computers.

- Janet does not know how chemicals interact if she is not a chemist.

- Janet is either a chemist or a mathematician if Janet goes to university.

- Janet goes to university as a computer science student.

- Janet is a chemist if and only if she is not a mathematician.

- Therefore, Janet does not know how chemicals interact.

We analyze logical arguments through two lenses: validity and soundness. An argument that is valid has premises that logically imply the conclusion. Though, what is a premise and conclusion, and what in the world does the phrase "logically imply" mean?

Form of an Argument

Firstly, statements that express a true or false claim/idea are *propositions*. For example, "The sky is blue", "$2 + 2 = 5$", "If $(n)^2 = 4$ then n is either -2 or 2". A proposition can be either true or false, but it must be a statement as opposed to an exclamatory, command, or question, as these do not have associated truth values.[1]

Premises are propositions that support an argument claim. In other words, a premise expresses truth or falsity. *Conclusions*, similar to premises, also express the truth of a claim, but serve as a judgment to the claim as a whole. A collection of premises either support or reject the judgment asserted by a conclusion. Such support is called a logical implication of a premise to a conclusion.

Before we discuss what it means for one premise to logically imply another, we must describe the notion of truth values. A truth value takes the form of true, i.e., $\top$, or false, i.e., $\bot$. Because of this, any proposition will, by default, have two possible values: $\top$ or $\bot$. As a corollary point, all propositions are either true or they are not true. As an example, "Either $2 + 2 = 5$ or $2 + 2 \neq 5$". In this example, the proposition is "$2 + 2 = 5$". This is clearly an absurdity, i.e., $2 + 2 = 5$ is $\bot$, but for the purposes of this claim, it does not matter, as it is true that $2 + 2 \neq 5$, and false that $2 + 2 = 5$. This style of argument is otherwise known as the law of excluded middle.

Defining truth in such a bivalent respect is a problem rooted deep in philosophy. Alfred Tarski coined the idea of using *schemata*, or formulae of our logic language, to provide a differentiation between the use of truth as a literal versus truth in the conceptual sense. In a broad sense, we state a claim in our language, then it is provided a truth value from our metalanguage. The classic example is, "Snow is white" is true if and only if snow is white.

In this text, we will represent propositions as lower-case letters, e.g., 'p', 'q', 'r', ..., 'z'.[2] To symbolize the above claim, let $p : $ "$2 + 2 = 5$". Now, let us substitute this into our statement: "Either p or $2 + 2 \neq 5$". We have run into a small roadblock; how do we represent the negation of a proposition? Negating propositions requires a connective, which we will now explain.

The Connectives

Every day we use connectives in our speech or text without realizing. *Connectives* link related phrases/words/ideas together with the intent of strengthening or weakening expressed statements.

---

[1] If this does not make sense so far, think of a command that you might tell someone, e.g., "Go to the store and buy a loaf of bread". Is it possible to express the truthiness of this command and, if so, what is it? Another example might be to ask someone, "What time is it?". How can a question, in and of itself, be true or false?

[2] Different authors describe different notation(s), or syntax, to represent the same semantic idea.

Negation

In most instances, for any proposition 'p', it is safe to use the phrase, "It is not the case that 'p' is true", to represent the *logical negation* of 'p'. This is rather cumbersome to spell out, however, so we symbolically use '$\neg p$' to denote the negation of proposition 'p'. Now, let us retry our substitution method from earlier: "Either 'p' or '$\neg p$' is **true**". Note that '$\neg p$' denotes "It is not the case that $2 + 2 = 5$ is true", which is semantically equivalent to $2 + 2 \neq 5$ (we may read this as "Two plus two is not equal to five"), but even this is still a bit awkward to read as we are intertwining logic and proposition symbols with English statements.

The issue with negation in natural language is that, often times, sentences do not have a straightforward binary conversion between non-negation and negation. For instance, suppose we have the two propositions, "Bob is happy", and "Bob is sad". Could we say that the latter is a mere negation of the former? In this case, we have to analyze what it means to be "not happy". Someone who is not happy may not necessarily be sad; they may be angry, neutral, or many other emotions. All we can express from the proposition that "Bob is happy" is that its negation is, "Bob is not happy", or equivalently as aforementioned, "It is not the case that Bob is happy".

English Equivalents. As we stated, negation in natural language is complicated at best and ambiguous at worst. Some equivalents of "negation" in natural language include "not" and "it is not the case that". Continuing with the explanation from the previous paragraph about converting a proposition into its negated counterpart, if we have the phrase "Bob is happy", we cannot prefix the phrase "happy" with "un-", as it does not indicate the negation of "happy". Furthermore, as we will see later on, negating quantified statements is also challenging. Suppose we have the following proposition: "Everyone is happy". Can we negate this by saying "Nobody is happy"? No, we cannot; the negation of "Everyone is happy" would be "It is not the case that everyone is happy", or more concisely, "Everyone is not happy". This suggests that there is someone that is not happy, but it does not suggest that nobody is happy. Negating statements takes practice and an understanding of English semantics.

Disjunction

"Either... or..." is the form of the first binary, or two-place, connective we will analyze. Symbolically, we represent this with $\vee$, also known as *logical disjunction* or alternation. Other non-symbolic representations of disjunction include, "or". Returning to the prior example, we can now use symbols to fully convert the previous example to symbolic logic: '$p \vee \neg p$'.

English Equivalents. Logical disjunction, as we stated, is most often conveyed in the word "or", e.g., "Jill may have cake or ice cream". Sometimes, it is implicitly used as part of an enumeration of choices, e.g., "Jill may have one of ice cream, cake, or donuts". There are other equivalents such as "otherwise" and "alternative", all of which convey inclusivity. Interestingly enough, in common speech, logical disjunction is often used in the exclusivity sense, i.e., a choice between options is mandatory, and nothing in between is permitted. In logic, we convey exclusive disjunction (also called exclusive or) commonly using "Either p or 'q' but not both (and not neither)". In a purely logical interpretation of propositions, however, both 'p' and 'q' being true is allowed. Considering one of the examples from before, if Jill has both cake and ice cream, this still expresses a true proposition, because they had at least one of cake and ice cream. If we introduce exclusivity via "Jill may have either ice cream or cake, but not both (and not neither)", if Jill has both desserts or neither of the desserts, the proposition is false.

Conjunction

Next, we will discuss conjunction, or the connection of propositions with non-symbolic words such as "and" and "but". A *logical conjunction* between schemata expresses the idea that each schema individually must be true in order for the conjunction to resolve as true. For example, consider the schemata 'p' and 'q'. If we know that both 'p' and 'q' are individually true, then we can say '$p \wedge q$' is true. Conversely, if either 'p' or 'q' are false, then '$p \wedge q$' is false. Symbolically, as we just demonstrated, this connective uses the inverted wedge ($\wedge$) to designate a logical conjunction.

English Equivalents. English equivalents of logical conjunction are used frequently in day-to-day speech. For example, "Steve is a cook and a swimmer" is a conjunction between the two propositions of Steve being a cook and Steve being a swimmer. Adverbs such as "additionally" and "moreover", in general, express the same idea as logical conjunction. So, "Steve is a swimmer. Additionally, he is a cook", and "Steve is a swimmer. Moreover, he is a cook" express semantically-equivalent propositions.

Example. Suppose we want to represent the statement, "John is a computer science major and Billy does not like to fish". Again, we assign the propositions to letters, e.g., p : "John is a computer science major", and q : "Billy does not like to fish". right? Not quite, in this scenario. When negating a schema, we use the $\neg$ symbol, e.g., '$\neg q$'. If we assign 'q' as we did, then there is no negation on the propositional letter. While this is not incorrect, it is correct and widely accepted to always assign the positive version of a proposition to a letter. Thus, instead, q : "Billy likes to fish", meaning when we attach a negation to the proposition via '$\neg q$' we get the statement, "It is not the case that Billy likes to fish", one that is semantically equivalent to the original. Finally, the symbolic logic expression is '$p \wedge \neg q$' since we must conjoin the two sub-schemata.

Logical Conditional

The *logical conditional* operator is the most complex connective that we will investigate in zeroth-order logic. Its semantic meaning in context is not always obvious. Conditionals are used in sentences where the following phrases exist: "if", "only if", "then", and "implies" (note that, as before, this is a non-exhaustive list of hints). Symbolically, this connective uses an arrow ($\rightarrow$) to designate a logical conditional. A point should be made about a logical conditional and its semantics: Logical conditionals are created, as we stated, with the arrow, e.g., '$p \rightarrow q$'. *Logical implication*, on the other hand, is a related concept but requires its own description: it ascribes the truth conditions between a collection of schemata and another individual schema. In summary, logical implication explains, in our system, how propositions imply one another, whereas the logical conditional (also sometimes referred to as the conditional with the "logical" dropped) is nothing more than a new syntactic connective.[1] We will use logical conditional in the following example.

English Equivalents. Conversion of the logical conditional into speech is more difficult because of its obtuse and confusing meaning. It is still possible, though, to translate using phrases such as those mentioned above. Time-based or action-based adverbs are also sometimes indicators of a conditional. "Whenever Joe is cooking, he smiles" expresses the idea that if Joe cooks, then he smiles. "When", "Given that" and "In the case of" all share the same sentiment of the conditional.

Example. Suppose we want to convert the following sentence into symbolic logic: "Katherine is not good at tennis only if she does not practice and she is not motivated to play". Let us first symbolize the propositions: We will assign the proposition p : "Katherine is good at tennis", q : "Katherine practices tennis", and r : "Katherine is motivated to play tennis". Notice how we took some liberties in substituting pronouns for names, as well as adding details to clarify the propositions. This is always acceptable and desired in symbolic logic; as long as it remains semantically equivalent to the original proposition, any translation is valid.

---

[1] Another way of reasoning about these contrasting ideas is to take two arbitrary schemata 'p' and 'q', then stick a conditional in between, i.e., '$p \rightarrow q$'. The existence of a logical conditional does not guarantee, or even necessarily suggest, that 'p' implies 'q'. Once we get to truth conditions, we will better understand why this is the case.

Logical Biconditional

Logical biconditional is often paraphrased as, "...if and only if...", "just in case", "iff", and symbolically represented as, $\leftrightarrow$ (note that this should not be conflated with "if" and "only if", as there is an important distinction with "if and only if"). For example, "Computers are necessary if and only if they are used by everyone in the world" uses the propositions p : "Computers are necessary" and q : "Computers are used by everyone in the world". Symbolically, '$p \leftrightarrow q$'. The important piece of this is hidden by the syntactic sugaring of $\leftrightarrow$; in actuality, a biconditional is nothing more than the conjunction of two conditionals: '$(p \to q) \wedge (q \to p)$'. In other words, two propositions must imply one another in order to represent a logical biconditional. Each sub-component of the expression, i.e., '$(p \to q)$' and '$(q \to p)$', corresponds to either the "if" or the "only if". The left-hand side represents "if", whereas the right-hand side represents "only if". We can, of course, convert any "if" expression to an "only if", although it may not be a valid expression at that point.

English Equivalents. Compared to other connectives, the biconditional is a bit harder to find variants of, besides the standard "if and only if". We want to use phrases that express equivalence of two ideas. So, "is equivalent to", "exactly when", and "necessary and sufficient" are good replacements for a biconditional in speech. The last example exemplifies the nature of the biconditional. That is, a proposition 'q' being necessary for 'p' is expressed by '$p \to q$', whereas a proposition 'q' being sufficient for 'p' is expressed by '$q \to p$'. Combining these together with a conjunction forms '$(p \to q) \wedge (q \to p)$'. A property of the biconditional is its slight ambiguity in mathematical proofs. The phrase "if and only if" may seem to connect directly with the previous schematization, but this is not the case. '$p \to q$' expresses, "q if p", or, "p only if q". This means that the left-hand side of the conjunction is, in actuality, the "only if" direction of the conditional, and the right-hand side refers to the "if" direction. Another interpretation of this is to say that the "if" refers to, "if p, then q", which suggests the ordering of the connectives is correct. Either way, because logical conjunction is commutative (i.e., '$p \wedge q$' is equivalent to '$q \wedge p$'), it matters not so much.

So, returning to the previous example, we now know what "only if" is symbolically, so we can convert the entire sentence into symbolic logic: '$(\neg q \wedge \neg p) \wedge \neg r$'.

Ambiguous Expressions

We can complicate things slightly by adding *ambiguity* into the equation. For example, let us convert the statement, "Samantha does not play video games or Ryan is a server and Paul is a pianist" into zeroth-order logic. Right away, we find an issue with our translation process: Firstly, there are three propositions instead of two. Thankfully, this does not hinder our progress significantly. What does, on the other hand, is the ambiguity of the expression. Similar to rules for operator precedence and associativity for basic mathematical operations such as addition and subtraction, logical connectives also have precedence values: We evaluate negations first, conjunctions second, disjunctions third, logical conditionals fourth, and biconditionals last. With this guideline in hand, we can now schematize the English sentence.

Example. Suppose p : "Samantha plays video games", q : "Ryan is a server", and r : "Paul is a pianist". Symbolically, this is equivalent to, '$\neg p \vee (q \wedge r)$'. According to our precedence rules, we evaluate the conjunction, i.e., "and" before "or". So, while it is not strictly necessary in this case since we laid out precedence rules, not all sources on symbolic logic provide a precedence list. In these instances, much like mathematical expressions, we insert parentheses to denote that an operator evaluation has higher priority. For example, '$\neg p \vee (q \wedge r)$'. For completeness, we can insert outer parentheses to group '$\neg p$' and '$q \wedge r$' with the $\vee$ operator, but it is unnecessary: '$(\neg p \vee (q \wedge r))$'.

Converting entire arguments, instead of individual sentences containing propositions, is fortunately very simple. The premises of a *valid* argument, when conjoined, imply the consequent. *Sound* arguments are both valid and have only true premises. We will construct a model for arguments. Let $A(P, c)$ denote an argument A with a collection of premises A_P and a conclusion A_c. So, suppose we have an argument A such that $A_P = \{a, b\}$ and $A_c = c$.[1] An argument can have zero or more premises, but it must have a conclusion. Thus, A is logically valid if and only if '$(a \wedge b) \to c$' is true. In a later section, we will investigate what it means for a proposition to be true or false.

We finally have all the tools necessary to convert the argument on page 21 into symbolic logic.

Example. Let p : "Janet knows how chemicals interact", q : "Janet is a chemist", r : "Janet is a mathematician", s : "Janet goes to university". We need to identify our premise set and conclusion. The conclusion of an argument is, in many instances, easy to identify if told outright. We can use conclusion word indicators, e.g., therefore, so, hence, thus, and more. In the argument, we are told, "Therefore, Janet does not know how chemicals react". So, our conclusion is, symbolically, $\neg p$. The remaining sentences are, as such, premises. Let us construct each premise piece by piece.

(i)   "Janet does not know how chemicals interact if she is not a chemistry student" is represented as '$\neg q \to \neg p$'.

---

[1]What we allude to, in regards to the representation of A_P, is called a *set*, and we will introduce them in the next section of this chapter.

(ii) "Janet is either a chemistry student or a computer science student if Janet goes to university" is represented as '$s \rightarrow (q \vee r)$'.

(iii) "Janet goes to university and is a computer science student" is represented as '$r \wedge s$'.

(iv) "Janet is a chemistry major if and only if she is not a computer science major" is represented as '$p \leftrightarrow \neg s$'.

Now that we have schematized each premise individually, we can combine them using the conjunction operator, then connect the resulting conjunction to the conclusion with the conditional: '$((((\neg q \rightarrow \neg p) \wedge (q \vee r)) \wedge (r \wedge s)) \wedge (p \leftrightarrow \neg s)) \rightarrow \neg p$'. Neither the validity nor soundness of this argument are of concern to us for now; we simply wanted to symbolize its premises and conclusion. The form of a symbolic logic formula was also of no concern since we only had small sentences.

Inductively Defining Zeroth-Order Logic

In order to properly parse and evaluate large ones, to ensure no errors are made, we need to inductively define valid expressions within our symbolic logic language. An inductive definition allows us to build the components of our language, which when combined together provide larger components.

1. All individual proposition letters, i.e., 'p', 'q', 'r', ..., 'z' are symbolic logic expressions.

2. If W is a symbolic logic expression defined by only a single proposition letter, i.e., (1), then $\neg W$ is a symbolic logic expression.

3. If W_1 and W_2 are symbolic logic expressions, then

    (a) $(W_1 \vee W_2)$ is a symbolic logic expression,

    (b) $(W_1 \wedge W_2)$ is a symbolic logic expression,

    (c) $(W_1 \rightarrow W_2)$ is a symbolic logic expression,

    (d) $(W_1 \leftrightarrow W_2)$ is a symbolic logic expression.

4. If W is a symbolic logic expression not defined by only a single proposition letter, i.e., (3), then $\neg W$ is a symbolic logic expression.

With this inductive definition and construction plan, we can also simplify certain expressions with redundant parentheses. For instance, we may omit the outer-most parentheses in an expression. As an example, '$((\neg s \wedge p) \leftrightarrow \neg (q \rightarrow \neg r))$' becomes '$(\neg s \wedge p) \leftrightarrow \neg (q \rightarrow \neg r)$' with this omission. Moreover, we often use the terms symbolic logic expression and schema interchangeably, which also holds true for their plurals: symbolic logic expressions and schemata.

Truth Assignment and Truth Tables

What does it actually mean for two propositions to be joined by a connective? We have seen quite a few examples of translation from English to symbolic logic, but we need to ascribe a meaning to argument validity. We can do this through truth values. Recall when we stated that all propositions are either true or false; verity (truth) and falsity are representable via a construct known as a *truth table*. Suppose we have a proposition 'p'; its possible truth values are either $\top$ or $\bot$. The left-hand column in the table below demonstrates this, whereas the right-hand column shows the result of an expression.

$$
\begin{array}{c|c}
p & p \\
\hline
\top & \top \\
\bot & \bot
\end{array}
$$

Figure 2.1: Truth Table of Proposition 'p'

Obviously, with a single proposition, the right-hand column is rather meaningless. What if we decide to use two propositions with a connective? When given a slightly more complex expression such as '$p \lor q$', how do we know its truth value?

First, when drawing a truth table, it is imperative to draw $n+1$ columns, where the first n columns correspond to how many distinct propositions are used in the provided expression. Next, we need to have rows for each possible *assignment*, or interpretation, of truth values to each proposition. Because we only have two possible input values for each proposition, this directly correlates to the number of rows in a truth table, namely being 2^n. Each row corresponds to a different, distinct truth assignment.

First, let us cover the simplest operator: unary negation. A negation flips all truth values of a proposition. Again, we use the '$\neg p$' to negate a proposition 'p'. Though, if we have more than one proposition to negate, e.g., if we wanted to negate the expression '$(p \lor q)$', we place a large dash on the outside of said expression: '$\neg(p \lor q)$'. This, appropriately, flips all truth values of the inner, nested expression.

$$
\begin{array}{c|c}
p & \neg p \\
\hline
\top & \bot \\
\bot & \top
\end{array}
$$

Figure 2.2: Truth Table of '$\neg p$'

Now we move into binary operators; or those operators that use two operands. With logical conjunction, the expression is true if and only if both operands are true. The idea is that, when we have two propositions combined with the conjunction connective, we wish to express the idea that 'p' is true at the same time that 'q' is true.

$$
\begin{array}{cc|c}
p & q & p \land q \\
\hline
\top & \top & \top \\
\top & \bot & \bot \\
\bot & \top & \bot \\
\bot & \bot & \bot \\
\end{array}
$$

Figure 2.3: Truth Table of '$p \land q$'.

Logical disjunction, or alternation, is true if and only if at least one of its operands is true. The idea is that, when we have two propositions combined with $\lor$, we wish to express the idea that at least 'p' ought to be true or 'q' ought to be true. So, if they are both false, then this idea is not expressed.

$$
\begin{array}{cc|c}
p & q & p \lor q \\
\hline
\top & \top & \top \\
\top & \bot & \top \\
\bot & \top & \top \\
\bot & \bot & \bot \\
\end{array}
$$

Figure 2.4: Truth Table of '$p \lor q$'.

Logical conditionals are true if and only if the antecedent, i.e., the left-hand operand, is not true and the consequent is not false. Conditionals are a tricky subject for many people, as the idea behind their meaning is unintuitive at first glance, not to mention the conflation of logical implication versus the conditional. Let us examine the rows which evaluate to true before the false row.

"$\top \to \top$ evaluates to $\top$" should, hopefully, be self-explanatory. If we state that, when some proposition, i.e., the antecedent, is true, another proposition, i.e., the consequent, is also true, then it is true that if the antecedent is true, then the consequent holds true.

"$\bot \to \top$ evaluates to $\top$" is a little trickier. Let us examine this with an example using two propositions. "If $2 + 2 = 5$ then $3 + 3 = 6$". Clearly, the antecedent is false whereas the consequent is true. The expression, therefore, evaluates to true because the conditional dictates only what happens when the antecedent is true; not when it is false.

"$\bot \to \bot$ evaluates to $\top$" is even trickier since both operands are false yet the expression somehow results in truth. If a false antecedent implies a false consequent, this suggests that, even though both expressions are false, it does not falsify the entire conditional since the original antecedent never promised, so to speak, that the consequent is true when the antecedent is false. As we have therefore demonstrated, false implies anything, whether it be true or false, resolves to true.

We may now investigate the only false case of the conditional: "$\top \to \bot$ evaluates to $\bot$" is the second easiest truth assignment to understand. Our conditional is somewhat akin to a promise, and by the antecedent being true alongside the presence of a false consequent, we are suggesting that the antecedent does not, in fact, imply the consequent. This is an absurdity, which falsifies the implicative.

A phrase to know about the relationship between the conditional and logical implication is, "Implication is the validity of the conditional". That is, a schema implies another schema if the conditional asserts their validity.

p	q	$p \to q$
$\top$	$\top$	$\top$
$\top$	$\bot$	$\bot$
$\bot$	$\top$	$\top$
$\bot$	$\bot$	$\top$

Figure 2.5: Truth Table of '$p \to q$'.

Finally, logical biconditional is also known as logical equivalence. This alternative name provides insight into its results; the expression '$p \leftrightarrow q$' is true if and only if 'p' and 'q' are identical in truth value.

p	q	$p \leftrightarrow q$
$\top$	$\top$	$\top$
$\top$	$\bot$	$\bot$
$\bot$	$\top$	$\bot$
$\bot$	$\bot$	$\top$

Figure 2.6: Truth Table of '$p \leftrightarrow q$'.

Like the conditional, the relationship between equivalence and the biconditional is stated as, "Equivalence is the validity of the biconditional". So, two schemata are equivalent just in case the biconditional expresses valid of those schemata.

After combining these newfound truth tables together, we can evaluate the truth of any expression defined within our logic language. We first, however, need to establish a notion of the "main operator" of an expression.

Main Operator

The *main operator* of a schema is the last operator that we investigate when performing a full truth analysis of the schema. Another definition is that the main operator is the first-parsed operator when evaluating a schema constructed through the inductive definition. What does this mean for us? Let us walk through an example to see.

Let us determine the main operator of '$\neg r \lor \neg((p \land q) \land (\neg r \leftrightarrow \neg p))$'. According to our rules for evaluation, we evaluate parenthesized expressions first. Inside the right-hand expression, i.e., '$\neg((p \land q) \land (\neg r \leftrightarrow \neg p))$', we see a conjunction of two expressions, one of which is another parenthesized expression, i.e., '$(\neg r \leftrightarrow \neg p)$'. The biconditional is broken down into two negated propositions, which resolve into their non-negated counterparts. If we start to rebuild this expression, we can quickly find the main operator. Combining the biconditional with the chain of conjunctions, i.e., '$p \land q$' gets us '$(p \land q) \land (\neg r \leftrightarrow \neg p)$'. This is then negated as '$\neg((p \land q) \land (\neg r \leftrightarrow \neg p))$'. Finally, we combine this with the disjunction operator where the left-hand operand is '$\neg r$'. Therefore the disjunction operator is the main operator.

Evaluation Trees

If we view the previous schema as an *evaluation tree*, it is even easier to understand, since each operator is broken into separate components for evaluation. Each branch describes a subexpression which, when combined via traversing up the tree, produces either a valid sub-expression or the original expression.

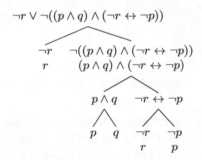

Figure 2.7: Evaluation Tree of '$\neg r \lor \neg((p \land q) \land (\neg r \leftrightarrow \neg p))$'

Evaluation trees break down the structure of something into sub-components for further evaluation. In the context of zeroth-order logic schemata, we decompose a schema in one of two ways: if the formula is negated, its subsequent formula is stacked. Otherwise, it produces a branch into two further evaluation trees. In the above example, the main operator is $\lor$, meaning it is split into '$\neg r$' and '$\neg((p \land q) \land (\neg r \leftrightarrow \neg p))$'. The left-hand side decomposes into 'r' because its main operator is $\neg$, indicating a stacked schema. After this, the left-hand parse tree can no longer decompose, meaning we proceed to the right-hand side. The schema '$\neg((p \land q) \land (\neg r \leftrightarrow \neg p))$', similarly, has a main operator of $\neg$, so we perform a similar operator removal. From there, the main operator is $\land$, indicating a branch with each sub-schemata. This process continues until all branches cannot be further reduced.

We could **also** describe evaluation trees via parse trees. *Parse trees* are fundamental **structures** not only in computer science, but also other fields such as (computational) linguistics, where parse trees provide the structure of sentences using parts-of-**speech**. Furthermore, parse trees express the contextual knowledge of the composition **of** an input schema. As an example, we might parse an arithmatic expression, e.g., '$2 + 4 \cdot 3$' as follows.[1]

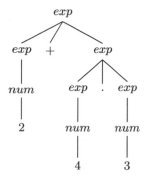

Figure 2.8: Parse Tree of '$2 + 4 \cdot 3$'

Expressions *exp* are comprised of two expressions and an operator in between. An *exp* can **lead towards** a *num*. In this example, the main operator so happens to be '$+$', meaning **we** add its left-hand expression 2 to its right-hand expression $4 \cdot 3$. Its resulting value **is,** therefore, 14. Let us consider another approach: what is stopping us from interpreting this as an expression whose main operator is multiplication? Nothing at **all! Let** us see the parse tree for an expression with multiplication as the last-to-**evaluate** expression instead.

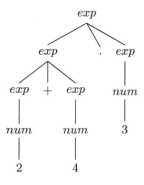

Figure 2.9: Ambiguous Parse Tree of '$2 + 4 \cdot 3$'

[1]The word "**parse**" stems from the Latin phrase "pars orationis".

From the above figures, we see that, if we change the order of evaluation, we get a completely different answer than the one that is most likely intended.[1] Evaluating the expression as such gives us a value of 24. In due time, parse trees will reappear, so if their purpose is not as clear at the moment as we hope, do not fret.

---

[1] "Intended" on the grounds that the standard order of operations, i.e., where multiplicatives are evaluated before additives, apply.

2.2   First-Order Logic

In the previous section, we created propositions that represented a collective idea or claim. We will quickly understand, however, that zeroth-order logic is rather weak in comparison to first-order logic. As a motivating example, suppose we want to represent the sentence, "All students go to college or school" in zeroth-order logic. There is really only one way to do so; because the disjunction connective exists, we can let p : "All students go to college", and q : "All students go to school". Symbolically, the schema is '$p \lor q$'. While this is feasible in our zeroth-order logic system, there is no possible way of adequately representing a *quantification* of variables, e.g., "All students", and therefore, we lose a large chunk of the semantics behind our statement. First-order logic rectifies this with the introduction of predicates, as well as three new connectives: the universal quantifier, the existential quantifier, and the identity symbol.

A *predicate* is a statement that provides context to some input variable(s). For example, we can let '$S(x)$' represent the idea that some 'x' is a student. Similarly, let '$C(x)$' represent the idea that some x go to college. Finally, let '$D(x)$' represent the idea that some 'x' goes to school. Using predicates in this fashion, i.e., with only one input variable is known as monadic first-order logic. Later, we will analyze polyadic first-order logic, i.e., first-order logic where predicates use more than one input variable.

The Quantifiers

Quantifiers are necessary in first-order logic for one reason: as their name suggests, they quantify, or provide numeric amounts to, some entity. There are two powerful quantifier connectives in first-order logic: the universal and existential quantifiers.

Universal

If we want to say, "All math majors are smart", then we are quantifying the proposition "math majors are smart" via "All". In other words, every *thing* that is a math major has the property of "smart". Additionally, we may claim that "No person who is not smart lives on Earth", which quantifies the proposition "smart people exist" via "No". In other words, anyone that lives on Earth is smart. We classify phrases and keywords as universal because they apply to an entire domain— nothing is excluded. In mathematical and logic contexts, the phrase, "For all", or "For every" is often utilized as an English representation of the *universal quantifier*. As an example, "For all integers x greater than one, x^2 is greater than $2x$". If we wanted to instead use symbols, this may be represented as "$\forall x \in \mathbb{Z}$ such that $x > 1$, $x^2 > 2x$".[1] This symbolage is not reserved only for the phrase "For all"; it is equivalently suited for "No", "Every", "None", etc. One key rule-of-thumb is that, when quantifying with a universal over some domain, use an implication to indicate a relationship. We will show an example of where this falls apart soon. This may seem obvious to some, but while the universal quantifier is rather straightforward, it quickly descends into madness after introducing its existential counterpart. Before doing so, let us write a few examples of translating natural language universal quantifiers into schemata.

Suppose we want to translate, "All intelligent beings are either from Earth or from Mars". We need three predicates: $I(x)$ meaning x is an intelligent being, $E(x)$ meaning x is from Earth, and $M(x)$ meaning x is from Mars. We need to express that, anything we choose from our domain, i.e., what we quantify over, if that thing is an intelligent being, then they are either from Earth or Mars. Thus we translate the sentence into the schema '$\forall x(I(x) \to (E(x) \lor M(x)))$'.

Let us consider an example of where not using an implication gets us into trouble. Suppose we want to translate, "All cats and dogs can fly." We need three predicates: $C(x)$ means x is a cat, $D(x)$ means x is a dog, and $F(x)$ means F can fly. Attempting to translate this proposition using only a conjunction connective gets us the schema '$\forall x(C(x) \land D(x) \land F(x))$', which expresses an incorrect proposition; namely that all things are cats and dogs and they fly. We, instead, should use the disjunction operator with an implication to express that, if something is either a cat or a dog, then it flies: '$\forall x((C(x) \lor D(x)) \to F(x))$'.

---

[1]The $\mathbb{Z}$ symbol denotes any integer. So, $\forall x \in \mathbb{Z}$ says, "for any integer" or equivalently "for every integer".

Existential

Unlike the universal quantifier whose scope is, as its name says, universal, the *existential quantifier* is simultaneously more and less specific. Take, for instance, "Not all cows have spots". It is important to understand that this claim does not say, "No cow has spots", nor something akin; it merely states that there exists a cow that does not have spots. What is more interesting about the existential quantifier is its power in representing propositions. Take, for instance, there exists an integer x such that x^2 is greater than $2x$. Symbolically, $\exists x \in \mathbb{Z}$ such that $x^2 > 2x$. Existentials do not express as strong of a statement as those expressed by its universal counterpart; indeed, an existential '$\exists x P(x)$' states the existence of at least one x that satisfies the predicate P. It does not, however, express that there is *only* one x, or exactly one x; the existential quantifier does not, in and of itself, denote an exact quantity of objects that satisfy a predicate. Therefore if we wanted to translate the proposition, "Most people are smart", we would use an existential quantifier via '$\exists x(P(x) \wedge S(x))$', where $S(x)$ means x is smart and $P(x)$ means x is a person. The determiners "Most", "Many", "Some", "A lot", "A", "An", "Any", all refer to the existential quantifier. "Any", however, becomes confusing, as does "every", when combined into a conditional. Let us see what this means via two examples.

First, suppose we want to schematize, "If Kate can solve any math problem, then she can solve every math problem". Of course, let k represent Kate, $S(x, y)$ to mean x solves y, and $M(x)$ to mean x is a math problem. One may believe that the use of "any" refers to a universal quantifier, resulting in '$\forall x(M(x) \wedge S(k, x)) \rightarrow \forall x(M(x) \rightarrow S(k, x))$'. This, however, is a tautological statement, because when the antecedent is true, the consequent is never false. We could also equivalently schematize this as '$\forall x((M(x) \wedge S(k, x)) \rightarrow (M(x) \rightarrow S(k, x)))$', since '$\forall x(P(x) \rightarrow Q(x))$' is logically equivalent to '$(P(x) \rightarrow \forall x Q(x))$'. We should, instead, treat this use of "any" as an existential quantifier, meaning that the proposition would unambiguously express that, "If Kate can solve at least one math problem, then she can solve every math problem". Schematizing such a proposition results in an existential quantifier in the antecedent: '$\exists x(M(x) \wedge S(k, x)) \rightarrow \forall y(M(y) \rightarrow S(k, y))$'. Note that the use of "any" in the antecedent suggests an existential quantifier, but what happens if we place it in the consequent?

Suppose we want to schematize, "If Kate can solve every math problem, then she can solve any math problem." Using the same schematization of predicates, we translate this as '$\forall x(M(x) \rightarrow S(k, x)) \rightarrow \exists x(M(x) \rightarrow S(k, x))$', right? If we apply the same idea insofar as using an existential quantifier for "any", we express, yet again, a tautology, but not for the same reason as before. It is true and hopefully apparent that the schema '$\forall x P(x) \rightarrow \exists x P(x)$' is tautological, because if everything satisfies P, then by definition, there is something that satisfies P. So, using an existential in the consequent leads us to a weaker assertion than our original desired proposition. We want to express that, because Kate can solve every math problem, then she can solve *any* math problem, where *any* means that, given an arbitrary math problem, Kate solves that problem. It should be clear that this is expresses the same proposition as the antecedent, leading us to instead use a universal quantifier in the consequent: "$\forall x(M(x) \wedge S(k, x)) \rightarrow \forall x(M(x) \wedge S(k, x))$".

Identity

Suppose we have two constants in our domain representing the individuals Alan Turing and Katherine Johnson as a and k respectively. We can definitively state that a and k do not refer to the same entity, and symbolically, we say '$\neg(a = k)$'. Perhaps we want to represent the North Star as n and Polaris as p, and because we know that the North Star is the same thing as Polaris, we write '$n = p$'.

Identity is a two-place predicate amongst variables and constants, as opposed to symbolic logic expressions like the other (unary and binary) connectives. Let us use identity inside a schema to show how it works: imagine we want to express the proposition that anyone who is the best computer scientist, is Katherine Johnson. To do so, we need a predicate $C(x)$ to indicate that x is a computer scientist, a predicate $B(x, y)$, denoting that x is better than y.[1] Our schema is, therefore, '$\forall x(C(x) \rightarrow \forall y((C(y) \land B(x, y)) \rightarrow x = k))$'.

Identity is also useful for determining uniqueness amongst objects in our domain. For instance, to say that there is at most one computer scientist, then we write the following schema: '$\forall x \forall y((C(x) \land C(y)) \rightarrow x = y)$', which suggests that any computer scientists that we choose from our domain must refer to the same computer scientist.

To say that there are at least two computer scientists, then we need to instead use existential quantification: '$\exists x \exists y((C(x) \land C(y)) \land \neg(x = y))$', which suggests that there are at least two computer scientists that we can poll from our domain that do not refer to the same computer scientist.

Combining these ideas together allows us to represent *exactness*; suppose we wish to express that there are exactly two computer scientists. We might use the following schema: '$\exists x \exists y((C(x) \land C(y)) \land \neg(x = y)) \land \forall z(C(z) \rightarrow (x = z \lor y = z))$', which first states that there are at least two computer scientists, but follows this with a restriction stating that any computer scientist chosen from our domain must be (identical to) either x or y.

Finally, let us translate the proposition "Alan Turing is a computer scientist who is smarter than Alonzo Church, but Katherine Johnson is the smartest" using predicates $S(x, y)$ to represent that x is smarter than y, and c to represent Alonzo Church. We schematize this proposition as '$(S(a, c) \land C(a)) \land \forall x(\neg(x = k) \rightarrow S(k, x))$' (note that we do not express the propositions that Alonzo Church or Katherine Johnson are computer scientists).

Inductively Defining First-Order Logic

Much like our definition for zeroth-order logic, we can inductively define first-order logic schemata. Note that our first-order logic system uses constants and variables, whereas some textbooks and introductions to the material omit constants altogether.

---

[1]There are, perhaps, arguments against our interpretation of someone being better than everyone else to mean they are the best.

1. Variables are defined as $t, u, v, \ldots, z, t', \ldots, z'$, but are themselves not symbolic logic expressions.

2. Constants are defined as $a, b, c, \ldots, s, a', \ldots, s'$, but are themselves not symbolic logic expressions.

3. All predicates, i.e., $A, B, C, \ldots, Z, A', \ldots, Z'$, followed by one or more variables or constants wrapped in parentheses and commas are symbolic logic expressions.

4. If W is a symbolic logic expression, then $\neg W$ is a symbolic logic expression.

5. If W is a symbolic logic expression and ω is a variable, then

    (a) '$\forall \omega W$' is a symbolic logic expression.

    (b) '$\exists \omega W$' is a symbolic logic expression.

6. If W_1 and W_2 are symbolic logic expressions, then

    (a) $(W_1 \vee W_2)$ is a symbolic logic expression.

    (b) $(W_1 \wedge W_2)$ is a symbolic logic expression.

    (c) $(W_1 \rightarrow W_2)$ is a symbolic logic expression.

    (d) $(W_1 \leftrightarrow W_2)$ is a symbolic logic expression.

7. If w_1 and w_2 are either variables or constants as defined in either (1) or (2), then $(w_1 = w_2)$ is a symbolic logic expression.

Once again, as we did with zeroth-order logic, we may drop the outer-most parentheses of an expression given that it does not ambiguate said expression. For instance, the schema '$(\forall x(\forall y(P(x) \rightarrow \neg Q(y))) \vee \exists z Q(z))$' becomes '$\forall x(\forall y(P(x) \rightarrow \neg Q(y))) \vee \exists z Q(z)$'. The scope of a quantifier extends over the schema to its immediate right, meaning that the x bound by '$\forall x$' has scope over the sub-schema '$\forall y(P(x) \rightarrow \neg Q(y))$'. Consequently, we could remove the parentheses surrounding the '$\forall y$' quantifier, producing a semantically-equivalent schema: '$\forall x \forall y(P(x) \rightarrow \neg Q(y)) \vee \exists z Q(z)$'.

2.3   Sets

Sets are a fundamental construct in computer science, mathematics, and many other fields. A *set* is a collection of objects, or elements, with arbitrary ordering.

Sets are delimited by braces, i.e., $\{\ldots\}$. Objects within a set are delimited by commas, i.e., $\{\ldots, \ldots\}$. For example, $A = \{9, 8, 1, 4\}$, $B = \{a, 2, 54, bd, e\}$, $C = \{\{7, 8, 9\}, -6, \{1, a, q\}, 9\}$ are all *proper sets* because they do not contain duplicate elements. $D = \{12, 12, -6, 80\}$ is what we will denote as an *improper set*, because it has duplicates. A set that contains duplicates is equivalent to the same set with all duplicates removed. For instance, $\{9, 8, 12, 12, 4, 9, 10, 12\}$ is equivalent to $\{9, 8, 12, 4, 10\}$.

We say that an element $x \in S$ if x is a member of S. With the preceding example, $9 \in A$, $\{12, abcd, qrst\} \in C$, but $10 \notin B$.

The size, or *cardinality*, of a set S is denoted as $|S|$. For example, in the preceding examples, $|A| = 4$, $|B| = 5$, and $|C| = 4$. Elements within a nested set of a set, as exemplified with set C, do not count towards the cardinality of a set. Duplicate elements also do not affect a set's cardinality; the set $E = \{a, a, a, a, a\}$ has $|E| = 1$ because there is only one distinct element, namely a, in E. Accordingly we also categorize E as improper.

A set can be empty, as denoted by the *empty set*, i.e., $\varnothing$. In other words, there does not exist an element x that is a member of $\varnothing$. Symbolically, $\forall x,\, x \notin \varnothing$.

S' is a *subset* of some set S if and only if every element of S' is a member of S. Symbolically, we represent subset as $S' \subseteq S$, and we can formulate our definition as '$\forall S \forall S' (S' \subseteq S \leftrightarrow \forall x((x \in S') \wedge (x \in S)))$'. S'' is a *proper subset* of S if and only if every element of S'' is a member of S, but $S'' \neq S$. In other words, S'' is not the same set as S. Symbolically, we represent this idea as '$\forall S \forall S'' (S'' \subset S \leftrightarrow \forall x(x \in S'') \wedge (x \in S) \wedge (S'' \neq S))$'. A way of remembering the difference comes through the appearance of the symbol. In algebra, we represent, "x is less than or equal to y" as $x \leq y$ with the bar underneath. The same idea holds for subsets; we represent "S' is a proper subset or equal to S" as "$S' \subseteq S$".

Two sets are *equivalent* if and only if they share the same elements. Note that this definition does not account for element ordering/positioning and duplicate elements, because these properties are irrelevant when working with sets. For instance, with the previous example, D is equivalent to the set $D' = \{12, -6, 80\}$, which is equivalent to the set $D'' = \{80, 12, -6\}$. We symbolize this as, '$\forall A \forall B (\forall x(x \in A \wedge x \in B) \rightarrow A = B)$'. To clarify, this says, for any two sets A and B, A is equal to B if every element x is both a member of A and B. Interestingly, we can create another definition using subsets to define equality as follows: '$\forall A \forall B((A \subseteq B) \wedge (B \subseteq A) \rightarrow A = B)$'.

We say S is the *union* of two sets A and B if and only if S contains all elements that are members of A or members of B. We use the "cup" to represent set union, i.e., $A \cup B$. Formalizing the definition, '$\forall A \forall B \forall S (\forall x((x \in S) \leftrightarrow (x \in A \vee x \in B)) \rightarrow S = A \cup B)$'. For example, let $A = \{5, 6, 7, 8, 9\}$ and $B = \{3, 4, 5, 6, 7\}$. Thus, $A \cup B = \{3, 4, 5, 6, 7, 8, 9\}$. Note that it is impossible for the union of two sets to be the empty set as long as $|A| + |B| > 0$.

We say S is the *intersection* of two sets A and B if and only if S contains all elements that are members of both A and B. We use the "cap" to represent set intersection, i.e., $A \cap B$. Formalizing the definition, '$\forall A \forall B \forall S (\forall x ((x \in S) \leftrightarrow (x \in A) \wedge (x \in B)) \rightarrow S = A \cap B)$'. For example, let $A = \{a, b, c, d, e, f\}$, and $B = \{q, r, s, c, d, t, u\}$. Thus, $A \cap B = \{c, d\}$. Another example is, let $C = \{12, 340, \{q, r, s\}, \{\{900\}\}\}$, and $D = \{\{q, s, r\}, \{\{900\}\}, 341\}$. Thus, $C \cap D = \{\{900\}\}$. Some may find it confusing that the nested set $\{q, r, s\}$ is not part of the intersection. Recall that the definition is that $\{q, r, s\}$ from C must be a member of D, which it is not, as $\{q, s, r\} \in D$. Finally, one more example is let $E = \{a, b, c\}$, and $F = \{d, e\}$. Thus, $E \cap F = \varnothing$. It should, hopefully, be apparent that the intersection of any set with the empty set always results in the empty set.

We say S is the *difference* of two sets A and B if and only if S contains all elements that are in A but not in B. We use the backslash, i.e., $\backslash$, to represent set difference, i.e., $A \backslash B$. Formalizing the definition, '$\forall A \forall B \forall S (\forall x ((x \in S) \leftrightarrow (x \in A) \wedge (x \notin B)) \rightarrow S = A \backslash B)$'. For example, let $A = \{a, b, c, d\}$, and $B = \{b, c, d, e\}$. Thus, $A - B = \{a\}$. Another example is, let $C = \{q, r\}$, and $D = \{q, r, s, t, u, v\}$. Thus, $C - D = \varnothing$. Finally, one more example is, let $E = \{1, 2, \{3, 4\}, 5\}$, and $F = \{\{4, 3\}, 2, 6\}$. Thus, $E - F = \{1, \{3, 4\}, 5\}$.

Common Mathematical Sets

There are several popularized sets in mathematics, each being referenced by a specific special symbol.

Integers

The set of *integers*, i.e., $\mathbb{Z}$, has all positive and negative whole numbers, including zero. Thus $\mathbb{Z} = \{\ldots, -2, -1, 0, 1, 2, \ldots\}$. The set of integers has no limit on either side and continues forever.

Natural Numbers

The set of *natural numbers*, i.e., $\mathbb{N}$, contains all positive integers and zero. In computer science, we generally define $\mathbb{N}$ as $\mathbb{N} = \{0, 1, 2, \ldots\}$. Defining the natural numbers like this is controversial, since some mathematicians consider zero to not be a natural number. A way around this approach is to consider the set of non-zero positive integers, i.e., $\mathbb{N}^+$ or even $\mathbb{Z}^+$.[1]

Rational Numbers

The set of *rational numbers*, i.e., $\mathbb{Q}$, contains all numbers that are representable as a ratio $\frac{p}{q}$ for some integers p and q.

---

[1]It is provable that mathematicians can never be pleased no matter the compromise.

Real Numbers

The set of *real numbers*, i.e., $\mathbb{R}$, contains all numbers that we know, including π, e, and is the only set, out of the four that we have described, which is *uncountably infinite*.[1] In essence, this means that we cannot find an end to the representation of a number. To exemplify this idea, imagine we have the real number 0.01. By the definition of $\mathbb{R}$, we also have 0.00000000000001 as a real number. But we also have $\frac{1}{10^{999999999}}$ as a real number. We can always add a zero to the decimal representation making the number smaller than it was previously. The general idea of *countably infinite* sets versus uncountably infinite sets is to create a pairing between a set and the natural numbers. For instance, we can create a mapping between $\mathbb{Z}$ and $\mathbb{N}$ by mapping all positive integers in $\mathbb{Z}$ to odd natural numbers in $\mathbb{N}$, and map all negative integers in $\mathbb{Z}$ to even natural numbers in $\mathbb{N}$. Because we can create this correspondence, we can formally prove that the set of integers is countably infinite. On the contrary, we cannot do this with the set of real numbers, because no matter what possible mapping we attempt, even if we mapped each added zero to $0.00\ldots 01$ to a natural number, we would never even get past this "first" real number. The notion of creating a correspondence, or map, between sets is described in further detail in the next section.

---

[1]By the phrase "that we know", we mean to exclude the set of imaginary numbers.

2.4   Functions

Functions are often introduced to students in middle or high school. Though, it is rare that curricula at this level discuss the theory behind what general function actually does. As an example, we can denote the square root of a number x via a function Sqrt.

A *function*, as an informal reintroduction, is a construct that receives some input, performs some operation, and returns an output. For example, we can write a function $f(x) = x^2$ to square a number x. In this definition, f is the function name, x is the input argument, and the body, i.e., the operation to-be performed is x^2. The data returned is the result after applying, or unwrapping, the value of x inside the operation. We can proceed through this derivation step-by-step to understand it better.

$$f(x) = x^2 \tag{2.1}$$
$$f(3) = x^2 \tag{2.2}$$
$$f(3) = 3^2 \tag{2.3}$$
$$f(3) = 9 \tag{2.4}$$

Line (2.1) simply repeats our function name, input variable name, and function body for convenience. Line (2.2) invokes a call to f with an input of 3. Line (2.3) shows the process of applying the values of the input variable x to every occurrence of x in the function body. Lastly, in (2.4), we compute the result of the expression.

Domain, Codomain, and Range

Functions are maps over sets. We *map* an element x from a set A to an element y of a set B if $f(a) = b$ for a function f. Let us narrow our set scope for a minute to get a better picture of function properties. The *domain D* of a function f is a set of its possible inputs. The *codomain D'* of a function f is a set of its possible outputs. The *range R* of a function f is the set of mapped values from D to D'. That is, if there exists x and y such that $f(x) = y$, then $y \in D'$. Let us see an example before continuing further.

Example. Let $D = \{a, b, c\}$ and $D' = \{1, 2, 3, 4\}$. Further suppose that a function g maps values from D to D', namely as $g(a) = 2$, $g(b) = 4$, $g(c) = 2$. The range of g is therefore $\{2, 4\}$.

Image and Pre-image

The *image* of a function f, denoted as $f(I)$, is a set such that, when given a set $I \subseteq D$, we get all elements mapped to those in I. The *pre-image* of a function f, denoted as $f^{-1}(I)$, is a set such that, when given a set $I \subseteq D'$, we get all mapping values from D. Again, we present an example.

Example. Using the definitions of D and D' from earlier, we can deduce multiple images and pre-images.

Possible images:

$$f(\{a\}) = \{2\}$$
$$f(\{b,c\}) = \{4,2\}$$
$$f(\{d\}) = \varnothing$$

Possible pre-images:

$$f^{-1}(\{1,2,3\}) = \{a,c\}$$
$$f^{-1}(\{1,4\}) = b$$
$$f^{-1}(\{1,3\}) = \varnothing$$

A good rule-of-thumb for images is to ask, "For these values of D, what values do I get from D'?", and for pre-images we ask, "For these values of D', what values map them from D?".

Importantly, functions must map one value to only one other value. Therefore a function f cannot map an input x to distinct outputs y and y'.

For a "square" function, its domain might be $\mathbb{Z}$ with its codomain as $\mathbb{N}$. The "square root" function, on the other hand, is a function only if we limit its codomain to the set of real numbers greater than or equal to zero because $\sqrt{x}$ maps input elements to multiple output elements in that its result can be either positive or negative. E.g., $\sqrt{25} = \pm 5$. Note that its domain might be the set of real numbers greater than or equal to zero; negative real numbers are undefined for the square root function.

The most commonly-presented functions throughout primary/secondary education are unary functions, i.e., functions of one input such as $f(x)$. Nothing is stopping us from defining a function that has multiple inputs. As an example, let $h(a,b) = 5$, where $a,b \in D$ and $5 \in D'$. Functions of two arguments are binary, and use ordered pairs to denote their inclusion in the domain. The set of possible inputs is defined as the cross product $D \times D \to D'$. We use binary functions almost, if not, daily without realizing. Suppose we define addition as a binary function Add over the set of natural numbers. We know that $\mathbb{N} \times \mathbb{N} = \{(0,0),(0,1),(0,2),\ldots\}$, and can define $\mathsf{Add}(m,n) = m+n$. Of course, we rely on the definition of addition from the $+$ symbol, but this simplification helps our discussion, since we can conclude that $m+n \in \mathbb{N}$. Ternary functions are also possible, requiring three inputs rather than one or two. We could go on, but any non-negative number of inputs to a function is definable.

Operations and Properties

Functions are sometimes called operations when they exhibit certain properties. Addition, or $+$, is an associative and commutative binary operation over the set of real numbers. An operation $\circ$ is *associative* over a set S if, for all elements $x, y, z \in S$, $x \circ (y \circ z)$ is equal to $(x \circ y) \circ z$. For instance, if $x, y, z \in \mathbb{Z}$, $(x + y) + z$ is equal to $(x + (y + z))$. An operation $\circ$ is *commutative* over a set S if, for all elements $x, y \in S$, $x \circ y$ is equal to $y \circ x$. For instance, if $x, y \in \mathbb{Z}$, $x + y$ is equal to $y + x$. Another example of an associative and commutative operation is multiplication over the set of real numbers. Subtraction, on the other hand, is neither commutative nor associative over the set real numbers. It is, however, both associative and commutative over the set $\{x, x, x, \ldots\}$ for any real number x. We can change the properties of an operation by modifying the set it is over. Classifying properties of operations in this way is not as interesting, since we most often care about larger sets such as the natural numbers, integers, or reals. We can categorize an operation $\circ$ and a set S as a *group* if $\circ$ is associative, there exists an element e such that $e \circ x = e$ for all $x \in S$, and there is a (not necessarily distinct) y such that $x \circ y = e$ for all $x \in S$. As an example, we can form a group G as $+$ over $\mathbb{Z}$ because addition is associative, any integer added to zero gets us that integer, and every integer has a negative counterpart we can add to get zero. Group theory and abstract algebra present these topics in far greater detail, so we will end the discussion here.

Recursive Functions

Recursive functions, and the idea behind recursion confuses many students and beginners to computer science, but a proper understanding is fundamental to programming and mathematics. A *recursive function* is a function f that calls itself. For example, the simplest recursive function may be defined as $f() = f()$, which states that f is a function that receives no arguments and calls itself. When we call a recursive function, we substitute the call with the function body. This is a bit difficult to visualize with a function of no arguments, so why not introduce a function $g(x)$ that receives some argument x whose definition adds x to a recursive call to g, i.e., $g(x) = x + g(x)$. When we evaluate the recursion, we see this resolves to $g(x) = x + x + x + \cdots + x$, for an infinite number of x's. Though, what is interesting about recursion is that we can define primitive operations, such as addition, via recursion. This form of recursion will be over the set of natural numbers. Hence we refer to recursive functions over $\mathbb{N}$ as *naturally-recursive* functions.

When we add two numbers, say, 3 and 2, we certainly know that their sum is 5. Though, what if we did not know how to add two numbers? Suppose that all we were given are two functions $\mathsf{add1}(x)$ and $\mathsf{sub1}(x)$, where $\mathsf{add1}(x)$ returns the next natural number after x, namely $x + 1$. $\mathsf{sub1}(x)$, on the contrary, returns the previous natural number before x, namely $x - 1$.[1] Assuming that these are the only two possible ways we can add numbers, we can write the function, $x + y$, using recursion.

---

[1] The range of the $\mathsf{sub1}$ function is only positive integers; meaning $\forall n \leq 1$, $\mathsf{sub1}(n) = 0$.

Because of our prior knowledge on elementary arithmetic, we can say, with absolute certainty, that $3 + 2$ is equal to $4 + 1$ which is equal to $5 + 0$. Conveniently enough, we know that $x + 0 = x$ for any number x. We can use this to determine a *terminating condition*, i.e., when to stop recursing. That is, when $y = 0$, we stop recursively adding values, since $x + 0$ is just x. Let us walk through the example step-by-step.

(i) Given $3 + 2$, we know that, with $x = 3$ and $y = 2$, y is not zero, so we can add one to x and subtract one from y. Namely, $\mathsf{add1}(3) + \mathsf{sub1}(2) = 4 + 1$.

(ii) We now have $4 + 1$, we know that, with $x = 4$ and $y = 2$, y is not zero, so we can add one to x and subtract one from y. Namely, $\mathsf{add1}(4) + \mathsf{sub1}(1) = 5 + 0$.

(iii) We now have $5 + 0$, we know that, with $x = 5$ and $y = 0$, y is equal to zero, so we simply return x, which is 5. Therefore, the correct result is obtained.

So, we continuously subtract one from y and continuously add one to x until y is zero. We can define this as a piece-wise function (recall the definition of such functions from the previous sections) where $\mathsf{add}(x, y)$ corresponds to $x + y$.

$$
\mathsf{add}(x, y) = \begin{cases} x & \text{if } y = 0 \\ \mathsf{add}(\mathsf{add1}(x), \mathsf{sub1}(y)) & \text{if } y > 0 \end{cases}
$$

As another example, we will add 10 and 4 using this recursive algorithm. Though, we will be a bit less verbose and not explicitly mention the values for x and y.

(i) We have $10 + 4$. Clearly, y is not zero, so we, instead, compute $\mathsf{add1}(10) + \mathsf{sub1}(4) = 11 + 3$.

(ii) We now have $11 + 3$. Clearly, y is not zero, so we compute $\mathsf{add1}(11) + \mathsf{sub1}(3) = 12 + 2$.

(iii) We have $12 + 2$. Clearly, y is not zero, so we compute $\mathsf{add1}(12) + \mathsf{sub1}(2) = 13 + 1$.

(iv) We now have $13 + 1$. Clearly, y is not zero, so we compute $\mathsf{add1}(13) + \mathsf{sub1}(1) = 14 + 0$.

(v) We now have $14 + 0$. Clearly, y is zero, so we return x, which is 14.

With addition out of the way, let us implement monus. No, that is not a spelling mistake—monus is a subtraction-like operation defined only for natural numbers. That is, $x \mathbin{\dot-} y$ is defined only for those x that are greater than or equal to y. Thus, $x \mathbin{\dot-} y \geq 0$. We need this notion of monus, and not minus, in order to write a recursive algorithm because again, we need a terminating condition. We know that $x \mathbin{\dot-} 0 = x$, so we can use this as our terminating condition. Namely, when $y = 0$, return x. Otherwise, call the function recursively. How can we do this using only add1 and sub1? Well, firstly, we need only to use sub1 because we know that, for instance, $5 \mathbin{\dot-} 3$ is equal to $4 \mathbin{\dot-} 2$ which is equal to $3 \mathbin{\dot-} 1$, which is equal to $2 \mathbin{\dot-} 0$. So, instead of adding one to x as part of the recursive step, we subtract one from both operands and only stop once y reaches zero. Let us walk through the example step-by-step.

(i) Given $5 \mathbin{\dot-} 3$, we know that y is not zero, so we can subtract one from x and subtract one from y. Namely, $\mathsf{sub1}(5) \mathbin{\dot-} \mathsf{sub1}(3) = 4 \mathbin{\dot-} 2$.

(ii) We now have $4 \mathbin{\dot-} 2$. y is not zero, so we can subtract one from both x and y. Namely, $\mathsf{sub1}(4) \mathbin{\dot-} \mathsf{sub1}(2) = 3 \mathbin{\dot-} 1$.

(iii) We now have $3 \mathbin{\dot-} 1$. y is not zero, so we can subtract one from both x and y. Namely, $\mathsf{sub1}(3) \mathbin{\dot-} \mathsf{sub1}(1) = 2 \mathbin{\dot-} 0$.

(iv) We now have $2 \mathbin{\dot-} 0$. y is zero, so we can return 2.

This completes the example. Let us define monus as a recursive piecewise function similar to our approach to addition. We will use $\mathsf{sub}(x\ y)$ to represent $x \mathbin{\dot-} y$.

$$
\mathsf{sub}(x, y) = \begin{cases} x & \text{if } y = 0 \\ \mathsf{sub}(\mathsf{sub1}(x), \mathsf{sub1}(y)) & \text{if } y > 0 \end{cases}
$$

What about multiplication over natural numbers? We can actually use our definition of addition in a definition for a recursive multiplication function. Let us take an example. Once again, because of our prior knowledge, we know that $5 \cdot 3$ is equal to 15. Though, we can represent this as follows. $5 \cdot 3 = 5 + (5 \cdot 2)$ which is equal to $5 + 5 + (5 \cdot 1)$ which is equal to $5 + 5 + 5$. So, we see that multiplication is nothing more than repeated addition. Instead of zero, however, we use one as our terminating condition, because $x \cdot 1 = x$. Thus, when $y = 1$ in $x \cdot y$, we return x. Let us walk through the example step-by-step.

(i) Given $5 \cdot 3$, we know that y is not one, so let us add x to the result of multiplying x by $\mathsf{sub1}(y)$. Namely, $5 + (5 \cdot \mathsf{sub1}(3)) = 5 + (5 \cdot 2)$.

(ii) We now must compute $5 \cdot 2$. y is not one, so let us add x to the recursive function call. Namely, $5 + (5 \cdot \mathsf{sub1}(2)) = 5 + (5 \cdot 1)$

(iii) We now must compute $5 \cdot 1$. y is clearly one, so we return 5.

At this point, we start a process called recursion unwinding. That is, we have the result of the base case, but we need to substitute these values in for the previous recursive calls. We evaluate these "recursive unwinds" from bottom-to-top.

(i) 5 is the base case for $5 \cdot 1$. We substitute 5 in for this expression in $5 + (5 \cdot 1)$ to get $5 + 5 = 10$, which is the value of $(5 \cdot 2)$.

(ii) We can substitute 10 in for the expression $5 + (5 \cdot 2)$ to get $5 + 10 = 15$, which is the value of $(5 \cdot 3)$, which is our answer.

With this example, we can write our recursive piece-wise definition for multiplication in terms of addition. We will use $\mathsf{mult}(x, y)$ to represent $x \cdot y$, or xy without the explicit symbol:

$$\mathsf{mult}(x, y) = \begin{cases} x & \text{if } y = 1 \\ \mathsf{add}(x, \mathsf{mult}(x, \mathsf{sub1}(y))) & \text{if } y > 1 \end{cases}$$

Now that we have explained recursion for simple arithmetic functions, we can move on to slightly harder concepts found in subsequent chapters. We will revisit and reintroduce natural recursion in Chapter 5 with the added benefit of implementing these rules in a programming language!

2.5   Proofs

What is a proof? A *proof* is a sequence of logical deductions from premises to a conclusion. When we prove something, we state facts in an attempt to convince ourselves, or **others**, that the conclusion is true. There are several methods of proof, and we will go through many examples.

When writing proofs, it is important to be diligent and careful with explanations. Similarly, stating things that are perhaps obvious to some, is always a good idea, e.g., definitions of even/odd numbers. In addition, all proofs should begin with *Proof:* and conclude with "QED", or a square $\square$. QED, or the square, symbolizes the Latin phrase, "Quod erat demonstrandum", which translates to, "which was to be stated". In other words, it designates the end of a proof.[1]

Direct Proofs

A direct proof takes the form of an implication, namely, "If p then q". When we prove such statements directly, we assume the antecedent p, and with this, we attempt to show that the consequent q cannot be false.

Example. "If x is even, then $(x)^2$ is even".

Proof. First, we assume the antecedent, namely "x is even", is true. Thus, x is an even number of the form $2k$ for some integer k. Now, we need to show that $(x)^2$ is also even. Let us plug in $2k$ for x to get $(2k)^2$. Expanding this out, we get $(2k \cdot 2k)$, which after factoring, we get $2(k + k)$. If we let $l = (k + k)$, we can substitute the parenthesized expression for l to get $2l$, which by definition is an even number. Therefore, if x is even, then $(x)^2$ is even.   QED.

Example. "If x and y are odd integers, then $x + y$ is even".

Proof. Assume that x and y are odd, meaning they are of the form $x = 2k + 1$ and $y = 2m + 1$ for some integers k and m. Substituting these in for $x + y$ gets us $(2k + 1) + (2m + 1) = 2k + 2m + 2$. Factoring gets us $2(k + m + 1)$. If we let $l = k + m + 1$, we can substitute the parenthesized expression for l to get $2l$, which by definition is an even number. Therefore, if x and y are odd integers, then $x + y$ is even.   QED.

Example. "The square of an odd integer is always odd".

Proof. Let us turn this statement into a conditional: "If x is an odd integer, then $(x)^2$ is odd". Now, assume x is odd, meaning $x = 2k + 1$ for some integer k. Thus, $(x)^2 = (2k+1) \cdot (2k+1) = 4k+4+1$. Factoring this result gets us $2(2k+2)+1$. Let $l = 2k + 2$, which after substituting gets us $2l + 1$, the definition of an odd integer. Thus, if x is an odd integer, then $(x)^2$ is odd.   QED.

---

[1]Formatting a proof in this fashion is largely a stylistic choice; as long as the argument and reasoning are clear, any variation is acceptable.

Example. "If $a \mid b$ and $b \mid c$, then $a \mid c$".

Recall the definition of $a \mid b$: $a \mid b$ means that $ax = b$ for some integer x. In other words, we can evenly divide b by a to get some integer x. Example: $3 \mid 6$ because $3(2) = 6$.

This proof asks us to prove the transitive property of division: if we can divide some number b by a, and we can further divide some number c by b, then we can divide c by a, i.e., a is a multiple of both b and c.

Proof. Assume that the antecedent is true, indicating $a \mid b$ and $b \mid c$. This claim means that $ax = b$ and $by = c$ for some integers x and y. We can substitute the value of b in $by = c$ with the former equation, i.e., $ax = b$, as follows: $(ax)y = c$. Now, because multiplication is associative, $(ax)y = a(xy)$. Thus, we get the form $a(xy) = c$, which, if we let $l = xy$, we get $al = c$. An equivalent representation is $a \mid c$. Therefore, if $a \mid b$ and $b \mid c$, then $a \mid c$.   QED.

Example. "If $x \mid y$ and y is odd, then x is odd".

Proof. We will prove that the two conditions $x \mid y$ and y imply that x is odd. First, assume the antecedent, which means that $xm = 2k + 1$ for some integers m and k. This implies that the product of x and m results in an odd integer. The product of two integers is odd only when one of its operands is odd. Therefore x must be odd. Hence, if $x \mid y$ and y are odd, then x is odd.   QED.

Proof by Contraposition

A conditional may be easier to prove if we use its contrapositive. That is, recall that, '$p \rightarrow q$' is equivalent to '$\neg q \rightarrow \neg p$'. This equivalence is particularly useful when the antecedent of an implication is complex and full of schemata.

Example. 'If x and y are integers and $x + y$ is even, then x and y have the same parity".

We will prove this by contraposition. Namely, the contrapositive of the statement is, "If x and y do not have the same parity, then $x + y$ is odd" (note that we do not negate the piece of the premise that states that x and y are integers).

Proof. Assume, by contraposition, x and y do not have the same parity. That is, one of the values is even and the other is odd. Without loss of generality, we can assume that if the consequent holds for when x is even and y is odd, we can conclude that it holds for when x is odd and y is even. So, assume x is even and y is odd, meaning $x = 2k$ and $y = 2l + 1$ for some integers k and l. Let us now substitute in these values for x and y in $x + y$: $(2k) + (2l + 1) = 2k + 2l + 1$. Factoring out 2 gets us $2(k + l) + 1$. If we let $m = k + l$, we get $2m + 1$, which is the definition of an odd integer. Therefore, by contraposition, if x and y are integers and $x + y$ is even, then x and y have the same parity.   QED.

Example. "If x and y are real numbers where xy is irrational, then either x or y must be irrational".

Proof. Assume, by contraposition, that neither x nor y are irrational. This means that we can write $x = p/q$ and $y = r/s$ where the fractions p/q and r/s are rational numbers written in their lowest terms. We wish to show that xy is rational. We can substitute in our fractions for xy to get $(p/q)(r/s) = pq/rs$ where $q \neq 0$ and $s \neq 0$. Thus, we can represent the product of x and y as a fraction, meaning it is rational. Therefore, by contraposition, if x and y are real numbers where xy is irrational, then either x or y must be irrational.   QED.

Proof by Contradiction

A proof by contradiction, as the name implies, is an attempt to show that two claims cannot exist at the same time and, by extension, the original statement is true. For instance, a contradiction is saying that an integer x is both even and odd. A proof by contradiction is also known as an indirect proof.

Proving a direct statement 'p' by contradiction assumes that '$\neg p$' is true and attempts to derive a contradiction via this assumption. We know that this schema is a logical contradiction because '$p \wedge \neg p$' is always false for any truth value of 'p'.

Proving an implication of the form '$p \rightarrow q$' by contradiction assumes that 'p' is true and '$\neg q$' is true. For the implication to hold, a contradiction must arise, because an implication of the form '$\top \rightarrow \bot$' is false. The reason we make the aforesaid assumptions is because the goal is to prove that '$-(p \rightarrow q)$' does not hold true. Pushing the negation inward and rewriting the implication into a disjunction gives us the schema '$(p \wedge \neg q)$'. Accordingly, if we demonstrate that '$\neg p$' or 'q' hold true, then this contradicts with the true value derived from the conjunction.

Example. "If $(x)^3$ is odd, then x is odd".

Proof. We will prove that, if $(x)^3$ is odd and x is even, then we arrive at a logical contradiction. Since x is even, we can write it as $2m$ for some integer k. Plugging this into $(x)^3$ gets us $(2m)^3 = (2m \cdot 2m \cdot 2m)$. We can factor 2 out to get $2(4mmm)$. If we let $l = 4mmm$, we can substitute this in to get $2l$, the definition of an even integer. But we assumed that x^3 is odd. Therefore, by contradiction, if x^3 is odd, then x is odd.   QED.

Example. "There does not exist a largest integer".

Proof. To the contrary, we assume that there is a largest integer, which we call N. Thus, for all n, $N > n$. Now, suppose $m = N + 1$. m is an integer because it is the sum of two integers. However, $m > N$, which contradicts our claim that N is the largest integer. Therefore, by contradiction, there does not exist a largest integer.   QED.

Example. "$\sqrt{2}$ is irrational".

Proof. Aiming for a contradiction, we assume that $\sqrt{2}$ is rational. This means we can write $\sqrt{2}$ as a rational number p/q in its lowest terms. Namely, $\sqrt{2} = p/q$. Squaring both sides gets us $(\sqrt{2})^2 = (p/q)^2 = 2 = p^2/q^2$. We can rewrite this in terms of p^2 to get $p^2 = 2q^2$. From our first direct proof example, we know that when an integer x is even, x^2 is also even. Thus, p must be even, meaning we can represent it as $p = 2k$ for some integer k. Let us substitute this back into the equation: $2 = (2k)^2/q^2$, and simplifying gets us $2 = 4k^2/q^2$. Rewriting this to isolate $4k^2$ results in $2q^2 = 4k^2$. Finally, dividing both sides by 2 gives $q^2=2k^2$. Again, since q^2 is even (notice the $2k^2$), q must be even. Since p and q are even, then we know $2 \mid p$ and $2 \mid q$. This contradicts our original assumption that p/q is written in its lowest terms. Therefore, by contradiction, $\sqrt{2}$ is irrational.   QED.

Proof by Cases

Sometimes, it is necessary to prove multiple parts, or sub-pieces, of a conditional. This usually occurs when there are obvious cases in which a condition only may occur. The idea is to assume the premise within the case is true, then derive that the consequent of the original statement must also be true. When we encounter such a situation, we preface each case, or scenario, with **Case #n**.

Example. "If y is odd and x is an integer, then $x(x + y)$ is even".

Proof. Assume that the antecedent is true, namely that y is odd and x is an integer, where $y = 2k + 1$ for some integer k. There are two cases: one in which x is even, and one in which x is odd. We will prove that the consequent holds true for both cases:

Case 1: Assume that x is even, where $x = 2l$ for some integer l. Then, we can substitute in our values for x and y into the consequent expression: $2l(2l + 2k + 1)$. If $m = 2l + 2k + 1$, we get $2m$, which is an even integer.

Case 2: Assume that x is odd, where $x = 2l + 1$ for some integer l. Then, we can substitute in our values for x and y into the consequent expression: $(2l + 1)(2l + 1 + 2k + 1) = (2l + 1)(2l + 2k + 2) = 4l^2 + 2lk + 6l + 2k + 2$. Factoring out 2 gets us $2(2l^2 + 3l/2 + k + 1)$. Let $m = 2l^2 + 3l/2 + k + 1$. Thus, we get the form $2m$, which by definition is an even integer (note that the fractional $3l/2$ cancels out when multiplying the expression by two).

This covers both cases where x is an integer. Therefore, if y is odd and x is an integer, then $x(x + y)$ is even.   QED.

If and Only If Proofs

If and only **if proofs** consist of two core components: proving the "if" direction, then proving the "only if" direction. Because an if and only if is comprised of two conjoined implications, namely $p \leftrightarrow q$ is equivalent to $(p \rightarrow q) \wedge (q \rightarrow p)$, we need to write proofs for two implications. When writing the subproofs, it is important to distinguish between the two. Therefore, writing **If:** or $\rightarrow$, and **Only if:** or $\leftarrow$. Remember that the rules for proving these implications remain the same, meaning we can prove the contrapositive of one implication but not the other and still achieve a correct and conclusive result. Note that for the following first example, we explicitly state the sub-implications. In future examples, we will only use the arrows to indicate the direction of the implication used in the subproof.

Example. "The sum of two integers x and y is odd if and only if exactly one of x or y is odd".

Proof.
($\rightarrow$) We will first prove the implication, "If $x + y$ is odd, then exactly one of x or y is odd". We will prove this by contraposition. Assume that it is not the case that exactly one of x or y is odd. This means that there are two cases:

Case 1: Assume that both x and y are odd. This means that $x = 2k + 1$ and $y = 2m + 1$ for some integers k and m. $x + y$ is, therefore, $(2k + 1) + (2m + 1) = 2k + 2m + 2 = 2(k + m + 1)$, which is by definition an even integer. Thus, $x + y$ is even.

Case 2: Assume that both x and y are even. This means that $x = 2k$ and $y = 2m$ for some integers k and m. $x + y$ is, therefore, $(2k) + (2m) = 2k + 2m = 2(k + m)$, which is by definition an even integer, meaning $x + y$ is even.

So, by cases and contraposition, if $x + y$ is odd, then exactly one of x or y is odd.

($\leftarrow$) We will now prove the converse, "If exactly one of x or y is odd, then $x + y$ is odd". Assume that exactly one of x or y is odd. Without loss of generality, we can assume that x is the odd integer. Thus, $x = 2k + 1$ for some integer k, meaning $y = 2m$ for some integer m (because y cannot be odd). So, $x + y = (2k + 1) + 2m = 2k + 2m + 1 = 2(k + m) + 1$, which is the definition of an odd integer. Thus, $x + y$ is odd.

We have **proved** both implications. Therefore, the sum of two integers x and y is odd if and only if exactly one of x or y is odd.   QED.

Example. "$x^3 - y^3$ is even if and only if $x - y$ is even".

Proof.

($\rightarrow$) We will prove this by contraposition, and assume that $x - y$ is odd. The only way that $x - y$ can be odd is if exactly one of x or y is odd. So, without loss of generality, we can assume that $x = 2k + 1$ and $y = 2m$ for some integers k and m. Plugging these into $x - y$ shows that the result is odd. Substituting these into $x^3 - y^3$ gets us $(2k + 1)^3 - (2m)^3$. Expanding this out results in $(8k^3 + 12k^2 + 6k + 1) - (2m \cdot 2m \cdot 2m)$ which simplifies to $2(4k^3 + 6k^2 + 3k) - 2(4mmm) + 1$. If we let $l = (4k^3 + 6k^2 + 3k) - 2(4mmm)$, our result is of the form $2l + 1$, which is the definition of an odd integer. Therefore, by contraposition, $x^3 - y^3$ is odd.

($\leftarrow$) Assume that $x - y$ is even. This occurs when x and y have the same parity. That is, either both x and y are even, or they are both odd. We can, therefore, use case analysis:

Case 1: Assume that x and y are even, in that $x = 2k$ and $y = 2l$ for any integers k and l. Thus, to reaffirm our assumption, $(2k) - (2l) = 2(k - l)$, an even integer. Moreover, $x^3 - y^3 = (2k)^3 - (2l)^3 = 2(4k^3 - 4l^3)$, an even integer. Therefore, $x^3 - y^3$ is even.

Case 2: Assume that x and y are odd, in that $x = 2k + 1$ and $y = 2l + 1$ for any integers k and l. Thus, to reaffirm our assumption, $(2k + 1) - (2l + 1) = 2(k - l)$, an even integer. Moreover, $x^3 - y^3 = (2k + 1)^3 - (2l + 1)^3 = 2(4k^3 - 4l^3 + 6k^2 - 6l^2 + 3k - 3l)$, an even integer.

So, by cases, $x^3 - y^3$ is even.

We have proved both implications. Therefore, $x^3 - y^3$ is even if and only if $x - y$ is even.   QED.

Example. Prove that $x + y$ is even if and only if $x - y$ is even for all integers x and y.

Proof.

($\rightarrow$) We will prove this directly and assume that $x + y$ is even. This means that $x + y = 2k$ where k is some integer. Let us write an equation in an attempt to substitute $2k$ into $x - y$:

$$x + y = 2k$$
$$x = 2k - y$$
$$x - y = (2k - y) - y$$
$$x - y = (2k - 2y)$$
$$x - y = 2(k - y)$$

Let $m = k - y$, which gets us $2m$ where m is some integer. Thus, if $x + y$ is even, then $x - y$ is even.

($\leftarrow$) We will **prove this** by contraposition, in which we have the statement if $x+y$ is odd, then $x-y$ is odd. Let us assume that $x+y$ is odd, meaning that $x+y = 2k+1$ where k is some integer. Let us again write an equation in an attempt to substitute $2k+1$ into $x-y$:

$$x + y = 2k + 1$$
$$x = 2k + 1 - y$$
$$x - y = (2k + 1 - y) - y$$
$$x - y = (2k + 1 - 2y)$$
$$x - y = 2(k - y) + 1$$

Let $m = k - y$, which gets us $2m + 1$ where m is some integer. Thus, if $x + y$ is odd, then $x - y$ is odd.

We have **proved** both conditionals. Therefore, $x + y$ is even if and only if $x - y$ is even.   QED.

2.6   Natural Deduction

Most proofs are completed via a sequence, or chain, of deductive steps to reach a logical conclusion. One such approach for proving statements is via *natural deduction*. While this method of proof has different names in slightly different contexts, the idea is to apply predefined rules and axioms to a set of premises to arrive at the desired conclusion. A benefit to using natural deduction is that its rules, in general, flow from what makes sense intuitively, hence the "natural" qualifier. For our purposes, we will apply natural deduction to both zeroth and first-order logic problems, starting with the former.

In a natural deduction proof, we have an argument $A(P,c)$, where P may be extended with premises and derivations towards the conclusion. Let us do a ton of examples to present this technique and its axioms. As we said, however, natural deduction is taught in numerous ways, applicable to many contexts; our technique will be similar with the exception of adding and removing axioms when necessary out of simplicity.

Example. $A(\{p \rightarrow q, p\}, q)$. When we begin a natural deduction style proof, we write down each premise one after another on separate lines with annotations to the right that state that they are, in fact, premises. Subsequent lines are derivations from these premises or other presumed assumptions (more on this later).

$$
\begin{array}{ll}
1 & p \rightarrow q \qquad \text{P} \\
2 & p \qquad\qquad \text{P}
\end{array}
$$

Where do we go from here? We want to prove 'q', and we know that '$p \to q$' and 'p' are true by the assertion that they are premises. Recall from its truth table that an implication is true if and only if it is not the case that the antecedent is true and the consequent is false. Therefore, because the antecedent, namely 'p', is true, it must be the case that 'q' is true. Intuitively, this idea should also make sense. So, we conclude that 'q' is true via *modus ponens*, or $\to$-elimination (abbreviated as $\to_{\text{elim}}$). In a natural deduction proof, after a derivation step, we specify the rule as well as the lines used in that rule.

$$
\begin{array}{ll}
1 \quad | \ p \to q & \text{P} \\
2 \quad | \ p & \text{P} \\
3 \quad | \ q & \to_{\text{elim}}, 1, 2 \\
\end{array}
$$

Because we reached the conclusion, this completes the proof. QED.

Example. $A(\{p \to q, q \to r\}, p \to r)$

$$
\begin{array}{ll}
1 \quad | \ p \to q & \text{P} \\
2 \quad | \ q \to r & \text{P} \\
\end{array}
$$

This proof is slightly more complicated because it brings rise to a new rule, namely $\to$-introduction (abbreviated as $\to_{\text{intro}}$). We want to show that, if '$p \to q$' is true and '$q \to r$' is true, then it holds that '$p \to r$' is true. Some may view this as a transitive implication, and that line of thought is exactly correct. Furthermore, this style of argumentation is, in fact, an axiom in many natural deduction systems called hypothetical syllogism. For us, however, we will prove the implication holds true through the notion of sub-proofs and $\to_{\text{intro}}$. The $\to_{\text{intro}}$ rule is defined as follows: if, by assuming φ we can derive ψ, then we can derive '$\varphi \to \psi$'. So, the first part of the $\to_{\text{intro}}$ rule is to assume the antecedent of the implication is true. Because we are trying to deduce that 'r' is true under the assumption that 'p' is true, we will indent this as a sub-proof.

$$
\begin{array}{ll}
1 \quad | \ p \to q & \text{P} \\
2 \quad | \ q \to r & \text{P} \\
3 \quad | \quad | \ p & \text{Ass.} \\
\end{array}
$$

Now we show that 'q' is true by $\to_{\text{elim}}$, and from this, show that r is true by the same logic.

$$
\begin{array}{ll}
1 \quad | \ p \to q & \text{P} \\
2 \quad | \ q \to r & \text{P} \\
3 \quad | \quad | \ p & \text{Ass.} \\
4 \quad | \quad | \ q & \to_{\text{elim}}, 1, 3 \\
5 \quad | \quad | \ r & \to_{\text{elim}}, 2, 4 \\
\end{array}
$$

We have shown that, if we assume 'p', we can deduce 'r'. Hence, we may conclude that '$p \to r$'. Because this completes the sub-proof, we un-indent its conclusion.

$$
\begin{array}{r|l l}
1 & p \to q & \text{P} \\
2 & q \to r & \text{P} \\
3 & \quad p & \text{Ass.} \\
4 & \quad q & \to_{\text{elim}}, 1, 3 \\
5 & \quad r & \to_{\text{elim}}, 2, 4 \\
6 & p \to r & \to_{\text{intro}}, 3\text{---}5 \\
\end{array}
$$

This, of course, completes the collective proof. QED.

Example. $A(\{p, q, p \land r\}, p \land (q \land r))$

$$
\begin{array}{r|l l}
1 & p & \text{P} \\
2 & q & \text{P} \\
\end{array}
$$

This next **proof** is incredibly simple and showcases two rules involving conjunction: $\land_{\text{intro}}$ and $\land_{\text{elim}}$. The former allows us to conjoin any two schemata that are currently "active". On the other hand, the latter rule allows us to prove either proposition of a conjunction. Recall that a conjunction is true if and only if both operands are true. So, if we want to create our desired conclusion, we should split '$p \land r$' to get 'r', then use the introduction rule twice.

$$
\begin{array}{r|l l}
1 & p & \text{P} \\
2 & q & \text{P} \\
3 & p \land r & \text{P} \\
4 & r & \land_{\text{elim}}, 3 \\
5 & q \land r & \land_{\text{intro}}, 2, 4 \\
6 & p \land (q \land r) & \land_{\text{intro}}, 1, 5 \\
\end{array}
$$

This completes the proof. QED.

Example. $A(\{t, (r \land \neg s) \to p, \neg s, t \to r\}, p \lor q)$

Let us put the rules that we have learned so far to the test and introduce a new rule: $\lor_{\text{intro}}$. $\lor_{\text{intro}}$ allows us to take any schema and affix any other arbitrary schema with disjunction. Recall that a disjunction is true if and only if at least one of its operands are true. So, if we know that an arbitrary schema φ is true, then it must be the case that '$\varphi \lor \psi$' is true for any schema ψ. In this proof, we must isolate 'p' so we may apply $\lor_{\text{intro}}$.

$$
\begin{array}{r|l l}
1 & t & \text{P} \\
2 & (r \land \neg s) \to p & \text{P} \\
3 & \neg s & \text{P} \\
4 & t \to r & \text{P} \\
5 & r & \to_{\text{elim}}, 1, 4 \\
6 & r \land \neg s & \land_{\text{intro}}, 6, 3 \\
7 & p & \to_{\text{elim}}, 2, 6 \\
8 & p \lor q & \lor_{\text{intro}}, 7 \\
\end{array}
$$

This completes the proof. QED.

Example. $A(\{p \lor q, p \to r, q \to r\}, r)$

$$
\begin{array}{r|ll}
1 & p \lor q & \text{P} \\
2 & p \to r & \text{P} \\
3 & q \to r & \text{P}
\end{array}
$$

A natural deduction proof technique that we have omitted until now is otherwise called an indirect proof or a proof by contradiction. We saw how this works for formal proofs with numbers and other statements, but we can generalize it with schemata. That is, assume '$\neg A$' for some schema A. Then, show that, by assuming '$\neg A$', we reach a contradiction. We are then allowed to conclude that '$\neg A$' must be true. Recall that we reach a contraction when, for any premise '$\neg A$', we deduce '$A \land \neg A$'. Let us try this out by proving another form of $\to_{\text{elim}}$, namely modus tollens: the law of contraposition. In addition, we will make use of two new rules: double negation elimination (DNE), which allows us to conclude a proposition A from '$\neg\neg A$', as well as double negation introduction (DNI), which allows us to conclude '$\neg\neg A$' from a proposition A.

Example. $A(\{p \to q, \neg q\}, \neg p)$

$$
\begin{array}{r|lll}
1 & p \to q & & \text{P} \\
2 & \neg q & & \text{P} \\
3 & & \neg\neg p & \text{Ass.} \\
4 & & p & \text{DNE, 3} \\
5 & & q & \to_{\text{elim}}, 1, 4 \\
6 & & q \land \neg q & \land_{\text{intro}} \\
7 & & \bot & \text{False, 6} \\
8 & \neg p & & \text{IP, 3–7}
\end{array}
$$

This completes the proof. QED.

Example. $A(\{p \lor q, \neg p\}, q)$

Let us prove disjunctive syllogism (DS). Though, there is one extra rule that we must introduce in order to complete this proof: the explosion principle. In summary, it says that from a contradiction, we may infer any premise at all. Note that this is different from an indirect proof/proof by contradiction where we explicitly assume '$\neg A$' to derive a contradiction that produces A. If we find a contradiction without any previous assumptions that aim toward a contradiction, any formula is provable (including the conclusion itself!). The proof of disjunctive syllogism may look a little funky because we nest a proof by cases inside; we need to show that by assuming 'p' and assuming 'q' separately, we deduce 'q'. The latter case is obvious, but the former requires the explosion principle.

1	$p \lor q$	P
2	$\neg p$	P
3	p	Ass.
4	$p \land \neg p$	$\land_{\text{intro}}$
5	$\bot$	False, 4
6	q	Explode, 5
7	q	Ass.
8	q	Rep, 7
9	q	Cases, 1–2, 3–6, 7–8

This completes the proof. QED.

Example. $A(\{p \to q, r \to s, p \lor r\}, q \lor s)$

Let us try another argument form: constructive dilemma. We will show that by assuming either antecedent of the provided implications, we can always derive the argument conclusion.

1	$p \to q$	P
2	$r \to s$	P
3	$p \lor r$	P
4	p	Ass.
5	q	$\to_{\text{elim}}$, 1, 4
6	$q \lor s$	$\lor_{\text{intro}}$, 5
7	$p \to (q \lor s)$	$\to_{\text{intro}}$, 4–6
8	r	Ass.
9	s	$\to_{\text{elim}}$, 2, 8
10	$q \lor s$	$\lor_{\text{intro}}$, 9
11	$r \to (q \lor s)$	$\to_{\text{intro}}$, 8–10
12	$q \lor s$	Cases, 1–3, 7, 11

This completes the proof. QED.

Example. $A(\{p \to q, r \to s, \neg q \lor \neg s\}, \neg p \lor \neg r)$

Up next, we shall prove destructive dilemma: the dual to constructive dilemma.

1	$p \rightarrow q$	P
2	$r \rightarrow s$	P
3	$\neg q \vee \neg s$	P
4	p	Ass.
5	q	$\rightarrow_{\text{elim}}$, 1, 4
6	$\neg \neg q$	DNI, 5
7	$\neg s$	DS, 3, 6
8	$\neg r$	MT, 2, 7
9	$\neg p \vee \neg r$	$\vee_{\text{intro}}$
10	$p \rightarrow \neg p \vee \neg r$	$\rightarrow_{\text{intro}}$, 4–9
11	r	Ass.
12	s	$\rightarrow_{\text{elim}}$, 2, 11
13	$\neg \neg s$	DNI, 12
14	$\neg q$	DS, 3, 13
15	$\neg p$	MT, 1, 14
16	$\neg p \vee \neg r$	$\vee_{\text{intro}}$
17	$r \rightarrow \neg p \vee \neg r$	$\rightarrow_{\text{intro}}$, 11–16
18	$\neg p \vee \neg r$	Cases 1-3, 10, 16

This completes the proof. QED.

2.7 Numbering Systems

Binary

We, as the readers, use base ten numbering in our daily lives.[1] That is, we have ten
digits ranging from 0 to 9, which form base ten numbers. After 9, we wrap around
to 10, proceeding to 19, and rolling right into 20. This continues until we run out of
"tens" decimal places at 99, hence we roll over to 100, repeating ad nauseam. Base
ten is convenient because we can represent a very large number with only a few
digit positions. Compare this to the base two system that computers use, otherwise
called *binary*. In base ten, or decimal, we have digits, whereas in binary we have
bits, or binary digits. Each bit is either 0 or 1, hence the base two name. Similar
to base ten, we wrap around and introduce a new bit once we exhaust all possible
values. Let us take a look at a table to better visualize the concept.

Base 10	Base 2
0	0
1	1
2	10
3	11
4	100
5	101
6	110
7	111

Figure 2.10: Base Ten and Base Two Equivalents from Zero to Seven

Hopefully, the pattern is evident. We will also note of a type of notation used
to distinguish between bases: we use a subscript x_{10} to indicate that x is written in
base ten, whereas y_2 is used to indicate a binary base. In general, we adopt the style
z_b to designate that the number z is in base b. Some may beg the question as to why
computers do not work with base ten, since it is the system we, as humans, rely on
daily. The answer boils down to the fact that computers use electricity and circuits;
electricity in a system either flows or it does not. This binary representation is ideal
for designing logic gates since we only work with two possibilities. Of course, this
raises another point: how do we convert from base ten to base two, or vice-versa?
Let us walk through this by a few examples, and then we can devise an algorithm.

Example. Convert 17_{10} into base two.

To convert 17_{10} into base two, we will continuously divide the number by 2,
taking the remainder and pushing it in an output space. We continue to divide our
number until its quotient is zero.

---

[1] This claim is made under the assumption that we do not switch numbering systems, or a new species
introduces us to something superior.

Input	Quotient	Remainder	Output
17	8	1	1
8	4	0	01
4	2	0	001
2	1	0	0001
1	0	1	10001

At each step, we compute the quotient, its remainder, and push the resulting remainder to the output. $17_{10} = 10001_2$. There is a simple verification method to check our work, but we will save this until we get to the section on converting from base two to base ten.

Example. Convert 63_{10} into base two.

Input	Quotient	Remainder	Output
63	31	1	1
31	15	1	11
15	7	1	111
7	3	1	1111
3	1	1	11111
1	0	1	111111

$63_{10} = 111111_2$.

Example. Convert 101_{10} into base two.

Input	Quotient	Remainder	Output
101	50	1	1
50	25	0	01
25	12	1	101
12	6	0	0101
6	3	0	00101
3	1	1	100101
1	0	1	1100101

$101_{10} = 1100101_2$.

Example. Convert 724_{10} into base two.

Input	Quotient	Remainder	Output
724	362	0	0
362	281	0	00
181	90	1	100
90	45	0	0100
45	22	1	10100
22	11	0	010100
11	5	1	1010100
5	2	1	11010100
2	1	0	011010100
1	0	1	1011010100

$724_{10} = 1011010100_2$.

In each of these examples, we perform the same steps to reach the desired outcome. Consequently, we can write an algorithm to convert between base ten to base two as a procedure:

---

(1) Store input into N.

(2) Store N/A into *Result*.

(3) **If** N is greater than zero **GoTo** (4), **Else GoTo** (7)

(4) Append (N mod 2) to front of *Result*.

(5) Set N to the quotient of N and 2.

(6) **GoTo** (3)

(7) **Display** *Result*.

Converting from base two to base ten is even simpler than the other way around. First, let us reason about what a decimal number is, at its core, and how its digit positions interplay. For instance, consider the number 342_{10}. If we didn't know that 342_{10} *is* 342 in base ten, we could check by multiplying each digit by its position as a power of ten, then summing the result. Thus, our answer is

$$= 3 \cdot 10^2 + 4 \cdot 10^1 + 2 \cdot 10^0$$
$$= 3 \cdot 100 + 4 \cdot 10 + 2 \cdot 1$$
$$= 300 + 40 + 2$$
$$= 342$$

This exact principle is shared among any base and not exclusive to base ten. To demonstrate, let us convert the base two values from the previous exercises back into base ten.

Example. Convert 10001_2 to base ten.

Like we said, we can use the principle that each bit corresponds to a power of two, multiply them by the bit at that position, and sum the results.

$$= 1 \cdot 2^4 + 0 \cdot 2^3 + 0 \cdot 2^2 + 0 \cdot 2^1 + 1 \cdot 2^0$$
$$= 1 \cdot 16 + 0 \cdot 8 + 0 \cdot 4 + 0 \cdot 2 + 1 \cdot 1$$
$$= 16 + 0 + 0 + 0 + 1$$
$$= 17$$

So, $10001_2 = 17_{10}$.

Example. Convert 111111_2 to base ten.

$$= 1 \cdot 2^5 + 1 \cdot 2^4 + 1 \cdot 2^3 + 1 \cdot 2^2 + 1 \cdot 2^1 + 1 \cdot 2^0$$
$$= 1 \cdot 32 + 1 \cdot 16 + 1 \cdot 8 + 1 \cdot 4 + 1 \cdot 2 + 1 \cdot 1$$
$$= 32 + 16 + 8 + 4 + 2 + 1$$
$$= 63$$

So, $111111_2 = 63_{10}$.

Example. Convert 1100101_2 to base ten.

$$= 1 \cdot 2^6 + 1 \cdot 2^5 + 0 \cdot 2^4 + 0 \cdot 2^3 + 1 \cdot 2^2 + 0 \cdot 2^1 + 1 \cdot 2^0$$
$$= 1 \cdot 64 + 1 \cdot 32 + 0 \cdot 16 + 0 \cdot 8 + 1 \cdot 4 + 0 \cdot 2 + 1 \cdot 1$$
$$= 64 + 32 + 0 + 0 + 4 + 0 + 1$$
$$= 101$$

So, $1100101_2 = 101_{10}$.

Example. Convert 1011010100_2 to base ten.

$$= 1 \cdot 2^9 + 0 \cdot 2^8 + 1 \cdot 2^7 + 1 \cdot 2^6 + 0 \cdot 2^5 + 1 \cdot 2^4 + 0 \cdot 2^3 + 1 \cdot 2^2 + 0 \cdot 2^1 + 0 \cdot 2^0$$
$$= 1 \cdot 512 + 0 \cdot 256 + 1 \cdot 128 + 1 \cdot 64 + 0 \cdot 32 + 1 \cdot 16 + 0 \cdot 8 + 1 \cdot 4 + 0 \cdot 2 + 0 \cdot 1$$
$$= 512 + 0 + 128 + 64 + 0 + 16 + 8 + 4 + 0 + 0$$
$$= 724$$

So, $1011010100_2 = 724_{10}$.

Hexadecimal

The last non-decimal numbering system that is important to us as computer scientists (that we mention, at least) is hexadecimal. Using context clues, we can infer that the prefix '*hexa*' means six, and the prefix '*deci*' means ten. Therefore hexadecimal has sixteen possible values, ranging from 0 to 9, then A to F, representing 10 to 15 respectively. Converting between binary and hexadecimal is amazingly trivial. Because this is the case, we will not describe the approach to converting directly to and from base ten to hexadecimal since it is more cumbersome and largely resembles the conversion from decimal to binary, just with base 16 powers rather than base two. Hexadecimal has interesting uses in computer programming, including a compact representation for colors, and memory address layout numbering.

Example. Convert $8A_{16}$ into base two.

To convert $8A_{16}$, we split the number character-by-character, and convert each hexadecimal character individually. 8_{16} is 1000_2, and A_{16} is 10_{10}, which is 1010_2. From there we conjoin the two binary numbers to get $8A_{16} = 10001010_2$.

Example. Convert $94C0B53_{16}$ into base two.

Although this number is rather large, the process is the same as before, just more laborious. $9_{16} = 1001_2$, $4_{16} = 0100_2$, $C_{16} = 1100_2$, $0_{16} = 0000_2$, $B_{16} = 1011_2$, $5_{16} = 0101_2$, $3_{16} = 0011_2$. Conjoining each sub-binary number gets us $94C0B53_{16} = 1001010011000000101101010011_2$.

Let us go the other direction and convert a binary number into hexadecimal. Fortunately the process brings nothing new to the table, although it begins to feel mundane.

Example. Convert 100011_2 to hexadecimal.

Converting 100011_2 into hexadecimal may seem scary at first because the number of bits is not divisible by four. Worry not, though, because we can just pad leading zeroes to the front of the number if we so choose without losing any semantic detail. So, $0010_2 = 2_{16}$ and $0011_2 = 3_{16}$, meaning $100011_2 = 23_{16}$.

Example. Convert 1100010111010001101_2 to hexadecimal.

Again, we split the binary number into groups of four bits as follows: $0110_2 = 6_{16}$, $0010_2 = 2_{16}$, $1110_2 = E_{16}$, $1000_2 = 8_{16}$, and $1101_2 = D_{16}$. Thus we arrive at the result $1100010111010001101_2 = 62E8D_{16}$.

3   Data Structures

Bad programmers worry about the code. Good programmers worry about data structures and their relationships.

—Linus Torvalds

3.1   Motivation for Data Structures

Our discussion of data structures will be one that is language-agnostic. In other words, we shall cover the theoretical aspects of data structures rather than implement them in a specific programming language. The lessons we take from this, however, will be invaluable later on, particularly once we start programming and writing our interpreters. For now, though, we will use mostly descriptions, diagrams, and *pseudocode*—a dialect that mimics real programming code. The benefit of using pseudocode is that we do not need to worry about the syntax or intricacies of any particular language.

3.2   Arrays

Arrays are contiguous blocks of storage where each block contains space for n elements of a given type.[1] For example, we may declare an array of size 10 to hold integers. Arrays can store only one type of value and are not resizable. The locations of elements in an array are called *indices*, which range from 0 to $(n-1)$. Thus, the first element in an array is at index 0, while the last is at index $n-1$.[2]

An advantage to using arrays are their quick access times. Because an array is a contiguous block of slots in memory, we can retrieve an element at a requested index instantly. A disadvantage of arrays is, as we stated, they are not resizable, their size must be known before creation, and can store only one type of element. For instance, we cannot store strings and integers, together, in an array.

---

[1] *Types*, for our purposes, categorize certain values, e.g., integers, floating-point numbers, strings, and so forth.

[2] Some programming languages do not abide by this widely-used convention, e.g., Matlab, FOR-TRAN, and Lua, instead opting to index from 1 to n inclusive.

3.3   Lists

Lists are possibly the most frequently-used data structure due to their versatility and accessibility. There are two broad types of lists: *array-based lists*, or *array lists*, as well as *linked lists*. We will cover each in great detail.

Array Lists

Like arrays, *array lists* store elements of a type. Unlike arrays, however, array lists are resizable, meaning we can remove and add elements as we please. Think of an array list like a collection of items needed by a shopper when at the grocery store; each time the shopper finds an item, they cross it off the list, and if they suddenly think of another item they need which is not presently on the list, it (the new item) gets added to the bottom of the list. Inserting elements only at the rear/bottom of an array list is not mandatory; insertion between other elements is possible.

Array lists are commonly used as wrappers around arrays. What this means is, when we use array lists, the underlying structure is just an array of some static size n. If we want to increase the capacity of our array list, the underlying array is re-created of the new size, and its preexisting elements are copied over.

Some advantages to array lists are their accessibility and ease of use; most implementations are quick to set up and understand which leads to their widespread usage compared to other data structures. Additionally, like arrays, they have instant element-access times, and unlike arrays, are resizable. This feature comes with a caveat, however, in that array resizing or element deletion are not as quick of operations. Though, the way that most array lists are used, these disadvantages are often severely overshadowed and matter much less than one may expect. On the other hand, suppose that we have a situation where we need to constantly remove elements from the front of an array list. Recall that arrays are not resizable, meaning that each time we delete an element at the front of an array, we have to copy over all elements from index $[1, (n-1)]$ to a new array of size $n-1$. Doing this repeatedly induces severe performance penalties. There are performance optimizations and workarounds to prevent these types of slowdowns, but the better choice would be to use a data structure that is not restricted to a statically-sized array.

Linked Lists

Linked lists remove us from the shackles of array-based data structures, in that, as their name implies, they are a series of *nodes*, or elements, linked together in a chain of sorts. These nodes need not be adjacent in memory, but rather reference each other to find what comes next in the chain/list. For instance, if we create a linked list, it has a *front/head* element that always references, or points, to the first element in the list (upon initialization, the head refers to nothing). If we add a new element, the head now points to this first element. Subsequent additions to the list continue growing the chain and links. Namely, element 1 points to element 2, element 2 to 3, and so on.

Elements, of course, have an associated index and value, but unlike array lists, are not necessarily restricted to using values of the same type.[1] They are also not constrained to a static size even in the underlying implementation! So, we can add and remove links from the chain whenever we please with no shuffling of values around aside from links from within the chain.

Of course, these advantages are not without their disadvantages. Reading and modifying elements are slower operations than the array counterparts since the elements are not contiguous blocks in memory. Adding and removing elements are "faster" in the sense that, as we stated, copying values over to a new array is out of the question. Because of this, though, we need to iterate/traverse through the list each time we wish to reference a provided index. The same goes for inserting elements into the list. Adding or removing elements from the front or rear of the list, on the other hand, are instant operations since we keep track of the first element of the list (and we can, similarly, keep track of the last!). Linked lists are also the backbone of many other data structures as we will soon see.

3.4   Stacks

Imagine you are washing dishes, by hand, at the kitchen sink. These dishes are assorted in a single stack to your left. A dish cannot be removed from anywhere but the top of the stack because displacement anywhere else will destroy the stack. Additionally, further imagine that people are, to your dismay, adding more dishes to the stack. Again, dishes cannot be added anywhere else but the top of the stack.

The *stack* data structure is as simple as it sounds—a collection of elements that operate on the principle of last-in-first-out, or LIFO. In other words, the last thing that we enter is the first thing removed. Stack implementations contain at least the following operations: POP and PUSH, where the former removes the top-most element from the stack (if one exists), and the latter adds a new element to the top of the stack. There may also exist an operation to view, but not remove, the top-most element via PEEK.

Stacks have the advantages of instant insertion and removal times but are obviously not as flexible as an array or linked list. A practical example of a stack data structure would be an "undo" function in a document-editing program—whenever an action is made, it is pushed to an event stack. An "undo" event would resemble popping an action off this stack. We illustrate this concept in Figure 3.1.

---

[1]Using identical types throughout a data structure is *highly recommended!* That is, mixing data such as strings and numbers causes interpretation issues when we need to analyze those values in a data structure.

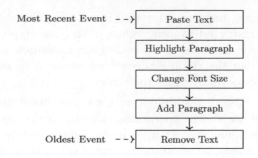

Figure 3.1: Example of "Undo" Event Stack in Text-Editing Program

3.5 Queues

Imagine you are in line at an amusement park for the most intense roller coaster in the world. Another, perhaps more generic term for a "line" is a *queue*. In this metaphor, riders enqueue the line at the back and board the roller coaster (and hence dequeue from the line) at the front.

What we have described is a practical example of the queue data structure. In a queue, elements are enqueued, or inserted, to the back of the line and are dequeued, or removed, from the front. Queues operate on the principle of first-in-first-out, or FIFO. The implementation of a queue data structure may contain different names for their operations, but at their core should contain operations for inserting an element to the back of the queue (e.g., ENQUEUE) and removing an element from the front of the queue (e.g., DEQUEUE).

Like the operations on a stack, these are also constant-time, since we may always keep a reference to the front and rear elements of a stack. Queues share similar drawbacks to stacks in that elements are not randomly accessible, in that we only know what exists at the front of a queue. Figure 3.2 demonstrates the task queue of a printer, which has a sequence of files to print one after the other.

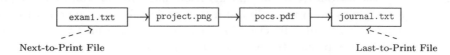

Next-to-Print File   Last-to-Print File

Figure 3.2: Example of Printer Task Queue

3.6   Sets

Sets are similar to array, with the restriction that sets cannot contain duplicate elements. Moreover, unlike arrays, there is no defined ordering of elements to a set. Thus, questions such as "What is the first/last element in the set?" are rather meaningless; the property of position is, in effect, non-existent for the users of the set data structure. Supported operations include adding and removing elements from the set, determining membership, and cardinality. We discussed sets from a mathematical perspective in Chapter 2.

3.7   Maps/Dictionaries

Dictionaries or *maps* associate *keys* with *values*. We can think of this as if we have a bunch of physical keys to physical boxes. Opening a box with its associated key retrieves its contents. Noteworthy functions include GET, which retrieves a value for a given key, PUT which adds an association, SIZE which returns the number of associations, and CONTAINSKEY which, as its name suggests, returns whether a key has an association. Figure 3.3 illustrates a mapping of *names* to *ages*, where "*Quine*" maps to 46, "*Carnap*" maps to 30, and both "*Gödel*" and "*Putnam*" map to 25.

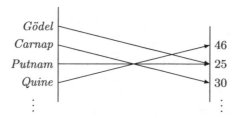

Figure 3.3: Mapping of *names* to *ages*.

3.8   Trees

Trees are fundamental data structures in computer science. Trees share a similar structure to linked lists, with the exception that elements may have multiple associated links. Trees have a *root* element, or *node*, and have branches that lead to other nodes in the tree. The nodes at the bottom of a branch are called *leaves*. Unlike trees in real life, however, trees grow from top-to-bottom, wherein the root exists at the top and leaves are at the bottom.[1]

---

[1] Many presume that trees in computer science contexts grow top-down because computer scientists never go outside. There is some partial truth to this claim.

Trees are recursive data structures because the elements of a tree are trees themselves. A popular variant of a tree is a binary tree, which is a tree that has at most two children. Being that trees are recursive data structures, it means that these children have at most two children, and so on through the tree. Below is an example of a binary tree that stores integers. In addition to integers, we may also store any data type we wish in tree nodes.

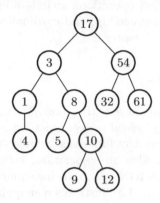

Figure 3.4: Example of Binary Tree.

3.9   Graphs

Graphs, in computer science, are not what students traditionally learn about in elementary geometry and algebra courses. In abstract math and computer science, a *graph* is a tuple $\langle V, E \rangle$, where V is the set of *vertices*, or nodes, and E is the set of edges. Edges are tuples, which serve as links between vertices. For example, Figure 3.5 shows a graph G_1 whose vertices $V = \{a, b, c, d, e, f\}$ and whose edge set $E = \{\langle a, b \rangle, \langle b, a \rangle, \langle b, c \rangle, \langle b, d \rangle, \langle b, f \rangle,$
$\langle c, b \rangle, \langle c, e \rangle, \langle d, b \rangle, \langle d, e \rangle, \langle e, c \rangle, \langle e, d \rangle, \langle e, f \rangle, \langle f, b \rangle, \langle f, e \rangle\}.$

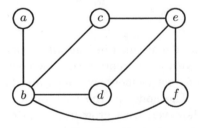

Figure 3.5: Illustration of Graph G_1

Edges can have a direction or be bidirectional. We see that G_1 has all bidirectional edges, since none use (directed) arrows to point towards a vertex. Directions on an edge disallow travel along the edge in the opposite direction. Moreover, if a graph G has an edge $\{v_1, v_2\}$ and also has the edge $\{v_2, v_1\}$, then that edge is bidirectional. Figure 3.6 shows an example of a graph G_2 using a directed edge set $E = \{\langle a, b \rangle, \langle b, d \rangle, \langle c, b \rangle, \langle d, e \rangle, \langle e, c \rangle, \langle f, b \rangle, \langle f, e \rangle\}$.

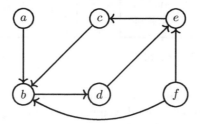

Figure 3.6: Illustration of Graph G_2

In addition to directions, edges in a graph may also be either *weighted* or *unweighted*, denoting a "cost", so to speak, to travel along an edge from one vertex to another. The edge set of a weighted graph contains triples $\langle v_1, v_2, k \rangle$, where $k \in \mathbb{R}$ is the cost from v_1 to v_2. Unweighted graphs have a constant edge weight k of one (or any other number). Figure 3.7 is an example of a graph with weights on the (directed) edges whose edge set $E = \{\langle a, b, 6 \rangle, \langle b, d, 9 \rangle, \langle c, b, 3 \rangle, \langle d, e, 4 \rangle, \langle e, c, 2 \rangle, \langle f, b, 8 \rangle, \langle f, e, 5 \rangle\}$.

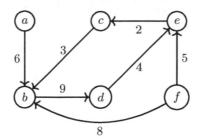

Figure 3.7: Illustration of Graph G_3

Representing graphs with the tuple/triple notation is cumbersome and prone to errors. To compensate, we can use *adjacency matrices* or *adjacency lists*. Adjacency matrices are matrices, or two-dimensional grids, where each entry corresponds to an edge between vertices. These entries contain either an edge distance or, if the graph is fully undirected, "1" indicates the existence of an edge, and "∞" indicates no edge. If a node does not have a "self-loop", its distance to itself is zero. The matrix row and column labels are the graph vertices, in which we read the entries as $\langle i, j \rangle$ for the ith row and the jth column.

	a	b	c	d	e	f
a	0	1	∞	∞	∞	∞
b	∞	0	∞	1	∞	∞
c	∞	1	0	∞	∞	∞
d	∞	∞	∞	0	1	∞
e	∞	∞	1	∞	0	∞
f	∞	1	∞	∞	1	0

Table 3.1: Adjacency Matrix of G_1

	a	b	c	d	e	f
a	0	6	∞	∞	∞	∞
b	∞	0	∞	9	∞	∞
c	∞	3	0	∞	∞	∞
d	∞	∞	∞	0	4	∞
e	∞	∞	2	∞	0	∞
f	∞	8	∞	∞	5	0

Table 3.2: Adjacency Matrix of G_3

Compare this with the adjacency list representation, which uses a linked list-esque model to designate edges and weights. For unweighted graphs, each vertex points to a list of nodes to represent connections. For weighted graphs, each vertex points to a list of tuples $\langle v, k \rangle$ where v is the linked vertex and k is the edge weight.

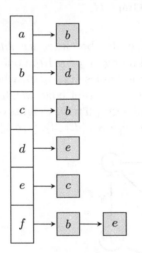

Figure 3.8: Adjacency List for G_1

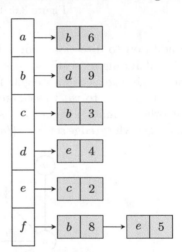

Figure 3.9: Adjacency List for G_3

Graphs are important because they provide a powerful tool for modeling and analyzing relationships between objects or entities. For one, they provide a concise and intuitive way to depict connections, interactions, dependencies, and patterns among different elements. Interestingly, many real-world problems can be mapped to graph problems, such as finding the shortest path, identifying connected components, or optimizing routes.

4   Formal Languages

The ultimate outcome of [syntactic] investigations should be a theory of linguistic structure in which the descriptive devices utilized in particular grammars are presented and studied abstractly with no specific reference to particular languages.

—Noam Chomsky

Much of our time together thus far has consisted of discussions about the history of computer science, formal logic, and elementary discrete mathematics. In this chapter, we will shift even further away from "practical" computer science in favor of explaining the fundamentals of languages and, more specifically, formal languages.

4.1   Languages

To talk about languages, we first need to define an alphabet. *Alphabets* are sets, Σ, where each element is a distinct *symbol* or a grouping of symbols. For example, $\Sigma = \{a,\ b,\ c,\ 1,\ 2,\ \pi,\ \gamma\rho\sigma\}$ is an alphabet containing seven members. Alphabets may, in theory, be infinite, but in practice are of a fixed size, or carnality.

We define a *language L* over an alphabet Σ as a subset of Σ where each element is an arrangement, or a permutation, of the letters in Σ. An arrangement of letters in an alphabet is denoted as a *word* or a *string*. For instance, if we assume L is the language over alphabet $\Sigma = \{a,\ b,\ c\}$, a word w in L may be *abc*, *ac*, *bc*, *cba*, *ccc*, *ccccccba*, and so on. An example of a word that does not belong in L is *dcba*, because $d \notin \Sigma$. Sometimes, it is useful to represent a string of no length, called the *empty string*, symbolically written as ε or λ (in this text we will use ε for canonical purposes). The empty string, ε, is by default not included in an alphabet; we include its usage via an asterisk, i.e., Σ^*, also known as the Kleene star. Namely, $\Sigma^* = \Sigma \cup \{\varepsilon\}$, meaning Σ is a subset of Σ^*.

Languages may also have constraints and rules that define the "well-formed" property of the language. That is, a language's constraints construct its valid words.

Grammars

Grammars describe the syntax of a language. Generally, we consider the grammar of the English language when determining if a sequence of words forms a sentence in accordance to the grammar rules. We will reconsider this as an example in due time, but to start off simple, we restrict our language to a very small set of strings. We define a grammar G as a set of terminals T, a set of non-terminals T', and a set of production rules R. A *terminal* is an atomic literal result of a production rule. A *non-terminal* is a set of possible paths that a string can take in a production rule. Finally, *production rules* combine and define the relationship between terminals and non-terminals. Let us see an example. Consider a language that has sentences of the form "*Subject* ' ' *Verb* ' ' *Object*". Take note that in between *Subject* and *Verb* as well as between *Verb* and *Object*, we have exactly one space in each spot.

```
T    ::=   "John" | "Alan" | "Siobahn" | "Katherine"
     |     "likes" | "enjoys" | "loathes" | "despises"
     |     "books" | "video games" | "clothes" | "food"
T'   ::=   R* S V O
```

Figure 4.1: Partial Grammar for S-V-O Language

We define T as the set of terminals, which includes several strings of subjects, verbs, and objects. The terminal set T does not place terminals into subsets; its sole purpose is to describe all possible terminals in a grammar. T' has four non-terminals: S, V, O, and R^*, designating subjects, verbs, objects, and the root production.[1] These on their own have no semantic meaning, but when combined with R, we begin to see the possible strings of this grammar.

```
T    ::=   "John" | "Alan" | "Siobahn" | "Katherine"
     |     "likes" | "enjoys" | "loathes" | "despises"
     |     "books" | "video games" | "clothes" | "food"
T'   ::=   R* S V O S
V    ::=   "likes" | "enjoys" | "loathes" | "despises"
O    ::=   "books" | "video games" | "clothes" | "food"
R*   ::=   S WS V WS O
```

Figure 4.2: Complete Grammar for S-V-O Language

Every grammar must have the non-terminal R^*, referencing the starting non-terminal, i.e., where the grammar starts for input strings. The production rule "X ::= Y Z | W" says that the left-hand non-terminal X produced the right-hand expression Y followed by Z, or the right-hand expression W, but not both. The expressions Y, Z, and W could all be terminals or non-terminals; it does not matter when describing the syntax of production rules.

---

[1] We also include a non-terminal WS, which defines a single (blank) space for separating productions.

Grammars, as we said, form the syntax of some language, wherein it validates strings as either part of or not part of the language. For example, using the prior definition of G, we may test the input string "Siobahn likes books" for presence in the language. To do so, we perform a sequence of substitution steps of the production rules for terminals and non-terminals. When checking a terminal against a non-terminal, we verify that the string is in the set of terminals produced by the non-terminal. Let us see the derivation of the string "Siobahn likes books":

$R* ::= S\ WS\ V\ WS\ O$

$R* ::=$ "Siobahn" $\in \{$ "John", ..., "Katherine"$\}\ WS\ V\ WS\ O$

$R* ::=$ "Siobahn" " " $\in \{$" "$\}\ V\ WS\ O$

$R* ::=$ "Siobahn " "likes" $\in \{$"likes", ..., "despises"$\}\ WS\ O$

$R* ::=$ "Siobahn likes" " " $\in \{$" "$\}\ O$

$R* ::=$ "Siobahn likes " "books" $\in \{$"books", "clothes", "food", "video games"$\}$

$R* ::-$ "Siobahn likes books"

Because we reach the end of the production rule and our input string has been fully examined, we conclude that the string "Siobahn likes books" is in the language described by G.

Let us write a counter example to show a non-present string, e.g., "Doug enjoys food".

$$R ::=\ \text{"Doug"} \notin \{\text{John}, ..., \text{Katherine}\}\ WS\ V\ WS\ O$$

Because "Doug" is not in the terminals produced by the non-terminal S, we reject "Doug enjoys food" from the language.

What we describe as grammars follows a specification called *Backus-Naur Form* (BNF) grammars, also sometimes referred to as its extended counterpart: *Extended Backus-Naur form* (EBNF) grammars. EBNF grammars use certain symbols to ascribe repetition or options to a production rule. As an example, the use of the Kleene closure says that a preceding expression is used zero or more times.

The potential of grammars far exceeds what we mention in this section. A grammar can be defined recursively wherein non-terminals refer to themselves. Let us see the grammar for a prefix notation arithmatic expression language.

This grammar describes a language that accepts prefix notation arithmatic expressions, e.g., '(+ 2 (* 4 5))'. For the most part, this is relatively straightforward; expressions are built in terms of themselves via *EXPR* or *NUM* non-terminals. Let us show an abbreviated derivation of the example string we provided.

```
T       ::=   "0" | "1" | ... | "9" | "+" | "-" | "*" | "/"
T'      ::=   R* WS NUM OP EXPR
WS      ::=   " "
NUM     ::=   ("0" | "1" | ... | "9")+
OP      ::=   "+" | "-" | "*" | "/"
EXPR    ::=   "(" OP WS EXPR WS EXPR ")"
        |     NUM
R*      ::=   EXPR
```

Figure 4.3: (EBNF) Grammar for Prefix Notation Arithmetic Expression Language

$R* ::= EXPR$

$R* ::= \text{``(''} \in \{\text{``(''}\}\ OP\ WS\ EXPR\ WS\ EXPR\ \text{``)''}$

$R* ::= \text{``(''}\ \text{``}+\text{''} \in \{\text{``}+\text{''},\ \text{``}-\text{''},\ \text{``}*\text{''},\ \text{``}/\text{''}\}\ OP\ WS\ EXPR\ WS\ EXPR\ \text{``)''}$

$R* ::= \text{``}(+\text{''}\ \text{``}\ \text{''} \in \{\text{``}\ \text{''}\}\ EXPR\ WS\ EXPR\ \text{``)''}$

$R* ::= \text{``}(+\ \text{''}\ \text{``}2\text{''} \in \{\text{``}0\text{''},\ \text{``}1\text{''},\ \ldots,\ \text{``}9\text{''}\}\ EXPR\ WS\ EXPR\ \text{``)''}$

$\vdots$

$R* ::= \text{``}(+\ 2\ (*\ 4\ 5))\text{''}$

One piece that is easy to omit is the use of a '+' and parentheses around the choices of the non-terminal *NUM*. The parentheses indicate a grouping of symbols, similar to how parentheses operate in traditional expressions. The plus sign without quotes, on the other hand, indicates that in order to successfully match the group, there must be at least one of the group bound to the '+'. In English, the non-terminal *NUM* refers to any sequence of digits. In contrast to the Kleene star, '+' is sometimes called the *Kleene plus*, indicating one or more matches as opposed to zero or more. Namely, we may define the Kleene plus in terms of the Kleene star as $\Sigma^+ = \Sigma\Sigma^*$. None of this answers the question of what features distinguish a Backus-Naur form grammar from an extended Backus-Naur form grammar. Grammars defined in BNF are not allowed to use these special symbols. In essence, EBNF grammars are much more expressive in their syntax; EBNF and BNF grammars are semantically equivalent and any idea expressed in the former is possible in the latter. We will describe these special symbols, e.g., Kleene star and others after we discuss regular expressions and finite automata; the latter of which takes precedence over the former.

4.2   Finite Automata

Finite automata are, in essence, very weak computers, or models of computation. Finite automata describe *transitions* between *states* in some model. To be specific, a state is an **identifier** referring to a "location" or property. The common example people refer to when explaining finite automata is a light switch. That is, a light switch has a **set of states** $Q = \{\mathsf{ON}, \mathsf{OFF}\}$, and a transition function δ describing the paths between each state, as well as the input used to get between states. Each transition requires data to "traverse" the transition, so to speak. Finite automata use input symbols belonging to an alphabet Σ. Imagine that this light switch finite automaton has the symbols $\Sigma = \{0, 1\}$. We may have a transition that goes from OFF to ON using the input 1. Moreover, we may have another transition from ON to OFF using the input 0. Thus, our transition function is a binary function $Q \times \Sigma \to Q$, mapping inputs of a state and a symbol to another state. The above example, therefore, has a transition function of two inputs: $\delta(\mathsf{OFF}, 1) = \mathsf{ON}$ and $\delta(\mathsf{ON}, 0) = \mathsf{OFF}$. A finite automaton such as this is *non-deterministic*, because it is unknown what to do if the machine receives a 1 symbol while in the ON state. In other words, $\delta(\mathsf{ON}, 1)$ does not have a mapped output. To make this *deterministic*, we need an output for every input possibility. Accordingly, each state q must have $|\Sigma|$ transitions, meaning that for a deterministic finite automaton, $|\delta| = |Q| \cdot |\Sigma|$. Transition functions do not necessarily need to lead to distinct states. Indeed, to complete the transition function, we may define $\delta(\mathsf{ONE}, 1) = \mathsf{ONE}$, and $\delta(\mathsf{OFF}, 0) = \mathsf{OFF}$. Drawing the automaton would reveal itself as follows.

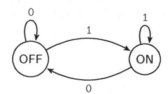

Figure 4.4: Light Switch Encoded as Finite Automaton

This, however, is not a complete (deterministic) finite automaton, as it misses a few key elements. First, all finite automata have a single starting state q_s. A starting state indicates where input begins reading into the automaton. Additionally, we need a set of **final states** F. A final state $f \in F$ determines whether an input is accepted or rejected. A rejected input is one that ends on a state $q \notin F$. Each time we traverse a path in the automaton, a symbol is consumed from the input string. If, by the time we reach the end of the input, we are on a final state, we accept the input string. So, a deterministic finite automaton D is a quintuple $(Q, \Sigma, \delta, q_s, F)$ whose values are those described above. Let us complete the light switch analogy automaton by adding a start state, say $q_s = \mathsf{OFF}$, as well as adding ON to F.

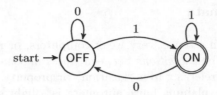

Figure 4.5: Complete Light Switch Encoding as DFA

As we said, though, finite automata consume strings of input. So, let us assume the light switch automaton receives the input string $s = 100101$, to see the terminating state. We can imagine this as the light switch being turned on, then off, then attempting to turn it off again, back on, then off, then finally on again. When we "attempt" to turn it off when it is in the off state, we loop back. Similarly, attempting to turn on a light that is already on loops back around. Because we end on a final state (i.e., when $|s| = 0$, the current state $q \in F$), the input is accepted.

We can model most devices with state using finite automata, such as elevators, transmission systems, and more practical, "real world" examples. Though, finite automata are commonly implemented to recognize languages of strings.

Example. Let us consider a deterministic finite automaton that recognizes all odd integers represented as binary strings. Such a DFA needs only two states $Q = \{\text{EVEN}, \text{ODD}\}$. We know from Chapter 2 that all binary numbers whose least-significant bit is 1 is odd. So, we can design a DFA that transitions from EVEN to ODD if it reads a 1 symbol. ODD should, therefore, be an accepting state, belonging to F. If we read a zero while on the ODD state, we travel back to EVEN.

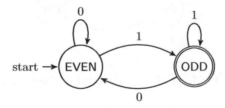

Figure 4.6: Finite Automaton Accepting Odd Binary Strings.

What a coincidence; this DFA accepts the same language as the one from our light switch automaton!

Example. Let us design a DFA that accepts strings of the form aaa whose length is a multiple of three. The language of this DFA is, therefore, $\mathcal{L} = \{\varepsilon,\ aaa,\ aaaaaa,\ \dots\}$. Assume that the input alphabet is $\Sigma = \{a,\ b\}$. If the automaton reads any b symbols, it automatically rejects the string. The thing is, there is no notion of "automatically rejecting" a string with a DFA. The way to simulate this is to use a "dead state". A dead state is a non-accepting state in which all transitions out are loops back onto itself, meaning that once we reach this state, there is no way out. We use $\varnothing$ to indicate a dead state.

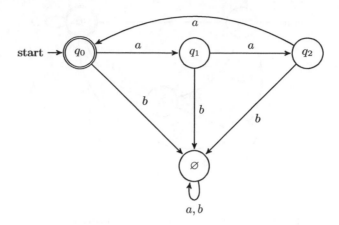

Figure 4.7: Finite Automaton Accepting String Multiples of *aaa*.

Example. Let us design a DFA that accepts strings that are either *a* or *bb*, and are sequences of **either** of these strings, possibly interleaved. We can once again assume $\Sigma = \{a, b\}$. So, $\mathcal{L} = \{a, bb, aa, abb, aabb, bba, bbaa, \ldots\}$. We need a dead state to represent the **transition** from q_1 when we read an *a*, since strings of the form *ba* are not possible. **Further** note the inclusion of q_0 to exclude the empty string from our language $\mathcal{L}$.

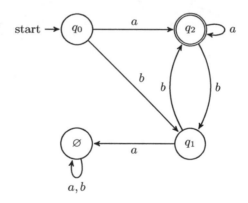

Figure 4.8: Finite Automaton Accepting Substrings of *a* or *bb*.

Example. Let us **ramp** up the difficulty and design a DFA that accepts strings representing all **integers**. To complicate things, imagine our alphabet contains special characters, **digits,** and letters (both upper and lower-case) designated by the sets SC, D, and L respectively. So, $\Sigma = \{SC \cup D \cup L\}$. A positive integer consists of an optional sign, i.e., $+$ or $-$, followed by at least one digit. Any other characters send us to a dead state. Any character aside from a digit or a sign sends us to the dead state from the **initial** state, which we will denote as the set $ND = \Sigma \setminus \{-, +\} \cup D$. The set $\Sigma \setminus D$ represents the set of alphabet symbols that are not digits.

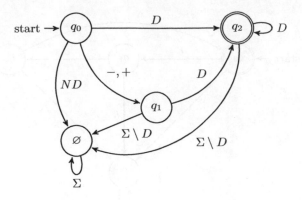

Figure 4.9: Finite Automaton Accepting Integers.

Example. Let us design a DFA that accepts any decimal number. This requires only a few changes to our previous DFA. Those changes include allowing for a single decimal symbol after an optional symbol, followed by any number of digits. The alphabet is the same as before. Further assume that $BC = \Sigma \setminus \{-, +, .\} \cup D$, where BC (standing for *Bad Character*) is the set of any character that is not a sign, decimal, or digit.

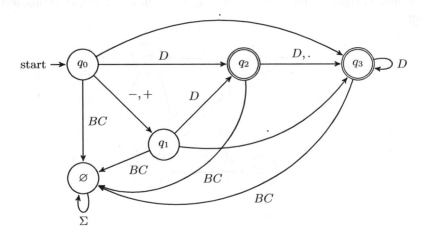

Figure 4.10: Finite Automaton Accepting Decimal Numbers.

Example. Let us design a DFA that accepts any infix expression. An infix expression consists of numbers and/or operations, e.g., $4 + 5$, 9, $6 \cdot 10 - 9 \cdot 12$. There are no parenthesized expressions. Assume that our alphabet $\Sigma = OP \cup NUM$, where NUM is the DFA that we designed in the previous example (for decimal numbers), and $OP = \{+, -, \cdot, /\}$. So, we can say that the infix expression is any amount of numbers (zero or more) followed by operations, followed by a required number. The required number is twofold: first, if we enter a string without an operator, then the first part of the grammar is omitted. Second, it allows us to continuously define numbers and operators, only stopping after we do not add an operator past the last number.

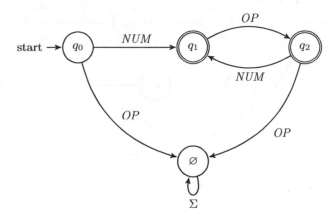

Figure 4.11: Finite Automaton Accepting Infix Expressions

Example. Let us design a DFA that accepts a few "keywords" from a programming language: `main`, `int`, and `char`, separated by underscores. We can assume that the alphabet is any lowercase letter. This DFA begins to show the power of a DFA for recognizing words, albeit while taking a bit of time to construct. To condense the DFA, we will omit any transitions to the dead state, since each transition is simply the difference between Σ and the letter on the other transition(s).

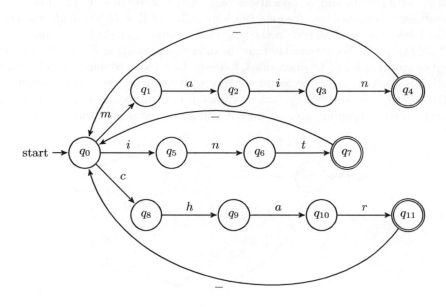

Figure 4.12: Finite Automaton Accepting Some Keywords.

Exercise 4.1. (⋆⋆)
Design a DFA that accepts a language consisting of strings with an even number of 'a' symbols, followed by an even number of 'b' symbols.

Exercise 4.2. (⋆⋆)
Design a DFA that accepts a language consisting of strings over the alphabet $\Sigma = \{0, 1\}$ that represent binary numbers divisible by eight.

Exercise 4.3. (⋆⋆)
Design a DFA that accepts a language consisting of strings over the alphabet $\Sigma = \{0, 1\}$ that represent binary numbers with an odd number of '0' symbols and '1' symbols.

Exercise 4.4. (⋆⋆)
Design a DFA that accepts a language consisting of strings over the alphabet $\Sigma = \{a, b\}$ that start and end with the same symbol.

Exercise 4.5. (⋆⋆⋆)
Design a DFA that accepts a language consisting of strings over the alphabet $\Sigma = \{a, b\}$ such that each string is $a^n b^m$, where $m, n \geq 0$, and $m - n$ is even.

Exercise 4.6. (⋆⋆⋆)
Design a DFA that accepts a language consisting of strings over the alphabet $\Sigma = \{a, b, c\}$ such that all strings begin with c and end with b, but do not contain either substrings cac, bab, or aaa.

Exercise 4.7. (★★★)
Design a DFA over the alphabet of digits, upper and lowercase letters, and the following symbols: '+', '−', '*', '/', '(', ')', '_', '\$', '−', '%', '^', '\', '@', '#', and '&'. The language describes valid variable identifiers for the *Java* programming language. A variable identifier in Java must start with a non-digit, and contain only uppercase and lowercase letters, digits, '\$', and underscores '_'. Any other inputs should be rejected.

Regular Expressions

Regular languages are languages recognized by a deterministic finite automaton. We describe regular languages using *regular expressions*, or regex(es), for short. Regexes are more compact than DFAs, and are used extensively in computer science. Any DFA can be converted into a regular expression and vice versa. In future chapters, we will make extensive use of regexes, so learning them now is extremely beneficial.

Regular expressions are constructed using symbols, which denote properties of the recognizing language. Let us explain some of these symbols specific to regexes.

To say that a regex accepts any sequence of some symbol, we use the Kleene star, or the asterisk, which we briefly explained at the start of this chapter. As an example, the language of any number of a's is $a^* = \{\varepsilon, a, aa, aaa, ...\}$. Sometimes, though, we want to exclude the empty string from the language, which we do via '+'. E.g., if $\Sigma = \{a\}$, then $L^+ = \{a, aa, aaa, ...\}$. If we want to choose between regexes, we use the vertical bar '|'. E.g., the language of zero or more a or bb is '$(a \mid bb)*$'. To designate grouping, we utilize parentheses, just as we would in mathematical equations.

Regular expressions, as noted, are translatable into equivalent DFAs, and vice versa. So, let us translate a few language descriptions into regular expressions.

Example. Write a regex for the language consisting of one or more a's followed by one b. The solution is simple: 'a^+b'.

Example. Write a regex for the language consisting of any number of a's or b's, preceded and followed by exactly three c's. We will group the "a or b" portion using parentheses and a Kleene star, and add the c's before and after. $ccc(a \mid bb)^*ccc$.

Example. Write a regex for the language consisting of an even number as a binary string, followed by an odd number as a binary string. As we saw with the respective DFA, all even binary numbers end with a zero, and all odd binary numbers end with a one. So, let us encode this into a regex: '$(0 \mid 1)^*0(0 \mid 1)^*1$'.

Example. Write a regex for the language consisting of all positive integers, as binary strings, divisible by two. For this example, we must recognize that any binary number divisible by two ends in a zero. Note that this problem is equivalent to asking if n mod 2 is zero and therefore the regular expression is '$(0 \mid 1)^*0$'.

Example. Write a regex for the language consisting of all integers. To condense our solution, we will make use of *character classes*, which are substitutes for large chains of "choice" operators. To demonstrate, the character class of any digit is represented as [0-9], which is semantically equivalent to $(0 \mid 1 \mid 2 \mid ... \mid 9)$. Additionally, we need a way of representing "optional" symbols or groups, i.e., whether something occurs exactly zero or one times. This is represented by a '?'. We need this to designate that the sign in front of an integer is optional: '$(+ \mid -)?[0-9]^{+}$'.

Example. Write a regex for the language consisting of any real, or decimal, number. Fortunately, this is just a re-telling of the corresponding DFA we designed earlier: '$(+ \mid -)?[0-9]^{*}(.[0-9]^{*})?$'.[1]

Example. Write a regex for the language consisting of strings of lower-cased vowels. '$(a \mid e \mid i \mid o \mid u)^{+}$'.

Example. Write a regex for the language consisting of infixed expressions. To make our lives easier, we will reuse the "decimal number" regular expression as "*num*", and "*op*" is the regular expression $(+ \mid - \mid * \mid /)$: $(num\ op)^{*}num$.

Lexical Analysis

Lexical analysis involves assigning meaning to sequences of characters. For example, in a string containing "1+23·41", we might *tokenize* these lexemes by assigning the token **Number** to the lexemes '1', '23', and '41'. Similarly, we could characterize '+' and '·' as **Operator** tokens. As suggested, *tokens* are categorizations of *lexemes*, which are members *of* those categorizations. We use lexical analysis primarily when designing the grammar of a programming language. Notice that, with regular expressions, we designed the tokens *num* and *op* to match against numbers and operators respectively. We then use these tokens for further syntactic and semantic analysis.

---

[1]Note the inclusion of the wildcard symbol '.' inside the regular expression; we do not include the period that ends the sentence in the regular expression and hence use quotes to surround the regex.

4.3   Syntactic Analysis

Syntactic analysis, also called *parsing,* is determining whether a sequence of tokens conform to a language grammar. When parsing tokens, we build data structures called parse trees, which are then converted into abstract syntax trees. *Parse trees,* as we referred to them in Chapter 2, are hierarchical representations of tokens. For instance, in Figure 4.13 we have a grammar for simple postfix-style arithmatic expressions. Parsing the expression '(1 (23 41 ·) +)' produces the parse tree shown in Figure 4.14.

```
exp      ::=   '(' (exp exp op) ')'
         |     num
op       ::=   '+' | '-' | '·' | '/'
num      ::=   digit+
digit    ::=   [0-9]
```

Figure 4.13: (EBNF) Grammar for Postfix Notation Arithmetic Expression Language

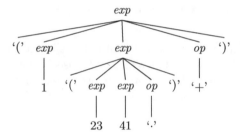

Figure 4.14: Parse Tree of '(1 (23 41 ·) +)'

Whereas parse trees describe the syntactic structure of an input, *abstract syntax trees* explains the relationships between subtrees. Moreover, abstract syntax trees strip extraneous characters such as separators that do not contribute to a node in the tree. As an example, consider the expression '((9 8 +) (17 81 −) ·)', whose parse tree contains the parentheses to indicate grouping. The abstract syntax tree counterpart removes these since they contribute nothing to the overall tree structure; the addition and subtraction subtrees already enforce the groups.

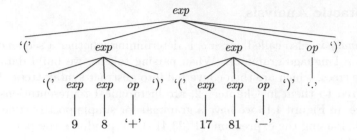

Figure 4.15: Parse Tree of '((9 8 +) (17 81 −) ·)'

Figure 4.16: Abstract Syntax Tree of '((9 8 +) (17 81 −) ·)'

We will make prolific use of abstract syntax trees in later chapters, so while they may appear to be nothing more than a theory-focused concept/data structure, they play extensive roles in practice! Furthermore, other textbooks and sources delve into the theory and intricacies of parsing, offering a wealth of additional information.

4.4   Analyzing λ-Calculus

Alonzo Church created the lambda calculus, or the λ-calculus in the early 1930s as an abstract machine for modeling computation in the scope of mathematics. Traditional lambda calculus, so to speak, is rather limiting in what it provides on the surface, but it helps lay the groundwork for several fundamental computer science concepts, including variables, function declaration, and function application.

Church's lambda calculus, much like classical logic, builds its schemata/well-formed formulas in terms of induction. The smallest unit is a *variable*, i.e., a lower-case letter usually beginning at x. Variables represent parameters or some kind of value. Next, we have the idea of *function abstraction*. Function abstractions are, in effect, function definitions, i.e., $(\lambda x.M)$, where M is any lambda calculus term. Function abstractions define a function that receives some argument, e.g., x, and has a body M. Finally, because we have function abstraction, we need a way of "invoking" a function. Thus, we have *function application*, i.e., $(M\ N)$ where M and N are arbitrary lambda calculus terms. For function application to make sense semantically, M must be some term that reduces to a function abstraction. Let us see a few examples of lambda calculus schemata.

- x

- y

- $(\lambda z.z)$

- $(((\lambda x.(\lambda y.x))\ z)\ w)$

- $((\lambda x.(x\ x))(\lambda x.(x\ x)))$

The lambda calculus also concerns us with the "scope" of variables, i.e., whether a variable is bound, free, or neither. A variable x in a lambda-calculus term is *bound* if and only if there exists a function abstraction M whose formal parameter is x and x occurs somewhere (as a non-formal parameter) in the body of M. An example is $(\lambda y.(\lambda z.y))$, where y is bound because it is the formal parameter of the outer-most function abstraction, and exists as a non-formal parameter in the inner function application. A *free* variable is the opposite of a bound variable in that a free variable x is one that exists without being the formal parameter to a function abstraction. An example is $(\lambda x.y)$, where y is free because it occurs without a matching function application.

α-substitution is a substitution principle in which we can substitute letters in a λ-calculus term for any non-bound letter. E.g., $\lambda x.x$ is α-equivalent to $\lambda y.y$ if we substitute x for y.

β-reduction is a substitution principle closely related to function application. We know that function application entails applying a function or operator to its arguments. As we saw in 2, for a function $f(x)$, we apply a function f to an argument by substituting the formal parameter x for the argument in the body of f. E.g., $f(x) = x{+}5$, $f(5)[x \mapsto 5]$, $f(5) = 5{+}5$, thus, $f(5) = 10$. This idea holds true for λ-calculus abstractions and applications; we β-reduce function applications by substituting the formal parameter of a lambda abstraction by its argument operand.

Example. β-reduce the following term: $((\lambda x.x)\ y)$

$$= y$$

Example. β-reduce the following term: $((\lambda x.(\lambda y.(x\ y))(\lambda z.x))(\lambda x.x))$

$$= ((\lambda y.((\lambda x.x)\ y))\ z)$$
$$= ((\lambda x.x)\ z)$$
$$= z$$

We can extend the syntax of the λ-calculus to make it more convenient to humans to use. What makes this formalism interesting, though, is that such an extension is entirely unnecessary–we can represent *any* algorithm with only the presented syntax and semantics. This includes arithmetic, decision structures, recursion, and everything else. For examples, numbers, i.e., natural numbers are representable by sequential lambda abstraction and application. Namely, zero is encoded as $\lambda f.\lambda x.x$, designating that we never apply the given function f to x. One is encoded as $\lambda f.\lambda x.(f\ x)$. Two is encoded as $\lambda f.\lambda x.(f\ (f\ x))$, and so on ad infinitum. In essence, we apply a function f, n times, where n is the natural number we wish to represent. It is important to understand that the lambda abstraction itself represents the natural number; not the evaluation of said lambda abstraction. What is more is that we can even represent, say, successor and addition with this encoding of natural numbers. Let us look at how to encode successor first as it is simpler. Recall that the successor function succ receives a natural number n and returns $n+1$. If we encode numbers as we have described, each number is represented as a function compositionally applied to an argument x. Thus, we can define succ as applying a function f to some given x, n times.

$$\text{succ}(n) = \lambda n.\lambda f.\lambda x.(f\ ((n\ f)\ x))$$

As this shows, the successor function is a function of three (curried) arguments: the input n to compute the successor of, the function f to use, and x which we apply f onto.

Example. Suppose we want to compute succ(3):

$$3 = \lambda f.\lambda x.(f\ (f\ (f\ x)))$$
$$\text{succ}(3) = (\lambda n.\lambda f.\lambda x.(f\ ((n\ f)\ x)))(\lambda f.\lambda x.(f\ (f\ (f\ x))))$$
$$= \lambda f.\lambda x.(f\ (((\lambda f.\lambda x.(f\ (f\ (f\ x))))\ f)\ x))$$
$$= \lambda f.\lambda x.(f\ ((\lambda x.(f\ (f\ (f\ x))))\ x))$$
$$4 = \lambda f.\lambda x.(f\ (f\ (f\ (f\ x))))$$

We can also compute the sum of two church numbers m and n. The addition of m and n as natural numbers boils down to computing n successors of m. For instance, consider $4+3$:

$$4+3 = 3+\text{succ}(0)+\text{succ}(0)+\text{succ}(0)+\text{succ}(0)$$

Zero, or 0, in our instance, is roughly symmetrical with x. So, we apply n to the successor function f to get n copies. From there, we get a function that we can apply to m.

$$\mathsf{Add}(x, y) = \lambda m.\lambda n.\lambda f.\lambda x.((n\ \mathsf{succ})\ m)$$

Of course, computing these λ−calculus reductions manually is repetitive and prone to errors. We describe some implementation of traditional arithmetic in this language as a baseline for function definition and application at a fundamental level. For instance, as numbers, we may represent boolean values, i.e., $\top$ and $\bot$, as well as conditionals, i.e., *if* x is true, then y, else z. For example, consider representing $\top$ as a two-argument (curried) function that returns its first argument.

$$\top = \lambda x.\lambda y.x$$

Closely related, suppose we represent $\bot$ as a two-argument (curried) function that returns its second argument.

$$\bot = \lambda x.\lambda y.y$$

Remember the crucial thing about church encoding: these values, *themselves*, represent their encoded value; not their evaluated forms.

5   Programming and Design

Computer Science is a science of abstraction-creating the right model for a problem and devising the appropriate mechanizable techniques to solve it.

—Alfred Aho

5.1   Recitation of Elementary Arithmetic

Suppose that you are back in elementary school, around the age of ten or so. You were just given that night's math homework on the order of operations and asked to evaluate expressions. Confident as ever, you race to pick up your pencil to begin the first question. It reads:

Evaluate the following expression:
$$3 - ((7 \cdot -9) + (6 - (-3\,/\,2)))$$

Hopefully, you are not overwhelmed by the length of the problem, and you gracefully touch the pencil to the paper and sketch the solution. Assuming you really *are* confident in your memory of the order of operations, you write the answer "58.5". As you wipe the sweat from your forehead, you notice some small words in italics which read, *"Show all work!"*.

If this did not send shivers down your spine, then great! Otherwise, you certainly remember being required to write out verbose solutions to seemingly simple problems that you could solve instantly with a calculator (or your head!). Begrudgingly, you would pick up the pencil and begin to solve each expression from the inside out:

$$
\begin{aligned}
&= 3 - ((7 \cdot -9) + (6 - (-3\,/\,2))) \\
&= 3 - (-63 + (6 - (-1.5))) \\
&= 3 - (-63 + 7.5) \\
&= 3 - -55.5 \\
&= 58.5
\end{aligned}
$$

We imagine that, for our intended readers, solving an expression of this caliber is of little difficulty (if it is, do not necessarily fret, though). Let us take a step back and think about this though, even if it seems unnecessary. How, actually, are we solving this? Depending on where you live(d), you learned the order of operations differently, but it is largely standardized as follows: parentheses are evaluated first, then exponents, then from left to right: multiplication and division, and lastly again from left to right: addition and subtraction. Such a standardization introduces the concepts of precedence, i.e., a decision of which operator is evaluated before another, and associativity, i.e., which direction to evaluate an operator.[1] One detail that is almost always omitted in these discussions, though, is the style of said expressions. We classify expressions such as these using the "infix" term. *Infix expressions* place the operator between its operands. As an example, 5+6 is an infix expression. Contrastingly, we can write an equivalent expression without this infix limitation. As a proof of concept, suppose we want to represent this with the operator written before the operands! This seems rather simple at first glance, and we can do so as follows: + 5 6. Of course, with this toy example, it is trivial, but what if we ramp up the difficulty with the expression from before: $3-((7 \cdot -9) + (6-(-3/2)))$. How do we write this as a prefix expression? Fortunately, it is similarly trivial! Here's the general procedure:

1. Determine the "main" operator of the expression.[2] This is the one that you would evaluate last in the standard infix notation. If there is no operator, i.e., it is a number, just keep the number.

2. Put the left-hand operand immediately after the operator from step 1, and put the right-hand operand after the left-hand.

3. Repeat step 1, but on the left and right operands.

Notice that, in using this procedure, we did exactly that with our toy 5+6 expression. The "main" operator is addition, +, and our left-hand operand is 5, whereas the right-hand operand is 6. Thus, we write + 5 6. Let us apply this rule to the complex expression:

(i) $-3 ((7 \cdot -9) + (6 - (-3 / 2)))$

(ii) $-3 + (7 \cdot -9) (6 - (-3 / 2))$

(iii) $-3 + \cdot 7 -9 (6 - (-3 / 2))$

(iv) $-3 + \cdot 7 -9 - 6 (-3 / 2)$

(v) $-3 + \cdot 7 -9 - 6 / -3 2$

---

[1] Recall our discussion on associativity as it relates to binary operators and groups from Chapter 2.
[2] Recall the "main" operator in zeroth/first-order logic schemata; the idea is shared here.

One detail that we omitted was the notion of parentheses; what exactly is the purpose of parentheses in arithmetic? In the standard infix notation, they group expressions we wish to evaluate before others. Expressions written in prefix notation, though, remove this inherent limitation. We always evaluate prefix expressions from left-to-right. The thing is, though, we also use parentheses to "clean up" an expression. While a prefix expression does not necessarily need parentheses, it is a good idea to group operations together for readability and, as we will investigate later, the ease of parsing:

   (i) (−3 ((7 · −9) + (6 − (−3 / 2)))))

   (ii) (−3 (+ (7 · −9) (6 − (−3 / 2)))))

   (iii) (−3 (+ (· 7 −9) (6 − (−3 / 2)))))

   (iv) (−3 (+ (· 7 −9) (−6 (−3 / 2)))))

   (v) (−3 (+ (· 7 −9) (−6 (/ −3 2)))))

If we want to dictate this expression with words in English, we could easily do so as, "The difference of 3 and a sub-expression containing the sum of a sub-expression containing the product of 7 and −9, and a sub-expression containing the difference of 6 and a sub-expression containing the quotient of −3 and 2". If we chose to do so, we could write this expression another way, using multiple lines, to clarify evaluation:

```
(−3
   (+
      (· 7 −9)
      (−6
         (/ −3 2)))))
```

Now, again, let us think about how we would actually evaluate this expression, from the ground up. Assuming we know *how* to evaluate an operator such as + or −, what is the algorithm?

   1. Determine if the expression is of the form (<OP> <EXPR1> <EXPR2>), or <NUMBER>.

   2. If the expression is a <NUMBER>, just display the NUMBER.

   3. Otherwise, evaluate OP using EXPR1 as the left-hand operand using step (1) and EXPR2 as the right-hand operand using step (1).

Fortunately for us, evaluating prefix expressions is significantly easier for a computer than evaluating infix expressions (at least in terms of writing the "how-to" component). This algorithm is only three steps long, and thankfully, computers are fully aware of how to compute expressions via the primitive arithmetic operations, so it is now only a matter of deciding how we are going to instruct the computer to do so.

What Language for Our Language?

Programming can be seen as an art, where programming languages serve as a kind of paintbrush. There are several languages, or paintbrushes, we could use, e.g., Python, Java, C++, Rust, and others, but we will use the C programming language. C is what many consider a "medium-level" language: one that is higher-level than mnemonic-driven instructions and binary encoding, but lower-level insofar as its close interaction with the computer hardware. Experienced computer scientists and programmers may view our decision to use C as rather odd, since it allows beginners to fall into bad programming practice traps and is significantly more "dangerous" than many others of its kind.[1] We argue, however, that C is a simple and small programming language, containing few keywords and programming abstractions. Furthermore, C is a *procedural* programming language, which means that it follows a step-by-step execution model. This aligns well with how beginners generally think and approach problem solving. Procedural programming allows beginners to grasp the concept of sequential execution, making it easier to understand the logic behind their programs. Finally, C serves as a solid foundation for learning other programming languages, as many modern languages, such as those we listed above, have C as their underlying influence.

In this section, we finally start writing code! In addition, we will reintroduce some concepts that we discussed from Chapters 2, 3, and 4. This time, however, we emphasize their relationships to programming as opposed to focusing solely on their theoretical potential.

Hello World!

Every programming introduction uses the famous, "Hello World!" program of some variety, and our textbook is no exception. Refer to Appendix 11.3 to set up your programming environment.

Listing 5.1—Hello World Program (main.c)

```
1    #include <stdio.h>                          Hello, world!
2
3    int main(void) {
4      printf("Hello, world!");
5      return 0;
6    }
```

What does this program do? We will go line-by-line in our analysis.

Line 1 includes functions from the standard input and output library in C. This contains several functions that allow programmers to output information to the console, files, as well as read information from the user.

---

[1] By "dangerous", we mean its security vulnerabilities.

Line 3 declares a function called `main` that has no arguments which returns a value of type `int`. A function, as we can recall from Chapter 2, is a series of computations to perform a task. In C, every program needs a `main` function. There are some slight variations that `main` may take the form, but for now, we consider those irrelevant. There is also an opening curly brace {. All functions in C require a pair of opening and closing braces {, } to designate the *body* of a function, i.e., where the steps to perform a task resides.

Line 4 calls the `printf` function with the string argument "Hello, world!". The `printf` function formats output information to the console, and can be a bit complex for people to wrap their heads around initially. We will explore this function a bit more later in our C primer, but for now, we can just make note of the fact that it outputs a string to the console.

Line 5 says that the `main` function returns a value of 0. For all intents and purposes of our adventure in this textbook, the fact that `main` returns a value at all is somewhat superfluous. For completeness, however, we will say that `main` returns an integer value based on the "state" of the program. In other words, returning a value of 0 from `main` indicates that the program, or `main` function for that matter, terminated successfully. If by chance there was an error that occurred somewhere, we could return a nonzero integer such as 1 or -1.

Finally, line 6 has the closing brace for the `main` function.

Natural Recursion

In Chapter 2, we introduced the notion of *recursive functions*, i.e., functions that call themselves. To gently introduce the notion of recursive functions in the C programming language, we will write some primitive operations via *natural recursion*. Natural recursion is a type of recursion that operates over the natural numbers, i.e., $\mathbb{N}$, or numbers from $\{0, 1, 2, 3, ...\}$. Since such a concept is rather abstract at first glance, let us illustrate this with what appears to be a simple example: $\mathsf{Add}(x, y)$.

Addition with Natural Recursion

How do we add two natural numbers x and y? If we actually sit down and think about how addition works, there are almost certainly some shortcuts people take. For instance, if $x = 19$ and $y = 43$, we can say that x is very close to 20, so we can simply add 20 to y and subtract one. Though, we are still missing this notion of addition. If we wish to think about this problem recursively, it would be wise to introduce a base case.

What happens if we add zero to any natural number? We simply get back the natural number. So, this can be treated as our base case. What about the recursive step? Let us assume, for the sake of constructing the solution to a larger problem, that we understand the idea behind adding exactly one to a value and subtracting exactly one to a value. If we have two natural numbers x and y, we can recursively compute the sum of x and y by taking the successor of x and subtracting one from y. The successor of some natural number n is equal to $n + 1$, using the function Succ. E.g., $\mathsf{Succ}(5) = 6$. So, our definition of addition, $\mathsf{Add}(x, y) = \mathsf{Succ}(\mathsf{Add}(x, y - 1))$.

Base case: If y is 0, return x.

Recursive step: Return $1+\mathsf{Add}(x, y - 1)$

Like always, a good motivation for understanding comes through an example. Using the preceding base case and recursive step, let us add $x = 9$, and $y = 3$.

(i) First, we call $\mathsf{Add}(9, 3)$. Is 3 equal to 0? Clearly not, so we do not return 9. We return $1+\mathsf{Add}(9, 2)$.

(ii) Is 2 equal to 0? Clearly not, so we do not return 9. We return $1+\mathsf{Add}(9, 1)$.

(iii) Is 1 equal to 0? Clearly not, so we do not return 9. We return $1+\mathsf{Add}(9, 0)$.

(iv) Is 0 equal to 0? Clearly, so we return 9. We now begin the process of reversing through the recursive calls since we reached our base case.

(v) Previously, we had $1+\mathsf{Add}(9, 0)$. We now know that $\mathsf{Add}(9, 0) = 9$, so we return $1+9 = 10$.

(vi) Previously, we had $1+\mathsf{Add}(9, 1)$. We now know that $\mathsf{Add}(9, 1) = 10$, so we return $1+10 = 11$.

(vii) Previously, we had $1+\mathsf{Add}(9, 2)$. We now know that $\mathsf{Add}(9, 2) = 11$, so we return $1+11 = 12$.

(viii) We are out of recursive calls, so our final result is 12.

As shown above, the function returns 12 for $x = 9$ and $y = 3$, which is correct, as $9+3 = 12$. Let us now write some C code to replicate this algorithm. Note that we will only list the function and not the main function or headers.

Listing 5.2—Naturally-Recursive Addition (`main.c`)

```
1   int add(int x, int y) {
2     if (0 == y) { return x; }
3     else { return 1 + add(x, y - 1); }
4   }
```

An important note about computing $\mathsf{Add}(x, y)$ via natural recursion is that this algorithm does not work if y is any negative integer. Our base case checks to see if y is equal to zero. The current approach subtracts one from y every time we recursively call Add. This means that y will never be zero, and is therefore stuck in infinite recursion.

Multiplication with Natural Recursion

Now that we understand the notion of natural recursion with addition, we should write a program to multiply two natural numbers. When we multiply two natural numbers x and y using natural recursion, we define multiplication in terms of addition. Namely, we add x to itself y times. Our base case is trivial: any number multiplied by zero results in zero. Then, we add recursively add n to the result of invoking Mult.

Base case: If y is 0, return 0.

Recursive step: Return $\mathsf{Add}(x, \mathsf{Mult}(x, y-1)))$

Again, let us use a simple example. Suppose we wish to multiply $x = 8$ and $y = 4$.

(i) First, we call $\mathsf{Mult}(8, 4)$. Is 4 equal to 0? Clearly not, so we do not return 0. We return $\mathsf{Add}(8, \mathsf{Mult}(8, 3))$.

(ii) Is 3 equal to 0? Clearly not, so we do not return 0. We return $\mathsf{Add}(8, \mathsf{Mult}(8, 2))$.

(iii) Is 2 equal to 0? Clearly not, so we do not return 0. We return $\mathsf{Add}(8, \mathsf{Mult}(8, 1))$.

(iv) Is 1 equal to 0? Clearly not, so we do not return 0. We return $\mathsf{Add}(8, \mathsf{Mult}(8, 0))$.

(v) Is 0 equal to 0? Clearly, so we return 0. We now begin the process of reversing through the recursive calls since we reached our base case.

(vi) Previously, we had $\mathsf{Add}(8, \mathsf{Mult}(8, 0))$. We now know that $\mathsf{Mult}(8, 0) = 0$, so we return $8+0 = 8$.

(vii) Previously, we had $\mathsf{Add}(8, \mathsf{Mult}(8, 1))$. We now know that $\mathsf{Mult}(8, 1) = 8$, so we return $8+8 = 16$.

(viii) Previously, we had $\mathsf{Add}(8, \mathsf{Mult}(8, 2))$. We now know that $\mathsf{Mult}(8, 2) = 16$, so we return $8+16 = 24$.

(ix) Previously, we had $\mathsf{Add}(8, \mathsf{Mult}(8, 3))$. We now know that $\mathsf{Mult}(8, 3) = 24$, so we return $8+24 = 32$.

(x) We are out of recursive calls, so our final result is 32.

Listing 5.3—Naturally-Recursive Multiplication (main.c)

```
1   int mult(int x, int y) {
2     if (0 == y) { return 0; }
3     else { return add(x, mult(x, y\;-\;1)); }
4   }
```

Exponentials with Natural Recursion

We will derive another naturally-recursive function: $\mathsf{Pow}(x, y)$, which is equivalent to x^y, or x multiplied by itself y times. As before, we need a base case and a recursive step. Assuming x and y are natural numbers, then $x^0 = 1$ should certainly be our base case. The recursive step is fortunately only slightly harder: $x^y = x \cdot x^{(y - 1)}$. Written out formally, we can, and should, express exponentiation in terms of Mult:

Base case: If y is 0, return 1.

Recursive step: Return $\mathsf{Mult}(x, \mathsf{Pow}(x, y - 1))$.

And the code is just a retailing of the formal definition:

Listing 5.4—Naturally-Recursive Exponentiation (`main.c`)

```
1   int pow(int x, int y) {
2     if (0 == y) { return 1; }
3     else { return mult(x, pow(x, y - 1)); }
4   }
```

Factorial with Natural Recursion

Let us ramp things up a bit more and write a slightly harder function, which `main` will invoke, i.e., call. We saw $\mathsf{fact}(n)$, a function that computes the factorial of a positive integer n, in Chapter 2. We noted the base case and the recursive step of fact.

Base case: If $n \leq 1$, return 1.

Recursive step: Return $n \cdot \mathsf{fact}(n-1)$

In C, it is quite trivial to replicate this behavior! We can use the conditional if to mimic the base case. Unlike the section on natural recursion, we will first write the code to compute $\mathsf{fact}(n)$, then walk through a computation example.

Listing 5.5—Naturally-Recursive Factorial (`main.c`)

```
1    #include <stdio.h>                                  The factorial of
2                                                        6 is 720
3    int fact(int n) {
4      if (n <= 1) { return 1; }
5      else { return n * fact(n - 1); }
6    }
7
8    int main() {
9      int x = 6;
10     printf("The factorial of %d is %d\n", x, fact(x));
11     return 0;
12   }
```

Inside the `main` function, we declare an integer x with the value of 6. Variables serve as placeholders for a value. This means that wherever we refer to x, the program will interpret this as the integer 6.

Our `printf` statement looks a bit complex now, so what did we do? Fear not, however, as even though it appears difficult to understand, its behavior is entirely predictable. The first argument to `printf` is what we call a format string. A format string is a string that has placeholders for data. These placeholders can represent anything: integers, floating-point values, characters, strings, memory addresses, or whatever we desire! In this case, we are printing out the characters "The factorial of ", then we encounter a %d. This is a placeholder for a value. Since it is the first placeholder in this string, it is going to search through the rest of the arguments to `printf`, i.e., x and `fact(x)`, and display the value of the first argument, being the value of x. It then prints the characters " is ", followed by another placeholder %d.[1] Since this is the second placeholder, it will extract the value of $\mathsf{fact}(x)$ This, however, is a function, so it will need to compute the value of $\mathsf{fact}(x)$ before printing it out.

Let us trace through a computation of $\mathsf{fact}(3)$ to clarify some certainly-present confusion about recursion.[2]

(i) First, we call $\mathsf{fact}(3)$ from `main`. We ask, "Is 3 less than or equal to 1?" Clearly not, so we do not execute the code inside the `if` body. We compute $3 \cdot \mathsf{fact}(2)$.

(ii) $\mathsf{fact}(2)$ is called. We ask, "Is 2 less than or equal to 1?" Clearly not, so we do not execute the code inside the `if` body. We then compute $2 \cdot \mathsf{fact}(1)$.

(iii) $\mathsf{fact}(1)$ is called. We ask, "Is 1 less than or equal to 1?" Clearly this is true, so we execute the code inside the `if` body. We return 1. We now begin the process of reversing through the recursive calls since we reached our base case.

(iv) Previously, we had $2 \cdot \mathsf{fact}(1)$. We now know $\mathsf{fact}(1) = 1$, so we return $2 \cdot 1 = 2$.

(v) Previously, we had $3 \cdot \mathsf{fact}(2)$. We now know $\mathsf{fact}(2) = 2$, so we return $3 \cdot 2 = 6$.

(vi) We are out of recursive calls, so our final result is 6.

As shown above, the function returns 6 for $n = 3$, which is correct, as $3! = 3 \cdot 2 \cdot 1 = 6$.

Computing Catalan Numbers with Natural Recursion

The *catalan numbers* are a sequence of natural numbers that fall "nicely" into a recursive formula. This formula may look a little scary, but it is nothing more than another form of natural recursion.[3]

$$C_0 = 1$$
$$C_n = \frac{2(2n-1)}{n+1} \cdot C_{n-1}$$

---

[1] Note that there is another special character '\n' This causes the program to return to the next line. It is akin to pressing "Enter".

[2] We use 3 instead of 6 to shorten the redundancy of the explanation.

[3] While their uses are not important for us, we note that they aid in combinatorics, i.e., permutations.

Listing 5.6—Naturally-Recursive Catalan Numbers (`main.c`)

```
1   int catalan(int n) {
2     if (n == 0) { return 1; }
3     else { return (int) ((2.0 * (2 * n - 1)) / (n + 1)) * catalan(n - 1); }
4   }
```

Interestingly, we use `2.0` for the first 2 in our formula. We do so because, otherwise, C will treat our division as integer division, thereby truncating any decimal places. For example, `5 / 2 = 2` according to integer division, but if either operand has a decimal, it will correctly give us `2.5`.[1]

Ackermann's Function

The Ackermann function is a fundamental recursive function in a subfield of computer science called computability theory. Regardless, its definition is the most complex that we have seen thus far.

$$A(0, n) = n+1 \quad \forall n \geq 0$$
$$A(m, 0) = A(m - 1, 1) \quad \forall m > 0$$
$$A(m, n) = A(m - 1, A(m, n - 1)) \quad \forall m, n > 0$$

Ackermann's function, A, is a binary function of two arguments. Second, its second argument in case 3 is, itself, a recursive call to A. Therefore, while it may not appear as such, the output of A grows astronomically fast even in very small changes of m and n. Let us write the function in C and investigate some inputs.

Listing 5.7—Ackermann's Function (`main.c`)

```
1   int A(int m, int n) {                              5
2     if (m == 0) { return n + 1; }                    7
3     else if (n == 0) { return A(m - 1, 1); }         5
4     else { return A(m - 1, A(m, n - 1)); }           13
5   }                                                  29
6                                                      61
7   int main(void) {                                   125
8     printf("%d\n", A(2, 1));                          13
9     printf("%d\n", A(2, 2));
10    printf("%d\n", A(3, 0));
11    printf("%d\n", A(3, 1));
12    printf("%d\n", A(3, 2));
13    printf("%d\n", A(3, 3));
14    printf("%d\n", A(3, 4));
15    printf("%d\n", A(4, 0));
16    return 0;
17  }
```

If we try to evaluate `A(4, 1)`, we see that the function takes around twenty or so seconds to give the result 65533.[2] We advise not evaluating `A(4, 2)`, because even though we know its result to be $2^{65533}-3$, a modern machine cannot realistically compute this value on its own within a reasonable time frame.

---

[1] We use the *casting operator* (`int`) to convert the result from a `double` to an `int`. We can cast types to other types, but information is not always preserved. For instance, casting a `double` to an `int` truncates its decimal.

[2] This time was recorded on a 2021 MacBook Pro with the M1 Pro chip.

Function Intricacies

Functions in **C** must be declared before they are invoked. For instance, if we write a function f, which calls a function g, then g must be defined above f. What if, however, g mutually-recurses on f? That is, g calls f, and f calls g? In this instance it is impossible for one function to be fully defined above the other. *Function prototypes* serve as the silver bullet; a function prototype is the signature of a function without its body. Function prototypes in a source file should be defined above every other function.

Listing 5.8—Function Prototypes (main.c)

```
1    // Function prototypes.
2    int f( );
3    int g( );
4
5    int f( ) {
6      ...
7      g();
8    }
9
10   int g( ) {
11     ...
12     f();
13   }
```

We will make extensive and full-fledged use of function prototypes in the sections and chapters to come.

Exercise 5.1. (⋆⋆)

The Collatz conjecture questions whether every positive integer, if given to the following recursive function, always converges to one [Lagarias, 1985].

$$\text{Collatz}(n) = \left\{ \begin{array}{ll} \lfloor n/2 \rfloor, & \text{if } n \text{ is even} \\ 3n{+}1, & \text{if } n \text{ is odd} \end{array} \right\}$$

Write the collatz function, which receives a positive integer n and prints out each number in the Collatz sequence generated by $\text{Collatz}(n)$.

Listing 5.9—Collatz Conjecture Skeleton Code (main.c)

```
1    void collatz(int n) { // TODO. }     |  10
2                                         |  5
3    int main(void) {                     |  16
4      collatz(10);                       |  8
5      return 0;                          |  4
6    }                                    |  2
                                          |  1
```

Counting with Natural Recursion

We have been using natural recursion to "count down" so to speak to a base case condition. Let us write a program that will actually interact with the user and print out some information, via natural recursion. Our goal is to allow the user to enter a number n, and the program will output a sequence of digits starting from n down to 0, followed by "Blast off!". We will call this function Countdown(n). Unlike our previous examples, however, our recursive calls will not return a numeric value. Instead, we are simply performing an action at each step of the computation. We can illustrate this with the formal definitions:

Base case: If n is 0, Print Blast off!

Recursive step: Print n, and call Countdown($n - 1$).

In the C language, we can imitate the behavior of "Print" using the format print function printf, as we did with the factorial example. Let us now write the corresponding code.

Listing 5.10—Countdown with Natural Recursion (main.c)

```
1  void countdown(int n) {
2    if (n > 0) {
3      printf("%d ", n);
4      countdown(n - 1);
5    } else {
6      printf("Blast off!");
7    }
8  }
```

With this example, we slightly amended our recursive definition. We check to see if n is greater than 0, and if so, we print the corresponding value of n, followed by a call to countdown with a value of n - 1. What is new is the else keyword and block. An else block is always paired with if. We can read it as, "If expr true, evaluate the if body. Otherwise, evaluate the else body", where expr is some expression that is true or false. This differs in one significant way from the code examples laid out before: when the program is in the "reversing the recursion" process, if our if body does not have a return statement, execution resumes outside the body of the if statement. Consider the following code:

Listing 5.11—Incorrect Implementation of countdown (main.c)

```
1  void countdown(int n) {
2    if (n > 0) {
3      printf("%d ", n);
4      countdown(n - 1);
5    }
6    printf("Blast off!");
7  }
```

If we try **to call** this function with a value of 3, it will print 3 2 1 Blast
off!Blast off!Blast off!. Assuming you have not accidentally already made
this mistake, its behavior might surprise the uninformed. When we return from
a block of code, execution completely terminates from that function forever in the
scope of that recursive call. If we omit return or do not insert an else block, once
the recursive call unwinds, it will resume execution after the function call. Because
it is at the end of the if statement body, we return to outside the if and execute
code from there. For completeness, as a technicality, even when we include the else
statement in the Countdown example, the reversal of the recursion still returns to
the point of calling countdown. The only noteworthy difference is that there is
no other code to execute in the body of the function, since an else body is only
executed when the preceding if expression is false.

Conditionals

Our natural recursion primer showed several examples of *conditional operators*.
Conditionals, in C, redirect program control. To illustrate, if we want to print out
the square of some integer x only when x is even, we can use an if/else statement
chain. The code inside the parentheses of an if is called a predicate and, if the
predicate is true, the corresponding body (i.e., code immediately following the if) is
executed. In the event that the predicate is false, the else block body is executed.
For the following example, we print the value of x if it is odd.

Listing 5.12—If/Else Statements (main.c)

```
1   #include <stdio.h>                                          x^2 = 64
2
3   int main(void) {
4     int x = 8;
5     if (x % 2 == 0) { printf("x^2 = %d\n", x * x); }
6     else { printf("x = %d\n", x); }
7     return 0;
8   }
```

We can compare variables, constants, and function calls against one another.
We can even assign variables inside the predicate of an if statement. In C, any
non-zero value is "truthy", so if we assign x to be the constant 5 as the predicate, it
evaluates x after the assignment and determines the "truthiness" of x. Comparing
a variable against the constant zero opens the possibility for an egregious mistake
by not using the double equals '==' comparison operator in favor of accidentally
using the assignment '=' operator.

Listing 5.13—Assigning Values Inside a Conditional

```
1    #include <stdio.h>                                         x is 5...
2                                                               Always here!
3    int main(void) {
4      int x = 8;
5      if (x = 5) { printf("x is 5...\n"); }
6      else { printf("How did we get here?\n"); }
7
8      if (x = 0) { printf("Not possible!\n"); }
9      else { printf("Always here!\n"); }
10     return 0;
11   }
```

When making comparisons of *l-values*, i.e., variables, against *r-values*, i.e., non-variables, it is an encouraged practice to place the constant/r-value on the left-hand side of the expression. This way, the compiler produces an error stating that assignment to an r-value is not possible if we accidentally use the assignment operator where we intend to use the logical equals comparison operator.

Listing 5.14—L-Values vs. R-Values (`main.c`)

```
1   #include <stdio.h>                                    How did we get here?
2                                                         Not possible!
3   int main(void) {
4     int x = 8;
5     if (5 == x) { printf("x is 5...\n"); }
6     else { printf("How did we get here?\n"); }
7
8     if (0 == x) { printf("Not possible!\n"); }
9     else { printf("Always here!\n"); }
10    return 0;
11  }
```

Comparisons are not always binary; sometimes we want to use multiple conditionals to solve some problem. For instance, suppose we want to write the **signum** function,[1] which returns −1 if the input number is negative, 0 if it is zero, and 1 if it is positive. In such instances, we take advantage of the `else if` construct. Just in case a preceding `if` condition is false, the succeeding `else if` condition is evaluated.

Listing 5.15—If, Else-If, Else

```
1   #include <stdio.h>                                    1
2                                                        -1
3   int signum(int n) {                                   0
4     if (0 == n) { return 0; }
5     else if (n < 0) { return -1; }
6     else { return 1; }
7   }
8
9   int main(void) {
10    printf("Signum of 5 is %d\n", signum(5));
11    printf("Signum of -5 is %d\n", signum(-5));
12    printf("Signum of 0 is %d\n", signum(0));
13    return 0;
14  }
```

Of course, what is to stop us from using a sequence of `if` statements rather than `else if`, or omitting an `else`? All of these are possibilities in real-world programs. Consider the following two code segments:[2]

Listing 5.16—If vs. Else-If (`main.c`)

```
1   #include <stdio.h>                      #include <stdio.h>
2
3   int main(void) {                        int main(void) {
4     int x = 0;                              int x = 0;
5     int y = 0;                              int y = 0;
6     if (0 == x) { printf("x=0"); }         if (0 == x) { printf("x=0"); }
7     else if (0 == y) { printf("y=0"); }    if (0 == y) { printf("y=0"); }
8     else { printf("x,y non-zero"); }       printf("x,y non-zero");
9     return 0;                              return 0;
10  }                                       }
```

---

[1] We read "signum" as *the sign of a number.*

[2] We omit the new-line character \n and condense the output messages to preserve horizontal space.

In the left-hand version, we use an `if`, `else if`, then an `else`. As such, the `if` predicate is evaluated and, because it is true, only "x is zero!" is printed. Clauses inside an `else if` or `else` are evaluated only when their preceding conditionals are false. Compare this to the right-hand side which uses an `if` followed by another `if`, without an `else`. The `else if` principle does not apply in this scenario, and thus not only does the program output "x=0" and "y=0" but it also outputs "x,y non-zero" because this line is not within the body of a conditional.

We can combine predicates together using the logical comparison operators "&&" and "||" denoting logical and/logical or respectively. These operators obey the same rules as the propositional logic conjunction and disjunction connectives, but have a peculiar difference: the ability to short-circuit. Consider the following code segments:

Listing 5.17—Short-Circuit Evaluation (`main.c`)

```
1    #include <stdio.h>                          x=0,y=0
2
3    int main(void) {
4      int x = 0;
5      int y = 0;
6      if (0 == x || 5 == y) {
7        printf("x=%d, y=%d\n", x, y);
8      }
9      if (5 == y && 0 == x) {
10       printf("y=5 and x=0\n");
11     }
12     return 0;
13   }
```

In the first `if` condition, we check to see if x is equal to zero or if y is equal to five. Because x is equal to zero, and we are using, effectively, the disjunction connective, only one operand must be true. As a consequence, the predicate 5 == y is never evaluated. Comparatively, the second `if` condition checks to see if y is equal to 5 and if x is equal to zero. Because both operands of a conjunction must be true for the connective to resolve to true, the predicate 0 == x is never evaluated because y is, in fact, not equal to five. Hence, the body of the second conditional is not executed.

Let us consider the following sloppy code that adds an assignment statement to the mix, hence the use of the sloppy adjective.[1]

Listing 5.18—Sloppy Code via Short-Circuiting (`main.c`)

```
1    #include <stdio.h>                          x=0, y=0
2                                                 x=0, y=5
3    int main(void) {
4      int x = 1;
5      int y = 0;
6      if (0 == x || (y = 5)) {
7        printf("x=%d, y=%d\n", x, y);
8      }
9      if (0 == x && (y = 5)) {
10       printf("x=%d, y=%d\n", x, y);
11     }
12     return 0;
13   }
```

---

[1]Interestingly, we have to *try* to make this code sloppy since the precedence of || is higher than assignment, so we add parentheses around the assignment.

We consider the previous code as sloppy because of the conditionally-evaluated assignment operation. The value of y changes based on the logical comparison operator we use due to short-circuiting. Furthermore, assignments statements inside a conditional should be used with caution; their use is sometimes perfectly warranted and we will demonstrate such instances. Introducing these nested assignment conditionals when unnecessary hurts code readability and makes it harder to debug. Many real-world C programming projects outright disallow this as a coding style.

One-armed `if` statements, which are `if` statements without an `else` clause, are highly discouraged if at all possible due to the potential for bugs.[1]

Exercise 5.2. (⋆)
Write conditional statements that determines if an integer n is greater than 100. If so, output n divided by two. If the number is less than 50, output n divided by 5. In any other case, print the string "N/A".

Exercise 5.3. (⋆)
Given an integer variable *age* in years, write conditional statements to determine if the age is able to vote in the United States. For reference, someone may legally once they turn eighteen years old. Output a relevant message string using `printf`.

Exercise 5.4. (⋆)
Write conditional statements to output the number of days that are in a given *month* represented as an integer from 1 (January) to 12 (December). Do not use more than three conditional statements. You can consider February to always have exactly 28 days.

Exercise 5.5. (⋆⋆)
Given a *year*, output whether or not it is a leap year. Leap years are years that are divisible by four or if the year is divisible by 400, but if the year is divisible by 100 and not divisible by 400, it is not a leap year. As an example, 1996 is a leap year because 4 | 1996, 2000 is a leap year because 400 | 2000, whereas 1900 is not a leap year because 100 | 1900 and 400 ∤ 1900.

Exercise 5.6. (⋆⋆)
Write conditional statements to determine if a quadratic of the form ax^2+bx+c has real solutions.[2] Assume that there exist `double` variables a, b, and c with arbitrary values. Use the quadratic formula. You will need to include the `math.h` header to access the square root function.

$$\frac{-b \pm \sqrt{b^2-4ac}}{2a}$$

Your solution should print "2" if the quadratic has two real solutions, "1" if the solutions are equivalent, and "0" if there are no real solutions.

Exercise 5.7. (⋆⋆)
Write a function `max` that returns the maximum of three integers a, b, and c. Do not use any built-in (C library) functions.

---

[1] We make this assertion under the assumption that new programmers should strictly consider the alternative case(s).

[2] A "real solution" means that $x \in \mathbb{R}$.

Exercise 5.8. (⋆⋆)
Write conditional statements to determine the letter grade of a given integer grade.
Namely, if the grade is greater than 90 and less than or equal to 100, output "A". If
it is greater than 80, output "B". If it is greater than 70, output "C". If it is greater
than 60, output "D". Otherwise, output "F". Note that, for instance, if the grade is
74", the program should **not** output "ABC"; only "C" should be displayed.

Iteration

Recursion allows us to execute code multiple times until we arrive at some condition.
For example, in the case of factorial, we recurse until n is less than or equal to one.
Unfortunately, recursion often falls short of the silver bullet image it projects; in
some instances, a recursive pattern is spotted rather easily. For other scenarios,
however, the recursive solution may be ridiculously convoluted. More often than
not, *iteration* can be used to effectively solve the same problem. Iteration allows us
to repeat a segment of code until some condition is met (does that sound familiar?).
Let us convert the recursive factorial function into its iterative counterpart:

Listing 5.19—Recursive vs. Iterative Factorial (main.c)

```
1   int fact(int n) {                    int fact(int n) {
2     if (n <= 1) { return 1; }            int result = 1;
3     else { return n * fact(n - 1); }     while (n > 1) {
4   }                                        result = result * n;
5                                            n = n - 1;
6                                          }
7                                          return result;
8                                        }
```

We use the while construct for iteration. A while loop receives a predicate and,
if it is true, we execute the body of the loop. If it is false, execution jumps from the
predicate to immediately after the loop body. For the factorial example, we declare
a local variable result to store the intermediary factorial calculation. For each
iteration, or pass through the loop body, we multiply result by n, then decrement
n by one. The recursive version does these exact operations, just through a different
lens, metaphorically speaking. If the function receives a value less than or equal to
one, the body of the loop never executes, because n starts off as not being greater
than one, hence the predicate is false. Let us convert another recursive function
from earlier in the chapter such as integer exponentiation:

Listing 5.20—Recursive vs. Iterative Exponentiation (main.c)

```
1   int expt(int b, int n) {             1   int expt(int n, int b) {
2     if (0 == n) { return 1; }          2     int result = 1;
3     else { return b * expt(b, n - 1); } 3     while (0 != b) {
4   }                                     4       result = result * n;
                                          5       b = b - 1;
                                          6     }
                                          7     return result;
                                          8   }
```

Much like factorial, this example accumulates the result, while a counter, namely b, decrements down to zero. The issue with this approach is that it is not very idiomatic; while loops are best reserved for indeterminately-timed conditions. Knowing that the loop terminates after a finite number of steps (in the case of factorial this is n) serves as a good indication to use a for loop. for loops have three components: an initializer, a predicate, and a stepper. Let us view this with an example:[1]

Listing 5.21—Factorial with For Loop (main.c)

```
1   int fact(int n) {
2     int result = 1;
3     for (int i = 1; i <= n; i++) {
4       result *= i;
5     }
6     return result;
7   }
```

As we said, for loops contain three components. In the previous listing, we initialize the integer i to 1. Any variables declared in the initializer, which may be more than one delimited by a comma, are local to the loop body.[2] Each pass through the loop, we check to ensure the predicate (e.g., i <= n) is true and, if so, we execute the loop body. Afterwards, we execute the "step" statement. A step statement is, in general, used to lead towards making the predicate false. In the factorial example, i approaches n, which eventually results in i being greater than n, thus falsifying the condition. All for loops can be written in terms of while loops and vice-versa. We will also convert the exponential function to use a for loop, which we see is slightly simpler than the factorial function because we only use i as a means to an end, rather than using its value in the loop body:

Listing 5.22—Exponentiation with For Loop (main.c)

```
1   int expt(int n, int b) {
2     int result = 1;
3     for (int i = 1; i <= b; i++) {
4       result *= n;
5     }
6     return result;
7   }
```

---

[1]We make use of the *= operator, also called the *augmented assignment operator*, to produce an expression equivalent to result = result * i;.

[2]An example of declaring more than one variable in a for loop initializer is for (int i = 0, j = 0; ...; i++, j++).

Loop variables, as we will refer to them, need not to always start from 1. In fact, a declaration is not mandatory, nor is any other part of the loop! Indeed, we can create an infinite for loop using the construct for (;;).[1] Let us write a for loop to determine if a number is prime.[2] We know that a number n is prime if and only if it cannot be divided by any positive integer other than one and itself. A for loop needs only to check up to the square root of n for primality. To do so, we include the math.h header, which includes the square root and ceiling functions. We include a check at the top of the function for the inputs 0 and 1 because, mathematically speaking, they are not prime.[3]

Listing 5.23—Determining Primality with For Loop (main.c)

```
1   #include <math.h>
2   #include <stdbool.h>
3
4   bool is_prime(int n) {
5    if (n < 2) { return false; }
6    else {
7     int bound = (int) ceil(sqrt(n));
8     for (int i = 2; i <= bound; i++) {
9      if (0 == n % i) { return false; }
10    }
11    return true;
12   }
13  }
```

We can also nest loops inside other loops! For instance, let us write a loop that computes a basic multiplication table of the integers 1 to 12:

Listing 5.24—For Loop to Draw Multiplication Table (main.c)

```
1   void multiplication_table(void) {          1 * 1 = 1
2    for (int i = 1; i <= 12; i++) {           1 * 2 = 2
3     for (int j = 1; j <= 12; j++) {
4      printf("%d * %d = %d\n", i, j, i * j);      .
5     }                                            .
6    }                                          12 * 11 = 132
7   }                                           12 * 12 = 144
```

Notice that, for every iteration of the i loop, there are 12 iterations of the j loop.[4] Therefore, there are a total of $12 \cdot 12 = 144$ iterations.

Exercise 5.9. (⋆)

Use a loop to compute the integer sum from a given integer a to a given integer b. Operate under the assumption that a is strictly less than b, where $a, b \in \mathbb{Z}$.

---

[1] This is rarely necessary since while (true) is more idiomatic and serves the same purpose.

[2] We include the stdbool.h header to define the true and false boolean datatype.

[3] Even though it seems sensible for ceil to return an int, it returns a double to account for the fact that taking the ceiling of the largest possible int should still produce a valid number.

[4] The use of "for" here was entirely intentional.

Pointers

Pointers often confuse many beginning programmers, but fortunately, the definition of a pointer is simple to grasp. A *pointer* is a memory address. Pointers, as their name suggests, point to a location in memory. If we wish to declare a pointer to the address of some value, we affix an asterisk '*' after the type declaration. As an example, suppose we want a pointer to point to the address of an integer variable val. We first declare a pointer ptr as int *ptr;, then declare our variable var: int var = 10;. Finally, we assign the pointer by retrieving the address of val. To get the address of a variable, prefix the variable name with the ampersand &, i.e., ptr = &val;. A pointer can point to nothing at all per the NULL keyword, which is literally address zero.

Listing 5.25—Basic Pointer Example (main.c)

```
1   int main(void) {
2     int *ptr = NULL;
3     int val = 10;
4     ptr = &val;
5   }
```

Initially, ptr points to nothing, i.e., NULL, but by reassigning ptr to the address of val, ptr points to val's address in memory. To print out this address via printf, use the format specifier %p, e.g., printf("%p", ptr);. We can replicate this via the ampersand operator on val to see that ptr correctly identifies the address of val, i.e., printf("%p", &val);. How do retrieve the value of the address pointed to by the pointer? In other words, what if we want to see the data *at* an address instead of the address itself? To answer this question, let us first consider the significance and necessity of pointers, since this motivation is often unclear. Suppose we want to write a program to swap the values of two variables.

Listing 5.26—Swapping by Value (main.c)

```
1   void swap(int x, int y) {
2     int temp = x;
3     x = y;
4     y = temp;
5   }
6
7   int main(void) {
8     int x = 5;
9     int y = 10;
10    printf("Before swapping: x=%d, y=%d\n", x, y);
11    swap(x, y);
12    printf("After swapping: x=%d, y=%d\n", x, y);
13    return 0;
14  }
```

One may be tempted to think that this works, but unfortunately, it does not go as expected. Both calls to output x and y output the same data: 5 and 10 respectively. We, instead, want it to output 10 and 5. C is a *pass-by-value* programming language, which means all values are copied before being passed to arguments. Thus, the values of 5 and 10 retrieved inside swap are copies and not the original variables declared inside main. What we want to do is change *those* variable values. We use pointers for this very paradigm; if we want to mutate/modify a value from one function inside another, we want to pass it by pointer. So, let us first adjust our swap function to instead receive two integer pointers instead of two integers. Then, we need to update the call to swap inside main. We want to pass the memory address of x and y to swap, and we now know that to get the address of a value, we use the ampersand operator:

Listing 5.27—Swapping by Pointer (main.c)

```
1   void swap(int *x, int *y) {
2     int temp = x;
3     x = y;
4     y = temp;
5   }
6
7   int main(void) {
8     int x = 5;
9     int y = 10;
10    printf("Before swapping: x=%d, y=%d\n", x, y);
11    swap(&x, &y);
12    printf("After swapping: x=%d, y=%d\n", x, y);
13    return 0;
14  }
```

We must now update the code inside swap. Right now, we are swapping the values of the pointers and not the data inside the pointer. To get the data pointed to by a pointer, i.e., the values of x and y, we use the *dereference operator*, which confusingly enough is also the asterisk. We can use the dereference operator to mutate the value stored at a pointer.

Listing 5.28—Examining swap (main.c)

```
1   void swap(int *x, int *y) {
2     int temp = *x;
3     *x = *y;
4     *y = temp;
5   }
```

We first dereference x to retrieve its value, then store it inside temp. Then, we again use dereferencing to set the value at the pointer to x to the value at the pointer to y. Finally, we set the value at the pointer to y to temp.

The pointers we have shown are comparatively simple to the pointers that many new C programmers fear. We said that pointers are nothing more than memory addresses, and pointers declared within the body of a function only exist within that body. As an example, in the following code segment, the pointer to x exists only inside the scope of ptr_function.

Listing 5.29—Pointer Lifetime (main.c)

```
1   int *ptr_function(void) {
2     int *x;
3     return x; // Invalid!
4   }
```

What if we want to create a pointer that lives beyond the scope of a function while still being declared within that function? This requires us to use *dynamic memory allocation* via malloc from the stdlib.h library. The malloc function allocates a chunk of memory and returns a pointer to the address of the chunk. malloc receives a parameter denoting the size of the chunk in bytes, and we can use the sizeof operator to correctly allocate a pointer.

Listing 5.30—Pointer via malloc (main.c)

```
1   #include <stdlib.h>
2
3   int *ptr_function(void) {
4     int *x = malloc(sizeof(int));
5     return x;
6   }
```

The memory chunk pointed to by the pointer x is the size of an int, which is usually 32 bits, or four bytes. More importantly, though, we can reference this address outside of ptr_function. Take the following program; it declares an integer pointer, stores the value 5000 at the address location, and returns the pointer from ptr_function. We see that the program correctly prints 5000 as the value stored at the pointer, and we can change this value as we please in the main function (or any other function).

Listing 5.31—Transferring Dynamically-Allocated Pointers (main.c)

```
1   int *ptr_function(void) {            value at ptr=5000
2     int *x = malloc(sizeof(int));      value at ptr=2500
3     *x = 5000;
4     return x;
5   }
6
7   int main(void) {
8     int *y = ptr_function();
9     printf("value at ptr=%d\n", *y);
10    *y = *y / 2;
11    printf("value at ptr=%d\n", *y);
12    return 0;
13  }
```

One thing to note is that any and all dynamically-allocated memory should be freed via free. Freeing allocated chunks, in essence, reclaims the memory, meaning it can be reused elsewhere by the program if necessary. So, because ptr_function dynamically allocates a pointer, we shall free this pointer when we are done using its contents.

Listing 5.32—Freeing Dynamically-Allocated Pointer (main.c)

```
1   int *ptr_function(void) {
2     int *x = malloc(sizeof(int));
3     *x = 5000;
4     return x;
5   }
6
7   int main(void) {
8     int *y = ptr_function();
9
10    free(y);
11    return 0;
12  }
```

Finally we note the potential for failure among malloc: if the program cannot allocate any memory for the requested chunk, malloc returns NULL. Consequently we should always check the return value of a call to functions that dynamically allocate memory such as malloc.

Listing 5.33—Error-Checking malloc Function (main.c)

```
1   int *ptr_function(void) {
2     int *x = malloc(sizeof(int));
3     if (NULL == x) {
4       fprintf(stderr, "ptr_function: malloc failed\n");
5       exit(EXIT_FAILURE);
6     } else {
7       return x;
8     }
9   }
```

In C, pointers are an absolutely crucial concept to understand. We will explore pointers and how to use them in greater detail/applications in the following sections.

Arrays

Playing with numbers can be enjoyable, but would not it be even more entertaining to have a collection of numbers for interactive exploration? Arrays make this a possibility.

An *array*, as we mentioned in our discussion on data structures, is a sequence of contiguous elements, or things. For example, $\{3, 4, 5, 6\}$ is an array of integers. Arrays can store any number of elements, including no elements. Arrays also may store duplicate elements, unlike a mathematical set. Lastly, all elements in a set must be of the same type. As an example, if we declare A as an array of integers, $A = \{3, 3.14, 5\}$ is not a valid array in C since 3.14 is a floating-point/decimal value and not an integer. On the contrary, if we declare B as an array of floating-point values, $B = \{3.213, -98.123, 0, 0, 6, -7\}$ is a valid array because all integers are floating-point values by definition. Though, what is interesting is how C handles storing an integer in a floating-point context. As an example, storing the integer 0 in an array of floating-point values automatically results in its conversion into 0.0.

Arrays are *indexable*, meaning we can retrieve and modify an element by its location in the array. Arrays, at least in the C language, always have a starting index of 0. We access array elements using brackets []. For example, using the definition of B, $B[0] = 3.213$, $B[3] = 0$, $B[5] = -7$. All indices of an array are represented as (discrete) integers, meaning that using a floating-point value as an index, e.g., B[0.5] fails to compile. Mathematically, the maximum index for any array is defined as its length minus one. Negative indices are invalid and are deemed out-of-bounds. It is common to think of indices as addresses. As an example, the value 3.213 "lives" at the address specified by $B[0]$ (though, this breaks down quickly if the array has duplicate values).

In C, we declare an array using the following syntax: type id[size];. For example, we can declare an array of integers that holds five elements, A, as int A[5];. To initialize an array of integers to preset values, we can use a construct called an initializer list as follows: int B[5] = {4, 3, 0, -3, 12};. We can pass arrays to functions, but in doing so we must also pass the size of the array. For instance, if we want to write a function that returns the sum of an array of double elements, we would write the following:[1]

Listing 5.34—Passing Arrays to Functions (main.c)

```
1   double sum_array(double arr[], const int size) {
2     double sum = 0;
3     for (int i = 0; i < size; i++) { sum += arr[i]; }
4     return sum;
5   }
6
7   int main(void) {
8     const int SIZE = 3;
9     double vals[SIZE] = {10.5, 11.25, 9.85};
10    double sum = sum_array(vals, SIZE);
11    return 0;
12  }
```

Imagine a scenario in which we do not know the size of the array prior to program execution, i.e., *compile-time*. In these instances, we can take advantage of our newly-acquired dynamic memory allocation function malloc. If we want to allocate n elements, each of which is the size of an int, we can do so as follows:

Listing 5.35—Passing Arrays to Functions (main.c)

```
1   int main(void) {
2     // We do not know the value of n.
3     int n = ...
4     int *vals = malloc(n * sizeof(int));
5     if (NULL == vals) {
6       fprintf(stderr, "main: malloc failed\n");
7       exit(EXIT_FAILURE);
8     }
9     return 0;
10  }
```

---

[1]Values may be passed to functions as const parameters, which indicates that they are not modified inside the function; only referenced/read. Most of the time, declaring a parameter as const helps to indicate that the value should not (and, by definition, cannot) be mutated.

Notice the use of an asterisk in the array declaration instead of brackets on line 4. Interestingly, arrays are nothing more than pointers at the end of the day; we can access pointer elements using brackets or through dereferencing the pointer and performing pointer arithmetic. For example, the following code segments are equivalent ways of accessing index four of an array of int values. Note that we omit the error check and headers for conciseness.[1]

Listing 5.36—Array Indexing via Brackets and Pointer Arithmetic (main.c)

```
1   int main(void) {                          int main(void) {
2     int n = ...                               int n = ...
3     int *vals = malloc(n * sizeof(int));      int *vals = malloc(n * sizeof(int));
4     printf("vals[4] = %d\n", vals[4]);        printf("vals[4] = %d\n", *(vals + 4));
5     free(vals);                               free(vals);
6     return 0;                                 return 0;
7   }                                         }
```

Pointer arithmetic answers the question of "Why do we index from zero instead of one?"; we see that if we were to add zero onto a pointer followed by a dereference, that would be equivalent to only a dereference operation.

Exercise 5.10. (⋆)

Write a function that receives an array of double values *aod* and its corresponding length *l*. Compute and return the product of this array.

Exercise 5.11. (⋆⋆)

Write a function that receives an array of int values *aoi* and its corresponding length *l*. Compute and return the sum of all prime numbers.

Exercise 5.12. (⋆⋆⋆)

Jagged arrays are multi-dimensional arrays whose element-arrays do not have a uniform length.[2] For example, consider the following array:

$$\{\{4, 3, 1\}, \{2, 3\}, \{88, 9, 31, 23\}, \{100\}\}$$

This array has four sub-arrays, where each have differing sizes. We can create a jagged array in C by declaring a one-dimensional array of one-dimensional values. To do so without using dynamic memory allocation, e.g., malloc, we must specify the number of sub-arrays. Note that we cannot use initializer lists for jagged sub-arrays.

Listing 5.37

```
1   int main(void) {
2     int arr1[3] = {4, 3, 1};
3     int arr2[2] = {2, 3};
4     int arr3[4] = {88, 9, 31, 23};
5     int arr4[1] = {100};
6     int *jagged_arr[4] = {arr1, arr2, arr3, arr4};
7     return 0;
8   }
```

---

[1]Pointer arithmetic accounts for the size offset of a datatype, so there is no need to perform a multiplicative offset.

[2]Some may question the need for jagged arrays. In many circumstances, they are unnecessary, but one example of their usefulness comes through sparse matrices; a (two-dimensional) matrix may often have empty (zeroed) elements, meaning that allocating the space for an entire two-dimensional array is often wasteful.

If we want to write a function that processes such jagged arrays, we have to pass another array containing the lengths of the sub-arrays, as well as the number of jagged arrays.

Listing 5.38

```
1   int main(void) {
2     int arr1[3] = {4, 3, 1};
3     int arr2[2] = {2, 3};
4     int arr3[4] = {88, 9, 31, 23};
5     int arr4[1] = {100};
6     int *jagged_arr[4] = {arr1, arr2, arr3, arr4};
7     int *jagged_arr_lens = {3, 2, 4, 1};
8     int num_jagged_arrs = 4;
9     return 0;
10  }
```

Write the `flatten_jagged_array` function, which receives an array of jagged arrays of integers, an array of jagged array lengths, and the number of jagged arrays. Return a new one-dimensional array of integers containing all elements from the collection of jagged arrays. You will need to dynamically-allocate the flattened array.

Listing 5.39

```
1   /**
2    * Prints a 1D-array of integers of the form
3    * [x, y, z, ...]
4    *
5    * @param int * - array of values.
6    * @param int - number of values in array.
7    */
8   void print_int_array(int *arr, int n) { ... }
9
10  int *flatten_jagged_array(int *jagged_arr[],
11                            int *jagged_arr_lens,
12                            int num_jagged_arrs) {
13    // TODO.
14  }
15
16  int main(void) {
17    ...
18    int *flattened_arr =
19      flatten_jagged_array(jagged_arr,
20                           jagged_arr_lens,
21                           num_jagged_arrs);
22    print_int_array(flattened_arr, 10);
23    free(flattened_arr);
24    return 0;
25  }
```

```
[4, 3, 1, 2, 3,
88, 9, 31, 23, 100]
```

Strings

The previous two sections discussed arrays and pointers, as well as their dual relationship. Furthermore, in Chapter 4, we described strings and languages as they relate to theoretical computer science. Fortunately, strings in C are very similar and, overall, less complicated.

Strings, as we know, are arrays of characters. In C, there are two broad types of strings: strings declared as arrays/pointers and string literals. To allocate memory for a string declared as an array or pointer, we use either a static array or the `malloc` function. For instance, what follows are two possible ways of storing a string:[1]

Listing 5.40—Two Ways to Create Strings (main.c)

```
1   int main(void) {
2     char str1[128];
3     char *str2 = malloc(128);
4     ...
5     free(str2);
6     return 0;
7   }
```

The variable `str1` is declared on the stack, since it does not use `malloc`, whereas the memory pointed to by `str2` is stored on the heap. To store some arbitrary string in the array, however, we must copy it into the array one character at a time by virtue of the fact that strings are merely character arrays. An additional caveat concerning strings is that they are terminated using the NUL-byte, i.e., \0.[2]

Listing 5.41—Assigning Characters One-by-One (main.c)

```
1    int main(void) {
2      char str1[128];
3      char *str2 = malloc(128);
4
5      // Copy "Hello!" into str1.
6      str[0] = 'H';
7      str[1] = 'e';
8      str[2] = 'l';
9      str[3] = 'l';
10     str[4] = 'o';
11     str[5] = '!';
12     str[6] = '\0';
13     free(str2);
14     return 0;
15   }
```

We could do the same with `str2`. The benefits of using `malloc` over a statically-allocated array include the ability to dynamically create a string without knowing its length a priori. Though, copying a string character by character is cumbersome at best. We will revisit this topic after discussing string literals.

String literals are declared using double quotes. We have been using string literals for a while now when invoking `printf`. String literals are a special case of strings because they cannot be mutated. In addition, string literals are implicitly NUL-terminated. We can declare a string literal in a variable as follows:

Listing 5.42—String Literal Assignments (main.c)

```
1   int main(void) {
2     char str1[128] = "Hello!";
3     char *str2 = "Hello!";
4     return 0;
5   }
```

---

[1]We omit the `malloc` error checks out of a desire for conciseness.

[2]In subsequent listings, we will only #include headers as they are introduced to preserve vertical code listing space.

What we cannot do, however, is change a character at a given index. So, the following code crashes upon execution.

Listing 5.43—Manipulating String Literals is Not Allowed (main.c)

```
1  int main(void) {
2    char str1[128] = "Hello!";
3    str1[2] = 'L';
4    return 0;
5  }
```

Recall, from earlier, the painful process of copying characters into a string. To circumvent this, we can make use of a function from the string.h header, namely strcpy.

Listing 5.44—Using strcpy for Strings (main.c)

```
1  #include <string.h>
2
3  int main(void) {
4    char str1[128];
5    strcpy(str1, "Hello!");
6    return 0;
7  }
```

The convenient thing about strcpy is that it automatically NUL-terminates the string. The above code copies the string literal "Hello!" into the string str1. Now, we may modify str1 since it is not a string literal.

Listing 5.45—Modifying a String Literal after strcpy (main.c)

```
1  int main(void) {
2    char str1[128];
3    strcpy(str1, "Hello!");
4    str[2] = 'L';
5    return 0;
6  }
```

There are several useful functions inside string.h; one of which is strdup: a function that duplicates the supplied string. strdup dynamically allocates memory when invoked, so using it should consequently imply the existence of a corresponding free.

Listing 5.46—Dynamically Copying Strings with strdup (main.c)

```
1  int main(void) {
2    char *str1 = strdup("Hello!");
3    free(str1);
4    return 0;
5  }
```

Determining equality between strings is handy, and the perfect function for this task is `strcmp`; it performs a lexicographic comparison of strings. Some may be surprised by the fact that we can compare strings as we do with numbers, but remember that the characters of a string are, at the end of the day, numbers. Thus, it is possible for a letter to be, e.g., "less than" another. A general rule of thumb to follow is the SNUL pattern: Special (Characters), Number, Uppercase, Lowercase. This pattern indicates that special characters, e.g., punctuation, are "less than" numbers, uppercase, and lowercase letters. For instance, `"HELLO"` is less than `"hello"` because it contains all uppercase letters. As another example, `"heLlo"` is greater than `"heLLo"` because the second 'l' in the former string is greater than the second 'L' in the latter string. `strcmp` returns a negative integer if its first string argument is less than its second, 0 if they are equal, and a positive integer if its first string argument is greater than its second. The exact value returned by `strcmp` depends on the lexicographical character difference. That is, the strings `"a"` and `"e"` have a character separated by four letters, meaning `strcmp("a", "e")` returns −4, since 'e' is four characters ahead of 'a'. `strcmp` is an incredibly helpful function that we will make extensive use of later on.[1]

Listing 5.47—Comparing Strings Lexicographically (`main.c`)

```
1   int main(void) {                              1
2     char *str1 = "heLlo";                       0
3     char *str2 = "heLLo";
4     printf("%d\n", strcmp(str1, str2));
5
6     char *str3 = "hi there";
7     char *str4 = "hi there";
8     printf("%d\n", strcmp(str3, str4));
9     return 0;
10  }
```

Retrieving the length of a string via `strlen` is also incredibly beneficial. The length of a C string is determined by the location of the NUL-termination byte. For instance, `strlen("Hello, world!")` returns 13 because all string literals are implicitly NUL-terminated. Conversely, suppose `foo` is declared as follows:

Listing 5.48—Prematurely NUL-terminating Strings (`main.c`)

```
1   int main(void) {
2     char foo[128];
3     strcpy(foo, "Hello\0, world!");
4     return 0;
5   }
```

Despite the implicit NUL-termination character at the end of the string literal, invoking `strlen` on `foo` returns 5. Again, the length of the string is defined as the number of non NUL characters that occur before the first NUL byte. Though, what happens if we copy characters into an array of `char`s but forgo a NUL byte?

---

[1]Interestingly, the C programming language standard states that only the sign of the return value from `strcmp` is important, i.e., whether it is positive, negative, or zero. Moreover, if the compiler sees that a `strcmp` operation can be optimized into a constant like those shown in the following listing, it will only return −1, 1, or 0. We can disable these optimizations, should we choose to do so, via the `-O0` compilation flag.

Listing 5.49—Do Not Forget to NUL-terminate! (`main.c`)

```
1   int main(void) {
2     char foo[128];
3     foo[0] = 'H';
4     foo[1] = 'e';
5     foo[2] = 'l';
6     foo[3] = 'l';
7     foo[4] = 'o';
8     return 0;
9   }
```

Can we guarantee that `strlen(foo)` is 5? No, we cannot! The reason is that we do not know what data is at `foo[5]`. Declaring `foo[128]` only guarantees that we have 128 bytes of available space to use. It makes no assumptions or presuppositions about said space, meaning that there may be preexisting "junk" at those memory addresses. If want to circumvent this issue, we may decide to use `memset`, from `string.h`, as follows:

Listing 5.50—Clear Stack-Allocated Memory for String (`main.c`)

```
1   int main(void) {
2     char foo[128];
3     memset(foo, 0, sizeof(foo));
4       ...
5     return 0;
6   }
```

From here, if we copy the characters from the string `"Hello"` into `foo`, we do not need to explicitly add a NUL-termination character since we already have via the call to `memset`. As a brief description, `memset` allows us to set the values of an array. For example, if we wanted to set each value of some array of 256 characters called `foo` to the letter `'A'`, we may use `memset(foo, 'A', 256)`.

Finally, we will discuss `strcat`: a function for concatenating, or conjoining, strings. Suppose we declare a string array, then want to copy into it multiple string literals. We may use `strcat` to append a string onto the end of another string. It looks for the first NUL byte in the destination string, then sets the next n characters to those characters in the source string of length n. It also adds a NUL-termination character to the end of the string, meaning it copies $n + 1$ characters into the destination string.

Listing 5.51—Concatenating Strings with `strcat` (`main.c`)

```
1   int main(void) {                             Hello, world! How are you?
2     char str[128];
3     // Clear out string.
4     memset(str, 0, 128);
5     strcpy(str, "Hello, world!");
6     strcat(str, " How are you?");
7     printf("%s\n", str);
8     return 0;
9   }
```

There are several other handy functions in the `string` header, but we will describe them as they are used in the future.

Exercise 5.13. (⋆)

Write your own implementation of strlen that does not use the built-in strlen function. Hint: use a while loop.

Exercise 5.14. (⋆)

Write your own implementation of strcmp that does not use the built-in strcmp function. Hint: this function receives two strings; there are two cases: when the strings are of unequal length and when they are of equal length.

Exercise 5.15. (⋆)

Write the streq function that receives two strings and returns true if they are lexicographically equivalent and false otherwise. This should be extremely simple, and we will make use of this function throughout the book.

Exercise 5.16. (⋆⋆)

The strcpy function is infamous due to its security weaknesses. In the code below, the problem is that strcpy has no bounds checking and, even if the destination array cannot store all characters in the source, it will copy them anyways, potentially overwriting preexisting data! The strncpy function exists to serve as a "safe alternative" to strcpy by requiring a "maximum length" n, meaning it copies exactly n characters from the source string into the destination.[1] Unfortunately, if the source string does not have any NUL characters, strncpy will not add a NUL byte to the end of the destination string. Write your own implementation of strncpy that does not use the built-in strcpy nor strncpy functions, and NUL-terminates the destination string.

Listing 5.52—strcpy is Unsafe! (main.c)

```
1   int main(void) {
2     char buffer[8];
3     strcpy(buffer, "Hello world how are you doing?");
4     return 0;
5   }
```

Exercise 5.17. (⋆⋆)

Like strcpy, strcat falls victim to the same security weakness. Fortunately, its strncat counterpart does, in fact, NUL-terminate the destination string. Write your own implementation of strncat that does not use the built-in strcat nor strncat functions.[2]

Exercise 5.18. (⋆⋆)

Write your own version of strdup that does not use the built-in strdup function.

Exercise 5.19. (⋆⋆)

Write a function strreverse that returns a reversed version of the given string. This string should be dynamically-allocated.

---

[1] If the source string has less than n characters, the destination string is padded with NUL-byte characters.

[2] Hilariously (or not so much, depending on your perspective), even strncat fails to be a safe counterpart to strcat. It *always* writes the NUL-byte character to the destination buffer, meaning that if we write n characters to a buffer containing n elements, strncat egregiously writes $n+1$ bytes due to the NUL-termination character!

Exercise 5.20. (★★★)

Write a function `most_frequent_char` that returns the most frequently-occurring character in a given string. Hint: use an array to keep track of each character's "count".

Enumerations

When we *enumerate* something, we typically associate it with the act of counting. An enum, in C, is a wrapper, of sorts, that provides meaning to values that otherwise have no discernible meaning. For instance, suppose we want to write a program that allows the user to pick between different preset colors. We may use an enum to represent the possible colors. To create an instance of an enumeration, we simply declare a variable of the given enumeration type. Then, to assign it a particular color, we can simply reference the enumeration values.

Listing 5.53—Color Enumeration & Assignment (`main.c`)

```
1   enum Color { RED, BLUE, GREEN, YELLOW, ORANGE, PURPLE, BLACK, WHITE };
2
3   enum Color my_clr = BLUE;
```

If we want to display an enum, we can, of course, use `printf`, but what is the format specifier? Recall that we said an enumeration is a form of counting. Under the hood, C associates integers from zero to the number of enumeration values minus one to a given enum. This means that `my_color` has a value of 1 since `BLUE` is the second enumeration value listed in the `Color` enum. We can compare enumeration values just like numbers and other data types. Though, at the same time, because enumerations are nothing but "named numbers", we can compare values that are entirely distinct enum declarations and return a true result—a potentially undesired outcome.

Listing 5.54—Comparison of Different Enumerations (`main.c`)

```
1    enum Color { ... };                              Color: 1
2    enum Suit { HEARTS, SPADES, CLUBS, DIAMONDS };   Suit: 1
3                                                     BLUE == SPADES? 1
4    int main(void) {
5      enum Color my_clr = BLUE;
6      printf("Color: %d\n", my_clr);
7      enum Suit my_st = SPADES;
8      printf("Suit: %d\n", my_st);
9      printf("BLUE == SPADES? %d\n", my_clr == my_st);
10     return 0;
11   }
```

Structs

Imagine that we are writing a program to process pairs of Cartesian coordinates, i.e., (x, y). How can we represent this in C? One cumbersome method is to declare two arrays: one for the x-coordinate and another for the y-coordinate, where each index corresponds to one pair. E.g., $x[0] = 3.14$ and $y[0] = 2.718$ represents the pair $(3.14, 2.718)$. As one can see, having to keep track of two separate values in two distinct arrays is annoying at best and problematic at worst. The solution is to define a structure.

A *structure*, or a `struct`, is a grouping of data. Structs give meaning to values. For instance, we can declare a point struct with two `double` variables `x` and `y` to represent a single point. Each datum declared in the struct is called a *field*. If we want to initialize a point, we declare it like any other variable. To modify the fields in a struct, we use the dot operator "`.`" as follows:

Listing 5.55—Declaring a point Struct (`main.c`)

```
1   struct point {
2     double x;
3     double y;
4   };
5
6   int main(void) {
7     struct point p1;
8     p1.x = 3.14;
9     p1.y = 2.718;
10    return 0;
11  }
```

We can also use an initializer list, similar to arrays, to initialize the fields in one fell swoop. Note that the order of values in an initializer list matches to the fields of the struct.

Listing 5.56—Quickly Initializing a Structure (`main.c`)

```
1   int main(void) {
2     struct point p1 = { 3.14, 2.718 };
3     return 0;
4   }
```

If the struct variable is declared as a pointer, we use the arrow "`->`" operator. Note that the pointer must point to valid, allocated memory via, e.g., `malloc`. We cannot use an initializer list with a struct pointer.

Listing 5.57—Dynamically-Allocated point Structure (`main.c`)

```
1   int main(void) {
2     struct point *p1 = malloc(sizeof(struct point));
3     p1->x = 3.14;
4     p1->y = 2.718;
5     return 0;
6   }
```

If we want to have a collection of structs, we can always declare an array where the struct is the type. Remember that we can store any variable type in an array, including pointers to structs.

Listing 5.58—Initializing an Array of Structures (`main.c`)

```
1   int main(void) {
2     struct point array_of_points[10];
3     // Set the x-coordinate to be the value of i.
4     for (int i = 0; i < 10; i++) {
5       array_of_points[i].x = i;
6       array_of_points[i].y = 0;
7     }
8     return 0;
9   }
```

Furthermore, suppose we do not know how many structures we wish to allocate at compile-time, i.e., before the program is compiled. Just like with arrays, we may use the dynamic memory allocation technique. What is more is that we can allocate an array of structure pointers where each element is a pointer.[1] to a dynamically-allocated structure.[2]

Listing 5.59—Dynamically-Allocated Array of `struct point *` *(main.c)*

```
1   int main(void) {
2    const size_t SIZE = 10;
3    struct point **points_arr = malloc(SIZE * sizeof(struct point *));
4
5    // Set the x-coordinate to be the value of i.
6    for (int i = 0; i < SIZE; i++) {
7     points_arr[i] = malloc(sizeof(struct point));
8     points_arr[i]->x = i;
9     points_arr[i]->y = 0;
10   }
11
12   // Free each individual point first.
13   for (int i = 0; i < SIZE; i++) {
14    free(points_arr[i]);
15   }
16
17   // Free the overall array.
18   free(points_arr);
19   return 0;
20  }
```

We can pass structs to functions either by value or by pointer. It is almost always better to pass a struct by pointer since, when passed by value, the entire struct, including fields, are copied to the function. Furthermore, if we modify the struct inside the function, the original struct is not modified if we pass by value. We will first demonstrate pass-by-value. The programs outputs a seemingly erroneous result.

Listing 5.60—Passing Structures by Value (main.c)

```
1   void add_scalar_to_point(struct point pt, int s) {      New coordinates:
2    pt.x += s;                                             (3.14, 2.718)
3    pt.y += s;
4   }
5
6   int main(void) {
7    struct point p = { 3.14, 2.718 };
8    add_scalar_to_point(p, 1.618);
9    printf("New coordinates: (%d, %d)\n", p.x, p.y);
10   return 0;
11  }
```

Compare this with the pass-by-pointer example, which outputs the following (now correct) result:

---

[1]Notice that, inside `malloc`, each element is of size `struct point *` and **not** `struct point`. This is a crucial distinction to understand. Sometimes it is appropriate to use the former and other times the latter.

[2]The double asterisks `**` indicates an array of pointers; that is all!

Listing 5.61—Passing Structures by Pointer (main.c)

```
1   void add_scalar_to_point(struct point *pt, int s) {      New coordinates:
2     pt->x += s;                                              (4.758, 4.336)
3     pt->y += s;
4   }
5
6   int main(void) {
7     struct point p = {3.14, 2.718};
8     add_scalar_to_point(&p, 1.618);
9     printf("New coordinates: (%d, %d)\n", p.x, p.y);
10    return 0;
11  }
```

The only **difference** between the two examples is the use of the "address-of" operator '&' and the modification to the signature of add_scalar_to_point. We could, similarly, declare the struct in main as a pointer, then pass it to the function.

Listing 5.62—Altering a Passed Structure inside a Function (main.c)

```
1   void add_scalar_to_point(struct point *pt, int s) {
2     pt->x += s;
3     pt->y += s;
4   }
5
6   int main(void) {
7     struct point *p = malloc(sizeof(struct point));
8     p->x = 3.14;
9     p->y = 2.718;
10    add_scalar_to_point(p, 1.618);
11    printf("New coordinates: (%d, %d)\n", p.x, p.y);
12    free(p);
13    return 0;
14  }
```

What if we **want** to write a function that initializes the coordinates of a point to the x,y origin? An unassuming programmer may be inclined to write the following function:

Listing 5.63—Dynamically Allocating Struct in Function (main.c)

```
1   struct point *point_create(void) {
2     struct point *p = malloc(sizeof(struct point));
3     p->x = 0;
4     p->y = 0;
5     return p;
6   }
7
8   int main(void) {
9     struct point *p1 = point_create();
10    // Some further use of p1.
11  }
```

Such a `point_create` function largely works as intended, but it restricts the caller to only having a dynamically-allocated struct. Moreover, the programmer now has to explicitly free the pointer returned by `point_create`, despite no real indication of the need to do so. These types of functions are sometimes referred to as *constructor* functions, in that they create a struct in memory while also potentially initializing its corresponding fields. An alternative solution is to pass a pointer to a `struct point` and have the function *only* initialize the fields. This refactoring decouples the allocation responsibility from the point representation and places it onto the programmer, with the added benefit that a struct passed to the function needs not to be allocated dynamically. On the other hand, the constructor function *must* dynamically allocate its struct so it lives beyond the scope of the function.

Listing 5.64—Better Point Initialization Function (`main.c`)

```
1   void point_init(struct point *p) {
2     p->x = 0;
3     p->y = 0;
4   }
```

Exercise 5.21. (⋆)
Design a `string` struct that stores the contents of a string as well as its length. This serves as an optimization because we no longer need to call `strlen` on the backing `char *` whenever we need to reference its size.

Exercise 5.22. (⋆⋆)
Design an `int-array` struct that stores an integer array as a pointer as well as its length. This serves as an optimization and quality-of-life improvement to the programmer because we no longer need to pass its length, explicitly, to a function.

Type Definitions

Much like integers, characters, doubles, floats, and structs, we can define our own type using the `typedef` construct. Type definitions are comprised of two "components": a base type and the type identifier. For example, suppose we want to shorten `unsigned char` to instead be referred to as a `byte`. To do so, we write the following:

Listing 5.65—Type Definition Example (`main.c`)

```
1   typedef unsigned char byte;
2
3   int main(void) {
4     // The following lines are equivalent:
5     byte x = 7;
6     unsigned char y = 7;
7     return 0;
8   }
```

Redefining built-in types is not as interesting, though. We most often use type definitions in conjunction with structs. When declaring a struct, we must use the `struct` keyword. If we affix the struct definition with a `typedef`, however, we can omit `struct` when declaring a variable of that type:

Listing 5.66—Using Type Definitions with Structs (main.c)

```
1    typedef struct point {
2      double x;
3      double y;
4    } point;
5
6    int main(void) {
7      point pt1 = { 10, 20 };
8      return 0;
9    }
```

As we see, the "base type" is the struct point definition, and its type identifier is point.

Unions

Structs are useful for gathering several components together into one collective identity. For example, a point has two possible components: an x-coordinate and a y-coordinate. Both fields are accessible and mutable at any time. *Unions*, on the other hand, provide access to one (and only one) field at a time. Namely, if a union has n fields, only one of those n fields is properly-accessible[1] Let us use a simple example to illustrate the use of unions.

Listing 5.67—Union of Multiple Fields (main.c)

```
1    union data {
2      char cval; double dval; int ival; char *sval;
3    };
```

We declare a union (type) called data with four fields. Unions, internally, create enough space to hold the largest possible data type within the union. In this instance, data is eight bytes long, because pointers are eight bytes in size. When working with data, if we want to store an integer, we access the ival field.

Listing 5.68—Accessing One Field of a Union (main.c)

```
1    union data {
2      char cval; double dval; int ival; char *sval;
3    };
4
5    int main(void) {
6      union data d;
7      d.ival = 10;
8      return 0;
9    }
```

This stores an integer value 10 in the union d. Because integers are four bytes long, four of the eight possible bytes are filled by the populated ival field. The rest of the space is thereby unused.

Additionally, union data fields are *aligned* on eight-byte boundaries. This simply means that, if the size of the largest field is not a multiple of eight, the compiler automatically increases the size of the union. Suppose we have the following union definition:

---

[1]We use the terminology "properly-accessible" to later present a problem with union.

Listing 5.69—Size Alignment of Unions (main.c)

```
1   union data {                              16
2     char cval;
3     double dval;
4     int ival;
5     char sval[10];
6   };
7
8   int main(void) {
9     union data d;
10    printf("Size of data union: %zu\n",
11           sizeof(union data));
12    return 0;
13  }
```

At first glance, we are inclined to believe that the union is ten bytes in size, because the largest field is a char array of ten elements. This is incorrect, however, because the compiler resizes this union to be the next largest multiple of eight.

Suppose we set d.ival to 10. If we were to access the other fields, e.g., dval, sval, or cval, the program would certainly compile, but it would either crash or print a potentially invalid result. Let us see what happens if we, instead, populate the sval array of ten characters, then try to access ival.

Listing 5.70—Accessing Multiple Union Fields (main.c)

```
1   union data {                              ABCDEFGHI
2     char cval;                              1145258561
3     double dval;
4     int ival;
5     char sval[10];
6   };
7
8   int main(void) {
9     union data d;
10    strcpy(d.sval, "ABCDEFGHI");
11    printf("sval: %s\n", d.sval);
12    printf("ival: %d\n", d.ival);
13    return 0;
14  }
```

We get the desired output of sval, but what in the world is going on with ival, and more confusingly, what is that large number? Recall that when we erroneously access ival, we also inadvertently access other data (fields) within the union. In this case, because integers are four bytes in size, it accesses the first four bytes of the sval array and attempts to view them as an integer. The first four bytes of the string "ABCD" are stored as 41_{10}, 42_{10}, 43_{10}, and 44_{10} in base ten respectively. Converting these into binary and then base ten results in 1094861636_{10}, but that is not the number that we see in the output window! Indeed, the most popular computer architectures, i.e., ARM and Intel x86, store bytes using the *little endian* system. *Endianness* refers to the ordering of bytes in memory [Bryant and O'Hallaron, 2010].[1] Little endian systems store bytes in reverse order, meaning that instead of storing our four byte string in our specified order of 41424344_{16}, it reverses the byte ordering thereby producing 44434241_{16}. We can convert this value to base ten, which results in the output value.

---

[1]Danny Cohen, in his *On Holy Wars and a Plea for Peace*, coined the use of "endianness" and categorized those who support the most-significant byte as being first are "Big-Endians", whereas those who support the least-significant byte as being first are "Little Endians".

Linked Lists

In one of the previous sections, we discussed arrays and their usefulness for storing a determinate amount of data. What if, on the other hand, we do not know how many values to store ahead of time? The *linked list* data structure, from Chapter 3, allows us to add, insert, remove, and lookup elements without the need to worry about array size constraints. Conceptually, a linked list is a chain of pointers, where each node in the chain stores two values, the first of which is the data at the block, and the second of which is a pointer to the next node in the list. Linked lists are held together in a chain. Thus, if a link is broken, it loses reference to the data after the chain break. The simplest linked list node implementation is one that contains an associated value (we will use an integer) and a "next" pointer.

Listing 5.71—Node Structure for Linked List (`main.c`)

```
1   struct node {
2     int value;
3     struct node *next;
4   };
```

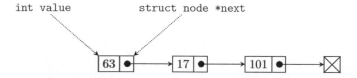

Figure 5.1: Linked List Example with Annotated Struct Fields

Linked lists are dynamically-allocated, meaning we have to use `malloc`. This is because, at compile-time, we do not know, for certain, the length of a linked list; we can add and remove nodes in the chain dynamically. So, let us write a helper function that initializes an arbitrary node with an argument-specified value.[1]

Listing 5.72—Creating a Node (`main.c`)

```
1   struct node *node_create(int value) {
2     struct node *n = malloc(sizeof(struct node));
3     n->value = value;
4     n->next = NULL;
5     return n;
6   }
```

Every non-empty linked list contains a head element, i.e., a node that starts the linked list. So, to create the linked list in the previous diagram, we access the `next` pointer of the root to add a node with value 63. Then, we access that node's `next` pointer to add a node with value 17, and so on. Of course, because we allocate nodes, we must accompany those allocations with invocations to `free`.

---

[1] We recognize and acknowledge that we are breaking our "only initialize; never create" paradigm; for these small code segments, consider such an egregious act as acceptable. Plus, this principle is, in general, applicable to code library maintainers and developers whose code will be used by *other* developers.

Listing 5.73—Manually Adding Nodes to Linked List (main.c)

```
1   int main(void) {
2     struct node *head = node_create(63);
3     head->next = node_create(17);
4     head->next->next = node_create(101);
5     head->next->next->next = node_create(217);
6     head->next->next->next->next = node_create(42);
7
8     free(head->next->next->next->next);
9     free(head->next->next->next);
10    free(head->next->next);
11    free(head->next);
12    free(head);
13
14    return 0;
15  }
```

If we want to print out a linked list, we can recurse from the head and, as long as we have not encountered a NULL node, we print its value and recursively print the rest of the list.

Listing 5.74—Recursively Printing a Linked List (main.c)

```
1   void list_print(struct node *head) {        63 17 101 217 42
2     if (head != NULL) {
3       printf("%d ", head->value);
4       list_print(head->next);
5     }
6   }
7
8   int main(void) {
9     ...
10    list_print(head);
11    ...
12  }
```

We can also compute the length of a linked list via the same recursive pattern; that is, if the current node is NULL, we return 0. Otherwise, recursively add one. Printing out the list from before produces the expected length of 5.

Listing 5.75—Naturally-Recursive Linked List Length (main.c)

```
1   int list_length(struct node *head) {
2     if (NULL == head) {
3       return 0;
4     } else {
5       return 1 + list_length(head->next);
6     }
7   }
8
9   int main(void) {
10    ...
11    printf("Length of linked list: %d\n", list_length(head));
12    ...
13  }
```

Recursion is not always the best tool to solve a problem; if our list grows to be hundreds of elements in size, the recursive solution falls apart in terms of efficiency for reasons we will explain in subsequent chapters. Let us rewrite list_length to instead use a loop.[1]

---

[1] We declare a temporary node pointer so that as we reassign the pointer variables through the loop, the original head remains pointed to the linked list head.

Listing 5.76—Loop-Based Linked List Length (`main.c`)

```
1   int list_length(struct node *head) {
2     int len = 0;
3     struct node *tmp = head;
4     while (NULL != tmp) {
5       len++;
6       tmp = tmp->next;
7     }
8   }
```

Adding values to the end of a list is rather cumbersome since we have to access deeper and deeper next pointers. Therefore, we can write a function that adds an integer value to the end of a given head. The algorithm is as follows: if the next pointer of the provided head is NULL, create a node with the argument-specified value.

Listing 5.77—Add Value to Linked List (`main.c`)

```
1   void list_add(struct node *head, int value) {
2     if (NULL == head->next) {
3       head->next = node_create(value);
4     } else {
5       list_add(head->next, value);
6     }
7   }
```

Now, we can invoke `list_add` to add numbers instead of painstakingly accessing next pointers.

Listing 5.78—Adding Elements to Linked List (`main.c`)

```
1   int main(void) {                            63 17 101 217 42
2     struct node *head = node_create(63);
3     list_add(head, 17);
4     list_add(head, 101);
5     list_add(head, 217);
6     list_add(head, 42);
7     list_print(head);
8
9     return 0;
10  }
```

Freeing a linked list is also cumbersome with our current setup since it requires knowing exactly how many links are declared. Let us write a `list_free` function. Freeing a list opens up a world of potential mistakes because the order in which it is freed is significant. We need to recursively traverse to the end of the chain and `free` from the end to the head.

Listing 5.79—Recursively Freeing a Linked List (main.c)

```
1   void tree_free(struct node *t) {
2    if (t != NULL) {
3      tree_free(t->next);
4      free(t);
5    }
6   }
7
8   int main(void) {
9    struct node *head = node_create(63);
10   list_add(head, 17);
11   list_add(head, 101);
12   list_add(head, 217);
13   list_add(head, 42);
14   list_print(head);
15   tree_free(head);
16   return 0;
17  }
```

Exercise 5.23. ($\star$)
Write two functions: list_min and list_max, which compute the minimum and maximum values of a list respectively.

Exercise 5.24. ($\star$)
Write a function list_contains that returns true if the provided list contains the specified value and false otherwise.

Exercise 5.25. ($\star\star$)
Write a function list_remove that removes the first occurrence of a specified value from a list. Be aware of edge cases, i.e., removing the head element or the end element of a list!

Exercise 5.26. ($\star\star$)
Write a function that removes the largest value from a list. Hint: Utilize the two functions alluded to in the preceding exercises.

Exercise 5.27. ($\star\star\star\star$)
The linked list data structure we have come to know and appreciate is referred to as *singly-linked*, as designated by each node having one link to its next node. *Doubly-linked lists*, on the other hand, have not only links to the next node, but also its predecessor. Correspondingly, it is possible to traverse a doubly-linked list forwards and backwards. Implement doubly-linked lists as a structure, then design functions to add/insert/remove nodes, and delete said lists. Which functions are now simpler to design in comparison to singly-linked lists?

Exercise 5.28. (⋆⋆⋆⋆⋆)

A popular problem in the field of natural language processing concerns the similarity of sentences. We can, primitively, measure the similarity between two sentences s_1 and s_2 by computing the *cosine similarity* of the words in the sentence [Singhal, 2001]. The words of a two sentences s_1 and s_2, where words are strings separated by spaces, form vectors v_1 and v_2, where each element represents the frequency of that word in the sentence. For instance, consider the two sentences s_1: "peter piper likes to pick plenty of peppers" and s_2: "peppery piper loves to eat tons of peppers". We create a (unioned) word vector w = {peter, piper, likes, to, pick, plenty, of, peppers, peppery, loves, tons}. Then, we define v_1 and v_2 as vectors whose elements act as counters, which map to elements of w. So, v_1 = {1, 1, 1, 1, 1, 1, 1, 1, 0, 0, 0}, and v_2 = {0, 1, 0, 1, 0, 0, 1, 1, 1, 1, 1}. Using these vectors, we compute their similarity using the following formula:[1]

$$\cos(\theta) = \frac{\sum_{i=1}^{n} A_i \cdot B_i}{\sqrt{(\sum_{i=1}^{n}(A_i)^2) \cdot (\sum_{i=1}^{n}(B_i)^2)}}$$

The reason we call this the cosine similarity is because we measure the angle between the two generated vectors. Namely, the closer the result is to one, the similar the sentences. This means that, if θ is one, then the sentences share all their words. Conversely, when θ is zero, then there are no shared words.[2] Implement the cosine_similarity function, which receives two strings and returns the cosine similarity. It is to your benefit to write several helper functions when solving this exercise.

Trees

A *tree*, as we discussed in Chapter 3, is a chain similar to that of a linked list. The difference, however, is that trees may have multiple attached links. Namely, trees have a root as well as children. Let us visualize a tree.

The tree in the figure above has a *root node* whose associated value is 31 with two children. Its left child has a value of 2, and its right child has a value of 39. The children of trees are themselves trees. Accordingly, we can treat 2 as the root of another tree which has its own children. Similarly, 39 is the root of another tree. In this example, however, neither 2 nor 39 have children, so they are denoted as *leaves*.

---

[1]The dot in between $A_i \cdot B_i$ is a multiplication sign.

[2]This basic cosine similarity algorithm only measures syntactic similarity between sentences, but even this syntactic characteristic is only extended to the words themselves and not their ordering.

Trees have an inherent relationship to recursive algorithms. Think about it: if we have a tree, and its children are also trees, any algorithm we run on the tree's root is applicable to that tree's children! For instance, suppose we have the following tree and wish to know if the tree contains any element whose value is between 13 and 19 inclusive.

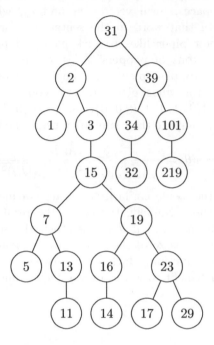

How might we design a recursive algorithm to compute such a result? Well, the idea could be to determine if the current element's value is in this interval and if so, return true. Otherwise, we, recursively, check the children of said element using the same algorithm. For simplicity, we will assume that the tree is a binary tree, i.e., a tree that has at most two children. Thus, the recursive algorithm is as follows: if the current element's value is within the interval, return true. Otherwise, check the left and right subtrees and, if either tree returns true, return true (and false otherwise).

Before we tackle this problem, let us design a tree struct and write some code to initialize trees.

Trees, much like linked lists, are generally dynamically-allocated.[1] Thus, we must use `malloc` to construct trees. So, we can write a helper function to allocate a tree structure and assign it a value, The preferred approach, though, is to pass a pointer to a `tree` struct which may or may not be dynamically-allocated (the point is to defer that responsibility away from `tree_init`). We should also write a `tree_free` function that recursively frees the elements of a dynamically-allocated tree.

---

[1] We attach the "generally" qualifier because trees may be backed by a static/fixed-size array, although this method of implementation is much less common.

Listing 5.80—Tree Structure and Creation (main.c)

```
1   struct tree {
2    int value;
3    struct tree *left;
4    struct tree *right;
5   };
6
7   void tree_init(struct tree *t, int value) {
8    t->value = value;
9    t->left = NULL;
10   t->right = NULL;
11  }
12
13  void tree_free(struct tree *t) {
14   if (t->left != NULL) { tree_free(t->left); }
15   if (t->right != NULL) { tree_free(t->right); }
16   free(t);
17  }
18
19  int main(void) {
20   struct tree *root = malloc(sizeof(struct tree));
21   tree_init(root, 3);
22
23   tree_free(root);
24   return 0;
25  }
```

Now, if we want to assign children to root, we can directly access and modify them. This more clearly demonstrates how each child is, itself, a tree and nothing more. At this point, manually recreating the tree from above is trivial, albeit a bit time-consuming.

Listing 5.81—Manual Leaf Creation in Binary Tree (main.c)

```
1   int main(void) {
2    struct tree *root = malloc(size(struct tree));
3    root->left = malloc(sizeof(struct tree));
4    root->right = malloc(sizeof(struct tree));
5
6    tree_init(root, 31);
7    tree_init(root->left, 2);
8    tree_init(root->right, 39);
9    tree_free(root);
10   return 0;
11  }
```

Now we can write a few functions that act on this, and similar, trees. Let us begin by writing the function that returns whether or not the tree contains a number between 13 and 19 inclusive.

Listing 5.82—Recursive Implementation of Tree Interval Check (main.c)

```
1   bool tree_has_between_interval(struct tree *t) {
2    if (NULL == t) {
3     return false;
4    } else if (t->value >= 13 && t->value <= 19) {
5     return true;
6    } else {
7     return tree_has_between_interval(t->left)
8          || tree_has_between_interval(t->right);
9    }
10   return false;
11  }
```

So, we see that, if the passed tree is NULL, this means that we have not encountered a value between the stated interval, and as such return false. If the value is between the interval, we of course return true. Otherwise, we check both subtrees and return true if at least one subtree has a valid value somewhere within the tree. For practice, we can also write a function to compute the number of leaf elements in a tree. We know that a leaf element is one that has no children, i.e., node->left == NULL and node->right == NULL. So, whenever we encounter a leaf node, we return 1 and sum these values together, similar to natural recursion for summation!

Listing 5.83—Naturally-Recursive Binary Tree Leaf Counting (main.c)

```
1   int count_leaf_elements(struct tree *t) {
2     if (NULL == t) { return 0; }
3     else if (NULL == t->left && NULL == t->right) { return 1; }
4     return count_leaf_nodes(t->left) + count_leaf_nodes(t->right);
5   }
```

Using the complex tree from before, we visually see that there are exactly eight leaf nodes. Running the tree through the program gets us the expected output of eight. How does this work, though? Recall that trees contain either subtrees or nothing at all. So, for instance, when one tree has one leaf, its parent tree must have at least one leaf element. Let us write three procedures to print the values in a binary tree in three orders: pre-order, in-order, and post-order. That is, a *pre-order traversal* prints the current node, then recurses down the left and right subtrees. The right sub-figure is a pre-order traversal of the large tree.

Listing 5.84—Pre-order Binary Tree Traversal (main.c)

```
1   void tree_print_preorder(struct tree *t) {        31 2 1 3 15 7 5 13 11 19
2     if (NULL == t) { return; }                       16 14 23 17 29 39 34 32
3     else {                                           101 219
4       printf("%d ", t->value);
5       tree_print_preorder(t->left);
6       tree_print_preorder(t->right);
7     }
8   }
```

An *in-order traversal* is only slightly different. Instead of immediately printing the value of the current element, we traverse down the left subtree and *then* print the node. Then, we traverse the right subtree. The neat property of an in-order traversal is if the tree holds a certain property, then the elements of the tree are printed in sorted increasing-order.

Listing 5.85—In-order Binary Tree Traversal (main.c)

```
1   void tree_print_inorder(struct tree *t) {         1 2 3 5 7 11 13 15 14 16
2     if (NULL == t) { return; }                       19 17 23 29 31 32 34 39
3     else {                                           101 219
4       tree_print_inorder(t->left);
5       printf("%d ", t->value);
6       tree_print_inorder(t->right);
7     }
8   }
```

Finally, a *post-order traversal* consists of traversing down the left and right subtrees and only then printing the value of the current element. Therefore, all subtrees are printed before printing the root of a tree. E.g., 31 is the last-printed element since it is the root of the entire tree.

Listing 5.86—Postorder Binary Tree Traversal (`main.c`)

```
1  void tree_print_postorder(struct tree *t) {        1 5 11 13 7 14 16 17 29
2   if (NULL == t) { return; }                        23 19 15 3 2 32 34 219
3   else {                                            101 39 31
4    tree_print_postorder(t->left);
5    tree_print_postorder(t->right);
6    printf("%d ", t->value);
7   }
8  }
```

Exercise 5.29. (⋆⋆)
Write a function `tree_size` that returns how many elements are in a given tree.

Exercise 5.30. (⋆⋆)
Write a function `tree_sum` that returns the sum of the values of each element in a given tree.

Exercise 5.31. (⋆⋆)
Write a function `tree_average` that returns the average of the values of each element in a given tree. Hint: use the two functions from the previous exercise.

Exercise 5.32. (⋆⋆)
Write a function `tree_is_balanced` that returns true if the left and right subtrees of a tree contain the same number of elements, and false otherwise.

Exercise 5.33. (⋆⋆)
Write a function `tree_is_sum_balanced` that returns true if the left and right subtrees of a tree sum to the same number, and false otherwise.

Exercise 5.34. (⋆⋆)
Write a function `tree_increment` that adds five to the value of each element in the tree.

Exercise 5.35. (⋆⋆)
Write a function `tree_overwrite_root` that replaces the value of the root if a tree with the largest valued element in the tree. Note that this does not mean we swap any elements; rather, just overwrite the value of the root with the largest value found in the tree.

Exercise 5.36. (⋆⋆⋆)
Write two functions `tree_min` and `tree_max` that return the minimum and maximum values in a tree respectively. It may be tempting to use a global variable to keep track of the "current" minimum and maximum, but try to do this without a global variable. Hint: these functions should always return a number. If an element is a leaf then it, of course, just returns its value. If it has any children, return the minimum and maximum of those via a post-order traversal. When implementing these functions, we must ensure that the passed tree is never NULL, since a NULL element has no value. How can we do that? Finally, if a tree has only one child, what do we do? Implementing one of these two functions correctly effectively implements both; the only difference being an operator flip.

Exercise 5.37. (★★★)

Write a function `tree_mirror` that mirrors the elements of a binary tree. That is, if we have a binary tree t and it has two subtrees l and r, l becomes r and r becomes l. Apply this process recursively throughout the binary tree. Hint: apply the algorithm one step at a time; draw examples of mirrored binary trees to help the visualization. Perform this operation in a post-order fashion. An indicator of success is if the in-order traversal of the now-mirrored tree is reversed.

Function Pointers

Sometimes, it is convenient to have a pointer to some instructions. In other words, we may want to pass around a function for later evaluation. As we will later see, this concept in functional programming is called the use of *first-class functions*, or the equivalent treatment of data and functions. In C, we can emulate this behavior via *function pointers*. Despite the somewhat frightening name, the concept is straightforward. A function pointer, as the name suggests, points to a function. It can then invoke the function that it points to with some arguments. Let us look at an example. Suppose that we want to store a pointer to a function that adds two numbers.

Listing 5.87

```
1   int add(int x, int y) { return x + y; }
2
3   int main(void) {
4     int (*function_ptr)(int, int) = &add;
5   }
```

We first create a function `add` that receives two integer arguments, x and y, and returns their sum.[1] Next, we declare a pointer to a function that receives two integers as parameters and returns an integer. Notice that the pointer type declaration matches the signature of the intended function. Further, note the use of parentheses around the pointer name; this, alongside the immediately-following type parameters, is what designates `function_ptr` as a function pointer. We then assign it to be the address of `add`. We can, thereafter, invoke `function_ptr` as if it were any standard function.

Listing 5.88

```
1   int add(int x, int y) { return x + y; }
2
3   int main(void) {
4     int (*function_ptr)(int, int) = &add;
5     int sum = (*function_ptr)(10, 20);
6     printf("The sum of %d and %d is %d.\n", 10, 20, sum);
7   }
```

Function pointers can be stored in structs, passed as parameters, and even returned from other functions. This is the whole idea behind treating functions as data—just as we can pass around variables, e.g., doubles and integers, we can do the same with function pointers. Let us write a function that receives a function pointer as a parameter.

---

[1]Ignore the fact that such a function is superfluous.

Listing 5.89

```
1   int name_length(const char *str) { ... }
2
3   int compute(const char *name, int (*fn)(const char *)) {
4     return (fn)(name);
5   }
```

Here we declare a function `name_length` whose body is, for our purposes, irrelevant. What is relevant is the next function, `compute`. It receives a `const char *`, as well as a pointer to a function `fn` that receives one `const char *` as an argument and returns an integer. So, we can invoke `fn` with the first argument. Note that, with function pointers, it is optional to add variable names to the formal parameters of a function pointer. This is because a function pointer needs not to store the names of the formal parameters of the function it points to; that is the job of the function itself. So, when the function is invoked, it has the job of finding the provided formal parameters.

Headers and Source Files

Thus far, all of our programs have been inside a single *source file* (.c). Larger programs require more files for modularity purposes. Header and source files provide a sense of abstraction among function and struct implementations. In essence, *header files* (.h) define *function prototypes* for functions whose implementation lies in a corresponding source file.

Imagine we want to design a line struct that we can use across multiple files. We can define the relevant struct inside the header file, then include said header file in another file, e.g., `main.c`. Unlike C library functions, however, header files that *we* define, use double quotes "" instead of < and > in their include directives. While it is compiler-dependent, in general, the use of double quotes tells the C preprocessor to look at locally-defined header files before searching through system files, i.e., where pre-defined headers are located [ISO, 1999].

Listing 5.90—Line Header File (line.h)

```
1   typedef struct line {
2     int x1, y1, x2, y2;
3   } line;
```

Listing 5.91—Using Line Header in Main Source File (main.c)

```
1   #include "line.h"
2
3   int main(void) { ... }
```

This is nice, but what if we want to add functionality to the `line` struct? For instance, perhaps we want to define a `distance` function to compute the distance from both endpoints of the line. We may want a function that returns a boolean based on whether the line passes through a given point. The purpose of a header file is to tell the "includer" of what definitions exist and are available to use. Header files do not provide function definitions; only signatures of available functions. This design philosophy suggests that an "includer" may *use* the functions, but should not concern themselves with their (function) definitions. These definitions must exist somewhere though, and indeed, we place them inside the `line.c` source file after including the `line.h` header.

Listing 5.92—Adding Functions to Line (`line.h`)

```
1   typedef struct line {
2     int x1, y1, x2, y2;
3   } line;
4
5   void line_init(line *l, int x1, int y1, int x2, int y2);
6   double line_distance(const line *l);
7   bool line_contains_point(const line *l, int x1, int y1);
```

Listing 5.93—Line Function Definitions (`line.c`)

```
1   #include "line.h"
2
3   void line_init(line *l, int x1, int y1, int x2, int y2) {
4     l->x1 = x1;
5     l->y1 = y1;
6     l->x2 = x2;
7     l->y2 = y2;
8   }
9
10  double line_distance(const line *l) {
11    double xsq = (l->x1 - l->x2) * (l->x1 - l->x2);
12    double ysq = (l->y1 - l->y2) * (l->y1 - l->y2);
13    return sqrt(xsq + ysq);
14  }
15
16  bool line_contains_point(const line *l, int x1, int y1) {
17    int slope = (double) ((l->y2 - l->y1) / (l->x2 - l->x1));
18    double y_int = l->y1 - slope * l->x1;
19    double exp_y = slope * x1 + y_int;
20    return exp_y == y1;
21  }
```

The C *preprocessor*, in effect, looks at include statements, and copies the code from those headers into the source file. In the end, a C compiler only sees one giant "file" of code and has no knowledge of files. This begs the question of what happens if multiple files include the same header, and indeed, this happens all the time; if our `main.c` source file includes the `line.h` header file, which itself is included by `line.c`, there would exist repeated definitions. The solution to this situation lies in header guards. Header/include guards are preprocessor directives that establish a symbol and, only if the symbol has not been defined before, we proceed to define it along with the remaining content of the header. Otherwise, the definition is bypassed. It can be compared to employing a conditional statement and a boolean flag, except in this case, these definitions remain hidden from the compiler and serve as a clever technique to avoid duplicate symbol definitions.

To create a header guard, begin by choosing a unique symbol name that will serve as the identifier for the header guard. It is common practice to use the header file name in uppercase, replacing any dots or dashes with underscores. At the beginning of the header file, before any code or declarations, we add a preprocessor directive to check if the symbol has been defined. This is typically done using the #ifndef (standing for "if not defined") directive, followed by the symbol name. Immediately after the #ifndef directive, insert a corresponding #define directive to define the symbol. This effectively marks the beginning of the header guard. Any and all code that belongs to the header should, at this point, be added. Finally, at the end of the header file, add a closing preprocessor directive using #endif to mark the end of the header guard.

Listing 5.94—Header Guard Example (line.h)

```
1   #ifndef LINE_H
2   #define LINE_H
3

4      .
5
6   #endif // LINE_H
```

We can now safely include line.h in both line.c and main.c without the compiler displaying duplicate symbol errors.

On the topic of functions in source files, *static functions* are locally-defined functions. That is, by declaring a function as static, we limit its visibility to the file in which it is defined. This helps in encapsulating/hiding the implementation details of the function and prevents it from being accessed by other files. It promotes information hiding and allows you to control access to certain functions, keeping them private to the file in which they are defined. This is particularly useful when you have helper functions or internal implementation details that should not be exposed to the outside world, so to speak.

Exercise 5.38. (★★★)
Design a "stack" data structure to store integers. Given your knowledge on trees and, in particular, linked lists, this should be fairly straightforward. We provide a sample header file alongside function stubs and comments in the source file to guide your implementation.[1]

Listing 5.95—Stack Header File (stack.h)

```
1    #ifndef STACK_H
2    #define STACK_H
3
4    typedef struct stack stack;
5
6    void stack_init(stack *stk);
7    void stack_push(const stack *stk, int v);
8    int stack_pop(stack *stk);
9    int stack_peek(stack *stk);
10   int stack_num_elements(const stack *stk);
11   void stack_destroy(stack *stk);
12
13   #endif // STACK_H
```

---

[1]Some may question the type definition in the stack header file without its body. This is done to constrain access to the structure fields to only those functions inside the corresponding source file.

Listing 5.96—Stack Source File (`stack.c`)

```
1   #include "stack.h"
2
3   typedef struct stack_node {
4     int value;
5     struct stack_node *next;
6   } stack_node;
7
8   typedef struct stack {
9     int num_elements;
10    stack_node *top;
11  } stack;
12
13  /**
14   * Receives a pointer to a stack and instantiates its fields.
15   * @param stack * ptr to stack.
16   */
17  void stack_init(stack *stk) { // TODO. }
18
19  /**
20   * Pushes a new node to the top of the stack.
21   * @param stack *stk - stack to modify.
22   * @param int v - value to push.
23   */
24  void stack_push(stack *stk, int v) { // TODO. }
25
26  /**
27   * Removes the top node from the stack.
28   * @param stack *stk - stack to pop from.
29   * @return int - top of stack.
30   */
31  int stack_pop(stack *stk) { // TODO. }
32
33  /**
34   * Returns, but does not remove, the top node from the stack.
35   * @param const stack *stk - stack to peek from.
36   * @return int - top of stack.
37   */
38  int stack_peek(const stack *stk) { // TODO. }
39
40  /**
41   * Returns the number of values/nodes in the stack.
42   * @param const stack *stk - stack to determine the size of.
43   */
44  int stack_num_elements(const stack *stk) { // TODO. }
45
46  /**
47   * Prints the values in the stack from top-to-bottom.
48   * @param const stack *stk - stack to print.
49   */
50  void stack_print(const stack *stk) { // TODO. }
51
52  /**
53   * De-allocates all nodes in the given stack.
54   * @param const stack *stk - stack to free elements from.
55   */
56  void stack_destroy(stack *stk) { // TODO. }
```

Listing 5.97—Testing Stack Implementation (`main.c`)

```
1   #include "stack.h"                      [15, 10, 5]
2                                           Previous top=15
3   int main(void) {                        Current top=10
4     stack stk;                            [10, 1, 25, 10, 5]
5     stack_init(&stk);
6     stack_push(&stk, 5);
7     stack_push(&stk, 10);
8     stack_push(&stk, 15);
9     stack_print(&stk);
10    printf("Previous top=%d\n",
11          stack_pop(&stk));
12    printf("Current top=%d\n",
13          stack_peek(&stk));
14    stack_push(&stk, 25);
15    stack_push(&stk, 1);
16    stack_push(&stk, 10);
17    stack_print(&stk);
18    stack_destroy(&stk);
19    return 0;
20  }
```

Exercise 5.39. (★★★)

Design a "queue" data structure to store strings. This should require only a few changes to the stack data structure aside from the identifiers and structure definition, which includes changing the structure from last-in-first-out to first-in-first-out. When storing strings in a data structure, be sure to duplicate the string due to possibly passing a string literal to the enqueue function.

Exercise 5.40. (★★★)

Rework the previous stack and queue implementations to use an array-backed representation rather than a linked list. That is, instead of dynamically-allocating a node whenever pushing/enqueueing a new value, you can simply insert a value into the next-available slot, and resize the backing array when necessary. Compare and contrast the different approaches.

Exercise 5.41. (★★★★)

Suppose we want to have a stack data structure that stores, say, characters, floats, doubles, or some other structure. With the current implementation, we would need to modify the existing type stored inside the `stack` structure. In doing so we break any code that makes use of the old `int`-based stack. The solution is, instead of storing `int` or any other specific data type, we can make our approach by using the generic `void *` data type. When initializing stack, we need to pass to it a function that de-allocates the data stored at a node. For example, if our stack stores dynamically-allocated `point` structures, we must tell the stack how to destroy a `point` when clearing the stack.[1] Note that `stack_print` is not possible without passing a `to_string` function that converts its input to a string representation. We provide an abridged version of the source file to showcase some of the necessary changes, as well as a test file.[2][3]

---

[1]The passed function pointer may, in fact, be `NULL` if the stored data is not dynamically-allocated.

[2]Our test suite passes references to `int` variables. This is done so we are able to properly type-cast and dereference the data stored at a node on the stack.

[3]Casting from a `void *` to an `int` requires us to cast the `void *` to an integer pointer, i.e., `int *`, which can then be de-referenced via the asterisk `*` operator. Pay careful attention to the order of operations!

Listing 5.98—Generic Stack Source File (`stack.c`)

```
1   #include "stack.h"
2
3   typedef struct stack_node {
4     void *value;
5     stack_node *next;
6   } stack_node;
7
8   typedef struct stack {
9     int num_elements;
10    stack_node *top;
11    void (*dfree)(void *);
12  } stack;
13
14  /**
15   * Receives a pointer to a stack and instantiates its fields.
16   * @param stack * ptr to stack.
17   */
18  void stack_init(stack *stk, void (*dfree)(void *)) { // TODO. }
```

Listing 5.99—Testing Generic Stack Implementation (`main.c`)

```
1   #include "stack.h"                              Previous top=15
2                                                   Current top=10
3   int main(void) {
4     int v1 = 5; int v2 = 10; int v3 = 15;
5     int v4 = 25; int v5 = 1; int v6 = 10;
6     stack stk;
7     stack_init(&stk, NULL);
8     stack_push(&stk, (void *) &v1);
9     stack_push(&stk, (void *) &v2);
10    stack_push(&stk, (void *) &v3);
11    printf("Previous top=%d\n",
12          *((int *) stack_pop(&stk)));
13    printf("Current top=%d\n",
14          *((int *) stack_peek(&stk)));
15    stack_push(&stk, (void *) &v4);
16    stack_push(&stk, (void *) &v5);
17    stack_push(&stk, (void *) &v6);
18    stack_destroy(&stk);
19    return 0;
20  }
```

Macros

Macros in C are used for symbolic replacement of code. For example, if we want to create a macro that determines the maximum of two values, we might write the following:

Listing 5.100—C Macro Example (`main.c`)

```
1   #define MAX(x, y) (((x) < (y)) ? (y) : (x))
```

Then, to reference/use the macro, we pass (to it) arguments like an ordinary function. The difference between macros and ordinary functions, however, is that the C preprocessor takes the macro definition and inserts it directly into wherever it was invoked. It should be stated, however, that macros are textual substitution, and nothing more, and do not necessarily need to be formed as "functions".[1] This consequently results in a lack of type-checking as well as the potential ambiguity of expressions due to no enforcement of operator precedence. We present these as examples in the following listing:

Listing 5.101—Preprocessor Macro Expansion (`main.c`)

```
1   #define MULT(x, y) ((x) * (y))        1   #define MULT(x, y) ((x) * (y))
2   #define BAD_MULT(x, y) (x * y)        2   #define BAD_MULT(x, y) (x * y)
3                                         3
4   int main(void) {                      4   int main(void) {
5     int x = 6;                          5     int x = 6;
6     int y = 3;                          6     int y = 3;
7     printf("%d\n",                      7     printf("%d\n",
8           MULT(x + 1, y + 1));          8           ((x + 1) * (y + 1)));
9     printf("%d\n",                      9     printf("%d\n",
10          BAD_MULT(x + 1, y + 1));      10          (x + 1 * y + 1));
11    return 0;                           11    return 0;
12  }                                     12  }
```

While it is a bit silly to write a macro that expands out (to) a multiplicative expression, this demonstrates a problem with writing macros the wrong way; BAD_-MULT does not add parentheses around the inner x and y variables, meaning that instead of $x+1$ being multiplied by $y+1$, y is incorrectly multiplied by one. Therefore the program prints $(6+1){\cdot}(3+1) = 28$ followed by $(6+1{\cdot}3+1) = 10$.

Despite their shortcomings, macros are useful in shortening redundant code that is not necessarily best served as a function. Furthermore, because macros are verbatim text replacements, they have zero overhead compared to function invocations, with the added cost of increased code size at compile-time. Multi-line macros are possible with the backslash \ symbol. For the sake of an example, let us create a macro that asserts whether or not a given value is NULL and, if so, prints to standard error and exits the program.

Listing 5.102—Conditionals Within Macros (`main.c`)

```
1   #define ASSERT_NON_NULL(ptr) \
2   if (NULL == ptr) { \
3     fprintf(stderr, "ptr is null\n"); \
4     exit(1); \
5   }
6
7   int main() {
8     int *ptr = NULL;
9     ASSERT_NON_NULL(ptr);
10    return 0;
11  }
```

---

[1]Indeed, we may write constants as preprocessor (macro) definitions, and we will do so throughout the rest of the text.

Exercise 5.42. (⋆⋆)

Many times in this text we will write to the standard error stream to display an error message. The *standard error stream* is a location for programs to output error messages (as opposed to standard output, where printf messages are sent). We do this via fprintf(stderr, msg). This is ever-so-slightly cumbersome to repeatedly type when we know exactly where the message is to be sent and its format. Implement the EPF macro, which receives a format-string message to display and outputs the message to standard error using fprintf. Recall, though, that fprintf is a variadic function, meaning it takes as many arguments as necessary. You will need to make use of the __VA_ARGS__ and the special __VA_OPT__-function macros; the former is a stand-in for the variadic arguments passed to the macro, and the latter specifies that, if the macro invocation contains no variadic arguments, then it expands to nothing. We provide the skeleton code and two test cases in the following listing. Fill in (a), (b), and (c).

Listing 5.103—EPF Macro Skeleton (main.c)

```
1  #define EPF((a)) \
2         (b)((c), fmt __VA_OPT__(,) __VA_ARGS__)
3
4  int main(void) {
5    EPF("Unknown file %s\n", "in.txt");
6    EPF("Invalid input!\n");
7    return 0;
8  }
```

Exercise 5.43. (⋆⋆)

We know that malloc returns a pointer to newly-allocated memory. We also know that it has the potential to fail as indicated by a NULL return value. Having to constantly check these return values can clutter up a code-base quickly. Write the ASSERT_ALLOC macro which, given a pointer to memory and a string, does nothing if the pointer is non-NULL. If, however, it is NULL, the program writes to stderr with a message saying the allocation failed, with the supplied string, and terminates the program. An example of this is as follows:

Listing 5.104—Example of Assertion Allocation Macro Failing

```
1  #define ASSERT_ALLOC(ptr, msg) // TODO.        main: allocation failed!
2
3  int main(void) {
4    int *ptr = malloc(1024);
5    // Assuming this fails, we get the output:
6    ASSERT_ALLOC(ptr, "main");
7    return 0;
8  }
```

User Input

Computer programs are powerful in their own right insofar as the ability to crunch numbers and make decisions quickly. We limit the potential of a program's usability, though, if we do not allow users to interact with that program. As programmers, we can write a function to compute the factorial of some predefined variable, but suppose we want to let non-programmers (who do not have access to the program source code) to use the calculator for themselves. We shall discuss two different ways of retrieving data from the user: standard input and terminal arguments.

Reading from Standard Input. There are many methods for receiving input while a program is running; some are good, whereas others are not so good. First, let us discuss ways to read a line from standard input. Standard input is, in general, where keyboard input is read from in a terminal application, acting as the dual to standard output. We use either fgets or getline, the former of which reads into a pre-allocated char buffer, and the latter dynamically allocates memory, as needed, to fill a buffer. Like fgets, the getline function may receive a pre-allocated buffer, but if it is not large enough to store the entered string, the buffer is resized accordingly. When the input buffer is NULL, getline simply allocates enough memory to the given pointer. Both fgets and getline are referred to as *blocking* input functions, which refers to how they stop program execution until it receives data or some indication to continue.

Listing 5.105—Reading Standard Input via fgets and getline (main.c)

```
1    int main(void) {
2      char buff_fgets[2048];
3      char *ret_fgets = fgets(buff_fgets, sizeof(buff_fgets), stdin);
4      if (NULL == ret_fgets) {
5        EPF("main: fgets failed to read data\n");
6        exit(EXIT_FAILURE);
7      }
8
9      char *buff_getline = NULL;
10     size_t n = 0;
11     size_t ret_getline = getline(&buff_getline, &n, stdin);
12     if (-1 == ret_getline) {
13       EPF("main: getline failed to read data\n");
14       exit(EXIT_FAILURE);
15     }
16
17     free(buff_getline);
18     return 0;
19   }
```

Both functions return values indicating success or failure. fgets returns a pointer to its input argument if it successfully read data, and NULL otherwise. getline, on the contrary, returns the number of read characters, and −1 if it failed to read any data. Interestingly, getline also receives a pointer to a size_t variable; in the event that the input buffer is not large enough, the passed size_t value is modified to reflect the new size of the buffer. Moreover, because the input buffer is modified (i.e., its pointer is re-allocated as necessary), we must pass a reference to the string, rather than just the string itself. Similar to malloc, we should always check the returned value(s).

Neither functions are sufficient, on their own, to help us with our problem of allowing the user to enter a number to compute its factorial because we can only read strings. Hence we introduce the sscanf function, which receives a string and, much like printf, uses format specifiers to search for desired contents. Unlike printf, however, sscanf stores the extracted data *into* variables rather than *out of* variables. Let us see how to extract an integer from a string using sscanf:[1]

Listing 5.106—Using sscanf to Extract Integer from String (main.c)

```
1   int main(void) {
2     char *buff_getline = NULL;
3     size_t n = -1;
4     size_t ret_getline = getline(&buff_getline, &n, stdin);
5
6     int fact_value = 0;
7     size_t tokens = sscanf(buff_getline, "%d", &fact_value);
8     if (1 != tokens) {
9       EPF("main: sscanf failed to read a number\n");
10      exit(EXIT_FAILURE);
11    }
12    return 0;
13  }
```

To extract, or tokenize, an integer from a string, we use the %d format specifier. We also pass a reference to the variable we want to hold the integer. sscanf returns the number of extracted tokens, and EOF if the input is only whitespace or empty.

Many C programming tutorials offer two ways to read user input: gets and scanf. The former looks eerily similar to fgets; it reads strings only from standard input, but falls victim to *buffer overflow* vulnerabilities. scanf, on the other hand, also reads data only from standard input, but also is susceptible to buffer overflow. Consider the following code:[2]

Listing 5.107—Buffer Overflow Example

```
1   int main(void) {
2     int y = 500;
3     char buff_gets[10];
4     gets(buff_gets);
5
6     printf("%s, %d, %x\n", buff_gets, y, y);
7     return 0;
8   }
```

The gets function reads all data from standard input and stores these characters, excluding the newline yet including a NUL-terminator, into the given buffer. Imagine the user enters a string that is fourteen characters long. Our buff_gets buffer only stores up to ten characters, but that data has to go somewhere, meaning the last four characters override whatever, if any, data was located at the memory addresses of those trailing characters. In our case, because we declare buff_gets immediately after declaring the integer y, those four remaining characters populate where 500 is stored. Let us see the output for a few different test cases:

---

[1]The error check for getline is omitted out of conciseness.

[2]Note the inclusion of the format specifier %x to output the hexadecimal representation of an integer.

Listing 5.108—Testing Buffer Overflow Program

```
> "Hello"↩                      | Hello, 500, 1f4
> "Helloworl"↩                  | Helloworl, 500, 1f4
> "Helloworld"↩                 | Helloworld, 256, 100
> "Helloworld1234"↩             | Helloworld, 875770417, 34333231
> "Helloworld1"↩                | Helloworld, 49, 31
```

Case one is simple: we enter a string of five characters excluding the NUL-terminator, which all fit inside our buffer. Case two fills the buffer entirely with ten characters including the NUL-terminator. Case three overfills the buffer by one character because of the NUL-terminator. Thus the corresponding numeric value for the NUL-terminator is 0_{10}, which as an 8-bit binary number is just 0_2. Recollecting our knowledge of little endianness from the section on unions, we know that 500_{10} is stored as the 32-bit integer $11110100\ 00000001\ 00000000\ 00000000_2$. Overwriting the first byte with 0_2 in little endian gets us $00000000\ 00000001\ 00000000\ 00000000_2$, which converts to 100_{16}. Case four fills the buffer five characters past the limit including the NUL-terminator, resulting in the value of y being changed to the representation of the string "1234" in binary. Each of these characters correspond to 31_{16}, 32_{16}, 33_{16}, and 34_{16}. Again, because the computer uses little endian, we flip these values to get a hexadecimal representation of 34333231_{16}. Case five over-fills the buffer by two bytes including the NUL-terminator. Because it takes only two bytes to represent 500_{10}, we overwrite these two bytes with the numeric values corresponding to "1" and the NUL-terminator, getting us the hexadecimal number 31_{16}.

Understanding *why* these two functions are dangerous is important, but not as much as simply not using them in favor of their safer `fgets` and `getline` counterparts. So do not be discouraged if the above discussion went a bit over your head. In fact, `gcc` emits a warning for any use of `gets` in a C program.

Reading Terminal Arguments. The `main` function that we have presented is secretly deceiving; as a matter of fact, it actually receives two arguments, rather than void:

Listing 5.109—Main Function Signature (`main.c`)

```
1   int main(int argc, char *argv[]) { ... }
```

We see that `main` receives a number of arguments, specified by `argc`, and an array of strings, specified by `argv`. These arguments correspond to those given to the program upon its execution. For instance, if we want to pass three numbers and a string as arguments to a program, we would use the following:

Listing 5.110—Terminal Arguments Example (`main.c`)

```
./program 5 10 1000 "This is a string argument"
```

Then inside the respective `main` function, `argc` is equal to five, and each element of `argv` is populated with the arguments we provide. This seems to contradict what we pass to the executable because we only specify four arguments: 5, 10, 15, and "This is a string argument". Omitting the program name, i.e., `program`, as the first argument is a common mistake. The name of the program is always included as the first argument, and therefore if we provide n arguments, the value of `argc` is $n+1$.

With our understanding of string data extraction from the last section, we are very easily able to extract a number from a string terminal argument:

Listing 5.111—Converting Argument Two to an Integer

```
1   int main(int argc, char *argv[]) {
2     int val = 0;
3     size_t tokens = sscanf(argv[1], "%d", &val);
4     return 0;
5   }
```

Exercise 5.44. (⋆⋆)
Write a small program that computes and prints the sum of all integers given as terminal arguments. You will need to write a function that determines if a string *is* an integer.[1] Below are some sample inputs and outputs:

Listing 5.112

```
1   > ./sum 5 10 15 20                    50
2   > ./sum 5 10 Hello 20                 35
3   > ./sum Hiya 10 Hey 20                30
4   > ./sum Hello Hi Howdy                0
```

Exercise 5.45. (⋆⋆)
Write a program that computes the factorial of all odd integers given, and the nth Fibonacci number of all even integers given. You do not need to consider cases when the input is a non-positive integer. Print each result on new lines with some indication of which function was used for the given input.

Listing 5.113

```
1   > ./fact-or-fib 5 6 10 11 24          5! = 120
                                          fib(6) = 8
                                          fib(10) = 55
                                          11! = 39916800
                                          fib(24) = 28657
```

Exercise 5.46. (⋆⋆⋆)
Redo the sum exercise, but this time, use recursion (if you used recursion in the previous exercise, then use a loop instead). That is, write a recursive function `sum`, which receive no arguments itself, but calls a local helper function `sum_helper`. Your helper function should have no local variables defined.

---

[1]Once you have some practice writing C functions, you may take advantage of the `strtod` standard library function.

Exercise 5.47. (★★★)
Design a program that allows the user to enter a sequence of integers from standard input. The program should output a "sequence sum" of the entered values, as well as any adjacent duplicate values. If there are no adjacent duplicates, output the string "No duplicates.". As an added challenge, do not use any integer arrays or other data structures for storing the numbers. To print the results all at once, construct two char[] buffers for the output result. Below are some sample tests.

Listing 5.114

> 1 7 8 9	1 8 16 25 No duplicates.
> 11 11 11 5 5 6 5 3 5 5	11 22 33 38 43 49 54 57 62 67 11 5 5
> 11 12 11 12	11 23 34 46 No duplicates.
> 5 5 5 5 5 5 5 5 5 5 5	5 10 15 20 25 30 35 40 45 50 55 5

Exercise 5.48. (★★★)
A *keylogger* is an application that records a user's input strokes/key presses. Most often, unfortunately, keyloggers are designed for nefarious purposes, such as stealing passwords. An infected user may be tempted to "scramble" their input if they, for whatever reason, know that the keylogger is active. For instance, suppose they type some text into a password field; the keylogger picks up the following keystrokes (as integers):

100 97 119 **107** 108 8 8 8 112 51 52 8 8 8 8 8 98 111 107 102 8 8 75 9
51 52 8 8 8 8 **97** 100 112 107 102 109 8 8 8 97 107 102 109 52 49 50 8
8 112 108 **109** 102 122 8 8 8 8 8 8 8 8 8 115 115 57 52 56 112 102 107
8 8 8 8 8 8 **119** 69 87 8 8 111 82 8 114 42 38 36 8 8 68 100 100 8 8 8
100 49 49 **49** 49 8 8 8 8 50 51 50 51 8 8 9 9 52 53 101 8 8 8 8 8 8 51

To the untrained eye, this looks like gibberish! The keylogger is able to decipher this into the victim's password: "badpassword"! How did they decipher the absolutely amazing encryption scheme? Design the decrypt function, which unscrambles a given array of characters.[1] Hint: the decimal 8 represents the backspace character.

Exercise 5.49. (★★★★)
Many programming courses/textbooks present an exercise that asks students to write a "calculator" application to the following effect:

---

[1]Note that decrypt must also receive the number of read characters.

1. Addition
2. Subtraction
3. Multiplication
4. Division

Enter an operation:
> 3
Enter your first number:
> 7
Enter your second number:
> 12

Your result is 84. Do you want to continue (Y/n)?
> n

This is a rather verbose program; an improved alternative would be to design a program that receives operands and operators to perform some computation.

```
> 4 + 3
7
> 81 * 9
729
> 325.25 / 45
7.22777778
> sin 45
0.8509
```

Design such a program. The more (correctly-implemented) features you include, the better, so be creative!

Exercise 5.50. ($\star\star\star\star\star$)
The *definite integral* of a function f, defined as $\int_a^b f(x)dx$, produces the area under the curve of f on the interval $[a, b]$. The thing is, though, integrals are defined in terms of *Riemann summations*, which provide estimations on the area under a curve. Riemann sums approximate the area by creating rectangles of a fixed width Δ, as shown in 5.2 for an arbitrary function f. Left-Riemann, right-Riemann, and midpoint-Riemann approximations define the focal point, i.e., the height, of the rectangle. Notice that, in Figure 5.2, we use a midpoint-Riemann sum with $\Delta = 0.2$, in which the collective sum of all the rectangle areas is the Riemann approximation. Your job is to use this idea to approximate the area of a circle.

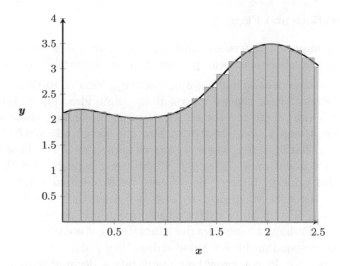

Figure 5.2: Midpoint-Riemann Approximation of a Function

Allow the user to enter a radius r and a delta Δ, then compute a left/right-Riemann approximation of the area of a circle. Hint: if you compute the left/right-Riemann approximation of one quadrant, you can very easily obtain an approximation of the total circle area. We illustrate this hint in Figure 5.3 where $\Delta = 0.5$ and its radius $r = 2$. Note that the approximated area will vary based on the chosen Riemann approximation.[1] Further note that no calculus knowledge is necessary to solve this exercise.

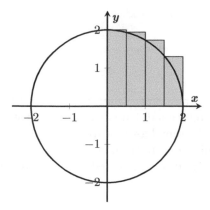

Figure 5.3: Right-Riemann Approximation of a Function

---

[1] A left-Riemann sum under-approximates the area, whereas a right-Riemann sum provides an over-approximation. A midpoint approximation uses the average between the left and right approximations. It should be noted that, in the general case, these statements do not hold as they depend on the interval we integrate our function over.

Bitwise Operations and Flags

At their core, computers understand nothing more than zeroes and ones, i.e., *binary values*. Decimal numbers are nothing more than an abstraction for humans.

For instance, consider the number 5_{10}, where n_{10} informs us that n is a base ten number, or decimal. How can we represent the same idea, but in binary? Recall from Chapter 2 that there are ten digits: 0 to 9. In binary, there are only two possible values: 0 and 1. So, intuitively, how can we encode zero? The simplest answer is to say that $0_{10} = 0_2$, where n_2 lets us know that n is a base two number, or binary. What about one? $1_{10} = 1_2$. We run into a problem with 2_{10} because 2 is not a valid value in binary! So, like we do in decimal when we reach ten, we simply roll the next value over by one and reset the right position to zero. Thus, $2_{10} = 10_2$. This pattern cycles ad infinitum, and so therefore $5_{10} = 101_2$. $35_{10} = 100011_2$. Perhaps we should write a function that converts a positive decimal value into a corresponding binary value string. E.g., $35_{10} =$ "100011". Though, there is an issue: we do not know how many bits a decimal number uses, right? Wrong! Logarithms are to the rescue. If we take $\log_2 35$, we get approximately 5.192. We saw that it takes six bits, or binary digits, to represent 35_{10} in binary. It may be tempting to round our decimal value to the next closest integer with the ceiling function. This will not work, however, because it fails to account for exact powers of two. E.g., $\lceil \log_2 16 \rceil = 4$, but $16_{10} = 10000_2$, meaning we should add one, then take the floor of the result, i.e., $\lfloor \log_2 n + 1 \rfloor$. We use the math.h header for the relevant functions.

Listing 5.115—Positive Decimal Values to Binary Function Stub (main.c)

```
1   char *decimal_to_binary(int n) {
2     // Negatives are impossible with this function.
3     if (0 > n) {
4       EPF("decimal_to_binary: n must be > 0!\n");
5       exit(EXIT_FAILURE);
6     }
7     // Handle zero case.
8     else if (0 == n) { // TODO. }
9     else { // TODO. }
10      return NULL;
11    }
```

This function should return a dynamically-allocated string representing the converted value in binary. The (any base) logarithm of zero is undefined, so we need to manually account for this case. Returning a string literal is not appropriate since string literals are not dynamically-allocated; a duplicated string literal is therefore warranted!

Listing 5.116—Handling Zero Case in Decimal-to-Binary Conversion (main.c)

```
1   char *decimal_to_binary(int n) {
2    char *result = NULL;
3
4    // Negatives are impossible with this function.
5    if (0 > n) {
6     EPF("decimal_to_binary: n must be > 0!\n");
7     exit(EXIT_FAILURE);
8    }
9    // Handle zero case.
10   else if (0 == n) {
11    result = strdup("0");
12   } else { // TODO. }
13
14   return result;
15  }
```

Now comes the interesting case. Using the logic on logarithms and bits from earlier, we know how many elements should be in our string: the number of required bits plus one for the NUL-termination character.

Listing 5.117—Handling Zero Case in Decimal-to-Binary Conversion (main.c)

```
1   char *decimal_to_binary(int n) {
2    char *result = NULL;
3     ...
4    if (0 > n) { ... }
5    // Handle zero case.
6    else if (0 == n) { ... }
7    else {
8     int no_bits = (int) floor(log2(n) + 1);
9     result = malloc(no_bits + 1);
10    ...
11   }
12   return result;
13  }
```

We now need to traverse through the number and determine, at each binary digit, whether it is a one or zero, and concatenate the relevant character. How do we do this? We need to introduce bitwise operators, or operations that act on bits, as the name suggests.[1]

First, we will discuss bitwise OR, denoted as '|'. When we take the bitwise OR of two integer values m and n, we create a result whose bits are set if the corresponding bit is set in at least m or n. For instance, take 145_{10} | 91_{10}. The binary representation of these values is 10100001_2 | 01011011_2. All we need to do is see if a bit is set at each position in the binary value, leading to 11011011_2 or 219_{10}.

Up next is bitwise AND, denoted as '&'. Bitwise AND is similar to OR with the exception that the corresponding bit must be set in both m and n. Using the numbers from before, 145_{10} & 91_{10} is 10001_2 or 17_{10}.

Now, there is bitwise XOR, denoted as '^'. Bitwise XOR has its corresponding bits set if exactly one of m or n has the bit set. Thus, 145_{10} ^ 91_{10} is 11001010_2 or 202_{10}.

---

[1] We could use the modulo operation, but that is not as fun!

Finally, we have bitwise NOT, otherwise known as one's complement denoted by '~'. Bitwise NOT flips all bits in a number, meaning it is a one-place operator. Though, bitwise NOT has a very special property that must be explained: it does not account for only the bits used in its representation, but rather also leading zeroes.[1] For instance, suppose we store 91 in a 32-bit int. This, to the program/-computer, looks like $00000000\ 00000000\ 00000000\ 01011011_2$. When we perform a bitwise NOT on said value, we flip all bits, including any leading zeroes. Thus, we end up with $11111111\ 11111111\ 11111111\ 10100100_2$, which is a number over four billion, right? Technically yes, but according to C, this is not correct. According to the program, we stored this value as a *signed integer*, meaning it has a single bit denoting whether it is positive or negative. The sign bit is the most-significant bit, i.e., the "farthest-left bit". So, rather than representing numbers from 0 until $2^{32} - 1$, we represent numbers from -2^{31} until $2^{31} - 1$. Though, this still does not necessarily answer the question—what is ~91? "It certainly is not negative two billion", is a correct response. In order to accurately represent a negative number, C uses the two's complement representation. We stated that bitwise NOT uses one's complement, which simply flips every bit. Two's complement, on the other hand, flips every bit except the sign bit and adds one to the result. Thus, taking the previous result of $11111111\ 11111111\ 11111111\ 10100100_2$ and flipping every bit except for the sign bit results in $10000000\ 00000000\ 00000000\ 01011011_2$. Finally, we add one to the number to get $10000000\ 00000000\ 00000000\ 01011100_2$, which is equivalent to -92_{10}. An astute reader may notice that this is just adding one to 91_{10} and negating the result. Once again, this is a correct observation! Thus, bitwise NOT adds one and negates its value.

Let us briefly return to the decimal_to_binary function. We know that we can use bitwise AND to determine whether the least significant bit is set via n & 1. Though, how can we test the next bit, i.e., the second-least significant bit, and so on? That brings us to the topic of bit-shifting operators.

Bitwise shifting is very intuitive from both a computer's and human's perspective. When we bit shift a number, it means that we take its binary digits and, literally, shift them either to the left or to the right. As an example, $110111101_2 = 477_{10}$ bit shifted to the left becomes $1110111010_2 = 944_{10}$. Conversely, bit shifting to the right becomes $11101110_2 = 238_{10}$. Thus, shifting left adds a trailing zero and shifting right adds a leading (but implicit) zero.[2], which is -1_{10} after performing two's complement arithmetic. Another perspective is to say that shifting a positive integer to the left by one multiplies said integer by two, and shifting to the right divides said integer by two (using integer division). It is better to say, though, that shifting either multiplies or divides the number by a power of two. E.g., shifting by three multiplies or divides the value by $2^3 = 8$.

---

[1]While all bitwise operators operate on the entire operand, we were operating under the assumption that our values were stored as 8-bit integers in the preceding examples and explanations on the binary bitwise operators.

[2]Bitwise right-shifting throws a wrench into the complexity by dealing with sign-extension. That is, suppose we bitwise right-shift a negative number. The sign bit is set, and as such, we carry that into the shifted result. E.g., -64_{10}, as a 32-bit integer, is $11111111\ 11111111\ 11111111\ 11000000_2$, but shifting it to the right by 2_{10} gets us $11111111\ 11111111\ 11111111\ 11110000_2$, or -16_{10}. Moreover, if we shift a positive integer to the left, we might accidentally overwrite the sign bit with a one! E.g., 16_{10}, as a 32-bit integer, is $00000000\ 00000000\ 00000000\ 00010000_2$, but shifting it to the left by twenty eight bits gets us $10000000\ 00000000\ 00000000\ 00000000_2$

Using this logic, we can finish our decimal_to_binary function. That is, we check each bit of our number using bit shifting and bitwise AND. If the corresponding bit is set, we add the character '1' to the character array and otherwise add '0'.

Listing 5.118—Integrating Bitshifting (main.c)

```
1   char *decimal_to_binary(int n) {
2    char *result = NULL;
3     ...
4    else {
5     int no_bits = (int) floor(log2(n) + 1);
6     result = malloc(no_bits + 1);
7     for (int i = 0; i < no_bits; i++) {
8      if (0 == ((n >> i) & 1)) {
9       result[i] = '1';
10      } else {
11       result[i] = '0';
12      }
13     }
14     result[no_bits] = '\0';
15    }
16    return result;
17   }
```

Interestingly, these bitwise operations are applicable to boolean values as well. E.g., true | true is nothing more than 1 | 1. Similarly, false & true is nothing more than 0 & 1 = 0. A purpose of using bitwise operations, however, is to combine multiple boolean values into one integer. Consider a file on a computer. Files have different permission properties, i.e., information that says who can access and mutate a file or its contents. Suppose our computer has three user classifications: file owners, groups, and others. The user who created a file, as its name suggests, is the file owner. We categorize a collection of individuals under some identifier, e.g., "students" or "faculty" as a group. Finally, there are others, which accounts for all users that are not the owner nor part of a group. Further imagine that a file has three permission types: read, write, and execute. If we had to keep track of individual booleans, we would have to worry about altering the state of nine booleans for every file! Even if we store these in an array, it is still cumbersome. Bitwise operations are our friend. If we use a "short" data type, we have sixteen bits to work with—more than enough. We designate the three least significant bits for "other user" permission, the next three are for "group" permission, and the following three bits are for "owner" permission. Correspondingly, we use define to give names to these bit positions.

Listing 5.119

```
1    #define OTHER_EXEC 0x0001
2    #define OTHER_WRITE 0x0002
3    #define OTHER_READ 0x0004
4
5    #define GROUP_EXEC 0x0008
6    #define GROUP_WRITE 0x0010
7    #define GROUP_READ 0x0020
8
9    #define OWNER_EXEC 0x0040
10   #define OWNER_WRITE 0x0080
11   #define OWNER_READ 0x0100
```

Because each permission has exactly one set bit, as demonstrated by using powers of two, we can combine file permissions. For instance, if we want to say that a file can be read, written, and executed by only the owner, we use a bitwise OR to set the three respective constants.

Listing 5.120

```
perm = OWNER_READ | OWNER_WRITE | OWNER_EXEC;
```

Which translates, in hexadecimal, to perm $= 0001_{16} \mid 0002_{16} \mid 0004_{16} = 01C0_{16}$.

If we want to check to see if a file has a certain permission, we use bitwise AND to check if the corresponding bit is set. Essentially, we want to see if the result of a bitwise AND with the relevant position is a non-zero value (because if we bitwise AND two numbers, only sharing set bits are set in the result). For example, checking "perm" to see if GROUP_EXEC is set looks like (perm & GROUP_-EXEC). In C, as we have mentioned, a conditional resolves non-zero values as true, meaning that as long as this is a non-zero value, it indicates that the flag is set. To set a flag, we use bitwise OR: perm = perm | GROUP_EXEC, or the less verbose augmented assignment operator: perm |= GROUP_EXEC. To disable a flag, we use bitwise AND combined with bitwise NOT: perm = perm & ~GROUP_EXEC, or perm &= ~GROUP_EXEC. The reason this works is because, if GROUP_EXEC is 0008_{16}, then ~GROUP_EXEC $= FFF7_{16}$. So, bitwise AND-ing any number with this bit toggled will disable it, and if it is already disabled, nothing happens. To "toggle" a bit, we use bitwise XOR: perm ^= GROUP_EXEC. Again, if the bit is set in perm, because GROUP_EXEC's bit is always trivially set, that bit in perm is disabled due to the properties of XOR. If it is disabled because of XOR properties, it becomes set (i.e., $0 \char`^ 1 = 1$).

Another reason to work with bitwise operations comes through how colors are (typically) represented in computers. Most often, computers store colors as *alpha-red-green-blue* integers, since as we have repeatedly mentioned, computers only understand numbers at their core. Namely, a 32-bit integer stores the data associated with a color where the most-significant byte stores the alpha channel, the next byte stores the red channel, the next stores the green, and the least-significant byte stores the blue channel. A channel, as suggested, is a value between 0 and 255 inclusive. Often times, colors are represented using hexadecimal as a means of shortening the notation. E.g., 0xffff00ff represents a color whose alpha channel is 255, red is 255, green is 0, and blue is 255. It may be tempting to say that this is a fully-opaque purple color since mixing red and blue colors gets us purple. In terms of ARGB, though, this is not correct! It is, in fact, magenta. Why do we care about this, though? We can extract individual channels of an ARGB value using bitshifting and bitwise AND. For instance, to extract the red channel from an ARGB value c requires us to bit shift the value down by 24 and perform a bitwise AND on 255, i.e., $(c \gg 24)$ & 255.

Exercise 5.51. (☆☆☆☆☆)

Jef Poskanzer invented the PPM image file format in the late 1980's [Henderson, 2019]. Its advantages over other image file formats include its listing of pixel data as explicit RGB values. PPM files also specify the image dimensions. For example, the following lines describe a 2×3 (pixel) image with red, green, and blue pixels in the first row, followed by blue, green, and red pixels in the second.

```
P3
2 3
255
255 0 0 0 255 0 0 0 255
0 0 255 0 255 0 255 0 0
```

Write two functions: `compress` and `decompress`. The former receives a two-dimensional array of integers corresponding to the RGB pixels of a PPM file. Its job is to create a new two-dimensional array that condenses these byte values into 32-bit integers. For instance, the color values 255 0 0 are compressible into $ff0000_{16}$ using bitwise operations. Use the following macro to retrieve the corresponding value of given RGB channels:

Listing 5.121

```
1    #define COLOR_RGB(R, G, B) \
2        ((((R) << 16) & 0xff0000) \
3        | (((G) << 8) & 0x00ff00) \
4        | ((B) & 0x0000ff))
```

The latter `decompress` function, on the other hand, does the opposite; it receives an array of integers and expands their values into separate red, green, and blue channels, returning a new two-dimensional array. Use the following macros to extract each color channel of an integer:

Listing 5.122

```
1    #define GET_RED(C) ((((C) >> 16) & 0xff)
2    #define GET_GREEN(C) ((((C) >> 8) & 0xff)
3    #define GET_BLUE(C) ((C) & 0xff)
```

The following exercises will use an image of a praying mantis as shown in Figure 5.4.[1]

Exercise 5.52. (⋆)

Design a `struct image` to hold (integer) pixel data, as well as its (the image) corresponding width and height. The pixel data should be the "compressed" integers as described previously. We provide a template as follows:

Listing 5.123

```
1    typedef struct image {
2        // TODO (you fill this in!).
3    } image;
```

Exercise 5.53. (⋆⋆⋆)

Write a function `zero_red`, which receives an image and returns a new image where the red channel of all pixels is set to zero (see Figure 5.5).

---

[1]The image is authored by Rick van der Haar, provided by unsplash.

Figure 5.4: Praying Mantis   Figure 5.5: No Red Channel

Exercise 5.54. (⋆⋆⋆)
Write a function `negative`, which receives an image and returns a new image where each color is converted to its negative counterpart. The negative of a color is the color created when each channel is subtracted from 255 (see Figure 5.6).

Exercise 5.55. (⋆⋆⋆)
Write a function `grayscale`, which receives an image and returns a new image where each color is converted to its grayscale counterpart. The grayscale of a color is the average of its color channels (see Figure 5.7).

Figure 5.6: Negative Image   Figure 5.7: Grayscale Image

Exercise 5.56. (⋆⋆⋆)
Write a function `swap_red_green`, which receives an image and returns a new image where each color has its red and green channels swapped (see Figure 5.8). Then, write another function `swap_green_blue`, which swaps the green and blue channels of a given image (see Figure 5.9).

Figure 5.8: Red & Green Swapped   Figure 5.9: Green & Blue Swapped

Exercise 5.57. (⋆⋆⋆)
Write functions `mirror_vert` and `mirror_horz`, which return new images where the pixels are flipped along the y and x axes respectively (see Figures 5.11 and 5.10).

Figure 5.10: Mirror Along y-axis   Figure 5.11: Mirror Along x-axis

Exercise 5.58. (★★★)

Brightness and contrast are two properties of images, where brightness describes how close each pixel is to their maximum values, and contrast describes the distance between pixels in the image. In essence, the more contrast, the brighter the bright colors, and the darker the dark colors. These two properties are described by $f(x) = \alpha x + \beta$, where α and β represent contrast and brightness respectively. Contrast α is a multiplicative value, wherein an $\alpha \in (0, 1)$ lowers the contrast, and an $\alpha > 1$ increases the contrast. Brightness, on the other hand, is a linear additive value, wherein positive values of β increase the brightness, and negative values decrease the brightness. The variable x is a color channel. For this exercise, write a function `alter_brightness_contrast` that receives an α and β, modifying the corresponding components. You will need to write a function that "clamps" a value between 0 and 255 (see Figures 5.12 and 5.13).

Figure 5.12: Brightness −50 Decrease   Figure 5.13: Contrast 2X Increase

Exercise 5.59. (★★★★)

Write a function `clockwise` that receives an image and returns a new image where its pixels are rotated clockwise (see Figure 5.14).

Exercise 5.60. (★★★★)

Write a function `clockwise_four` that receives an image and returns a new image containing the pixel data of the original image rotated four times. The top-left quadrant should contain the original (image), the top-right is one clockwise iteration, the bottom-right is two clockwise iterations, and the bottom-left is three clockwise iterations (see Figure 5.15).

Figure 5.14: Clockwise Rotation   Figure 5.15: Four Cloclwise Rotations

Exercise 5.61. ($\star\star\star\star\star$)

Benoît Mandelbrot discovered the *Mandelbrot set* in the very early 1980's [Mandelbrot, 1980].[1] To even begin discussing what the Mandelbrot set is, we need to very quickly introduce complex numbers.

Complex numbers have a real and imaginary component, in which the imaginary component is multiplied by the imaginary constant i, or $\sqrt{-1}$. For example, $4 + 3i$ has a real component 4 and an imaginary component i. We can add/subtract and multiply complex numbers as follows:

$$(a + bi) \pm (c + di) = (a \pm c) + i(b \pm d)$$
$$(a + bi)\cdot(c + di) = (ac - bd) + i(ad + bc)$$

Because this exercise is so involved, we will expand it into several sub-exercises.

Exercise 5.62. ($\star\star\star$)

First, design a struct for working with complex numbers. This should, of course, contain two fields: a `double` for the real and a `double` for the imaginary.[2] Then write the addition and multiplication functions over complex numbers. Finally, design the `abs` function, which returns the distance to the complex number in the plane from the origin. The absolute value of a complex number c is the square root of the sum of its squared real and imaginary components, i.e., $abs(c) = \sqrt{real(c)^2 + imag(c)^2}$.

---

[1]There is a common debate between which researcher(s) discovered the set; even though it is named after Mandelbrot himself, Brooks and Matelski published a paper with the equation and a text-representation of the fractal prior to Mandelbrot's publications [Brooks and Matelski, 1981].

[2]The i that accompanies the imaginary component is only present if we print the complex number; you should not store this value in any way inside the structure definition.

Listing 5.124—Skeleton Code for Complex Numbers Implementation

```
1   typedef struct complex {
2     // TODO.
3   } complex;
4
5   /**
6    * Initializes the given complex number with the given
7    * real and imaginary components.
8    */
9   void complex_create(complex *c, double re, double im) { ... }
10
11  /**
12   * Adds the complex number b to the complex number a.
13   * We modify the components of a.
14   */
15  void complex_add(complex *a, const complex *b) { ... }
16
17  /**
18   * Multiplies the complex number b with the complex number a.
19   * We modify the components of a.
20   */
21  void complex_mult(complex *a, const complex *b) { ... }
22
23  /**
24   * Returns the absolute value of the given complex number.
25   * This distance is from the complex components to (0, 0i).
26   */
27  double complex_abs(const complex *a) { ... }
```

Exercise 5.63. (⋆⋆)

Design an exponentiation function over complex numbers. This may be defined using natural recursion. The exponent argument must be a positive integer.

Exercise 5.64. (⋆⋆)

Later on, we will need to normalize values from one interval to another. Namely, the Mandelbrot set exists between the values $[-2, 2]$ on both axes of the complex plane. Design the normalize function, which receives five double values: a number to normalize, an old range, and a new range. The idea is, given a value $x \in [m, n]$ where $n \geq m$, we want to determine what value x would be if it were between another range $[m', n']$. We present a sequence of examples as follows:

Listing 5.125—Normalization Function Examples

```
1   /**                                                    0
2    * Normalizes a given value from one range to another. 0.25
3    */                                                    75
4   double normalize(double n, double old_min,
5                    double old_max, double new_min,
6                    double new_max) { ... }
7
8   int main(void) {
9     printf("%f\n", normalize(5, 1, 10, -1, 1));
10    printf("%f\n", normalize(2.5, 1, 10, 0, 1));
11    printf("%f\n", normalize(2.5, -5, 5, 1, 100));
12    return 0;
13  }
```

With these details now covered, we can begin our discussion. The Mandelbrot set is a set of complex numbers such that, if we iterate over every point in the complex plane using some function $f(c)$, if c diverges (to infinity), it is not part of the set. Conversely, if $f(c)$, after repeated iteration, appears to converge to a value, then it is in the set. We can then plot these points onto an image. The function f that we are discussing is actually the following recursive definition, where c is the complex number that we are iterating: $z_{n+1} = z_n + c$.

Exercise 5.65. (★★)

Design the `mandelbrot_iterate` function, which receives two complex numbers: z and c, as well as an integer m denoting the maximum number of possible iterations. Continuously apply the preceding recursive definition onto z until we either exceed m or the absolute value of z is less than two. The former case means the value diverges, whereas the latter means the value converges and is, therefore, in the set. Return the number of iterations used to plot c. Note that, the higher value of m we use, the more precise the Mandelbrot set.

Exercise 5.66. (★★★★)

Design the `mandelbrot` function, which receives four `double` values representing the minimum and maximum values along the complex plane. For instance, to draw the entire fractal, we should pass -2, -2, 2, 2.[1] Our `mandelbrot` function normalizes the received x and y coordinates to the provided argument ranges, then invokes the iteration function. If the returned number of iterations exceeds the allowed maximum, set the pixel color to white. Otherwise, set it to black. Return these pixel values in an `image` struct. The desired image dimensions are up to you.

---

[1] When we say "the entire fractal", we mean as opposed to a zoomed-in section of the fractal.

Listing 5.126—Mandelbrot Skeleton Code

```
1   #define IMAGE_WIDTH ___
2   #define IMAGE_HEIGHT ___
3   #define MAX_ITERATIONS ___
4
5   /**
6    * Iterates the Mandelbrot set function using the given complex
7    * values of z and c. We iterate at most m times.
8    */
9   int mandelbrot_iterate(complex *z, complex *c, int m) {
10    for (int i = 0; i < m; i++) {
11      if (___) { return ___; }
12      else { z = ___; }
13    }
14    return ___;
15  }
16
17  /**
18   * Constructs a PPM image of the Mandelbrot set. The parameters
19   * specify the starting and ending coordinates of the fractal "canvas".
20   */
21  image *mandelbrot(double mincx, double mincy,
22                    double maxcx, double maxcy) {
23    image *img = ___;
24    // Initialize the img fields accordingly.
25
26    for (int x = 0; x < img->w; x++) {
27      for (int y = 0; y < img->h; y++) {
28        double cx = normalize(x, 0, IMAGE_WIDTH, ___, ___);
29        double cy = normalize(y, 0, IMAGE_HEIGHT, ___, ___);
30
31        complex z, c;
32        complex_create(&z, cx, cy);
33        complex_create(&c, cx ,cy);
34        int num_it = mandelbrot_iterate(___, ___, MAX_ITERATIONS);
35        img->pixels[y][x] = ___;
36      }
37    }
38    return img;
39  }
```

Interestingly, we can map colors to the Mandelbrot fractal using a variety of techniques. We present one possible to show what is possible with enough creativity in Figure 5.16.

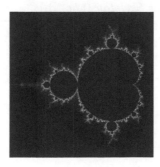

Figure 5.16: Colored Mandelbrot Fractal

Exercise 5.67. (⋆⋆⋆⋆⋆)
Digital data is transmitted via network communication. While it might seem
straightforward to send an image to a friend, the process actually involves significant complexity on the networking end. In the upcoming exercises, we will
replicate a basic networking system where hosts have the ability to exchange data
with other hosts (this simulation grossly oversimplifies the complexities of network
programming, but serves as a nice programming exercise).

We will be working with bits and bytes in this exercise, even more so than before.
The standard C datatypes are subject to change based on the architecture and C
compiler, which means that an int may not always store 32 bits. On the other
hand, the uint32_t type is guaranteed by the stdint.h library to always store
the necessary bits for an unsigned 32-bit integer.

A *host*, in our network, has an identifier id specified by a 32-bit integer. Hosts
send and receive data *packets*, which contain a header and a data field. Hosts store
a stack of packet pointers, which reference packets where they (the specified host)
are the intended recipient. The *header* of a packet stores a preamble, a start-of-data
byte, a destination host identifier, a source host identifier, and a length-of-packet.
The preamble is a sequence of three bytes containing 00110011 11001100 00110011,
followed by the start-of-data 11001101. The destination and source host identifiers
are four-byte integers, and the length-of-packet is a two-byte value corresponding to
the total number of bytes used for the given packet. The idea is that any arbitrary
host will continuously read sequences of data and, if it intercepts a packet, it stores
the packet in its stack only if it is the intended host. All packets are broadcasted
to every device on the network, but are "dropped" if they are not the intended
destination host.

Exercise 5.68. (⋆⋆)
Design a host structure and type definition as specified above. Create the host_-
init function, which receives a pointer to a host structure to initialize with a given
identifier. In the interest of time, also write the host_add_packet function that
adds a packet to the host's stack of packets.

Listing 5.127—Host Header Skeleton (host.h)

```
1    #ifndef HOST_H
2    #define HOST_H
3
4    #include <stdint.h>
5
6    typedef struct host host;
7
8    void host_init(uint32_t id);
9    void host_add_packet(host *h, packet *pkt);
10
11   #endif // HOST_H
```

Listing 5.128—Host Source Skeleton (host.c)

```
1   #include "host.h"
2
3   typedef struct host {
4     ___;
5     ___;
6   } host;
7
8   /**
9    * Initializes a host with the given identifier.
10   */
11  void host_init(host *h, uint32_t id) {
12    // TODO.
13  }
14
15  /**
16   * Adds a packet to the given host's message stack.
17   */
18  void host_add_packet(host *h, packet *pkt) {
19    // TODO.
20  }
```

Exercise 5.69. (★★)

Design the packet structure and type definition. It should include a nested structure definition for a header. From there, write the packet_init function, which receives a pointer to a packet, a sender, a receiver, as well as an array of uint8_t data, and initializes its fields as specified. Do not return the packet; only initialize the required fields. Remember to initialize the preamble and start-of-packet fields.

Listing 5.129—Packet Header Skeleton (packet.h)

```
1    #ifndef PACKET_H
2    #define PACKET_H
3
4    #include <stdint.h>
5
6    typedef struct packet packet;
7
8    void packet_init(packet *pkt, uint32_t send, uint32_t recv,
9                     uint8_t *data, uint16_t size_of_data);
10
11   #endif // PACKET_H
```

Listing 5.130 (packet.c)

```
1   #include "packet.h"
2
3   typedef struct packet {
4     struct header {
5       ___ preamble; ___ start_of_data; ___ send;
6       ___ recv; ___ size_of_data;
7     } hdr;
8     ___ data;
9   };
10
11  /**
12   * Initializes a packet with the given data and the other required fields.
13   */
14  void packet_init(packet *pkt, uint32_t send, uint32_t recv,
15                   uint8_t *data, uint16_t size_of_data) { // TODO. }
```

Exercise 5.70. (★★★)

Using the skeleton code in Listing 5.131, write the forward function, which receives a packet and forwards it, appropriately, to the intended recipient. The forward function should also receive an array of hosts and the number of hosts on the network.

Listing 5.131—Skeleton Code for Networking Exercise (network.c)

```
1    #include "host.h"
2    #include "packet.h"
3
4    #define NUM_HOSTS 5
5
6    void forward(packet *pkt, host *hosts, size_t num_hosts) {
7      for (int i = 0; i < num_hosts; i++) {
8        host curr_host = ___;
9        if (___) {
10         host_add_packet(___, ___);
11       }
12     }
13   }
14
15   int main(void) {
16     // Declare 5 hosts.
17     struct host hosts[NUM_HOSTS];
18     host_init(&hosts[0], 3232238081);
19     host_init(&hosts[1], 3232238126);
20     host_init(&hosts[2], 3232238131);
21     host_init(&hosts[3], 3232238224);
22     host_init(&hosts[4], 3232238292);
23
24     // A random packet with data.
25     packet pkt;
26     uint8_t data[15] = {72, 101, 108, 108, 111, 44, 32, 104,
27                         111, 115, 116, 32, 52, 54, 33};
28     packet_init(&pkt, 3232238224, 3232238081, data, sizeof(data) + HEADER_SIZE);
29
30     // Forward the packet.
31     forward(&pkt, hosts, NUM_HOSTS);
32
33     return 0;
34   }
```

Exercise 5.71. (★★★★)

Write an interface, either through standard input or terminal arguments, for the end-user to connect to a host and view its stored messages in the following format:

```
Message 1/1
Sender: 192.168.10.144
Receiver: 192.168.10.1

Hello, host 46!
```

To do this, write three functions: get_host_id, get_msg, and print_message. The two former functions receive pointers to strings and store the host identifier and message in those strings. The latter receives three strings representing the sender and receiver addresses, the message itself as a string, the message number, and how many messages the host who calls print_message has stored inside its packets stack. The host identifier is printed as an *IPv4* address, which is nothing more than a 32-bit integer separated into four octets.

Listing 5.132—Skeleton Code for Utility Functions in Networking Exercise (network.c)

```
1   void print_msg(char *send, char *recv, char *msg,
2                  size_t n, size_t msg_count) { // TODO. }
3
4   /**
5    * Populates the pointer buffer with a string representing
6    * the "IPv4 address" of the given value.
7    * E.g., if id=3232238224, then *ptr="192.168.10.144"
8    */
9   void get_ip(char **ptr, uint32_t id) {
10    int ret = -1;
11    if (NULL == *ptr) { ret = asprintf(ptr, ___, ___); }
12    else { ret = sprintf(*ptr, ___, ___); }
13    if (0 > ret) {
14     EPF("get_ip: failed to output host id to string\n");
15     *ptr = NULL;
16    }
17  }
18
19  /**
20   * Populates the pointer buffer with the data contents. If
21   * ptr is passed as NULL, allocate to it the number of
22   * characters necessary to store the data.
23   */
24  void get_msg(char **ptr, uint8_t *data, size_t len) {
25    if (NULL == *ptr) { *ptr = calloc(___, 1); }
26    for (int i = 0; i < len; i++) {
27     (*ptr)[i] = ___;
28    }
29  }
```

5.2 $\mathcal{L}_{\text{PF1}}$: **Our First Language**

For our first language, we will write a program that evaluates simple prefix arithmetic expressions such as those we discussed in the previous section. This basic language will use only four operators: $+$, $-$, $\cdot$, and $/$, representing n-ary addition, subtraction, multiplication, and division, respectively. An expression can contain parenthesized expressions, such as $(+ \ 3 \ (\cdot \ 5 \ 4))$, or be as simple as a number. We will also include unary plus and negation operators. A number x is a NUMBER if $x \in \mathbb{R}$. As examples, 3, 4.5, -123, -19.345123 are all of type NUMBER. To serve as a quick preview, our program will evaluate expressions such as $(+ \ (- \ 9 \ 1) \ (\cdot \ (- \ 5 \ 3) \ (\cdot \ 2 \ 10)))$ and return the correct mathematical result, which in this case is 48.

As discussed in Chapter 4, the problems of lexical, syntactical, and semantic analysis are complex enough on their own. Accordingly, we will not write our own lexer and parser. Instead, we will utilize a small yet powerful library, *mpc*: "Micro Parser Combinators".

Generating Grammars

The *mpc* library allows us to write parsers for language grammars. The language that we will design bears resemblance to Scheme/Racket/other LISP-esque languages. These types of languages are otherwise known as *symbolic expression*, or s-expression, languages and utilize the prefix notation of operator/operand placement as described earlier in this chapter. Designing a programming language from the ground up is complicated. There are many elements and factors to consider, such as lexical/dynamic scoping, static/dynamic typing, should it be object-oriented, functional or imperative, and several others.[1] For larger languages, and as we will discuss further in the chapter on compilation, it is also important to determine the target architecture or back-end framework. For example, whether we should target x86/64, ARM, the JVM, LLVM, MIPS, and so on.[2] In this section and chapter, we will write a very small interpreter at first, then gradually expand its functionality and implementation into a language that is rather practical for a good subset of elementary-to-intermediate terminal-based projects.

We will now describe the grammar of our first interpreter and language: $\mathcal{L}_{\text{PF1}}$, an acronym for, "PreFix 1". This language will support only numbers, basic arithmetic operations, and comments, but even this will keep us busy for a while; designing the internal representation of structures, functions, numbers, symbols, etc., is a not-so-easy task. Below are some examples of inputs for $\mathcal{L}_{\text{PF1}}$ and their corresponding outputs.

---

[1]Understanding what these terms mean or their related significance is unimportant for the time being.

[2]These categories are "back-ends" for a programming language; compilers often target specific *architectures* with differing instruction sets and capabilities.

Listing 5.133

```
> 5                              5
> (+ 2 3)                        5
> (* (+ 6 7) (- 11 8 (- 6)))     117
> (- (+ (* 3.05 (- 3.14 5)))     -6.6835263157
     (* (/ 12 (* 9.5 1.25)))))
```

As we can see, $\mathcal{L}_{\text{PF1}}$ supports four *n*-ary operations: addition, subtraction, multiplication, and division. These operators are dubbed *n*-ary because we can apply them to any **positive**, non-zero number of arguments. Each operation is applicable to floating-point numbers of type `long double` in C (note that, in a later section, we will extend the language to support arbitrarily large numbers). As with the style of prefix notation expressions, we always preface a function application with parentheses, followed by the operator, followed by its operands. Additionally, an application can be invoked with brackets [] or curly braces {} so long as they are balanced (e.g., (...] is invalid). This notation will help us distinguish between conjoined applications.

Chapter 4 described the idea behind EBNF grammars. We will use EBNF grammars to describe each of our languages, starting with $\mathcal{L}_{PF1}$.[1] In addition, we will design a few "helper" supplemental rules to make our grammar easier to understand.

```
upcase     ::=   [A-Z]
downcase   ::=   [a-z]
special    ::=   [+-*/_=!?<>]
digit      ::=   [0-9]
symchar    ::=   upcase | downcase | special
```

Figure 5.17: EBNF Grammar for "Helpful Productions"

```
expr          ::=   application
              |     datum
              |     comment
application   ::=   '(' expr* ')'
              |     '[' expr* ']'
              |     '{' expr* '}'
datum         ::=   number
              |     symbol
comment       ::=   ';' (. - '\n')*
number        ::=   ('+'|'-')? (digit)+ ('.' (digit) *)?
symbol        ::=   symchar (symchar | number)*
pf1           ::=   expr+
```

Figure 5.18: EBNF Grammar for $\mathcal{L}_{PF1}$

The root rule of our language is *pf1*, which states that a program in *pf1* consists of at least one expression.

An *expr* is either an *application*, i.e., the invocation of an operator, a *datum*, i.e., a number, a symbol, or a comment.

Applications are, again, surrounded by parentheses; the left-hand argument is the operator expression, which is followed by zero or more expressions.

A *number* must contain at least one digit, and may or may not have a floating-point/decimal component (note: representing numbers like this causes issues with the internal C type representation, which we will address later). Additionally, numbers have an optional sign, e.g., -5, +7, and 7 are all valid numbers according to the parser.

---

[1]It is important to recognize the limitations of symbol and number length in C, which our EBNF grammar does not consider.

Finally, a *symbol* starts with a letter, an underscore, plus, minus, asterisk, forward slash, less than, equal to, greater than signs, an exclamation point, or a question mark, followed by the same symbols with the addition of numbers. We cannot start symbols with a number, as this will cause the grammar to get confused and possibly misrepresent a number as a symbol or vice-versa. We will come back to comments, but for now, comments are a semicolon followed by any non-newline character.

Let us now embed this into C with *mpc*. Again, the internal representation of input through *mpc* is converted into a traversable abstract syntax tree. We can use the AST to extract vital information, then choose how to evaluate it according to our language.

Embedding our grammar into *mpc* is simple, yet easy to mess up if one is not careful. First, create two files: parser.c and parser.h. We need to initialize our grammar rules as global variables so we can share access across separate functions. Inside parser.h, we will declare two functions for initializing and cleaning up *mpc* parser functionality.

Listing 5.134—Parser Header File (parser.h)

```
1   #ifndef PARSER_H
2   #define PARSER_H
3
4   void parser_init(const char *filename);
5   void parser_cleanup(void);
6
7   #endif // PARSER_H
```

Then, inside parser.c, we need to declare these functions as well as the *mpc* parser rules. We will declare the latter as static since they should be invisible to outside modules. In addition, we will write two static functions for initializing parser rules and deciding what to do with input. We will call said functions inside parser_init:

Listing 5.135—Initial Parser Source File (parser.c)

```
1   #include "parser.h"
2   #include "mpc.h"
3
4   /* Static function prototypes. */
5   static void parser_read(const char *filename);
6   static void parser_init_rules(void);
7
8   /* Global parser rule declarations. */
9   static mpc_parser_t *expr_rule;
10  static mpc_parser_t *application_rule;
11  static mpc_parser_t *datum_rule;
12  static mpc_parser_t *comment_rule;
13  static mpc_parser_t *number_rule;
14  static mpc_parser_t *symbol_rule;
15  static mpc_parser_t *pf1_rule;
16
17  void parser_init(const char *filename) {
18   parser_init_rules();
19   parser_read(filename);
20  }
21
22  void parser_cleanup(void) { // TODO. }
23  static void parser_init_rules(void) { // TODO. }
24  static void parser_read(const char *filename) { // TODO. }
```

Thus far, we created four functions and seven parser rules. The latter corresponds directly to our grammar, whereas the former consists of two "helper" functions, and two that will be called outside this module.

Let us now skip down to `parser_init_rules` to write our grammar, since this is the hardest and easiest to incorrectly write part. While we are in this section of the code, we can add the one line to `parser_cleanup` needed to clean and free parser rules generated by *mpc*.[1]

Listing 5.136—Defining Grammar Rules in mpc (`parser.c`)

```
1    void parser_cleanup(void) {
2      mpc_cleanup(7, expr_rule, application_rule, datum_rule,
3                 comment_rule, number_rule, symbol_rule, pf1_rule);
4    }
5
6    static void parser_init_rules(void) {
7      /* First, define/instantiate the rules. */
8      expr_rule = mpc_new("expr");
9      application_rule = mpc_new("application");
10     datum_rule = mpc_new("datum");
11     comment_rule = mpc_new("comment");
12     number_rule = mpc_new("number");
13     symbol_rule = mpc_new("symbol");
14     pf1_rule = mpc_new("pf1");
15
16     /* Now, define the grammar: */
17     mpc_err_t *error = mpca_lang(MPCA_LANG_DEFAULT,
18       "expr        : <application>                       \n"
19       "             | <datum>                            \n"
20       "             | <comment>                      ; \n"
21       "application: ('('<expr>*')')                      \n"
22       "             | ('{'<expr>*'}')                    \n"
23       "             | ('['<expr>*']')                ; \n"
24       "datum       : <number>                            \n"
25       "             | <symbol>                       ; \n"
26       "comment     : ';'/[^\\n]*/                    ; \n"
27       "number      : /(+-)?[0-9]+(\\.[0-9]+)?/       ; \n"
28       "symbol      : /[a-zA-Z\\-\\+_\\*<=>\\/!\\?]    \n"
29       "              [a-zA-Z0-9\\-\\+_\\*<=>\\/!\\?]*/ ; \n"
30       "pf1         : <expr>+                         ; \n",
31       expr_rule, application_rule, datum_rule, comment_rule,
32       number_rule, symbol_rule, pf1_rule, NULL);
33
34     if (NULL != error) {
35       mpc_err_print(error);
36       exit(EXIT_FAILURE);
37     }
38   }
```

Notice how each rule consists of its name, a colon, then the body of the rule. The bodies are consistent with the earlier EBNF grammar specification. To create a language with *mpc*, we use the `mpca_lang` function which accepts a language "type", a string representing the grammar, followed by the parser rules. Again, it is imperative that the code is written exactly as stated, or the parser will display errors since it cannot interpret an incorrectly-specified grammar. If an error is encountered, we store it inside a `mpc_err_t` struct. On the other hand, if error is NULL, this means an error did not occur and we can safely continue. Otherwise, we display the error using the library function `mpc_err_print`, then quit the program altogether.

---

[1] We use a slightly different typography style for the font in the following code listing to preserve horizontal space and alignment within each rule.

We now have our grammar specification for $\mathcal{L}_{\text{PF1}}$, and all we must do in parser.c is write parser_read. Depending on how the user runs the program, they may want to evaluate input they enter through the terminal or the contents of a file. Passing a *file name* allows such interchangeability. If the file name that is sent to the function is NULL, then we should interpret that as the user wishing to type expressions in the terminal. Anything else we can, at the very least, try to interpret as a file. In C, we wrap files with a construct called FILE. To open a file, we call fopen(filename, mode); with a given file name and "mode of access", which returns a FILE *. For example, FILE *fp = fopen("test.txt", "r"); says that we wish to open test.txt for reading (hence the "r"), and we want to store the value of the opened file inside the pointer fp. Importantly, this does *not* mean that we have read anything from the file; it only means that we have a FILE * available to manipulate depending on the mode.

Fortunately, *mpc* provides two useful functions for reading the contents of a file and a standard string: mpc_parse_file and mpc_parse respectively.

Listing 5.137—Reading Content into Parser (parser.c)

```
1   void parser_read(const char *filename) {
2     // We need to keep track of what is parsed.
3     mpc_result_t result;
4     int code;
5
6     // If the file is null or empty, we read from the terminal.
7     if (NULL == filename || streq(filename, "")) {
8       code = mpc_parse_pipe("<stdin>", stdin, pf1_rule, &result);
9     } else {
10      FILE *fp = fopen(filename, "r");
11      // If an error occurs with the file, NULL is returned.
12      if (NULL == fp) {
13        EPF("Error opening file");
14        exit(EXIT_FAILURE);
15      } else {
16        code = mpc_parse_file(filename, fp, pf1_rule, &result);
17      }
18
19      // Close all file handles after opening.
20      fclose(fp);
21    }
22
23    // Check to make sure we parsed correctly!
24    if (0 > code) {
25      mpc_err_print(result.error);
26      mpc_err_delete(result.error);
27    } else {
28      mpc_ast_print(result.output);
29      mpc_ast_delete(result.output);
30    }
31  }
```

Hopefully, the above code is not too overwhelming. First, we declare two variables to keep track of our result abstract syntax tree and "code". A "code" is simply a number representing success or failure. Many C functions return values depending on if they succeed or fail. As examples, both fopen and mpc_parse_-file return "codes" to indicate success or failure. Often, a code of zero, NULL, or a negative number indicates failure, but this is, unfortunately, not a gold standard. Additionally, C functions might set the global errno constant to a specific value. This constant is defined and accessible from errno.h. As an example, malloc will set errno to the preprocessor definition ENOMEM if it fails to allocate memory.

Listing 5.138—Checking the Value of errno *Constant* (main.c)

```
1   int main(void) {                                    Cannot allocate memory (12)
2    // Clear out existing check.
3    errno = 0;
4    int *ptr = malloc(10000000000000000);
5    if (0 != errno) {
6     printf("%s (%d)\n", strerror(errno),
7                         errno);
8    } else {
9     free(ptr);
10   }
11   return 0;
12  }
```

After these declarations, we check to see if the file passed is either NULL or the empty string, and if so, we intend to only parse contents from the terminal. The question now is, "How do we read content from the terminal?" We will answer this question in a bit. Jumping down to the else block indicates that there is something in the filename variable. We attempt to interpret said variable as a file name via fopen. If, for example, the variable does not contain a valid file name, or a file name at all, e.g., a number, then fopen returns a value of NULL. Otherwise, we know that the file opened successfully and we can read/parse its contents with mpc_parse_file. This function, similarly, returns a code. If the input content is not well-formed according to the grammar, then the function returns a value less than or equal to zero, indicating an error. If an error is found, we display the error, then delete the result. Otherwise, we print the abstract syntax tree generated by the parser followed immediately by its deletion.[1]

Let us now write the code to initialize and construct the abstract syntax tree. Create a main.c file with the following contents:

Listing 5.139—Initialize and Cleanup Parser (main.c)

```
1   #include "parser.h"
2
3   int main(int argc, char *argv[]) {
4    parser_init("program1.pf1");
5    parser_cleanup();
6    return 0;
7   }
```

So, we can finally write a test program! Open a new file called program1.pf1 and add the text (+ 2 3). Upon executing the program, the terminal should produce a complex yet digestible output.

Listing 5.140

```
expr|>
 application|>
  char:1:1 '('
  expr|datum|symbol|regex:1:2 '+'
  expr|datum|number|regex:1:4 '2'
  expr|datum|number|regex:1:6 '3'
  char:1:7 ')'
```

---

[1]In future iterations of the interpreter, we will not want to delete intermediate abstract syntax trees as they may contain declarations/expressions used later in the program!

What does this output mean? We can trace through it as a parse tree to get a better idea. The program begins at the root node of the tree and parses an expression. An expression consists of either an application or a datum. Since our input file contains an application of + to the values 2 and 3, it chooses the former rule. This particular application contains five pieces: the opening parenthesis, a symbol, i.e., '+', a number, i.e., '2', another number, i.e., '3', and a closing parenthesis. Notice how the parser creates the syntax tree–we designate an application to consist of the outer parentheses, an expression representing the operator, and any number of operand expressions. In this example, we include two operands for the + operator.

Congratulations! These are the beginning steps of writing the interpreter for basic arithmetic expressions.

Let us try a complicated expression, such as the one that we created when describing the grammar. Store it in a file program2.pf1. Save the file, and change main.c to read from this file instead of program1.pf1. Recompile your code, and run the output executable. With any luck, the output should look like the following:

Listing 5.141

```
(- (+ (* 3.05 (- 3.14 5)))          |  expr|>
   (* (/ 12 (* 9.5 1.25)))))        |   application|>
                                    |    char:1:1 '('
                                    |    expr|datum|symbol|regex:1:2 '-'
                                    |    expr|application|>
                                    |     char:1:4 '('
                                    |     expr|datum|symbol|regex:1:5 '+'
                                    |     expr|application|>
                                    |      char:1:7 '('
                                    |      expr|datum|symbol|regex:1:8 '*'
                                    |      expr|datum|number|regex:1:10 '3.05'
                                    |      expr|application|>
                                    |       char:1:15 '('
                                    |       expr|datum|symbol|regex:1:16 '-'
                                    |       expr|datum|number|regex:1:18 '3.14'
                                    |       expr|datum|number|regex:1:23 '5'
                                    |       char:1:24 ')'
                                    |      char:1:25 ')'
                                    |     char:1:26 ')'
                                    |    expr|application|>
                                    |     char:2:1 '('
                                    |     expr|datum|symbol|regex:2:2 '*'
                                    |     expr|application|>
                                    |      char:2:4 '('
                                    |      expr|datum|symbol|regex:2:5 '/'
                                    |      expr|datum|number|regex:2:7 '12'
                                    |      expr|application|>
                                    |       char:2:10 '('
                                    |       expr|datum|symbol|regex:2:11 '*'
                                    |       expr|datum|number|regex:2:13 '9.5'
                                    |       expr|datum|number|regex:2:17 '1.25'
                                    |       char:2:21 ')'
                                    |      char:2:22 ')'
                                    |     char:2:23 ')'
                                    |    char:2:24 ')'
```

Whoa! That is a lot of information to unfold! Indeed, that is correct. The thing, though, is that *mpc* only outputs the parse tree of an expression and not the abstract syntax tree. Recall that a parse tree shows all parts that comprise a rule, including constant literals such as parentheses. An abstract syntax tree, on the other hand, removes small details and focuses on the semantics of a node, as shown in Figure 5.19.

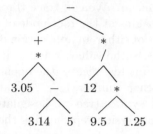

Figure 5.19: Abstract Syntax Tree of Arithmetic S-Expression

Representation Independence with Respect to Abstract Syntax Trees

All interpreters and languages we write in this book will use the *mpc* library. Though, what if, down the road, we want to modify which library we use? We would need to go through and change every instance of *mpc* to this new library. For parser, we do not have much of a choice but to rely heavily on the functionality built into *mpc* because of its grammar construction rules. What we can do, however, is create a ubiquitous abstract syntax tree representation and helper functions for accessing components of an abstract syntax tree. This way our interpreters will only access the helper functions without relying or worrying about how they work. Moreover, if we want to swap *mpc* for another library, we need not to touch the interpreter–only the abstract syntax tree representation and parser should be modified. This is a programming paradigm known as *abstraction* or *representation independence*.

First, let us create a representation for abstract syntax trees and some helper functions for accessing fields. Let us assume that any abstract syntax tree will have a list of nodes/children, a "number of children", and a string identifier. Additionally, there are several abstract syntax tree functions to write, including initialization, destruction, child access, size access, and tag access. It may seem odd to write these "accessor" functions when we can directly access fields within a struct. Though, it would be greatly beneficial if we could create the type-defined struct inside the source file and omit any outside sources directly accessing these fields to prevent accidental modification. Then, in the corresponding source file, we define those aforesaid functions.

Listing 5.142—Abstract Syntax Tree Header (ast.h)

```
1   #ifndef AST_H
2   #define AST_H
3
4   #include <stdlib.h>
5   #include <string.h>
6
7   typedef struct ast ast;
8
9   void ast_init(ast *t, void *data, char *tag, size_t children_num, char *contents);
10  ast *ast_child(const ast *tree, const size_t idx);
11  size_t ast_children_num(const ast *tree);
12  char *ast_tag(const ast *tree);
13  bool ast_is_type(const ast *tree, const char *tag);
14  void ast_print(const ast *tree);
15  char *ast_contents(const ast *tree);
16  void ast_destroy(ast *tree);
17
18  #endif // AST_H
```

Listing 5.143

```
1   #include "ast.h"
2
3   #include "mpc.h"
4
5   typedef struct ast {
6    size_t children_num;
7    struct ast **children;
8    char *tag;
9    char *contents;
10   size_t row;
11   size_t col;
12  } ast;
13
14  static void ast_print_helper(ast *tree, int indent);
```

Listing 5.144—Abstract Syntax Tree Initialization Function (ast.c)

```
1   void ast_init(ast *tree, void *data, char *tag,
2                  size_t children_num, char *contents) {
3    // Copy tag and contents.
4    tree->tag = strdup(tag);
5    tree->contents = strdup(contents);
6
7    // Allocate children.
8    tree->children_num = children_num;
9    tree->children = calloc(tree->children_num, sizeof(ast *));
10   ASSERT_ALLOC(tree->children, "ast_init");
11   mpc_ast_t *tdata = (mpc_ast_t *) data;
12
13   // Copy the children over.
14   for (int i = 0; i < tdata->children_num; i++) {
15    mpc_ast_t *curr = tdata->children[i];
16    tree->children[i] = malloc(sizeof(ast));
17    ASSERT_ALLOC(tree->children[i], "ast_init");
18    ast_init(tree->children[i], curr, curr->tag,
19            curr->children_num, curr->contents);
20   }
21
22   // Copy over the row and column positions of the tree.
23   tree->row = tdata->state.row;
24   tree->col = tdata->state.col;
25  }
```

Listing 5.145—Abstract Syntax Tree Attribute Accessor Functions (ast.c)

```
1   ast *ast_child(const ast *tree, const size_t idx) {
2     if (0 > idx || idx >= tree->children_num) {
3       EPF("ast_child: tried to index %zu in tree of size %zu\n",
4           idx, tree->children_num);
5       exit(EXIT_FAILURE);
6     }
7     return tree->children[idx];
8   }
9
10  size_t ast_children_num(const ast *tree) { return tree->children_num; }
11  char *ast_tag(const ast *tree) { return tree->tag; }
12  char *ast_contents(const ast *tree) { return tree->contents; }
13  void ast_print(ast *tree) { ast_print_helper(tree, 0); }
```

Listing 5.146—Abstract Syntax Tree Destructor and Printer Functions (ast.c)

```
1   void ast_destroy(ast *tree) {
2     // Free the children first, then its contents.
3     for (int i = 0; i < tree->children_num; i++) {
4       ast_destroy(tree->children[i]);
5     }
6     free(tree->children);
7     free(tree->tag);
8     free(tree->contents);
9   }
10
11  static void ast_print_helper(ast *tree, int indent) {
12    if (NULL == tree) { return; }
13    for (int i = 0; i < indent; i++) { printf(" "); }
14
15    printf("%s", tree->tag);
16    if (strlen(tree->contents) > 0) {
17      printf("%lu:%lu '%s'", tree->row + 1, tree->col + 1, tree->contents);
18    }
19    printf("\n");
20
21    for (int i = 0; i < tree->children_num; i++) {
22      ast_print_helper(tree->children[i], indent + 1);
23    }
24  }
```

Most of this should be rather self-explanatory. The void pointer in the ast_-init function is perhaps a little perplexing. When we create an abstract syntax tree, the creation function does not need to know what kind of tree "data" it is given, i.e., whether it is an mpc_ast_t tree or something else. Thus, a void pointer says that there exists a pointer to something, i.e., some kind of data; the function just does not know what. The "what" is abstracted away by our abstract syntax tree type, and is inaccessible to the programmer, at least on the interpreter side. Another point of confusion is the ast_print function. It is recursive and calls a static helper function ast_print_helper. In essence, we print out the abstract syntax tree one node (i.e., its contents) at a time. Then, we recursively print its children at an increased indentation level to indicate that the child is one-level deeper.[1] Let us modify parser_read to create one of our abstract syntax trees and pass it along to eval_ast in the interpreter.

---

[1] Understanding the entirety of ast_print_helper is not necessary—we add it for the sake of completeness, since we will repeatedly print the abstract syntax trees for the purposes of debugging.

Listing 5.147—Adding Abstract Syntax Trees to Parser (`parser.c`)

```
1    #include "ast.h"
2
3    void parser_read(const char *filename) {
4      ...
5      else {
6        mpc_ast_print(result.output);
7        // Extract the fields out from the library AST. This is unavoidable.
8        mpc_ast_t *mpc_ast = (mpc_ast_t *) result.output;
9        ast *my_ast = malloc(sizeof(ast));
10       ASSERT_ALLOC(my_ast, "parser_read");
11       ast_init(my_ast, result.output, NULL, NULL, NULL);
12       ...
13       ast_destroy(my_ast);
14       free(my_ast);
15     }
16   }
```

Right now, we are not doing anything with the abstract syntax tree—we create it, then immediately after it is destroyed.

Another thing that is important about the abstract syntax tree initialization is its decoupling from the external representation of the abstract syntax tree. Namely, after we create our version of the abstract syntax tree, i.e., ast, we stop using mpc altogether.

In our root evaluator, we extensively use strstr to determine the type of the abstract syntax tree to evaluate. As part of our representation independence, we should hide the implementation of tags by writing ast_is_type. This function receives the abstract syntax tree and a string tag and returns true if the AST has the provided tag and false otherwise. We can then replace all calls to strstr for determining tags with this function. We use strstr (to search for the desired tag) rather than strcmp (to compare for the desired tag) because the *mpc* library supplements matches with additional information about the data, which we do not strictly need to analyze. We will show an example of such information in a few paragraphs.

Listing 5.148—Hiding Tag Determination for ASTs (`eval.c`)

```
1    bool ast_is_type(const ast *tree, const char *tag) {
2      return strstr(tree, tag) != NULL;
3    }
```

Evaluation and Application

We would like our program to actually evaluate a given expression instead of this large and complex syntax tree mess. Before we write the code to do this, however, we need to discuss the nature of evaluation and application.

Evaluation is the process by which we compute the value of an expression. Often, this is in tandem with application, i.e., function application. For example, numbers evaluate to numbers.

Application is the process of interpreting a function and, as its name suggests, applying it to a set of arguments. For example, we can apply the function + to the arguments 1, 2, 4, and 10 to get a result of $1+2+4+10 = 17$.

One important step we must do before worrying about evaluation and application is to handle s-values. An *s-value*, or a *symbolic expression*, is an expression that resolves to some value. For example, the s-value 3 resolves to the literal 3, and the s-value + resolves to the literal symbol +. This may seem rather intuitive at first, but we need to construct a way of representing and interpreting different s-values, since the way we interpret, say, a number, is different than how we interpret symbols. We will do this via a structure.

Let us create a file sval.h to represent an s-value struct. We now must decide what an s-value should store. One particular field should be its type. As suggested, different s-values can represent different values, e.g., symbols or numbers. We can create an enum to categorize the possible s-value types.

Listing 5.149—S-value Header File (sval.h)

```
1    #ifndef SVAL_H
2    #define SVAL_H
3
4    enum sval_type { SVAL_NUMBER, SVAL_SYMBOL };
5
6    struct sval {
7      enum sval_type type;
8      union data {
9        long double number;
10       char *symbol;
11     } data;
12   };
13
14   struct sval *sval_number_create(long double value);
15   struct sval *sval_symbol_create(char *symbol);
16   void sval_destroy(struct sval *sv);
17
18   #endif // SVAL_H
```

So far, this should look familiar. We are declaring an enum called sval_type with two possibilities: SVAL_NUMBER and SVAL_SYMBOL. From there, we declare a struct of type sval which stores an sval_type to keep track of, as its name suggests, its s-value type. As of now, we will only use two s-value types, but this will grow as we expand our language.

Finally, we get to the oddball of the bunch: the nested union. Recall that a union is simply a decision-based data definition—namely, we can set an s-value to contain either a long double number or a char * symbol, but not both. This definition differentiation proves to be extremely helpful later when we evaluate s-values.

Now, let us write the corresponding source file, sval.c. In this file, we will create the three functions specified by the header: sval_number_create, sval_-symbol_create, and sval_destroy. The former two create s-values for given numbers and symbols respectively, whereas the latter frees any associated memory from an s-value. We need the 'creator' because we have to allocate s-values such that they are available for reference in other functions. Analogously, we need the 'destroyer' to remove, or free, said allocated memory. We once again break the "only initialize; never create" principle of struct allocation on the grounds that, because we control the life cycle and pipeline of s-values, we will not worry about when and where they are allocated.

Inside sval.c, we will write a static helper function, sval_create which receives an s-value type, then allocates and returns the memory for an sval pointer. Notice that we are using the calloc function instead of malloc; we use it because our struct definition for s-values contains many fields, some of which (later on) need to be zero-initialized.

Listing 5.150—S-value Source File (sval.c)

```
1    #include <stdio.h>
2    #include <stdlib.h>
3
4    #include "sval.h"
5
6    struct sval *sval_number_create(long double number) {
7      struct sval *sv = sval_create(SVAL_NUMBER);
8      sv->data.number = number;
9      return sv;
10   }
11
12   struct sval *sval_symbol_create(char *symbol) {
13     struct sval *sv = sval_create(SVAL_SYMBOL);
14     sv->data.symbol = strdup(symbol);
15     return sv;
16   }
17
18   void sval_destroy(struct sval *sv) {
19     if (SVAL_SYMBOL == sv->type) {
20       free(sv->data.symbol);
21     }
22     free(sv);
23   }
24
25   static struct sval *sval_create(const enum sval_type type) {
26     struct sval *sv = calloc(1, sizeof(struct sval));
27     ASSERT_ALLOC(sv, "sval_create");
28     sv->type = type;
29     return sv;
30   }
```

Modularity is a big component of program design, and we will begin good practices early. We want to abstract, or hide, most of the details of the data union from the rest of the program, as it does nothing but complicate the implementation. Additionally, we wrap the allocation of struct sval pointers in a function to adhere to the DRY: Do not Repeat Yourself, principle.

The number creation function, i.e., sval_number_create, is simple to read, but what is with the strdup function? Well, strings and pointers in C are, as we have mentioned many times, weird and unintuitive. Since we may not always have access to the contents of the abstract syntax tree, we need to guarantee that we have access to the contents of this tree, namely, its symbol. *mpc* stores the contents as a string, or char *. If we lose access to the data inside symbol, and we do not copy its content memory over, we, therefore, lose access to the symbol data as well. strdup creates a copy of its passed string and returns a pointer to its location. We store this inside our data union. Since this function creates a copy of the string, we know that it is allocated and, thus, must be destroyed. Fortunately, we have a function for destroying s-values, so all we need to do is amend its definition to destroy symbols.

We now have a representation of s-values! Now, the fun begins: we need to evaluate a given $\mathcal{L}_{PF1}$ program, which may be as simple as a single number or symbol, and as complex as a large chain of arithmetic expressions. Let us first create two pairs of files: a source/header pair for eval, and a source/header pair for apply. As previously mentioned, the purpose of eval is to recursively evaluate a $\mathcal{L}_{PF1}$ program. The latter will apply a function to given arguments. We will start with evaluation. Fortunately, eval.h is straightforward—we only need one global, or public, accessible function, eval_ast. This function receives an abstract syntax tree representing the program, or expression, to evaluate. Inside this function, we will break down the tree into children and evaluate each one piece by piece.

Listing 5.151—Preliminary Evaluation Header (eval.h)

```
1   #ifndef EVAL_H
2   #define EVAL_H
3
4   #include "ast.h"
5
6   void eval_ast(ast *ast);
7
8   #endif // EVAL_H
```

Listing 5.152—Preliminary Evaluation Source File (eval.c)

```
1    #include "eval.h"
2    #include "sval.h"
3
4    void eval_ast(ast *ast) {
5      for (int i = 0; i < ast->children_num; i++) {
6        struct sval *sv = eval(ast->children[i]);
7      }
8    }
9
10   static struct sval *eval(ast *ast) {
11     if (ast_is_type(ast, "number")) { return eval_number(ast); }
12     else if (ast_is_type(ast, "symbol")) { return eval_symbol(ast); }
13     else if (ast_is_type(ast, "comment")) { return NULL; }
14     else { return NULL; }
15   }
16
17   static struct sval *eval_number(ast *number) { // TODO. }
18   static struct sval *eval_symbol(ast *symbol) { // TODO. }
```

This may look like a lot of complex code, but let us break it down. Since the header file defines `eval_ast`, we better declare it in this file! This function iterates over the children of the passed abstract syntax tree and calls `eval` on each child. What is `eval`, though? We want a way to evaluate different types of abstract syntax trees through their tags. Tags, in the *mpc* library, are similar to the types of s-values with the exception that tags are strings and not enums. So, in this function, for numbers, we check to see if the tag of the passed abstract syntax tree contains `"number"`, and if so, we call the `eval_number` function. Correspondingly, if the tag contains `"symbol"`, we call the `eval_symbol` function. Comments are the simplest—since we want the interpreter to ignore comments, we just return NULL to advance onto the next expression to interpret, if any exist. This notion begs the question, "Why not just check to see if the tag is equal to the string instead of checking to see if it contains `"number"` or `"symbol"`? Well, if we did this, we would rarely, if ever, evaluate a number or symbol. The reasoning is not so clear at first glance, but recall the abstract syntax tree generated from a single number. Namely, the tag for such a tree is "expr|datum|number|regex", which is obviously not equal to the string `"number"`, but it does contain said string. We use the function `strstr` to see if one string is a sub-string of another. Though, note that we abstracted this function away into `ast_is_type` when making our abstract syntax trees representation-independent.

Now, we move to two important evaluation functions: `eval_number` and `eval_symbol`. Since the two functions are very similar, we can write their definitions together.

Listing 5.153—Evaluating Numbers and Symbols (eval.c)

```
1    static struct sval *eval_number(ast *number) {
2      struct sval *num = NULL;
3      // TODO extract the contents, i.e., the number, from the ast.
4      return num;
5    }
6
7    static struct sval *eval_symbol(ast *symbol) {
8      struct sval *sym = NULL;
9      // TODO extract the contents, i.e., the symbol text, from the ast.
10     return sym;
11   }
```

Both functions declare a `struct sval *` with an initial value of NULL. Right before we return from the functions, we will invoke the relevant `sval_create` function, i.e., either the one for symbols or numbers. The differences in the code (aside from variable names) begin at this point. `eval_number` must interpret the contents of `number` to see if it is a number and, if so, store it in the `data` union. The definition of a number, at this time, is a C `long double`. We make use of the `sscanf` function to see if the tree contains a valid number.

Listing 5.154—Number Evaluation (`eval.c`)

```
1   static struct sval *eval_number(ast *number) {
2     struct sval *num = NULL;
3     long double num_value;
4     int scanned = sscanf(ast_contents(number), "%Lf", &num_value);
5     if (0 == scanned) {
6       EPF("eval_number: unrecognized input\n");
7       exit(EXIT_FAILURE);
8     }
9     num = sval_number_create(num_value);
10    return num;
11  }
```

Let us now transition to symbol evaluation, which overall is significantly easier to digest than number evaluation. The symbol *is* the contents of the corresponding abstract syntax tree. We should only free the symbol char * if it has an associated (non-NULL) value. Numbers, of course, do not have a symbol because they are not symbols, and we cannot free non-allocated memory.

Listing 5.155—Symbol Evaluation (`eval.c`)

```
1   static struct sval *eval_symbol(ast *symbol) {
2     return sval_symbol_create(ast_contents(symbol));
3   }
```

Listing 5.156—Destructor Function for S-values (`eval.c`)

```
1   void sval_destroy(struct sval *sv) {
2     if (SVAL_SYMBOL == sv->type) { free(sv->data.symbol); }
3     free(sv);
4   }
```

Excellent! Our code successfully evaluates numbers and symbols. Though, we are still not sure how to display said numbers and symbols in the output window. *mpc* provides a nice abstract syntax tree printing function, so it would be great if we had a similar function but for s-values; let us write one!

Listing 5.157—Printing Number & Symbol S-values (`eval.c`)

```
1   void sval_print(const struct sval *sv) {
2     if (SVAL_NUMBER == sv->type) {
3       printf("%Lg\n", sv->data.number);
4     } else if (SVAL_SYMBOL == sv->type) {
5       printf("%s\n", sv->data.symbol);
6     } else {
7       EPF("sval_print: invalid sval: %d\n", sv->type);
8     }
9   }
```

This function checks the type of the s-value and prints out the appropriate data from the union. If we somehow encounter an s-value that is not part of our definition (which is impossible at the moment), we display an error and exit the program. Note: be sure to add the function prototype to `sval.h`!

Now, let us update `eval_ast` to print the s-value if one exists. At the moment, it is impossible for an s-value to not exist, but we do not always want to immediately exit the program when one does not exist, so to prevent any confusion down the road, we throw in a NULL check.

Listing 5.158—Root Evaluation Function (eval.c)

```
1  void eval_ast(ast *ast) {
2    for (int i = 0; i < ast->children_num; i++) {
3      struct sval *sv = eval(ast->children[i]);
4      if (NULL != sv) { sval_print(sv); }
5    }
6  }
```

Finally, we need to change parser_read to evaluate the resulting abstract syntax tree instead of simply printing it out. Then, at the end, we destroy our abstract syntax tree, as well as the *mpc* abstract syntax tree.

Listing 5.159—Sending AST from Parser to Evaluator (eval.c)

```
1    ...
2    // Check to make sure we parsed correctly!
3    if (code < 0) {
4      mpc_err_print(result.error);
5      mpc_err_delete(result.error);
6    } else {
7      ...
8      eval_ast(my_ast);
9      ast_destroy(my_ast);
10     mpc_ast_delete(result.output);
11   }
```

As a brief aside, it may be a bit perplexing to have two separate functions for destroying our abstract syntax tree and the *mpc* variant. Since we wrapped *mpc* inside our ast struct, why not delete the associated *mpc* tree when we invoke ast_destroy? The problem revolves around toys. Imagine that a teacher of an elementary school represents the root abstract syntax tree. Each teacher has children to manage, and each child has a "toy". Whenever we create a new abstract syntax tree via ast_create, we are creating a new, literal child. This child has a toy, i.e., part of the *mpc* abstract syntax tree, that it can "play with", i.e., use. Now, when it is time to clean up the toys, the teacher is very particular about the process and controls the entire pipeline, meaning they (the teacher) go around to each child and manually put up their toy. If a child puts up their toy before the teacher proclaims that it is clean-up time, the universe collapses in on itself. This analogy is rather comical, but it helps to understand why an abstract syntax tree cannot free its *mpc* abstract syntax tree. If we do, then we end up free-ing a piece of the tree that, when we call mpc_ast_delete on the root, it will see the associated data is freed, then try to free it anyways! Thus, we encounter a double-free bug.[1]

Returning to our interpreter, if we try to run a simple program that has only one value, we, to our dismay, receive a blank output. What went wrong? Well, the issue is that eval_ast expects a tree with at least one child. With our current grammar structure, combined with the inner working of *mpc*, having only one simple s-value produces an abstract syntax tree with zero children. In this instance, we need only to evaluate the root of the tree. Otherwise, we recursively evaluate its children. When executing the program, we finally receive some output!

---

[1] If we dug into the *mpc* library, we could add a clause that only frees non-NULL abstract syntax trees, and simply set the pointer to NULL upon freeing our version of the representation-independent abstract syntax tree.

Listing 5.160—Recursively Evaluating ASTs (eval.c)

```
1   void eval_ast(ast *ast) {                                              173
2     // If there are no children,
3     // we simply evaluate that ast.
4     if (0 == ast_children_num(ast)) {
5       struct sval *sv = eval(ast);
6       if (NULL != sv) { sval_print(sv); }
7       else {
8         // Otherwise, evaluate the children recursively.
9         for (int i = 0; i < ast_children_num(ast); i++) {
10          struct sval *sv = eval(ast_child(ast, i));
11          if (NULL != sv) { sval_print(sv); }
12        }
13      }
14    }
15  }
```

Awesome! $\mathcal{L}_{\mathrm{PF1}}$ now prints out numbers, only when we provide it with a single number. This may not seem exciting, but we only have to make a few more additions to complete $\mathcal{L}_{\mathrm{PF1}}$, so we have come a long way! Let us now add function application.

The core of function application lies in apply, but we need first must write a new function in eval to invoke the application process.

Listing 5.161—Evaluation Function Stems (eval.c)

```
1   #include "apply.h"
2   #include "eval.h"
3
4   static struct sval *eval(ast *ast);
5   static struct sval *eval_number(ast *number);
6   static struct sval *eval_symbol(ast *symbol);
7   static struct sval *eval_application(ast *application);
8
9   void eval_ast(ast *ast) { ... }
10  static struct sval *eval(ast *ast) { ... }
11  static struct sval *eval_number(ast *number) { ... }
12  static struct sval *eval_symbol(ast *symbol) { ... }
13  static struct sval *eval_application(ast *application) {
14    // TODO evaluate the function, its arguments, then apply.
15  }
```

What *is* a function application? Consider the expression (+ 2 (- 5 4)). A function application takes the function, + and applies it to its arguments, namely 2 and (- 5 4). What about the nested application? Well, it is evaluated before we apply +: We take the function - and apply it to its arguments, namely 5 and 4. This cycle is known as an evaluation-application loop. In order to apply a function, we must first evaluate its arguments. For $\mathcal{L}_{\mathrm{PF1}}$, this means that an arithmetic expression must evaluate any nested expressions before applying the function. How do we do this? We first need to dive into the structure of an application abstract syntax tree to extract the needed elements. Consider the abstract syntax tree of the above expression.

```
expr|>
 application|>
  char:1:1 '('
  expr|datum|symbol|regex:1:2 '+'
  expr|datum|number|regex:1:4 '2'
  expr|application|>
   char:1:6 '('
   expr|datum|symbol|regex:1:7 '-'
   expr|datum|number|regex:1:9 '5'
   expr|datum|number|regex:1:11 '4'
```

```
char:1:12 ')'
char:1:13 ')'
```

With any **function** application, we have a few invariants, i.e., properties that never change: the first character, or node, in the tree is always an opening parenthesis. Immediately after is the function we wish to use. Any subsequent nodes except the last (which is the closing parenthesis) are arguments to this function. Let us define this inductively; a function application with this setup must have at least three children: the opening parenthesis, function symbol, and the closing parenthesis (note that this means some functions may not have any arguments, which is acceptable!). Since we know that the function application is always the second child, we can represent this as a constant in `eval.c`: `APPLICATION_FUNCTION_IDX` with a value of 1. Any arguments are in the indices $[2, ..., n-2]$ where n represents the number of children in this abstract syntax tree. Remember that the $n-1^{th}$ child of the tree is the closing parenthesis. So, any arguments to the function can exist at these and only these indices.

We have finished our evaluation description; we just have to translate it into code. Let us recap: we want to first evaluate the function "symbol", i.e., the symbol which encodes the function. So, we resolve this first. Then, we iterate through the arguments and evaluate each one in succession. Finally, we apply the function to these evaluated arguments.

Listing 5.162—Function Application Stem (`eval.c`)

```
1   static struct sval *eval_application(ast *application) {
2     struct sval *function = eval(ast_child(application, APPLICATION_FUNCTION_IDX));
3     for (...) {
4       // TODO evaluate each argument.
5     }
6     // TODO apply the function to its arguments.
7   }
```

We have run into a small roadblock, unfortunately. How do we evaluate a function with an indeterminate amount of arguments at runtime? In other words, addition, i.e., + evaluates as many arguments as it is provided. We cannot say for certain how many arguments it needs to evaluate, right? Wrong! We already know how many arguments it has by the aforementioned `for` loop! We simply take the number of children in the tree and subtract four. This will give us the number of arguments to evaluate.

Our problem does not stop there, however; we still have the issue of storing each evaluated s-value, so what do we do? The answer to this problem is a dynamically-allocated list. Recall that static array sizes must be known at compile-time, and since we do not know the number of arguments in a tree until it is parsed, we cannot use a statically-allocated list.[1] If we want to declare an array of, say, n integers with dynamic allocation, we use the following code:

Listing 5.163—Dynamically-Allocated Integer Array

```
1   int *array = malloc(n * sizeof(int));
```

[1]Certain C compilers offer support for *variable-length arrays* (VLA): stack-based arrays of variable length [Kochan, 2004].

This code says that we wish to allocate n spaces of memory, each of size int. Though, our program uses struct sval *, and not int, so what do we do? Simple: we just replace int with struct sval *.

Listing 5.164—Double Pointer of S-values

```
1   struct sval **arguments = malloc(n * sizeof(struct sval *));
```

The above declaration says that arguments is a pointer to an array of n slots to store struct sval *. This is precisely what we are after! For example, suppose we wish to apply + to the arguments 125, 94 and 101. We have three arguments to the function and therefore need to store three struct sval *. Thus, arguments is assigned malloc(3 * sizeof(struct sval *)).

The final question is, "How do we evaluate the arguments?" Conveniently enough, we have a nice function, eval, to evaluate any expression! Let us simply call that when evaluating the arguments to an application.

Listing 5.165—Recursive Argument Evaluation (eval.c)

```
1   static struct sval *eval_application(ast *application) {
2     struct sval *function = eval(ast_child(application, APPLICATION_FUNCTION_IDX));
3
4     // Number of arguments to use.
5     size_t num_args = application->children_num - 3;
6
7     // Allocate an array of arguments.
8     struct sval **arguments = malloc(num_args * sizeof(struct sval *));
9     ASSERT_ALLOC(arguments, "eval_application");
10
11    // Evaluate each argument.
12    for (int i = 0; i < num_args; i++) {
13      arguments[i] = eval(ast_child(application, i + 2));
14    }
15
16    struct sval *result = apply(function, arguments, num_args);
17
18    // Delete the allocated arguments array.
19    free(arguments);
20    return result;
21  }
```

Not a whole lot has changed; we allocate the correct number of arguments, iterate over the children of the abstract syntax tree, evaluate each argument, and store its computed result inside the arguments array.[1] Then, we call a mystery function apply with the function, its arguments, and the number of arguments. Finally, we free the array of arguments since it is no longer necessary, then return the result. Evaluation is complete! Now, let us dive deep into the apply header and source files.

---

[1] The offset of i + 2 in the abstract syntax tree list of children may seem bizarre, but remember the structure of an application abstract syntax tree

Listing 5.166—Function Application Header (`apply.h`)

```
1   #ifndef APPLY_H
2   #define APPLY_H
3
4   #include "sval.h"
5
6   struct sval *apply(const struct sval *function, struct sval **arguments,
7                      const size_t num_args);
8
9   #endif // APPLY_H
```

Fortunately, the `apply.h` header is not too complex—we define the prototype for the `apply` function so it is visible to `eval.c`. Let us now jump into `apply.c`. Before we begin coding, however, let us take a step back and think about what arithmetic operations $\mathcal{L}_{PF1}$ supports. For now, it is addition, subtraction, multiplication, and division. Thus, we need to declare four static functions: `apply_-addition`, `apply_subtraction`, `apply_multiplication`, and `apply_division`. Each of these functions will receive an array of arguments, i.e., an array of `struct sval *`, similar to the "root" `apply` function. Analogous to how `eval` works, `apply` will check the function we pass and call the appropriate static function.

Listing 5.167—Function Application Source File (`apply.c`)

```
1   #include "apply.h"
2
3   struct sval *apply(const struct sval *function, struct sval **args,
4                      const size_t num_args) {
5     char *fn = function->data.symbol;
6     if (streq(fn, "+")) { return apply_add(args, num_args); }
7     else if (streq(fn, "-")) { return apply_sub(args, num_args); }
8     else if (streq(fn, "*")) { return apply_mul(args, num_args); }
9     else if (streq(fn, "/")) { return apply_div(args, num_args); }
10    else {
11      EPF("apply: unknown function");
12      return NULL;
13    }
14  }
15
16  static struct sval *apply_add(struct sval **args, const size_t nargs) {// TODO.}
17  static struct sval *apply_sub(struct sval **args, const size_t nargs) {// TODO.}
18  static struct sval *apply_mul(struct sval **args, const size_t nargs) {// TODO.}
19  static struct sval *apply_div(struct sval **args, const size_t nargs) {// TODO.}
```

`apply`, as we can see, grabs the symbol representing the function "identifier", i.e., the string that says what this function is called. We then check to see if it is one of the four arithmetic operators supported by $\mathcal{L}_{PF1}$, and if so, we call its respective apply function. Let us finally write the code to apply an arithmetic operation to some arguments. We will do addition and subtraction together.

Inside `apply_addition`, we have two arguments: the evaluated s-values, and a number representing how many arguments to which we apply addition. So, we first create a `long double` to represent the current sum. Then, we loop over the arguments array and add the data, i.e., the value inside the `data` union, to the data in our running sum. Finally, we create a new s-value containing the sum.

Listing 5.168—Addition Application (`apply.c`)

```
1  static struct sval *apply_add(struct sval **args, size_t num_args) {
2    long double current_sum = 0;
3    for (int i = 0; i < num_args; i++) {
4      current_sum += args[i]->data.number;
5    }
6    return sval_number_create(current_sum);
7  }
```

We can write very similar code for applying subtraction to a list of arguments. The only difference (no pun intended) is that, because subtraction is not commutative, we have to subtract from left to right. For example, (- 4 5 6 7) evaluates to -14 because $4-5-6-7 = -14$. Thus, we cannot start the difference at zero as we did for "sum". Moreover, we cannot start our loop from 0 because this would mean that we subtract our first number from the first number; a redundant operation. Finally, we have to make a small adjustment to account for unary negation: if there is only one argument, e.g., (- 4), we negate and return that value.

Listing 5.169—Subtraction and Unary Negation Application (`apply.c`)

```
1  static struct sval *apply_sub(struct sval **args, size_t num_args) {
2    long double difference = args[0]->data.number;
3    // Unary negation.
4    if (1 == num_args) { difference = -difference; }
5    // Subtraction.
6    for (int i = 1; i < num_args; i++) {
7      difference -= args[i]->data.number;
8    }
9    return sval_number_create(difference);
10 }
```

The code for multiplication and division evaluation is trivial:

Listing 5.170—Multiplication & Division Application (`tester.c`)

```
1  static struct sval *apply_mul(struct sval **args, size_t num_args) {
2    long double product = 1;
3    for (int i = 0; i < num_args; i++) { product *= args[i]->data.number; }
4    return sval_number_create(product);
5  }
6
7  static struct sval *apply_div(struct sval **args, size_t num_args) {
8    long double quotient = args[0]->data.number;
9    for (int i = 1; i < num_args; i++) {
10     long double value = args[i]->data.number;
11     quotient /= value;
12   }
13   return sval_number_create(quotient);
14 }
```

Last but certainly not least, to complete our implementation of $\mathcal{L}_{PF1}$, we need to add a line to the eval function that interprets function applications:

Listing 5.171—Adding Application Evaluation (`tester.c`)

```
1  static struct sval *eval(ast *ast) {
2    if (ast_is_type(ast, "number")) { return eval_number(ast); }
3    else if (ast_is_type(ast, "symbol")) { return eval_symbol(ast); }
4    else if (ast_is_type(ast, "application")) { return eval_application(ast); }
5    else { return NULL; }
6  }
```

Treading and Testing

Excellent! Let us run this code on, say, a simple expression, e.g., (+ 4 3). This
should produce 7. Now, let us try some slightly harder examples:

Listing 5.172

```
> (+ 2 (- 5 4))                                 |  3
> (* 3 1 4)                                      |  12
> (* 3 1 (- 2 4))                                |  -6
> (+ 2.05 9.5)                                   |  11.55
> (- (+ (* 3.05 (- 3.14 5)))                     |  -6.68353
    (* (/ 12 (* 9.5 1.25))))                     |
> (- 4 5 6 7)                                    |  -14
> (- 3 (+ (* 7 (- 9))                            |  58.5
    (- 6 (/ -3 2)))))                            |
> (+ (- 9 1)                                     |  48
    (* (- 5 3)                                   |
       (* 2 10)))                                |
> (/ 5 0)                                        |  inf
```

Though, what happens if we try to compute mathematical heresy, i.e., division-
by-zero? It looks like C handles division-by-zero by labeling it as infinity, but is
this the true answer? Mathematically, division-by-zero is undefined, as so in C. So,
we should adjust our interpreter, namely apply_division, to account for division
by zero.

Listing 5.173—Accounting for Divide-by-Zero (tester.c)

```
1   static struct sval *apply_div(struct sval **args, size_t num_args) {
2     long double quotient = args[0]->data.number;
3     for (int i = 1; i < num_args; i++) {
4       long double value = args[i]->data.number;
5       if (0 == value) {
6         EPF("apply_div: attempted to divide by zero\n");
7         return sval_number_create(0);
8       } else { quotient /= value; }
9     }
10    return sval_number_create(quotient);
11  }
```

If we retry division by zero, we receive "Div by zero". Next, let us see what
happens if we input a symbol for one of the operands of an expression:

Listing 5.174

```
> (+ 4 5 jdkaw)                                  |  9
```

This produces a "correct" answer, but would it not be better if we instead
displayed an error? How do we do that? jdkaw is a symbol as defined by our
language grammar. So, we can insert a check for each arithmetic operation that
ensures each argument is a SVAL_NUMBER, and if not, we display an error message.

Listing 5.175—Type-checking Arithmatic Functions (apply.c)

```
1   static struct sval *apply_add(struct sval **args, size_t num_args) {
2    long double current_sum = 0;
3    for (int i = 0; i < num_args; i++) {
4     if (SVAL_NUMBER != args[i]->type) {
5      EPF("+ expected number; did not receive number\n");
6      exit(EXIT_FAILURE);
7     } else { current_sum += args[i]->data.number; }
8    }
9    return sval_number_create(current_sum);
10   }
```

We can propagate this check to each function since all four expect only numeric arguments. Re-running the test produces the expected error message.

Right now, these error messages are a little vague—it would serve the programmer better if, for example, they knew exactly what the function received instead of a number. Also, all of our errors thus far "terminate-on-error", meaning that as soon as an error is encountered, the entire program ends. If we attempt to divide by zero, it may be beneficial to continue running the interpreter and simply not evaluate the erroneous expression. We will explore these ideas later on.

Faster and Stronger Tests. Testing programs as they are built is essential to computer programmers. So far, our system allows us to specify a file as input representing a program in $\mathcal{L}_{PF1}$. As our interpreter grows and the languages become ever more complex, we will need to test more programs. Doing this one test at a time is inefficient and prone to errors. In this section, we will write a module for testing a series of programs in our interpreter.

Firstly, when we run a program through $\mathcal{L}_{PF1}$, we expect some output (assuming it does not crash or otherwise produce a non-sensical answer). Then, as humans, we compare this output to the expected, or intended, output. Automating this process would greatly reduce the possibility of overlooking a bug or accidentally introducing one when implementing new language features.

Ideally, we want a program that compares the output of executing a program in our language to the expected output. The input programs use the extension of the language, e.g., .pf1, whereas the output files have the extension .out. We can create a directory tests at the same level as the src directory that contains each test and its corresponding expected output file. For instance, program1.pf1 may contain 3, and the expected output file program1.out also contains 3.

Let us create a file tester.c. This file has its own main function as its existence is disjoint from the existence of $\mathcal{L}_{PF1}$ or any of its respective code. When we run tester, we want to specify how many tests to run. We extract out this value from the terminal arguments array argv[1] using sscanf:

Listing 5.176—Using Terminal Arguments to Read Data (tester.c)

```
1   int main(int argc, char *argv[]) {
2     if (2 != argc) {
3       EPF("usage: tester [number of tests]\n");
4     } else {
5       size_t number_of_tests = 0;
6       sscanf(argv[1], "%zu", &number_of_tests);
7       for (int i = 0; i < number_of_tests; i++) {
8         ...
9       }
10    }
11    return 0;
12  }
```

We now need to iterate through each possible test, execute it, and determine if it passes or not. There are two file names we need to examine: the input and output files. To store these, we use the asprintf function. asprintf formats its given arguments, similar to printf, into a char *. Recall that printf formats its given arguments into a format string char *, which is sent to standard output. asprintf, on the other hand, formats its arguments into a saved char *, which is dynamically-allocated if the given char * is NULL. Note that we must pass a reference, i.e., a double pointer, to the char * since the function modifies its contents. Each file contains the words program followed by a number as a "test identifier", and the extension.

Listing 5.177—Formatting Test Input and Expected Output Files (tester.c)

```
1   int main(int argc, char *argv[]) {
2     ...
3     for (int i = 0; i < number_of_tests; i++) {
4       char *in_file = NULL;
5       char *out_file = NULL;
6       asprintf(&in_file, "tests/program%zu.pf1", i + 1);
7       asprintf(&out_file, "tests/program%zu.out", i + 1);
8       ...
9       free(out_file);
10      free(in_file);
11    }
12    return 0;
13  }
```

We now have both file names available. Ideally, we want a function, e.g., test_-file, that returns true if the program output matches the expected output, and false otherwise. When a program fails to match, however, we should specify what the program received as well as what it expected. This brings up the point that, sometimes, we want to modify parameters as they are passed to a function. Passing a pointer to the object to modify is the only way to do this within an arbitrary function. Recall from our discussion on pointers that, when we wish to swap the values at two integers, we must pass them by pointer to a swap function. The same is true for char * values; all we need to do is pass these by pointer and we are good to go. Though, it is a bit confusing for newcomers to the C programming language because char * is already being passed as a pointer. Remember that char * is synonymous with "string", and passing a char * by value means that we only modify a local copy of the string and not the original. Accordingly, in addition to the two file names, test_file receives two more parameters: one to populate the expected output, and another to populate the actual output of the program.

Listing 5.178—Test Evaluation (`tester.c`)

```
1  int main(int argc, char *argv[]) {
2    ...
3    for (size_t i = 0; i < number_of_tests; i++) {
4      char *in_file = NULL;
5      char *out_file = NULL;
6      char *expected_output = NULL;
7      char *actual_output = NULL;
8      ...
9      bool passes = test_file(in_file, out_file,
10                             &expected_output, &actual_output);
11   }
12   return 0;
13 }
```

Listing 5.179—Implementing `test_file` (`tester.c`)

```
1  bool test_file(const char *in_file, const char *out_file,
2                 char **expected_contents, char **actual_contents) {
3    FILE *out_file_fp = fopen("out_file", "r");
4    if (NULL == out_file) {
5      EPF("test_file: failed to open expected output file %s\n", out_file);
6    }
7  }
```

So, we have opened the expected output file. We now need a way of running a command, i.e., `./pf1`, through C. A *pipe* allows us to implement this feature. We will not discuss the intricacies of pipes at the moment, so just know that they are a way of sending and receiving data between programs. In addition, we will also read the contents of the expected output file.

Listing 5.180—Read Actual and Expected Program Outputs (`tester.c`)

```
1  bool test_file(const char *in_file, const char *out_file,
2                 char **expected_contents, char **actual_contents) {
3    ...
4    /* Open the command for reading. */
5    char *cmd = NULL;
6    asprintf(&cmd, "./pf1 %s", in_file);
7    fp = popen(cmd, "r");
8
9    size_t sz;
10   getline(actual_contents, &sz, fp);
11   size_t sz2;
12   getline(expected_contents, &sz2, outfile);
13   ...
14   return false;
15 }
```

At this point, `actual_contents` and `expected_contents` have strings that we can compare directly for equality. If they match, then the test program succeeded in producing a correct result. Otherwise, something is amiss, and we must return false. Because both `getline` and `asprintf` dynamically-allocate data, we need to free these variables before returning a result from `test_file`.

Listing 5.181—Store Comparison Data in Argument Pointers (tester.c)

```
 1  bool test_file(const char *in_file, const char *out_file,
 2                 char **expected_contents, char **actual_contents) {
 3    ...
 4    bool c = true;
 5    if (!streq(*expected_contents, *actual_contents)) { c = false; }
 6    pclose(fp);
 7    fclose(outfile);
 8    free(cmd);
 9    return c;
10  }
```

Returning to main, we can now use the result obtained by calling test_file. If the boolean value is true, we print an "ok" status report. Otherwise, we display an error message that states what the output ought to be and what it (that is, the program input) actually produced.

Listing 5.182—Tester Source File (tester.c)

```
 1  int main(int argc, char *argv[]) {
 2    ...
 3    printf("Test %zu: ", i + 1);
 4    if (passes) { printf("OK\n"); }
 5    else {
 6     printf("FAILED");
 7     printf("\t\tExpected %s; Received: %s\n",
 8           expected_output, actual_output);
 9    }
10    ...
11    return 0;
12  }
```

Because asprintf is used not only in this function but also across test_file, we must free those four variables in every iteration of the for loop. To execute this program, we need to first compile $\mathcal{L}_{\text{PF1}}$ using make, then compile tester via gcc.[1]

Listing 5.183—Tester Source File (tester.c)

```
 1  int main(int argc, char *argv[]) {             Test 1: OK
 2    ...                                          Test 2: OK
 3    for (size_t i = 0; i < number_of_tests; i++) {  Test 3: OK
 4     printf("Test %zu: ", i + 1);                Test 4: OK
 5     if (passes) { printf("OK\n"); }             Test 5: OK
 6     else {
 7      printf("FAILED");
 8      printf("\t\tExpected %s; Received: %s\n",
 9            expected_output, actual_output);
10     }
11     free(expected_output);
12     free(actual_output);
13     free(in_file);
14     free(out_file);
15    }
16    return 0;
17  }
18
19  ./tester.o 5
```

---

[1] We could also add tester as a target in our Makefile.

5.3 $\mathcal{L}_{PF2}$: Now With Environments

Our current language, $\mathcal{L}_{PF1}$, is nice and all, but adding variables to the language would help immensely. First, let us define a new language, $\mathcal{L}_{PF2}$, which is a superset of $\mathcal{L}_{PF1}$ with the addition of environments and variables. Now, let us discuss what a variable looks like in $\mathcal{L}_{PF2}$, and define this notion of environments.

By now, you certainly understand what variables are in the C programming language. Fortunately for us, variables in $\mathcal{L}_{PF2}$ are not so different. We define variables via define. For example, (define x 10) defines a variable x with a value of 10.

With this idea in mind, we need to update our language grammar to include the ability to define variables.

```
expr      ::=   define
          |     application
          |     datum;
define    ::=   '(' 'define' symbol expr ')'
pf2       ::=   expr+;
```

Figure 5.20: Extended BNF Grammar for $\mathcal{L}_{PF2}$

We amend two preexisting grammar rules and add one that is entirely new. Expressions are now either definitions, function applications, or a type of data. Definitions are similar to function applications, except that define always contains two arguments: the first being a symbol and the second being an expression that is bound to the symbol. Finally, we change all existing instances of $\mathcal{L}_{PF1}$ to $\mathcal{L}_{PF2}$, and we declare that a program in $\mathcal{L}_{PF2}$ consists of one or more expressions. Such a modification allows us to define multiple variables and evaluate multiple expressions.

Let us begin by testing some basic programs in $\mathcal{L}_{PF2}$ to determine their abstract syntax trees.

Listing 5.184—Assignment and Addition Expressions

```
(define x 10)                        expr|define|>
                                       char:1:1 '('
                                       string:1:2 'define'
> (+ x 10)                             symbol|regex:1:9 'x'
                                       expr|datum|number|regex:1:11 '10'
                                       char:1:13 ')'
                                     expr|application|>
                                       char:2:1 '('
                                       expr|datum|symbol|regex:2:2 '+'
                                       expr|datum|symbol|regex:2:4 'x'
                                       expr|datum|number|regex:2:6 '10'
                                       char:2:8 ')'
```

If we try to evaluate this program, our interpreter will completely ignore the definition on the first line. Following this, it finds that x is not a number and hence displays the error, `"+ expected number; did not receive number"`. What we would like for our interpreter to do is resolve the variable x to its numeric representation and substitute it for x.

An *environment* is an association between symbols, i.e., variables, and values, i.e., s-values. For instance, with the preceding example, we associate the symbol x with the value 10. Whenever we define a new symbol, it and its value are stored in the current environment. So, how can we represent this structure? With a C struct, of course! We create a source/header pair for an env where the header is the following:

Listing 5.185—Environment Header (env.h)

```
1   #ifndef ENV_H
2   #define ENV_H
3
4   #include "sval.h"
5
6   struct env_pair {
7     char *key;
8     struct sval *value;
9     struct env_pair *next;
10  };
11
12  struct environment {
13    struct environment *parent;
14    struct env_pair *head;
15    size_t num_associations;
16  };
17
18  struct environment *environment_create(struct environment *parent);
19  struct sval *environment_lookup(struct environment *env, const char *key);
20  void environment_put(struct environment *env, char *key, struct sval *value);
21  void environment_destroy(struct environment *env);
22
23  #endif // ENV_H
```

An environment has four functions: one for creating an environment, one for looking up a symbol's value, one for inserting a new symbol and value into the environment, and one for deleting the environment from memory.

Notice that the first function, the creator, receives an environment as a parameter, called parent. This pointer is useless for us in $\mathcal{L}_{PF2}$, and we will revisit and explain its necessity in Chapter 6.

Next, we have a function for looking up a symbol in the environment and returning its associated s-value. For example, if we look up the value of x, we would receive 10.

Third, a function for inserting a symbol and its associated s-value exists. We need this to add symbol bindings to the environment.

Lastly, because we have a creation function, we need an accompanying destroyer function, which frees any memory associated with the environment.

Essentially, an environment consists of *association pairs*. Pairs map case-sensitive identifiers, i.e., symbolic names, to expressions. The environment association pairs contain an identifier and an expression. For instance, if we defined a variable x to the expression 10, the environment would contain a single association pair x:10, where the identifier is x and its corresponding expression is 10. Therefore, whenever we wish to reference x, its expression, namely 10, is returned. Since we do not know how many variables our environment will store at compile-time, using a linked-list data structure is a good idea. As we will mention in the next section, however, it matters little how we represent our pairs.

We choose to represent the environment, as we mentioned, as a linked list. Linked lists, as we know from Chapter 3 and earlier in this chapter, allow us to dynamically add new elements whenever, and particularly wherever, we please. Though, while it is quick to add a definition to the environment, it is slower to retrieve the value of a definition as the environment grows in size. Recall the GET function in a linked-list; it runs in *linear time*, compared to faster data structures such as trees.[1] Because we want our environments to be simple to implement at this time, however, such a trade-off is appropriately warranted.

Let us write each environment function one by one. First, we will create env.c with the template functions. Then, we will write the function to construct and return a new environment.

Listing 5.186—Environment Source File Function Stems (env.c)

```
1   #include "env.h"
2
3   struct environment *environment_create(struct environment *parent) { ...}
4   struct sval *environment_lookup(struct environment *env, const char *key) {...}
5   void environment_put(struct environment *env, char *key, struct sval *value) {...}
6   void environment_destroy(struct environment *env) {...}
```

Listing 5.187—Environment Constructor Function (env.c)

```
1   struct environment *
2   environment_create(struct environment *parent) {
3     struct environment *env = malloc(sizeof(struct environment));
4     ASSERT_ALLOC(env, environment_create);
5     env->head = NULL;
6     env->parent = parent;
7     env->num_associations = 0;
8     return env;
9   }
```

As always, we allocate memory for an environment, and since we have this lone parent pointer lying about, we will assign it as NULL for the time being.

Next, let us write the function for looking up the s-value of a symbol.

Listing 5.188—Symbol Lookup in Environment (env.c)

```
1   struct sval *environment_lookup(struct environment *env, const char *key) {
2     for (struct env_pair *curr; curr != NULL; curr = curr->next) {
3       if (streq(curr->key, key)) { return curr->value; }
4     }
5     return NULL;
6   }
```

---

[1]Linear time roughly indicates that an algorithm's performance scales proportionally to the input size.

In this function, we iterate over each association pair in the environment and determine if there is a key that shares the same name as the passed parameter key. If so, then we know that there is an associated value to return, which we retrieve from the environment list.

Now, we need a function for inserting association pairs into the environment. It should be noted that, if we attempt to redefine an existing symbol, the new binding takes precedence over the old one, hence *shadowing* the original definition.

Listing 5.189—Insert Symbol Binding in Environment (env.c)

```
1    void environment_put(struct environment *env, char *key, struct sval *value) {
2      struct env_pair *pair = malloc(sizeof(struct env_pair));
3      ASSERT_ALLOC(pair, "environment_put");
4      pair->key = strdup(key);
5      pair->value = value;
6
7      pair->next = env->head;
8      env->head = pair;
9      env->num_associations++;
10   }
```

Finally, we need a way of destroying an environment and its associated bindings. All we need to do is traverse the environment, find each environment pair (binding), then free its key and the node. Notice the parallels between this and the destruction of a linked-list.

Listing 5.190—Environment Destructor Function (env.c)

```
1    void environment_destroy(struct environment *env) {
2      while (env->head != NULL) {
3        struct env_pair curr = env->head;
4        env->head = env->head->next;
5        free(curr->key);
6        free(curr);
7      }
8      free(env);
9    }
```

Representation Independence with Respect to Environments

Our model of environments is a linked-list of association pairs, as we repeatedly emphasized. It is important to stress that this representation is merely a (pedagogical) design choice, and it may be a good idea to alter this representation down the road during development. For this reason, we want our environment to be *representation-independent*. In other words, when we designed the environment, we wrote several functions that act on an environment that are then called by our interpreter. It is not the responsibility of the interpreter to know how the environment works or its representation; its job is to *use* the environment for what it is worth.[1] Thus, creating a framework for a representation-independent environment that our interpreter can use is absolutely essential for good software and program design. If the structure of our environment changes, then the only functions that should require alteration under this paradigm are environment-labeled functions; the interpreter and any other modules that rely on environments should not need changing. Representation-independence is often referred to as a means of abstraction; we hide the implementation of something (in our case, the environment) and focus on using said something. Such a paradigm allows us to rely on "the what", rather than "the how".[2]

In future chapters, we will repeat this paradigm for several features in our interpreter. So, understanding its purpose and role in the project (and programming as a whole) is, in our opinion, crucial.

A Place to Call Home: Built-in Functions

In $\mathcal{L}_{PF1}$ and $\mathcal{L}_{PF2}$, we have four primitive arithmetic operations: +, -, *, and /, representing addition, subtraction, multiplication, and division respectively. The thing is, what if we want to add more functions? Suppose, for instance, that we want to add an operation that raises a base b to an exponent x, i.e., the power function. We, obviously, need to add a function to apply.c which performs this operation, but we also have to modify the non-static function apply to now account for power. We have to modify this function each and every time we add or remove functions. Would it not be better and more structured if we included a way of defining built-in functions that our interpreter and language automatically looks up? In our next language, we will do just that—our interpreter will keep track of a "base" environment with built-in functions, primitive operations, and constants. What is even better about this method is that it allows the programmer to override the default definition of these functions/constants. Case in point, if, for whatever reason, a programmer wanted to override + to store the value of 5 instead of a function, while certainly an odd decision, it is a possibility.

---

[1] Even with the wonderful idea of representation independence, we must be sure to construct an unambiguous definition that is abstract enough so as to not have to leak information into the object (i.e., the interpreter) using said model (i.e., the environment). A crucial example of this is the fact that our environment model semantics shadow previously-defined identifiers. Such behavioral semantics are required to effectively and correctly use a model and its underlying implementation.

[2] The term representation independence was established by John C. Mitchell in his *Representation independence and data abstraction* paper, as it relates to operations on the stack data structure and the λ-calculus [Mitchell, 1986]. Going even further back, David Parnas' paper describes encapsulation and modularity for designing and maintaining complex systems [Parnas, 1972].

First, we need to amend our definition of the sval struct to include the ability to store a function. Just like variables, we can store functions as data! In other words, we can create a function pointer, as noted earlier in the chapter, to store the location of instructions to perform a task. As an example, suppose we create an s-value to store the addition function. Within this s-value, we also store a function pointer to the apply-addition function. So, let us update our struct definition.

Listing 5.191—S-value Enumeration for Built-in Functions (sval.h)

```
1   enum sval_type { SVAL_NUMBER, SVAL_SYMBOL, SVAL_BUILTIN };
2
3   struct sval {
4     enum sval_type type;
5     union data {
6       long double number;
7       char *symbol;
8       struct sval *(*builtin)(struct sval **args, const size_t num_args,
9                               struct environment *env);
10    } data;
11  };
```

We made two alterations: the first is that we have a new SVAL type in our enum: SVAL_BUILTIN. Second, with the union inside our struct, we keep track of a function pointer called builtin. All applications receive an array of s-values, a number of arguments, and an environment in which the function is applied. One assumption we make with this function pointer is that any function we assign to it is a built-in function with a set definition ahead of time. For example, we know how the + operator should work, and we have pre-programmed this into apply_addition.

Now, inside apply, let us write a function builtin_functions_init which receives an environment to populate. Inside this function we declare s-values for each built-in operation, assign the relevant data (i.e., function pointers), and put them in the environment for later reference/look-up.

Listing 5.192—Built-in Function Table (apply.c)

```
1   void builtin_functions_init(struct environment *env) {
2     environment_put(env, "+", sval_builtin_create(apply_add));
3     environment_put(env, "-", sval_builtin_create(apply_sub));
4     environment_put(env, "*", sval_builtin_create(apply_mul));
5     environment_put(env, "/", sval_builtin_create(apply_div));
6   }
7
8   struct sval *apply(const struct sval *function, struct sval **args,
9                      size_t num_args, struct environment *env) {
10    if (SVAL_BUILTIN == function->type) {
11      return (function->data.builtin)(args, num_args, args);
12    } else {
13      EPF("apply: unknown function");
14      exit(EXIT_FAILURE);
15    }
16  }
```

To make this slightly easier to understand and cleaner, we wrote a helper function, sval_builtin_create inside sval.c that receives a function pointer and automatically creates a populated s-value.

Listing 5.193—Constructor for S-value Built-ins (sval.c)

```
1   struct sval *
2   sval_create_builtin(struct sval *(*builtin)(struct sval **args,
3                         size_t num_args, struct environment *env)) {
4       struct sval *sv = sval_create(SVAL_BUILTIN, NULL);
5       sv->data.builtin = builtin;
6       return sv;
7   }
```

One last addition: we need to modify eval_ast to initialize the global environment with the built-in functions.

Listing 5.194—Initializing Built-in Functions (eval.c)

```
1    void eval_ast(ast *ast) {
2     struct environment *global_env = environment_create(NULL);
3     builtin_functions_init(global_env);
4
5     // If there are no children, simply evaluate that ast.
6     if (0 == ast_children_num(ast)) {
7       struct sval *sv = eval(ast, global_env);
8       if (sv != NULL) { sval_print(sv); }
9     } else {
10    // Otherwise, evaluate its children recursively.
11      for (int i = 0; i < ast_children_num(ast); i++) {
12       struct sval *sv = eval(ast_child(ast, i), global_env);
13       if (NULL != sv) { sval_print(sv); }
14      }
15     }
16     environment_destroy(global_env);
17   }
```

Note: because add_builtin_functions has global scope, it needs to be added as a function prototype in apply.h.

Great! The apply function is now significantly easier to digest and, better yet, we need not modify its definition each and every time we add a new built-in function to our system. Let us execute the interpreter, and, we should see no change in functionality. One change we encourage is to update the s-value print function to account for s-value functions:

Listing 5.195—Printing S-value Built-ins (sval.c)

```
1    void sval_print(const struct sval *sv) {
2     if (SVAL_NUMBER == sv->type) {
3       printf("%Lg\n", sv->data.number);
4     } else if (SVAL_SYMBOL == sv->type) {
5       printf("%s\n", sv->data.symbol);
6     } else if (SVAL_BUILTIN == sv->type) {
7       printf("%s\n", "<function>");
8     } else {
9       EPF("sval_print: invalid sval");
10      exit(EXIT_FAILURE);
11     }
12   }
```

Thus, if the program contains, say, lone function, e.g., + or −, it will produce the following output:

Listing 5.196

```
> +                              | <function>
> -                              | <function>
```

Let us add **three** new built-in functions to our language: pow, floor, and ceil. pow receives **a base** number b and raises it to a given exponent x, i.e., b^x. floor rounds a floating-point value down to the nearest integer, e.g., floor(4.7) = 4. ceil, on the **other** hand, rounds a floating-point value up to the nearest integer, e.g., floor(4.01) = 5. We can use the C standard math library for these functions instead of writing them on our own.[1] As always, it is important to write proper error checks **and coherent** code.

Listing 5.197—Power Function (apply.c)

```
1   static struct sval *apply_power(struct sval **args, size_t num_args,
2                                    struct environment *env) {
3     // Check the number of arguments - pow expects 2.
4     if (2 != num_args) {
5      EPF("apply_power: pow expects two arguments but got %zu\n", num_args);
6      exit(EXIT_FAILURE);
7     }
8     // Pull the operands out of the args array.
9     struct sval *base = args[0];
10    struct sval *expt = args[1];
11
12    // Error checking.
13    if (SVAL_NUMBER != base->type) {
14     EPF("apply_power: pow expects argument 1 to be a number");
15     exit(EXIT_FAILURE);
16    } else if (SVAL_NUMBER != expt->type) {
17     EPF("apply_power: pow expects argument 2 to be a number");
18     exit(EXIT_FAILURE);
19    }
20
21    // Use the standard library function powl (pow with long doubles).
22    return sval_number_create(powl(base->data.number, expt->data.number));
23  }
```

Listing 5.198—Floor Function (apply.c)

```
1   static struct sval *apply_floor(struct sval **args, size_t num_args,
2                                    struct environment *env) {
3     // Check the number of arguments - floor expects 1.
4     if (1 != num_args) {
5      EPF("apply_floor: floor expects one argument but got %zu\n", num_args);
6      exit(EXIT_FAILURE);
7     }
8     // Pull the operands out of the args array.
9     struct sval *operand = args[0];
10
11    // Error checking.
12    if (SVAL_NUMBER != operand->type) {
13     EPF("apply_floor: floor expects argument 1 to be a number");
14     exit(EXIT_FAILURE);
15    }
16
17    // Use the standard library function.
18    return sval_number_create(floorl(operand->data.number));
19  }
```

---

[1]To remain **consistent** with our representation independence theme, we must explicitly specify the requirements of **function** arguments, e.g., the second argument of pow must be a positive integer.

Listing 5.199—Ceiling Function (`apply.c`)

```
1   static struct sval *apply_ceil(struct sval **args, size_t num_args,
2                                   struct environment *env) {
3     // Check the number of arguments - ceil expects 1.
4     if (1 != num_args) {
5       EPF("apply_ceil: ceil expects one argument but got %zu\n", num_args);
6       exit(EXIT_FAILURE);
7     }
8     // Pull the operands out of the args array.
9     struct sval *operand = args[0];
10
11    // Error checking.
12    if (SVAL_NUMBER != operand->type) {
13      EPF("apply_ceil: ceil expects argument 1 to be a number");
14      exit(EXIT_FAILURE);
15    }
16
17    // Use the standard library function.
18    return sval_number_create(ceill(operand->data.number));
19  }
```

And lastly, we must add these three to the global environment as they are predefined functions. We follow this addition up with some test cases:

Listing 5.200—Adding Other Math Built-ins (`apply.c`)

```
1   void builtin_functions_init(struct environment *env) {
2     ...
3     environment_put(env, "pow", sval_builtin_create(apply_power));
4     environment_put(env, "floor", sval_builtin_create(apply_floor));
5     environment_put(env, "ceil", sval_builtin_create(apply_ceil));
6   }
```

Listing 5.201

> (ceil 5.5)	6
> (floor 5.5)	5
> (ceil (* 3.14 12))	38
> (floor (* 3.14 12))	37
> (pow 2 8)	256
> (pow 2 (pow 2 2))	16
> (pow 3 (floor (- 3.5 1.125)))	9

We highly encourage the readers to design many more built-in (arithmatic) functions. Furthermore, in subsequent languages, we will add more functions that operate on more than just numbers, e.g., booleans, characters, and so on. Get creative!

In this chapter, we first reviewed elementary arithmetic in prefix notation, discussed the C programming language and its intricacies, and designed three prefix-based languages and interpreters. We also described environments and the idea behind representation independence with respect to environments.

There are **many** resources available for learning C. Thankfully, C has not changed too much since its original implementation. Compared to "modern" counterparts, C is a tiny programming language, which comes with associated advantages and drawbacks. The canonical resource for learning C is Brian Kernighan and Dennis Ritchie's [Kernighan and Ritchie, 1988] book commonly referred to as "K&R", although some of its examples and code style are antiquated compared to those typically exemplified today. K. N. King's [King, 2008] text on C is an excellent overview and academic perspective on the language, providing plentiful exercises. Finally, Peter van der Linden's book [van der Linden, 1994] is a more advanced book, hence the *Expert C* title, but it travels deep into the land of C, offering historical perspectives, security vulnerabilities, and miscellaneous tips and tricks on writing more complex C code. Because C is essentially everywhere we look in one way or another, there is no shortage of tutorials and references on the language, for both good and bad.

6   Interpretation

> *First, we want to establish the idea that a computer language is not just a way of getting a computer to perform operations but rather that it is a novel formal medium for expressing ideas about methodology.*

> —Hal Abelson & Gerald Jay Sussman

6.1 $\mathcal{L}_{\text{COND}}$: Conditionals and Decisions

Decision/control structures are a fundamental component of programming—we often need them in order to make a decision about what to do with data or values. In Chapter 5, we used conditionals extensively for natural recursion, error checking, and much more. For more information about writing conditional statements in C, please revisit Chapter 5.

In this chapter, we will start by writing $\mathcal{L}_{\text{COND1}}$: an extension of $\mathcal{L}_{\text{PF2}}$ that includes boolean variables and literals. Then, we will write $\mathcal{L}_{\text{COND2}}$: an extension of $\mathcal{L}_{\text{COND1}}$ to include decision-based arithmetic expressions. Afterward, we will write $\mathcal{L}_{\text{COND3}}$: a drastic jump from $\mathcal{L}_{\text{COND2}}$ which brings conditional expressions to the table.

Logical Expressions

Up until this point, all expressions in $\mathcal{L}_{\text{PF2}}$ compute a numeric result, e.g., addition, subtraction, power, ceiling, so on and so forth. What if we want to write expressions that are decision-based, or rather, return a true/false value? In C, we can write a statement to evaluate a boolean expression, e.g., `bool t = 5 < 4;`. It would perhaps be convenient if our language included such semantics. With that, it is time to introduce $\mathcal{L}_{\text{COND1}}$: now with boolean literals.

Implementing Boolean Values

A boolean, similar to C, is a true or false value. We represent true and false in $\mathcal{L}_{\text{COND1}}$ as #t and #f respectively. Let us extend our grammar to include our changes. Booleans, like numbers and symbols, are a type of data, or datum:

```
        datum       ::=    number
                      |     boolean
                      |     symbol
        boolean     ::=    '#' ('t' | 'f')
```

Figure 6.1: Extended BNF Grammar for $\mathcal{L}_{\text{COND1}}$

Listing 6.1—Extended mpc Grammar for $\mathcal{L}_{\text{COND1}}$

```
1    static void parser_init_rules(void) {
2        ...
3        boolean_rule = mpc_new("boolean");
4
5        mpc_err_t *error =
6            mpca_lang(MPCA_LANG_DEFAULT,
7                    "datum   : <number>          \n"
8                    "        | <symbol>          \n"
9                    "        | <boolean>         \n"
10                   "boolean: '#'('t'|'f')       ",
11                   ..., boolean_rule, NULL);
12       ...
13   }
```

That is all we need to do to our grammar; most of the changes come through the addition of a new s-value. We need to add a new enum to sval_type, and update the union inside the sval struct to include booleans. For our purposes, we will represent booleans as the C bool type.[1] We also need to add a creation function for boolean s-values.

Listing 6.2—Adding Boolean S-values (sval.h)

```
1    enum sval_type { ..., SVAL_BOOLEAN, ... };
2
3    struct sval {
4        ...
5        union data {
6            ...
7            bool boolean;
8            ...
9        } data;
10   };
11   ...
12   struct sval *sval_boolean_create(bool boolean);
```

Now, we need to modify sval.c to support the printing of booleans. We make the decision, out of consistency, to textually represent an output boolean identical to its input representation. That is, any boolean expression will output either #t or #f instead of, perhaps, true or false. Lastly, we need to add a function for processing boolean s-values.

---

[1] Make sure to include the stdbool.h header at the top of sval.h!

Listing 6.3—Constructor Function for Boolean S-values (`sval.c`)

```
 1  struct sval *sval_boolean_create(bool boolean) {
 2    struct sval *sv = sval_create(SVAL_BOOLEAN);
 3    sv->data.boolean = boolean;
 4    return sv;
 5  }
 6
 7  void sval_print(const struct sval *sv) {
 8    ...
 9    else if (sv->type == SVAL_BOOLEAN) {
10      printf("#%c\n", sv->data.boolean ? 't' : 'f');
11    }
12    ...
13  }
```

Listing 6.4—Evaluating Booleans (`eval.c`)

```
 1  static struct sval *eval(ast *ast, struct environment *env) {
 2    ...
 3    else if (ast_is_type(ast, "boolean")) {
 4      return eval_boolean(ast, env);
 5    }
 6    ...
 7  }
 8    ...
 9  static struct sval *eval_boolean(ast *boolean, struct environment *env) {
10    bool booll = streq(ast_contents(ast_child(boolean, 1)), "t");
11    return sval_boolean_create(booll);
12  }
```

You may be thinking to yourself, "That is all we had to write for `eval_-boolean`?" Yes, it is! Recall that `streq` returns a boolean—we check to see if the contents of the abstract syntax tree is identical to `"t"`. If so, then the data should be `true`, and `false` otherwise, but note that the only other possibility is `"f"`.

What may confuse some readers is the need to dive into the children of the boolean abstract syntax tree node. Would it not be simpler to just evaluate the contents of that node? Yes, it certainly is, but the problem is in the structure of our grammar rule for booleans. Let us investigate the output abstract syntax tree of a boolean.

Listing 6.5

```
> #t                        expr|datum|boolean|>
                              char:1:12 '#'
                              char:1:13 't'
```

As we can see, a boolean has two children: the first represents the `#` character, and the second represents the letter corresponding to true or false. As hinted, we only need to check the contents of the second child since the hash sign is always present (try and print out the contents of the boolean abstract syntax tree node; what do you see, or rather, what do you *not* see?).

Now, if we try to execute the program and define, then evaluate, a couple of booleans.

Listing 6.6

```
(define b1 #t)
(define b2 #f)

> b1                                          #t
> b2                                          #f
```

Our $\mathcal{L}_{\text{COND1}}$ language now understands booleans. Excellent! Though, having booleans on their own serves very little purpose other than to constantly beg for companioning logical operators!

As a motivating example, suppose we want to write a program that determines if two numeric values are equivalent. Sadly, $\mathcal{L}_{\text{COND1}}$ is incapable of doing so, since it has no way of comparing values.

Let us extend $\mathcal{L}_{\text{COND1}}$ to $\mathcal{L}_{\text{COND2}}$ via the addition of five numeric comparison operators: numeric equals =, <, <=, >, >=, and one boolean negation operator: not. All six operators will be implemented as functions, meaning their definitions, fortunately, reside only in apply.c.

```
expr            ::=    application | ...
application     ::=    boolexpr | ...
boolexpr        ::=    ('<'|'>'|'<='|'>='|'='|'not') ' ' expr+
```

Figure 6.2: Extended BNF Grammar for $\mathcal{L}_{\text{COND2}}$

First, let us write the six static function prototypes. Note that we have abbreviated the function names for spacing purposes.

Listing 6.7—Comparison Operator Application Functions (apply.c)

```
1    static struct sval *apply_num_eq(struct sval **args, size_t num_args);
2    static struct sval *apply_num_lt(struct sval **args, size_t num_args);
3    static struct sval *apply_num_leq(struct sval **args, size_t num_args);
4    static struct sval *apply_num_gt(struct sval **args, size_t num_args);
5    static struct sval *apply_num_geq(struct sval **args, size_t num_args);
6    static struct sval *apply_not(struct sval **args, size_t num_args);
```

The first five functions are similar in that they reference the number portion of the s-value's union, whereas apply_not instead references the boolean. We will write apply_num_eq and apply_not together, since after writing the former two, the remaining four are just as trivial and repetitive.

Numeric equals, i.e., '=' works as it does in traditional mathematics, with the exception that instead of restricting it to being a binary operator, it can be an n-ary operator. For instance, if we want to check whether several variables are numerically equivalent, we can use (= x y z a b). Unlike the arithmetic functions, however, these six functions return boolean s-values, i.e., s-values which represent a true or false value.

Listing 6.8—Numeric Equality Function Definition (apply.c)

```
1   static struct sval *apply_num_eq(struct sval **args, size_t num_args) {
2     if (num_args < 2) {
3       EPF("apply_num_eq: = expects at least two arguments but got %zu\n",
4           num_args);
5       exit(EXIT_FAILURE);
6     }
7
8     bool eq_result = true;
9     struct sval *curr_number = args[0];
10
11    // Iterate over each number and make sure they're equivalent.
12    for (int i = 1; i < num_args; i++) {
13      if (curr_number->data.number != args[i]->data.number) {
14        eq_result = false;
15        break;
16      }
17      curr_number = args[i];
18    }
19    return sval_boolean_create(eq_result);
20  }
```

Numeric **less than**, i.e., '<' is also not solely a binary operator—in fact, we can compare any **number** of, well, numbers, that we desire. The only requirement is that for less than to return true, all operands must be less than the next. For instance, (< 3 4 5) **returns** #t, but (< 3 1 5 7 9) returns #f. Identical to '=', '<' requires at least two **arguments**, as any fewer would be non-sensical.

Listing 6.9—Numeric "Less Than" Function Definition (apply.c)

```
1   static struct sval *apply_num_lt(struct sval **args, size_t num_args) {
2     if (num_args < 2) {
3       EPF("apply_num_lt: < expects at least two arguments but got %zu\n",
4           num_args);
5       exit(EXIT_FAILURE);
6     }
7
8     bool lt_result = true;
9     struct sval *curr_number = args[0];
10
11    for (int i = 1; i < num_args; i++) {
12      if (curr_number->data.number >= args[i]->data.number) {
13        lt_result = false;
14        break;
15      }
16      curr_number = args[i];
17    }
18    return sval_boolean_create(lt_result);
19  }
```

Logical **negation**, i.e., 'not' flips the given boolean operator, identical to how it works in C. That is, if we pass an expression that resolves to #t, applying not resolves to #f, **and** vice versa. The only remaining steps are to add the functions to the global **(built-in)** environment, and write test cases.[1]

---

[1] We make **use of the** ASSERT_ARITY macro, which allows us to quickly assert whether a function received the **correct number** of arguments. The macro only accounts for functions with a definitive arity and does not **work with** variadic functions, e.g., addition, numeric equals, and so forth.

Listing 6.10—Logical "Not" Function Definition (`apply.c`)

```
1   static struct sval *apply_not(struct sval **args, size_t num_args) {
2     ASSERT_ARITY("not", 1, num_args);
3     return sval_boolean_create(!args[0]->data.boolean);
4   }
```

Listing 6.11

```
(define x 5)
(define y (+ x 10))
(define z (- y 5))
(define w (+ (- z y) x))

> (= x y z w)                            | #f
> (< x y z w)                            | #f
> (= 2 2 2 (+ 2 (- 4 (+ 8 (- 4)))))     | #t
> (not (= 2 2))                          | #f
> (>= 9 8 7 6 x 4 3 2 1)                 | #t
> (> 9 8 7 6 5 x 4 3 2 1)                | #f
```

Lo and behold, we get the correct and sensible answers! Now that we have an adequate representation of boolean expressions and operators, we can jump right into the meat of this section: conditional, or case analysis, expressions.

Decision Structures via cond and if

We will write $\mathcal{L}_{COND3}$: the extension to $\mathcal{L}_{COND2}$ which includes two ways of representing case analysis expressions: `cond` and `if`. The former is similar to a series of `if`, `else if` chains in imperative languages, e.g., C, whereas `if` contains only one clause for truth case, and one clause for the false case.

```
expr           ::=   application | ...
application    ::=   cond | if | ...
cond           ::=   '(cond' cond-clause* else-clause ')'
cond-clause    ::=   '[' expr ' ' expr ']'
else-clause    ::=   '[' 'else' ' ' expr ']'
if             ::=   '(if ' expr ' ' expr ' ' expr')'
```

Figure 6.3: Extended BNF Grammar for $\mathcal{L}_{COND3}$

One key distinction between conditionals in $\mathcal{L}_{COND1}$ and those written in, say, C, is that both `cond` and `if` are expressions, i.e., when evaluated, they return values. Let us see an example:

Listing 6.12

```
> (if (< 10 20) 5 10)                    | 5
```

In C, we cannot write such expressions—the closest we come is via a function to emulate the "return style" behavior. Along this vein, consider the following code segment:

Listing 6.13

```
(define result
 (cond
  [(<= 10 (+ 5 2)) 800]
  [(= 20 (+ 5 2)) 700]
  [else 600]))
```

We see that the variable result uses a cond to determine its numeric value. Fortunately, thanks to the additions of $\mathcal{L}_{\text{COND2}}$, we have the operators to handle such comparisons.

We stated the grammar for $\mathcal{L}_{\text{COND3}}$, but it is important to discuss the particulars of both decision expressions. First off, both cond and if require "alternative" expressions. In other words, "one-armed if" expressions are not possible like they are in other languages, e.g., C. Consider the following code:

Listing 6.14

```
(define var1 5)
(define var2 (if (= var1 10) 50))
```

var1 is certainly not equal to 10, so the expression does not evaluate the "consequent"; rather, it resolves to nothing at all! So, it begs the question: what value is stored in var2? We do not really know, and to prevent such questions from arising in our language, we outright disallow such expressions. The same holds true for cond: it must contain at least one case analysis and end with an else case. As such, this means that it is possible for the only case in a cond clause to be else, but this would be pointless.

As suggested, $\mathcal{L}_{\text{COND3}}$ will recognize two conditional forms: cond and if. While cond is useful for instances of multiple conditions, if is best used when the outcome is binary, i.e., one of two possibilities. Additionally, we place some further restrictions on conditional expressions, namely that cond must contain an else clause, and if expressions must contain three expressions representing the predicate, consequent, and alternative outcome respectively.

What is rather convenient about these modifications is that we need not touch apply nor sval, nor even the grammar, as both case analysis forms are mere syntactic evaluations. Accordingly, let us begin to design their respective evaluation functions. cond and if are both *special forms* of application; the only difference to normal functions is that we evaluate these two differently. Thus, in eval_-application, we *could* add checks to see if the function (symbol) is one of these predefined forms:

Listing 6.15—Evaluating Conditionals (eval.c)

```
1   static struct sval *eval_application(ast *application,
2                                        struct environment *env) {
3     struct sval *function = eval(ast_child(application,
4                                            APPLICATION_FUNCTION_IDX),
5                                  env);
6
7     // First, check to see if "function" is one of the special forms.
8     if (streq(function->data.symbol, "cond")) {
9       return eval_cond(function->data.symbol, env);
10    } else if (streq(function->data.symbol, "if")) {
11      return eval_if(ast, env);
12    }
13    ...
14  }
15
16  static struct sval *eval_cond(ast *cond, struct environment *env) { // TODO. }
17  static struct sval *eval_if(ast *ifc, struct environment *env) { // TODO. }
```

Though, this would be rather cumbersome if we add more special forms like we certainly will in Chapters 7 and 8. Perhaps the better and more modular approach would be to write a lookup system, similar to environments, but for special forms. To do this, we first need a data structural representation of special forms. A special form has a keyword indicating the form, e.g., "if", and an evaluation function (pointer). Additionally, we need a pointer to the "next" special form since we will mimic the environment linked list structure.

Listing 6.16—Special Form Header File (sform.h)

```
1   #ifndef SFORM_H
2   #define SFORM_H
3
4   #include "ast.h"
5   #include "env.h"
6   #include "sval.h"
7
8   struct sform {
9     char *form;
10    struct sval *(*eval_form)(ast *ast, struct environment *env);
11    struct sform *next;
12  };
```

Now, much like environments, we need a "root" representation, i.e., a way to access all special forms. Environments store a head pointer, so we should store a similar pointer in, say, a forms table.

Listing 6.17—Special Form Table Definition (sform.h)

```
1   struct forms_table {
2     struct sform *head;
3   };
```

Now to design the necessary functions. We need four: one for creating a special form, one for lookup, one to determine if something is a valid special form, and one to destroy/free the special forms at the end of the program.

Listing 6.18—Special Form Function Prototypes (sform.h)

```
1   void special_forms_create(char *form,
2                             struct sval *(eval_form)
3                                 (ast *ast, struct environment *env));
4   struct sval *(*special_forms_lookup(char *form))(ast *, struct environment *);
5   bool special_forms_exists(char *form);
6   void special_forms_destroy(void);
```

The nice **part** about creating a special form is that we can, almost verbatim, reuse the code for storing a value in environments. This also holds true for destroying special forms.

Listing 6.19—Creation and Destruction of Special Forms (sform.c)

```
1   #include "sform.h"
2
3   static struct forms_table table;
4
5   void special_forms_create(char *form,
6                             struct sval *(eval_form)
7                                 (ast *ast, struct environment *env)) {
8     struct sform *f = malloc(sizeof(struct sform));
9     ASSERT_ALLOC(f, "special_forms_create");
10    f->form = strdup(form);
11    f->eval_form = eval_form;
12    f->next = table.head;
13    table.head = f;
14  }
15
16  bool special_forms_exists(char *form) { // TODO. }
17
18  struct sval *
19  (*special_forms_lookup(char *form))(ast *, struct environment *) { // TODO. }
20
21  void special_forms_destroy(void) {
22    struct sform *front = table.head;
23    while (NULL != front) {
24      struct sform *curr = front;
25      front = front->next;
26      free(curr->form);
27      free(curr);
28    }
29  }
```

Now we write the middle two functions. special_forms_exists is trivial because it uses the result from the lookup function; if it returns NULL, then the form is not a special form.

Listing 6.20—Determine if Special Form Exists (sform.c)

```
1   bool special_forms_exists(char *form) {
2     return NULL != special_forms_lookup(form);
3   }
```

Finally, we come to the weird-looking function whose return value is complex enough to drive some people mad. Do not let this discourage you because all this says is we are returning a pointer to a function that receives two arguments: an abstract syntax tree, and an environment. Hopefully, that structure is familiar, as all static functions within eval.c use that very signature. So, what do we do within this function? We iterate through each special form to find the one that we want, and return its stored function pointer if there is a match. Otherwise, we return NULL, indicating that the passed argument is not a special form.

Listing 6.21—Special Form Lookup Function (eval.c)

```
1   struct sval *
2   (*special_forms_lookup(char *form))(ast *, struct environment *) {
3     for (struct sform *curr = table.head; curr != NULL; curr = curr->next) {
4       if (streq(curr->form, form)) { return curr->eval_form; }
5     }
6     return NULL;
7   }
```

Let us jump over to eval.c and initialize some special forms. Let us declare a static function to do this. Inside, we will call special_forms_create and pass our two existing special forms, i.e., if and cond, alongside their evaluation functions.

Listing 6.22—Adding cond and if Special Forms (eval.c)

```
1   static void special_forms_init(void) {
2     ...
3     special_forms_create("if", eval_if);
4     special_forms_create("cond", eval_cond);
5   }
```

Only two more steps: initialize the special forms table in the root evaluation function, i.e., eval_ast, where the global environment is similarly established. At the end of this function, we invoke the destroyer to free the associated memory.

Listing 6.23—Initialization of Special Forms Table (eval.c)

```
1    void eval_ast(ast *ast) {
2      struct environment *global_env = environment_create(NULL);
3      builtin_functions_init(global_env);
4      special_forms_init();
5      ...
6      // Evaluation...
7      ...
8      special_forms_destroy();
9      environment_destroy(global_env);
10   }
```

Last, but certainly not least, in eval_application, we add a clause to determine if the function to be applied is one of the special forms and, if so, invoke its stored function pointer.

Listing 6.24—Checking for Special Forms in Application (eval.c)

```
1    static struct sval *eval_application(ast *application,
2                              struct environment *env) {
3      struct sval *function = eval(ast_child(application, APPLICATION_FUNCTION_IDX),
4                              env);
5
6      // First, check to see if "function" is one of the special forms.
7      if (special_forms_exists(function->data.symbol)) {
8        return special_forms_lookup(function->data.symbol)(application, env);
9      }
10     ...
11   }
```

This may seem like a lot of upfront work to invest compared to a chain of conditionals, but this mindset of modularity and abstraction goes a long way in the scalability of program and language design.

Returning to conditionals, because if uses a predictable and predefined syntax structure, we will analyze and design it before its cond counterpart.

Let us write a very simple example of an if expression in $\mathcal{L}_{\text{COND3}}$. This way, we can deconstruct the abstract syntax tree to determine where, when, and what we need to evaluate.

Listing 6.25

```
> (if (< 2 3) 10 20)                  | expr|>
                                      |   application|>
                                      |     char:1:1 '('
                                      |     expr|datum|symbol|regex:1:2 'if'
                                      |     expr|application|>
                                      |       char:1:5 '('
                                      |       expr|datum|symbol|regex:1:6 '<'
                                      |       expr|datum|number|regex:1:8 '2'
                                      |       expr|datum|number|regex:1:10 '3'
                                      |       char:1:11 ')'
                                      |     expr|datum|number|regex:1:13 '10'
                                      |     expr|datum|number|regex:1:16 '20'
                                      |     char:1:18 ')'
```

We know that if contains three valuable components: the predicate, the consequent case, and the alternative case. Scanning over the abstract syntax tree, we make note that the predicate is child 3 (index 2), the consequent is child 4 (index 3), and the consequent is child 5 (index 4). Since these numbers are somewhat arbitrary in design, we can refactor them as constants at the top of eval.c so we better understand their intention:

Listing 6.26—Defining Conditional Expression Indices (eval.c)

```
1   #include "mpc.h"
2
3   #define APPLICATION_FUNCTION_IDX 1
4   #define IF_PREDICATE_IDX 2
5   #define IF_CONSEQUENT_IDX 3
6   #define IF_ALTERNATE_IDX 4
```

Now, using these, we can actually evaluate if expressions, but in what order? First, we evaluate the predicate to see if it returns true and, if so, we evaluate the consequent (expression). On the contrary, we evaluate the alternate (expression). Upon adding if, we should write test cases.

Listing 6.27—Evaluation of if Expressions (eval.c)

```
1   static struct sval *eval_if(ast *ifc, struct environment *env) {
2     // First, evaluate the predicate.
3     struct sval *predicate_value = eval(ast_child(ifc, IF_PREDICATE_IDX), env);
4
5     // Depending on its result, either evaluate the consequent or alternate.
6     if (predicate_value->data.boolean) {
7       return eval(ast_child(ifc, IF_CONSEQUENT_IDX), env);
8     } else {
9       return eval(ast_child(ifc, IF_ALTERNATE_IDX), env);
10    }
11  }
```

Listing 6.28

```
> (if (> 3 2) (- 3 2) (+ 3 2))        | 1
> (if (< 2 3) 10 20)                  | 10
> (if (= (+ 10 20 30) (+ 30 20 9))    | 0
      (+ 90 60 30)
      (- 90 60 30))
```

From this framework we can easily implement cond. The neat thing about these (cond and if) constructs is that it is possible to implement one in terms of the other since they mimic behaviors. Our approach, though, will not take advantage of this interchangeability due to the structure of our abstract syntax trees. To start, let us see another example of cond:

Listing 6.29

```
(cond
  [(= 20 30) 40]
  [(< 20 15) 100]
  [else 60])
```

The cond form, as we have stated, evaluates each predicate listed as the first of two expressions written in brackets. So, $\mathcal{L}_{\text{COND3}}$ evaluates (= 20 30) to determine if it is true. If so, it returns 40. In the case it is not true, we skip evaluation of 40 and continue to the next case, repeating ad nauseam. The only exception to this specification is when all explicit predicates are false. When this occurs, similar to other languages, e.g., C, there is a "fall back" case that we evaluate. In other words, it serves as somewhat of a "last resort" clause. In our small code snippet, since neither of the preceding predicates resolves to true, we evaluate, then return, 60. Let us now view the abstract syntax tree of a sample cond expression. Recall that, as a special form, cond is merely an application with some fancy window dressing.

```
expr|>
  application|>
    char:1:1 '('
    expr|datum|symbol|regex:1:2 'cond'
    expr|application|>
      char:2:3 '['
      expr|application|>
        char:2:4 '('
        expr|datum|symbol|regex:2:5 '='
        expr|datum|number|regex:2:7 '20'
        expr|datum|number|regex:2:10 '30'
        char:2:12 ')'
      expr|datum|number|regex:2:14 '40'
      char:2:16 ']'
    expr|application|>
      char:3:3 '['
      expr|application|>
        char:3:4 '('
        expr|datum|symbol|regex:3:5 '<'
        expr|datum|number|regex:3:7 '20'
        expr|datum|number|regex:3:10 '15'
        char:3:12 ')'
      expr|datum|number|regex:3:14 '100'
      char:3:17 ']'
    expr|application|>
      char:4:3 '['
      expr|datum|symbol|regex:4:4 'else'
      expr|datum|number|regex:4:9 '60'
      char:4:11 ']'
    char:4:12 ')'
```

We can **break** a cond down into sub-components for easier analysis: A cond should have **at least** two applications, the second of which has a special form as its function **name**, namely else. Each application will consist of two further sub-components: **a predicate** and its pairing consequent. Because these two pieces are an application, the third child (index 2) is the predicate, and the fourth child (index 3) is its consequent. All we need to do is iterate through each clause and, once we evaluate a predicate that resolves to true, we evaluate, then return, its consequent. Because there exists the very likely possibility of traversing through each clause, **we need** to keep track of how many clauses are present in the cond expression. **Namely**, if a cond has n children in its abstract syntax tree, we know that three of **those** children are syntax and not part of the expression, i.e., the opening parenthesis, the cond string, and the closing parenthesis. Thus, there should be $n-3$ predicate/consequent clauses, where the last of which encompasses the alternative, i.e., else clause.

Listing 6.30—Evaluation of cond (eval.c)

```
1   #define COND_CLAUSE_IDX 2
2   #define COND_CLAUSE_COUNT 3
3   ...
4   static struct sval *eval_cond(ast *cond, struct environment *env) {
5     int num_clauses = ast_children_num(cond) - COND_CLAUSE_COUNT;
6
7     // For every clause (except the else), we grab it,
8     // determine if its true, and if so, return its consequent.
9     for (int i = 0; i < num_clauses - 1; i++) { // TODO. }
10
11    // If we get here, the else clause should be evaluated and returned.
12  }
```

Now, we **need to** keep track of two s-value positions: the current clause predicate, and the current **clause** consequent. We already have a number to keep track of where to start counting clauses from, so we should simply offset from that value!

Listing 6.31—Offset for cond Evaluation (eval.c)

```
1   static struct sval *eval_cond(ast *cond, struct environment *env) {
2     int num_clauses = ast_children_num(cond) - COND_CLAUSE_COUNT;
3
4     // For every clause (except the else), we grab it,
5     // determine if its true, and return its consequent.
6     for (int i = 0; i < num_clauses - 1; i++) {
7       ast *clause = ast_child(cond, COND_CLAUSE_IDX + i);
8       struct sval *predicate = eval(ast_child(clause, COND_PREDICATE_IDX), env);
9
10      if (predicate->data.boolean) {
11        return eval(ast_child(clause, COND_CONSEQUENT_IDX), env);
12      }
13    }
14    ...
15  }
```

We iterate **from** 0 up to the number of clauses minus one because we want to examine **every clause** except the last as it is of a special "form". Inside the body of the loop, **we retrieve** each clause, then extract and evaluate its predicate. If it returns true, i.e., **the** predicate is true, we then evaluate and return the consequent. All that is left **is** to analyze the else case. The cond abstract syntax tree has n children, and **we** know that child $n-1$ is the last closing parentheses. Therefore, the else clause **must** be at position $n-2$.

Listing 6.32—Evaluation of Last Child in cond (eval.c)

```
1  static struct sval *eval_cond(ast *cond, struct environment *env) {
2    ...
3    return eval(ast_child(ast_child(cond, ast_children_num(cond) - 2), 2), env);
4  }
```

But wait, we are not done quite yet! Recall that this child is also an application of a special form. Accordingly, we can unwrap and evaluate the clause here to simplify the procedure. An else clause, because it is an application, has m children, where child $m-1$ is the closing parentheses. Therefore, the alternate expression to evaluate is at index $m-2$. Let us write the code and at the same time refactor the code to use preprocessor definitions instead of magic numbers:

Listing 6.33—Refactoring Constants (eval.c)

```
1  #define COND_ELSE_OFFSET_IDX 2
2  #define COND_ELSE_CONSEQUENT_IDX 2
3    ...
4  static struct sval *eval_cond(ast *cond, struct environment *env) {
5    ...
6    return eval(ast_child(ast_child(cond,
7                      ast_children_num(cond) - COND_ELSE_OFFSET_IDX),
8                  COND_ELSE_CONSEQUENT_IDX), env);
9  }
```

That will do it! Now, let us write some test cases.

Listing 6.34

```
> (cond                              60
  [(= 20 30) 40]
  [(< 20 15) 100]
  [else 60])
```

Here is another test case that computes interest rate based on a given amount, then computes the sum of those values:[1]

Listing 6.35

```
(define amount 7500)
(define interest-rate
 (cond
  [(<= amount 1000) 0.040]
  [(<= amount 5000) 0.045]
  [(<= amount 10000) 0.055]
  [else 0.060]))

> (+ amount (* amount interest-rate))        7912.5
```

Exercise 6.1. (★★★)

Earlier, we implemented cond and if where the former must include an else as its last predicate, and the latter is not one-armed. Add the necessary functionality to make one-armed if expressions possible, as well as cond statements with no else. In the event that there is no true predicate, NULL should be returned instead of a populated s-value.

---

[1] If you are having trouble with executing the below program, make sure your decimal values have a leading zero!

Short-Circuiting with Logical Operators

As we explored in Chapter 5, there exist operators for evaluating multiple boolean expressions. For example, if we want to evaluate an expression only when three conditions are true, we can use "&&", e.g., if (x && y && z). Along those lines, if we want to evaluate an expression when at least one condition is true, we can use "||", e.g., if (x || y || z). $\mathcal{L}_{\text{COND3}}$ allows us to mimic such behavior via a chain of "cond" expressions:

Listing 6.36

```
(cond
 [x
  (cond
   [y
    (cond
     [z  ])])])
```

But, as we can see, this quickly diverges into chaos. Some may consider writing a built-in function that only evaluates an expression "e" when all its previous arguments are true. There are two problems with this approach: first, we do not know how many arguments will be passed to this mystery function, and second, which is a significantly worse problem, we cannot short-circuit evaluate the operator with this approach. Recall that, via function application, all arguments are evaluated prior to invoking the function. With boolean operators such as "and", and "or" that potentially short-circuit, it is impossible and irresponsible to preemptively evaluate the arguments. Thus, we need to introduce two new special forms: "and", and "or". Each special form will evaluate each passed expression one at a time from left to right. For "and", if we encounter a false condition, we immediately return false, and therefore stop the execution of the remaining clauses. On the other hand, for "or", if we encounter a true condition, we immediately return true, and therefore stop the execution of the remaining clauses.

Now, let us implement these short-circuit operators. As we said, each operator is a special form that we can add to our lookup table. Both definitions are similar in design, so if we implement one, we can copy it over to the other and make the necessary alterations.

Implementing Logical And/Or

First, we need to know how many clauses to evaluate. Similar to cond and if we have a minimum number of expected children in the abstract syntax tree. Namely, we have the pair of opening and closing parentheses, then the and/or keyword. Thus, if an abstract syntax tree contains n children, it contains $n-3$ clauses.

Listing 6.37—Evaluation of Logical And (eval.c)

```
1   #define LOGICAL_CLAUSE_IDX 3
2   #define LOGICAL_CLAUSE_OFFSET 2
3
4   static struct sval *eval_and(ast *and, struct environment *env) {
5     size_t num_clauses = ast_children_num(and) - LOGICAL_CLAUSE_IDX;
6     for (int i = 0; i < num_clauses; i++) {
7       struct sval *boolean_sval = eval(ast_child(and, i + LOGICAL_CLAUSE_OFFSET),
8                                         env);
9       if (!boolean_sval->data.boolean) {
10        return sval_boolean_create(false);
11      }
12    }
13    return sval_boolean_create(true);
14  }
```

The code largely annotates itself; we evaluate each argument of the logical operator. In the case of and, when we find an argument which resolves to false, and short-circuits, thereby returning false. Conversely, in the case of or, when we find an argument which resolves to true, or short-circuits, thereby returning true. For either operator, the "fall-through" case aligns with the intention of said operator. For instance, we return true when all arguments to and are true, and similarly, when all the arguments to or are false, we return false. Following this, we can finally test some more simple programs:

Listing 6.38

```
(define a 10)
(define b 20)
(define c 30)

> (and #t #t #t)                      #t
> (and (= a (+ 10 b)) (= (- c b)))    #f
> (and (= a b) (= b c) (= a c))       #f
> (or #f #f #f)                       #f
> (or #f #f #t #f #f)                 #t
```

With these operators, we can implement other logical operators, e.g., conditional, biconditional, and exclusive-or.

Exercise 6.2. ($\star$)
Add the apply_conditional function that receives two booleans and returns false if the first is true and the second is false, and true otherwise.

Exercise 6.3. ($\star$)
Add the apply_biconditional function that receives at least two booleans and returns true if they are all the same truth value, and false otherwise.

Exercise 6.4. ($\star$)
Add the apply_xor function that receives at least two booleans and XORs their values. Do *not* implement short-circuit evaluation for XOR.

6.2 $\mathcal{L}_{\text{LOCAL}}$: Local Identifiers and Values

Thus far, our programs have defined variables and expressions in what is known as global scope. In C, we often declare local variables inside functions, i.e., variables that are only visible inside the function in use. Right now, $\mathcal{L}_{\text{COND3}}$ does not have such a counterpart. In this section, we will write $\mathcal{L}_{\text{LOCAL}}$: an extension to $\mathcal{L}_{\text{COND3}}$ that includes the ability to use local environments for expressions.

Before we jump into our implementation of $\mathcal{L}_{\text{LOCAL}}$, we need to explain two paradigms of "scoping". The scope of a variable, as we explained, is the visibility of a variable in a piece of code. C is what we refer to as a *lexically-scoped* language. Lexical scoping is a type of variable binding that attaches value based on its location in code. Let us see what we mean by an example in C. We first assign a local variable x to be 20 inside main, then invoke bar with an argument of 30. This is followed by an invocation of foo that prints the global variable x, namely 10. Inside bar, its x variable references the one passed as an argument, namely 30, meaning the program outputs the following under lexical scoping:

Listing 6.39—Lexically-Scoped Variables

```
1    int x = 10;                                    x in foo: 10
2                                                   x in bar: 30
3    void foo(void) {
4      printf("x in foo: %d\n", x);
5    }
6
7    void bar(int x) {
8      foo();
9      printf("x in bar: %d\n", x);
10   }
11
12   int main(void) {
13     int x = 20;
14     bar(30);
15     return 0;
16   }
```

Another scoping paradigm is called *dynamic scoping*. Under dynamic scoping, a variable's value is determined by its most recent assignment rather than its location in code. Reusing the above code example, rather than printing 10 inside foo, it actually prints 30, which makes little sense intuitively; we assign x to be 20 only inside main, meaning foo should have no idea of this assignment. Though, under dynamic scope, this is exactly what happens![1] For this reason, many programming languages avoid the use of dynamic scope in favor of lexical scoping, and we will do the same in $\mathcal{L}_{\text{LOCAL}}$.

---

[1]Note that we cannot test this code because C uses lexical scoping.

```
expr          ::=    application | ...
application   ::=    let | letstar | ...
let           ::=    'let (' let-bndg+ ')' expr
letstar       ::=    'let* (' let-bndg+ ')' expr
let-bndg      ::=    id ' ' expr
```

Figure 6.4: Extended BNF Grammar for $\mathcal{L}_{\text{LOCAL}}$

let Expressions

As a motivating example for local variable definitions, suppose we have the following code:

Listing 6.40

```
(define x 5)
(define y 6)

> (+ x y)                              11
```

This, obviously, produces 11. Though, we have run into a pretty pertinent problem: x and y now populate global scope, i.e., the global environment, and we cannot change their values in $\mathcal{L}_{\text{COND3}}$. It would be rather convenient if we had a way of declaring local variables in the event that we do not wish to pollute the global environment.

Listing 6.41

```
(let ([x 5]
      [y 6])
  (+ x y))
```

Readers, take a minute to think about what this expression does. We see that we have something called let with what appears to be an application of applications of x and y to values. Instead, this binds x to the literal 5 and y to the literal 6. From there, we see a trivial application of addition to x and y. A let expression allows us to define, then use, local variables. Any declarations are visible only to the body of the let expression, and are, effectively, destroyed afterward. This begs the question: what happens if we define a variable to be in both global and local scope? Take the following code segment:

Listing 6.42

```
(define x 10)

(let ([x 20]
      [y 30])
  (if (= x 10)
      (* x 100)
      (* x 200)))

(if (= x 10)
    (* x 100)
    (* x 200))
```

The code first defines a variable x in global scope, then creates a let with two variables x and y. The body consists of a case analysis that checks to see if x is equal to 10. The thing is, which x does it reference? In this case, it references the x created by the let construct. Thus, the output of the let expression is 4000. This paradigm is known as *lexical scoping*. Lastly, we have a duplicate case analysis outside the let which references the x declared globally, meaning it outputs 1000.

We must consider what actually happens, in detail, when $\mathcal{L}_{\text{LOCAL}}$ encounters a let expression. Instead of adding variables to the global environment, it extends the current environment. That is, we create an environment that holds the values of variables declared within the let, which has a pointer, or link, to its parent environment. For instance, we know that the program contains a global parent environment, which we call e_0. When a let is evaluated, we create an extension of the current environment, say e_1. The environment e_1 contains the bindings of all declared variables. Then, once the body is evaluated, e_1 is destroyed. Symbolically, we will use $e_1 \rightsquigarrow e_0$ to designate that environment e_0 is the parent environment of e_1, or equivalently, environment e_1 chains to the environment e_0.

This again raises an important question: what happens if a symbol within a let is not declared within the let? Simple! We check the let environment for a declaration, and if it does not exist, it searches the parent environment. If we hit the (global) parent environment and the variable does not exist, we return NULL. Of course, this means we need to amend our env lookup function definition.

Listing 6.43—Parent Environment Lookup (env.c)

```
1   struct sval *environment_lookup(struct environment *env, const char *key) {
2     ...
3     if (NULL != env->parent) {
4       return environment_lookup(env->parent, key);
5     }
6     return NULL;
7   }
```

Until now, we had no need for the parent environment pointer that we introduced in Chapter 5, because all variables and expressions were declared in the global environment.

With the preliminary discussion out of the way, let us implement let in $\mathcal{L}_{\text{LOCAL}}$. Similar to cond and if, let is a special form, meaning it is a type of application. Accordingly, let us take a look at a sample abstract syntax tree:

```
expr|>
  application|>
    char:1:1 '('
    expr|datum|symbol|regex:1:2 'let'
    expr|application|>
      char:1:6 '('
      expr|application|>
        char:1:7 '('
        expr|datum|symbol|regex:1:8 'x'
        expr|datum|number|regex:1:10 '5'
        char:1:11 ')'
      expr|application|>
        char:2:7 '('
        expr|datum|symbol|regex:2:8 'y'
        expr|datum|number|regex:2:10 '6'
        char:2:11 ')'
      char:2:12 ')'
    expr|application|>
```

```
  char:3:3 '('
  expr|datum|symbol|regex:3:4 '+'
  expr|datum|symbol|regex:3:6 'x'
  expr|datum|symbol|regex:3:8 'y'
  char:3:9 ')'
char:3:10 ')'
```

As we see, `let` expressions contain two important components: variable/identifier bindings and its body. As previously described, `let` expressions introduce a new environment that extends its parent environment. Therefore we can establish some skeleton code for evaluating `let`:

Listing 6.44—Function Stub for `let` Evaluation (eval.c)

```
1  static struct sval *eval_let(ast *let, struct environment *env) {
2    struct environment *new_env = environment_create(env);
3    // TODO populate new_env with the let variable bindings.
4
5    // Evaluate the body with new_env.
6    return eval( ..., new_env);
7  }
```

We need a way of computing the number of bindings that we define within the `let`. Similar to how we compute the number of clauses within a `cond`, we will use the abstract syntax tree as a base. The third child (index two) of a `let` abstract syntax tree is where the variable binding nodes begin. So, we can use this sub-tree to compute the number of bindings. The application contains at least two children because of the opening and closing parentheses. Accordingly, if the subtree contains n children, then it has $n-2$ variable bindings.

Listing 6.45—Removing Constants (eval.c)

```
1   #define LET_BINDING_OFFSET_IDX 2
2   #define LET_ALL_BINDINGS_IDX 2
3   #define LET_BINDING_IDX 1
4   #define LET_SYMBOL_IDX 1
5   #define LET_EXPR_IDX 2
6   #define LET_BODY_OFFSET_IDX 2
7   ...
8   static struct sval *eval_let(ast *let, struct environment *env) {
9     // Initialize the new environment with env as its parent.
10    struct environment *new_env = environment_create(env);
11    ast *bindings = ast_child(let, LET_ALL_BINDINGS_IDX);
12    int num_bindings = ast_children_num(bindings) - LET_BINDING_OFFSET_IDX;
13
14    // Populate the environment with the variables and their evaluated expressions.
15    for (int i = 0; i < num_bindings; i++) {
16      ast *curr_binding = ast_child(bindings, LET_BINDING_IDX + i);
17      ast *sym_tree = ast_child(curr_binding, LET_SYMBOL_IDX);
18      struct sval *expr = eval(ast_child(curr_binding, LET_EXPR_IDX), env);
19      environment_put(new_env, ast_contents(sym_tree), expr);
20    }
21
22    // Evaluate the body with new_env.
23    return eval(ast_child(let, ast_children_num(let) - LET_BODY_OFFSET_IDX),
24                new_env);
25  }
```

Does this **look familiar**? It certainly should! It is almost identical to the code we wrote for cond **with** the exception that we introduce a new environment. There is, however, **another difference** that should be noted. When we evaluate the expression, notice that **we do not** evaluate the symbol. This is because if a binding already exists for said symbol, **its** evaluation resolves to its environment binding, which is not the desired outcome.

The only **remaining** item is to modify special_forms_init to accept our new special form:

*Listing 6.46—**Add** let Special Form* (eval.c)

```
1  static void special_forms_init(void) {
2    special_forms_create("if", eval_if);
3    special_forms_create("cond", eval_cond);
4    special_forms_create("and", eval_and);
5    special_forms_create("or", eval_or);
6    special_forms_create("let", eval_let);
7  }
```

Now, evaluating a simple let expression should produce the expected output:

Listing 6.47

```
> (let ([x 5]              11
        [y 6])
    (+ x y))
```

Let us try **nested** let expressions, as well as declaring the same variable in both global and **local scope**:

Listing 6.48

```
> (let ([x 20]            30000
        [y 30])
    (let ([z (+ x y)])
      (* x y z)))
```

Listing 6.49

```
(define x 10)

> (let ([x 20]            4000
        [y 30])
    (if (= x 10)
        (* x 100)
        (* x 200)))

> (if (= x 10)            1000
      (* x 100)
      (* x 200))
```

Fantastic, **it works** well! There is one small problem though: what happens if we want to **use definitions** inside of another definition? For instance, examine the following code:

Listing 6.50

```
(let ([x 20]
      [y 30]
      [z (+ x y)])
  (* x y z))
```

This, in a perfect world, outputs 30000, since we define z in terms of x and y. The problem is that these definitions of x and y are only visible to the body of the let expression. So, to the local declaration of z, it sees x and y as unbound symbols. One workaround is to use nested let expressions.

Listing 6.51

```
(let ([x 20])
  (let ([y 30])
    (let ([z (+ x y)])
      (* x y z))))
```

Thus, the body has access to all three variables, z has access to x and y, and y has access to x. It is somewhat inconvenient and cumbersome to have to write nested let expressions in this fashion. Let us rectify this issue with let*.

let* Expressions

There is an important environmental/scope distinction between let and let* expressions: a let evaluates all variable bindings with respect to the parent environment. On the other hand, let* initializes each binding in a separate environment where the environment of successive variables references the previous. To explain, we will use the previous "problematic" let example, but modify it to instead use let*.

Listing 6.52

```
(let* ([x 20]
       [y 30]
       [z (+ x y)])
  (* x y z))
```

First, assume that there exists a parent environment e_0 that the let* is declared within. When we evaluate the expression paired with x, we create an environment $e_1 \rightsquigarrow e_0$, which holds the value of the evaluated x. Likewise, we create an environment $e_2 \rightsquigarrow e_1$, which holds the value of the evaluated y. Lastly, we create an environment $e_3 \rightsquigarrow e_2$, which holds the value of the evaluated z. Then, the let* body is evaluated in e_3. So, let us add this as a special form to our language.

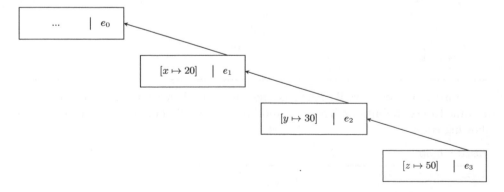

Figure 6.5: Environment Extension within let* Binding Expressions

Listing 6.53—Evaluation of `let*` (`eval.c`)

```
1   static struct sval *eval_letstar(ast *letstar, struct environment *env) {
2     struct environment *curr = env;
3     ast *bindings = ast_child(letstar, LET_ALL_BINDINGS_IDX);
4     int num_bindings = ast_children_num(bindings) - LET_BINDING_OFFSET_IDX;
5
6     for (int i = 0; i < num_bindings; i++) {
7       struct environment *new_env = environment_create(curr);
8       ast *curr_binding = ast_child(bindings, LET_BINDING_IDX + i);
9       ast *sym_tree = ast_child(curr_binding, LET_SYMBOL_IDX);
10      struct sval *expr = eval(ast_child(curr_binding, LET_EXPR_IDX), curr);
11      environment_put(new_env, ast_contents(sym_tree), expr);
12      curr = new_env;
13    }
14
15    return eval(ast_child(letstar, ast_children_num(letstar) - LET_BODY_OFFSET_IDX),
16               curr);
17  }
```

Conveniently enough, not much needs to be altered from our definition for `let` expressions. We first create a temporary variable to hold the "current" environment. We define the "current" environment to be the environment that is in use by the variable bindings. So, before the loop begins, the current environment is the passed environment, i.e., the environment wherein we define this `let*` expression. Upon entering the loop, we create a new environment whose parent is the "current" environment. After evaluating the current variable binding, we set the current environment to be the new environment we made so that we, effectively, create a chain of environments.

After adding the special form to the table, we can test the program:

Listing 6.54

```
> (let* ([x 20]              |  30000
         [y 30]              |
         [z (+ x y)])        |
    (* x y z))               |
```

6.3 $\mathcal{L}_{PROC1}$ & $\mathcal{L}_{PROC2}$: Recursive Procedures

Thus far, we have written several languages with support for variables, environments, conditionals, and local scope. The only important and fundamental currently-omitted feature is procedures. We have previously used procedures in $\mathcal{L}_{LOCAL}$ via applications of primitive procedures such as +. In this section, we will write $\mathcal{L}_{PROC1}$: an extension to $\mathcal{L}_{LOCAL}$ to include procedures and recursion.

```
expr          ::=   application | ...
application   ::=   proc | ...
proc          ::=   'lambda' '(' id* ')' expr
```

Figure 6.6: Extended BNF Grammar for $\mathcal{L}_{PROC1}$

Procedure Representation

We represent a procedure as a symbol enclosed by parentheses. Procedures may or may not have arguments. For example, if we want to define a procedure add that adds two natural numbers using natural recursion in $\mathcal{L}_{PROC1}$, we would use the following syntax.

Listing 6.55

```
; A NaturalNumber is an Integer greater than or equal to zero.

;; add : NaturalNumber NaturalNumber -> NaturalNumber
;; Recursively adds two natural numbers.
(define add
 (lambda (n m)
  (cond
   [(= n 0) m]
   [else (+ 1 (add (- n 1) m))]))))
```

We see that a procedure is represented similarly to a variable with the added exception that the definition consists of a lambda expression. The keyword lambda defines a function. We represent functions/procedures as (lambda $(p_1 \ p_2 \ ... \ p_n)$ body) where the second clause, i.e., $(p_1 \ p_2 \ ... \ p_n)$ are its formal parameters, and body refers to the function body.[1] Complex functions whose definitions are not as apparent contain *documentation comments* above their function signature.

---

[1]While there are semantic differences between procedures and functions, our text refers to them interchangeably.

Documentation comments have two parts: a type header, and a purpose statement. Type headers loosely describe the input and output data types of the function; they do not necessarily need to match the exact data type name. Types to the left of an arrow are function inputs, whereas the type to the right is its output. A function purpose statement explains why we want the function and its intended use; it should not serve as a verbatim retelling of the code. Note that, sometimes, we will include data definitions, as inspired from Felleisen's *How to Design Programs* [Felleisen et al., 2018], to give significance to names. For example, we can say that a **NaturalNumber** "is a" **Number** greater than or equal to zero, or a **Function** is $\{X\}\{Y\}[X \rightarrow Y]$ for any types X and Y. Brackets indicate a grouping of symbols, generally denoting a function or data structure (as we will show in Chapter 7. Braces describe generic types, meaning $\{X\}$ does not say that $\{X\}$ is a formal parameter, but is a placeholder for a type. As a look ahead, we will make significant use of data definitions in subsequent chapters. We restate that these documentation comments are for the programmer who reads (your) code and should therefore be clear, thorough, and concise.

Throughout the rest of this book, we will use λ to designate the keyword `lambda` when defining a procedure/function to conserve code listing space.

Let us write a few simple procedures to clean up our naturally recursive definition of add in an attempt to remove constant values, e.g., 1 and 0. Because of their suggestive identifiers, we will use these functions in place of comparisons against zero, adding one, and subtracting one whenever necessary to reduce redundancy.

Listing 6.56—Useful Arithmetic Functions

```
(define zero?
 (λ (n)
  (= n 0)))

(define add1
 (λ (n)
  (+ n 1)))

(define sub1
 (λ (n)
  (- n 1)))

(define add
 (λ (n m)
  (cond
   [(zero? n) m]
   [else (add1 (add (sub1 n) m))]))))
```

We are now ready to begin constructing procedures. First, let us create an s-value representation of procedures. A procedure has a list of symbols representing the formal parameters and a body. So, we can create a struct to represent a procedure, and insert it as part of the data union. Note that we already have an enum representing procedures, namely SVAL_BUILTIN, so we can create a new enum value: SVAL_PROCEDURE.

Listing 6.57—Procedure S-Value Representation (sval.c)

```
1    struct procedure {
2      char **formals;
3      size_t num_formals;
4      ast *body;
5    };
6
7    struct sval {
8      ...
9      union data {
10       ...
11       struct procedure *proc;
12     } data;
13   };
14     ...
15   struct sval *sval_procedure_create(char **formals, size_t num_formals, ast *body);
```

You may be wondering why does the procedure not store an identifier. Well, think about it—the procedure itself has no reason to store an identifier. Consider the following example:

Listing 6.58

```
(define add (λ (...) ...))
```

We bind the procedure to the name add. Therefore, it is superfluous to give a name to a lambda. It only makes sense to say that add, in this case, is bound to a lambda expression. In fact, because procedures are first-class, i.e., treated as data, providing a name complicates the structure even more.

Now, we should write the function to create the s-value for a lambda procedure.

Listing 6.59—S-value Procedure Creation (sval.c)

```
1    struct sval *sval_procedure_create(char **formals,
2                               size_t num_formals, ast *body) {
3      struct sval *sv = sval_create(SVAL_PROCEDURE);
4      struct procedure *proc = malloc(sizeof(struct procedure));
5      ASSERT_ALLOC(proc, "sval_procedure_create");
6      proc->num_formals = num_formals;
7      proc->formals = formals;
8      proc->body = body;
9      sv->data.proc = proc;
10     return sv;
11   }
```

Hopefully, nothing in the above code looks too foreign—we create the appropriate s-value, its corresponding procedure struct to store the number of formals, the formals themselves (represented as strings), and the body of the procedure represented as an abstract syntax tree.

Next, we should amend the sval_print function to now print both built-in and user-defined functions.

Listing 6.60—Printing Procedure S-values (sval.c)

```
1  void sval_print(const struct sval *sv) {
2    ...
3    else if (SVAL_PROCEDURE == sv->type || SVAL_BUILTIN == sv->type) {
4      printf("%s\n", "<function>");
5    }
6    ...
7  }
```

Finally, we update the sval_destroy function to free the data associated with the procedure, namely the array of formals (and each corresponding formal), and the body abstract syntax tree.

Listing 6.61—Procedure S-value Destruction (sval.c)

```
1   void sval_destroy(struct sval *sv) {
2     ...
3     else if (SVAL_PROCEDURE == sv->type) {
4     // Free the formals.
5     for (int i = 0; i < sv->data.proc->num_formals; i++) {
6       free(sv->data.proc->formals[i]);
7     }
8     // Free the procedure itself.
9     free(sv->data.proc);
10    }
11    ...
12  }
```

Now to head into the meat of this problem. In eval.c, we will write the code to first interpret a lambda. Afterward, we will update our function application code to handle both built-in functions and user-defined procedures.

Listing 6.62—lambda Evaluation Function Stub (eval.c)

```
1  static struct sval *eval_lambda(ast *lambda, struct environment *env) { // TODO. }
```

We now answer the question, "How do we interpret a lambda?" Fortunately, it is even simpler than, say, a let or cond expression! lambda is a special form, so it is a type of application, which consists of three primary parts: the lambda keyword, the list of formals, and the body. Let us look at a simple lambda expression and its abstract syntax tree:

Listing 6.63

```
(λ (x) (+ x 1))              expr|>
                              application|>
                               char:1:1 '('
                               expr|datum|symbol|regex:1:2 'lambda'
                               expr|application|>
                                char:1:9 '('
                                expr|datum|symbol|regex:1:10 'x'
                                char:1:11 ')'
                               expr|application|>
                                char:1:13 '('
                                expr|datum|symbol|regex:1:14 '+'
                                expr|datum|symbol|regex:1:16 'x'
                                expr|datum|number|regex:1:18 '1'
                                char:1:19 ')'
                               char:1:20 ')'
```

We see that the formals are also treated as an application subtree. Thus, if we extract and analyze this tree, we can determine how many formals are declared within this lambda. The application has at least two children, being the pair of parentheses. Thus, if the subtree has n children, there are $n-2$ declared formals. Moreover, we see that the abstract syntax tree of a lambda node starts with the opening parentheses, then the lambda keyword. Therefore, the formal declarations are always child 3 (index 2) of the lambda abstract syntax tree, both of which we can declare as constants.

Listing 6.64—Removing Constants (eval.c)

```
1  #define LAMBDA_FORMALS_IDX 2
2  #define LAMBDA_FORMALS_OFFSET 2
3    ...
4  static struct sval *eval_lambda(ast *lambda, struct environment *env) {
5    ast *formals_ast = lambda->children[LAMBDA_FORMALS_IDX];
6    size_t num_formals = formals_ast->children_num - LAMBDA_FORMALS_OFFSET;
7    // TODO.
8  }
```

Now, we need to extract each formal from the abstract syntax tree and store them in an array. Because we are declaring an array of strings, we should use a char **.

Listing 6.65—Allocation of Formals Array (eval.c)

```
1  static struct sval *eval_lambda(ast *lambda, struct environment *env) {
2    ...
3    char **formals = malloc(num_formals * sizeof(char *));
4    ASSERT_ALLOC(formals, "eval_lambda");
5    // TODO.
6  }
```

With this, we can copy over each formal string to its corresponding position in the array. In addition, we should also go ahead and extract the body from the tree. The body is one index behind the closing parentheses of the lambda tree. Thus, if the tree has n children, the body subtree is child $n-1$ (index $n-2$). Since we have the necessary pieces to create a procedure, all we need to do now is invoke, then return, sval_procedure_create.

Listing 6.66—lambda Evaluation (eval.c)

```
1  static struct sval *eval_lambda(ast *lambda, struct environment *env) {
2    ...
3    // Copy the formals over to the array.
4    for (int i = 0; i < num_formals; i++) {
5      formals[i] = strdup(formals_ast->children[1 + i]->contents);
6    }
7    ast *body = lambda->children[LAMBDA_BODY_IDX];
8    return sval_procedure_create(formals, num_formals, body);
9  }
```

That is all there is to interpreting a lambda expression (aside from adding the relevant special form to eval_application, of course). Now, if we create a sample program that defines one, $\mathcal{L}_{\text{LOCAL}}$ should correctly output that it is a function.

Listing 6.67

`(define identity (λ (x) x))`	
`> identity`	`<function>`

If we try to *invoke* identity, then, sadly, the program will not work, because $\mathcal{L}_{\text{LOCAL}}$ does not understand user-defined procedure application. It will soon, though, with the invention of $\mathcal{L}_{\text{PROC2}}$.

The only difference between $\mathcal{L}_{\text{PROC1}}$ and $\mathcal{L}_{\text{PROC2}}$ is that the latter understands how to apply a user-defined procedure to its arguments. We have seen how $\mathcal{L}_{\text{PF3}}$ does this with primitive built-in procedures, and the process for user-defined procedures is only slightly different.

How exactly do we apply a user-defined procedure to its arguments? We need to bind the formals of the procedure to the arguments. Take, for instance, the identity procedure from above:

Listing 6.68

`(define identity (λ (x) x))`

Suppose we invoke identity with the argument 10. Upon doing so, $\mathcal{L}_{\text{PROC2}}$ searches the current environment for the definition of identity and retrieves its stored formals and body, followed by a binding of the only formal parameter, x, to the argument 10. Subsequently, it evaluates the body with respect to the binding of x to 10. **Binding formal parameters to arguments is known as extending the current environment.** We will write a function in env.c to do this for us:

Listing 6.69—Environment Extension (env.c)

```
1   struct environment *environment_extend(struct environment *parent,
2                                           struct sval *procedure,
3                                           struct sval **arguments) {
4     struct environment *new_env = environment_create(parent);
5     struct procedure *proc = procedure->data.proc;
6
7     // Copy formals over.
8     for (int i = 0; i < proc->num_formals; i++) {
9       environment_put(new_env, proc->formals[i], arguments[i]);
10    }
11    return new_env;
12  }
```

We first create an environment that links itself to the parent environment, similar to how let works. Then, we retrieve the stored procedure and assign each formal (identifier) to the evaluated argument. Switching over to eval_application, we can see this in action:

Listing 6.70—Binding Formals to Arguments (eval.c)

```
1   static struct sval *eval_application(ast *application,
2                                        struct environment *env) {
3      ...
4      // If it is a built-in function, evaluate here.
5      struct sval *result = NULL;
6      if (function->type == SVAL_BUILTIN) {
7        result = apply(function, arguments, num_args);
8      } else {
9        // Otherwise, extend the current environment.
10       struct environment *new_env = environment_extend(env, function, arguments);
11       result = eval(function->data.proc->body, new_env);
12       environment_destroy(new_env);
13     }
14     ...
15   }
```

We need to amend this definition rather heavily, in that we first check to see if the function is either built-in or a user-defined procedure. If it is the former, then we call apply. Otherwise, we perform a more interesting evaluation. We extend the current environment with the formal bindings, then evaluate the body with respect to the new environment. Let us run and invoke identity:

Listing 6.71

(**define** identity (λ (x) x))	
> (identity 10)	10

Suppose we want to write a procedure that computes the sales tax of some dollar amount and then write another function that computes the total of a sale with the sum of the sales tax and amount:

Listing 6.72

(**define** sales-tax	
(λ (amt)	
(* 0.07 amt)))	
(**define** total	
(λ (amt)	
(+ (sales-tax amt) amt)))	
> (total 50)	53.5
> (total 49.99)	53.4893
> (total 149.99)	160.489
> (total 299.99)	320.989

With these additions, we now have a very respectable language and interpreter! One thing we want to try out, though, is the use of recursion with our procedures.

Recursive Procedures

$\mathcal{L}_{\text{PROC2}}$ is smart enough to understand and correctly interpret recursive procedures. Below are a few examples:

Listing 6.73

```
(define zero?
  (λ (n)
    (= n 0)))

(define sub1
  (λ (n)
    (- n 1)))

(define fact
  (λ (n)
    (cond
      [(zero? n) 1]
      [else (* n (fact (sub1 n)))])))

> (fact 5)                                120
```

Exercise 6.5. (⋆)
Design the f2c function, which receives a temperature in Fahrenheit and converts it to Celsius.

Exercise 6.6. (⋆)
Design the combineDigits function, which receives two digits, as numbers, and returns a number representing their conjunction. For example, (combineDigits 2 4) resolves to 24.

Exercise 6.7. (⋆⋆)
Design the sub function, which defines subtraction over natural numbers using sub1.

Exercise 6.8. (⋆⋆)
Design the mult function, which defines multiplication over natural numbers using add and sub1 .

Exercise 6.9. (⋆⋆)
Design the expt function, which defines exponentiation over natural numbers using mult and sub1.

Exercise 6.10. (⋆⋆)
Design the tetr function, which defines tetration: a lesser-known operation that represents repeated exponentiation. For instance, (tetr 2 3) represents 2^{2^2}, which is equivalent to $(2^2)^2$, which is 16.

Exercise 6.11. (⋆⋆)
Video games often deal with collision detection between objects, which determines when two objects overlap, or collide, with one another. Three-dimensional games are extremely complex, so we will dial our scope back to "Pong-esque" (two-dimensional) games, where all objects were rectangular. Write the rect-collide? function in $\mathcal{L}_{PROC2}$, which receives two rectangle definitions and returns true if they overlap and false otherwise. A rectangle definition consists of an (x, y) coordinate pair, as well as a width and height. In Figure 6.7, the left-hand two rectangles overlap, but the right-hand two rectangles do not overlap.

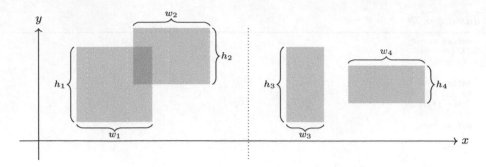

Figure 6.7: Collision Detection Between Rectangles.

Exercise 6.12. (★★)

The Haskell programming language uses the following grammar to denote (anonymous) lambda functions.

```
lambda  ::=  '\ ' vars expr
vars    ::=  '(' (symbol ' ')* symbol? ')'
```

Figure 6.8: Extended BNF Grammar for Haskell-esque Lambda

Add this as a syntactic extension to $\mathcal{L}_{\text{PROC2}}$. Below is an example of its intended usage.

Listing 6.74

```
(define !
  (\ (n)
    (cond
      [(zero? n) 1]
      [else (* n (! (sub1 n)))])))
```

Exercise 6.13. ($\star\star\star$)

We have seen that we can represent tetration in terms of exponentiation, with exponentiation in terms of multiplication, with multiplication in terms of addition, and with addition in terms of adding and subtracting one. We can continue this pattern indefinitely, even though the operations will quickly blow up to incredibly large numbers. For instance, pentation is repeated tetration. What if we want to write a generator that, when given a number, corresponds to returning a function that performs an operation. For instance, if we call generate with zero, we return an addition function. If generate receives one, we return a multiplication function. If generate receives two, we return an exponentiation function, and so on ad infinitum. Design the generate function. You should be inspired by your add, mult, expt, and tetr functions. As a hint, consider the observed patterns in the designs of those naturally-recursive functions. You should not call any other functions inside generate besides add1, sub1, and generate. We provide the skeleton code below, as well as examples.[1]

Listing 6.75—Skeleton Code for generate

```
; A NN is a NaturalNumber.

;; generate : NN -> [NN NN -> NN]
;; Returns a binary function corresponding to
;; the naturally-recursive arithmetic operation.
(define generate
 (λ (i)
  (λ (n m)
   (cond
    ; Base cases.
    [(zero? m)
     (cond
      [(zero? i) ___]
      [(zero? (sub1 i)) ___]
      [else ___])]
    ; Case analysis on i.
    [(zero? i) ___]
    [else ___])))))
```

Listing 6.76—Examples of generate

```
(define add (G 0))
(define mult (G 1))
(define expt (G 2))
(define tetr (G 3))

> (add 12 4)
> (mult 4 7)
> (expt 2 5)
> (tetr 3 2)
```

```
16
28
32
27
```

---

[1] This is Ackermann's *original* function; the one shown in Chapter 5 was a binary function, whereas this one receives three arguments.

$\mathcal{L}_{\text{LETREC}}$: **One More Time with** letrec

The recursive procedures we have written thus far are incredibly effective at writing meaningful programs. Though, it is sometimes to our advantages to write helper functions for recursive algorithms. For instance, suppose we want to write a function that computes the Fibonacci sequence in accumulator-passing style. This means that our procedure does not build a result via unwinding a series of recursive calls, but rather, the result is accumulated through parameter-passing. Let us write the associated Fibonacci function to accomplish this task.

We first need a function that gets the job done, i.e., computes the nth Fibonacci number. Recall that the nth Fibonacci number is the sum of its previous two Fibonacci numbers, starting from zero and one:

$$\text{Fib}(n) = \begin{cases} 0 & \text{if } n = 0 \\ 1 & \text{if } n = 1 \\ \text{Fib}(n-1) + \text{Fib}(n-2) \end{cases}$$

We can very easily translate this into $\mathcal{L}_{\text{PROC2}}$ by following the formula pattern:

Listing 6.77

```
(define fib
 (λ (n)
  (cond
   [(= n 0) 0]
   [(= n 1) 1]
   [else (+ (fib (- n 1))
            (fib (- n 2)))])))
```

The thing is, this is a very (and we mean *very*) inefficient way of computing Fibonacci numbers. Why? Consider the following computation of Fib(9). According to the above algorithm, Fib(9) is computed as the sum of Fib(8) and Fib(7). These recursive calls must be resolved themselves. Namely, Fib(8) is the sum of Fib(7) and Fib(6), whereas Fib(7) is the sum of Fib(6) and Fib(5), and so on. As we can see, multiple results are unnecessarily computed more than once! This scales *exponentially* as the input to Fib increases.

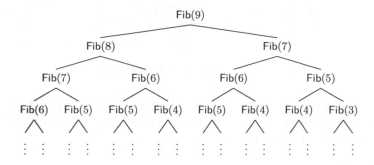

Figure 6.9: Exponential Recursive Blowup of Fib(9)

A better algorithm, as we previously stated, is to store previous results along the way and use those in further computations. What does this entail? Well, we need to store two values: a and b, as these represent the previous Fibonacci values. We also must store the current Fibonacci result. Lastly, we need to keep track of which Fibonacci number we are computing, let us say n. Therefore, each time we compute a new Fibonacci result, we subtract one from this value until it reaches one. Our base cases are, as described by the equation, when $n = 0$ or $n = 1$. Though, in this case, we do not want to return any direct result, but rather return the value we are accumulating through parameter-passing, i.e., res.

Listing 6.78

```
(define fib
  (λ (a b res n)
   (cond
    [(or (zero? n) (zero? (sub1 n))) res]
    [else
     (let ([new-fib (+ a b)])
       (fib b new-fib new-fib (- n 1)))])))
```

So, if we want to compute the nth Fibonacci number using this new algorithm, we must also pass three additional arguments: a, b, and *res*. Fib(0) = 0, and Fib(1) = 1, so those are our initial values for a and b. *res* also starts off as 0. The example below computes the tenth Fibonacci number, which resolves to 55.

Listing 6.79

```
> (fib 0 1 0 10)                              | 55
```

The problem is that we have exposed much of the internal algorithm to the caller of `fib`. It would be remarkable to have this fast-performing Fibonacci function that does not require the user to specify the starting values of a, b, and *res*. To solve this, we will write $\mathcal{L}_{\text{LETREC}}$: an extension to $\mathcal{L}_{\text{PROC2}}$ that adds the ability to define local recursive procedures.

```
expr         ::=  application | ...
application  ::=  letrec | ...
letrec       ::=  'letrec (' let-bndg+ ')' expr
```

Figure 6.10: Extended BNF Grammar for $\mathcal{L}_{\text{LETREC}}$

Here's the actual problem: let us say that we abstract the code that generates the Fibonacci sequence via a function, e.g., `fib-helper`. We then write `fib` to call `fib-helper` with the required initial values:

Listing 6.80

```
(define fib
 (λ (n)
  (fib-helper 0 1 0 n)))

(define fib-helper
 (λ (a b res n)
  (cond
   [(or (zero? n) (zero? (sub1 n))) res]
   [else
    (let ([new-fib (+ a b)])
     (fib-helper b new-fib new-fib (sub1 n)))])))

> (fib 10)                                          55
```

Doing this solves one of two issues, one of which is that the caller of `fib` needs not to worry about how Fibonacci values are computed. The bigger issue, however, is that `fib-helper` is still exposed as a top-level definition. A clever reader may think to define `fib` as we have, then internalize `fib-helper` as a `let` definition.

Listing 6.81

```
(define fib
 (λ (n)
  (let ([fib-helper
         (λ (a b res n)
          (cond
           [(or (zero? n) (zero? (sub1 n))) res]
           [else
            (let ([new-fib (+ a b)])
             (fib-helper b new-fib new-fib (sub1 n)))])])
   (fib-helper 0 1 0 n))))
```

This looks like it works, right? Well, unfortunately, there is a pretty big problem, namely how `let` operates. `let` creates definitional bindings only after the body of a variable has been evaluated. Thus, when attempting to evaluate the recursive `fib-helper` procedure, it does not see its existence in the current environment because `let` has not declared its existence. We can resolve this problem via a new language construct, namely `letrec`.

letrec adds the definitional identifier bindings for a variable *prior* to its body evaluation. Hence, when a recursive procedure is evaluated, its body recognizes the procedure name in its environment. To add letrec to our language, we can begin by declaring it as a special application form.

Listing 6.82—letrec Evaluation Function Stub (eval.c)

```
1  static struct sval *eval_letrec(ast *letrec, struct environment *env) { // TODO. }
2    ...
3  static void special_forms_init(void) {
4    ...
5    special_forms_create("letrec", eval_letrec);
6  }
```

Much like the standard let definition, we will retrieve the bindings and create a new environment. The difference is that, when evaluating the current binding, we evaluate it with respect to the newly-created environment. Note the similarity and important(!) differences to let*.

Listing 6.83—Evaluation of letrec (eval.c)

```
1   static struct sval *eval_letrec(ast *letrec, struct environment *env) {
2     // Initialize the new environment with env as its parent.
3     struct environment *new_env = environment_create(env);
4     ast *bindings = ast_child(letrec, LET_ALL_BINDINGS_IDX);
5     int num_bindings = ast_children_num(bindings) - LET_BINDING_OFFSET_IDX;
6
7     // Create the new bindings and store them in the new env.
8     for (int i = 0; i < num_bindings; i++) {
9       ast *curr_binding = ast_child(bindings, LET_BINDING_IDX + i);
10      ast *sym_tree = ast_child(curr_binding, LET_SYMBOL_IDX);
11      struct sval *expr = eval(ast_child(curr_binding, LET_EXPR_IDX), new_env);
12      environment_put(new_env, ast_contents(sym_tree), expr);
13    }
14
15    // Evaluate the body with new_env.
16    return eval(ast_child(letrec,
17                          ast_children_num(letrec) - LET_BODY_OFFSET_IDX), new_env);
18  }
```

At last, we can re-write our program to use letrec as opposed to lousy top-level definitions.

Listing 6.84

```
(define fib
 (λ (n)
  (letrec ([fib-helper
            (λ (a b res n)
             (cond
              [(or (zero? n) (zero? (sub1 n))) res]
              [else
               (let ([new-fib (+ a b)])
                (fib-helper b
                            new-fib
                            new-fib
                            (sub1 n)))])])
    (fib-helper 0 1 0 n))))

> (fib 10)                                           55
```

Let us get a bit more practice with letrec by writing fact using accumulative recursion. We will pass the accumulating product along as a parameter and when our number reaches zero, we return the product.

Listing 6.85

```
(define fact
 (λ (n)
  (letrec ([fact-helper
            (λ (m product)
             (cond
              [(zero? n) product]
              [else
               (fact-helper (sub1 m)
                            (* m product))]))])
   (fact-helper n 1))))

> (fact 5)                                                        120
```

If we did not have letrec, we would need to either use a different algorithm or expose the internals of fact-helper as a top-level definition. Neither of these outcomes are always acceptable solutions, though.

letrec allows for recursive function bindings, as we have demonstrated and implemented. Though, it is fundamental to state that letrec is not at all necessary for "recursion" inside a let binding! We can simulate recursion in an interesting way via the *U-combinator*. Recall that the issue with recursive bindings in a let block: the extended environment is only visible to the body of the let. So, trying to reference an identifier declared from within a let binding inside the binding itself quickly leads to trouble. What if, instead, we passed a function as an argument to our binding and invoke that recursively? There is nothing that says we cannot invoke a function argument onto itself. For instance, let us convert the factorial function from letrec to a let using this paradigm.

Listing 6.86—Letrec to Let Equivalence Conversion

```
(letrec                                  (let
 ([!                                       ([!
   (λ (n)                                    (λ (f)
    (cond                                     (λ (n)
     [(zero? n) 1]                             (cond
     [else                                      [(zero? n) 1]
      (* n (! (sub1 n)))]))])                   [else
 (! 5))                                          (* n ((f f) (sub1 n)))]))))])
                                          ((! !) 5))
```

As shown, we never invoke function identifier itself. Rather, we create a function that receives a function and returns another function expecting a value. We saw this idea in Chapter 4 with the λ-calculus, and it shows up here as well. The confusing part about all of this is that the initial invocation of the function in the let body is invoked on itself. Remember, though, that this returns a function expecting the input to the factorial, namely n. There is nothing special to what is going on, and the same thing happens when we make the "recursive call" to f by applying it onto itself. In reality, this is not recursion at all, because it simply passes a function to another function for continued evaluation. Still, it demonstrates that, although letrec is convenient, it is largely superfluous![1] Moreover, because we have support for multi-arity functions, we could simply pass the function and input as arguments to a two-argument function.

---

[1]By "superfluous", we mean to say that it is a form of *syntactic sugar*, which implies an abstraction.

Listing 6.87

```
> (let ([!
         (λ (f n)
          (cond                                        120
           [(zero? n) 1]
           [else (* n (f f (sub1 n)))])))])
    (! ! 5))
```

Exercise 6.14. (★★★★)

The Racket and Scheme programming languages provide a construct called the "named let", which allows the programmer to define a recursive function without the need for letrec or a top-level function. We provide an example as follows:

Listing 6.88

```
> (let loop ([i 10])        (10 9 8 7 6 5 4 3 2 1)
    (cond
     [(zero? i) '()]
     [else (cons i (loop (sub1 i)))]))
```

Implement named let bindings into $\mathcal{L}_{\text{LETREC}}$. Its syntax includes the let keyword, an identifier, and any number of variable bindings that act as formal parameters. The extended environment should contain the named let identifier as a procedure that is local only to that block.

$\mathcal{L}_{\text{CLOSURE}}$: Closures

Procedures in $\mathcal{L}_{\text{LETREC}}$ are rather simple so far. Though, in a "real Scheme", procedures are able to store and recall the environment used in their definition. Procedures like these are called closures. A *closure* stores a body and the environment used in its definition. Let us write $\mathcal{L}_{\text{CLOSURE}}$: an extension to $\mathcal{L}_{\text{LETREC}}$ that uses closures.

Right now, there is no true motivating example to explain the benefits of closures. In Chapter 8, when we introduce side-effects (and procedures that have side-effects), we shall explain the reason and significance of closures.

Because each procedure also stores a pointer to an environment, we need to amend our struct definition for procedures in sval.h. Similarly, we should update its creation function to take an environment as an argument.

Listing 6.89—Closure Representation (sval.c)

```
1   #include "env.h"
2   ...
3   struct procedure {
4     char **formals;
5     size_t num_formals;
6     ast *body;
7     struct environment *env;
8   };
9   ...
10  struct sval *sval_procedure_create(char **formals, size_t num_formals, ast *body,
11                          struct environment *env);
```

Now to update `eval_application` to instead use the closure's environment rather than the one passed as an argument. Warning, though: we still need to evaluate the arguments in the non-closure environment—we only evaluate the body of a procedure with the closure's extended environment.

Listing 6.90—Updating Function Application to Respect Closures (`eval.c`)

```
1   static struct sval *eval_application(ast *application,
2                                        struct environment *env) {
3       ...
4       else {
5         // Otherwise, extend the current environment.
6         struct environment *new_env = environment_extend(function->data.proc->env,
7                                                          function, arguments);
8         result = eval(function->data.proc->body, new_env);
9         environment_destroy(new_env);
10      }
11      ...
12  }
```

Exercise 6.15. (⋆⋆)

We represent procedures with `lambda`. Though, many Scheme interpreters also allow the usage of the following syntax to define procedures. Modify $\mathcal{L}_{\text{CLOSURE}}$ to allow both forms of procedure definitions. This should require no changes to the grammar or parser; only make changes in the evaluator.

Listing 6.91

```
(define (fact n)
 (cond
  [(zero? n) 1]
  [else (* n (fact (sub1 n)))]))
```

6.4   Working with Even More Data

Recursive procedures are exceedingly useful, but being limited to only numeric data is somewhat boring. In the following sections, we will write subsequent interpreters that introduce important and fundamental data types.

$\mathcal{L}_{\text{CHAR}}$: Characters and Character Operations

In this section, we will write $\mathcal{L}_{\text{CHAR}}$: a superset of $\mathcal{L}_{\text{CLOSURE}}$ that adds character literals.

A character literal is a single character, e.g., 'A', 'B', '4', '0'. In $\mathcal{L}_{\text{CHAR}}$, we will prefix character literals with a hash and backslash, i.e., #\, followed by the desired character, e.g., #\A represents the character 'A'. To add these into $\mathcal{L}_{\text{CHAR}}$, we need to modify our grammar to accept characters in this manner. As a corollary, characters are a type of datum, identical to numbers and booleans.

```
datum      ::=   number
           |     boolean
           |     symbol
           |     character;
character  ::=   '\''#' symchar;
```

Figure 6.11: Extended BNF Grammar for $\mathcal{L}_{\text{CHAR}}$

Now, to add this to our parser, we first add the pound sign. Then, we need to tell the parser to properly escape the backslash. As we discussed in our primer on C, there are certain characters that perform specific tasks when prefixed by a backlash, e.g., \n creates a line break. To display an actual backslash and not escape a character, we escape the backslash, i.e., \\. The parser that we are using allows us to escape characters as we have seen with symbols such as +. Because we want to insert the literal backslash to escape certain symbols in the parser, we have to escape the backslash in the grammar, i.e., \\+. Thus, we need to use four backslashes to indicate that we want to insert two backslash characters as part of the grammar rule, where the former backslash escapes the latter backslash. This is followed by any single character as allowed by our grammar.

Listing 6.92—Adding Character Parser Rule (`parser.c`)

```
1    static void parser_init_rules(void) {
2      ...
3      character_rule = mpc_new("character");
4      ...
5      mpc_err_t *error =
6        mpca_lang(MPCA_LANG_DEFAULT,
7          "datum    : <number>     \n"
8          "         | <boolean>    \n"
9          "         | <symbol>     \n"
10         "         | <character>  \n"
11         "character: '#''\\\\'/[a-zA-Z0-9\\-\\+_\\*<=>\\/!\\?]/;\n",
12         ..., character_rule, NULL);
13     ...
14   }
```

Now, let us look at the abstract syntax tree of a character:

Listing 6.93

```
> \#A                                         expr|datum|>
                                                character|>
                                                  char:1:1 '#'
                                                  char:1:2 '\'
                                                  regex:1:3 'A'
```

We can safely ignore the first two components of a character node and focus solely on the regular expression at child three (index 2). Let us add a character component to our s-values.

Listing 6.94—Character S-value Representation (`sval.h`)

```
1    enum sval_type { ..., SVAL_CHARACTER }
2    ...
3    struct sval {
4      ...
5      union data {
6        ...
7        char character;
8        ...
9      }
10   }
```

A limitation of the mpc library is that it does not support Unicode characters, meaning we are limited to the keys on a typical QWERTY keyboard, or more broadly, ASCII (American Standard Code for Information Interchange).[1] If, on the other hand, we were not restricted to this subset, we could use different symbols, e.g., λ instead of "lambda" to represent procedures. So, we use a simple char to hold our character data.[2] Now, let us write the corresponding s-value constructor function. At the same time, we should update the printer function. When displaying a character, we want to affix the backslash and the pound sign to the character.

---

[1]The Unicode standard is a character encoding that aims to support thousands of symbols across different languages and domains.

[2]The char datatype, as mentioned in Chapter 5, is defined by the C-standard to be at least one byte long. Unicode characters are designed to hold multiple bytes of information since Unicode characters are not representable with only one allotted byte. In these cases, we can use a string, i.e., char * to hold as many bytes of data as necessary to represent the Unicode character.

Listing 6.95—Printing Character S-values (sval.c)

```
1   struct sval *sval_character_create(char *character) {
2     struct sval *sv = sval_create(SVAL_CHARACTER);
3     sv->data.character = character;
4     return sv;
5   }
6     ...
7   struct sval *sval_print(sval *sv) {
8     ...
9     else if (SVAL_CHARACTER == sv->type) {
10      printf("#\\%c", sv->data.character);
11    }
12    ...
13  }
```

Now, all that we need to add is the respective character evaluation function.

Listing 6.96—Evaluation of Characters (eval.c)

```
1   static struct sval *eval(ast *ast, struct environment *env) {
2     ...
3     else if (ast_is_type(ast, "character")) {
4       return eval_character(ast, env);
5     }
6   }
7     ...
8   static struct sval *eval_character(ast *character, struct environment *env) {
9     char ch = ast_contents(ast_child(character, CHARACTER_IDX))[0];
10    return sval_character_create(ch);
11  }
```

Strings comprise the contents of an abstract syntax tree node. We know by our grammar that the contents of the third child of a character node consist of a single character. Since we are operating on a string, we need to extract the first character (at index 0).

$\mathcal{L}_{\text{STRING}}$: **String and String Operations**

In this section we will write $\mathcal{L}_{\text{STRING}}$: an extension of $\mathcal{L}_{\text{CHAR}}$ that adds a new data type: strings.

A string, as we recall from C, is a sequence of characters. We enclose strings by double quotes, e.g., "Hello, world!". We first must modify our grammar by adding the string rule. Strings contain any non-double-quote characters, including no characters at all, or completely blank characters.

```
datum    ::=   number
         |     boolean
         |     symbol
         |     character
         |     string
string   ::=   '"' symchar+ '"'
```

Figure 6.12: Extended BNF Grammar for $\mathcal{L}_{\text{STRING}}$

While this grammar rule may frighten some, it is all easily explainable—namely, as we stated, a string consists of any (hence the wildcard period character, i.e., ".".) non-double-quoted (hence the "[^"]" rule) characters, enclosed by double quotes.

Next, we must amend the mpc grammar. One noteworthy detail about embedding a "string" rule into the mpc library is that, internally, it creates rules that have a label of "string". So, to prevent name collisions, we should use a different name for our strings, perhaps, "mystring". Be aware that, much like the rule for symbols, it is imperative that the rule is copied verbatim.

Listing 6.97—Adding String Rule to Parser (sval.c)

```
1   static mpc_parser_t *string_rule;
2     ...
3   void parser_cleanup(void) {
4     mpc_cleanup(..., ..., string_rule);
5   }
6     ...
7   static void parser_init_rules(void) {
8     ...
9     string_rule = mpc_new("mystring");
10    ...
11    mpc_err_t *error =
12      mpca_lang(MPCA_LANG_DEFAULT,
13        "datum: <number>    \n"
14        "     | <boolean>   \n"
15        "     | <character> \n"
16        "     | <symbol>    \n"
17        "     | <mystring>; \n"
18        "mystring: /\\"(\\.|[^\"\\"])\\"/; \n",
19        ..., string_rule, NULL);
20    ...
21  }
```

Let us view the abstract syntax tree for the string "Hello, world!".

Listing 6.98

```
> "Hello, world!"          | expr|datum|>
                           |   mystring|>
                           |     char:1:1 '"'
                           |     regex:1:2 'Hello, world!'
                           |     char:1:15 '"'
```

Perfect! Just what we are looking for. Next, we need to modify both the s-value union and enumeration to account for strings, as well as add the appropriate constructor function.

Listing 6.99—Adding String S-value to Data Union (sval.h)

```
1   enum sval_type { ..., SVAL_STRING };*)
2   struct sval {
3     enum sval_type type;
4     union data {
5       ...
6       char *string;
7       ...
8     } data;
9   };
10    ...
11  struct sval *sval_string_create(char *string);
```

We will store a string as a char *, containing all characters used to create the string.

Listing 6.100—String S-value Creation (sval.c)

```
1  struct sval *sval_string_create(char *string) {
2    struct sval *sv = sval_create(SVAL_STRING);
3    sv->data.string = string;
4    return sv;
5  }
```

Last but not least, we add the recognition code within the evaluator. Here's where things get a bit tricky. String evaluation is a bit less straightforward than what one may expect at first glance. When the parser reads a string, it must be enclosed in double quotes. The string s-value, on the other hand, must only receive the string data itself and not its quotes. In subsequent sections when we manipulate and write functions on strings, we want those functions to work only on the string data itself and not the quotes. Though, when we display the string variable, we want to enclose it with quotes. Therefore, we add quotes around the string in sval_-print, but extract out the important contents in eval_string. The question, of course, is how can we copy every character except the first and last of a string? We dynamically allocate a string to store every character except the two quotes, as well as the NUL-byte. From there, we use strncpy to copy over the characters between the opening and closing quotes.

Listing 6.101—String Evaluation (eval.c)

```
1  static struct sval *eval(ast *ast, struct environment *env) {
2    ...
3    else if (ast_is_type(ast, "mystring")) {
4      return eval_string(ast, env);
5    }
6  }
7    ...
8  static struct sval *eval_string(ast *string, struct environment *env) {
9    char *str = ast_contents(string);
10   size_t slen = strlen(str) - 1;
11   // if the raw string has n >= 2 characters, we allocate n - 1 bytes.
12   char *new_str = malloc(slen);
13   strcpy(new_str, str + 1);
14   return sval_string_create(new_str);
15 }
```

Functions Operating on Strings

Strings are useful themselves, similar to characters, but perhaps we want to add some built-in functions that operate on strings. For instance, we may want to grab a specific character of a string, extract a substring, find the first occurrence of a substring, append strings together, or find the length of a string. We will the following five functions to apply.c:

- string-length receives a string s as an argument and returns the number of characters in s excluding the opening and closing double quotes. E.g., (string-length "Hello, world!") evaluates to 13.

- string-append receives at least two strings and returns a string where the resulting string is comprised of each argument string concatenated together. E.g., (string-append "Hello" "," " " "world!") evaluates to "Hello, world!".

- char-at receives a string s and an index i and returns the character at index i of s. E.g., (char-at "Hello, world!" 4) evaluates to \#o. If i is out-of-bounds, we return the NUL-byte character.[1]

- substring receives a string s and two indices, m, n, and returns the sub-string s' from indices m to n where n is exclusive. E.g., (substring "Hello, world!" 0 5) evaluates to "Hello". E.g., (substring "Hello, world!" 0 1) evaluates to "H". If $n > m$ or either m or n are out of bounds, the empty string is returned. A rule of thumb with this form of substring is that the number of characters returned is equal to n - m. Consequently, if $m = n$, then we return the empty string.

- index-of receives two strings s_1 and s_2 and returns the index of the first occurrence of s_2 in s_1. If s_2 never occurs in s_1, or the length of s_2 is greater than s_1, it returns -1. E.g., (index-of "Hello, world!" "world") evaluates to 7. E.g., (index-of "Hello, world!" "a") evaluates to -1. If s_2 is the empty string, we return zero.

Let us implement these built-in functions one by one. We will add the prototypes and the function pointers at the end.

First, note that we can always just take and return the length of the string since we do not store the double quotes of a string.

Listing 6.102—Built-in String Length Function (apply.c)

```
1   static struct sval *apply_string_length(struct sval **args,
2                                            size_t num_args,
3                                            struct environment *env) {
4     ASSERT_ARITY("string-length", 1, num_args);
5     return sval_number_create(strlen(args[0]->data.string));
6   }
```

Next up is string-append. We need to compute the length of each string, then dynamically allocate a string of said size plus one for the NUL-byte. Lastly, we copy each string and the NUL-byte into the newly-created string. This is then sent to a string s-value. Note the use of pointer arithmetic on the second instance of calling strcpy.[2]

---

[1] Out-of-bounds, in this context, means that i is negative or exceeds the length of the string.

[2] Pointer arithmetic allows us to directly apply an offset to a pointer. For example, if we have a pointer int *p = malloc(1024);, we can advance p to the next four-byte address by incrementing p, i.e., p++. Pointer arithmetic applies offsets based on the size of the datatype of the pointer, which means, in this context, adding one to p actually adds a four byte offset, since an int is four bytes. In fact, array indexing is syntactic sugar for arithmetic!

Listing 6.103—Built-in String Append Function (`apply.c`)

```
1  static struct sval *apply_string_append(struct sval **args,
2                                          size_t num_args,
3                                          struct environment *env) {
4    if (2 > num_args) {
5      EPF("apply_string_append: string-append expects at least
6          two arguments but got %zu\n", num_args);
7      exit(EXIT_FAILURE);
8    }
9    size_t l1 = strlen(s1);
10   size_t l2 = strlen(s2);
11   char *new_str = malloc(l1 + l2 + 1);
12   ASSERT_ALLOC(new_str, "apply_string_append");
13   strcpy(new_str, s1);
14   strcpy(new_str + l1, s2);
15   return sval_string_create(new_str);
16 }
```

Now we have `char-at`, which retrieves the character at a given index of a string.

Listing 6.104—Built-in Character "At" Function (`apply.c`)

```
1  static struct sval *apply_string_char_at(struct sval **args,
2                                           size_t num_args,
3                                           struct environment *env) {
4    ASSERT_ARITY("char-at", 2, num_args);
5    char *str = args[0]->data.string;
6    int idx = (int) args[1]->data.number;
7    if (idx < 0 || idx >= strlen(str)) { return sval_character_create('\0'); }
8    else { return sval_character_create(str[idx]); }
9  }
```

The `substring` function is up next, and it creates a new string out of the current string from index m, inclusive, to index n, exclusive, where $n > m$. The easiest solution is to allocate $n-m+1$ bytes of space for a new string, then copy the characters starting from the mth character up to but not including n. We again make use of `strncpy` to avoid the need for a redundant loop.

Listing 6.105—Built-in Substring Function (`apply.c`)

```
1  static struct sval *apply_string_substring(struct sval **args,
2                                             size_t num_args,
3                                             struct environment *env) {
4    ASSERT_ARITY("substring", 3, num_args);
5    char *str = args[0]->data.string;
6    size_t slen = strlen(str);
7    int m = (int) args[1]->data.number;
8    int n = (int) args[2]->data.number;
9
10   // Error checks!
11   if (m < 0 || n < 0 || m > n || m >= slen || n >= slen) {
12     return sval_string_create(strdup(""));
13   } else {
14     // Create a string of length n - m + 1 for NUL-byte.
15     size_t num_characters = n - m;
16     char *new_str = malloc(num_characters + 1);
17     ASSERT_ALLOC(new_str, "apply_string_substring");
18     strncpy(new_str, str + m, num_characters);
19     return sval_string_create(new_str);
20   }
21 }
```

The last built-in function we will write is index-of, which receives two strings s_1 and s_2 and returns the index of the first occurrence of s_2 in s_1, or -1 otherwise. We will, once again, make use of the strstr function (recall its initial usage was in the evaluator). strstr receives two strings and returns a pointer to the character that starts the substring. For instance, strstr("Hello, world!", "lo, w") returns a char * to the string starting at "lo, world!". Though, we need the index of this position and not the pointer. The simplest and most convenient solution is to do some pointer arithmetic. That is, if we subtract the returned substring pointer from the start of the string, we calculate an offset that amounts to the number of characters between the substring and the start of the string. Using the previous example, if we subtract the base string pointer from the substring pointer, we get 3. Note that if s_2 is not in s_1 or the length of $s_2 > s_1$, then strstr returns NULL. In this scenario, our index-of should evaluate to -1. Even more surprisingly, if s_2 is the empty string, then strstr returns a pointer to s_1. In this scenario, our index-of should return 0.

Listing 6.106—Built-in String Index Of Function (apply.c)

```
1   static struct sval *apply_string_index_of(struct sval **args,
2                                              size_t num_args,
3                                              struct environment *env) {
4     ASSERT_ARITY("index-of", 2, num_args);
5     char *s1 = args[0]->data.string;
6     char *s2 = args[1]->data.string;
7     char *sub = strstr(s1, s2);
8     if (NULL == sub) { return sval_number_create("-1"); }
9     else if (sub == s1) { return sval_number_create("0"); }
10    else { return sval_string_create(sub - s1); }
11  }
```

Now, to test, we must add these as function prototypes and as built-in procedures.

Exercise 6.16. ($\star$)
Write a predicate, both in $\mathcal{L}_{\text{STRING}}$ and in C, called string-empty? that returns true if the string has length zero and false otherwise.

Exercise 6.17. ($\star$)
Write a recursive function index-of-char that receives a string s and a character ch that returns the first index of ch in s. If ch is not in s, return -1.

Exercise 6.18. ($\star\star$)
In string-append, notice that we invoke strlen twice, once for each string. If we call string-append many times, we end up wasting a lot of time with strlen. Modify the sval struct such that, when a string s-value is created, its length is stored alongside. Strings are immutable anyways, so it is impossible for this field to change!

Exercise 6.19. ($\star\star$)
Write a recursive function string-replace* that receives a string s, a string k, and a string m. The function should recursively replace any occurrences of the string k with the string m, creating a new string. You do not need to consider inputs where k is a substring of m, which induce infinite replacements without proper safeguards. Though, if you do want to consider this as a challenge, increase the exercise difficulty to ($\star\star\star$) three stars.

Exercise 6.20. (★★)

Write a recursive function `string-trim` that receives a string s and removes leading and trailing whitespace, returning a new string. For instance, invoking `string-trim` on the string `" hello "` should resolve to `"hello"`.

Exercise 6.21. (★★★)

Write a recursive function `string-remove` that receives a string s and a string key k. The function should recursively remove all occurrences of k in s. For instance, in the string (`string-remove "abbababaabb" "ab"`) returns b, and (`string-remove "aaabbb" "ab"`) returns `""`. Hint: use `substring` and `index-of`.

Exercise 6.22. (★★★)

Write a function `string-search` that receives a string s and a string k. The function should return a string containing the surrounding characters of k if k exists in s. If there are multiple occurrences of k in s, return the first. By "surrounding characters", we mean twenty characters preceding k, and $20 + |k|$ characters succeeding k. If there are not enough characters on either side, take all of them on the respective side. Hint: `min` and `max` are useful functions!

Data Conversion

Suppose we have the string "34" embedded in our language somewhere, and we want to treat it as a numeric value. The converse is equally applicable; if we have a number, what if we wish to represent it as a string? What about representing booleans as strings and vice-versa? In this section, we will write a few helper functions to convert between data types.

- `number->string` converts a given number into its string counterpart. For example, (`number->string 57.85`) evaluates to `"57.85"`.

- `string->number` converts a given string into a number if it is possible to do so. E.g., (`string->number "200.325"`) evaluates to the number `200.325`, but on the contrary, (`number->string "Hello!"`) displays an error.

- `number->char` converts a number, as an integer, to its ASCII character counterpart, if it is possible to do so. E.g., (`number->char 80`) evaluates to `\#P`, but on the contrary, (`number->char -9`) displays an error.

- `char->number` converts a character into its integer counterpart if it is possible to do so. E.g., (`char->number \#P`) evaluates to 80, but on the contrary, the invocation of (`char->number 80`) displays an error.

Any other conversion functions, e.g., string->char, can be written in terms of these primitive functions. Fortunately, only one of these functions, apply_-number_to_string is a bit hard to understand. We need a way of converting a number to a string. One way to do this is to use the snprintf function which receives a format string and some data, to which it converts the provided data to a string and stores it in a string. The way we use it is relatively simple to understand: we declare a char * where the format string is allocated and stored. Then, we tell it the maximum number of characters to store. Finally, we give it the same arguments we would to printf: a format specifier for long double numbers and the value itself. We then send this string to sval_string_create. Though, we should not carelessly convert all numbers to a floating-point representation via the %lf format specifier. Instead, we will test numbers for "integerness" and format them as such in the output string.

Listing 6.107—Built-in Number-String Conversion Function (apply.c)

```
1   static struct sval *apply_number_to_string(struct sval **args,
2                                               size_t num_args,
3                                               struct environment *env) {
4     ASSERT_ARITY("number->string", 1, num_args);
5     char *str_num = NULL;
6     long double val = args[0]->data.number;
7     size_t nchars;
8     // Test for "integerness".
9     if (val == (int) val) {
10      nchars = asprintf(str_num, "%d" , (int) args[0]->data.number);
11    } else {
12      nchars = asprintf(str_num, "%lf" , args[0]->data.number);
13    }
14    return sval_string_create(str_num);
15  }
```

Listing 6.108—Built-in String-Number Conversion Function (apply.c)

```
1   static struct sval *apply_string_to_number(struct sval **args,
2                                               size_t num_args,
3                                               struct environment *env) {
4     ASSERT_ARITY("string->number", 1, num_args);
5     return sval_number_create(args[0]->data.string);
6   }
```

Listing 6.109—Built-in Number-Character Conversion Function (apply.c)

```
1   static struct sval *apply_number_to_char(struct sval **args,
2                                             size_t num_args,
3                                             struct environment *env) {
4     ASSERT_ARITY("number->char", 1, num_args);
5     return sval_character_create((char) (args[0]->data.number));
6   }
```

Listing 6.110—Built-in Character-Number Conversion Function (apply.c)

```
1   static struct sval *apply_char_to_number(struct sval **args,
2                                             size_t num_args,
3                                             struct environment *env) {
4     ASSERT_ARITY("char->number", 1, num_args);
5     struct sval *character = args[0];
6     return sval_number_create(character->data.character);
7   }
```

Now, we can test the examples from before.

Listing 6.111

```
> (number->string 57.85)          | "57.85"
> (string->number "200.325")      | 200.325
> (number->char 80)               | \#P
> (char->number \#P)              | 80
```

Exercise 6.23. (⋆)
Write a function in $\mathcal{L}_{\text{STRING}}$: string->boolean that converts a string into a boolean, e.g., (string->boolean "true") resolves to #t. Then, write another function, boolean->string that converts a boolean into a string, e.g., (boolean->string #f) resolves to "false".

Exercise 6.24. (⋆)
Write a function in $\mathcal{L}_{\text{STRING}}$: char->string that converts a character into a string, e.g., (char->string \#P) resolves to "P".

Exercise 6.25. (⋆⋆)
Write two predicates in $\mathcal{L}_{\text{STRING}}$: char-is-uppercase? that determines whether or not a character is a uppercase letter, and char-is-lowercase? that determines whether or not a character is a lowercase letter. If the input is not a letter, return false. Hint: use char->number.

Exercise 6.26. (⋆⋆)
Write two predicates in $\mathcal{L}_{\text{STRING}}$: char-is-digit? that determines whether or not a character is a digit, and char-is-special? that determines whether or not a character is a special character, i.e., any non-digit or letter.

Exercise 6.27. (⋆⋆)
Write a predicate in $\mathcal{L}_{\text{STRING}}$: string-integer? that determines whether or not the given string is an integer.

Exercise 6.28. (⋆⋆⋆)
Write a predicate in $\mathcal{L}_{\text{STRING}}$: string-number? that determines whether or not the given string is a number. Note that a number, by our definition, is any real number written in non-scientific notation. Refer to Chapter 4 for a deterministic finite automaton numeric recognizer.

$\mathcal{L}_{\text{EQUAL}}$: Equivalence and Equality

In this section we will write $\mathcal{L}_{\text{EQUAL}}$: an extension to $\mathcal{L}_{\text{STRING}}$ that adds the ability to check values for equality, their types, and other useful comparison functions.

$\mathcal{L}_{\text{EQUAL}}$, as of now, supports checking numbers for equality as well as comparison operators such as < and >. Comparing other data types would be extremely helpful as would the ability to determine the type of a value. We will first implement the latter as a predicate, then move on to comparing the other three data types at our disposal.

$\mathcal{L}_{\text{EQUAL}}$ adds five new type-determination predicates: number?, char?, string?, boolean?, and symbol?. Each predicate receives a value and returns true if it is of the type queried by the predicate and false otherwise.

Listing 6.112

> (number? 10)	#t
> (number? #f)	#f
> (string? 10)	#f
> (string? "10")	#t
> (string? "#f")	#t
> (boolean? "#t")	#f
> (boolean? (= 10 20))	#t

All five of these procedures are identical with the exception that each query the s-value type enum for a different type. As such, we will show only the implementation of `apply_number_predicate`.

Listing 6.113—Built-in Number Predicate Function (apply.c)

```
1  static struct sval *apply_number_predicate(struct sval **args,
2                                             size_t num_args,
3                                             struct environment *env) {
4    ASSERT_ARITY("number?", 1, num_args);
5    return sval_boolean_create(SVAL_NUMBER == args[0]->type);
6  }
```

Now, imagine we are writing a program to check whether two symbols or strings are equivalent. How might we do this? We have a general solution and a specific solution. The former is to write a function that determines if two values are equivalent, whereas the latter is to write separate functions for comparing each datum individually. We will implement the latter first, then write an equivalence checker in terms of individual datum checks.

We presently have a check to determine if two numbers are equivalent, namely via the function `apply_num_eq`. We need four more functions for checking symbol, string, character, and boolean equality. Each function receives at least two arguments and returns #t if and only if each argument is equal to one another according to some criteria. Strings are equivalent if and only if they are exact copies of one another. Symbols are equivalent if and only they are exact copies of one another. Booleans are equivalent if and only if they share the same truth value. Finally, characters are equivalent if and only if they share the same character value. We will implement `char=?` and `string=?` and leave it as an exercise to the reader to implement the other two predicates. Notice the striking parallels between these two functions and the comparison for numeric equality.

Listing 6.114—Built-in Character Equivalency Function (`apply.c`)

```
1   static struct sval *apply_char_eq(struct sval **args,
2                                     size_t num_args,
3                                     struct environment *env) {
4     if (2 > num_args) {
5       EPF("apply_char_eq: char=? expects at least two arguments; got %zu\n",
6           num_args);
7       exit(EXIT_FAILURE);
8     }
9
10    bool eq_result = true;
11    struct sval *curr_char = args[0];
12    for (int i = 1; i < num_args; i++) {
13      if (curr_char->data.character != args[i]->data.character) {
14        eq_result = false;
15        break;
16      }
17    }
18    return sval_boolean_create(eq_result);
19  }
```

Listing 6.115—Built-in String Equivalency Function (`apply.c`)

```
1   static struct sval *apply_string_eq(struct sval **args,
2                                       size_t num_args,
3                                       struct environment *env) {
4     if (2 > num_args) {
5       EPF("apply_string_eq: string=? expects >= 2 arguments; got %zu\n",
6           num_args);
7       exit(EXIT_FAILURE);
8     }
9
10    bool eq_result = true;
11    struct sval *curr_string = args[0];
12    for (int i = 1; i < num_args; i++) {
13      if (!streq(curr_string->data.string, args[i]->data.string)) {
14        eq_result = false;
15        break;
16      }
17    }
18    return sval_boolean_create(eq_result);
19  }
```

Recall that in C, characters are just numbers with some fancy coating, meaning we can compare them using, for example, == and !=. Strings, on the other hand, require iterative processing to check character-by-character or the use of a helper function, e.g., `strcmp` or `streq`.

With these four functions under our belt, we can now write a generalized eqv? function that determines if any two values are equivalent to one another. Accordingly, if we have two values, α and β, they are equivalent if and only if exactly one of the following holds true:

1. α and β are both expressions that resolve to numbers and resolve to the same number.

2. α and β are both expressions that resolve to booleans and share the same truth value.

3. α and β are both expressions that resolve to symbols and resolve to the same symbol.

4. α and β are both expressions that resolve to strings and resolve to strings that are equal in length and character placement.

5. α and β are both expressions that resolve to characters and resolve to the same character.

Therefore, eqv? can simply invoke the five equality checkers for each type and return their result. In any other case, we return #f.

Listing 6.116—Built-in Data Equivalency Function (apply.c)

```
1   static struct sval *apply_eqv_predicate(struct sval **args,
2                                             size_t num_args,
3                                             struct environment *env) {
4     ASSERT_ARITY("eqv?", 2, num_args);
5     // If they do not share the same type then they're automatically not eqv.
6     if (args[0]->type != args[1]->type) {
7      return sval_boolean_create(false);
8     } else {
9      switch (args[0]->type) {
10      case SVAL_NUMBER: return apply_num_eq(args, num_args, env);
11      case SVAL_BOOLEAN: return apply_boolean_eq(args, num_args, env);
12      case SVAL_CHARACTER: return apply_char_eq(args, num_args, env);
13      case SVAL_STRING: return apply_string_eq(args, num_args, env);
14      case SVAL_SYMBOL: return apply_symbol_eq(args, num_args, env);
15      default: return sval_boolean_create(false);
16      }
17     }
18   }
```

At last, we can check any given type against any other type.

Exercise 6.29. (⋆)
It is sometimes useful to know whether or not a given value is a procedure. Write apply_procedure_predicate that returns true if its argument is a procedure s-value and false otherwise.

Exercise 6.30. (⋆⋆)
Lisp and Scheme both provide the ability to compare pointer values via the eq? function. Its result on certain s-values depends on the implementation, but its intended output is to show whether two objects point to the same object in memory.[1] Implement this as a function in $\mathcal{L}_{\text{EQUAL}}$. We provide some example inputs and outputs.

---

[1]Literals or constants, e.g., 3, #f, are often thought to be eq? to themselves, and indeed, this is true in most Scheme/Lisp implementations. What differs, though, is the comparison against different types of numbers such as floating-point values/integers. Our eq? definition will treat these as if they are identical.

Listing 6.117—Use of eq? Predicate.

```
(define a 'a)                    #t
(define b a)                     #t
(define c 'b)                    #f
(define d 'a)                    #t
(define e #t)                    #t
                                 #t
> (eq? a a)                      #t
> (eq? a b)                      #t
> (eq? a c)                      #t
> (eq? a d)
> (eq? b d)
> (eq? 3 3.0)
> (eq? 3 3)
> (eq? #f #f)
> (eq? #t e)
```

Exercise 6.31. (⋆⋆⋆)

The *Levenshtein distance* between two strings s and t measures the number of required alterations on s to arrive at t, also called the *edit distance*.[1] For example, consider the strings *"numeric"* and *"nominal"*. To translate the former into the latter, we need to change the u to an o, the e to an i, the n to an r, the i to an a, and the c to an l. Thus we need to change five characters, which means the Levenshtein distance between *"numeric"* and *"nominal"* is five. Let us consider another example: *"pipeline"* and *"plurality"*. To translate the former into the latter, we need to change the i to an l, the (second) p to a u, the (first) e to an r, the l to an a, the n to a t, and add an additional y. Thus we need to change five characters and add one, which means the Levenshtein distance between *"pipeline"* and *"plurality"* is six. Below is a recursive algorithm to compute the Levenshtein distance of two strings s and t:

$$\text{leven}(s, t) = \begin{cases} |s| & \text{if } |t| \text{ is zero.} \\ |t| & \text{if } |s| \text{ is zero.} \\ \text{leven}(\text{substr}(s, 1), (\text{substr}(t, 1))) & \text{if } s[0] == s[1] \\ 1 + min \begin{cases} \text{leven}(\text{substr}(s, 1), t) \\ \text{leven}(s, (\text{substr}(t, 1))) \\ \text{leven}(\text{substr}(s, 1), (\text{substr}(t, 1))) \end{cases} & \text{otherwise} \end{cases}$$

The substr function corresponds to substring from earlier in this chapter. Implement this as a recursive algorithm. One thing to note, however, is that this is a horribly inefficient algorithm and will not be able to compute Levenshtein distances of strings longer than a few characters.

---

[1]Vladimir Levenshtein's interest in edit distances originated from the desire to transmit optimal correction codes for strings [Levenshtein, 1966].

7 Functional Programming

The ability to juggle with code is the beauty of functional programming, and once you get it, it will feel like second nature. Just like when you learn to juggle or ride a bicycle. But just as you cannot learn the latter two without actual practice and not just by reading a book or watching videos, you must write code to move to the next level.

—Erik Meijer

In Chapter 5, we introduced the C programming language and started to build our interpreter. Then, in Chapter 6, we continued on this adventure by adding procedures, conditionals, and other data types. In this chapter, we will implement more "functional" programming language features. By functional, we suggest the programming paradigm of function application and composition, rather than statefulness, reassignment, and sequence.[1]

7.1 Quotes, Pairs, Lists, and Quasiquotes

$\mathcal{L}_{\text{QUOTE}}$: Quoted Expressions

In our previous interpreters and languages, symbols were always evaluated. In other words, if we ask the interpreter to interpret the symbol x, it looks up the value of x with respect to its environment. What if, however, we do not want the interpreter to evaluate x, or for that matter any arbitrarily complex expression? Quoted expressions help us with this problem. In this section, we will write $\mathcal{L}_{\text{QUOTE}}$: an extension to $\mathcal{L}_{\text{CLOSURE}}$ that adds the ability to quote any expression.

```
expr    ::=   quoted | ...
quoted  ::=   ' ' expr
```

Figure 7.1: Extended BNF Grammar for $\mathcal{L}_{\text{QUOTE}}$

A *quoted expression* is any $\mathcal{L}_{\text{QUOTE}}$ expression that is prepended by a single quote, i.e., ' '. Quoted expressions resolve to data—not code. As with the above example, if we define a variable x, then wish to see the value of x, we would write the following code.

---

[1] "Statefulness" means rememberance of values/variables in a system across time.

Listing 7.1

(**define** x 10)	
> x	10

Though, there are times, as we will soon see, when the binding of a variable is wrapped in a quoted expression, meaning we can only retrieve the data of the symbol rather than the data at said symbol. For example, quoting x as 'x will display the literal x and not the associated value. There are a few exceptions to this rule. First, self-evaluating expressions, e.g., numbers, characters, strings, and booleans are evaluated even if they are quoted. So, quoting a number, e.g., '5 still resolves to the numeric value 5. Thus, we can write the following expressions.

Listing 7.2

(**define** x 100)	
> (+ x '5)	105

If we try to do this when quoting the symbol x, i.e., 'x, our interpreter will display an error saying that the plus operator expects a number.

Listing 7.3

(**define** x '5)	
> (+ 'x '5)	Error!

Let us add quoted expressions to our interpreter. Quoted expressions using "'" are not a special form, meaning they have to be added as a parser rule.[1] As we said, a quoted expression is just any expression with a quote prepended. Moreover, quoted expressions are a type of datum.

Notice that the quote is escaped because we want to insert the literal quote symbol in front of an expression. Now, time to add it into the evaluator.

Listing 7.4—Quoted Expression Evaluation (eval.c)

```
1   #define QUOTED_EXPR_IDX 1
2   static struct sval *eval_quoted(ast *quoted, struct environment *env) {
3    ast *quoted_expr = ast_child(quoted, QUOTED_EXPR_IDX);
4    char *quoted_sym = ast_contents(quoted_expr);
5    struct sval *sym = NULL;
6
7    if (ast_is_type(quoted_expr, "number")) {
8     sym = eval_number(quoted_expr, env);
9    } else if (ast_is_type(quoted_expr, "boolean")) {
10    sym = eval_boolean(quoted_expr, env);
11   } else if (ast_is_type(quoted_expr, "string")) {
12    sym = eval_string(quoted_expr, env);
13   } else if (ast_is_type(quoted_expr, "character")) {
14    sym = eval_boolean(quoted_expr, env);
15   } else {
16    sym = sval_symbol_create(quoted_sym);
17   }
18   return sym;
19  }
```

---

[1]We make this clarification for reasons listed in subsequent sections.

None of the cases should be particularly interesting. We simply evaluate the self-evaluating expressions, and otherwise, pass it forward as a symbol. Let us test this out.

Listing 7.5

```
> '5                                    |  5
> (+ '5 5)                              |  10
> (and '#f #t)                          |  #f
> '(if #t 1000 2000)                    |  (if #t 1000 2000)
```

Excellent—quoted expressions now work as intended. The thing is, via the special case of quoted applications, we are inadvertently building a storage system—we can store values inside a quoted application. What might this lead us towards?

$\mathcal{L}_{\text{LIST}}$: Pairs and Lists

Up until this point, our interpreter has no understanding of internal data structures such as arrays. In this section, we will write $\mathcal{L}_{\text{LIST}}$: an extension to $\mathcal{L}_{\text{QUOTE}}$ which adds pairs and lists, as well as several built-in functions. Note that we will take full advantage of the features we added in $\mathcal{L}_{\text{QUOTE}}$, so if you skipped that section, please go back!

```
expr          ::=    application | ...
application   ::=    cons
              |      cons-pred
              |      first
              |      rest
              |      list
              |      ...
cons          ::=    'cons ' expr expr
cons-pred     ::=    'cons? ' expr
first         ::=    'first ' expr
rest          ::=    'rest ' expr
```

Figure 7.2: Extended BNF Grammar for $\mathcal{L}_{\text{LIST}}$

Before discussing lists, we need to explain the concept of pairs. A *pair* of non-pair elements e_1 and e_2 is constructed using the cons function. So, calling (cons e1 e2) produces an s-value displayed as (e1 . e2). Every pair, in this style, has a first element referenced by first, and a second element referenced by rest (pronounced "rest"). Thus, if we define p1 to be the aforementioned pair, then invoke first and rest on p1, we get, respectively, e1 and e2. In the future, we will constantly reference data stored in pairs. Accordingly, we will refer to the functions using the "typewriter" font, e.g., first. When referencing the element(s) of a pair, we shall use italicized roman letters, e.g., *first*.[1] cons pairs may be defined in terms of themselves, e.g., (cons (cons 'x 'y) (cons 'z (cons 'w 'u))) is a perfectly valid *cons* pair. Moreover, we can functionally compose first and rest to get different elements in a nested pair. For instance, if we have the following pair:

Listing 7.6

```
(define p1 (cons (cons 'x 'y)
                 (cons 'z
                       (cons 'w 'u))))
```

We can access the elements 'x via (first (first p1)) (pronounced as "the first of the first") and 'y via (rest (first p1)) (pronounced as the rest of the first).

Let us write the s-value definition for a pair. We know that a pair has two parts: the first and the rest. These are, themselves, s-values. We can add the relevant enumeration to sval_type, as well as declare a construction function for pairs.

Listing 7.7—Pair S-value Representation (sval.h)

```
1    enum sval_type { ..., SVAL_PAIR };
2
3    struct pair {
4      struct sval *first;
5      struct sval *rest;
6    };
7
8    struct sval {
9      enum sval_type type;
10     union data {
11       ...
12       struct pair pair;
13     } data;
14   };
15
16   struct sval *sval_pair_create(struct sval *first, struct sval *rest);
```

As we stated, a pair receives two values representing the *first* and the *rest* respectively. So, its constructor definition does nothing more than initialize these fields.

---

[1] Interestingly, the original Lisp language did not use *first* and *rest*, but rather *car* and *cdr*. John McCarthy's original Lisp implementation was written on the IBM 704, which contained macros for retrieving the contents of the address part (*car*) of the register and the contents of the decrement part of the register (*cdr*). Registers, in this context, are synonymous with memory locations; the *car* and *cdr* macros loaded pointers to the elements of a *cons* cell. Each memory location stored 36 bits, with 15 bits each reserved for the first and second elements of a *cons* pair respectively. The remaining six bits encoded the operation type and indexing [McCarthy, 1962] [McCarthy, 1978]. Modern implementations of Lisp-esque languages, including our prefixed language, use the more conventional first and rest operations.

Listing 7.8—Pair S-value Creation (sval.c)

```
1  struct sval *sval_pair_create(struct sval *first, struct sval *rest) {
2    struct sval *sv = sval_create(SVAL_PAIR);
3    sv->data.pair.first = first;
4    sv->data.pair.rest = rest;
5    return sv;
6  }
```

Now, before we go any further with pairs, we need to make a detour into a discussion on lists and how they interconnect with pairs.

A *list* is one of two values: either the empty list or a *cons* pair whose *rest* is a list. This definition complicates things a bit because we now need to distinguish between pairs and lists, right? The answer is yes and no at the same time. We define a list in terms of pairs. For instance, (cons 1 (cons 2 (cons 3 '()))) is a list because it is recursively defined as *cons* pairs whose *rest* is either the empty list or another *cons* pair. The empty list is denoted by '(). In addition to this differentiation between lists and pairs, we also need to mention proper versus improper lists. A *proper list* is a list that ends with the empty list. An *improper list* is a list that is not a proper list. This seems a bit circular, but let us use an example to explain. (cons 1 (cons 2 (cons 3 4))) is not a proper list because it does not end with the empty list. On the other hand, (cons 1 (cons 2 (cons 3 '()))) is a proper list because it does end with the empty list. Interestingly, a list may itself be a proper list yet have elements that are improper. For instance, (cons (cons (cons 1 2) 3) (cons 4 '())) is a proper list, but (cons (cons 1 2) 3) is an improper nested list.

So we now know the distinction between lists and pairs, but do we really care about the distinction between a proper and improper list? Not at the interpretation level, no; we only care about this difference at the "printing level". In other words, a list needs only be *viewed* as improper if it is improper, but at the interpretation level, it is just seen as a list s-value. We will circle back to printing lists and pairs soon.

Let us now write the corresponding s-value constructor for lists. Since lists are just fancy pairs, we do not need to create a separate enumeration value nor add a field in the data union. A list receives many elements that are, themselves, s-values. Since we do not know how many elements a list may contain, we pass an array of s-values to the constructor.

How do we initialize a list from a sequence of s-values? It is relatively easy: we create a "blank pair" called curr where its *first* and *rest* are both NULL. Then, we iterate over the list of arguments, set the *first* of curr to be the ith argument, set its *rest* to be a "blank pair", then set curr to be its own *rest*. Finally, we return a pointer to the front of the list.

Listing 7.9—S-value List Creation Implementation (`sval.c`)

```
1   struct sval *sval_list_create(struct sval **args, size_t num_args) {
2     struct sval *curr = sval_pair_create(NULL, NULL);
3     struct sval *front = curr;
4     for (int i = 0; i < num_args; i++) {
5       curr->data.pair.first = args[i];
6       curr->data.pair.rest = sval_pair_create(NULL, NULL);
7       curr = curr->data.pair.rest;
8     }
9     curr->data.pair.rest = NULL;
10    return front;
11  }
```

When constructing a list, there are many possible values that are storable. Symbols in a list should be the literal symbol and not an evaluated symbol. This is the only exception to the rule—anything else to be added to a list should be evaluated.

Lists are somewhat complex to define at the meta-language level. We have seen that a *cons* pair allows us to conjoin two values, and a series of *cons* pairs where the *rest* of the final element is the empty list is a proper list. So, since we now understand the notion of *cons* pairs, we should define lists in terms of *cons* pairs. The algorithm is as follows: create a blank (i.e., where the *first* and *rest* are both NULL) *cons* pair p. For each element e in the list abstract syntax tree, evaluate e according to an algorithm A, producing $A(e)$. Then, set the *first* of p to $A(e)$. Initialize the *rest* of p to a new blank *cons* pair. Finally, assign p to be the *rest* of p.

Listing 7.10—List Evaluation (`eval.c`)

```
1   static struct sval *eval_list(ast *list, struct environment *env) {
2     // Create a pair object and iterate through the chain to create firsts/rsts.
3     struct sval *curr = sval_pair_create(NULL, NULL);
4     struct sval *front = curr;
5     size_t num_elements = ast_children_num(list) - QUOTED_ELEMENTS_OFFSET;
6
7     // Each time we find a pair, add the data as first and new pair as rst.
8     for (int i = 0; i < num_elements; i++) {
9       struct sval *curr_sym = NULL;
10      ast *next = ast_child(list, i + QUOTED_CONTENT_OFFSET);
11      curr_sym = eval_list_element(next, env);
12
13      curr->data.pair.first = curr_sym;
14      curr->data.pair.rest = sval_pair_create(NULL, NULL);
15      curr = curr->data.pair.rest;
16    }
17    return front;
18  }
```

We made note of a mysterious algorithm A, so what does that do? A corresponds to `eval_list_element` in the above listing. The evaluation of element e in the list depends on its type. For example, symbols do not resolve to values—they resolve to the symbol themselves. E.g., `'(x y)` resolves to the list `(x y)` and not the values of x and y, assuming they are bound/defined. Additionally, a syntactic application within a list is simply another list. By syntactic, we mean, e.g., `'((3 4) 5)`, the parser recognizes the inner list `(3 4)` as an application, but it is in fact a list. So, we evaluate that child as if it were a list. Otherwise, we want to evaluate elements as they are. For instance, numbers can resolve to the numbers themselves.

Listing 7.11—List Element Evaluation (eval.c)

```
1   static struct sval *eval_list_element(ast *element, struct environment *env) {
2     struct sval *curr_sym = NULL;
3     if (ast_is_type(element, "application")) {
4       curr_sym = eval_list(element, env);
5     } else if (ast_is_type(element, "symbol")) {
6       curr_sym = sval_symbol_create(ast_contents(element));
7     } else {
8       curr_sym = eval(element, env);
9     }
10    return curr_sym;
11  }
```

There is little point in having pairs and lists without a way of retrieving their internal data. In $\mathcal{L}_{\text{LIST}}$, we will add a few built-in functions: first, rest, cons, null?, and cons?. The first three are functions we have repeatedly described, but we relist them for emphasis.

- first receives a pair/list as an argument and returns the first element of a pair/list. For instance, (first '(1 2 3 4)) returns 1.

- rest receives a pair/list as an argument and returns everything except the first element of a pair/list. For instance, (rest '(1 2 3 4)) returns (2 3 4).

- cons receives two arguments and creates a pair where the first operand is the *first*, and the second operand is the *rest*. For instance, (cons 2 5) returns (2 . 5).

- null? receives an argument and returns true if and only if it is a pair/list and both its *first* and its *rest* are NULL.

- cons? receives an argument and returns true if and only if it is a valid *cons* pair. If the list/pair is empty, it is not valid, and thus the function returns false.

Implementing these functions is relatively straightforward. As such, we will only show the implementations of first, null?, and cons.

Listing 7.12—Built-in first Function (apply.c)

```
1   static struct sval *apply_first(struct sval **args, size_t num_args,
2                                   struct environment *env) {
3     ASSERT_ARITY("first", 1, num_args);
4     struct sval *sv = args[0];
5     return sv->data.pair.first;
6   }
```

Listing 7.13—Built-in null *Predicate Function* (apply.c)

```
1   static struct sval *apply_null_predicate(struct sval **args, size_t num_args,
2                                             struct environment *env) {
3     ASSERT_ARITY("null?", 1, num_args);
4     bool null_result = false;
5
6     // The predicate needs to be a list and have zero elements for null? to be true.
7     if (SVAL_PAIR == args[0]->type
8         && NULL == args[0]->data.pair.first
9         && NULL == args[0]->data.pair.rest) {
10      null_result = true;
11    }
12    return sval_boolean_create(null_result);
13  }
```

Listing 7.14—Built-in cons *Function* (apply.c)

```
1   static struct sval *apply_cons(struct sval **args, size_t num_args,
2                                   struct environment *env) {
3     ASSERT_ARITY("cons", 2, num_args);
4     return sval_pair_create(args[0], args[1]);
5   }
```

One last alteration is necessary. Inside eval_quoted, we need to add a clause for evaluating lists. Lists are a special type of application. Thus, whenever we encounter, e.g., '(...), we pass the application child forward as a list to eval_-list.

Listing 7.15—Evaluating Pseudo-Application in Quoted Expressions (eval.c)

```
1   static struct sval *eval_quoted(ast *quoted, struct environment *env) {
2     ...
3     if (ast_is_type(quoted_expr, "application")) {
4       sym = eval_list(quoted_expr, env);
5     }
6     ...
7   }
```

At long last, we return to the problem of printing pairs and lists, which is the only time we must distinguish between the two (as well as the notion of proper versus improper lists).

First, we need a way of determining if a list is proper or not. If a list is proper, it does not contain dots. Note that a list may contain a sublist that is improper and hence has dots. Recall that a list is proper if and only if it is a list terminated by the empty list. So, all we need to do is recursively check the given s-value to determine one of two properties:

1. If either the s-value or its *first* are NULL, it is a proper list.

2. If the *first* is non-NULL and its *rest* is not a list, it is not a proper list.

All other cases recursively check the *rest* of the given list.

Listing 7.16—Determining If A Pair is Proper (sval.c)

```
1   static bool is_proper_list(const struct sval *ls) {
2     if (NULL == ls || NULL == ls->data.pair.first) { return true; }
3     else if (NULL != ls->data.pair.first
4              && NULL != ls->data.pair.rest
5              && SVAL_PAIR != ls->data.pair.rest->type) { return false; }
6     else { return is_proper_list(ls->data.pair.rest); }
7   }
```

We now have a case analysis. Let us handle the easier case first: if the list is not proper, then we print its *first* and *rest* with a dot separator '.' encased in parentheses.

Listing 7.17—Printing S-value Pair (sval.c)

```
1    void sval_print(struct sval *sv) {
2      ...
3      else if (SVAL_PAIR == sv->type) {
4        printf("(");
5        if (is_proper_list(sv)) {
6          struct sval *curr = sv;
7          // TODO...
8        } else if (NULL != sv) {
9          sval_print(sv->data.pair.first);
10         printf(" . ");
11         sval_print(sv->data.pair.rest);
12       }
13       printf(")");
14     }
15   }
```

Next, we iteratively print the *first* of the list, keeping track of a curr pointer that is constantly updated.

Listing 7.18—Printing S-value Pair (sval.c)

```
1    void sval_print(struct sval *sv) {
2      ...
3      else if (SVAL_PAIR == sv->type) {
4        printf("(");
5        if (is_proper_list(sv)) {
6          struct sval *curr = sv;
7          // If the list is null then it is automatically proper.
8          if (curr->data.pair.first != NULL) {
9            while (curr->data.pair.rest->data.pair.rest != NULL) {
10             sval_print(curr->data.pair.first);
11             curr = curr->data.pair.rest;
12             printf(" ");
13           }
14           sval_print(curr->data.pair.first);
15         }
16       } else if (NULL != sv) {
17         sval_print(sv->data.pair.first);
18         printf(" . ");
19         sval_print(sv->data.pair.rest);
20       }
21       printf(")");
22     }
23     ...
24   }
```

Recognition, evaluation, and s-value construction of pairs and lists are now complete. Let us write a few tests.

Listing 7.19

```
(define l1 '(1 2 3 4))
(define l2 (cons (cons 1 2) (cons 3 (cons 4 5))))
(define l3 (cons 1 (cons 2 (cons 3 (cons 4 '())))))

> (first l1)                                          1
> (first l2)                                          (1 . 2)
> (first l3)                                          1
> (rest l1)                                           (2 3 4)
> (rest l2)                                           (3 . (4 . 5))
> (rest l3)                                           (2 3 4)
> (first (rest l2))                                   (1 . 2)
> (first (rest l3))                                   2
```

Notice that we composed a `first` operation immediately following from a `rest` invocation. We can write a function that hides the explicit function composition as follows:

Listing 7.20

```
(define second
(λ (l)
  (first (rest l))))
```

Be aware that retrieving the *second* of a list that has no *second* crashes the program.

One supplemental change we need to make is to the built-in `eqv?` function. Namely, we need to ensure that `eqv?` returns true if both of its arguments are the empty list. Some may consider implementing the functionality to recursively compare lists, but this is not necessary; we can write a language-level function to determine if lists are recursively equivalent.

Listing 7.21

```
> (eqv? '() '())                                      #t
> (eqv? '(10) '(10))                                  #f
> (eqv? '(a b) '(a))                                  #f
```

Because we had no intuition of lists in $\mathcal{L}_{\text{QUOTE}}$, we omitted a small yet noteworthy language feature: quoted expressions that are, themselves, quoted! Consider the following expression: `''(+ 2 3)`. What might this evaluate to? Well, we should think of this as a list whose *first* is `'` and whose *rest* is `(+ 2 3)`. This approach generalizes to any number of quotes, e.g., `''''(+ 2 3)` is converted into the following:

Listing 7.22

```
(quote (quote (quote (+ 2 3))))
```

We, without much reasoning, introduced this new function "quote". This is simply another method of writing a quoted expression. Furthermore, it allows us to visualize the fact that this is a list whose *first* is a quote and whose *rest* is another arbitrary expression. How can we represent this in our interpreter? First, we need to amend the definition of `eval_quoted` to check for quoted expressions. If we find one, we create a two-element list (note that it is *not* a *cons* pair) whose *first* is the symbol `quote` and whose *rest* is the "sub" quoted expression.

Listing 7.23—Creating a Quoted S-Value (`sval.c`)

```
1   struct sval *sval_quote_create(struct sval *rest) {
2     struct sval **args = malloc(2 * sizeof(struct sval *));
3     struct sval *s = sval_symbol_create("quote");
4     args[0] = s;
5     args[1] = rest;
6     struct sval *sym = sval_list_create(args, 2);
7     free(args);
8     return sym;
9   }
```

Listing 7.24—Quoted Expressions That Are Quoted (`eval.c`)

```
1    static struct sval *eval_quoted(ast *quoted, struct environment *env) {
2      ast *quoted_expr = ast_child(quoted, QUOTED_EXPR_IDX);
3      char *quoted_sym = ast_contents(quoted_expr);
4      struct sval *sym = NULL;
5      ...
6      else if (ast_is_type(quoted_expr, "quoted")) {
7        struct sval *rest = eval_quoted(ast_child(quoted_expr, 1), env);
8        sym = sval_quote_create(rest);
9      }
10   }
```

Fortunately, since we already have the mechanism for printing lists, there is nothing left to do. Let us write a few tests (this is, admittedly, a lot of test cases, but we want to convey the structure of quoted expressions):

Listing 7.25

```
(define qexp '''(+ 2 3))

> (first qexp)                                       quote
> (rest qexp)                                        ((quote (+ 2 3)))
> (first (rest qexp))                                (quote (+ 2 3))
> (rest (rest qexp))                                 ()
> (first (first (rest qexp)))                        quote
> (first (rest (first (rest qexp))))                 (+ 2 3)
> (first (first (rest (first (rest qexp)))))         +
> (rest (first (rest (first (rest qexp)))))          (2 3)
```

With the notion of the `quote` special form and the `'` symbol, we want them to be treated, semantically, the same. In other words, we also want the programmer to be able to invoke `quote` as if they were using its symbolic counterpart. So, one way to circumvent any issues is to write two "helper functions", `eval_quoted_symbol` and `eval_quoted_form` that pass different children of their abstract syntax trees to `eval_quoted`. This means that `eval_quoted` only has to care about how to deal with its expression rather than extracting it from the abstract syntax tree.

Listing 7.26—Quoted Special Form (`eval.c`)

```
1    #define QUOTE_SYMBOL_EXPR_IDX 1
2    #define QUOTE_FORM_EXPR_IDX 2
3    static struct sval *eval_quoted_symbol(ast *quote_symbol,
4                                           struct environment *env) {
5      return eval_quoted(ast_child(quote_symbol, QUOTE_SYMBOL_EXPR_IDX), env);
6    }
7
8    static struct sval *eval_quoted_form(ast *quote_form,
9                                         struct environment *env) {
10     return eval_quoted(ast_child(quote_form, QUOTE_FORM_EXPR_IDX), env);
11   }
```

Two pieces of the puzzle remain: modify `eval_quoted` function to operate on the passed abstract syntax tree rather than a child, and update the root `eval` function to instead call `eval_quoted_form`. Note that the simplest way to make the former change is to rename the abstract syntax tree formal parameter and remove the declaration of a separate variable inside the function.

Listing 7.27—Evaluating Quoted Expression (eval.c)

```
1    static struct sval *eval(ast *ast, struct environment *env) {
2      ...
3      else if (ast_is_type(ast, "quoted")) {
4        return eval_quoted_symbol(ast, env);
5      }
6    }
7
8    static struct sval *eval_quoted(ast *quoted_expr, struct environment *env) { ... }
```

Exercise 7.1. (⋆)
Write a function `third` that retrieves the third element of a list using only `first` and `rest`. Assume that the input list contains at least three arguments.

Exercise 7.2. (⋆)
Write a function `init` to compute a list of all elements, except the last, of a list. If the list is empty, return the empty list.

Exercise 7.3. (⋆)
Write a function `last` to retrieve the last element of a list. If the list is empty, return the empty list. Hint: the last element of the list must have an empty *rest*.

Exercise 7.4. (⋆)
Write a function `append` to append two lists `ls1` and `ls2` Hint: think about how to solve this recursively; if `ls1` is empty, return `ls2`. Otherwise, return a list where the *first* of `ls1` is cons'd onto `ls2`.

Exercise 7.5. (⋆)
Write a function `loc->string` that receives a list of characters and returns a string that results when conjoining, or concatenating, each character. As an example, `(loc->string '(#\h #\e #\l #\l #\o #\w #\o #\r #\l #\d))` resolves to "helloworld".

Exercise 7.6. (⋆⋆)
In Chapter 5, we referenced the Collatz conjecture as an exercise to be implemented as a C function. Design the `collatz` function in $\mathcal{L}_{LIST}$, only this time, accumulate the Collatz intermediary values in a list.

Listing 7.28

> (collatz 10)	(10 5 16 8 4 2 1)

Exercise 7.7. (⋆⋆)
Write a function n-in-a-row*? to determine if a list contains some value v, n times sequentially. For example, calling `(n-in-a-row*? ls 'a 3)` returns true when *ls* is `'(a a b c a a a b b)` and false for `(n-in-a-row*? ls 'b 3)`.

Exercise 7.8. (⋆⋆)
Write a function `collect-seq`, which receives a list ls and a value v, returning a list of the same values, except where the longest sequence of v is within its own nested list. For instance, if ls is '(a a b c a a a b b) and v is 'a, then `collect-seq` returns (a a b c (a a a) b b).

Exercise 7.9. (⋆⋆)
Write a function `contiguous-str?`, which receives a list of strings and determines if the list is "contiguous". A list of strings is contiguous if each string has its first character equal to the last character of its predecessor string. For example, if ls is '("aa" "ab" "bccd" "df"), then `contiguous-str?` returns true. On the other hand, if ls is '("ab" "cd"), then `contiguous-str?` returns false. Consider this problem as a sequence of case analyses. If the list is empty or contains only one element, it cannot be contiguous.

Exercise 7.10. (⋆⋆)
Design the `combineDigits*` function, which receives a list of digits and combines them into one number. For example, (combineDigits* '(2 5 8 1)) returns 2581.

Exercise 7.11. (⋆⋆⋆)
The Scheme and Racket programming languages have a "case dispatch" keyword conveniently named `case`.[1] It receives an expression e to evaluate and a sequence of clauses similar to `cond`. Each clause contains two expressions: a comparison expression c_i and a resulting expression r_i. Unlike `cond`, however, each c_i must be a quoted expression. If c_i is a self-evaluating expression and it is `eqv?` to e, its corresponding r_i is evaluated. If c_i a list, its elements are compared against e and, if any are `eqv?` to e, the corresponding r_i is evaluated. If none of the preceding clauses have a comparison expression that matches against e, the result of the `else` clause is evaluated. We present some examples below. Add `case` to $\mathcal{L}_{\text{LIST}}$. Hint: use `sval_quote_create` to quote each comparison expression before evaluation. It may be helpful to write a recursive function, e.g., `sval_equals` that determines if two s-values are equivalent. It may also be helpful to write the `sval_-list_contains` function which receives a `SVAL_PAIR` list ls and another s-value v, returning true if v is in ls and false otherwise.

---

[1] Our description does not perfectly resemble either Scheme or Racket's implementation of `case`—we describe a hybrid between the two.

Listing 7.29

```
> (case (first '(f g))                    | consonant
    ['(a e i o u) 'vowel]                  |
    ['(w y) 'semi-vowel]                   |
    [else 'consonant])                     |
                                           |
> (case 5                                  | five
    ['1 'one]                              |
    ['2 'two]                              |
    ['3 'three]                            |
    ['4 'four]                             |
    ['5 'five]                             |
    [else 'something-else])                |
                                           |
> (case (* 1 5)                            | normal
    ['0 'non-existent]                     |
    ['(1 2 3) 'tiny]                       |
    ['(4 5 6) 'normal]                     |
    ['(7 8 9) 'large]                      |
    ['(10 11 12) 'huge]                    |
    [else 'gigantic])                      |
```

Exercise 7.12. ($\star\star\star\star\star$)

Antimetabole is a rhetorical device in which words in one half of the sentence are
reversed in the second half [Harris et al., 2018]. For example, consider the sentence
"We are one for all, but he is all for one." We see that "one for all" and "all for
one" form the antimetabole example. Implement a function antimetabole, which
receives two sub-sentences s_1 and s_2, and returns a list of words that exemplify
antimetabole. For example, (antimetabole s1 s2), where s_1 is "we are one for
all" and s_2 is "but he is all for one", should return ("one" "for" "all"). You
may assume that both sub-sentences contain contain only lowercase letters and
no punctuation. You may further assume that s_1 and s_2 indeed have exactly one
instance of antimetabole.

Exercise 7.13. ($\star\star\star\star\star$)

Parison is defined as parallelism between the parts-of-speech of a sentence [Harris
et al., 2018]. For example, "the fox jumped over the lazy dog, but the octopus
swam beneath the giant shark" exemplifies parison due to the syntactic similarity between s_1: "the fox jumped over the lazy dog" and s_2:"the octopus swam
beneath the giant shark". The parts-of-speech used are DT/the/the, NN/fox/octo-
pus, VBD/jumped/swam, IN/over/beneath, DT/the/the, JJ/lazy/giant, and NN/-
dog/shark.[1] The previous notation has the part-of-speech as the first value, the
corresponding word in s_1 as the second value, and the corresponding word in s_2 as
the third value. Design the parison function, which receives a string s and a list of
the parts-of-speech of each word in s. The function should identify the substrings
that comprise the parison example, and return a list of those substrings. Note
that an example of parison may consist of more than two sub-sentences. You may
assume that every provided sentence contains exactly one instance of parison and
that the words are all lowercase letters, contain no punctuation, and are separated
by spaces. We present an example as follows:

---

[1]Worrying about what these part-of-speech abbreviations mean is not part of this exercise.

Listing 7.30

```
(define s1
  "the fox jumped over the lazy
   dog but the octopus swam beneath
   the giant shark"
(define lopos
  '(DT NN VBD IN DT JJ NN CC
    DT NN VBD IN DT JJ NN))

> (parison s1 lopos)                    ("the fox jumped over the lazy dog"
                                         "the octopus swam beneath the
                                          giant shark")
```

$\mathcal{L}_{\text{QUASI}}$: **Quasiquotes**

We have seen how to define lists of data in $\mathcal{L}_{\text{LIST}}$, e.g., '(1 2 3 4) or (cons 1 2) or even '(1 x (3 y) 5 z). Let us investigate that last list for a moment. What is its resulting value? Under our current constraints, we receive the following output for the given input:

Listing 7.31

```
> '(1 x (3 y) 5 z)                      (1 x (3 y) 5 z)
```

Suppose that, instead of inserting the raw symbols x, y, and z, we want to give meaning to these values in a list. For example, if we define those variables as follows:

Listing 7.32

```
(define x 10)
(define y 30)
(define z 50)
```

And, similarly, with an input of (1 x (3 y) 5 z), we wish to output the following list:

Listing 7.33

```
(1 10 (3 30) 5 50)
```

How do we do this? In this section, we will write $\mathcal{L}_{\text{QUASI}}$: an extension of $\mathcal{L}_{\text{LIST}}$ to include the ability to evaluate parts of a list via quasiquotes.

Quasiquotes are almost identical to quotes, but come with the added ability to "unquote" portions of a list. Using the previous code as a base, we get the desired output using the code below:

Listing 7.34

```
`(1 ,x (3 ,y) 5 ,z)
```

The comma ',' is known as unquote; it evaluates the succeeding expression. As we said before, a quote is identical to a quasiquote, meaning the following code segments are equivalent:

Listing 7.35

```
'(1 x (3 y) 5 z)
`(1 x (3 y) 5 z)
```

Though, with the standard, non-quasiquote, we cannot unquote expressions. So, let us implement this feature! We first need to introduce two new datum rules to our grammar: quasiquoted and unquoted.

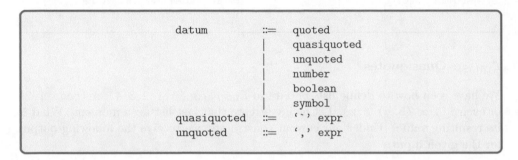

Figure 7.3: Extended BNF Grammar for $\mathcal{L}_{\text{QUASI}}$

Note that, with this grammar, this means we can unquote or quasiquote as many expressions as we want, even if it does not make sense. Our interpreter, for the time being, only handles valid input, so we will omit the discussion of semantic error-checking analysis for such rules. Embed these into the parser, and all we need to do is modify the code for evaluating standard quoted expressions. We can, thankfully, condense the quoted-expression handler to simply pass the expression forward to eval_quoted if we are not unquoting the data. In the previous section(s) on quoted expressions, however, we deferred handling multiple quoted expressions until after our discussion on lists and pairs. Since we now have a fundamental understanding, we will integrate the special form quasiquote and its symbolic counterpart directly into the interpreter. As before, we write two helper functions: eval_quasiquoted_symbol and eval_quasiquoted_form that both invoke eval_quasiquoted with the corresponding quasiquoted expression. Fortunately, we may reuse the constants defined for retrieving the correct index of the quoted expression in the abstract syntax tree.

Listing 7.36—Quasiquoted Expression Evaluation (eval.c)

```
1   static struct sval *eval_quasiquoted_symbol(ast *quasiquoted_symbol,
2                                       struct environment *env) {
3    return eval_quasiquoted(ast_child(quasiquoted_symbol, QUOTE_SYMBOL_EXPR_IDX),
4                            env);
5   }
6
7   static struct sval *eval_quasiquoted_form(ast *quasiquoted_form,
8                                     struct environment *env) {
9    return eval_quasiquoted(ast_child(quasiquoted_form, QUOTE_FORM_EXPR_IDX), env);
10  }
11
12  static struct sval *eval_quasiquoted(ast *quasiquoted_expr,
13                                      struct environment *env) {
14   char *quasiquoted_sym = ast_contents(quasiquoted_expr);
15   struct sval *sym = NULL;
16
17   if (ast_is_type(quasiquoted_expr, "application")) {
18     sym = eval_list(quasiquoted_expr, env);
19   } else if (ast_is_type(quasiquoted_expr, "unquoted")) {
20     sym = eval(ast_child(quasiquoted_expr, 1), env);
21   } else {
22     sym = eval_quoted(quasiquoted_expr, env);
23   }
24   return sym;
25  }
```

Notice we added only a single clause for handling unquotes (and removed the other redundant self-evaluating clauses). We need to check to see if the quasiquote contains an immediately following unquote, e.g., ` ,x. If so, we evaluate that node in the abstract syntax tree. Otherwise, we continue as we did previously. Let us look at a sample abstract syntax tree that matches this scenario:

```
>
 expr|define|>
  char:1:1 '('
  string:1:2 'define'
  symbol|regex:1:9 'x'
  expr|datum|number|regex:1:11 '10'
  char:1:13 ')'
 expr|datum|quasiquoted|>
  char:2:1 '`'
  expr|datum|unquoted|>
   char:2:2 '',
   expr|datum|symbol|regex:2:3 'x'
 expr|datum|symbol|regex:2:3 'x'
```

We see that, in an unquoted expression, the expression we wish to evaluate is always the second child (index 1). So, we can refactor that into a preprocessor definition.

Listing 7.37—Unquoted Expression Evaluation (eval.c)

```
1   #define QUASIQUOTED_EXPR_IDX 1
2   ...
3   static struct sval *eval_quasiquoted(ast *quasiquoted_expr,
4                                      struct environment *env) {
5     ...
6     else if (ast_is_type(quasiquoted_expr, "unquoted")) {
7       sym = eval(ast_child(quasiquoted_expr, QUASIQUOTED_EXPR_IDX), env);
8     }
9   }
```

Lastly, we update the root `eval` function. It is important to check for quasiquoted above quoted because both strings contain the substring quoted, meaning a quasiquoted expression will erroneously match a quoted expression. In addition, be sure to only invoke `eval_quasiquoted_form` rather than `eval_quasiquoted` for the aforementioned reasons.

Listing 7.38—Adding Quoted and Quasiquoted Expressions (`eval.c`)

```
1  static struct sval *eval(ast *ast, struct environment *env) {
2    ...
3    // Check for "quasiquoted" before "quoted" due to substring!
4    else if (ast_is_type(ast, "quasiquoted")) {
5      return eval_quasiquoted_form(ast, env);
6    } else if (ast_is_type(ast, "quoted")) {
7      return eval_quoted_form(ast, env);
8    }
9  }
```

Running a simple example produces the correct answer.

Listing 7.39

```
(define x 10)

> `,x                               10
> (quasiquote ,x)                   10
```

Unfortunately, we forgot to handle unquoted expressions within a list. Let us modify `eval_list_element` to account for this, and after testing, we should see our changes:

Listing 7.40—Evaluating Unquoted Expressions (`eval.c`)

```
1  static struct sval *eval_list_element(ast *element, struct environment *env) {
2    ...
3    else if (ast_is_type(element, "unquoted")) {
4      curr_sym = eval(ast_child(element, QUASIQUOTED_EXPR_IDX), env);
5    }
6  }
```

Listing 7.41

```
(define x 10)
(define y 30)
(define z 50)

> `(1 ,x (3 ,y) 5 ,z)              (1 10 (3 30) 5 50)
```

What is interesting about quasiquoting and unquoting is that the expression to unquote can be as complex or simple as we want. For instance, let us embed an arithmetic expression into our quasiquote list.

Listing 7.42

```
(define x 10)
(define y 30)
(define z 50)

> `(1 ,(* 5 x) (3 ,y) 5 ,(* z y))   (1 50 (3 30) 5 150)
```

Brilliant! We now have a way of representing unquoted data in $\mathcal{L}_{\text{QUASI}}$.

Exercise 7.14. (⋆)

In addition to the special form `quasiquote`, there is a similar special form `unquote`. Implement this into your interpreter.

Exercise 7.15. (⋆⋆⋆)

Many Scheme interpreters/dialects allow for the "unquote-splicing" operator. In summary, it allows us to embed the elements from a list inside a quasiquoted expression inside the resulting expression. We present an example below. Notice the difference between a standard unquote and the unquote-splice; the former simply sticks the list, as a symbol, inside the outer list. The latter, on the other hand, takes each element of the unquoted list, one by one, and inserts them into the outer list. Add unquote-splicing to your interpreter. Hint: you will need to modify the grammar, but you should only otherwise modify `eval_list` since you need access to the original list as well as the unquote-spliced list elements). As a note, unquote-splicing on a non-list element (or a variable that does not resolve to a list) should produce an error.

Listing 7.43

```
(define ls1 '(2 3 4))

> `(1 ,ls1 5)                    (1 (2 3 4) 5)
> `(1 ,@ls1 5)                   (1 2 3 4 5)
```

Exercise 7.16. (⋆⋆)

If you did not add the `unquote-splice` special form from the previous exercise, do so now.

A Shortcut for Pair Creation

Creating a *cons* pair is convenient for grouping two values together, or starting a list. Though, it may be slightly inconvenient to have to invoke the `cons` function each time we simply want to conjoin two values. For instance, suppose we have the following code:

Listing 7.44

```
(define x 5)
(define y 10)
(define pair (cons x y))

> pair                          (5 . 10)
```

Creating a *cons* pair defined only in terms of two values is a little cumbersome. Why not introduce a syntax that allows the programmer to form *cons* pairs without the need for `cons`? That is, we give the programmer control over where and what is the *first* and *rest* of the pair. We know that, for a *cons* pair, the dot "." separates the two aforementioned values. So, ideally, we might introduce a syntax that combines the dot notation with our newly-found quasiquoting: `` `(,x . ,y)``. Hence, this would be equivalent to `(cons x y)`. We first need to establish a rule about the "dot operator". A dot, when used in this context, can only occur within a list expression. In addition, there must be one and only one element following a dot. Lastly, there must be at least one element preceding the dot. So, where do we go in the interpreter? We need only to make a small change in `eval_list`: instead of immediately evaluating the list element according to `eval_list_element`, we must check the "ahead" element, i.e., the element one position ahead of the current to see if it is the dot. If so, we define *e* to be a *cons* pair where its *first* is the current element, and its *rest* is the element ahead of the dot.

Listing 7.45—Using Dots in Cons Pair (`eval.c`)

```
1   static struct sval *eval_list(ast *list, struct environment *env) {
2     ...
3     for (int i = 0; i < num_elements; i++) {
4
5       if (i < num_elements - 1 &&
6           streq(".", ast_contents(ast_child(list, 1 + i + QUOTED_CONTENT_OFFSET))))) {
7         curr->data.pair.first =
8           eval_list_element(ast_child(list, i + QUOTED_CONTENT_OFFSET), env);
9         curr->data.pair.rest =
10          eval_list_element(ast_child(list, 2 + i + QUOTED_CONTENT_OFFSET), env);
11        break;
12      }
13    }
14  }
```

The second piece of the conditional should make sense—we ensure that the element ahead of the current is a dot. Though, what about the former? Why do we need a check to keep 1 less than `num_elements - 1`? Simple! If we are on the last element of the list, then we cannot possibly check the "ahead" element because it is non-existent![1] Let us test this feature out:

Listing 7.46

```
(define dotted-list '(5 . 6))
(define cons-list (cons 5 6))

> dotted-list                              (5 . 6)
> cons-list                                (5 . 6)
```

So, as we stated, using the quote and dot operators is almost equivalent to using cons. We say almost because there is an important distinction between quoting and cons, and that distinction comes from argument evaluation. The function cons evaluates its arguments,[2] whereas a quoted dot pair does not. Let us look at the following example:

---

[1] Technically, it *is* possible, but this is otherwise known as an *out-of-bounds memory access* and should be avoided at all costs.

[2] Although Dan Friedman and David Wise vehemently disagree with this idea in their *CONS Should Not Evaluate its Arguments* paper [Friedman and Wise, 1976].

Listing 7.47

```
(define x 5)
(define y 6)
(define dotted-list '(x . y))
(define cons-list (cons x y))

> dotted-list                                    (x . y)
> cons-list                                      (5 . 6)
```

Notice how the former list declaration using the quote does not evaluate x and y—it instead inserts the literal symbols. If we want to equalize this with the behavior of a cons invocation, we must use quasiquoting and the comma to evaluate the values bound to the symbols x and y. We can, of course, use the pair operations first and rest to extract the contents of a dot-constructed pair.

Listing 7.48

```
(define x 5)
(define y 6)
(define dotted-list `(,x . ,y))
(define cons-list (cons x y))

> dotted-list                                    (5 . 6)
> cons-list                                      (5 . 6)
> (first dotted-list)                            5
> (rest dotted-list)                             6
```

Lastly, let us use our newly-built pair construct inductively. That is, we can define a dotted pair in terms of another pair:

Listing 7.49

```
(define double-dotted-list
 '((5 . 6) . 7))
(define double-cons-list
 (cons (cons 5 6) 7))

> double-cons-list                               ((5 . 6) . 7)
> double-dotted-list                             ((5 . 6) . 7)
> (first double-dotted-list)                     (5 . 6)
> (first (first double-dotted-list))             5
> (rest (first double-dotted-list))              6
> (rest double-dotted-list)                      7
```

We apply a general rule-of-thumb for using quasiquotes to construct pairs/lists: if it clutters the expression to use quasiquotes, prefer to use *cons*. On the other hand, if we want to unquote several variables at once to form a list, then quasiquotes/unquotes are the better choice.[1]

---

[1]We will demonstrate examples of these instances when we introduce association lists.

7.2   Variadic Arguments

When writing a procedure definition, we may not always know a priori how many arguments it should receive. If we want to process any given number of values in a function call, we need to introduce the idea of *variadic arguments*. For instance, suppose we are writing a function foo, which we wish to define as using variadic arguments. This consequently implies that we can invoke foo with any number of arguments.

Listing 7.50

```
(foo 1 2 3 4 5)
(foo)
(foo 1 2 3)
```

Though, how do we address this in our interpreter? Right now, when writing a procedure, we use the notion of formal parameters to specify the names of a parameter to a function. The problem is that variadic arguments do not know ahead of time how many arguments to expect. Representing variadic arguments as lists is the solution. Thus, if we want to compute the number of arguments to a variadic function, we first need a function to compute the length of a list.

Listing 7.51

```
(define length
  (λ (ls)
    (cond
      [(null? ls) 0]
      [else (add1 (length (rest ls)))])))
```

From here, we can define the syntax and semantics of variadic-argument functions via $\mathcal{L}_{\text{VARIADIC}}$: an extension of $\mathcal{L}_{\text{QUASI}}$.

```
expr          ::=   application | ...
application   ::=   proc | proc-var | ...
proc          ::=   'lambda' '(' id* ')' expr
proc-var      ::=   'lambda-var' '(' id ')' expr
```

Figure 7.4: Extended BNF Grammar for $\mathcal{L}_{\text{VARIADIC}}$

We will say that a function that receives any number of arguments is defined as a lambda-var, where its formal parameter is a single list. For instance, consider the following code segment:

Listing 7.52

```
(define process-any-args
  (λ-var (args)
    (length args)))
```

Thus we, internally, treat args as a list. So, we may invoke process-any-args with, as its name says, any number of arguments:

Listing 7.53

> (process-any-args 1 2 3 (+ 4 5) 6 7)	6
> (process-any-args)	0

Note that, with variadic-argument functions, each argument is individually evaluated before passing the result forward. Additionally, the argument defined in the procedure is bound to the list created by evaluating each argument. In other words, args is bound to '(1 2 3 (+ 4 5) 6 7). Fortunately, we do not need to make any alterations to the grammar—we only need to add a special form to account for lambda-var and update function application. Let us work on the former task first.

Listing 7.54—Evaluation of Variadic Lambdas (eval.c)

```
1   #define LAMBDAVAR_FORMALS_IDX 2
2   #define LAMBDAVAR_SYMBOL_IDX 1
3
4   static struct sval *eval_lambdavar(ast *lambdavar, struct environment *env) {
5     ast *formal_ast = ast_child(lambdavar, LAMBDAVAR_FORMALS_IDX);
6     char **formals = malloc(sizeof(char *));
7     ASSERT_ALLOC(formals, "eval_lambdavar");
8     char *formal_name = ast_contents(ast_child(formal_ast, LAMBDAVAR_SYMBOL_IDX));
9     formals[0] = strdup(formal_name);
10    return sval_procedure_create(formals, 1, ast_child(lambdavar, LAMBDA_BODY_IDX),
11                                 env, true);
12  }
```

What is going on here? Like normal, non-variadic-argument procedures, we need to keep track of the formal parameter listings. In this case, we only have one formal parameter, namely the list of arguments. So, we allocate space for one formal, then create the procedure as normal. One change we also made is the addition of a "flag" in the procedure struct that notes whether or not a procedure uses variadic arguments. Hence, the inclusion of true as the last argument to the modified sval_procedure_create function.

Now, let us jump down to function application. The changes here are more important and potentially more difficult to understand.

Listing 7.55—Handling Variadic Arguments in Function Application (eval.c)

```
1   static struct sval *eval_application(ast *application, struct environment *env) {
2     ...
3     struct sval *result = NULL;
4     if (SVAL_BUILTIN == function->type) {
5       result = apply(function, arguments, num_args, env);
6     } else {
7       // If it is variadic, we need to create a list out of the arguments.
8       if (function->data.proc->is_variadic) {
9         struct sval *list = sval_list_create(arguments, num_args);
10        arguments = realloc(arguments, sizeof(struct sval *));
11        ASSERT_ALLOC(arguments, "eval_application");
12        arguments[0] = list;
13      }
14      // Otherwise, extend the current environment.
15      struct environment *new_env =
16        environment_extend(function->data.proc->env, function, arguments);
17      result = eval(function->data.proc->body, new_env);
18    }
19    ...
20  }
```

In the `else` block, we have a second `if` clause that accounts for variadic functions. We already have an array of evaluated arguments, so we can simply create an s-value to represent a list.[1] We still need to use an array of arguments to store the newly-initialized list, so we should reuse that space via `realloc`. The first, and only argument, is a pointer to the list (of given arguments). Lastly, we evaluate the function body as normal via environment extension. Let us now try the "length" example from before:

Listing 7.56

```
(define length
 (λ (ls)
  (cond
   [(null? ls) 0]
   [else (add1 (length (rest ls)))])))

(define process-any-args
 (λ-var (args)
  (length args)))

> (process-any-args 1 2 3 4 5 6)            6
> (process-any-args 1 2 3)                  3
> (process-any-args)                        0
```

A benefit of writing variadic functions is that we can implement generalized "helper" functions. For instance, it would be nice to have, say, a "list" function that creates a list of its evaluated arguments (note the distinction between this and a quoted list). We must write a helper function to extract each element from the variadic argument which creates a list of *cons* pairs:

Listing 7.57

```
(define list
 (letrec ([list-helper
           (λ (ls)
            (cond
             [(null? ls) '()]
             [else
              (cons (first ls)
                    (list-helper (rest ls)))]))])
  (λ-var (args)
   (list-helper args))))

> (list (+ 2 3) 4 5 6 7 (- 8 3))            (5 4 5 6 7 5)
```

Exercise 7.17. ($\star\star$)
Redesign the `combineDigits*` function to be variadic rather than receiving a list of digits.

Exercise 7.18. ($\star\star$)
The *Racket* programming language supports variadic arguments in functions, but with a slightly different syntax than our `lambda-var` implementation. `args`, in the following left-hand code listing, is an array of arguments passed to `foo`. Though, Racket similarly supports defining functions using a form of syntactic sugar that abstracts away the `lambda` which we demonstrate in the right-hand code listing. Remove λ-var and replace it with the "non-syntactic sugar'd" Racket variant. Hint: the formal parameter, in this instance, is not a special form!

---

[1]This function is equivalent to applying the built-in `list` procedure. We abstracted away the procedure to minimize redundancy.

Listing 7.58

`(define foo`
`(λ args`
`...))`
	`(define (foo . args)`
	`...)`

Exercise 7.19. (★★)

Implement the second "syntactic sugar'd" Racket variant of variadic-argument procedures. This relies on the successful implementation of "syntactic sugar'd" functions, which was a previous exercise.

Exercise 7.20. (★★★)

In addition to specifying variadic argument functions, we can specify functions that receive "at least n" arguments. For instance, the below function requires that `foo` receive at least two arguments when invoked. The first two are bound to `arg1` and `arg2`, and any subsequent arguments are stored as a list in `argl`. We will designate these as n-variadic argument functions. Implement n-variadic argument functions first as the non-syntactic sugared variant, and second as the syntactic sugar'd variant.

Listing 7.59

```
(define foo
  (λ (arg1 arg2 . argl)
    ...))
```

7.3   First-Class and Higher-Order Functions

Variables are, for all intents and purposes, data. That is, a variable encapsulates information about some particular value. With this notion of data, we often manipulate data through functions by passing them as arguments. Functions, contrastingly, are often viewed as constructs that receive, then return, data, wherein some claim that functions themselves are not data. For instance, many programming languages do not support the ability to "store" or pass functions around as arguments. C, funnily enough, mimics this behavior via function pointers. Our languages, on the other hand, fully support *first-class functions*, i.e., treating variables and functions equivalently as data. So, we can pass functions to other functions as arguments just like we can with numbers, symbols, et. cetera. Along those lines, functions may return other functions. As an example, let us write a function `perform`, in $\mathcal{L}_{\text{QUASI}}$, which receives three arguments: a binary function f, and two expressions e_1 and e_2. `perform` returns the result of applying f to e_1 and e_2.

Listing 7.60

```
(define perform
 (λ (f e1 e2)
  (f e1 e2)))
```

The above code may appear redundant, since, because f is a function, we can invoke it on e_1 and e_2. But alas, this code demonstrates the potential of first-class functions—because functions are data, we are able to pass them as arguments and return functions from functions. Another example, one that returns a function, is defined below.

Listing 7.61

```
(define return-function
 (λ ()
  (λ (x) (+ x 10))))
```

What happens if we invoke this function? Because it receives no arguments, we invoke it via (`return-function`). The output window should say that this function returns a function, which is correct! We can, therefore, apply the return value of this function to any numeric value.

Listing 7.62

```
(define return-function
 (λ ()
  (λ (x) (+ x 10))))

> (return-function)              <function>
> ((return-function) 20)         30
```

Functions that return other functions requiring arguments is commonplace in functional programming. In fact, Haskell Curry helped develop the concept of *currying*, which reduces functions of multiple arguments into functions of only one argument. For example, consider the following equivalent functions, where the left-hand definition receives four arguments, and the right-hand definition receives one but returns a sequence of functions wherein each receive one argument as well. Currying helps translate functions to the λ-calculus for analysis of their properties.

Listing 7.63—Function Currying

```
(define sum-of-squares           (define sum-of-squares
  (λ (x y z w)                      (λ (x)
    (+ (* x x)                        (λ (y)
       (* y y)                          (λ (z)
       (* z z)                            (λ (w)
       (* w w))))                           (+ (* x x)
                                               (* y y)
                                               (* z z)
                                               (* w w)))))))
```

Additionally, function currying allows us to partially define a function, then perhaps extend its capabilities down the line without the need to rewrite its invocations. Consider a sequence of functions where we pass the desired tip percentage of a restaurant bill, the tax percentage, and finally two values representing the bill subtotal and non-taxable service fees. The use of first-class functions means we can return and store a function that always computes, say, fifteen percent gratuity:

Listing 7.64—Restaurant "Bill" Calculator

```
(define compute-bill
  (λ (tip-pt)
    (λ (tax-pt)
      (λ (sub serv)
        (let ([tax-amt
               (+ sub
                  (* sub
                     (/ tip-pt 100)))])
          (+ (+ tax-amt
                (* (/ tax-pt 100)
                   tax-amt))
             serv))))))

(define t15 (compute-bill 15))
(define t15x7 ((compute-bill 15) 7))

> (((compute-bill 30) 8.5) 127.50 25)      204.84
> ((t15 9.5) 99.95 15)                     140.86
> (t15x7 65.00 5)                          84.98
```

The concept of higher-order functions is a fundamental concept in functional programming. A *higher-order function* is a function that intentionally receives a function(s) as arguments. One popular example is map: it receives a function and a list, then applies the function to every element of the list, resulting in a new (returned) list.

Listing 7.65

```
(define map
  (λ (f ls)
    (cond
      [(null? ls) '()]
      [else (cons (f (first ls))
                  (map f (rest ls)))])))

(define ls1 '(1 2 3 4 5)

> (map (λ (x) (* x x)) ls1)                (2 4 6 8 10)
```

Another higher-order function example is filter, which removes elements that do not satisfy a given predicate *p*. In other words, all elements *e* such that $(p\ e)$ returns true are collected.

Listing 7.66

```
(define filter
 (λ (p ls)
  (cond
   [(null? ls) '()]
   [(p (first ls))
    (cons (first ls)
          (filter p (rest ls)))]
   [else (filter p (rest ls))])))

(define ls '(1 2 3 4 5 6))

> (filter even? ls)                        (2 4 6)
> (filter odd? ls)                         (1 3 5)
> (filter zero? ls)                        ()
```

A third example is `foldr`: a function that receives a binary function, an accumulator, and a list of values. `foldr` applies the function to both the accumulator and the *first* of the list, stores this result back into the accumulator, and continues until the list is empty.[1]

Listing 7.67

```
(define foldr
 (λ (f acc ls)
  (cond
   [(null? ls) acc]
   [else (foldr f
                (f (first ls) acc)
                (rest ls))])))

(define ls1 '(10 2 49 1))
(define ls2 '("Hello, " "Jane"))

> (foldr + 0 ls1)                          62
> (foldr string-append "" ls2)             "Hello, Jane"
> (foldr max (first ls1) (rest ls1))       49
```

A fourth example is `zipf`, which receives a binary function and two lists. It then applies the binary function to each element of the two lists, returning a new list in the process. Our version of `zipf` only considers lists that are of the same length.

Listing 7.68

```
(define zipf
 (λ (f ls1 ls2)
  (cond
   [(null? ls) '()]
   [else
    (cons
     (f (first ls1) (first ls2))
     (zip f (rest ls1) (rest ls2)))])))

(define ls1 '(1 3 5 7 9 11))
(define ls2 '(2 4 6 8 10 12)

> (zipf + ls1 ls2)                          (3 7 11 15 19 23)
```

Exercise 7.21. (★★)

Implement the higher-order function `andmap`, which receives a predicate and a list. `andmap` returns #t if all elements of the given list satisfy the predicate, and #f otherwise.

---

[1]The `max` function receives two numbers and returns the larger of the two.

Exercise 7.22. (⋆⋆)
Implement the higher-order function `ormap`, which receives a predicate and a list. `ormap` returns #t if at least one element of the given list satisfies the predicate, and #f otherwise.

Exercise 7.23. (⋆⋆)
Implement the higher-order function `compose2`, which receives two functions and returns a function representing their composition. Recall that the composition of two functions f and g is $f{\circ}g$, or g applied to its argument x, which is then passed to f, i.e., $\lambda x.(f(g(x)))$.

Exercise 7.24. (⋆⋆⋆)
Implement the higher-order function `compose`, which receives at least two functions and returns a function representing their collective composition. You will need to use a variadic argument function. For instance, if `compose` receives functions f, g, h, and i, compose returns a function $\lambda x.(f(g(h(i(x)))))$. Hint: a variant of `foldr`, namely `foldl`, is incredibly helpful in making this solution as clean and concise as possible.

Exercise 7.25. (⋆⋆⋆⋆)
Recall the cosine similarity exercise from Chapter 5. Repeat the exercise, only this time, implement your algorithm at the $\mathcal{L}_{\text{VARIADIC}}$ level. We present this exercise in this section due to the relevancy of `foldr`, `map`, and `zip` and how they help to simplify the problem.

7.4   Evaluation and Application at the Interpreter Level

Our languages perform expression evaluation and function application at the meta-interpreter level, i.e., in the interpreter (C) code. It is extremely important to allow the programmer to use eval and apply as functions at the interpreter level, whose motivation follows shortly. In this section, we will write $\mathcal{L}_{\text{EVAL}}$: an extension to $\mathcal{L}_{\text{VARIADIC}}$ that introduces eval and apply as functions.

```
expr         ::=   application | ...
application  ::=   eval | apply | ...
eval         ::=   'eval ' expr
apply        ::=   'apply ' expr
```

Figure 7.5: Extended BNF Grammar for $\mathcal{L}_{\text{EVAL}}$

First, let us discuss what eval and apply should do at the interpreter level. eval takes an expression and evaluates it as code rather than data. This means that, if the program generates an s-expression at runtime, rather than one we type in the code editor, we may use eval to produce the value of that s-expression data as if it were executable code. For example, if we supply eval with the following inputs, we receive the corresponding outputs:

Listing 7.69

```
(define x 5)
(define y 6)

> (eval 5)              5
> (eval '(+ 2 3))       5
> (eval ''y)            y
> (eval (eval ''y))     6
> (eval `(+ ,x ,y))     11
```

Its apply counterpart, on the other hand, receives two arguments: a function and a list of arguments to the function. As its name may suggest, it applies the function to all elements *inside* the provided list. See the below examples.

Listing 7.70

```
> (apply + '(1 2 3 4 5))          15
> (apply * '(1 2 3 4 5))          120
> (apply cons '(1 2))             (1 . 2)
> (apply append '((a b c) (d e f)))   (a b c d e f)
> (apply (λ (x) (+ 5 x)) '(100))  105
```

Importantly, apply does not return a list; its return value is entirely dependent on the provided function.

There are a couple of ways we could implement these two functions into our language, and we will start with `eval`. The simplest approach may be a bit inefficient, but it is the most intuitive. A naive approach to our problem is to call the root `eval` function on the result of evaluating the argument. We quickly realize, though, that `eval` requires an abstract syntax tree as input, not an s-value! So, instead of writing a function from s-values to s-values, let us take a "backdoor approach" by using our parser, since that gives us the desired abstract syntax tree.

The result of any evaluated expression is some s-value printed to the terminal via `sval-print`. What if, instead, we wrote code to first evaluate the argument to `eval`, then convert the corresponding s-value result to a string, and feed *that* into the parser? This gives us the following process diagram:

$$\to s = \text{eval\_eval}(...)$$
$$\to s' = \text{sval\_tostring}(s)$$
$$\to t = \text{parser\_create\_ast}(s')$$
$$\to \text{eval}(t)$$

`eval_eval` is the special form evaluation function. We begin by evaluating the argument to `eval`. From there, we take the resulting s-value and convert it to a string.

Listing 7.71—Function to Evaluate `eval` *(eval.c)*

```
1    static struct sval *eval_eval(ast *eval_ast, struct environment *env) {
2      struct sval *sv = eval(ast_child(eval_ast, EVAL_EXPR_IDX), env);
3      char *sv_str = sval_tostring(sv);
4      return NULL;
5    }
```

The `sval_tostring` function is not difficult (to write), but requires some refactoring. Right now, `sval_print` outputs the string representation to standard output. We want the representation to be stored as a string! To do this without having to rewrite a ton of code, we will create a new function: `sval_fprint`, which receives an s-value and a `FILE *` destination. Fortunately, all we need to do is go through the code for `sval_print` and change any `printf` invocation to `fprintf`. In making this change, we will redefine `sval_print` to call `sval_fprint` with `stdout` as the `FILE *` input stream.

Listing 7.72—Abstracting From `sval_print` *Definition* `(sval.c)`

```
1    void sval_print(struct sval *sv) {
2      sval_fprint(sv, stdout);
3    }
4
5    static void sval_fprint(struct sval *sv, FILE *stream) { ... }
```

This, in and of itself, does not solve our problem of outputting the s-value as a char *. To do so, we will write another function: sval_tostring which receives an s-value and returns the desired char *. What is more interesting about this function is *how* we output the s-value to a string. Recall that sval_fprint also receives a FILE *; we can use the open_memstream function to direct data written to the stream into the provided char *.

Listing 7.73—Converting S-Value to char * (sval.c)

```
1   char *sval_tostring(struct sval *sv) {
2     char *buffer = NULL;
3     size_t buffer_size = 0;
4     FILE *stream = open_memstream(&buffer, &buffer_size);
5     sval_fprint(sv, stream);
6     fclose(stream);
7     return buffer;
8   }
```

Now that we have the necessary char *, we can invoke the parser! Though, we need a function that receives an input string and returns an abstract syntax tree–something we currently do not have because the logic/function for parsing an abstract syntax tree lies within parser_parse.

Listing 7.74—Create an AST From String (parser.c)

```
1   ast *parser_create_ast(const char *contents) {
2     mpc_ast_t *mpc_ast = parser_open(contents, PARSE_STRING);
3     ast *tree = malloc(sizeof(ast));
4     ASSERT_ALLOC(tree, "parser_create_ast");
5     ast_create(tree, mpc_ast, mpc_ast->tag,
6             mpc_ast->children_num, mpc_ast->contents);
7     return tree;
8   }
```

Finally, inside eval_eval, we free the string returned by sval_tostring because it was dynamically allocated by open-memstream. Then, we may call the root evaluation eval function and pass it the newly-made abstract syntax tree.

Listing 7.75—Evaluating New AST (eval.c)

```
1   static struct sval *eval_eval(ast *eval_ast, struct environment *env) {
2     struct sval *sv = eval(ast_child(eval_ast, EVAL_EXPR_IDX), env);
3     char *sv_str = sval_tostring(sv);
4     ast *new_ast = parser_create_ast(sv_str);
5     free(sv_str);
6     return eval(new_ast, env);
7   }
```

Running the tests from before prove to be successful.

Let us switch gears from evaluation and move into function application. As we stated, apply receives a function and a list of arguments. The provided function must be of the same arity as the number of elements in the list. For instance, + in (apply + '(1 2 3 4)) requires at least one argument. Another example is (apply append '((a b c) (d e f))); append requires two arguments and the provided argument list has two elements which, themselves, are lists. We begin by writing eval_apply where we extract and evaluate the function and its list of arguments respectively. The goal of this function is to apply the function to an array of s-value arguments (notice the similarity to eval_application!).

Listing 7.76—Initial Evaluation of `apply` (eval.c)

```
1   #define APPLY_ARGS_IDX 3
2   #define APPLY_FUNCTION_IDX 2
3
4   static struct sval *eval_apply(ast *apply_ast, struct environment *env) {
5     struct sval *function = eval(ast_child(apply_ast, APPLY_FUNCTION_IDX), env);
6     struct sval *loargs = eval(ast_child(apply_ast, APPLY_ARGS_IDX), env);
7     ...
8   }
```

From here, we initialize the array of s-value arguments and traverse through our list of arguments to the function. Since the s-value must be a list, we can traverse it as if we were traversing any other list with a relevant *first* and *rest*.

Listing 7.77—Converting Elements into List of S-Values (eval.c)

```
1   static struct sval *eval_apply(ast *apply_ast, struct environment *env) {
2     ...
3     struct sval **arguments = NULL;
4     struct sval *curr = loargs;
5
6     // Since it is a list, we go element-by-element.
7     int i = 0;
8     while (true) {
9       arguments = realloc(arguments, (i + 1) * sizeof(struct sval *));
10      ASSERT_ALLOC(arguments, "eval_apply");
11      arguments[i] = curr->data.pair.first;
12      if (NULL == curr->data.pair.rest) { break; }
13      i++;
14      curr = curr->data.pair.rest;
15    }
16    ...
17  }
```

Finally, we can apply the function to its arguments. Though, instead of painstakingly copying or rewriting the code we already have inside `eval_application`, we should abstract from this and write a function that both `eval_application` and `eval_apply` can call. This new function: `eval_function_application`, receives an s-value representing the function, an array of s-value arguments, the number of arguments passed, and the environment to apply the function inside. Because its definition is identical to the latter half of the previous implementation of `eval_-application`, we will omit the details.

Listing 7.78—Abstracting from Identical Code in Function Application (eval.c)

```
1   static struct sval *eval_apply(ast *apply_ast, struct environment *env) {
2     ...
3     return eval_function_application(function, arguments, num_args, env);
4   }
5
6   static struct sval *eval_application(ast *application, struct environment *env) {
7     ...
8     return eval_function_application(function, arguments, num_args, env);
9   }
10
11  static struct sval *eval_function_application(struct sval *function,
12                                                struct sval **arguments,
13                                                size_t num_args,
14                                                struct environment *env) { ... }
```

Rerunning the previous tests also pass as expected.

7.5   Constructive Recursion

Accumulator-Passing Style

We have repeatedly seen examples of recursive functions, many of which are singly recursive, in which we break a problem down into smaller problem(s) and invoke recursive calls. Let us consider the factorial function as an example. So long as $n >$ 0, we multiply n by a recursive call with '$n-1$'. That is, we started with the problem of computing '$n!$', and we decomposed it into '$n \cdot (n-1)!$'. This problem is then potentially broken down into a step further, thereby resolving to '$n \cdot (n-1) \cdot (n-2)!$'.[1] In this section, we will introduce the concept of *accumulator-passing style*, which serves to optimize recursive functions.

A component of accumulator-passing style functions is the fact that a function of this form is, by definition, *tail recursive*. A tail recursive function is a function where the last operation performed is a single recursive function call. Consider the following definition of length:

Listing 7.79

```
(define length
 (λ (ls)
  (cond
   [(null? ls) 0]
   [else (add1 (length (rest ls)))])))
```

Let us analyze the recursive stack trace of this function using the input list ' (5 10 15 20).

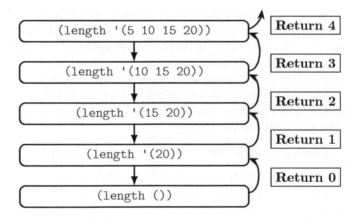

We see that, in the second cond clause, the outermost expression is add1 and not a recursive call. Therefore, this version of length is not tail recursive and, therefore, does not use accumulator-passing style. We also know this because the recursion unwinds—that is, the arrows to the right-hand side correspond to the recursive unwinding process. Recall that the last step in the function of the non-base case is an addition operation of 1 and the sum of the next recursive call. Let us now take a look at a version that keeps track of the length via an argument to the recursive call.

---

[1] We use the word "potentially" because this depends on the input number.

Listing 7.80

```
(define length
  (letrec ([length-helper
             (λ (ls n)
               (cond
                 [(null? ls) n]
                 [else (length-helper (rest ls) (add1 n))]))])
    (λ (ls)
      (length-helper ls 0))))
```

Let us once again analyze the recursive trace of this function using the input list '(5 10 15 20):

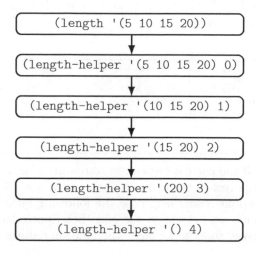

Once our tail recursive solution reaches the base case, i.e., an empty list, we immediately return n, which in this example is 4. It is, therefore, more efficient to use the tail recursive version as opposed to non-tail recursive. For those skeptical readers who question our claim, consider the sum of the number of recursive calls made plus the number of unwindings versus the number of tail-recursive calls. When processing larger lists, the performance benefits of accumulator-passing style begin to shine brighter than it may originally appear. Of course, accumulator-passing style functions, in general, should be written with a helper function to accommodate the additional passed parameter(s) so as to not burden the function caller with remembering their initial values. Another amazing property of tail recursive functions is their direct correspondence to iterative structures, e.g., loops. Any tail recursive function may be converted into a function that uses some loop, bypassing the need for recursion at all.

Continuation-Passing Style

Before we gravitate into a discussion on continuations and the need for continuation-passing style as a whole, let us begin with a motivating example. Suppose we have the following function that computes the product of a list of numbers (assuming that an empty list returns 1):

Listing 7.81

```
(define product-lon
 (λ (ls)
  (cond
   [(null? ls) 1]
   [else (* (first ls) (product-lon (rest ls)))])))
```

This works as intended, but what happens if one of our elements is a zero? The entire product resolves to zero, of course! The core issue is slightly less subtle, however: when we encounter a zero, the product of the remaining numbers in the list is still computed, despite it always resulting in zero. What if there was a way to circumvent this issue? In C, for instance, we have explicit return statements that terminate a procedure early.[1]

Listing 7.82

```
1  long double product-lon(long double *lon, size_t n) {
2    long double product = 1;
3    for (int i = 0; i < n; i++) {
4      if (0 == lon[i]) { return 0; }
5      else { product = product * lon[i]; }
6    }
7    return product;
8  }
```

We check to see if the current element is zero and, if so, immediately return 0 thereby cancelling the rest of the loop. We are, sadly, not afforded this luxury in our languages. A curious reader may pose the following question: "Could we not just add an additional cond clause to the mix that resolves to zero if the *first* of lon is 0?" For instance, suppose we made the following alteration:

Listing 7.83

```
(define product-lon
 (λ (ls)
  (cond
   [(null? ls) 1]
   [(zero? (first ls)) 0]
   [else (* (first ls) (product-lon (rest ls)))])))
```

Would this not work as intended? While it would allow us to break out of the current recursive step, it would do nothing to prevent the unnecessary recursive unwinding. This alternative base case is treated identically to the null? base case, meaning that when it is reached, the program unwinds the recursion up to that point if it exists (which, for our example, clearly does!). Continuations allow us to implement this behavior.

A *continuation* is, in effect, the next "step" of a computation. More specifically, it denotes where the result of a previous computation is sent. So, using the word in its definition, it allows us to see where we continue evaluation. Continuations are somewhat meaningless without the notion of *continuation-passing style*. A function written in CPS receives one extra argument: a continuation k, which is sent the result of a computation.[2] Let us write a very simple example where we convert addition into continuation-passing style.

---

[1] Instead of using a recursive algorithm, we will use the iterative approach since it is simpler to implement and understand in a C context.

[2] We intentionally do not further elaborate on the continuation representation.

Suppose we have a binary function add that we want to convert to continuation-passing style.

Listing 7.84

```
(define add
 (λ (n m)
  (+ n m)))
```

The first step is to rename the function with an affixed -cps. This is not mandatory, but it helps to distinguish it from its non-CPS'd counterpart:

Listing 7.85

```
(define add-cps
 (λ (n m)
  (+ n m)))
```

Next, we must add an extra formal parameter to the function: the continuation k:

Listing 7.86

```
(define add-cps
 (λ (n m k)
  (+ n m)))
```

Finally, everywhere there exists a "simple" operator we wrap in an invocation to k. For the time being, we assume that continuations are functions:

Listing 7.87

```
(define add-cps
 (λ (n m k)
  (k (+ n m))))
```

So, what exactly is going on in this example? We add the numbers n and m and send the result of the computation to the continuation k. The question that is likely on everyone's mind at this point is, "What *is* the continuation?". The answer is *anything*! An answer like this is somewhat disappointing since it may not clarify anything, but let us continue with the example and see if it fills in the gaps.

We want to designate the *empty continuation*, i.e., the "base" continuation. This continuation, since we are using a functional representation of continuations, is just the identity function.

Listing 7.88

```
(define empty-k
 (λ ()
  (λ (v) v)))
```

So, when we invoke empty-k, we receive a function whose input is echoed back out. Let us see what this looks like in the context of our add-cps function. Recall that it now takes three arguments: two numbers and a continuation. Upon its invocation, we supply said numbers and the empty continuation.

Listing 7.89

```
(define add-cps
 (λ (n m k)
  (k (+ n m))))

(define empty-k
 (λ ()
  (λ (v) v)))

> (add-cps 5 10 (empty-k))                    15
```

Let us magnify this a bit to see how it works. Invoking add-cps resolves its arguments as follows:

Listing 7.90

```
(add-cps 5 10 (λ (v) v))
((λ (v) v) (+ 5 10))
((λ (v) v) 15)
15
```

Invoking (empty-k) evaluates to the identity function. Therefore passing the expression (+ 5 10) resolves to itself, which reduces to 15.

An example with only addition is not very fun nor enlightening, so let us now apply our knowledge to the original problem. We want to bail out of the product-lon function early. We can implement this behavior by sending a value to a continuation which, in effect, breaks the chain of recursive calls and prevents unwinding. Recall that a continuation is the next step of a computation, or the next thing to do, so to speak. When invoking a continuation, everything, i.e., function invocations, etc., performed before the continuation is stopped. Therefore, this behavior is exactly what we are after—if we encounter a 0 in our list of numbers, we know that the product can never not be zero from that point forward, meaning that we should simply invoke the continuation with 0. Let us start by converting our product-lon function into continuation-passing style:

Listing 7.91

```
(define product-lon-cps
 (λ (ls k)
  (cond
   [(null? ls) ...]
   [(zero? (first ls)) ...]
   [else ...])))
```

We took the liberty of affixing -cps to the function name as well as adding k to the formal parameter list. Now, we have three cases; the first two of which are trivial. Numbers are "simple", meaning that all we need to do is invoke the continuation in these cases.

Listing 7.92

```
(define product-lon-cps
 (λ (ls k)
  (cond
   [(null? ls) (k 1)]
   [(zero? (first ls)) (k 0)]
   [else ...])))
```

The recursive case, unfortunately, is not "simple". A characteristic (and, by definition, a **requirement**) of all functions written in continuation-passing style is that they are **tail recursive**, akin to accumulator-passing style. With this in mind, let us write the corresponding skeleton code:

Listing 7.93

```
(define product-lon-cps
 (λ (ls k)
  (cond
   [(null? ls) (k 1)]
   [(zero? (first ls)) (k 0)]
   [else (product-lon-cps (rest ls) ...)]))))
```

The first **argument**, ls, is the same as before, meaning we pass the *rest* of ls. Our second argument, i.e., the continuation, is more complex. Recall that we assume our continuation representation are functions of one argument. This assumption allows us to write more into the skeleton. The second argument is a function of one argument, say v:

Listing 7.94

```
(define product-lon-cps
 (λ (ls k)
  (cond
   [...]
   [else (product-lon-cps
          (rest ls)
          (λ (v)
           ...))]))))
```

What is v, one should ask? It is the result of computing (product-lon-cps (rest ls)). Therefore, whatever result is returned from this recursive function invocation is "stored" in v. Remember that k is a function and, by invoking it, we pass the argument *to* the function. In all cases aside from the empty continuation, this will be the (λ (v) ...) function we declare. So, what do we do with v? Well, what does the original function do? We multiply the result of the recursive call (which in this instance is v) with the *first* of ls, and we can do the same thing here!

Listing 7.95

```
(define product-lon-cps
 (λ (ls k)
  (cond
   [...]
   [else (product-lon-cps
          (rest ls)
          (λ (v)
           (* v (first ls))))]))))
```

Are we **done** yet? Almost! We absolutely must not forget to apply k to the result of the **passed** continuation function. Otherwise, the correct result will never be computed and sent to future continuations. Remember that we can only apply the continuation to "simple" values. Fortunately, a multiplication * is simple, so we are safe to **invoke** the continuation on the result:

Listing 7.96

```
(define product-lon-cps
 (λ (ls k)
  (cond
   [(null? ls) (k 1)]
   [(zero? (first ls)) (k 0)]
   [else (product-lon-cps
          (rest ls)
          (λ (v)
           (k (* v (first ls)))))])))
```

Invoking our function with the empty continuation from before gives us delightful (albeit predictable) results:

Listing 7.97

```
> (product-lon-cps                                   0
   '(5 8 0 17 2 1 8 2 8 1 27 81 82 72 27 17 61 623)
   (empty-k))
> (product-lon-cps                                   20646452185344
   '(73 81 62 83 76 18 62 8)
   (empty-k))
```

This looks identical to what it would look like if we did not bother with continuations and continuation-passing style. Indeed, the output perfectly mirrors said counterpart. What is obscured by our changes, however, is the performance gain when using very large lists or lists that have, say, a zero near the front of the list.

Practicality of Continuation-Passing Style

We now present another topic that benefits from continuation-passing style semantics: exceptions. Consider the following function to divide a number n by m:

Listing 7.98

```
(define divide
 (λ (n m)
  (/ n m)))
```

Of course, if we set $m = 0$, the program crashes because dividing by zero is undefined. Though, what if we did not want the program to crash? We may, instead, want to return a message to the programmer. We could, therefore, implement the following code:

Listing 7.99

```
(define divide-or-error
 (λ (n m)
  (cond
   [(zero? m) "div/0"]
   [else (/ n m)])))
```

While this solves our problem, it is a bit cumbersome. Furthermore, it now carries an assumption that the programmer must deal with: if the function has an error, it returns a string. Otherwise, a number is returned. It would be nice to give the function caller a say in how errors are handled. This is, again, where we may use continuations. Imagine that we have two different "pipelines", so to speak, where we dedicate the former pipeline for errors and the latter for "successful" functions, i.e., those that do not error. We have seen that we can pass values to continuations, so we can implement these pipelines as continuations! Thus, if a function errors, it sends a value to the "error continuation" and otherwise sends the function result to the "success continuation". Let us rewrite the function using these ideas:

Listing 7.100

```
(define divide-or-error
 (λ (n m err-k succ-k)
  (cond
   [(zero? m) (err-k "div/0")]
   [else (succ-k (/ n m))])))
```

Then, we may invoke the function with continuations (as functions themselves) that handle received values differently. For instance, if the function sends a value to the error continuation, we may want to print it using `printf`. On the other hand, if the function does not error, we should just resolve to the value itself.

Listing 7.101

```
> (divide-or-error 5 0              | "ERR: div/0"
   (λ (err) (printf "ERR: ~a~n" err))  |
   (λ (succ) succ))                    |
> (divide-or-error 66.5 7           | "9.5"
   (λ (err) (printf "ERR: ~a~n" err))  |
   (λ (succ) succ))                    |
```

We could wrap this behavior in another function, e.g., `divide`, that abstracts away the explicit continuation definitions.

Listing 7.102

```
(define divide
 (λ (n m)
  (divide-or-error n m
   (λ (err) (printf "ERR: ~a~n" err))
   (λ (succ) succ))))
```

Aside from programming language constructs such as exception-handling, is there another reason why converting functions into continuation-passing style is worth the hassle? Of course; any function can be converted into continuation-passing style. Consequently, a CPS'd function is in tail position. We can eliminate tail calls as a form of program optimization, whose benefits shall soon become apparent.

Exercise 7.26. (★★★)

Properties of functions are sometimes deterministic, and other times not. In general, though, it is impossible to write an algorithm that solves non-trivial semantic properties of functions.[1] Fortunately for us, determining if a (simple) function is tail-recursive is neither non-trivial nor a semantic property! Write the `tail-recursive?` predicate that determines whether a quoted function is tail-recursive. Account for cond, if, lambda, zero?, add1, sub1, as well as the two-argument + and * functions. You may assume that the expression mimics a locally-recursive function definition. We present a few examples to guide your design.

Listing 7.103

```
(define f1
 '(! (lambda (n)
     (cond
       [(zero? n) 1]
       [else (* n (! (sub1 n)))])))))

(define f2
 '(!-tr (lambda (n acc)
       (cond
         [(zero? n) acc]
         [else (!-tr (sub1 n) (* n acc))])))))

(define f3
 '(fib (lambda (n)
       (cond
         [(zero? n) 0]
         [(zero? (sub1 n)) 1]
         [else (+ (fib (sub1 n))
                 (fib (sub1 (sub1 n))))])))))

> (tail-recursive? f1)                                    #f
> (tail-recursive? f2)                                    #t
> (tail-recursive? f3)                                    #f
```

A Flavor of Tail-Call Optimization

We have discussed both accumulator-passing and continuation-passing styles, but why not put them to use? In this section, we will explore the need for accumulator-passing style and how it plays a role in *tail-call optimization*.

---

[1] All thanks to Henry Gordon Rice.

We now understand why tail recursion is significant when dealing with recursive functions, so what if we simply translate every function that uses non-tail recursion into ones that do use tail recursion? This is possible and many compilers/implementations do this, but it is quite complicated. Moreover, the manual translation of a large function may drastically increase in complexity when converting it to its tail recursive counterpart. Fortunately, in "real" Scheme implementations, tail-call optimization is a requirement, which means the procedure call stack will never overflow from a function that otherwise might (e.g., from a non-tail recursive function use). Our interpreter does not use tail recursion nor does it perform any optimizations to do such. This, unfortunately, implies that writing a function that uses tail recursion in our language poses minimal performance benefits.[1] Consider the following recursive trivial recursive implementation of the factorial function; testing this function on a small number produces expected results. Though, if we try a rather large number, e.g., 15000, gives us a segmentation fault.

Listing 7.104

```
(define !
 (λ (n)
  (if (zero? n)
      1
      (* n (! (- n 1)))))))

> (! 5)                                 120
> (! 15000)                             Segmentation fault.
```

First, we need to know *why* this segmentation faults with a large number as input. Let us look at the Valgrind output to determine the problem:[2]

```
==93175== Stack overflow in thread #1: can't grow stack to 0x1ffe801000
==93175==
==93175== Process terminating with default action of signal 11 (SIGSEGV)
==93175== Access not within mapped region at address 0x1FFE801E60
==93175== Stack overflow in thread #1: can't grow stack to 0x1ffe801000
==93175== at 0x495EE6C: ??? (in /usr/lib/aarch64-linux-gnu/libgmp.so.10.4.1)
==93175== If you believe this happened as a result of a stack
==93175== overflow in your program's main thread (unlikely but
==93175== possible), you can try to increase the size of the
==93175== main thread stack using the --main-stacksize= flag.
```

Valgrind states that the interpreter crashed, most likely, due to a stack overflow. Recursive functions written in a non-tail recursive manner push activation records, continuously, onto the call stack. There is a limit to how many activation records can go on the call stack at a time. So, rewriting ! into t-tr is as follows:

---

[1] Testing the recursive versus tail recursive factorial functions prove to show a difference in favor of the tail recursive solution by only a few milliseconds.

[2] Valgrind is a program that allows programmers to debug C memory problems and crashes.

Listing 7.105

```
(define !-tr
  (λ (n)
    (!-tr-helper n 1)))

(define !-tr-helper
  (λ (n acc)
    (if (zero? n)
        acc
        (!-tr-helper (sub1 n)
                     (* n acc)))))

> (!-tr 5)                        120
> (!-tr 15000)                    2746599...
> (!-tr 30000)                    Segmentation fault.
```

Sadly, this also causes a stack overflow, albeit allowing for a slightly higher input value, as we see that the second test case works. What is the problem? Our interpreter is written in such a way that does not account for tail recursive functions. Recall how the function `eval_application` works: we recursively evaluate the arguments to a function, then recursively evaluate the function body. The last sentence is the issue we need to resolve. Let us take this one step at a time, however, and analyze a very small interpreted language: one that supports global definitions, `if`, and non-variadic function application. We, of course, need to allow numbers, booleans, and symbols.

The reason we care about tail-call optimization in the first place is that we can represent tail recursive function calls as infinite loops! That is, instead of recursing on the body of the function upon function application, why not create some global static variables that keep track of the current expression to evaluate? Namely, if we create two pointers: `ast *` and `struct environment *env`, we can continuously reassign them when evaluating.

Listing 7.106—Creating Global Variables for TCO (`eval.c`)

```
1   static ast *ast_out = NULL;
2   static struct environment *env_out = NULL;
```

From here, we need to update `eval_application` to assign values to the global "out" variables. Again, these designate the "next" abstract syntax tree and environment to evaluate in a non-recursive context.

Listing 7.107 (`eval.c`)

```
1    static struct sval *eval_application(ast *application,
2                                         struct environment *env) {
3      ...
4      if (SVAL_BUILTIN == function->type) {
5        result = apply(function, arguments, num_args, env);
6      } else {
7        ast_out = function->data.proc->body;
8        env_out = environment_extend(function->data.proc->env, function, arguments);
9      }
10     ...
11   }
```

Inside the root `eval` function, we first wrap the body inside an infinite loop:

Listing 7.108—Adding Infinite Loop to Root Evaluation (eval.c)

```
1   static struct sval *eval(ast *expr, struct environment *env) {
2     while (true) {
3       ...
4       else {
5         EPF("eval: Unknown ast: %p, tag: %s\n", expr, ast_tag(expr));
6         exit(EXIT_FAILURE);
7       }
8     }
9   }
```

Up next we reassign the expr and env arguments in the root evaluation function. This presents an issue, though: eval_application returns an s-value whenever we apply a builtin function and NULL otherwise. The solution is to return said s-value if and only if it is non-NULL.

Listing 7.109 (eval.c)

```
1    static struct sval *eval(ast *expr, struct environment *env) {
2      while (true) {
3        ...
4        else if (ast_is_type(expr, "application")) {
5          struct sval *sv = eval_application(expr, env);
6          if (NULL != sv) { return sv; }
7          else {
8            expr = ast_out;
9            env = env_out;
10         }
11       }
12       ...
13     }
14   }
```

It is tempting to try out the tail recursive factorial program now, but there is another issue: special forms may or may not return NULL with this setup! Namely, eval_if no longer return a meaningful s-value since we assign ast_out to be either the consequent or alternative abstract syntax tree. To account for all special forms, we should create a global static flag cont that, when enabled, continues the loop and, when disabled, returns the provided s-value. We need to always disable the flag after the NULL check.

Listing 7.110 (eval.c)

```
1   static bool cont = false;
2   ...
3   static struct sval *eval(ast *expr, struct environment *env) {
4     while (true) {
5       ...
6       else if (ast_is_type(expr, "application")) {
7         struct sval *sv = eval_application(expr, env);
8         if (NULL != sv || !cont) { return sv; }
9         else {
10          expr = ast_out;
11          env = env_out;
12        }
13        cont = false;
14      }
15      ...
16    }
17  }
18
19  static struct sval *eval_if(ast *ifc, struct environment *env) {
20    struct sval *predicate_value = eval(ast_child(ifc, IF_PREDICATE_IDX), env);
21    bool pv = predicate_value->data.boolean;
22    ast_out = ast_child(ifc, pv ? IF_CONSEQUENT_IDX : IF_ALTERNATE_IDX);
23    cont = true;
24    return NULL;
25  }
```

Finally, we must disable the flag if we apply a builtin function and enable it otherwise. Returning an s-value after applying a builtin function is never NULL unless an error occurs.

Listing 7.111 (eval.c)

```
1   static struct sval *eval_application(ast *application,
2                                        struct environment *env) {
3     ...
4     struct sval *result = NULL;
5     if (SVAL_BUILTIN == function->type) {
6       cont = false;
7       result = apply(function, arguments, num_args, env);
8     } else {
9       cont = true;
10      env_out = environment_extend(...);
11      ast_out = function->data.proc->body;
12    }
13
14  }
```

And that is it! We now have an interpreter that respects tail recursion. We did not have to modify the signatures for any functions at all. Let us write an infinite recursive "loop" function as an example of our not-so-difficult work.

Listing 7.112

```
(define inf
(λ ()
 (inf)))
```

Of course, this never terminates.[1] In the old implementation, this would quickly result in a segmentation fault. Trying a very large input on the tail recursive factorial function also no longer immediately segfaults.

---

[1] It does eventually crash because we are liberal with how we free dynamic memory.

Exercise 7.27. (★★)
Implement tail-call optimization for cond expressions.

Exercise 7.28. (★★)
Implement tail-call optimization for let, let*, and letrec expressions.

Environment Memoization

In the previous section we implemented tail-call optimization for function applications, leaving conditionals and local bindings as exercises. One thing to note is that our program does eventually crash with a SIGSEGV. We exemplify this with the inf program from before.

Listing 7.113

```
(define inf
 (λ ()
  (inf)))

> (inf)                                      SIGSEGV
```

The reason this occurs, as our footnote stated, is because we constantly allocate memory. Though, it is somewhat unclear as to where this occurs. Upon investigation, we notice that, whenever we call a function, we extend the environment to include new formal parameter bindings. This is fine for most functions, but consider what happens if the arguments do not change in between recursive calls? Would it not be more efficient to "share" environments rather than creating one that is exactly the same as a previous function call? Indeed, this is the case. Though, to do so, we need two important details: how to compare s-values and environments for equality.

S-value equality requires checking both s-value types and their internal values. We have functions/operators to compare characters, booleans, numbers, and strings/symbols, so the only s-value type we must consider is SVAL_PAIR. Two pairs are equivalent if both their *first* and *rest* are equivalent. Note that we implemented almost this exact behavior when adding eqv? to our language; the difference being that sval_equals only returns a bool rather than a boolean s-value and for comparing exactly two s-values.

Listing 7.114—S-Value Equality (sval.c)

```
1   bool sval_equals(struct sval *sv1, struct sval *sv2) {
2     if ((NULL == sv1) ^ (NULL == sv2)) { return false; }
3     else if (sv1->type != sv2->type) { return false; } else {
4       switch (sv1->type) {
5         case SVAL_NUMBER:
6           return bignum_equal(sv1->data.number, sv2->data.number);
7         case SVAL_SYMBOL:
8           return 0 == strcmp(sv1->data.symbol, sv2->data.symbol);
9         case SVAL_BOOLEAN:
10          return sv1->data.boolean == sv2->data.boolean;
11        case SVAL_CHARACTER:
12          return sv1->data.character == sv2->data.character;
13        case SVAL_STRING:
14          return 0 == strcmp(sv1->data.string, sv2->data.string);
15        case SVAL_PAIR:
16          if (NULL == sv1->data.pair.first && NULL == sv2->data.pair.first) {
17            return true;
18          } else if (sval_equals(sv1->data.pair.first, sv2->data.pair.first)) {
19            return sval_equals(sv1->data.pair.rest, sv2->data.pair.rest);
20          } else {
21            return false;
22          }
23        default:
24          return false;
25      }
26    }
27  }
```

In comparing memoized environment bindings, we only want to check if the memoized environment *itself* is equal to the new formal parameter bindings made by the recursive call. Recall that environment_lookup recursively checks its parent environment is a binding is not found. The solution is to write a helper function environment_lookup_one that searches only the provided environment for a binding. With this, we can rewrite environment_lookup to invoke this procedure.

Listing 7.115—Refactoring Environment Lookup Functions (env.c)

```
1   struct sval *environment_lookup(struct environment *env, const char *key) {
2     struct sval *value = environment_lookup_one(env, key);
3     if (NULL == value && NULL != env) {
4       return environment_lookup(env->parent, key);
5     } else {
6       return value;
7     }
8   }
9   ...
10  static struct sval *environment_lookup_one(struct environment *env,
11                                             const char *key) {
12    if (NULL == env) { return NULL; }
13    for (struct env_pair *curr = env->head; NULL != curr; curr = curr->next) {
14      if (streq(curr->key, key)) { return curr->value; }
15    }
16    return NULL;
17  }
```

Now that we have environment_lookup_one, we can write a function to compare an environment *e* against the formal parameters to a function *f*. We can memoize the environment to a function's formal parameters and new argument bindings if

1. The environment *e* has bindings to all of the formal parameters of *f* and only those formal parameters.

2. The environment e's bindings are equal to f's given arguments.

Listing 7.116—Memoized Environment Equality (env.c)

```
1   static bool environment_equals(struct environment *e, struct sval *f,
2                               struct sval **args) {
3     if (NULL == e) { return false; }
4     struct procedure *proc = f->data.proc;
5     if (e->num_associations != proc->num_formals) { return false; }
6     ...
7   }
```

There is one additional problem we must account for: procedure differentiation. If one procedure calls another procedure that has the same environment bindings, then the environment memoizer will assume it is the same procedure as before and erroneously return the memoized environment. The easy solution is twofold: store the previously-called procedure alongside the memoized environment and check to determine if the one passed to environment_extend is (via pointer comparison) the memoized procedure.

Listing 7.117—Environment Extension Modifications (env.c)

```
1   struct environment *environment_extend(struct environment *e, struct sval *f,
2                               struct sval **args) {
3     // Determine if the parent has the same bindings as the new env.
4     if (procedure->data.proc == memo.proc
5      && environment_equals(memo.menv, procedure, arguments)) {
6       return memo.menv;
7     }
8     struct environment *new_env = environment_create(parent);
9     struct procedure *proc = procedure->data.proc;
10
11    // Copy formals over.
12    for (int i = 0; i < proc->num_formals; i++) {
13      environment_put(new_env, proc->formals[i], arguments[i]);
14    }
15    memo.menv = new_env;
16    memo.proc = proc;
17    return new_env;
18  }
```

And voilà, we have an interpreter that can run truly infinite programs without segmentation faulting or receiving a kill signal. The obvious disadvantage to this approach is that we can only infinitely recurse on functions whose arguments are constant.

7.6   Nested Interpreters

Right now, we have written several interpreters in C to parse and evaluate a subset of the Scheme programming language. Now, because our language is powerful enough, we will move away from writing in C to writing in the language of our latest interpreter to write an interpreter! This may seem like madness, but worry not, we will start out small.

First off, how can we even evaluate expressions in our interpreter? Do we not need a complex lexer and parser? As a matter of fact, we have all the necessary ingredients to parse complicated programs already available. Imagine we have a function called value-of, which computes the value of (hence the name!) some arbitrary expression. What would that function look like? Or, more importantly, what would the input data look like? We have a representation of storing an indeterminate number of items: lists. If we wanted to compute the value of, e.g., '(3 + 4), what would we do? Well, we might start by extracting each piece of the list into variables.

Listing 7.118

```
(define input '(3 + 4))
(let ([lhs-rand (first input)]
      [rator (second input)]
      [rhs-rand (third input)])
  ...)
```

Extracting an element via first is familiar, but what are second and third? Each is a mere composition of first and rest. Thus, (second ls) is equivalent to (first (rest ls)), and (third ls) is equivalent to (first (rest (rest ls))). This allows us to extract specific elements from a list of determined values. At this point, we may be tempted to apply the rator to the arguments lhs-rand and rhs-rand. Though, we need to stop and think about what we are evaluating. Right now, rator is *not* a procedure; it is a symbol inside a list. We need a method of mapping between symbols and corresponding procedures. For example, we want to be able to map the symbol '+ to the procedure +. Fortunately, we can achieve this via association lists. In Chapter 5, we discussed association lists as a representation for environments, and we will use them here as our environment representation (for the time being, our environments will not be representation independent). Thus, we can create an environment e_0 to contain a list of *cons* pairs, where the *first* is the symbol, and the *rest* is the associated primitive procedure. For the moment, we will define the global environment as containing the primitive operations for addition and subtraction. To maintain representation independence, we should design extend-env and empty-env alongside the global environment:

Listing 7.119

```
(define extend-env
 (λ (x arg env)
  (cons (cons x arg) env)))

(define empty-env
 (λ ()
  `()))

(define global-env
 (extend-env '+ +
  (extend-env '- -
   (empty-env))))
```

The *cons* pairs denote that the *first* represents the symbol to search for in the environment, and the *rest* is the its bound value. In the case of '+ and '-, the bound values are the addition and subtraction procedures respectively. Now, we need a function to lookup the value of symbol in the environment. Suppose we call this function apply-env, which receives two arguments: a symbol to lookup, v, and an environment, env. apply-env recursively searches the environment for a *cons* pair *p* where the *first* of *p* matches v. If one exists, we return the rest of the first of the pair, i.e., the corresponding mapped value. Note that, because we are using *cons* pairs, we do not need to wrap the rest invocation in a call to first.

Listing 7.120

```
(define apply-env
 (λ (v env)
  (cond
   [(null? env) 'error]
   [(eqv? (first (first env)) v) (rest (first env))]
   [else (apply-env v (rest env))]))))
```

We are on our way there! Let us continue by writing some of the value-of procedure. Some expressions are simple and do not require further evaluation, e.g., numbers. Symbols need to be resolved/looked up in the environment.

Listing 7.121

```
(define value-of
 (λ (expr env)
  (cond
   [(number? expr) expr]
   [(symbol? expr) (apply-env expr env)]
   [else 'error])))
```

Interestingly enough, this interpreter, as it stands, is all that is necessary to write a *very* simple program; one that outputs the same number that it is provided. This is rather boring; why not spice it up by adding arithmatic expressions?

Listing 7.122

```
> (value-of '5 global-env)                    5
```

Recognizer and Reducer Functions

We classify a *nested interpreter* as an interpreter for a language specification that we write in the language *of* our interpreter.[1] The languages that we have been designing so far use the fancy $\mathcal{L}$ with a subscript serving as the name of the language (extension). Nested interpreters also use subscript identifiers, but include a superscript asterisk, i.e., $\mathcal{L}^*$. In essence, any and all code written for these languages is nested inside the C-written interpreter, hence its name.

The nested interpreters that we will design throughout the rest of this book, in general, utilize two categorizations of functions: recognizers and reducers. A *recognizer function*, or recognition function, is a predicate that determines whether a given expression resembles a form. For example, to determine if an arbitrary s-expression is a prefixed binary addition operator, we can design the recognizer add?, which verifies that the s-expression is a list containing three elements, and its *first* is the '+ symbol.

Listing 7.123—Example of add? *Recognizer Function*

```
(define add?
 (λ (exp)
  (and (cons? exp)
       (= (length exp) 3)
       (eqv? (first exp) '+))))
```

Every recognizer function has an accompanying reducer function that describes how to process or evaluate the form determined by the recognizer. In the add example, we may write the value-of-add reducer to add its two components together. Note that we often recursively evaluate components of a form via a root reduction dispatch function, such as value-of. We also extract the form components into local variables to aid in our discussion of the reducer.

Listing 7.124—Example of value-of-add *Reducer Function*

```
(define value-of-add
 (λ (exp)
  (let ([lhs (value-of (second exp))]
        [rhs (value-of (third exp))])
   (+ lhs rhs))))
```

Recognition and reduction functions go hand-in-hand, and we will generally combine them into one listing (frame) to condense the vertical space as necessary. Recognition functions will always have the name <name?> whereas reducers will always have the name <value-of-name>.

---

[1] John Reynolds uses the term "definitional interpreter" to illustrate the same concepts [Reynolds, 1972].

$\mathcal{L}^*_{\text{INFIX}}$: An Infix Calculator

A few chapters ago, we began our journey by exploring prefix arithmetic expressions. In this and subsequent sections, we will begin our journey of writing interpreters within our interpreter. Each interpreter will have a suffixed asterisk (*) to designate that it is a *nested interpreter*. So, in this section, we will write $\mathcal{L}^*_{\text{INFIX}}$: a language to parse simple binary infix expressions.

In the previous section, we implied that some readers may feel inclined to define three variables for the three components of an infix binary operator, those being the lhs-rand, rator, and rhs-rand. Interestingly enough, this is part of what we need to do in order to parse infix expressions. First, we have to be able to recognize a binary infix expression. A binary infix expression contains the three aforementioned components in a list, and the rator is a symbol. We can write a function, e.g., binop? to test if an expression is a binary infix expression. We will need to write a helper function, length, to compute the length of a list. We also need to write and define second, and third (which we will omit in the listings). All that is remaining is evaluation of a binary infix expression. Similar to those interpreters we have written in C, as a function application, we evaluate the arguments before applying. So, let us write a function, e.g., value-of-binop, which receives an expression and an environment, and evaluates the arguments then applies the respective binary operator. Following these additions, we should create a few relevant test cases.

Listing 7.125

```
(define binop?                          (define value-of-binop
  (λ (expr)                               (λ (expr env)
    (and (cons? expr)                       (let ([lhs-rand (first expr)]
         (= (length expr) 3)                      [rator (second expr)]
         (symbol? (second expr)))))             [rhs-rand (third expr)])
                                            ((value-of rator env)
                                             (value-of lhs-rand env)
                                             (value-of rhs-rand env)))))
```

Listing 7.126

```
(define value-of
  (λ (expr env)
    (cond
      [(number? expr) (value-of-number expr)]
      [(symbol? expr) (apply-env expr env)]
      [(binop? expr) ...]
      [else 'error])))
```

Listing 7.127

```
> (value-of '(3 + 4) global-env)                    7
> (value-of '((3 + 4) + (9 - 6)) global-env)        10
```

Is this not absolutely invigorating? We have written a series of (increasingly-difficult) interpreters in C, wherein the last one is now powerful enough that we can write an interpreter within the interpreter.

Exercise 7.29. (⋆⋆⋆⋆⋆)

In many instances, infix expressions come across as intuitive to those of us who use them regularly compared to prefix, as we have demonstrated. Though, one downside of $\mathcal{L}^*_{\text{INFIX}}$ is its requirement of parentheses to force precedence and associativity. Modify $\mathcal{L}^*_{\text{INFIX}}$ to allow for expressions that use the following precedence and associativity rules: parenthesized expressions are evaluated first, then exponents, then multiplication/division, and finally addition/subtraction. Multiplication, division, addition, and subtraction are all left-associative, whereas exponents are right-associative. We present some test cases below.

Listing 7.128

```
> (value-of '(2 - 3 - 4 - 5) global-env)              -10
> (value-of '(2 * 4 + 3 * 5 - 9 * 8) global-env)      -49
> (value-of '(2 + 3 * 4 - 5) '() global-env)          9
> (value-of '(1 + 2 + 3 + 4) '() global-env)          10
> (value-of '(2 * 4 + 3 - 5 * 9) global-env)          -34
> (value-of '(2 * (4 * 7 + 5) * 9) global-env)        594
> (value-of '(2 - (4 + 7 + 5) * 9) global-env)        -142
> (value-of '(2 * 4) global-env)                      8
> (value-of '(3 - 9 + 8 - 7 + 6) global-env)          1
```

Hint: write a `flatmap*` function that recursively applies a function f to all sublists of a list *ls*. Take the following invocations for examples of how this function might be used.

Listing 7.129—"Flat Map" Skeleton Code and Examples

```
; A MaybeList is one of:
; - X
; - (cons X MaybeList)

;; flatmap : {X} {Y} [[ListOf X] -> Y]
;;                    [ListOf [MaybeList X]]
;;                    -> [ListOf Y]
;; Applies a function f over lists to a list potential
;; lists. If an element is a sublist, it is flattened
;; and f is applied to it. If an element is any other
;; value, it is copied over to the resulting list.
(define flatmap*
 (λ (f ls)
  (cond
   [(null? ls) ___]
   [(cons? (first ls)) ___]
   [else ___])))

> (flatmap* length '(1 (2) ((3)) (4 ((5 6 7)) 8)))      (1 1 1 3)
> (flatmap* length '(((1 2) 3 (4 ((5) (6)) 7)) 8 9))    (3 8 9)
> (flatmap* length '(1 (((((2 3 4 5) (6)))) 7) 8 9))    (1 2 8 9)
```

$\mathcal{L}^*_{\text{COND}}$: **Booleans and Conditionals**

In this section we will extend $\mathcal{L}^*_{\text{INFIX}}$ to include boolean literals and conditionals via if in the $\mathcal{L}^*_{\text{COND}}$ language.

First, we need a way of recognizing boolean values. So, similar to numbers, we can simply add a clause in value-of that checks to see if a value is a boolean using the predefined predicate. Similar to the number and symbol counterparts, we do not need a recognizer for the primitive boolean type, meaning we just write its reducer.

Listing 7.130

```
(define value-of-boolean
  (λ (expr env)
    expr))
```

After this addition to the root evaluation function, we can now evaluate boolean literals.

Listing 7.131

```
> (value-of '#f global-env)          #f
> (value-of '#t global-env)          #t
```

Now that our nested interpreter understands boolean values, let us switch our interpreter to use prefixed expressions instead of infix. In doing this, we will want to redefine our arithmetic expressions. We shall create two procedures for evaluating addition and subtraction of arbitrary numbers. These expressions, therefore, will be of type "add" and "sub" respectively. Each expression consists of an operator and the two operands. Conveniently enough, both decision predicates are almost identical—the only distinction being the predicate name and the symbol to check. Let us also write two reducer functions for computing the value of addition and subtraction expressions.

Listing 7.132

```
(define add?                      (define value-of-add
  (λ (expr)                         (λ (expr env)
    (and (cons? expr)                 (let ([lhs-rand (second expr)]
         (= (length expr) 3)                [rhs-rand (third expr)])
         (eqv? (first expr) '+))))       (+ (value-of lhs-rand env)
                                            (value-of rhs-rand env)))))
```

Listing 7.133

```
(define sub?                      (define value-of-sub
  (λ (expr)                         (λ (expr env)
    (and (cons? expr)                 (let ([lhs-rand (second expr)]
         (= (length expr) 3)                [rhs-rand (third expr)])
         (eqv? (first expr) '-))))       (- (value-of lhs-rand env)
                                            (value-of rhs-rand env)))))
```

Listing 7.134

```
(define value-of
 (λ (expr env)
  (cond
   [(number? expr) (value-of-number expr env)]
   [(symbol? expr) (apply-env expr env)]
   [(boolean? expr) (value-of-boolean expr env)]
   [(add? expr) (value-of-add expr env)]
   [(sub? expr) (value-of-sub expr env)]
   [else 'error])))
```

Now, we can execute a few test cases.

Listing 7.135

```
> (value-of '(- 10 3) global-env)          7
> (value-of '(+ 2 3) global-env)           5
```

With this, we can add a couple of special yet familiar procedures to our interpreter: sub1, add1, and zero?. Their recognition and reducer functions are similar to the binary add and sub functions.

Listing 7.136

```
(define zero?                          (define value-of-zero
 (λ (expr)                              (λ (expr env)
  (and (cons? expr)                      (let ([rand (second expr)])
       (= (length expr) 2)                (= (value-of rand env) 0))))
       (eqv? (first expr) 'zero?))))
```

Listing 7.137

```
(define add1?                          (define value-of-add1
 (λ (expr)                              (λ (expr env)
  (and (cons? expr)                      (let ([rand (second expr)])
       (= (length expr) 2)                (+ (value-of rand env) 1))))
       (eqv? (first expr) 'add1))))
```

Listing 7.138

```
(define sub1?                          (define value-of-sub1
 (λ (expr)                              (λ (expr env)
  (and (cons? expr)                      (let ([rand (second expr)])
       (= (length expr) 2)                (- (value-of rand env) 1))))
       (eqv? (first expr) 'sub1))))
```

Now, all that is left is to add these forms to value-of.

Listing 7.139

```
(define value-of
 (λ (expr env)
  (cond
   [(number? expr) (value-of-number expr env)]
   [(symbol? expr) (apply-env expr env)]
   [(boolean? expr) (value-of-boolean expr env)]
   [(add1? expr) (value-of-add1 expr env)]
   [(sub1? expr) (value-of-sub1 expr env)]
   [(zero? expr) (value-of-zero expr env)]
   [(add? expr) (value-of-add expr env)]
   [(sub? expr) (value-of-sub expr env)]
   [else 'error])))
```

As always, let us test the modifications.

Listing 7.140

> (value-of '(add1 (add1 (add1 (add1 (add1 0))))) global-env)	5
> (value-of '(+ (add1 (add1 10)) (sub1 9)) global-env)	20
> (value-of '(zero? 10) global-env)	#f
> (value-of '(zero? (sub1 (sub1 (sub1 (sub1 4)))) global-env)	#t

Next, we should add support for conditionals. This is simple enough—a conditional in $\mathcal{L}^*_{\text{COND}}$ takes the form of a list where the *first* is if, the *second* is the predicate to test, the *third* is the consequent, and the *fourth* is the alternative. As we did in $\mathcal{L}_{\text{COND3}}$, we first evaluate the predicate and, if it resolves to true, we evaluate the consequent. Otherwise, we evaluate the alternative.

Listing 7.141

```
(define if?                          (define value-of-if
  (λ (expr)                            (λ (expr env)
    (and (cons? expr)                    (let ([predicate (second expr)]
         (= (length expr) 4)                   [consequent (third expr)]
         (eqv? (first expr) 'if))))          [alternative (fourth expr)])
                                         (if (value-of predicate env)
                                             (value-of consequent env)
                                             (value-of alternative env)))))
```

Now, once again, we test.

Listing 7.142

> (value-of '(if (zero? 0) (+ 5 5) (+ 10 10)) global-env)	10
> (value-of '(if (zero? (sub1 (sub1 (+ 1 2)))) 100 200) global-env)	200

$\mathcal{L}^*_{\text{PROC}}$: **Procedures and Variables**

Because the interpreter is rather small, we will limit the scope of procedure and variable definitions by a considerable amount. We define this limit to be a super-set of the λ-calculus. For instance, our interpreter will be able to correctly evaluate the following expressions.

Listing 7.143

```
'((lambda (x) x) 5)

'((lambda (x) (if (zero? x) 20 30)) 0)

'(let ([x 10]) (+ x 20))

'(let ([z 10]) (let ([y 500]) (if (zero? (- y y)) z (add1 z))))
```

So, this means our interpreter should understand lexically-scoped variables via one-binding `let` declarations, and one-argument lambda procedures. Implementing the former is a bit easier than the latter, so we will begin from there.

Recall, from Chapters 5 and 6, the notion of environment extension. When we extend an environment e_0, we create a new environment e_1 which has a pointer to e_0 alongside any new variable bindings (i.e., $e_1 \rightsquigarrow e_0$). So, when we create, for instance, a `let` binding, we create a new environment, then add the variable name and associated value to said environment. In our interpreter, we first want to recognize `let` expressions of one variable binding. A `let` expression has three components: the `let` symbol itself, a variable binding, and the body. Because we want our `let` declarations to mimic ones from our implementing language, the bindings are stored within a list of a list, e.g., ([x 10]). Thus, the symbol to bind is the first of the first of the second, i.e., x, and the expression to evaluate, i.e., 10, then bind to x is the second of the first of the second. A complete example is (let ([x 10]) x). So, let us now write the code for evaluating a `let` expression. We need to evaluate the variable binding expression first, then use that evaluation in the body of the `let`. Furthermore, we need to extend the current environment to support the new variable binding.

Listing 7.144

```
(define let?                          (define value-of-let
  (λ (expr)                             (λ (expr env)
    (and (cons? expr)                     (let* ([lobindings (second expr)]
         (= (length expr) 3)                     [binding (first lobindings)]
         (eqv? (first expr) 'let)               [var (first expr)]
         (symbol?                                [res-var (second expr)]
          (first                                 [body (third expr)])
           (first (second expr))))))))     ...)))
```

We are going to go step-by-step to show exactly what is happening in this evaluation. We first extract the three components of the `let` declaration. Now, we need to evaluate the body in an environment that contains the new symbol. Remember that in Chapters 5 and 6, we introduced extend-env: a procedure to add a new symbol and expression to an environment *as a new environment*. Extending the environment, as we have seen previously, returns a new environment with the appended symbol binding.

Listing 7.145

```
(define value-of-let
 (λ (expr env)
  (let* ([lobindings (second expr)]
         [binding (first lobindings)]
         [var (first expr)]
         [res-var (second expr)]
         [body (third expr)])
   (value-of body (extend-env var (value-of res-var env) env)))))
```

Here's the deal: our environment, right now, uses an association list as its representation. Fortunately, our interpreter is already representation independent because there are no references to environments other than apply-env (which abstracts the code to find a symbol binding). The only thing that is left is to write extend-env and update value-of. We might also consider rewriting global_-env to use extend-env rather than relying on the non-representation-independent association list representation.

Listing 7.146

```
(define extend-env
 (λ (x arg env)
  (cons (cons x arg) env)))

(define value-of
 (λ (expr env)
  (cond
   [...]
   [(let? expr) (value-of-let expr env)]
   [...])))
```

Let us see how the tests that use let fair with our changes.

Listing 7.147

```
> (value-of '(let ([x 10])                  | 30
              (+ x 20))                      |
            global-env)                      |
> (value-of '(let ([z 10])                  | 10
              (let ([y 500])                 |
               (if (zero? (- y y))           |
                   z                         |
                   (add1 z))))               |
            global-env)                      |
```

Awesome! Lexical bindings now work beautifully. Let us now tackle the monster that is lambda procedures (which is not actually a monster).

A lambda procedure has three components akin to let: the lambda symbol, a formal parameter as a list element, i.e., (x), and the body. Let us write the code to determine if an arbitrary expression is a lambda expression.

Listing 7.148

```
(define lambda?
 (λ (expr)
  (and (cons? expr)
       (= (length expr) 3)
       (eqv? (first expr) 'lambda)
       (symbol? (first (second expr))))))
```

Now, we need to write the code for evaluating a `lambda` expression. How do we do this? A `lambda` is a procedure, so it should certainly return one! In this procedure, once invoked, we evaluate the body with respect to the formal parameter. Thus, when the function is invoked, it receives one argument which is then bound, in a new environment, to the listed formal parameter. In the code listing, the argument passed to the `lambda` is `arg`, which is bound to the formal parameter specified by `param`.

Listing 7.149

```
(define value-of-lambda
 (λ (expr env)
  (let* ([loparams (second expr)]
         [param (first loparams)]
         [body (third expr)])
   (λ (arg)
    (value-of body (extend-env param arg env))))))
```

Lastly, we must add function application. There is little use in having lambda functions without any way of invoking them somehow. A function application has two components represented as elements of a list: an operator, or "rator" for short, and an operand, or "rand" for short. A "rator" is either a symbol, a lambda function, or another application (notice the recursive definition). The former is only possible when said symbol is defined as a lambda procedure, e.g., in a lexical scoped environment, i.e., `let`. The "rand" can be any possible value, so long as it is a valid argument to the procedure.

Listing 7.150

```
(define application?
 (λ (expr)
  (and (cons? expr)
       (= (length expr) 2)
       (or (symbol? (first expr))
           (lambda? (first expr))
           (application? (first expr))))))
```

Now to evaluate function applications. Fortunately, this component is significantly easier than the application step in the previous interpreters! All we need to do is evaluate both the "rator" and "rand", then invoke "rator" as a function with "rand" as its argument.

Listing 7.151

```
(define value-of-application
 (λ (expr env)
  (let ([rator (first expr)]
        [rand (second expr)])
   ((value-of rator env) (value-of rand env)))))
```

Tying everything together gets us the following.

Listing 7.152

```
(define value-of
 (λ (expr env)
  (cond
   [...]
   [(lambda? expr) (value-of-lambda expr env)]
   [(application? expr) (value-of-application expr env)]
   [...])))
```

Let us see some test cases! To make things slightly more interesting, we added a binary multiplication operator to $\mathcal{L}^*_{PROC}$.

Listing 7.153

```
> (value-of '((lambda (x) x) 5)                                     5
          global-env)
> (value-of '((lambda (x) (add1 x)) 5)                             6
          global-env)
> (value-of '(let ([! (lambda (x) (* x x))])                       60
          (let ([! (lambda (n)
                  (if (zero? n)
                   1
                   (* n (! (sub1 n)))))])
           (! 5)))
          global-env)
> (value-of '(let ([y (* 3 4)])                                    80
          ((lambda (x) (* x y)) (sub1 6)))
          global-env)
```

This mini-interpreter and $\mathcal{L}^*_{PROC}$ are now so powerful that they recognize and correctly evaluate recursive procedures. How amazing is that?

Representation Independence With Respect to Closures

Our interpreter is representation-independent with respect to environments. That is, the interpreter calls the environment helper functions apply-env, extend-env, and empty-env. Using these functions instead of manipulating/accessing the environment directly allows us greater flexibility in our representation of the environment. At the moment, this is not the case for closures. Closures are created when we declare a lambda function, and are applied when invoking the function, i.e., value-of-lambda and value-of-application respectively. Our current interpreter assumes that closures use a functional representation; value-of-lambda returns a function, and value-of-application applies the evaluated operator onto its evaluated operand. An improved approach is to use representation-independent closures. In this short section, we will implement two helper functions to achieve this goal.

What functions do we need to get representation-independence with respect to closures? Well, there are only two cases in which closures are used: when they are created and when they are applied. So, we should aptly call these create_closure and apply_closure respectively.

`create_closure` receives two arguments: a body and an environment. It is up to the implementation of the closure to decide how it wants to represent the closure. For instance, we may choose to represent it using functions, as we currently do, or we may choose to use a data-structural representation such as a tagged list. To showcase the differences between the two, we shall implement closures with tagged lists. Let us begin by writing the function stub.

Listing 7.154

```
(define create-closure
 (λ (body env)
  ...))
```

Because we choose to represent closures as tagged lists, we create a list whose first element (*first*) is `'create-closure`, whose second element (*second*) is the formal parameter to the closure, whose third element (*third*) is the body to evaluate, and whose fourth element (*fourth*) is the environment to evaluate the closure within. Handily, this is easily doable with quasiquotes.

Listing 7.155

```
(define create-closure
 (λ (x body env)
  `(create-closure ,x ,body ,env)))
```

Now, the "true" wizardry is upon us with `apply-closure`. `apply-closure` receives an operator and an operand. By definition, the operator must be a `create-clo sure` tagged list. Before, the operator must have been a function since we were using a non-representation-independent, functional representation of closures. So, we can extract out the values from the tagged list using a `let`, then evaluate the body with respect to its extended environment. Recall that we have to bind the formal parameter x to the operand passed to `apply-closure`.

Listing 7.156

```
(define apply-closure
 (λ (rator rand)
  (let ([x (second rator)]
        [body (third rator)]
        [env (fourth rator)])
   (value-of body (extend-env x rand env)))))
```

Remember the whole motivation behind representation independence: it is not the job of the interpreter to know *how* we choose to implement environments or closures. That is, it sees these structures as black boxes, accessible or mutable through the helper functions. Therefore, if we decide to change the representation of one or both structures, the interpreter works the same (assuming we correctly implement the underlying representation, of course!). Let us finally add these two functions to the interpreter to make it truly representation-independent. The only two functions we need to update are `value-of-lambda` and `value-of-application`. After doing so, the previous tests should work as expected.

Listing 7.157

```
(define value-of-lambda
  (λ (expr env)
    (let* ([loparam (second expr)]
           [param (first loparam)]
           [body (third expr)])
      (create-closure param body env))))

(define value-of-application
  (λ (expr env)
    (let ([rator (first expr)]
          [rand (second expr)])
      (apply-closure rator rand))))
```

Lexical Scoping Implementation

The previous nested interpreter added local bindings via `let`. Because we continuously pass the environment inside to the expression body, these bindings use lexical scoping. If we want to add recursive bindings via `letrec`, we need to amend our interpreter to explicitly use lexical scoping wherein we return the environment used in the evaluation of an arbitrary expression. This translation propagates through the entire interpreter. So, to pass two values as the result of some evaluation, we use a *cons* pair. Returning pairs from an expression is nothing new, but it is significantly more convenient to update our representation of both closures and environments to work with a similar representation. Closures use a functional representation whereas environments use association lists. We will convert both to use a tagged list representation. Tagged lists are data whose *first* is some identifying "tag", or symbol, denoting the purpose of the list contents. So, in particular, we need to update our definition of `apply-env` to recognize each environment tag and perform the appropriate dispatch. Closures, conveniently, are somewhat simpler compared to their functional counterparts, omitting the need for the additional lambda expression to check for the argument to the closure.

Listing 7.158—Tagged List Representation for Closures and Environments

```
(define empty-env
 (λ ()
  `(empty-env)))

(define extend-env
 (λ (x arg env)
  `(extend-env ,x ,arg ,env)))

(define apply-env
 (λ (y env)
  (let ([tag (first env)])
   (cond
    [(eqv? tag 'empty-env) 'unknown-identifier]
    [(eqv? tag 'extend-env)
     (let ([x (second env)]
           [arg (third env)]
           [env^ (fourth env)])
      (cond
       [(eqv? y x) arg]
       [else (apply-env y env^)]))]
    [else #f]))))

(define make-closure
 (λ (x body env)
  `(make-closure ,x ,body ,env)))

(define apply-closure
 (λ (rator rand env)
  (let ([tag (first rator)])
   (cond
    [(eqv? tag 'make-closure)
     (let ([x (second rator)]
           [body (third rator)]
           [env^ (fourth rator)])
      (value-of body (extend-env x rand env^)))]
    [else #f]))))
```

Now, in the (interpreter) reducer functions, we need to update each place where we return a value to return a *cons* pair whose *first* is the evaluated expression and whose *rest* is the environment in which that expression was evaluated. For certain expressions that recursively call value-of, there is no need to wrap it in such a pair because the resulting expression is *already* wrapped. It is also important to account for the fact that each call to value-of will return a pair, meaning that in cases where said value is significant, e.g., when evaluating (+ x y), x and y are extracted out and used in the subsequent pair. In most cases, the lexically-scoped environment returned is irrelevant, meaning we will omit its extraction. Moreover, because many of these changes are purely mechanical, we will only show a couple of recognizer/reducer pairs.

Listing 7.159—Lexically-Scopifying Our Interpreter

```
(define value-of-number
 (λ (exp env)
  (let ([n exp])
   `(,n . ,env))))

(define value-of-zero?
 (λ (exp env)
  (let ([n (second exp)])
   (let* ([pair-n (value-of n env)] [res-of-n (first pair-n)])
    `(,(= res-of-n 0) . ,env)))))

(define value-of-mul
 (λ (exp env)
  (let ([x (second exp)] [y (third exp)])
   (let* ([pair-x (value-of x env)] [res-of-x (first pair-x)]
          [pair-y (value-of y env)] [res-of-y (first pair-y)])
    `(,(* res-of-x res-of-y) . ,env)))))

(define value-of-if
 (λ (exp env)
  (let ([p (second exp)] [c (third exp)] [a (fourth exp)])
   (let* ([pair-p (value-of p env)] [res-of-p (first pair-p)])
    (if res-of-p
        (value-of c env)
        (value-of a env))))))

(define value-of-let
 (λ (exp env)
  (let ([x (first (first (second exp)))] [binding (second (first (second exp)))] [body (third
        exp)])
   (let* ([pair-binding (value-of binding env)]
          [res-of-binding (first pair-binding)])
    (value-of body (extend-env x res-of-binding env))))))
```

We can throw a few tests at the updated to show its changes. Doing so demonstrates that our result is, of course, a pair. To get the result, all we would need to do is retrieve the *first*. Additionally, we see the tagged list representation in action.[1]

---

[1]Some may question the lack of parentheses upon invoking extend-env for the first time in the tagged list representation. This is because of how we print lists–if the list generated by extend-env ends in the empty list, which it does, then it is treated as *cons*'ing onto a *cons* cell, thus removing parentheses.

Listing 7.160

```
> (value-of '5                             '(5 empty-env)
          (empty-env))

> (value-of '(lambda (x)                   '((make-closure x
             (lambda (y)                       (lambda (y) (+ x y))
                (+ x y)))                      (empty-env))
             (empty-env))                    empty-env)

> (value-of '(((lambda (x)                 '(11 extend-env y 6
              (lambda (y)                     (extend-env x 5 (empty-env)))
                 (+ x y)))
              5)
              6)
             (empty-env))

> (value-of '(let ([add                    '(15 extend-env y 10
                 (lambda (x)                   (extend-env x 5 (empty-env)))
                 (lambda (y)
                    (+ x y)))])
              ((add 5) 10))
             (empty-env))

> (value-of                                '(6 extend-env y 3
  '(let ([f (lambda (x) x)])                  (extend-env
   (let ([g (lambda (y) (+ (f y) 3))])        f
   (let ([f (lambda (z) (+ 3 z))])            (make-closure x x (empty-env))
      (g 3))))                                (empty-env)))
  (empty-env))
```

With this brief detour put to bed, we can now implement `letrec` into our system. This version of `letrec` is harder than the one we defined at the interpreter (C) level because we do not have side-effects in our language. That form of `letrec` declared all variable identifiers in an environment prior to evaluating their respective bindings. As each binding was "uncovered", so to speak, its respective value was changed in the environment via `environment-set!`. We have no such environment alteration capabilities, so we will need another approach. A not-very-well-known but classic method is through "half-closures". Closures, as we know, store an expression to evaluate and the environment in which it was created. The problem with `letrec` is that a binding is allowed to be recursive, meaning that an identifier is referenceable within the binding. Consider the following definition of factorial that uses `letrec`. Note that this code is, at the moment, only executable outside the nested interpreter.

Listing 7.161—Implementation of Factorial using `letrec`

```
> (letrec ([!                              120
           (λ (n)
            (if (zero? n)
              1
              (* n (! (sub1 n)))))])
     (! 5))
```

We somehow need a way of telling our interpreter that `letrec` contains an identifier whose binding is referenced only when it (i.e., the identifier) is referenced.

So, let us first add the recognizer, reducer, and clause to the interpreter for `letrec` expressions. The magic comes not from any of these, but in fact from `apply-env` which we will amend shortly. In writing the corresponding reducer function, we need to communicate to `apply-env` that the environment passed to the `letrec` body evaluation is special since it contains a half-closure. Thus, we will write a `make-letrec-env` function that has a unique tag identifier.

Listing 7.162

```
(define make-letrec-env
  (λ (1/2-closure env)
   `(letrec-env ,1/2-closure ,env)))

(define letrec?
  (λ (exp)
   (and (cons? exp)
        (= (length exp) 3)
        (eqv? (first exp) 'letrec))))

(define value-of-letrec
  (λ (exp env)
   (let ([1/2-closure (second exp)] [body (third exp)])
     (value-of body (make-letrec-env 1/2-closure env)))))

(define value-of
  (λ (exp env)
   (cond
    [...]
    [(letrec? exp) (value-of-letrec exp env)]
    [(application? exp) (value-of-application exp env)]
    [else 'error])))
```

As we said, the heart of the logic lies within `apply-env`. It encompasses three (meaningful) clauses: `empty-env`, `extend-env`, and now `letrec-env`. We first extract the necessary fields from the tagged list. We then retrieve the binding associated with the identifier in the half-closure using `assv` and `second`. This binding is evaluated with respect to the environment referenced by y. Again, because this result is a *cons* value/environment pair, we return the result defined by its *first*.

Listing 7.163

```
(define apply-env
  (λ (y env)
   (let ([tag (first env)])
    (cond
     [...]
     [(eqv? tag 'letrec-env)
      (let* ([1/2-closure (second env)] [env^ (third env)])
       (let* ([p (assv y 1/2-closure)]
              [1/2-closure-binding (second p)]
              [pair-1/2-closure (value-of 1/2-closure-binding env)]
              [res-of-1/2-closure (first pair-1/2-closure)])
        res-of-1/2-closure))]
     [else #f]))))
```

This modification allows us to evaluate the ! expression from before in our nested interpreter.

Listing 7.164

```
> (value-of                                                    120
   '(letrec ([!
             (lambda (n)
               (if (zero? n)
                   1
                   (* n (! (sub1 n)))))])
      (! 5))
   (empty-env))
```

On the other hand, suppose that the half-closure binding is not used recursively. These instances inherently question the use of letrec in the first place. Regardless, our interpreter should appropriately handle such cases as if they were recursive. If we, for example, declare an identifier num to bind the expression 10, the half-closure is ((num 10)). Whenever we reference num in the body of our letrec, we invoke apply-env to see that, of course, the corresponding environment is tagged as make-letrec-env. From there, we evaluate the bound expression with respect to this environment to see that its value is not a closure, but instead a constant paired with a "letrec environment". Note that this idea propagates to defining functions that are not recursive in a letrec environment; the only difference is that instead of a constant being returned from the environment, a closure is returned that is simply not called within its body.

Listing 7.165

```
> (value-of                        '(20
   '(letrec ([num 10])               letrec-env ((num 10)) (empty-env))
      (+ num num))
   (empty-env))
> (value-of                        '(#f extend-env n 71
   '(letrec ([even?                   (letrec-env
             (lambda (n)               ((even?
               (zero?                   (lambda (n)
                 (remainder n 2)))])    (zero?
      (even? 71))                        (remainder n 2)))))
   (empty-env))                       (empty-env)))
```

$\mathcal{L}_{\text{LOOP}}^*$: Iteration Through Obscured Recursion

In this section, we will write $\mathcal{L}_{\text{LOOP}}^*$: an extension to $\mathcal{L}_{\text{PROC}}^*$ that adds a "non-recursive" loop to our language. We say "non-recursive" with quotes because the implementing language, i.e., $\mathcal{L}_{\text{LOOP}}^*$ will use recursion to emulate the loop. In essence, $\mathcal{L}_{\text{LOOP}}^*$ abstracts the recursion away from the programmer.

In Chapter 8, we will explore loops in greater detail in the non-nested interpreter. For the moment, in this section, we will add a special form to our nested interpreter called do. As a look-ahead, the do form in non-functional chapter is significantly easier to digest than the one we are about to implement simply because the capability of our form is limited by our language "toolset".

A do loop is represented as a list with four elements: the first (*first*) is the symbol do, the second (*second*) is a condition c, the third (*third*) is a "step expression" s, and the last (*fourth*) is the body to evaluate. The do loop executes the body until c is false. Each time the loop repeats, we evaluate three expressions in the following order: c, s, and the body. If c is false, neither s nor the body are evaluated. Programming languages with explicit iteration statements, e.g., C, introduce "side-effects", because the last component of a for loop, in most instances, modifies the value of a variable directly. As an example, consider the following loop in C:

Listing 7.166

```
1    for (int i = 10; i > 0; i--) {  ...  }
```

The body of this for loop is irrelevant and is, therefore, grayed out by ellipses. Rather, focus on the last component: i--. Such an expression decrements the value of i by one, then stores it back into i. Because we modify the state of i, we say that the loop has a side-effect. Our language, in its current state, does not have side-effects, so we need to circumvent the problem of explicit variable updates. A simple and effective solution is to shadow variables. Suppose we have the following code:

Listing 7.167

```
(value-of '(let ([i 10])
             (do [(zero? i) 0]
                 (- i 1)
                 (display i)))
          global-env)
```

Notice that we specify four components: the variable declaration, the condition, step, and the loop body expressions. First off, the condition consists of two sub-components: the condition to continue iteration, and the terminating expression. Before executing the loop body, we first evaluate the if which, correspondingly, checks to see if i is zero. When i finally reaches zero, the do expression resolves to the terminating expression, which in this instance is 0. The step expression says that, each time the body of the loop is executed, we decrement i by one. Again, we cannot directly mutate the value of i. So, what we can do is add i with its new value, namely i-1, to the environment, then pass it forward to subsequent expression evaluations.[1] Finally, we evaluate the body of the do expression.

Let us get to work! We must start by writing the code to recognize, or parse, a do expression. Again, the first (*first*) is the do symbol, the second (*second*) is an expression which resolves to true or false, the third (*third*) is an expression that alters the value of some symbol, and the last (*fourth*) is the do-body. Revisiting the expression extracted by *third*, when we say it "alters the value of some symbol", we restrict the possibilities of said expression. Namely, the expression should be a binary operator where the first operand is a symbol and the second is an arbitrary expression. E.g., (+ i 1), (- i 1), and so on.

Listing 7.168

```
(define do?
 (λ (expr)
  (and (cons? expr)
       (= (length expr) 4)
       (eqv? (first expr) 'do)
       (symbol? (sthird expr)))))
```

The last expression in the and chain may look a bit complex, but tracing through a simple do expression will hopefully reduce any induced stress. Now, let us write the accompanying value-of-do. Be warned that this function is more complicated than any form we have seen so far, so we need to take it one step at a time. To start, let us extract the four components from the expression: the condition, the terminating expression, the step, and the body. Then, we certainly need a letrec to simulate the iteration. Within the letrec, we declare a function repeat that is invoked as long as condition resolves to true.

Listing 7.169

```
(define value-of-do
 (λ (expr env)
  (let* ([locondition (second expr)]
         [condition (first locondition)]
         [term (second locondition)]
         [step (third expr)]
         [body (fourth expr)])
   (letrec ([repeat
              (λ (...)
                ...)])
    (repeat ...)))))
```

[1]This code example also integrates display which calls the built-in display function. We omit its implementation due to its simplicity. In essence, all it does is calls sval_tostring on the given argument.

So, what should we pass to repeat? Recall the intended behavior of do: evaluate the condition expression, and as long as it is true, evaluate the body and extend the environment to include the updated step value. If the condition is false, return the terminating expression. So, to keep track of the extended environment, we should pass it as an argument to repeat. But recall that we also want to evaluate the body of the loop. Since we are only allowed one expression in the body of a lambda, we should wrap the invocation of evaluating the body into the recursive call as an argument.

Listing 7.170

```
(define value-of-do
 (λ (expr env)
  (let* ([locondition (second expr)]
         [condition (first locondition)]
         [term (second locondition)]
         [step (third expr)]
         [body (fourth expr)])
   (letrec ([repeat
              (λ (prev-expr prev-env)
                )])
    (repeat body env)))))
```

What is next? We evaluate the condition expression and when it is true, invoke repeat with an evaluated body and extended environment.

Listing 7.171

```
(define value-of-do
 (λ (expr env)
  (let* ([locondition (second expr)]
         [condition (first locondition)]
         [term (second locondition)]
         [step (third expr)]
         [body (fourth expr)])
   (letrec ([repeat
              (λ (prev-expr prev-env)
                (cond
                  [(value-of condition prev-env)
                   (repeat
                    (value-of body prev-env)
                    (extend-env (second step) (value-of step prev-env) prev-env))]
                  [else term]))])
    (repeat body env)))))
```

When extending the environment, we have a couple of guarantees. The first is that step is a list. The second is that step is represented as a binary operator application where the first operand is a symbol. So, we can extract the symbol with second, evaluate the step expression, then store this result into the new environment. This is passed along to the recursive call to repeat for subsequent evaluations. Let us try out the do loop from the preceding example.

Listing 7.172

```
> (value-of '(let ([i 10])          109876543210
              (do [(if (zero? i) #f #t) 0]
                  (- i 1)
                  (display i)))
           global-env)
```

As expected, the loop body outputs the numbers in decreasing order from ten down to one. Then, the loop resolves to 0 once the provided condition is false.

$\mathcal{L}^*_{\text{LOGIC}}$: A Logical Formula Interpreter

In Chapter 2, we introduced propositional logic, namely logical connectives, atoms, satisfiability, and proofs. In this section, we will write $\mathcal{L}^*_{\text{LOGIC}}$: a nested interpreter to parse and evaluate propositional logical expressions.

As a refresher, a propositional logic formula contains connectives and atoms. These connectives include logical conjunction, disjunction, implication, equivalence, and negation. Our connectives will take the form of tagged lists, where the tag is a connective identifier, and the rest of the elements represent propositional formulas. Additionally, atoms will also be tagged lists where the tag is atom. Let us look at a few examples.

Listing 7.173

```
(define p1 `(atom p))
(define p2 `(atom q))
`(and ,p1 ,p2)
`(or ,p1 (atom r))
`(imp ,p2 (not (atom p)))
`(iff (not (and ,p1 ,p2))
      (imp (not ,p2) (not ,p1)))
```

Right now, these formulas are not very interesting because there are no associated truth values. In our previous interpreters, we used environments to store the corresponding values of symbols. In this language, environments will store either #t or #f to each atom as an association list. E.g., suppose we define an environment env as follows.

Listing 7.174

```
(define env `((p . #t) (q . #f) (r . #f)))
```

Let us begin! We will first create the data definition for a schema. Then, we can write the basic evaluator and make the implementation representation-independent.

Listing 7.175

```
; An AtomSchema is an 'atom

; A UnaryConnective is a 'not

; A BinaryConnective is one of:
; - 'and
; - 'or
; - 'imp
; - 'iff

; A Schema is one of:
; - (ListOf AtomSchema Atom)
; - (ListOf UnaryConnective Schema)
; - (ListOf BinaryConnective Schema Schema)

;; value-of : Schema Environment -> Schema
;; Evaluates a zeroth-order logic schema according to an
;; assignment of truth values in the environment.
(define value-of
  (λ (exp env)
    ( ...)))
```

Each logical connective needs a recognition predicate as well as an evaluation procedure. We can go ahead and fill the gaps inside `value-of` to streamline our design.

Listing 7.176

```
(define value-of
 (λ (exp env)
  (cond
   [(negation? exp) (value-of-negation exp env)]
   [(conjunction? exp) (value-of-conjunction exp env)]
   [(disjunction? exp) (value-of-disjunction exp env)]
   [(implication? exp) (value-of-implication exp env)]
   [(biconditional? exp) (value-of-biconditional exp env)]
   [else 'error])))
```

Now let us write the recognition predicates. Again, all we need to do is verify the number of operands and the list tag. Each recognition predicate is almost identical to one another; the only difference being the tag and required list length. After this, we evaluate each of the five connectives according to their logical rules.

Listing 7.177

```
(define negation?
 (λ (exp)
  (and (eqv? (first exp) 'not)
       (= (length exp) 2))))
```

```
(define value-of-negation
 (λ (exp env)
  (let
   ([vexp (value-of (second exp) env)])
   (if vexp #f #t))))
```

Listing 7.178

```
(define conjunction?
 (λ (exp)
  (and (eqv? (first exp) 'and)
       (= (length exp) 3))))
```

```
(define value-of-conjunction
 (λ (exp env)
  (let*
   ([lhs (value-of (second exp) env)]
    [rhs (value-of (third exp) env)])
   (and lhs rhs))))
```

Listing 7.179

```
(define disjunction?
 (λ (exp)
  (and (eqv? (first exp) 'or)
       (= (length exp) 3))))
```

```
(define value-of-disjunction
 (λ (exp env)
  (let*
   ([lhs (value-of (second exp) env)]
    [rhs (value-of (third exp) env)])
   (or lhs rhs))))
```

Listing 7.180

```
(define implication?
 (λ (exp)
  (and (eqv? (first exp) 'imp)
       (= (length exp) 3))))
```

```
(define value-of-implication
 (λ (exp env)
  (let*
   ([lhs (value-of (second exp) env)]
    [rhs (value-of (third exp) env)])
   (or (not lhs) rhs))))
```

Listing 7.181

```
(define biconditional?
 (λ (exp)
  (and (eqv? (first exp) 'iff)
       (= (length exp) 3))))
```

```
(define value-of-biconditional
 (λ (exp env)
  (let*
   ([lhs (value-of (second exp) env)]
    [rhs (value-of (third exp) env)])
   (eqv? lhs rhs))))
```

Notice that we recursively evaluate the operands before applying the "connective" as the operator. Now, the only remaining pieces of the puzzle are atom?, value-of-atom, and lookup. The former reducer simply invokes lookup on the atom symbol (which is represented as (second exp)), whereas the latter traverses through the environment to find the corresponding truth value.

Listing 7.182

```
(define atom?                              (define value-of-atom
  (λ (exp)                                   (λ (exp env)
    (and (eqv? (first exp) 'atom)             (let ([aexp (second exp)])
         (= (length exp) 2))))                 (apply-env aexp env))))
```

Listing 7.183

```
(define lookup
  (λ (y env)
    (let ([binding (first env)])
      (cond
        [(eqv? (first binding) y) (rest binding)]
        [else (lookup y (rest env))]))))
```

Last but certainly not least, we need some test cases!

Listing 7.184

```
> (value-of                                 #t
    '(atom q)
    '((p . #t) (q . #t)))
> (value-of                                 #t
    '(and (atom p) (atom q))
    '((p . #t) (q . #t)))
> (value-of                                 #t
    '(and (or (atom p) (not (atom q)))
          (not (atom r)))
    '((p . #f) (q . #f) (r . #t)))
```

So, we can use this interpreter to parse simple propositional logic formulas! Let us make it representation-independent with respect to environments. Fortunately, we only need one helper function: apply-env. Because it is impossible to add new atoms to a formula after the start of evaluation, we need not extend the environment.

$\mathcal{L}^*_{\text{CNF}}$: **Conjunctive Normal Form Constructor**

Continuing with the trend of formal logic, in this section we will write $\mathcal{L}^*_{\text{CNF}}$: an interpreter for converting propositional logic formulas into conjunctive normal form.

Let us start off with some definitions before proceeding into a discussion on the importance of conjunctive normal form schemata. A propositional logic schema S is in *conjunctive normal form*, or CNF, if and only if it is a conjunction of disjunctive sub-schemata, composed of only simple schemata, i.e., negated or non-negated atoms.

'$p \wedge (q \vee r)$'

'$\neg q$'

'$((\neg p \vee \neg q) \vee \neg r) \wedge (p \vee (\neg q \vee \neg r))$'

Figure 7.6: Examples of Schemata in CNF

A schema in CNF cannot contain any connective other than logical conjunction, disjunction, and negation. A schema S is a k-CNF schema if each sub-schema S' contains k simple schemata. As an example, the previous schema '$((\neg p \vee \neg q) \vee \neg r) \wedge (p \vee (\neg q \vee \neg r))$' has two sub-schemata as operands of the (main operator) conjunction: '$((\neg p \vee \neg q) \vee \neg r)$' and '$(p \vee (\neg q \vee \neg r))$'. The former of these schemata is comprised of the sub-schemata '$\neg p$', '$\neg q$', and '$\neg r$', all of which are only (negated) atoms. Similarly, the latter of these schemata is comprised of the sub-schemata 'p', '$\neg q$', and '$\neg r$', all of which are only (negated) atoms. Moreover, these sub-schemata each have three simple schemata as operands. Therefore if we assume that we only have p, q, and r as propositional letters in our language, this is a 3-CNF schema.

Why do we even care about conjunctive normal form? Every propositional logic schema can be converted into an equivalent CNF. is useful for reducing the complexity and size of logic circuitry, as it relates to propositional logic. Standardizing, or normalizing, a representation for schemata helps quickly test software that rely on boolean schemata. Moreover, boolean satisfiability is a fundamental computer science problem, and converting a schema into its CNF equivalent allows us to quickly determine a falsifying assignment (should one exist). To do so, we look at an arbitrary clause of a CNF schema and assign $\perp$ to all negated atoms and $\top$ to all non-negated atoms. Because every conjunct of a CNF schema must be true for the overarching schema to be true, a falsifying interpretation of a conjunct falsifies the overarching schema (missing atoms from the sub-schema can be assigned arbitrary values).

Example. Determine a falsifying truth value assignment for the CNF schema '$(p \lor \neg r) \land (\neg q \lor \neg p)$'. First we pick a schema at random and assign truth values using the aforementioned rules. Let 'p'=$\bot$ and '$\neg r$'= $\top$. Thus, '$(\bot \lor \bot)$' resolves to $\bot$. Because 'q' is not at all used in the sub-schema, we can say that there are at least two falsifying assignments: 'p'=$\bot$, 'q'=$\top$, 'r'= $\bot$, and 'p'=$\bot$, 'q'=$\bot$, 'r'= $\bot$. So we quickly conclude that this schema is *not* a tautology.

Interestingly, a schema that is in full-CNF may be quickly assessed for satisfiability. A schema is in *full-CNF* if it is in k-CNF where k is equal to the number of atoms in the language. A full-CNF schema S is a *tautology* if there are 2^k clauses, meaning every possible (truth value) interpretation is a clause in the full-CNF schema. A full-CNF schema S is *unsatisfiable* if, after removing logically-contradicting schemata from the conjunction, the schema is empty. A full-CNF schema S is *satisfiable* if it is not unsatisfiable.

Example. Determine if the full-CNF schema '$((\neg p \lor \neg q) \lor \neg r) \land (p \lor (\neg q \lor \neg r))$' is satisfiable, assuming a language containing the atoms 'p', 'q', and 'r'. Because the schema contains no logical contradictions, there are no schemata to remove. Therefore this schema is satisfiable.

With the theory background taken care of, let us write a nested interpreter! Not quite, because we need to implement the conversion procedure! Given a schema, we convert it to CNF using the following steps (not necessarily in this order):

1. Remove all conditionals, i.e., '$p \to q$' converts into '$\neg p \lor q$'.

2. Remove all biconditionals, i.e,. '$p \leftrightarrow q$' converts into '$(p \land q) \lor (\neg p \land \neg q)$'.

3. Distribute negations inward using equivalences.

    (i) '$\neg\neg p$' converts into 'p'.
    (ii) '$\neg(p \lor q)$' converts into '$\neg p \land \neg q$'.
    (iii) '$\neg(p \land q)$' converts into '$\neg p \lor \neg q$'.
    (iv) '$\neg(p \to q)$' converts into '$(p \land \neg q)$'.
    (v) '$\neg(p \leftrightarrow q)$' converts into '$(p \land \neg q) \lor (\neg p \land q)$'.

4. Distribute '$\lor$' over '$\land$'.

We will use the previous connective recognizers from $\mathcal{L}^*_{\text{LOGIC}}$, only needing to modify the reducers. We do make one modification in that atoms are now represented as symbols rather than a tagged list.[1] The root reducer serves as a standard dispatch function.

[1]The former representation was (atom a) where a was a symbol. Our current representation omits the tag and list.

Listing 7.185

```
(define value-of-cnf
 (λ (wff)
  (cond
   [(atom? wff) wff]
   [(negation? wff) (value-of-negation wff)]
   [(conjunction? wff) (value-of-conjunction wff)]
   [(disjunction? wff) (value-of-disjunction wff)]
   [(implication? wff) (value-of-implication wff)]
   [(biconditional? wff) (value-of-biconditional wff)]
   [else #f])))
```

Let us start by writing `value-of-conjunction`, which converts both operands of the conjunction, recursively, to CNF.

Listing 7.186

```
(define value-of-conjunction
 (λ (wff)
  (let ([lhs (value-of-cnf (second wff))]
        [rhs (value-of-cnf (third wff))])
   `(and ,lhs ,rhs))))
```

Up next we write `value-of-implication` and `value-of-biconditional`, which convert the schemata using the equivalence rules as previously specified. These newly-constructed schemata are then passed to the CNF conversion function.

Listing 7.187

```
(define value-of-implication
 (λ (wff)
  (let ([lhs (second exp)]
        [rhs (third exp)])
   (value-of-cnf `(or (not ,lhs) ,rhs)))))
```

Listing 7.188

```
(define value-of-biconditional
 (λ (wff)
  (let ([lhs (second wff)]
        [rhs (third wff)])
   (value-of-cnf `(or (and ,lhs ,rhs)
                      (and (not ,lhs) (not ,rhs)))))))
```

Now we must handle negation via `value-of-negation`. There are two types of negated schemata: simply and complexly. Simply-negated schemata are of the form $\neg\neg S$ for any schema S, in which we remove the negations. Complexly-negated schemata are any negated binary connective. In either case, every negated schema has a *second* representing the negated schema that we denote as *val*. If *val* is an atom, we do nothing except return the original expression, since an atom cannot be converted further. If *val* is a negated schema, we recursively convert the sub-schema of *val*, thereby removing the double negation. If *val* is either a conditional or biconditional, we recursively convert the equivalent translation.[1]

---

[1] If we pre-processed the input schema into *negated normal form*, or NNF, we would not need these clauses. We present this as an exercise.

Listing 7.189

```
(define value-of-negation
 (λ (wff)
  (let ([val (second wff)])
   (cond
    [(atom? val) wff]
    [(negation? val)
     (value-of-cnf (second val))]
    [(implication? val)
     (value-of-cnf `(and ,(second val) (not ,(third val))))]
    [(biconditional? val)
     (value-of-cnf `(or (and ,(second val) (not ,(third val)))
                        (and (not ,(second val)) ,(third val))))]
    [...]))))
```

We now consider negated conjunctions and disjunctions, which prepend a negation in front of both operands of the connectives. Since this is a repeated process where the only difference lies in the connective, we will write a function
distribute-negation, which affixes a negation connective onto the operands. Using this, we create a connective that is the dual of the one that is negated.

Listing 7.190

```
(define distribute-negation
 (λ (exp)
   (map (λ (wff) (list 'not wff)) exp)))
```

Listing 7.191

```
(define value-of-negation
 (λ (wff)
  (let ([val (second wff)])
   (cond
    [...]
    [(disjunction? val)
     (value-of-cnf (cons 'and (distribute-negation (rest val))))]
    [(conjunction? val)
     (value-of-cnf (cons 'or (distribute-negation (rest val))))]))))
```

Last but certainly not least we come to value-of-disjunction. We know
that we need to distribute logical disjunction over logical conjunction, but we
only do this in the event where at least one operand is a conjunction. Let us
write distribute-disjunction: it receives two expressions, which represent the
operands of a disjunction, and recursively performs a distribution. If neither operand
is a conjunction, then we return the schemata as operands of a disjunction (effectively reconstructing the original schema). Without loss of generality, we consider
the case where the left-hand schema is a conjunction. So, we need to distribute
the right-hand schema over the left-hand. For example, such a schema may be
'$(p \land q) \lor r$'. To correctly distribute the connective, we take the right-hand schema
and recursively distribute a disjunction with 'p' as the left-hand schema and 'r'
as the right-hand, forming '$p \lor r$'. We then distribute over the other operand,
resulting in '$q \lor r$'. We then collapse these schemata into a conjunction, i.e.,
'$(p \lor r) \land (q \lor r)$', which is in CNF.

Listing 7.192

```
;; distribute-disjunction : Schema Schema -> Schema
;; Distributes logical disjunction over logical conjunction.
(define distribute-disjunction
  (λ (lhs rhs)
    (cond
      [(conjunction? lhs)
       (list 'and
         (distribute-disjunction (second lhs) rhs)
         (distribute-disjunction (third lhs) rhs))]
      [(conjunction? rhs)
       (list 'and
         (distribute-disjunction lhs (second rhs))
         (distribute-disjunction lhs (third rhs)))]
      [else (or-wff lhs rhs)])))
```

We realize this explanation is a bit hard to follow, so we supplement it with two examples.

Example. Distribute $\lor$ over $\land$ in '$(p \land \neg s) \lor (\neg q \land \neg r)$'.

$$= \text{'}[(p \land \neg s) \lor \neg q] \land [(p \land \neg s) \lor \neg r]\text{'}$$
$$= \text{'}[(p \land \neg q) \land (\neg s \lor \neg q)] \land [(p \lor \neg r) \land (\neg s \lor \neg r)]\text{'}$$

Example. Distribute $\lor$ over $\land$ in '$((q \land r) \land s) \lor (\neg r \land \neg s)$'.

$$= \text{'}[(\neg r \land \neg s) \lor s] \land [(\neg r \land \neg s) \lor (q \land r)]\text{'}$$
$$= \text{'}[(s \lor \neg r) \land (s \lor \neg s)] \land \{[(\neg r \land \neg s) \lor q] \land [(\neg r \land \neg s) \lor r)]\}\text{'}$$
$$= \text{'}[(s \lor \neg r) \land (s \lor \neg s)] \land \{[(q \lor \neg r) \land (q \lor \neg s)] \land [(r \lor \neg r) \land (r \lor \neg s)]\}\text{'}$$

Because disjunction and conjunction are both commutative operations, the order in which we check the operands of a logical disjunction is irrelevant. Therefore there are multiple logically correct and equivalent answers to every CNF; the order we choose is purely coincidental, although applying heuristics to this decision could lower the size of the output (CNF) schema. We present some of these condensing operations as exercises.

We can finally put the pieces together and implement `value-of-disjunction`, which receives a schema and recursively converts its operands into CNF as arguments to the disjunction distribution function.

Listing 7.193

```
(define value-of-disjunction
  (λ (wff)
    (let ([lhs (second exp)]
          [rhs (third exp)])
      (distribute-disjunction
        (value-of-cnf lhs)
        (value-of-cnf rhs)))))
```

Let us test few schemata to see the results. We will use the examples that we converted, including schemata that use conditionals and biconditionals.

Listing 7.194

`> (value-of-cnf` `   '(or p (and q r)))`	`(and (or p q) (or p r))`

`> (value-of-cnf`
`   '(or (and p (not s))`
`       (and (not q)`
`            (not r))))`
	`(and (and (or p (not q))`
	`           (or p (not r)))`
	`      (and (or (not s) (not q))`
	`           (or (not s) (not r))))`

`> (value-of-cnf` `   '(imp p (and p q)))`	`(and (or (not p) p) (or (not p) q))`

`> (value-of-cnf`
`   '(imp (or (not p) (not q))`
`        (not (not q))))`
	`(and (or p q) (or q q))`

`> (value-of-cnf`
`   '(iff (or p q) r))`
	`(and (and (and (or (or p q) (not p))`
	`                (or (or p q) (not q)))`
	`           (or (or p q) (not r)))`
	`      (and (and (or r (not p))`
	`                (or r (not q)))`
	`           (or r (not r))))`

Converting the output into a readable format shows they are, indeed, in CNF.[1]

$`(p \vee q) \wedge (p \vee r)`$

$`(p \vee \neg q) \wedge (p \vee \neg r) \wedge (\neg s \vee \neg q) \wedge (\neg s \vee \neg r)`$

$`(\neg p \vee p) \wedge (\neg p \vee q)`$

$`(p \vee q) \wedge (q \vee q)`$

$`(p \vee q \vee \neg p) \wedge (p \vee q \vee \neg q) \wedge (p \vee q \vee \neg r) \wedge (r \vee \neg p) \wedge (r \vee \neg q) \wedge (r \vee \neg r)`$

Exercise 7.30. (★★★)
Implement a pp-cnf function that receives a schema in prefix notation and converts it to infix. As an example, the schema '(and (or q r) (imp (not s) (not r))) might be "pretty printed" as ((q + r) & (~s -> ~r)).

Exercise 7.31. (★★★)
As we see, converting a schema into CNF can blow up the output schema due to redundant and tautological clauses. Add an optimization to the interpreter that removes redundant clauses, i.e., '$p \leftrightarrow p$', '$p \rightarrow p$', '$p \vee p$', and '$p \wedge p$' all reduce to 'p'. Then, add a pass that removes tautological clauses, e.g., '$p \vee \neg p$', or '$(q \vee \neg r) \vee \neg(q \vee \neg r)$'.

Exercise 7.32. (★★★★)
Using variadic-argument logical conjunction and disjunction removes redundant connectives in the final CNF schema. Implement this behavior into the interpreter. Such a modification requires altering the corresponding recognizers and distribution functions. This is tricky to get right, which is why we label it as a four star problem.

---

[1]To condense the representation, we will assume the logical conjunction and disjunction connectives are n-ary rather than binary. Such an assumption provably preserves the semantic behavior.

Exercise 7.33. (★★★★)
First-order logic adds variables, constants, predicates, and quantifiers to zeroth-order logic, whilst removing atoms. Design a nested interpreter to process first-order logic schemata. The root reducer function should return whether the schema is well-formed. A first-order logic schema is well-formed if it conforms to the inductive definition from **Chapter 2**.

Exercise 7.34. (★★★★★)
Using the previous exercise as a basis, write an algorithm that rewrites a first-order logic schema in *prenex normal form* (PNF).[1] A first-order logic is in PNF if it is of the form $Q_1V_1Q_2V_2...Q_nV_nM$, where $Q_1...Q_n$ are quantifiers, $V_1...V_n$ are variables, and M is a quantifier-free schema called the *matrix*. Schemata in PNF obey similar rules to those in CNF schemata, namely that there are no conditionals or biconditionals, and negations are pushed inwards using equivalence rules as listed in Figure 7.7. Quantifiers are extracted using equivalence rules as listed in Figure 7.8.[2] Additionally, PNF schemata variables are rewritten so no shadowing occurs. For example, the x bound by '$\exists x$' shadows the x bound by '$\forall x$' in the schema '$\forall x(P(x) \rightarrow \exists xQ(x, a))$'. We rewrite this using a new variable '$\forall x(P(x) \rightarrow \exists yQ(y, a))$'. The PNF schema is '$\forall x(\exists y(\neg P(x) \lor Q(y, a)))$'. Hint: you will need to keep track of which variables are used where (and when) in the schema. Solving this problem in steps, as we did for the CNF nested interpreter, is a good approach. Those steps include removing conditionals and biconditionals, pushing negations inward, renaming shadowed quantifiers and variables, then pulling quantifiers outward.

$$\neg\forall x P(x) \leftrightarrow \exists x\neg P(x)$$
$$\neg\exists x P(x) \leftrightarrow \forall x\neg P(x)$$

$$(\phi \lor \forall x\psi) \leftrightarrow \forall x(\phi \lor \psi)$$
$$(\phi \lor \exists x\psi) \leftrightarrow \exists x(\phi \lor \psi)$$
$$(\phi \land \forall x\psi) \leftrightarrow \forall x(\phi \land \psi)$$
$$(\phi \land \exists x\psi) \leftrightarrow \exists x(\phi \land \psi)$$

Figure 7.7: Negation of Quantifiers   Figure 7.8: Negation of Quantifiers

---

[1] Why do we care about PNF schemata? Similar to CNF schemata, it serves as a normal form for first-order logic automatic theorem proving software.

[2] The variable being quantified over within $\forall x\psi$ must not be free in ϕ so as to avoid accidental variable capture.

$\mathcal{L}^*_{\text{BOUND}}$: **Bound Variable Determiner**

In the λ-calculus, lambda terms contain two pieces: the formal parameter declaration, and a body. Knowing what variables are bound versus those that are free is often useful. In this section, we will write an interpreter to recognize simple lambda calculus expressions whose main purpose is to count the number of bound variables. Recall that, in a lambda calculus expression, a bound variable is one that occurs as a formal parameter and also occurs in the body of said expression. For instance, in (lambda (x) (...x...)), x is bound. The complexity of the inner expression is irrelevant—as long as the variable occurs, it is bound. Conversely, in ((lambda (y) x) y), y is not bound because it is not in the body of the lambda declaration.

As before, we will write a procedure to parse such an expression. Our interpreter accepts three forms: a symbol, a lambda declaration, and function application. Because their functionality is identical, we will reuse lambda? and application? from the previous interpreters.

Listing 7.195

```
(define bound-count
 (λ (exp env)
  (cond
   [(symbol? exp) ...]
   [(lambda? exp) ...]
   [(application? exp) ...]
   [else 'error])))
```

Environments will have a different representation than they did in the former interpreter. Namely, an environment is nothing more than a list of symbols that were declared as formal parameters. Each time we encounter a lambda expression, we extract the symbol and add it to this list for later lookup. Along those lines, once we find a symbol, we search the environment for the variable and, if it exists, we return 1 and otherwise 0. As we recurse over the different parts of the lambda expression, we will continue counting variables—particularly, in the case of function application, we add the result of recursively invoking bound-count on the operator and operand. Let us go from the bottom-up and work on the application case first.

Listing 7.196

```
(define application-bound-count
 (λ (exp env)
  (let ([rator (first exp)]
        [rand (second exp)])
   (+ (bound-count rator env)
      (bound-count rand env)))))

(define bound-count
 (λ (exp env)
  (cond
   [(symbol? exp) (symbol-bound-count exp env)]
   [(lambda? exp) (lambda-bound-count exp env)]
   [(application? exp) (application-bound-count exp env)]
   [else 'error])))
```

Next, we will work with a lambda declaration. We need to extract the formal parameter, store in the environment, and recursively evaluate the body. Because this form of an interpreter is significantly different from the previous, we will not make the environments representation-independent. Moreover, the interpreter does not evaluate any expressions; rather, it returns a single number and nothing more.

Listing 7.197

```
(define lambda-bound-count
 (λ (exp env)
  (let ([formal (second exp)]
        [body (third exp)])
    (bound-count body (cons formal env)))))
```

Lastly, let us evaluate symbols. If exp is a symbol, we need to search for it in the environment. We can write a helper function, member?, which returns true if a value is in the given list and false otherwise.

Listing 7.198

```
(define member?
 (λ (obj ls)
  (cond
   [(null? ls) #f]
   [(eqv? (first ls) obj) #t]
   [else (member? obj (rest ls))])))
```

Listing 7.199

```
(define symbol-bound-count
 (λ (exp env)
  (cond
   [(member? exp env) 1]
   [else 0])))
```

Let us throw a few lambda expressions at this to test!

Listing 7.200

```
> (bound-count '(lambda (x) x) '())              1
> (bound-count '(lambda (y) x) '())              0
> (bound-count '((((lambda (x)                   5
                 (lambda (y)
                  (x (lambda (z) (y z)))))
                 (lambda (q) (r s)))
                (lambda (t) u))
               (lambda (v)
               (lambda (w)
                (w (lambda (x) (x x))))))
              '())
```

$\mathcal{L}^*_{\text{SETS}}$: Set Operations Interpreter

In Chapter 2, we discussed sets as well as their accompanying operations and details on proving properties of sets. In this section, we will write $\mathcal{L}^*_{\text{SETS}}$: a nested interpreter for computing properties of sets.

Our language will be completely functional; wherein we may define local variables via let bindings. Sets are defined as lists whose *first* is the symbol set and whose *rest* is a list of arbitrary values. Let us begin by writing a root reducer: value-of. From there, we will write each recognizer and reducer side-by-side. Namely, each recognizer and reducer correspond to a set operation, variable declaration, or set definition. The only recognizer and reducer pair that we will not write are those for numbers and variables (represented as symbols), which are trivial to handle.[1]

Listing 7.201

```
(define value-of
 (λ (exp env)
  (cond
   [(number? exp) exp]
   [(symbol? exp) (apply-env exp env)]
   [(set? exp) (value-of-set exp env)]
   [(let? exp) (value-of-let exp env)]
   [(member-set? exp) (value-of-member-set exp env)]
   [(union? exp) (value-of-union exp env)]
   [(intersection? exp) (value-of-intersection exp env)]
   [(difference? exp) (value-of-difference exp env)]
   [(subset? exp) (value-of-subset exp env)]
   [(proper-subset? exp) (value-of-proper-subset exp env)]
   [(set-equal? exp) (value-of-set-equal exp env)]
   [(firstdinality? exp) (value-of-cardinality exp env)]
   [(complement? exp) (value-of-complement? exp env)]
   [(firsttesian-product? exp) (value-of-cartesian-product exp env)]
   [(power-set? exp) (value-of-power-set? exp env)]
   [else 'error-unknown-set-operation])))
```

For simplicity, we will only implement the first six recognizers and reducers and leave the remaining as exercises to the reader.

To start, we need a way of recognizing a set declaration. As we stated, a set is defined as a list with a *first* tag. E.g., (set 4 3 2) is a valid set declaration. Let us write the accompanying recognizer and reducer, neither of which are non-trivial. Reducing a set is as simple as returning the defined set (list).

Listing 7.202

```
(define set?                        (define value-of-set
 (λ (exp)                            (λ (exp env)
  (and (cons? exp)                    (second exp)))
      (= (length exp) 2)
      (eqv? (first exp) 'set))))
```

Let us now write the let recognizer and reducer. All we need to do is, when encountering a let, we evaluate the variable binding and evaluate the expression being bound to the identifier. We then evaluate the body of the let with respect to an extended environment containing a binding from the identifier to its corresponding expression.

---

[1] $\mathcal{L}^*_{\text{SETS}}$ does not account for duplicate values in a set, meaning these reducers may produce incorrect results when a set contains duplicates.

Listing 7.203

```
(define let?                       (define value-of-let
  (λ (exp)                           (λ (exp env)
    (and (cons? exp)                   (let* ([lobindings (second exp)]
         (= (length exp) 3)                   [binding (first lobindings)]
         (eqv? (first exp) 'let))))          [id (first binding)]
                                             [S (value-of
                                                 (second binding)
                                                 env)]
                                             [body (third exp)])
                                       (value-of body
                                                 (extend-env id S env)))))
```

This allows us to write expressions of the following format, e.g., we declare two sets A and B as such. Note that, to keep with the general theme of set initialization, we use braces to denote the elements of a set.

Listing 7.204

```
> (value-of                        (1 2 3 4 5)
   '(let ([A (set {1 2 3 4 5})])
      (let ([B (set {3 5 7 9})])
        A)))
```

Now that we have a notion of constructing sets and variables via local bindings, we can begin to write operations that act on sets. We shall start with the simplest: set membership, i.e., '$\in$'. An element $x \in S$ where S is some set if and only if x is a member of S. Fortunately for us, we wrote member? when designing $\mathcal{L}^*_{\text{BOUND}}$, so we should reuse its definition in $\mathcal{L}^*_{\text{SETS}}$.

With member? in hand, we can write the membership recognizer and reducer. $\mathcal{L}^*_{\text{SETS}}$ uses infix operators rather than prefix, meaning that we must check the *second* of an expression list for its operator rather than its *first*. Because our interpreter does not support special characters, i.e., '$\in$', we will encode set membership as the symbol in. For instance, we may ask '(5 in (set 4 2 5 8)), which should, of course, return #t. The reducer evaluates the argument, i.e., x, as well as the set argument, i.e., S, then invokes the utility member? function.[1]

Listing 7.205

```
(define member-set?                (define value-of-member-set
  (λ (exp)                           (λ (exp env)
    (and (cons? exp)                   (let ([x (value-of (first exp) env)]
         (= (length exp) 3)                  [S (value-of (third exp) env)])
         (eqv? (second exp) 'in))))    (member? x S))))
```

Now, let us write a difficult operation: set union, i.e., '$\cup$'. Recall that the union of two sets A and B, denoted by $A \cup B$, is the set of elements that are in either A or B. Our recognizer will use a capital U to denote union (which we will omit in our listings due to redundancy). The reducer is a bit more complicated because it should receive an expression and an environment, but compute the union of the two set arguments. Consequently, we define a local recursive procedure union via letrec, and extract then evaluate the set arguments via let. The object that is returned from union, however, is *not* a "set" according to our definition, meaning we should wrap it in quasiquotes.

---

[1] We must affix -set to the recognizer and reducer names so as to not conflict with our earlier (and distinct) definition of member?.

Listing 7.206

```
(define value-of-union
  (letrec ([union
            (λ (sA sB)
              (...))])
    (λ (exp env)
      (let ([sA (value-of (first exp) env)]
            [sB (value-of (third exp) env)])
        (cons 'set (union sA sB))))))
```

Thinking about union algorithmically, we have three cases to consider, where the first is trivial. If the first set is empty, we return the second. Now, we need to do something based on the element at the *first* of sA which we will denote as *e*. If *e* ∈ sB, then we should *not* add it to the recursively-constructed set because it will be added in the fourth case to consider. So, we just call union with (rest sA) and sB.

Listing 7.207

```
(define value-of-union
  (letrec ([union
            (λ (sA sB)
              (cond
                [...]
                [(member? (first sA) sB) (union (rest sA) sB)]
                [else ...]))])
    ...))
```

The last case is, of course, when *e* ∉ sB. If this is true, then we want to add it to the recursively-constructed set since this is the only time that we will be able to add *e* as sets do not contain duplicate values. Therefore, we create a *cons* pair whose *first* is *e* and whose *rest* is the result of recursively applying union on (rest sA) and sB.

Listing 7.208

```
(define value-of-union
  (letrec ([union
            (λ (sA sB)
              (cond
                [...]
                [else (cons (first sA) (union (rest sA) sB))]))])
    ...))
```

Here's the idea: if *e* ∈ sB, we skip over *e*. Eventually, sA will be the empty set, meaning we can conjoin the remaining elements in sB onto the end of sA, hence the base case. Let us write a test case.

Listing 7.209

```
> (value-of                        (set (1 2 3 4 5 7 9))
   '(let ([A (set {1 2 3 4 5})])
      (let ([B (set {3 5 7 9})])
        (A U B)))
   (empty-env))
```

Let us now write the recognizer and reducer for set difference. Recall that the difference between two sets A and B, denoted by "\" consists of all elements that are in A but not in B. In many programming languages, though, the backslash is a reserved special character for representing other types of characters, therefore we choose for set difference to use the arithmetic difference dash -. Much like the reducer for set union, value-of-difference has a local recursive definition to compute the intended result after extracting the sets via let.

Listing 7.210

```
(define difference?                    (define value-of-difference
  (λ (exp)                               (letrec ([diff
    (and (cons? exp)                                 (λ (sA sB)
         (= (length exp) 3)                           (cond
         (eqv? (second exp) '-))))                     [...])])
                                          (λ (exp env)
                                            (let ([A (value-of (first exp) env)]
                                                  [B (value-of (third exp) env)])
                                              (cons 'set (diff A B)))))))
```

Again, let us consider the algorithm for computing set difference. We have two base cases: when sB is empty and when sA is empty. In the former case, we return sA, whereas for the latter, we return the empty list (because $\varnothing - S = \varnothing$ for any set S). Next, we check to see if the *first* of sA is in sB and, if so, do not add it to the recursively-constructed set. Otherwise, *cons* the *first* of sA onto the result of recursively invoking diff with a trimmed sA. Notice the striking similarity to the definition of value-of-union. In fact, the only differences include the extra base case and call to (rest sB) in the third cond clause.

Listing 7.211

```
(define value-of-difference
  (letrec ([diff
             (λ (sA sB)
               (cond
                 [(null? sB) sA]
                 [(null? sA) '()]
                 [(member? (first sA) sB) (diff (rest sA) (rest sB))]
                 [else (cons (first sA) (diff (rest sA) sB))]))])
    (λ (exp env)
      ...)))
```

Let us throw a few tests at this, using different sets for each run.

Listing 7.212

```
(define s1 '(set {3 4 5 6 7}))
(define s2 '(set {1 2 3 4}))
(define s3 '(set {1 4 7 10}))
(define s4 '(set {2 3 4 5 6}))
(define s5 '(set {1 2 3 4 10 12}))
(define s6 '(set {}))

> (value-of                                              (set {5 6 7})
    `(let ([A ,s1]) (let ([B ,s2]) (A - B)))
    (empty-env))
> (value-of                                              (set {1 7 10})
    `(let ([C ,s3]) (let ([D ,s4]) (C - D)))
    (empty-env))
> (value-of                                              (set {1 2 3 4 10 12})
    `(let ([E ,s5]) (let ([F ,s6]) (E - F)))
    (empty-env))
> (value-of                                              (set {})
    `(let ([G ,s2]) (let ([H ,s5]) (G - H)))
    (empty-env))
```

Exercise 7.35. (⋆)

The cardinality function, which we will denote in code as 'size', returns the number of elements in a set. Write the recognizer/reducer pair card?/value-of-card.

Exercise 7.36. (⋆)

The intersection function, which we will denote in code as '^', returns a set of elements that are in both A and B. For instance, (set {1 2 3 4}) ^ (set {2 3 5 7}) resolves to (set {2 3}). Write the recognizer/reducer pair for computing set intersections, i.e., inter?/value-of-inter.

Exercise 7.37. (⋆)

The proper subset function, which we will denote in code as '<', returns #t if all elements of a set A are in a set B but A is *not* equal to B. For instance, (set {1 2 3 4}) < (set {1 2 3 4 5}) resolves to #t, but (set {1 2 3}) < (set {1 2 3}) resolves to #f. Write the proper-subset?/value-of-proper-subset recognizer and reducer pair.

Exercise 7.38. (⋆)

The subset function, which we will denote in code as '=<', returns #t if all elements of a set A are in a set B **or** if A is equal to B. For instance, (set {1 2 3 4}) =< (set {1 2 3 4 5}) resolves to #t and (set {1 2 3}) =< (set {1 2 3}) also resolves to #t. Write the recognizer/reducer pair subset?/value-of-subset.

Exercise 7.39. (⋆⋆)

The set equality function, which we will denote in code as '=', returns #t if two sets A and B share the same elements and #f otherwise. Write the recognizer/reducer pair set-equal?/value-of-set-equal. Hint: two sets are equal if they are subsets of each other.

Exercise 7.40. (⋆⋆)

The complement function, which we will denote in code as 'not', returns the set of all elements that are in a *universe set U* and are not in a set A. Suppose that 'not' is a binary operator where the set we want to compute the complement of is the right-hand argument and the universe set is the left-hand argument. For instance, (set {1 2 3 4 5 6 7 8 9 10}) not (set {2 3 4 5}) returns (set {1 6 7 8 9 10}). Write the recognizer/reducer pair comp?/value-of-comp.

Exercise 7.41. (★★★)
The cartesian product, which we will denote in code as 'X', is for our purposes a
binary operator that computes a set of pairs such that for two sets A of n elements
and B of m elements, A X B resolves to the set with $n \cdot m$ resolves to the set:

$$\{(a_1, \ b_1), \ (a_2, \ b_2), \ \ldots, \ (a_n, \ b_1), \ \ldots, \ (a_n, \ b_n)\}$$

For instance, ((set $\{1 \ 2\}$) X (set $\{a \ b \ c\}$)) resolves to (set $\{(1 \ a) \ (1 \ b)$
(1 c) (2 a) (2 b) (2 c)$\}$). Write the recognizer/reducer pair cart-prod?/
value-of-cart-prod.

Exercise 7.42. (★★★★)
The power set, which we will denote in code as 'pset', computes a set of all possible
subsets of a set A. For instance, (pset (set $\{1 \ 2 \ 3\}$) resolves to

$$\text{(set } \{(\text{set } \{\}) \ (\text{set } \{1\}) \ (\text{set } \{2\}) \ (\text{set } \{3\}) \ (\text{set } \{1 \ 2\})$$
$$(\text{set } \{1 \ 3\}) \ (\text{set } \{2 \ 3\}) \ (\text{set } \{1 \ 2 \ 3\})\})$$

Write the recognizer/reducer pair pset?/value-of-pset.

$\mathcal{L}^*_{\mathrm{BST}}$: A Functional Binary Search Tree and Sorting Algorithms

In Chapter 3, we discussed trees and, in particular, binary search trees. This section is dedicated to writing a binary search tree, for numbers, in our interpreted language.

A binary search tree, as we recall, consists of a node with at most two children: a left and right child. Binary search trees have the *invariant*, i.e., a property that is forever true, that all values to the left of a node are less and all values to the right are greater.[1] Before we begin to work with values inside the tree, let us write the definition for constructing an empty tree.

Listing 7.213

```
; A BinarySearchTree is one of:
; - '()
; - (ListOf Number BinarySearchTree BinarySearchTree)

(define bst-create-empty
 (λ ()
  '()))

(define bst-create
 (λ (val l r)
  (list val l r)))
```

The data definition and accompanying constructor functions are no trouble at all—we define a binary search tree as a list. Namely, a binary search tree is either empty, i.e., the empty list, or is a list whose *first* is a number, whose *second* is the left-hand child, and whose *third* is the right-hand child.

Determining if a binary search tree is empty is an even easier task—we just check if it is null?, meaning we can define a variable as the null? function as follows.

Listing 7.214

```
(define bst-empty? null?)
```

Up next is adding values to the binary search tree. Inserting values is, effectively, a binary search procedure; if the given tree is null, we create a binary search tree with the given value and empty children.

Listing 7.215

```
;; bst-add : BinarySearchTree Number -> BinarySearchTree
;; Adds a value into the binary search tree.
(define bst-add
 (λ (t val)
  (cond
   [(bst-empty? t) (bst-create val (bst-create-empty) (bst-create-empty))]
   [...]
   [else #f]))))
```

---

[1]Depending on the purpose, some implementations of binary search trees will mirror this invariant.

The other cases are slightly more interesting. If t's value *is* insert, then we just return t because we cannot insert a preexisting value into a binary tree. In the likely event that the number is not part of the tree, we check to see if it is less than the current subtree root and, if so, recurse on the left-hand tree. Otherwise, we recurse on the right-hand side.[1] To simplify the implementation, we created (but do not show) three helper functions: bst-value, bst-left, and bst-right, which retrieve the value, left child, and right child of a provided binary search tree respectively.

Listing 7.216

```
(define bst-add
 (λ (t val)
  (cond
   [(bst-empty? t) (bst-create val (bst-create-empty) (bst-create-empty))]
   [(= (bst-value t) val) t]
   [(< (bst-value t) val) (bst-create (bst-value t)
                                      (bst-left t)
                                      (bst-add (bst-right t) val))]
   [(> (bst-value t) val) (bst-create (bst-value t)
                                      (bst-add (bst-left t) val)
                                      (bst-right t))]
   [else #f])))
```

Now that we can add values into a binary search tree, we should write a function that looks up/determines the existence of values. Its template is very similar to value insertion with the exception that we never create a binary search tree—we instead recurse down either side of the tree depending on the input value. If we find the value, we return true and, if the tree is empty, we return false.

Listing 7.217

```
;; bst-search : BinarySearchTree Value -> Boolean
;; Determines if a number exists in a binary search tree.
(define bst-search
 (λ (t val)
  (cond
   [(bst-empty? t) #f]
   [(= (bst-value t) val) #t]
   [(< (bst-value t) val) (bst-search (bst-right t) val)]
   [(> (bst-value t) val) (bst-search (bst-left t) val)]
   [else #f])))
```

Next, we may want a function that computes the height of a binary search tree. The height h of a tree t is the longest path from the root to a leaf. Because there are two possible heights in a tree due to its left and right children, we take the largest of the two computed values.

Listing 7.218

```
;; bst-height : BinarySearchTree -> Number
;; Returns the height of a binary search tree, which is the maximum length
;; from the root to a leaf node.
(define bst-height
 (λ (t)
  (cond
   [(bst-empty? t) 0]
   [else (add1 (max (bst-height (bst-left t))
                    (bst-height (bst-right t))))])))
```

---

[1] In our implementation, the logic is the same with the exception that our comparison is swapped; if the current subtree root is less than the value, we recurse on the right-hand side and vice versa.

Suppose we want a function that converts a list of numbers into a binary search tree. This seems like it would be easy, and indeed the approach is not complicated, but we will discuss a few key ideas about binary search trees alongside the implementation. An arbitrary list of numbers may or may not be sorted. Values in a binary search tree are inherently sorted. What this means is, we may write a function `list->bst` that receives a list *l* and recursively constructs a binary search tree from each value in the tree. We consider two cases: when the list is empty and when it is non-empty. The empty case is trivial—an empty list corresponds directly to an empty binary search tree. Otherwise, we create a binary search tree whose value is the *first* of *l*.

Listing 7.219

```
(define list->bst
 (λ (lon)
  (cond
   [(null? lon) (bst-create-empty)]
   [else
    (let ([val (first lon)]
          [rest (rest lon)])
     (make-bst val ... ...))])))
```

From here, we must add the two children to our new binary search tree. We know by the binary search tree invariant that each value in a node's left subtree is less than that node's value. Correspondingly, all values in the right subtree are greater than that node's value. So, we can filter these values out via `filter` and λ expressions.

Listing 7.220

```
(define list->bst
 (λ (lon)
  (cond
   [(null? lon) (bst-create-empty)]
   [else
    (let ([val (first lon)]
          [rest (rest lon)])
     (bst-create val
                 (list->bst (filter (λ (x) (< x val)) rest))
                 (list->bst (filter (λ (x) (> x val)) rest))))])))
```

While this is a convenient function to write, it suffers from a performance issue. Binary search trees are used to search for values quickly. With our implementation of `list->bst`, though, we end up creating a binary search tree that mirrors a linked list *if* the values in the list are sorted. Linked lists require linear time to search, whereas a binary search tree should, optimally, require only *logarithmic time*. How can we resolve this predicament? Such a problem occurs when the input list is sorted or is close to being sorted (in either ascending or descending order). So, why not guarantee that the list is sorted, then create the binary tree from that list of values? The only difference with our approach would be to insert values from the *middle* of the list and create the respective left and right subtrees.

To start, we need a function that sorts a list of numbers. There are a dozen-plus ways to sort a list of objects. Some algorithms are much faster, others require extra space, and some are performant under certain circumstances. We will implement the *insertion sort*: a sorting algorithm that works as follows:

Algorithm 1 Pseudocode for Insertion Sort Algorithm

---

   procedure INSERT(e, ls)
      if ls is empty **then**
         return $cons(e$, empty$)$
      else if e is less than $first(ls)$ **then**
         return $cons(e$, $ls)$
      else
         return $cons(first(ls)$, INSERT$(e$, $rest(ls)))$
      end if
   end procedure

   procedure ISORT(ls)
      if ls is empty **then**
         return empty
      else
         return $foldr$(INSERT, empty, ls)
      end if
   end procedure

We fold the INSERT function on the given input list.[1] INSERT receives an element e and a list ls and returns a new list where e is "properly inserted" into ls. Importantly, the ls passed to INSERT is sorted. Implementing this is straightforward from the pseudocode, so we will use it without reiterating its implementation verbatim. We will now write `list->bst-better` which sorts the input list of numbers and constructs a *balanced* binary search tree.[2] This is achieved by retrieving the middle element of the list and recursively constructing left and right subtrees.[3]

Listing 7.221

```
;; list->bst-helper : [ListOf Number] -> BinarySearchTree
;; Constructs a "balanced" binary search tree from a list of numbers.
(define list->bst-better
 (letrec ([list->bst-helper
            (λ (lon low high)
              (cond
               [(>= low high) (bst-create-empty)]
               [else (let* ([mid (quotient (+ low high) 2)]
                            [mide (list-ref mid lon)])
                       (bst-create mide
                                   (list->bst-helper lon low mid)
                                   (list->bst-helper lon (add1 mid) high)))])))])
  (λ (lon)
    (let* ([slon (i-sort lon)]
           [len (length slon)])
      (list->bst-helper slon 0 len)))))
```

Testing a few binary search trees with our new approach demonstrates immediate improvements.

---

[1] Note that we could write this without the higher-order *foldr* function using natural recursion.

[2] We sort using `i-sort` whose definition is omitted.

[3] The "middle element" of a list is found by computing left and right indices of the sub list—each subtree acts only on a given sub list. In the end, we use `list-ref`, which itself is a linear time function, but this loss in performance is alleviated after the binary search tree is constructed.

Listing 7.222

```
(define ls1 '(1 2 3 4 5))

> (list->bst ls1)                          (1 ()
                                              (2 ()
                                                 (3 ()
                                                    (4 ()
                                                       (5 () ()))))))
```

Listing 7.223

```
(define ls2 '(6 10 5 8 3 2 1 9 4 7))

> (list->bst ls2)                          (6 (5 (3 (2 (1 () ())
                                                       ())
                                                    (4 () ()))
                                                 ())
                                              (10 (8 (7 () ())
                                                     (9 () ()))
                                                  ()))
```

Listing 7.224

```
(define ls1 '(1 2 3 4 5 6 7 8 9 10))

> (list->bst-better ls1)                   (6 (3 (2 (1 () ()) ())
                                                 (5 (4 () ())
                                                    ()))
                                              (9 (8 (7 () ())
                                                    ())
                                                 (10 () ())))
```

Listing 7.225

```
(define ls2 '(6 10 5 8 3 2 1 9 4 7))

> (list->bst-better ls2)                   (6 (3 (2 (1 () ()) ())
                                                 (5 (4 () ())
                                                    ()))
                                              (9 (8 (7 () ())
                                                    ())
                                                 (10 () ())))
```

Imagine calling the former `list->bst` function on a list with, say, one million elements. If the list was sorted, there would be no performance gains over just linearly searching through the original list! Furthermore, notice that `list->bst-better` returns the same binary search tree for both `ls1` and `ls2` which is expected behavior.

The insertion sort algorithm we chose is simple to implement. Along these lines, we will demonstrate another easy-to-understand sorting algorithm: the *selection sort*. Selection sort first extracts, and removes, the minimum element e from a list l. This means that $l - e = l'$ and $|l'| = |l| - 1$, so the list always shrinks. From this, it constructs a new list where e is the *first*, and we recursively selection sort l' as the *rest*. So, let us write two helper functions: `list-min` and `list-remove`.[1,2]

---

[1] We will omit the definition of min as it is trivial to write.

[2] Note the use of the higher-order function `foldr`. Writing `list-min` without `foldr` is certainly possible, but requires either a helper function or an extra parameter. Can you explain why?

Listing 7.226

```
;; list-min : [NEListOf Number] -> Number
;; Finds the minimum number in a list of numbers.
(define list-min
 (λ (ls)
  (foldr min (first ls) ls)))

;; list-remove : [NEListOf Number] Number -> [ListOf Number]
;; Removes the first occurrence of some number in a list.
(define list-remove
 (λ (ls m)
  (cond
   [(null? ls) '()]
   [(eqv? (first ls) m) (rest ls)]
   [else (cons (first ls) (list-remove (rest ls) m))])))
```

Now we have everything we need to implement s-sort. Its body uses our auxiliary functions and recursively constructs a sorted list.

Listing 7.227—Selection Sort Implementation

```
;; s-sort : [ListOf Number] -> [ListOf Number]
;; Selection sorts a list of numbers.
(define s-sort
 (λ (ls)
  (cond
   [(null? ls) ls]
   [else
    (let* ([min-e (list-min ls)]
           [n-ls (list-remove ls min-e)])
     (cons min-e (s-sort n-ls)))])))
```

As we have stated, both the insertion and selection sorts make the most sense intuitively but suffer from poor performance as the input list grows in size. A better alternative, in most circumstances, is the *merge sort*: a popular divide-and-conquer algorithm. It first subdivides a list into two lists (down the middle) and recursively sorts those. These two lists are then merged (hence the name!) into one sorted list. Consider sorting the following list: '(-1 5 -2 6 3 -7 -6 5).[1]

---

[1]Thanks, Steve Tate, for requiring us to draw this out in the UNC Greensboro algorithm analysis course.

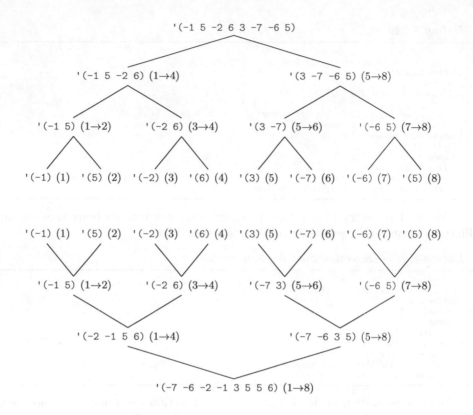

Figure 7.9: Merge Sort Illustration

As the diagram shows, we first divide the input list into sublists recursively, then merge them together. All inputs to the *merge* part of the merge sort are already sorted, so it is a simple linear time operation. Let us start by writing a function that splits a list in half by returning the left half as the *first* of a *cons* pair and the right half as the *rest*. This in and of itself, however, requires two helper functions: take and drop. The former receives a list and an integer n and returns a list with the first n elements of the list. The latter on the other hand receives a list and an integer n and returns a list *without* the first n elements. We will show a few examples of these functions but leave them as exercises to the reader to implement.

Listing 7.228

```
> (take '(1 2 3 4 5 6 7 8 9) 5)        (1 2 3 4 5)
> (drop '(1 2 3 4 5 6 7 8 9) 5)        (6 7 8 9)
> (take '(1 2 3 4 5 6 7 8 9) 0)        ()
> (drop '(1 2 3 4 5 6 7 8 9) 0)        (1 2 3 4 5 6 7 8 9)
```

Using these two functions, we can now implement split:

Listing 7.229

```
;; split : {X} [ListOf X] -> (cons [ListOf X] [ListOf X])
;; Returns a cons pair whose fst is the left-half
;; of the list and whose rst is the right-half.
(define split
  (λ (ls)
    (let ([len (length ls)]
          [mid (quotient len 2)])
      (cond
        [(<= len 1) (cons '() ls)]
        [else (cons (take ls mid) (drop ls mid))]))))
```

Up next is the merge function–it receives two sorted lists of elements and combines their elements in sorted order.

Listing 7.230

```
;; merge : {X} [ListOf X] [ListOf X] -> [ListOf X]
;; Combines two sorted lists.
(define merge
  (λ (ls1 ls2)
    (cond
      [(null? ls1) ls2]
      [(null? ls2) ls1]
      [(< (first ls1) (first ls2))
       (cons (first ls1) (merge (rest ls1) ls2))]
      [else
       (cons (rest ls2) (merge ls1 (rest ls2)))])))
```

Lastly, we combine these functions to write m-sort. All we do is recursively call m-sort on the left and right split lists and merge their contents.

Listing 7.231

```
;; m-sort : [ListOf Number] -> [ListOf Number]
;; Merge sorts a list of numbers.
(define m-sort
  (λ (ls)
    (let ([len (length ls)])
      (cond
        [(<= len 1) ls]
        [else (let* ([mid (quotient len 2)]
                     [spair (split ls len mid)]
                     [lhs (first spair)]
                     [rhs (rest spair)])
                (merge (m-sort lhs) (m-sort rhs)))]))))
```

Finally, we will discuss the *quicksort*: another divide-and-conquer sorting algorithm. Fortunately, this function is the easiest to write since it requires writing only one function. Quicksort returns the empty list if its input is empty. Otherwise, we choose a *pivot* p, i.e., an element of the list. We then subdivide the list into three partitions: l_1, l_2, and l_3. l_1 contains all elements that are strictly less than the pivot, l_2 contains all elements that are equal to the pivot, and l_3 contains all elements that are strictly greater than the pivot. This is easily achievable by using the filter function:[1]

---

[1]It must be noted that writing an *optimal* quicksort algorithm is difficult, since the best value of p would be to pick the middle element of the data set (wherein there are roughly one-half of the elements on either side of p), which is not easily computable without sorting the list!

Listing 7.232—Quicksort Filtering

```
(define q-sort
 (λ (ls)
  (cond
   [(null? ls) '()]
   [else (let* ([pivot (first ls)]
                [ltpart (filter (λ (x) (< x pivot)) ls)]
                [eqpart (filter (λ (x) (= x pivot)) ls)]
                [gtpart (filter (λ (x) (> x pivot)) ls)])
          ...)])))
```

From here, we need to recursively sort the left and right partitions (note that we do not sort eqpart as that is nonsensical). This is followed up by appending each sublist to the resulting list.

Listing 7.233—Quicksort Implementation

```
;; q-sort : [ListOf Number] -> [ListOf Number]
;; Quicksorts a list of numbers.
(define q-sort
 (λ (ls)
  (cond
   [(null? ls) '()]
   [else
    (let* ([pivot (first ls)]
           [ltpart (filter (λ (x) (< x pivot)) ls)]
           [eqpart (filter (λ (x) (= x pivot)) ls)]
           [gtpart (filter (λ (x) (> x pivot)) ls)])
     (let ([ltl (q-sort ltpart)]
           [gtl (q-sort gtpart)])
      (append ltl (append eqpart gtl))))])))
```

Interestingly enough, there exist data structures that automatically balance a binary search tree called *height-balancing trees*, e.g., AVL, red-black, and B-trees.

$\mathcal{L}^*_{\text{TRIE}}$: A Compression Technique

Data compression is prominent and ever-present in computer science. Part of this field is to find new and innovative ways to take data, in any arbitrary form, and shrink it as much as possible while retaining some resemblance of the original data. This measure of resemblance is traditionally broken down into two categories, namely lossless versus lossy compression.

In this section, we will focus on a *lossless compression*[1] technique for strings by implementing a string compression data structure called a *trie*. This is not to be confused with "tree", even though a trie is a kind of tree, also sometimes referred to as a prefix tree.

---

[1]Lossless data compression refers to the fact that the compression technique preserves all data when compressing, and decompressing recovers the original data. Lossy compression, on the other hand, loses some (generally insignificant) data upon compression.

Prefix trees, as we stated, store strings and characters. Consider the following repetitive sentence: "Peter Piper picked a peck of pickled peppers". A trie decomposes this sentence into prefix nodes. Each node corresponds to a letter in the sentence, starting from the root of the trie, where each path from the root to a leaf reconstructs a word in the original sentence. Decomposing the example sentence (treating upper and lower-case letters the same) produces three nodes from the root containing the letters 'a', 'o', and 'p'. The 'a' subtrie has no children since the only word that starts with 'a' is the word 'a' itself. The 'o' subtree has one child, namely 'f', which has no children since the only word beginning with 'o' is "of". Finally, we come to the most complex of the collection: words starting with 'p'. 'p' has two children: 'e' and 'i'. Each of these have their own subtries containing letters 'c', 'p', and 't' for 'e', and 'c', 'p' for 'i' respectively, which further recursively decompose until no more letters remain.

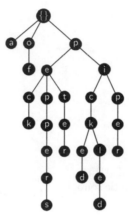

Figure 7.10: Trie Derivation of "Peter Piper picked a peck of pickled peppers".

In addition to keeping track of which letters form what words, nodes that denote the end of a word have a leaf "quantity" node. For example, the sentence "Hungry Harry alphabetizes his alphabetic soup with alphabet letters" contains the prefix "alphabet" three times, but the word "alphabet" itself appears only once (see Figure 7.11). Similarly, the sentence "Hungry Harry alphabetizes his alphabetic soup" contains the prefix "alphabet", but does not have alphabet as a word (see Figure 7.12).

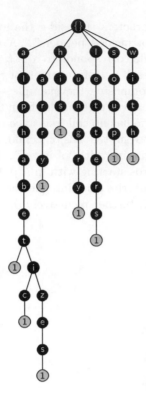

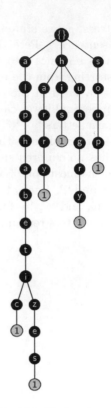

Figure 7.11: Trie Derivation of "Hungry Harry alphabetizes his alphabetic soup with alphabet letters"

Figure 7.12: Trie Derivation of "Hungry Harry alphabetizes his alphabetic soup"

With these examples, let us begin to write a trie implementation. First, we need to understand the structure of a trie. We will say that a `Trie` is a non-recursive data structure, being either a tagged list representing a leaf (containing a count as its *second*) or a list of what we will call `TrieNodes`. A `TrieNode`, on the other hand, is a recursive structure; trie nodes are tagged lists with a character as its *second* and a list of trie node children as its *third* (its *first* is the associated tag symbol):

Listing 7.234—Data Definition for Trie and TrieNode

```
; A Trie is one of:
; - (trie-leaf NaturalNumber)
; - [ListOf TrieNode]
;
; A TrieNode is (trie-node Char [ListOf Trie])

(define trie-char snd)
(define trie-children third)
(define leaf-count snd)
```

Listing 7.235—Trie Recognizers and Constructors

```
(define trie?
 (λ (t)
  (eqv? (first t) 'trie-node)))

(define leaf?
 (λ (t)
  (eqv? (first t) 'trie-leaf)))

(define (make-trie ch trie-forest)
  (list 'trie-node ch trie-forest))

(define (make-leaf)
  (list 'trie-leaf 1))
```

Let us write a function that takes a word and inserts it into a trie node containing said word and only that word. We recursively traverse the inner string contents, letter by letter, starting with a `make-trie`, then ending with a `make-leaf`. Because we want to receive a list of characters as input rather than just a string, we will use the auxiliary `string->loc` function, which converts a string to a list of characters.

Listing 7.236

```
; A Word is a [ListOf Char]          (trie-node #\h
                                      ((trie-node #\u
;; word->trienode : Word -> TrieNode    ((trie-node #\n
;; Adds a word into an empty trienode.    ((trie-node #\g
(define word->trienode                     ((trie-node #\r
 (λ (w)                                      ((trie-node #\y
  (cond                                        ((trie-leaf 1)))))))))))))))
   [(empty? w) (make-leaf)]
   [else (make-trie
           (first w)
           (list (word->trienode
                   (rest w))))]))))

> (word->trienode
   (string->loc "hungry"))
```

We now need a function that inserts a word into a preexisting trie. Such a function will use two mutually-recursive locally-defined functions that insert one letter at a time into the trie: `trienode-insert` and `trie-insert-helper`. Both functions receive a word, whereas the former receives a trie and the latter receives a list of trie nodes. The latter has two base cases, the first of which handles when the list of trie nodes is empty, meaning we just return a list whose sole element is the word inserted into a trie node. This case occurs when the trie does not have a character as a child node. The second base case happens when we reach the end of the word and the trie is a leaf node, in which we increment its counter by one, meaning the word already exists in the trie. Let us write these two cases and the starter code for both functions. `make-leaf-add1` receives a leaf node and increments its count by one, returning a new leaf in the process.

Listing 7.237

```
(define (make-leaf-add1 lf)
  (list 'trie-leaf (add1 (leaf-count lf))))

;; trie-insert : Word Trie -> Trie
;; Inserts a word into the trie. If the word is already in
;; the trie, its leaf counter is incremented.
(define trie-insert
  (letrec ([trienode-insert
            (λ (w t)
              ...)]
           [trie-insert-helper
            (λ (w f)
              (cond
                [(null? f) (list (word->trienode w))]
                [(and (null? w) (leaf? (first f)))
                 (list (make-leaf-add1 (first f)))]))])
    trie-insert-helper))
```

Of course, these two cases do not handle the necessarily interesting piece of the puzzle, that being when we insert a letter in a trie that already contains the given letter. In such instances, there are three possibilities:

1. If the word (list) is empty and there is not currently a leaf element at the list of trie nodes, then we need to create one via make-leaf and cons. This occurs when adding words that are prefixes of preexisting words.

2. If the *first* of the word is equivalent to the trie-char of the *first* of our list of trie nodes, we recurse deeper into the trie by *cons*'ing the result of calling trienode-insert on w with the trie node and the *rest* of the list of trie nodes.

3. Otherwise, we recursively create a pair out of the rest of the list of trie nodes.

Listing 7.238

```
(define trie-insert
  (letrec ([...]
           [trie-insert-helper
            (λ (w f)
              (cond
                [...]
                [(null? w) (cons (make-leaf) f)]
                [(eqv? (first w) (trie-char (first f)))
                 (cons (trienode-insert w (first f)) (rest f))]
                [else
                 (cons (first f) (trie-insert-helper w (rest f)))]))])
    trie-insert-helper))
```

Let us now write trienode-insert, which receives a word and inserts it into a non-empty trie.

Listing 7.239

```
(define trie-insert
  (letrec ([trie-node
            (λ (w t)
              (make-trie (trie-char t)
                         (trie-insert-helper (rest w) (trie-children t))))]
           [...])
    ...))
```

These two functions are all we need to create a trie. Let us see an example using the sentence from earlier.

Listing 7.240

```
(define t1
  (trie-insert
    (string->loc "hungry") '()))
(define t2
  (trie-insert
    (string->loc "harry") t1))
(define t3
  (trie-insert
    (string->loc "alphabetizes") t2))
(define t4
  (trie-insert
    (string->loc "his") t3))
(define t5
  (trie-insert
    (string->loc "alphabetic") t4))
(define t6
  (trie-insert
    (string->loc "soup") t5))
(define t7
  (trie-insert
    (string->loc "with") t6))
(define t8
  (trie-insert
    (string->loc "alphabet") t7))

> t8
```

```
'((trie-node #\h
   ((trie-node #\u
     ((trie-node #\n
       ((trie-node #\g
         ((trie-node #\r
           ((trie-node #\y
             ((trie-leaf 1)))))))))))
    (trie-node #\a
     ((trie-node #\r
       ((trie-node #\r
         ((trie-node #\y
           ((trie-leaf 1)))))))))
    (trie-node #\i
     ((trie-node #\s
       ((trie-leaf 1)))))))
  (trie-node #\a
   ((trie-node #\l
     ((trie-node #\p
       ((trie-node #\h
         ((trie-node #\a
           ((trie-node #\b
             ((trie-node #\e
               ((trie-node #\t
                 ((trie-leaf 1)
                  (trie-node #\i
                   ((trie-node #\z
                     ((trie-node #\e
                       ((trie-node #\s
                         ((trie-leaf 1)))))))
                    (trie-node #\c
                     ((trie-leaf 1)))))))))))))))))))
    (trie-node #\s
     ((trie-node #\o
       ((trie-node #\u
         ((trie-node #\p ((trie-leaf 1)))
          ))))))
    (trie-node #\w
     ((trie-node #\i
       ((trie-node #\t
         ((trie-node #\h ((trie-leaf 1)))
          )))))))
```

Searching for words in a trie is now a trivial and quick task! We pay, up front, the price of creating a trie, but we recuperate most of those costs when querying the inserted words.

Exercise 7.43. (★★)
Write the `trie-word-count` function that returns the number of times a word appears in a trie. This should not involve any arithmatic operations.

Exercise 7.44. (★★)
Write the `trie-contains?` predicate which returns true if the given word exists in the given trie and false otherwise. Assuming you wrote `trie-word-count`, this should be trivial.

Exercise 7.45. (★★★)
Write a `list->trie` function that converts a list of strings into a trie by inserting each string into the trie one after another.

Exercise 7.46. (★★★)
Write a `trie->list` function that converts a trie into a list containing the words from the given trie. Ensure that words are inserted into the list as many times as they exist in the trie.

Exercise 7.47. (★★★)
Write a `trie->remove` function that removes a given word from the given trie. If the word does not exist, then nothing is done. Breaking this problem up into sub-problems may be helpful, e.g., if the trie contains the word and has a count greater than one, if the trie contains the word and has a count equal to one, and if it is non-existent in the trie.

$\mathcal{L}^*_{\text{DFA}}$: Deterministic Finite Automaton Recognizer

In Chapter 4, we discussed finite automaton and regular expressions as methods of symbol recognition in lexical analysis. In this section, we will write a deterministic finite automaton recognizer and tester. While this stems away from our use of the term "nested interpreter", it is a useful program and allows us to explore how one of these seemingly abstract machines works.

First, recall that a DFA has five components: a set of states Q, an alphabet Σ, a transition function δ, a start state q, and a set of final states F. We will design a DFA handler, which receives a description of some DFA, and returns a function that allows us to test input strings for acceptance.

Though, how should we build this handler, and namely, how might we want to structure our input data? We will write our DFA as a constructor closure that receives a list of data. Managing the data is the complicated piece due to what all we need to store. A DFA, as we said, contains a set of states Q, as well as a transition function δ. Our handler will bring these units together. Namely, a state in our DFA will be a tagged list where the tag, or the *first*, is a state identifier. A state also contains an association list of pairs representing the transition function (these pairs are structured such that the *first* is the input symbol and the *rest* is the destination state). Finally, the third element of the set list is a list of state properties. A state can be either a starting state (s), a final state (f), both (s f), or neither (). We present an example as follows:

Listing 7.241

```
'((q0 ((a . q1) (b . q2)) (s))
  (q1 ((a . q1) (b . q2)) ())
  (q2 ((a . q2) (b . q2)) (f)))
```

The above DFA corresponds to the following diagram:

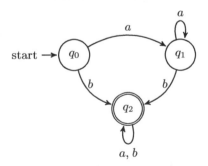

Figure 7.13: Simple DFA Example #1.

Now, let us write the recognizer. As we said, we want this to be a function that receives a list of state data (as described previously), then returns a function that should receive, then test, a string.

Listing 7.242

```
(define dfa
 (λ (los)
  (let ([states los])
   (λ (input)
    ...))))
```

Right now, `dfa` is a function of one argument: a list-of-states which assigns a field `states` to be the value of `los` just for book-keeping purposes. Inside the `let` block, we want to write a recursive procedure that iterates over each symbol in the input and traverses through the DFA. Let us walk through a simple example.

Suppose we want to determine if the list of symbols `'(a a a b b)`, representing the string `"aaabb"`, is in the language defined by the above DFA.

(i) The starting state is q_0. The next symbol is a. We transition to q_1 using (a, q_1).

(ii) The next symbol is a. We transition to q_1 using (a, q_1).

(iii) The next symbol is a. We transition to q_1 using (a, q_1).

(iv) The next symbol is b. We transition to q_2 using (b, q_2).

(v) The next symbol is b. We transition to q_2 using (b, q_2).

(vi) We have no more symbols to scan. Because q_2 is a final state, we accept the input.

With this in mind, what do we need to do? We want a recursive function that receives a symbol and the current state, which then scans the list of states, retrieves the state of interest, then scans its transition function for the correct next state. Let us write the template code for such a procedure.

Listing 7.243

```
(define dfa
 (λ (los)
  (let* ([states los])
   (letrec ([test
              (λ (sym curr-state)
               ...)])
    (λ (input)
     ...)))))
```

Out of simplicity, we can assume that the first state in the list of states denotes the start state. So, let us store this in a variable.

Listing 7.244

```
(define dfa
 (λ (los)
  (let* ([states los]
         [start (first states)])
   (letrec ([test
              (λ (sym curr-state)
               ...)])
    (λ (input)
     ...)))))
```

In addition to the start state, we should write a procedure that, when given a state, determines if it is a final state or not. We can do this by checking its state property field, or element, for the symbol 'f.

Listing 7.245

```
(define dfa

(letrec ([final-state?
          (λ (state)
            (member? 'f (third state)))]
         [test
          (λ (sym curr-state)
            ...)])))
```

Now, let us write the hardest part: test. As we said, it receives two arguments: a symbol and a state. First, we can write the base case. That is, if the symbol is null, we can just query the current state to see if it is final, which in turn accepts or rejects the input.

Listing 7.246

```
(define dfa

(letrec ([final-state? ...]
         [tester
          (λ (sym curr-state)
            (cond
              [(null? sym) (final-state? curr-state)]))])
  ...))
```

Otherwise, we extract the transitions from the current state, and at the same time, find the next state. We can use a helper function assv, which receives a symbol and an association list. For example:

Listing 7.247

```
(define assv
  (λ (obj ls)
    (cond
      [(null? ls) #f]
      [else
       (let ([binding (first ls)])
         (cond
           [(eqv? (first binding) obj)
            binding]
           [else (assv obj (rest ls))]))])))

> (assv 'b '((a . 1) (b . 2) (c . 3)))          (b . 2)
> (assv 'z '((a . 1) (b . 2) (c . 3)))          #f
```

Therefore, we make the necessary changes in the dfa local definition of tester:

Listing 7.248

```
(define dfa

  (letrec ([...]
          [tester
           (λ (sym curr-state)
            (cond
             [(null? sym) (final-state? curr-state)]
             [else
              (let* ([transitions (second curr-state)]
                     [next (assv (first sym) transitions)])
                ...)])])])
    ...))
```

With these fields, we can re-invoke `tester` with the next symbol and state respectively.

Listing 7.249

```
(define dfa

  (letrec ([...]
          [tester
           (λ (sym curr-state)
            (cond
             [(null? sym) (final-state? curr-state)]
             [else
              (let* ([transitions (second curr-state)]
                     [next (assv (first sym) transitions)])
                (tester (rest sym) (assv (second next) states)))])])])
    ...))
```

Notice that `next` is the transition pair, of the form `'(sym state)`, used to get to the subsequent state from `curr-state`. Finally, in the invocation to `tester`, we call `assv` on the snd of `next`, which is a state identifier. The recursive calls continue until `s` is empty. The last piece of the puzzle is to add a lambda function into the body of the `letrec` which invokes `tester` with the input argument and the start state `start`.

Listing 7.250

```
(define dfa
  (λ (los)
   (let* ([states los]
          [start (first states)])
    (letrec ([final-state?
              (λ (state)
               (member? 'f (third state)))]
            [tester
             (λ (sym curr-state)
              (cond
               [(null? sym) (final-state? curr-state)]
               [else
                (let* ([transitions (second curr-state)]
                       [next (assv (first sym) transitions)])
                  (tester (rest sym) (assv (second next) states)))])])])
     (λ (input)
      (tester input q0))))))
```

Now, let us construct the DFA from earlier, using the familiar syntax.

Listing 7.251

```
(define d1 (dfa '((q0 ((a . q1) (b . q2)) (s))
                  (q1 ((a . q1) (b . q2)) ())
                  (q2 ((a . q2) (b . q2)) (f)))))
```

If we output d1, we see it displays as a function, which makes sense because the returned expression is the lambda which receives input and invokes tester. So, let us invoke this with a few tests.

Listing 7.252

```
> (d1 '(a))                    | #f
> (d1 '(b))                    | #t
> (d1 '(a b))                  | #t
> (d1 '(a a a a a a a))        | #f
> (d1 '(b a a a b a b))        | #t
> (d1 '(a a a a a a b))        | #t
```

We can, visually, explain the language described by this DFA. It is the language of a's and b's such that the input contains at least one b. This is evident by test cases 1 and 4. As another example, let us write the code to represent the following DFA:

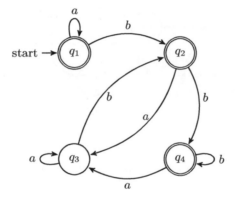

Figure 7.14: Simple DFA Example #2.

Going from a diagram, it is trivial to describe the transitions and state properties. We quickly run into a severe problem, though! The start state is also a final state, which means that the DFA accepts the empty string. So, what do we do in this case? Our code currently runs under the assumption that the first state is guaranteed to be the start state. So, why do we need a property that says if it is the starting state? It is, effectively, superfluous. So, if the starting state is also a final state, we can simply mark it as final and be rid of the 's tag.

With this modification, an accurate description of the DFA is possible.

Listing 7.253

```
(define d2
  (dfa '((q1 ((a . q1) (b . q2)) (s f))
         (q2 ((a . q3) (b . q4)) (f))
         (q3 ((a . q3) (b . q1)) ())
         (q4 ((a . q3) (b . q4)) (f)))))

> (d2 '())                    #t
> (d2 '(a b))                 #t
> (d2 '(b a))                 #f
> (d2 '(a a a a a))           #t
> (d2 '(b b a a))             #f
> (d2 '(b b a a b))           #t
> (d2 '(b b a b b a))         #f
> (d2 '(a a a b b))           #t
```

Hopefully, the pattern in the accepted language is apparent—this DFA accepts all strings that are either empty, only contain a's, or end with b.

Exercise 7.48. (⋆)
Describe the language of strings that the following automaton accepts, then encode it into the interpreter.

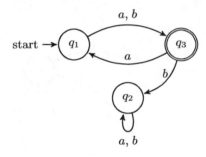

Figure 7.15: Simple DFA Example #3.

$\mathcal{L}^*_{\text{TURING}}$: **Simulating a Turing Machine**

It is astounding how little computing power is necessary to do "heavy-duty" tasks. Of course, said tasks may take a seemingly infinite amount of time to complete, but nonetheless, given enough time, they terminate. In this section, we will minimize our programming syntax and semantics to support only two symbols, natural numbers, and small data stores called registers. This language will be aptly named after Alan Turing: $\mathcal{L}^*_{\text{TURING}}$. While not an exact replicate of the formal definition of a Turing machine, its capabilities mimic the power of one.

$\mathcal{L}^*_{\text{TURING}}$ recognizes two symbols: '+' and '-'. These are the only storable symbols. Said symbols are storable in *registers*, identified by positive integers, e.g., 1, 2, and so on. For example, to add a '+' to register 1, we use the command (1 (+)). If we want to store the symbols '-', '-', '+', '-', '-' in register 2, we use (2 (- - + - -)). Each insertion is issued as a *cons* pair whose *first* is the identifying register and whose *second* is a list of symbols to add to the end of the register contents. Instructions are executed sequentially, and each instruction is stored in a list. Take the following program which stores a binary representation of the corresponding register identifier in the register for registers 1 to 5, interpreting '+' as one and '-' as zero. The output window shows the environment representation, which is nothing more than an association list of registers mapped to their contents.

Listing 7.254

'((1 (+))
  (2 (+ -))
  (3 (+ +))
  (4 (+ - -))
  (5 (+ - +)))
	((1 . (+)) (2 . (+ -)) (3 . (+ +))
	  (4 . (+ - -)) (5 . (+ - +)))

As it would appear, this program does nothing all too interesting because it has nothing to divert program flow. Therefore, we introduce two new commands: a program counter decrementer and a program counter incrementer. The program counter is a natural number corresponding to the currently-executing instruction. After each statement is executed, the program counter increments by one, hence the sequential nature of $\mathcal{L}^*_{\text{TURING}}$. To jump successive instructions, we use the '>' operator. For example, to jump three instructions ahead, we use (> > >) as follows.

Listing 7.255

'((1 (+))
  (> > >)
  (2 (+ -))
  (3 (+ +))
  (4 (+ - -))
  (5 (+ - +)))
	((1 . +) (4 . + - -) (5 . + - +))

As demonstrated, we jump from instruction 2 to instruction 5. We will call this a type of redirection operator, namely a "forward redirection". Going the other way allows us to mimic looping semantics from other programming languages. For example, if we want to transfer control from instruction 5 back to the start of the program, we use the "backward redirection" operator, i.e., <.

Listing 7.256

```
'((1 (+))                          ⊥
  (2 (+ -))
  (3 (+ +))
  (4 (+ - -))
  (< < <)
  (5 (+ - +)))
```

This program, as expected, never terminates; it continuously sets the values in registers 1, 2, 3, and 4. So, redirection operators serve little purpose without augmenting our language with decision structures. Our machine interprets question marks as case analyses on a register, based on its contents. We will perform case analysis via (N ?) where N is a register. If the register contains no symbols, control flow continues to the next sequential instruction. If the first value in the register is '+', the symbol is removed and we jump two instructions ahead. Lastly, if the first value in the register is '–', the symbol is removed and we jump three instructions ahead. The fact that we pop symbols off a register provides the potential to continuously make decisions that lead to a program that terminates. Of course, even though we have such a small set of operators, it remains easy to accidentally wind up in an infinite loop, just as it is in any other programming language. See Figure 7.16 for a condensed explanation of the case analysis algorithm.

First of (N ?)	Register Behavior	Instruction Jump
'()	none	Go To Next
'+	Remove + from N	Jump 2 Instructions
'–	Remove – from N	Jump 3 Instructions

Figure 7.16: Case Analysis Operations in $\mathcal{L}^*_{\text{TURING}}$

Let us write a $\mathcal{L}^*_{\text{TURING}}$ that transfers the contents from register 1 to register 2 using our new syntax and semantics. Because programs in $\mathcal{L}^*_{\text{TURING}}$ are somewhat offputting to non-computer readers of the language, we will supplement the program with adjacent comments. To begin, we will store an arbitrary set of input symbols inside register 1.

Listing 7.257

```
'((1 (+ - - - + - - + - +))          ((1)
  (1 ?)          ; Case analysis on R1.       (2 . + - - - +
  (> > > > > >)  ; If |R1|=0 goto end.              - - + - +))
  (> > >)        ; If R1 has + goto (2 (+))
  (2 (-))        ; Add - to R2.
  (< < < <)      ; Back to (1 ?).
  (2 (+))        ; Add + to R2.
  (< < < < < <)) ; Back to (1 ?).
```

On the other hand, if we want to *copy* the values from register 1 into register 2, we need to use an auxiliary register that transfers contents from register 1 to register 3 while also inserting symbols into register 2. Afterwards, we remove all symbols from register 3 and insert them back into register 1 using the same idea. We cannot simply add symbols to the end of register 1 as that would cause an infinitely looping program.

Listing 7.258

```
'((1 (+ - - - + - - + - +))
  ;; First, move R1 into R2.
  (1 ?)                     ; Cases on R1.
  (> > > > > > > > >)       ; Go to R3 copy.
  (> >)
  (> > > >)
  (3 (+))                   ; Push + to R3.
  (2 (+))                   ; Push + to R2.
  (< < < < < <)             ; Back to R1 case.
  (3 (-))                   ; Push - to R3.
  (2 (-))                   ; Push - to R2.
  (< < < < < < < <)         ; Back to R1 case.
  ;; Now copy over from r3 back to r1.
  (3 ?)                     ; Cases on R3.
  (> > > > > > >)           ; Go to end.
  (> >)
  (> > >)
  (1 (+))                   ; Push + to R1.
  (< < < < <)               ; Back to R3 case.
  (1 (-))                   ; Push - to R1.
  (< < < < < < <)))         ; Back to R2 case.
```

```
((1 . + - - - +
      - - + - +)
 (3)
 (2 . + - - - +
      - - + - +))
```

Notice that register 3 shows up in the output window, just without any contents. We could implement a procedure to remove auxiliary registers like these, i.e., registers that are used during program execution, but are empty at program termination time.

$\mathcal{L}^*_{\text{DERIVATIVE}}$: **A Symbolic Differentiator**

In calculus, the notion of the derivative of a function comes up quite frequently. Computing the derivative of a function by hand is a laborious task often reserved for introductory students. In this section, we will write a symbolic differentiator, which uses basic rules from calculus to find the derivative of a given function. *Note: even if the reader has not taken a course in elementary calculus, we present the topic in a way that does not require knowledge of concepts from calculus.*

The target outcome is to be able to take the derivative of a function represented as an s-expression, e.g., $x^2 + \cos(\sqrt{x})$ is represented as (+ (expt x 2) (cos (sqrt x))). Actually understanding what the derivative of a function is, is beyond the scope of this textbook. We, on the other hand, will apply simple rules of calculus to find the derivative of simple functions. Then, we can apply those rules on a larger problem and break it down into sub-components.

First, we need to write a evaluation function that receives expressions/functions and computes their derivative. We shall name this function deriv-of. For now, it just returns #f since there are no dispatch clauses.

Listing 7.259

```
(define deriv-of
 (λ (exp)
  (cond
   [else #f])))
```

Now, let us take the derivative of the simplest possible function: a constant number.

Derivative of a constant: If we have a function $f = c$ where c is any number, the derivative of f is always zero. E.g., (deriv-of 5) resolves to 0. We need to write the recognition and derivative evaluation functions for a constant.

Listing 7.260

```
(define constant?              (define deriv-of-constant
 (λ (exp)                       (λ (exp)
  (number? exp)))                0))
```

Derivative of a variable: The second-simplest function to differentiate is when the function is a single variable, e.g., $f = \phi$, where ϕ is any variable, e.g., x, y. The derivative of these functions is always one. E.g., (deriv-of 'x). The recognition and evaluation functions are just as trivial as those for differentiating constants.

Listing 7.261

```
(define variable?              (define deriv-of-variable
 (λ (exp)                       (λ (exp)
  (symbol? exp)))                1))
```

Derivative of a Sum/Difference: To compute the derivative of the sum/difference of two functions f and g, namely $f \pm g$, we differentiate f and g independently, then either add or subtract the values. E.g., (deriv-of '(+ (+ (+ x x) x) (+ 5 x))) resolves to 8 because the derivative of (+ (+ x x) x) is 3, and the derivative of (+ 5 x) is 1. When differentiating a sum/difference, we need to create a sum/difference expression. We can create two local functions make-sum and make-difference that receive two expression functions f and g, and resolves them based on their values. We can utilize useful properties of addition and subtraction to "fold" the expressions. For instance, (+ x 0) is equivalent to x. Another example is (- 13 6) which resolves to 7. If we cannot "fold" an expression, we just return it as a sum/difference list.

Listing 7.262

```
(define sum?
 (λ (exp)
  (and (cons? exp)
       (= (length exp) 3)
       (eqv? (first exp) '+))))
```

```
(define deriv-of-sum
 (λ (exp)
  (let ([f (deriv-of (second exp))]
        [g (deriv-of (third exp))])
   (let
    ([make-sum
      (λ (f g)
       (cond
        [(and (number? f) (zero? f)) g]
        [(and (number? g) (zero? g)) f]
        [(and (number? f) (number? g))
         (+ f g)]
        [else `(+ ,f ,g)]))])
    (make-sum f g)))))
```

Listing 7.263

```
(define difference?
 (λ (exp)
  (and (cons? exp)
       (= (length exp) 3)
       (eqv? (first exp) '-))))
```

```
(define deriv-of-difference
 (λ (exp)
  (let ([f (deriv-of (second exp))]
        [g (deriv-of (third exp))])
   (let
    ([make-difference
      (λ (f g)
       (cond
        [(and (number? f)
              (number? g)
              (zero? f))
         (- g)]
        [(and (number? g) (zero? g)) f]
        [(and (number? f) (number? g))
         (- f g)]
        [else `(- ,f ,g)]))])
    (make-difference f g)))))
```

Listing 7.264

```
> (deriv-of '(+ (+ (+ x x) x) (+ 5 x)))     8
> (deriv-of '(- 5 x))                        1
```

Derivative of a Product: Differentiating a product, e.g., $f \cdot g$, is ever-so-slightly more difficult than sum and difference derivatives. The derivative of such a product is $(f \cdot g') + (f' \cdot g)$ where f' and g' are the derivatives of f and g respectively. So, we can write the relevant recognition and reducer pair. Just like `make-sum` and `make-difference`, we will create a `make-product` that folds constants, zeroes out expressions that multiply by zero, and eliminates multiplications by one. With these, we can write `deriv-of-product`, which makes use of the previously-implemented functions.

Listing 7.265

```
(define product?                          (define deriv-of-product
 (λ (exp)                                   (λ (exp)
  (and (cons? exp)                           (let ([f (second exp)]
       (= (length exp) 3)                          [g (third exp)])
       (eqv? (first exp) '*))))             (let
                                             ([make-product
                                               (λ (f g)
                                                (cond
                                                 [(and (number? f) (zero? f)) 0]
                                                 [(and (number? g) (zero? g)) 0]
                                                 [(and (number? f) (= f 1)) g]
                                                 [(and (number? g) (= g 1)) f]
                                                 [(and (number? f) (number? g))
                                                  (* f g)]
                                                 [else `(* ,f ,g)]))])
                                              (make-sum
                                               (make-product (deriv-of f) g)
                                               (make-product (deriv-of g) f))))))
```

Listing 7.266

```
> (deriv-of '(- (* 5 x) (* 11 x)))           -6
> (deriv-of '(+ (* (* 3 x) x) (* 9 x)))      (+ (+ (* 3 x) (* 3 x))
                                                9)
```

Derivative of a Quotient: Opposite to products, we will now differentiate division, or quotients. The derivative of a quotient, f/g, is $((f \cdot g') - (f' \cdot g))/(g^2)$. So, as we can see, it is eerily similar to differentiating a product with two modifications: we subtract the right-hand side from the left (instead of addition), and divide the difference by g squared, or $g \cdot g$. Let us write the recognition/reducer functions as well as `make-quotient`.

Listing 7.267

```
(define quotient?
 (λ (exp)
  (and (cons? exp)
       (= (length exp) 3)
       (eqv? (first exp) '/))))
```

```
(define deriv-of-quotient
 (λ (exp)
  (let* ([f (second exp)]
         [g (third exp)]
         [df (deriv-of f)]
         [dg (deriv-of g)])
   (let
    ([make-quotient
      (λ (f g)
       (cond
        [(and (number? f) (zero? f)) 0]
        [(and (number? f) (number? g))
         (/ f g)]
        [else `(/ ,f ,g)]))])
    (make-quotient
     (make-difference
      (make-product df g)
      (make-product dg f))
     (make-product g g))))))
```

Listing 7.268

```
> (deriv-of '(/ 1 x))
> (deriv-of '(/ 1 (make-product x x)))
```

```
(/ -1 (* x x))
(/ (- 0 (+ x x))
   (* (* x x)
      (* x x)))
```

Derivative of a (Simple) Exponent: The last function "class" that we will implement is a simple exponential. A simple exponential takes the form ϕ^n where ϕ is any variable and n is any integer. E.g., (expt x 2) is a simple exponent, but (expt (cos x) 4) is not. The derivative of a simple exponential is $n \cdot x^{n-1}$. E.g., the derivative of x^5 is $5 \cdot x^4$. Let us write the accompanying recognition/reducer pair and "make" function. Note that we can make use of some simple algebraic rules to fold exponentials, e.g., $x^0 = 1$, $x^1 = x$, and $0^n = 0$ for any $n > 0$.

Listing 7.269

```
(define expt?
 (λ (exp)
  (and (cons? exp)
       (= (length exp) 3)
       (symbol? (second exp))
       (eqv? (first exp) 'expt))))
```

```
(define deriv-of-expt
 (λ (exp)
  (let ([base (second exp)]
        [power (third exp)])
   (let
    ([make-expt
      (λ (f g)
       (cond
        [(and (number? f) (zero? f)) 0]
        [(and (number? g) (zero? g)) 1]
        [(and (number? g) (= g 1)) f]
        [(and (number? f) (number? g))
         (expt f g)]
        [else `(expt ,f ,g)]))])
    (make-expt
     (make-product power base)
     (sub1 power))))))
```

Listing 7.270

```
> (deriv-of '(expt x 3))              (expt (* 3 x) 2)


> (deriv-of '(* 4 (expt x 3)))        (* (expt (* 3 x) 2) 4)


> (deriv-of '(/ (* 2 x) (expt x 2)))  (/ (- (* 2 (expt x 2))
                                            (* (* 2 x) (* 2 x)))
                                         (expt (expt x 2) 2))

> (deriv-of '(/ (- (* 3 x) 4)         (/ (- (* 3 (- (* 2 (expt x 2)) 1))
               (- (* 2 (expt x 2))       (* (* (* 2 x) 2)
                  1)))                       (- (* 3 x) 4)))
                                         (expt (- (* 2 (expt x 2)) 1) 2))
```

Exercise 7.49. (⋆⋆)

Write two functions: `deriv-of-sqrt` and `deriv-of-log`, which take the derivative of square roots and base ten logarithms respectively. The derivative of a square root function is $(1/2) \cdot (f'/\sqrt{(f)})$ where f is some function. The derivative of a base ten logarithmic function is f'/f where f is some function.

Exercise 7.50. (⋆)

Write two functions: `deriv-of-sin` and `deriv-of-cos`, which take the derivative of the sine and cosine functions respectively. The derivative of the sine function is $f' \cdot \cos(f)$, where f is some function. The derivative of the cosine function is $f' \cdot -\sin(f)$.

Exercise 7.51. (⋆⋆)

Write a function: `deriv-of-tan` which takes the derivative of the tangent function. The derivative of the tangent function is $1 + \tan^2(f) \cdot f'$, where f is some function.

Exercise 7.52. (⋆⋆)

Turn the addition and subtraction functions, namely + and − into functions that use any number greater than or equal to two of arguments. That is, allow differentiation of functions such as (deriv-of (+ 5 6 7 8 ...)).

$\mathcal{L}^*_{\text{PROOF}}$: Natural Deduction Proof Checker

In Chapter 2, we dedicated an entire section to propositional logic and its significance in the world of computer science. Along those lines, we also discussed proof techniques, one of which was natural deduction. In this section, we will write $\mathcal{L}^*_{\text{PROOF}}$: a nested interpreter that determines whether or not a given natural deduction propositional logic proof is valid.

Let us look at a sample PL proof to see what we are getting into. We will then explain our encoding scheme to translate the proof into a representation understandable by $\mathcal{L}^*_{\text{PROOF}}$.

1.	$p \vee q$	Premise	
2.	$\neg p$	Premise	
3.	$q \rightarrow r$	Premise	
4.	q	1, 2	DS
5.	r	3, 4	MP
6.	$q \wedge r$	4, 5	$\wedge$-Intro

A natural deduction proof, as we have shown, contains premises and derivation steps. At each step, we may apply a rule that follows from previous steps. Let us envision a prefix encoding of this proof:

Listing 7.271

```
'(proof
  ((or (atom p) (atom q)) () Premise)
  ((not (atom q)) () Premise)
  ((implies (atom q) (atom r)) () Premise)
  ((atom q) (1 2) DS)
  ((atom r) (3 4) MP)
  ((and (atom q) (atom r)) (4 5) ConjIntro))
```

We encode a proof as a list of elements described by steps. Namely, a step is a list that contains three elements: the *first* is the proposition declared by the step, the *second* is a list of (previous) steps used in the derivation of its proposition, and the *third* is the step "type". Our goal is to take a proof written in this format and output whether it is a valid proof or not. An invalid proof is one that, at some point, incorrectly defines a step.

To start, we should implement a large evaluation function, i.e., `check`, which receives a step using the aforementioned format and delegates evaluation of each component via case analysis. It also receives the proof as a whole. We will come back to explain the motivation behind this choice soon.

Listing 7.272

```
(define check
 (λ (step proof)
  (cond
   [(rule-premise? step) (check-rule-premise step proof)]
   [(rule-mp? step) (check-rule-mp step proof)]
   [...]
   [else #f])))
```

Now, we can write the accompanying recognition functions. We will categorize our recognition functions based on the type of recognizer. Namely, we have propositions and rules. Rules consist of propositions, meaning we should write the proposition recognizers first. For simplicity, we will only show the implementation of two recognizers. As a data definition, we say that propositions are implemented as a list where the *first* is the "type" of proposition, i.e., an implication, conjunction, atom, and so on. The remaining elements are arguments to the connective or proposition type.

Listing 7.273

```
(define prop-atom?
 (λ (p)
  (and (cons? p)
       (= (length p) 2)
       (eqv? (first p) 'atom))))

(define prop-implies?
 (λ (p)
  (and (cons? p)
       (= (length p) 3)
       (eqv? (first p) 'implies))))
```

Next, we can write the "rule" recognizers. Rules act as derivation steps in a proof, as we described earlier. Fortunately, these are almost identical to the prop-recognizers.

Listing 7.274

```
(define rule-premise?
 (λ (step)
  (and (cons? step)
       (= (length step) 3)
       (eqv? (third step) 'Premise))))

(define rule-mp?
 (λ (step)
  (and (cons? step)
       (= (length step) 3)
       (= (length (second step)) 2)
       (eqv? (third step) 'MP))))
```

Note that we do not implement reducers for prop- recognizers as there is no need; we simply use these recognizers in tandem when invoking check-rule- reducers. Speaking of those reducers, let us write those! check-rule- reducers return a boolean value that designates whether the rule was applied correctly or incorrectly. Premises are trivial and are always, by definition, applied correctly. So, we will jump directly to check-rule-mp. All reducers receive two arguments: the step that it evaluates on, and the entire proof as a list. We need this because we must verify that derivation steps were applied correctly. So, when we reference a step in the *second* list, we retrieve it from the proof using a naturally recursive function get-proof-step.

Listing 7.275

```
(define get-proof-step
 (λ (step proof)
  (cond
   [(null? proof) #f]
   [(= step 1) (first proof)]
   [else (get-proof-step (- step 1) (rest proof))])))

(define check-rule-mp
 (λ (mp proof)
  (let* ([steps (second mp)]
        [s1 (first (get-proof-step (first steps) proof))]
        [s2 (first (get-proof-step (second steps) proof))])
   ...)))
```

We verify three properties when determining if a MP rule was correctly applied: if s1 is an implication, if the antecedent of s1 is equal to s2, and if the consequent of s2 is equal to the proposition defined by the step. Consider the following example.

Listing 7.276

```
'(((implies (atom p) (atom q)) () Premise)
 ((atom p) () Premise)
 ((atom q) (1 2) MP)))
```

When we encounter the final step of this proof, we see that it uses MP. So, we look up the steps used in its derivation, namely 1 and 2. One thing that we have yet to define is prop-=?: a predicate that determines if two propositions are the same. Two prop-atom? are the same if they share the same proposition atom. Two prop-implies? are the same if, according to prop-=?, their antecedents are equivalent and their consequents are equivalent.

Listing 7.277

```
(define prop-=?
 (λ (p1 p2)
  (cond
   [(and (prop-atom? p1) (prop-atom? p2))
    (eqv? (second p1) (second p2))]
   [(and (prop-implies? p1) (prop-implies? p2))
    (and (prop-=? (first p1) (first p2)) (prop-=? (second p1) (second p2)))]
   [else #f])))
```

We may now use this equality checker in check-rule-mp.

Listing 7.278

```
(define check-rule-mp
 (λ (mp proof)
  (let* (...)
   (and (prop-implies? s1)
        (prop-=? (second s1) s2)
        (prop-=? (third s1) (first mp))))))
```

Finally, we need a way of traversing through the proof to analyze each rule one at a time sequentially. As we have repeatedly seen, the best approach is to use `letrec` that localizes the recursion. Recall that we want to return #t if the proof is correct and #f otherwise. Our base case is simple: if we have reached the end of the proof, then every step prior must be correct, so the collective proof is correct. We then check each step in succession. If we encounter a check that returns #t, we continue checking the remaining steps. Upon encountering an incorrectly-applied rule, we return #f.

Listing 7.279

```
(define check-proof
  (letrec ([checker
            (λ (step proof)
              (cond
                [(null? step) #t]
                [(eqv? (check (first step) proof) #t)
                 (checker (rest step) proof)]
                [else #f]))])
    (λ (proof)
      (checker proof proof))))
```

Let us try a very simple example: one that only uses atoms as the antecedent and conclusion of an implication.

Listing 7.280

```
(define pf1
  '(((implies (atom p) (atom q)) () Premise)
    ((atom p) () Premise)
    ((atom q) (1 2) MP)))

> (check-proof pf1)                                        #t
```

$\mathcal{L}^*_{\text{CONTINUATION}}$: A Continuation-Passing Style Interpreter

In a prior section, we mentioned the intricacies of continuations and continuation-passing style. In this section, we will revise and extend $\mathcal{L}^*_{\text{PROC}}$ into $\mathcal{L}^*_{\text{CONTINUATION}}$: a language that supports continuations and the illustrious call/cc operator.

Our discussion on continuations was driven entirely by manual continuation development. What we mean by this is that we wrote functions in explicit continuation-passing style to exhibit the potential of continuations. Some languages, however, come with built-in support for working with continuations. Scheme is one of these languages with the call/cc, or call-with-current-continuation operator. Unlike our current implementation of continuations, call/cc allows us to "jump out" of a piece of code, terminating any subsequent expressions. For instance, consider the following code:

Listing 7.281

```
(define foo-callcc
 (+ 2 (call/cc
       (λ (k)
        (* 2 (k 3) 5)))))
```

call/cc inserts a "hole", of sorts, into the outer addition expression, producing (+ 2 ???). The ??? is a call/cc invocation. So, we look inside its definition to see if the continuation, namely k, is invoked with an expression. If so, the ??? is replaced by this value. Since we call k with 3, we substitute ??? by 3, resulting in (+ 2 3), which is of course 5. What is significant about call/cc is, like our continuation-passing style exception-handling technique, it stops all subsequent expression evaluation. In the above example, the body of the function passed to call/cc is a multiplication of 2, (k 3), and 5. Because we invoke the continuation, the multiplication step never finishes.

So, can we write a nested interpreter to implement call/cc? Certainly! We first need to rewrite our previous interpreter, namely $\mathcal{L}^*_{\text{PROC}}$, in continuation-passing style.

All functions written in CPS must be tail recursive, as we previously described. So, let us start by supporting a subset of $\mathcal{L}^*_{\text{PROC}}$ and working our way up. To start, all functions that are written in CPS must receive the extra continuation argument.

Listing 7.282

```
(define value-of-cps
 (λ (exp env k)
  (cond
   [(number? exp) ...]
   [(symbol? exp) ...]
   [(add? exp) ...]
   [(lambda? exp) ...]
   [(application? exp) ...])))
```

The idea is to apply the continuation k wherever the original interpreter resolves to a value. For example, in the number? clause, it resolves to exp, meaning we should apply k to exp, treating the continuation as a function.

Listing 7.283

```
(define value-of-cps
 (λ (exp env k)
  (cond
   [(number? exp) (k exp)]
   [...])))
```

As a quick preview, let us write a test case to see what this design paradigm entails. The initial call to `value-of-cps` should receive the empty continuation, i.e., the identity function.

Listing 7.284

```
> (value-of-cps '5 (empty-env) (λ (v) v))                              5
```

Analyzing the trace of this function shows that when we arrive at the number? case, we apply the continuation to the expression, resulting in ((lambda (v) v) 5), thus resolving to 5.

Symbol evaluation works the same—apply the continuation onto the result of calling `apply-env`.

Addition is where things get a bit more complicated. Recall that we said a function written in CPS must be tail recursive. Well, `value-of-add-cps` is not directly tail recursive, but is what we will refer to as mutually-tail recursive. In essence, `value-of-cps` calls `value-of-add-cps`, which calls `value-of-cps`. We could, technically, inline the recognizer `value-of-add-cps` into the root evaluator; we choose not to out of code cleanliness.

First, we extract the two operands of + out of the expression and evaluate them in accordance to continuation-passing style semantics.

Listing 7.285

```
(define value-of-add-cps
 (λ (exp env k)
  (let ([v1 (second exp)]
        [v2 (third exp)])
   (value-of-cps v1 env
    (λ (res-v1)
     (value-of-cps v2 env
      (λ (res-v2)
       (k (+ res-v1 res-v2)))))))))
```

The lambda reducer applies the continuation to a function of *two* arguments rather than one. We must explicitly pass a continuation in addition to the function argument. Otherwise, everything is the same as the non-CPS'd interpreter.

Listing 7.286

```
(define value-of-lambda-cps
 (λ (exp env k)
  (let* ([loparam (second exp)]
         [x (first loparam)]
         [body (third exp)])
   (k
    (λ (arg k^)
     (value-of-cps body (extend-env x arg env) k^))))))
```

Application reduction, to the surprise of some readers, does not invoke the continuation. The reason is simple: function application ultimately reduces to one of the other cases that apply the continuation on its result. Therefore, applying the continuation onto the result of an application is redundant.

Listing 7.287

```
(define value-of-application-cps
 (λ (exp env k)
  (let ([rator (first exp)]
        [rand (second exp)])
   (value-of-cps rator env
    (λ (rat)
     (value-of-cps rand env
      (λ (ran)
       (rat ran k)))))))))
```

Let us throw a few tests at this interpreter:

Listing 7.288

```
> (value-of-cps                                          80
   '(+ ((lambda (x) (+ x x)) 10)
       ((lambda (x) (+ x (+ x x))) 20))
   (empty-env)
   (λ (v) v))

> (value-of-cps                                          60
   '((((lambda (x)
        (lambda (y)
         (lambda (z) (+ x (+ y z)))))) 10) 20) 30)
   (empty-env)
   (λ (v) v))
```

The interpreter works as intended. It is now time, at long last, to implement call/cc. Let us write a few tests that show how it works:

Listing 7.289

```
> (value-of-cps                                      | 5
    '(call/cc (lambda (k) (+ 2000000 (k 5))))        |
    (empty-env)                                      |
    (λ (v) v))                                       |
                                                     |
> (value-of-cps                                      | 60
    '(+ 10                                           |
        (+ (call/cc (lambda (k)                      |
                       (+ 10 (+ (k 20) 30))))        |
           30))                                      |
    (empty-env)                                      |
    (λ (v) v))                                       |
                                                     |
> (value-of-cps                                      | 100
    '(+ 10                                           |
        (+ (call/cc (lambda (k) (+ 10 (+ 20 30))))   |
           30))                                      |
    (empty-env)                                      |
    (λ (v) v))                                       |
                                                     |
> (value-of-cps                                      | 40
    '(+ 10                                           |
        (call/cc                                     |
          (lambda (k)                                |
            (+ (call/cc                              |
                 (lambda (k^)                        |
                   (+ 10 (+ 20 (k 30)))))            |
               9000))))                              |
    (empty-env)                                      |
    (λ (v) v))                                       |
                                                     |
> (value-of-cps                                      | 60
    '(+ 10                                           |
        (call/cc                                     |
          (lambda (k)                                |
            (+ 20 30))))                             |
    (empty-env)                                      |
    (λ (v) v))                                       |
```

Let us begin by writing the recognizer; all we need to check for is that the *first* is call/cc.

Listing 7.290

```
(define callcc?
  (λ (exp)
    (and (cons? exp)
         (= (length exp) 2)
         (eqv? (first exp) 'call/cc))))
```

Its reducer is the most complex we have seen yet. Here's the idea: the expression to call/cc is a procedure of one argument representing the continuation. Evaluating this function (body) in CPS gets us, of course, a continuation k^. We should apply said continuation onto a procedure of two arguments: some value and a new continuation k^^. At this point, the current continuation is k^^. Though, we do not want to invoke k^^ on the passed value, but rather we want to invoke the continuation *provided at the time of evaluating the body*, namely k.

Listing 7.291

```
(define value-of-callcc-cps
  (λ (exp env k)
    (let ([body (second exp)])
      (value-of-cps body env
        (λ (f)
          (f (λ (v k^^) (k v)) k))))))
```

Running the above tests gets us the correct output as desired. Though, this code is very difficult to understand at first (and staring at it for hours on end rarely improves anything), so let us slow down and analyze each piece of this puzzle. To do this, we need to also take a look at `value-of-lambda-cps` and `value-of-application-cps`:

Listing 7.292

```
(define value-of-lambda-cps
  (λ (exp env k)
    (let* ([loparam (second exp)]
           [x (first loparam)]
           [body (third exp)])
      (k (λ (arg k^)
           (value-of-cps body (extend-env x arg env) k^))))))

(define value-of-application-cps
  (λ (exp env k)
    (let ([rator (first exp)]
          [rand (second exp)])
      (value-of-cps rator env
        (λ (rat)
          (value-of-cps rand env
            (λ (ran)
              (rat ran k)))))))) 
```

Let us clarify something that we somewhat glossed over when defining these two functions. Our `lambda` case returns a procedure of two arguments: `arg` and `k^`, meaning that whenever we invoke `rat`, or the operator of an application, we must give it two operands: the operand to the function (which we have repeatedly seen and is no different from the non-CPS'd counterpart) and the continuation to use in subsequent evaluations.

With this understanding under our belt, let us analyze the `call/cc` reducer. Because it is written in continuation-passing style, we evaluate the body of the expression which, by definition, must be a procedure representing a continuation, e.g., `(call/cc (lambda (k) ...))`. Accordingly, the expression will always invoke the lambda reducer and return a procedure of two arguments. As such, we call this procedure `f` to denote its existence *as* a procedure.

Next, we call f and pass to it two arguments (as it should expect): a function of two arguments (v and k^) and the current continuation k. Note that, because f is returned by the lambda reducer, it binds the function of two arguments to the formal parameter arg and the continuation to k^. Inside of our language, whenever we decide to invoke the continuation, e.g., (call/cc (lambda (k) (+ 2 (k 3)))), we, as the programmer, give the continuation one argument which in this instance is 3. The other argument, namely the continuation, is passed *by the interpreter* within function application reduction. What matters, however, is what expression is bound to k. During evaluation of the call/cc's lambda, we extend its environment to include a binding of x to arg. x is the continuation formal parameter, and arg is the two-argument (lambda (v k^^) ...). Finally, we run into two cases: either we invoke the continuation or we do not. In the former case, the continuation from when the function was defined, i.e., k, is called with a value v, sending v out of the current context. Therefore, any remaining expressions to evaluate are "terminated". In the latter case, k is never invoked, meaning we never call k on some value v. The environment still contains a binding of k to the continuation; we just never invoke it. Instead, the value is evaluated via value-of-cps and returned like any other expression.

If we wanted, we could implement the remaining features in $\mathcal{L}^*_{\text{PROC}}$, e.g., conditionals, local declarations, side-effects, and begin!, but we leave these as exercises to the reader.

Exercise 7.53. ($\star$)
As a preliminary exercise, update apply-env to include an extra parameter representing a continuation. In addition, update its definition to invoke the continuation on the returned association value. This, consequently, means the dispatch value-of function should no longer invoke k on the expression returned by apply-env.

Exercise 7.54. ($\star$)
Right now, this interpreter is not representation-independent with respect to closures; namely, we treat closures as functions. Write the helper functions create-closure and apply-closure. Note that apply-closure, like apply-env, should receive the continuation as a parameter. Then, update your value-of-lambda and value-of-application to call the closure helper functions.

Exercise 7.55. ($\star$)
In addition to making environments and closures representation independent, continuations ought to receive similar treatment. Our interpreter assumes that continuations are functions, but that representation is by definition not mandatory! Write the empty-k and apply-k helper functions and replace every instance of functional continuations with these new functions. The representation of continuations is, by definition, irrelevant, but a functional representation is certainly the easiest to understand and use.

Exercise 7.56. ($\star\star\star$)
Implement let/cc: a variant of call/cc that abstracts the lambda representation of continuations away. Think of it as a let binding but only for continuations. let/cc can be represented in terms of call/cc. For instance, the following two forms are equivalent.

Listing 7.293

| (let/cc k (+ 2 3 (k 4))) | (call/cc (lambda (k) (+ 2 3 (k 4)))) |

$\mathcal{L}^*_{\text{PARTIAL}}$: Partial Evaluation Interpreter

Consider the following expression: `((lambda (x y) (+ (+ x x) (+ y y))) 10)`. If we ran this in any of our current interpreters, the program would fail because the function expects two arguments, namely x and y, but received only one. It might be more beneficial, however, to have the program store the argument, namely x, inside a closure, and to return the closure for future evaluation. This form of evaluation is called *partial evaluation*. A function that does not receive all arguments necessary to perform function application will return another function expecting those which remain. In the case of the above example, a partial evaluator generates a closure containing `(+ (+ x x) (+ y y))`, the formal parameter y, and a binding of x $\mapsto$ 10 inside the stored environment. In this section, we will write $\mathcal{L}^*_{\text{PARTIAL}}$: a nested interpreter that implements a partial evaluator.

First, let us write the standard representation-independent (with respect to environments and closures) interpreter from earlier in this section. Our environment model is the same; we use an association list representation (because of this, we omit its inclusion in the listing). The closure model, though, differs because we will use a tagged list rather than a functional closure representation since we want access to formal parameter names. In addition to this change, we want our interpreter to support multi-arity functions, since there would be no partial evaluation with this exclusion. We will write a extend-env-bindings function that binds multiple formal parameters to multiple arguments using foldr.

Listing 7.294

```
;; extend-env-bindings : [ListOf Symbol] [ListOf Any] Environment -> Environment
;; Binds a list of formal parameters to the arguments in the given environment.
(define extend-env-bindings
 (λ (formals args env)
  (foldr (λ (formal arg acc-env)
          (extend-env formal arg acc-env))
        env
        formals
        args)))

(define create-closure
 (λ (vars body env)
  (list 'create-closure vars body env)))

(define apply-closure
 (λ (rator rands)
  (cond
   [(closure? rator) (value-of-closure rator rands)]
   [else #f])))
```

The key to this nested interpreter rests inside value-of-closure. We want to extract the values from the closure tagged list. If the number of formal parameters to the closure is equal to the number of given arguments, then we perform standard function application on the body. On the other hand, if the number of operands m is less than the number of required formals n, we return a new closure containing an extended environment with the first m formal parameters bound to each operand. We also "truncate" the required formals from the closure, leaving $n-m$ formals left to be passed to the closure when invoked. To retrieve the first m or last m elements of a list, we take advantage of the naturally-recursive take and drop functions.

Listing 7.295

```
(define value-of-closure
 (λ (rator rands)
  (let ([vars (second rator)]
        [body (third rator)]
        [env (fourth rator)])
   (cond
    [(= (length vars) (length rands))
     (value-of body (extend-env-bindings vars rands env))]
    [else
     (let ([n (length rands)])
      (create-closure (drop vars n)
                      body
                      (extend-env-bindings (take vars n) rands env)))])))))
```

Now, we can run the example from before. Let us pass one argument to the function, e.g., 10, which becomes bound in the generated closure. At the same time, let us doubly invoke the function to see what happens:

Listing 7.296

```
> (value-of                                      (create-closure (y)
  '((lambda (x y) (+ (* x x) (y y))) 10)          (+ (* x x) (y y))
  (empty-env))                                    ((x . 10)))

> (value-of                                      500
  '(((lambda (x y) (+ (* x x) (* y y))) 10) 20)
  (base-env))
```

When we call the function with only one argument, we receive a closure, as expected, with x bound to 10. In the second invocation, the function produces 500 because all its arguments are fulfilled with values. Partial evaluation is handy as it allows us to define functions without the need for explicit definitions of said functions. As an example, we can write add1 as a partial application of the previous procedure.

Listing 7.297

```
> (value-of                                      (create-closure (y)
  '((lambda (x y) (+ (* x x) (y y))) 1)           (+ (* x x) (y y))
  (empty-env))                                    ((x . 1)))

> (value-of                                      16
  '(((lambda (x y) (+ (* x x) (* y y))) 1) 15)
  (base-env))
```

We could also write the higher-order function map that creates a map-add1 function that, as its name suggests, returns a mapping function that adds one to each element of a list. First, let us write map in a let binding using the recursive lexical scoping technique from Chapter 6.

Listing 7.298

```
> (value-of                                              (2 3 4 5)
   '(let ([map
           (lambda (m f ls)
             (if (null? ls)
                 (quote ())
                 (cons (f (first ls))
                       (m m f (rest ls)))))])
      (map
       map
       (lambda (x) (+ x 1))
       (cons 1
        (cons 2
         (cons 3
          (cons 4
           (quote ())))))))
   (empty-env))
```

This is what we anticipated, but let us use partial evaluation to get the desired map-add1 procedure.

Listing 7.299

```
> (value-of                                              (2 3 4 5)
   '(let ([add1
           (lambda (x) (+ x 1))]
      (let ([map
             (lambda (m f ls)
               (if (null? ls)
                   (quote ())
                   (cons (f (first ls))
                         (m m f (rest ls)))))])
        (let ([map-add1 (map map add1)])
          (map-add1 (cons 1
                     (cons 2
                      (cons 3
                       (cons 4
                        (quote ())))))))))
   (empty-env))
```

7.7 Types and Type Systems

Types are a way of describing the categorical value associated with a variable or function. For example, we constantly use types in C with function signatures via return and formal parameters, function prototypes, and other such declarations. Contrastingly, our programming language does not allow for explicit type annotations. In other words, the type of an expression is known only at runtime rather than compile-time. Such a type system is called *dynamic*, whereas the type system for C is *static*. Static type systems allow for better compiler errors and provide less of an opportunity for a program to crash after starting execution. Dynamic type systems, on the other hand, are much more flexible in that the programmer needs not to know the type of an expression before its definition. Though, this can result in sometimes sloppy code. Consider the following code segment:

Listing 7.300

```
(define val (if #t 3 "Hello!"))
```

What is the type associated with val? A static type checker would see this expression and complain because the consequent and alternative cases of the conditional differ; the former is a number and the latter is a string. So, can we say that val is of type "number or string"? Some programming languages do explicitly allow for this annotation. Though, to mimic this behavior in C, the best we can realistically do is use a union inside a struct that assigns the according field.[1]

Listing 7.301

```
1   union data {
2     int n;
3     char *s;
4   };
5
6   int main(void) {
7     union data d;
8     if (true) { d.n = 3; }
9     else { d.s = "Hello"; }
10    return 0;
11  }
```

As shown, this is not the most elegant code and, even though the if is always true, we can assume an arbitrary instance where we do not know the fate of the conditional at compile-time.

To provide a sense of how basic type-checkers work, we will write a small type checker via $\mathcal{L}^*_{\text{TYPE-CHECK}}$. Type checking is a complex problem in computer science, but at its core uses straightforward rules to determine whether an expression is well-typed. For instance, given a function f : Number $\rightarrow$ Number, we can verify that applying f to some value x is correct depending on the type of x. This process is recursive in nature, meaning it works for expressions inside other expressions.

---

[1] This is not strictly the case due to generic void pointer assignment.

When we type check an expression, we do not evaluate the expression, but rather we determine if its type is correct. So, if we were to type check an `if` expression, we do not evaluate the `if` expression (namely the components it comprises). Instead, we determine if the predicate p is of type **Boolean** and its consequent c and alternative a share types. Normally, when evaluating an if expression, we only evaluate either the consequent or the alternative depending on the result of the predicate. Because we do not care about the result of the expression, we preemptively type check all three clauses.

Let us go piece by piece. We will say that a number corresponds to type **Number**, booleans correspond to type **Boolean**, and strings correspond to type **String**. Symbols look up their associated type in a *context*. Recall that, with previous interpreters, we associate symbols with values. In a type checker, though, symbols are associated with types in a context rather than an environment (though these two structures are nearly identical from a relational standpoint—even down to the empty-, extend-, and `apply-` representation-independence functions).

Listing 7.302

```
; A Type is an Atom

; A Context is an Environment

;; type-check : Expr Context -> Type
;; Determines if the given expression is well-typed.
(define type-check
 (λ (exp ctx)
  (cond
   [(number? exp) 'Number]
   [(boolean? exp) 'Boolean]
   [(string? exp) 'String]
   [(symbol? exp) (apply-ctx y ctx)]
   [...])))
```

To type check, say, an `if` expression, we follow the steps outlined above. Though, we need a way of determining if two types are equivalent. Because types are potentially recursive due to functions, a simple eqv? symbol comparison is not sufficient. We will write corresponding recognizer functions for **Number**, **Boolean**, and **String** types, but then take a brief junction to talk about function types as these are the only "recursive" types in our system.

A function f of one argument has an input type X and an output type Y denoted as a list whose first element is X, whose second element is ->, and whose third element is Y. Thus, the corresponding recognizer function is simple, but integrating it into a type-equivalence checker requires a recursive call to check that the *first* and *rest* of types t_1 and t_2 are equivalent.

Listing 7.303

```
(define type-number? (λ (s) (eqv? s 'Number)))
(define type-boolean? (λ (s) (eqv? s 'Boolean)))
(define type-string? (λ (s) (eqv? s 'String)))
(define type-function?
 (λ (s)
  (and (cons? s)
       (= (length s) 3)
       (eqv? (second s) '->))))

;; type-equals? : Type Type -> Boolean
;; Determines if two types are equal.
(define type-equals?
 (λ (t1 t2)
  (cond
   [(and (type-number? t1) (type-number? t2)) #t]
   [(and (type-boolean? t1) (type-boolean? t2)) #t]
   [(and (type-string? t1) (type-string? t2)) #t]
   [(and (type-function? t1) (type-function? t2))
    (and (type-equals? (first t1) (first t2))
         (type-equals? (third t1) (third t2)))]
   [else #f])))
```

Now, we **will integrate** conditional (if) expressions and functions into our type checker. The latter requires creating a function type representation and type-checking its body. There are two nuances to functions: First, functions require a type annotation for its formal parameter. A type annotation tells the type checker what is the type of an expression. Formal parameters need this annotation because, otherwise, there is no way to determine its type.[1]. So, our notation for a function will be (lambda (x : T) body) where the formal parameter is a list whose first element is the symbol, the second element is a colon, and the third element is the type of x.[2]

Listing 7.304—Type-Checking if *Expressions*

```
(define type-check-if
 (λ (exp ctx)
  (let* ([p (second exp)]
         [c (third exp)]
         [a (fourth exp)]
         [tp (type-check p ctx)]
         [tc (type-check c ctx)]
         [ta (type-check a ctx)])
   (if (and (type-boolean? tp) (type-equals? tc ta))
       tc
       'Type-Mismatch))))
```

Listing 7.305—Type-Checking lambda *Expressions*

```
(define type-check-lambda
 (λ (exp ctx)
  (let* ([fp (second exp)]
         [x (first fp)]
         [T (third fp)]
         [body (third exp)])
   (list T '-> (type-check body (extend-ctx x T ctx))))))
```

---

[1] There *is a way* around this that involves *type inferencing*. In summary, type inferring the body may prove that the formal parameter is used in another typed context, i.e., addition. So, the type inferencer can infer that the input type is a Number. This comes with the added benefit that a function can be *polymorphic*, e.g., the identity function can receive and return any type in a type inferencer!

[2] Note that we simply ignore the colon as it is a stylistic choice and not important to the semantics of a type annotation.

Tying these supplemental reducers into the type-checking function gives us the following:

Listing 7.306

```
(define type-check
 (λ (exp ctx)
  (cond
   [(number? exp) 'Number]
   [(boolean? exp) 'Boolean]
   [(string? exp) 'String]
   [(symbol? exp) (apply-ctx exp ctx)]
   [(if? exp) (type-check-if exp ctx)]
   [(lambda? exp) (type-check-lambda exp ctx)]
   [else 'Type-Mismatch])))
```

Let us test out a few expressions:

Listing 7.307

> (type-check '5 (empty-ctx))	Number
> (type-check '(if #t #f #t) (empty-ctx))	Boolean
> (type-check '(lambda (x : Number) x) (empty-ctx))	(Number -> Number)
> (type-check '(lambda (y : Boolean) (if y 5 10)) (empty-ctx))	(Boolean -> Number)
> (type-check '(lambda (z : Boolean) (if 10 #f z)) (empty-ctx))	Type-Mismatch

We will also add support for type-checking unary function application. Doing so is straightforward as well: we first check to ensure that the operator is a function. Then, we type-check the *first* of the function type against the type of the operand. If both of these checks succeed, we return the *third* of the function type.

Listing 7.308

```
(define type-check-application
 (λ (exp ctx)
  (let* ([rator (first exp)]
         [rand (second exp)]
         [trator (type-check rator ctx)]
         [trand (type-check rand ctx)])
   (cond
    [(and (type-function? trator) (type-equals? (first trator) trand))
     (third trator)]
    [else 'Type-Mismatch]))))

(define type-check
 (λ (exp ctx)
  (cond
   [...]
   [(application? exp) (type-check-application exp ctx)]
   [else 'Type-Mismatch])))
```

We also added a type-check-sum to type check for sum expressions where both arguments must be of type **Number**.

Listing 7.309

```
> (type-check '(lambda (x : Number) (+ x x))      (Number -> Number)
            (empty-ctx))


> (type-check '((lambda (x : Number) (+ x x)) 5)   Number
            (empty-ctx))


> (type-check '((lambda (b : Boolean)              Boolean
               (if b #f #t)) #f)
            (empty-ctx))

> (type-check '((lambda (f : (Number -> Number))   Number
                (f 10))
              (lambda (n : Number) n))
            (empty-ctx))
> (type-check '(lambda (f : (Number -> Number))    ((Number -> Number) ->
                (lambda (n : Number) (f n)))        (Number -> Number))
            (empty-ctx))

> (type-check '(((lambda (f : (Number -> Number))  Number
                (lambda (n : Number) (f n)))
              (lambda (n : Number) (+ n n))) 50)
            (empty-ctx))
```

Exercise 7.57. (★★★★)

Design a nested interpreter for a typed language that resembles a hybrid of $\mathcal{L}^*_{\text{PROC}}$ and $\mathcal{L}^*_{\text{TYPE-CHECK}}$. That is, given a typed expression, the nested interpreter should first verify that the types are correct, then evaluate its result. If an expression fails to type-check, then do not evaluate the expression. We present some test cases (and their expected outputs) to guide your design.

Listing 7.310

```
> (value-of '(((lambda (f : (Number -> Number))   100
              (lambda (n : Number) (f n)))
            (lambda (n : Number) (+ n n))) 50)
          (empty-env))

> (value-of '(let ([x 50])                        2500
             (let ([y #f])
              (if y x (* x x))))
          (empty-env))

> (value-of                                       #f
  '(let ([zero? (lambda (n : (Number -> Boolean))
               (= n 0))])
    (let ([x 0])
     (let ([y #f])
      (zero? (if y (+ x x) x)))))
  (empty-env))

> (value-of                                       'Type-Mismatch
  '(let ([zero? (lambda (n : (Number -> Boolean))
               (= n 0))])
    (let ([x #f])
     (let ([y 5])
      (zero? (if y (+ x x) x)))))
  (empty-env))
```

8 Imperative Programming

> *Nevertheless, I consider OOP as an aspect of programming in the large;*
> *that is, as an aspect that logically follows programming in the small*
> *and requires sound knowledge of procedural programming.*
>
> —Niklaus Wirth

8.1 Side-Effects

In this chapter, we will write a few languages that introduce *side-effects*. Almost all programming languages allow the programmer to redefine variables after their initial declaration. In C, this is easily achievable as follows:

Listing 8.1

```
1  int main(void) {
2    int x = 5;
3    x = 10;
4    return 0;
5  }
```

Until now, side-effects were impossible in our interpreter.

$\mathcal{L}_{\text{SET}}$: Assignment Statements

In this section, we will write $\mathcal{L}_{\text{SET}}$: an extension to $\mathcal{L}_{\text{QUASI}}$ which implements the three side-effect-inducing functions set!, set-first!, and set-rest!.

expr	::=	application | ...
application	::=	set | setfirst | setrest | ...
set	::=	'set! ' symbol expr
setfirst	::=	'set-first! ' symbol expr
setrest	::=	'set-rest! ' symbol expr

Figure 8.1: Extended BNF Grammar for $\mathcal{L}_{\text{SET}}$

First, set! (pronounced "set bang") takes two arguments: a symbol and an expression. It modifies/replaces the currently-stored value at the symbol's location in the environment. If the symbol does not exist, an error is thrown.

Next, set-first! takes two arguments: a list and an expression. It modifies/replaces the currently-stored *first* in the list inside the environment. If the first argument is not a list or the symbol does not exist, an error is thrown.

Lastly, set-rest! takes two arguments: a list and an expression. It modifies/replaces the currently-stored *rest* in the list inside the environment. If the first argument is not a list or the symbol does not exist, an error is thrown.

Unlike other built-in functions, these three are unique in that we do not strictly evaluate their arguments. Hence, we cannot put these functions inside apply; they are special forms and have their own respective eval functions.

Listing 8.2—Side-Effect Function Stubs (eval.c)

```
1  static struct sval *eval_set(ast *set, struct environment *env) {
2    // TODO.
3  }
4  static struct sval *eval_setfirst(ast *setfirst, struct environment *env) {
5    // TODO.
6  }
7  static struct sval *eval_setrest(ast *setrest, struct environment *env) {
8    // TODO.
9  }
```

Let us go through these one-by-one to examine how we update a variable or list in its environment.

set! looks up the given variable in its current environment and changes the value of the closest-bound variable with said name. To illustrate this point, consider the following code segment that initializes several variables, in let bindings, of the same name.

Listing 8.3

```
(let ([x 5])
  (let ([x 10])
    (let ([x 15])
      (set! x 20))))
```

The set! used only modifies the value of the inner-most x declaration, meaning that its value changes from 15 to 20. We also present, perhaps, a simpler example that makes the alteration more evident.

Listing 8.4

```
(define x 10)

> (* x x)                    100
> (set! x 15)
> (* x x)                    225
```

Conveniently, implementing set! is straightforward. We first need to add a function to our environment module: environment_set, which receives the environment to modify, a symbol, and its value to store. Much like environment_-lookup, we retrieve the association pair in the provided environment and overwrite its existing value if it exists. Otherwise, we recursively set the symbol value in the parent environment. If the symbol does not exist (meaning the parent environment is eventually NULL), then an error is displayed.

Listing 8.5—Environment Manipulation (env.h)

```
1  #ifndef ENV_H
2  #define ENV_H
3    ...
4  void environment_set(struct environment *env, char *key, struct sval *value);
5    ...
6  #endif // ENV_H
```

Listing 8.6—Writing Environment Manipulation Function (env.c)

```
1  void environment_set(struct environment *env, char *key, struct sval *sv) {
2    for (struct env_pair *p = env->head; p != NULL; p = p->next) {
3      if (streq(p->key, key)) {
4        p->value = sv;
5        return;
6      }
7    }
8
9    if (NULL != env->parent) {
10     environment_set(env->parent, key, sv);
11   } else {
12     EPF("environment_set: cannot set %s\n, key");
13     exit(EXIT_FAILURE);
14   }
15 }
```

Using this **newly**-created function, we write eval_set, which sets the value of the provided **symbol**. We, however, must first evaluate the expression to assign. It is crucial, **though,** to not evaluate the first argument, namely the symbol; resolving the symbol (**with** respect to the current environment) will produce a value, i.e., the currently-**bound** value to said symbol, which is certainly not what we are after. Therefore, all **that** we need to do is retrieve the relevant abstract syntax tree child and update the environment accordingly.

Listing 8.7—Evaluating set! (eval.c)

```
1  static struct sval *eval_set(ast *set, struct environment *env) {
2    // Do NOT evaluate the first argument, do evaluate the second.
3    ast *symbol = ast_child(set, 2);
4    struct sval *expr = eval(ast_child(set, 3), env);
5    environment_set(env, ast_contents(symbol), expr);
6    return NULL;
7  }
```

Next, we **will** implement set-first! and set-rest!. Similar to set!, they each receive **a** symbol to modify and an expression. Unlike set!, we must lookup the s-value **associated** with the provided symbol because we wish to alter its *first* and *rest* respectively. Thus, we need access to the s-value itself so we may change its data union **property.** The implementations of set-first! and set-rest! are almost identical; the only difference being the data field they update. Given this, we will only **show** the implementation of set-first! due to the relative ease of designing set-rest! afterwards.

Listing 8.8—Evaluating `set-first!` (eval.c)

```
1   static struct sval *eval_setfirst(ast *setfirst, struct environment *env) {
2     // First, check to see if the symbol exists in the environment.
3     ast *symbol = ast_child(setfirst, 2);
4     struct sval *res_symbol = environment_lookup(env, ast_contents(symbol));
5     if (NULL == res_symbol) {
6       EPF("eval_setfirst: unknown symbol\n");
7       exit(EXIT_FAILURE);
8     } else {
9       ASSERT_ARG("set-first!", 1, SVAL_PAIR, res_symbol->type);
10      res_symbol->data.pair.first = eval(ast_child(setfirst, 3), env);
11    }
12    return NULL;
13  }
```

Exercise 8.1. (⋆)

Certain functions that produce side-effects such as `set!` do not return a value, meaning their output is ignored by our evaluator. It is clearer, though, to say that the function returns (void). Plus, having an explicit function at the meta-interpreter level means we may specify that some piece of code returns no value. Implement the `void` function in $\mathcal{L}_{SET}$. Its definition is one line long; do not over-think the solution.

Purity versus Impurity

Purity describes a function's behavior and its interaction with the outside world, so to speak. A function is *pure* if it abides by the following two properties:

1. It has no side-effects. This means that it cannot alter any data outside of its definition.

2. Its output is deterministic. In other words, if we run the function with the same input, it should always produce the same output. That is, if $f(x) = y$ on some invocation of f, it should always produce y for any invocation of f.

Mutating non-local variable state is a side-effect, and is arguably the most common way for a function to be impure. Let us see some examples of C functions that violate this principle:

Listing 8.9

```
1   int x = 5;
2   int y = 0;
3   int z = 0;
4
5   void foo() { x = 98; }
6
7   void bar() { y++; }
8
9   int baz(int n) {
10    z += n;
11    return z;
12  }
13
14  int main(void) {
15    bar();
16    bar();
17    bar();
18  }
```

In the previous code listing, we invoke bar three times, where each call increments the global y variable. Because y changes in between calls to bar, it violates rule #1 of a pure function. Consider the following table, which labels the program variable environment in between function calls.

Execution Number of bar	Environment
0	$[x_G \mapsto 0,\, y_G \mapsto 0,\, z_G \mapsto 0]$
1	$[x_G \mapsto 0,\, y_G \mapsto 1,\, z_G \mapsto 0]$
2	$[x_G \mapsto 0,\, y_G \mapsto 2,\, z_G \mapsto 0]$
3	$[x_G \mapsto 0,\, y_G \mapsto 3,\, z_G \mapsto 0]$

Figure 8.2: Execution Environment Trace of Listing 8.9

To generalize Figure 8.2, any function that modifies a global variable (using a v_G subscript) is not pure. As we said, a pure function must have deterministic and predictable output for any arbitrary input. So, a function that calls a naturally-impure function results in "impurifying" the caller.

Some languages, e.g., Haskell, are purely functional, meaning programs written in that language produce no side effects. How is that even a possibility if we want to get any real work done? Reading in data from the user or files inherently produces side effects. The answer lies within monads.

Monads in Programming

Monad is a scary term for a not-so-scary concept, at least in the context of functional programming. A monad contains a value and some extra information about how to operate on that value. A very common example of using monads comes through exception-handling. Throwing an exception produces side-effects, meaning that in a purely functional languages, exceptions in the traditional sense cannot exist. Consider the following code:

Listing 8.10

```
1   double divide(double x, double y) {
2     return x / y;
3   }
```

Now, suppose we wish to compose divide with another pure function, say, add10.

Listing 8.11

```
1   double add10(double n) {
2     return n + 10;
3   }
```

Composing these two gets us something like add10(divide(x, y)). Here is the problem: what if y is zero? We cannot divide by zero! So, in C, we might display an error message saying that y must be non-zero and exit the program.

Listing 8.12

```
1  double divide(double x, double y) {
2    if (0 == y) {
3      EPF("divide: y cannot be zero");
4      exit(EXIT_FAILURE);
5    } else {
6      return x / y;
7    }
8  }
```

In a functional programming world, this solution is not practical. Instead, we want to keep running the program but somehow convey that an error was received and we return, effectively, nothing. Hence, we introduce the Maybe monad. Since we are in the land of C, we may construct Maybe as a struct of two fields: Just, or Nothing. Just wraps a value representing the result of the computation. Nothing, on the other hand, denotes that, whatever tried to compute the result of a Maybe, failed (somehow) and does not have an answer, thereby placing true for the bool nothing field. Normally, monads work on generic types, meaning they work with any arbitrary value. Since we are in C, however, we will write a "double" specific Maybe monad called MaybeDouble (we could make this generic with void *).

Listing 8.13— "Maybe" Monad

```
1  typedef struct {
2    double just;
3    bool nothing;
4  } maybe_double;
```

So, let us change divide to return a Maybe monad instead.

Listing 8.14

```
1  maybe_double divide(double x, double y) {
2    maybe_double res;
3    if (0 == y) { res.nothing = true; }
4    else { res.just = x / y; }
5    return res;
6  }
```

But here is the thing: the signature for add10 must receive a monad and we have to check whether the result of invoking divide caused a Just or Nothing. This quickly turns into a monotonous chore if there are more than a few functions to update. Plus, this approach is not at all flexible! It requires us to always check the state of the monad, namely, if nothing is false, we then may check the just field. It would be better if we had a way to compose functions that use MaybeDouble. Fortunately, if we follow the canonical monad design pattern, there exists such a thing: the bind function. bind receives a monad to act on, a function that acts on that monad, and returns a monad after applying said function to the given monad. bind is the "pipeline of choice", so to speak, for monads; it decides how to proceed with the given monad state. In the case of MaybeDouble, we know that if the given monad is Just, we should certainly continue program execution and, therefore, apply the provided function on the value encapsulated by the monad. On the other hand, if the given monad is Nothing, we just continue to return Nothing up the chain.

Let us redesign our `maybe_double` monad to include a function pointer for bind. As we stated, it receives a monad and a function that acts on that monad and returns a new monad.

Listing 8.15

```
1   typedef struct maybe_double {
2     // bind : [M A] [A -> M B] -> [M B]
3     struct maybe_double
4     (*bind)(const struct maybe_double md,
5             struct maybe_double (*f)(const double));
6
7     double just;
8     bool nothing;
9   } maybe_double;
```

Otherwise, everything remains the same. One additional problem we have is that we have no way of encapsulating a value in a monad. In other words, we need a function that receives some value and returns a monad of that value. In our case, we want a function to receive a double and return a MaybeDouble whose Just field is populated. This in monadic terms is called "`return`". Because we are programming in C, we cannot use the keyword "return" as a name. Thus, we use "`ret`".

Listing 8.16

```
1   typedef struct maybe_double {
2     // bind : [M A] [A -> M B] -> [M B]
3     struct maybe_double
4     (*bind)(const struct maybe_double md,
5             struct maybe_double (*f)(const double));
6
7     // ret : A -> [M A]
8     struct maybe_double (*ret)(const double v);
9
10    double just;
11    bool nothing;
12  } maybe_double;
```

So, let us write the two most important functions: `maybe_double_bind`, and `maybe_double_return`. The former, of course, receives a MaybeDouble and a function from a double to a MaybeDouble, and if the provided MaybeDouble is Just, we invoke the function on said Just. Otherwise, we return Nothing. The latter wraps the provided double in a MaybeDouble.

Listing 8.17

```
1   maybe_double maybe_double_bind(const maybe_double md,
2                                  maybe_double (*f)(const double)) {
3     // If the monad has a value, we invoke f on that value.
4     if (!md.nothing) {
5       return f(md.just);
6     } else {
7       return maybe_double_nothing();
8     }
9   }
10
11  maybe_double maybe_double_return(const double v) {
12    return maybe_double_just(v);
13  }
```

Now, let us write a few helper functions that create a "blank" MaybeDouble, a Just MaybeDouble, and a Nothing MaybeDouble. We will also write a function that outputs the value of a MaybeDouble. We know, however, that IO is side-effect-inducing, but we will allow it for pedagogical purposes.

Listing 8.18

```
1   maybe_double maybe_double_create(void) {
2     maybe_double md;
3     md.bind = maybe_double_bind;
4     md.ret = maybe_double_return;
5     return md;
6   }
7
8   maybe_double maybe_double_just(const double d) {
9     maybe_double md = maybe_double_create();
10    md.just = d;
11    md.nothing = false;
12    return md;
13  }
14
15  maybe_double maybe_double_nothing(void) {
16    maybe_double md = maybe_double_create();
17    md.nothing = true;
18    return md;
19  }
20
21  void maybe_double_print(const maybe_double md) {
22    if (!md.nothing) {
23      printf("Just %f\n", md.just);
24    } else {
25      printf("Nothing\n");
26    }
27  }
```

Finally, let us rewrite divide to return instances of this newly-designed MaybeDouble. Correspondingly, we should update add10 to return Just.

Listing 8.19

```
1   maybe_double divide(double x, double y) {
2     if (0 == y) { return maybe_double_nothing(); }
3     else { return maybe_double_just(x / y); }
4   }
5
6   maybe_double add10(double x) {
7     return maybe_double_just(x + 10);
8   }
```

At long last, here comes the time to use the monad. We can call divide with two arbitrary variables a and b and assign its result into a monad. Now, if we wish to compose the functions, we can do so. Moreover, to simulate the idea of repeated function composition, we will not constantly reassign the value of the "result".

Listing 8.20

```
1   int main(int argc, char *argv[]) {          Just 27.565217
2     double a = 174;
3     double b = 23;
4     maybe_double result =
5      maybe_double_bind(
6       maybe_double_bind(
7        divide(a, b), add10), add10);
8     maybe_double_print(result);
9     return 0;
10  }
```

174 divided by 23 gets us 7.565217, then composing add10 twice onto the result gets us the new value. What happens if we assign 0 to b? Nothing. As expected, we receive a **Nothing**; the division 'fails', meaning we return **Nothing**. Through bind, add10 never has to care about the result of a divide; only that if it receives a **Just** that it adds ten.

Let us write another monad that abstracts a powerful debugging tool: print statements. Of course, IO is a side-effect, so if we can send along debugging messages with the result of a computation rather than merely printing from a function, we would remove a violation of impurity. Hence, we introduce the **Writer** monad.

The **Writer** monad contains two values: a value representing the current computation, and a "log". The log keeps track of information written to the log over time. As an example, suppose we wish to print logging information about a chain of mathematical expressions, e.g., the series of binds from the **Maybe** monad.

We will, once again, write a **Writer** monad that receives a double as its "value". Its log, on the other hand, is a bit more complex. Working with strings in C is already difficult enough, so to simplify our implementation, we will assume that the log can only be up to a certain size, namely LINE_MAX, which is defined in the limits.h header. Everything else remains the same as its **Maybe** monad counterpart.

Listing 8.21

```
1   typedef struct writer_double {
2     // bind : [M A] [A -> M B] -> [M B]
3     struct writer_double
4      (*bind)(const struct writer_double wm,
5              struct writer_double (*f)(const double));
6     // ret : A -> [M A]
7     struct writer_double (*ret)(const double v, const char *log);
8
9     double value;
10    char log[LINE_MAX];
11  } writer_double;
```

Well, there is one additional change to make: writer_double_return receives not only a value but a string to append to its log. By "append", we mean strncpy.

Listing 8.22

```
1   writer_double writer_double_return(const double v, const char *log) {
2     writer_double wd = writer_double_create();
3     wd.value = v;
4     strncpy(wd.log, log, sizeof(wd.log) - 1);
5     return wd;
6   }
```

writer_double_bind is a bit more complex. Like maybe_double, we invoke the given function pointer on the value stored in the passed monad. Unlike Maybe, however, we work with two monads rather than one. bind receives Writer A, and we compute Writer B from invoking f on the value stored in A. Finally, we create one more monad that serves as the "return" monad. This return monad contains the logs of both A and B, where B's log is appended to the end of A's log. Using a series of strncat invocations is cumbersome and prone to errors. Therefore, we shall make use of snprintf: a format printer for strings. Using this function, we also insert a comma-separator between the log of A and the log of B.

Listing 8.23

```
1   writer_double writer_double_bind(const struct writer_double wd_a,
2                                   writer_double (*f)(const double)) {
3     // Apply f to the value in the writer monad.
4     writer_double wd_b = f(wd_a.value);
5
6     // Create a new writer to hold the new log.
7     writer_double wd_return;
8     wd_return.value = wd_b.value;
9
10    // Concatenate the logs of A and B onto the new log.
11    snprintf(wd_return.log, sizeof(wd_return.log), "%s,%s", wd_a.log, wd_b.log);
12    return wd_return;
13  }
```

Up next, we should write the Writer "helper" functions, i.e., create and print. One small detail to note about create is that we clear (i.e., set its values to zero) the memory allocated to the log. This is done to ensure that, when we concatenate new strings into a log, we are not copying text into uninitialized garbage or cause strncpy to fail due to there not being a NUL-byte. For print, we display the result and log using the syntax for *cons* out of familiarity.

Listing 8.24

```
1   writer_double writer_double_create(void) {
2     writer_double md;
3     memset(md.log, 0, sizeof(md.log));
4     md.bind = writer_double_bind;
5     md.ret = writer_double_return;
6     return md;
7   }
8
9   void writer_double_print(const writer_double md) {
10    printf("(%f . \"%s\")\n", md.value, md.log);
11  }
```

Amazingly, nothing needs to change inside main aside from renaming the monad type specifier. On the contrary, we should certainly modify the two functions that use the Writer monad. Instead of using divide, let us write a function that computes the square root of some value while also writing out to the log. add10 also reports this information to its log.

Listing 8.25

```
1   writer_double sqrt_write(double x) {
2    return writer_double_return(sqrt(x), "Square root");
3   }
4
5   writer_double add10(double x) {
6    return writer_double_return(x + 10, "Added 10 to value");
7   }
```

Rerunning `main` produces the following output:

```
(33.190906 . "Square root,Added 10 to value,Added 10 to value")
```

It may seem like a lot of work up front to implement monads by hand, and indeed, this is the case. In a purely functional language, however, many monads are predefined. Furthermore, the principle of referential transparency (and thus no side-effects) means that runtime errors are much less frequent and are, accordingly, deterministic.

Exercise 8.2. (⋆⋆)
Random number generation is a seemingly non-deterministic and non-functional process. On the contrary, computers generate *pseudo random numbers* by picking a *seed* numeric value and, through (typically) complex algorithms, are able to poll numbers that are "random enough" for most users.[1] Though, the ability to generate random numbers is a feature of most programming languages. The Portable Operating System Interface (POSIX) provides a set of random number generation functions. For instance, to generate a random integer in the interval $[0, 2^{31})$, we use `lrand48` in the first code segment below. Notice that we first call `srand48` with `time(NULL)` as its argument. This sets the random number generator seed to the current system time in seconds since January 1, 1970.[2] Because this value is always unique, i.e., generating a new number every second, choosing this as our seed works sufficiently enough. Generating a random number between values involves modulus and offsetting the value returned by `lrand48`. To generate a random integer between -50 and 50 inclusive, we use code shown in the second listing. Write a function, `random_int(int a, int b)`, that generates a random integer between $[a, b]$. Then, integrate a similar function in our $\mathcal{L}_{\text{SET}}$ language.

Listing 8.26

```
1   #include <time.h>
2
3   int main(void) {
4    srand48(time(NULL));
5    int r = lrand48();
6    return 0;
7   }
```

---

[1] By "random enough", we mean enough to "fool" a common user, but are poor from a security standpoint.
[2] This is also known as *epoch time*.

Listing 8.27

```
1    #include <time.h>
2
3    int main(void) {
4      srand48(time(NULL));
5      int lower_bound = -50;
6      int upper_bound = 50;
7      int r = lower_bound + (lrand48() % (upper_bound - lower_bound + 1));
8      return 0;
9    }
```

Exercise 8.3. (⋆)
Write a function, random, that generates a random double-precision value between
[0, 1). As a hint, use the mrand48() function. Then, integrate a similar function in
our $\mathcal{L}_{\text{SET}}$ language.

Exercise 8.4. (⋆)
Write a function srandom(int seed) that sets the srand48 seed to the given input.
Then, integrate a similar function in our $\mathcal{L}_{\text{SET}}$ language (we add this because the
programmer using $\mathcal{L}_{\text{SET}}$ may want to use a preset seed for random number generation). Finally, integrate another function, srandom-default, that sets the srand48
seed to the current system time.

Exercise 8.5. (⋆⋆)
Having a program terminate upon receiving malformed input or due to some other
error is handy, but introduces problems with control flow. Continuations, as we
have shown in Chapter 7, aid in the ability to exit a series of recursive calls in the
event of an error. Write a function at the C $\mathcal{L}_{\text{SET}}$ level called error, which receives
a string and outputs the string to standard error, followed by a call to exit(EXIT_-
FAILURE);. Indeed, we place this exercise in Chapter 8 under side-effects because
quitting the program upon receiving an error, in this fashion, has the side-effect
of quitting the program (as well as outputting the string message to the standard
error output stream)!

Exercise 8.6. (⋆⋆)
Similar to the previous exercise, write a function at the C $\mathcal{L}_{\text{SET}}$ level called exit,
which receives no arguments and calls exit(EXIT_SUCCESS);. Unlike error, which
outputs a message to stderr, the exit function simply quits the program.

8.2 $\mathcal{L}_{\text{BEGIN}}$: Sequential Expressions

Introducing side-effects to our languages added some unforeseen predicaments, such
as the fact that any set expression does not return a value. In our interpreter, the
corresponding evaluation functions return NULL, signifying that their return value
is irrelevant. We, indeed, could make it so the return value of a set expression is
the value of the updated variable. Though, this behavior would detract from the
primary purpose of having side-effect-inducing functions. So, what do we do when
we want to do more than just set the value of a symbol? In this section, we will
write $\mathcal{L}_{\text{BEGIN}}$: an extension to $\mathcal{L}_{\text{SET}}$ that allows the programmer to write sequential
expressions.

```
expr          ::=   application | ...
application   ::=   begin | ...
begin         ::=   'begin ' expr+
```

Figure 8.3: Extended BNF Grammar for $\mathcal{L}_{\text{BEGIN}}$

Where do we begin? Well, with the begin special form, of course! Let us first discuss its syntax. begin is a special form of function application that, when evaluated, evaluates each of its arguments in sequential order, then returns the value of the last expression. As an example, let us suppose we want to write code to set the value of some variable, say, n, then return n.

Listing 8.28

```
(define n 100)
(begin
 (set! n (+ n 100))
 n)
```

The above expression binds n to the value 100, then sets it to 200. After setting, we return n. In other words, the begin special form resolves to the last expression. Consider the following example, in which we amend the value of n prior to using it as the result of a cond case.

Listing 8.29

```
(define n 100)

> (cond                            'answer-is-200
   [(= (begin
        (set! n (+ n 100))
        n)
      200)
    'answer-is-200]
   [else 'answer-is-not-200])
```

Now, let us implement the special form! Fortunately, begin is simpler than some of the special forms, because all that is required of us is to determine the number of inner expressions, then evaluate each one by one, and return the value of the last expression. Because begin is a special form, it, by definition, has at least three children, namely the pair of parentheses, and begin. Therefore, any begin form has $n-3$ expressions to evaluate if we assume it has $n \geq 3$ children. Note that, when evaluating the inner expressions, we must offset by an index of 2 to account for the opening parenthesis and begin symbol. We can refactor this into a preprocessor definition. Similarly, we can refactor the 3 from $n-3$ into one as well.

Listing 8.30—Removing Constants from Begin Special Form (eval.c)

```
1   #define BEGIN_EXPR_COUNT 3
2   #define BEGIN_OFFSET 2
3
4   static struct sval *eval_begin(ast *begin, struct environment *env) {
5     size_t num_expr = ast_children_num(begin) - 3;
6     struct sval *return_expr = NULL;
7     for (int i = 0; i < num_expr; i++) {
8       return_expr = eval(ast_child(begin, BEGIN_OFFSET + i), env);
9     }
10    return return_expr;
11  }
```

Closures and Side-Effects

Back when we introduced closures and functions, we stated that the motivation behind closures was not quite as clear and we would present said motivation later. Now is later, so let us now see how we can use closures alongside side-effects. For example, imagine we want to create a "counter" function that increments a variable each time it is invoked. We want every separate created counter to be distinct. Before side-effects, we had no way of achieving this goal, since incrementing a local variable requires storing (and then later modifying) that local variable. The idea is to generate a local (let) environment that is encapsulated by a closure. Inside the closure body, we increment, then return, the variable. We generate the closure by creating a procedure of no arguments. The closure, itself, returns a closure because we want the act of re-invoking the closure to serve as a means of incrementing the local variable.

Listing 8.31—Incrementing Variables Inside a Closure

```
(define counter
 (λ ()
  (let ([v 0])
   (λ ()
    (begin
     (set! v (add1 v))
     v)))))

(define c1 (counter))
(define c2 (counter))

> (c1)                        1
> (c1)                        2
> (c1)                        3
> (c2)                        1
> (c2)                        2
```

Exercise 8.7. (★★)

Write a pay-bill function that receives a bill balance b and an amount to pay towards the balance m. If $m < b$, return another function that receives one argument, which will be used to pay more towards the remaining balance. If $m \geq b$, return true.

Exercise 8.8. (⋆⋆⋆)
Whenever we want to perform a sequence of expressions/statements, we must use begin. This can be quite cumbersome, however, especially when the most common action involves setting a variable and returning its updated value. To enhance the interpreter's functionality, it would be advantageous to integrate the behavior of begin directly. In other words, any code block should interpret all subsequent expressions instead of solely evaluating and returning the result of the first expression.

To achieve this, we can develop a function that sequentially evaluates each expression in an abstract syntax tree. Add this feature to $\mathcal{L}_{\text{BEGIN}}$. As a hint, we already did this for begin; changing its name to make it generic (e.g., eval_-sequence) is certainly a good idea, since every location where multiple blocks can occur will need to be amended.

Exercise 8.9. (⋆⋆⋆)
Mixing functional programming paradigms with imperative constructs is often a challenge. The higher-order function map receives a function and applies it to the elements of a list thereby returning a new list. Write the map-void! function that, given a function f, a base case expression b, and a list ls, applies f to every element of ls. If ls is empty, then evaluate the base case expression. Note that this function produces a value corresponding to b's type; such value is meaningless, since we only care about executing f on a list of elements, where f may or may not be pure.

Listing 8.32—Example of map-void *Invocation with* display *Function*

```
> (map-void!                    | 1
   (λ (x)                       | 4
    (display (* x x))           | 9
     '(1 2 3 4 5)               | 16
                                | 25
```

8.3 $\mathcal{L}_{\text{OUT}}$: Fancier Output

Until now, we have used the built-in "print" functionality to retrieve the result of some arbitrary expression. In this section, we will write $\mathcal{L}_{\text{OUT}}$: an extension to $\mathcal{L}_{\text{BEGIN}}$ that adds a format-printing construct.

```
expr         ::=   application | ...
application  ::=   printf | ...
printf       ::=   'printf' expr expr*
```

Figure 8.4: Extended BNF Grammar for $\mathcal{L}_{\text{OUT}}$

C, alongside many other languages, allows the programmer to use format-strings to output data. Recall from Chapter 4 that format string consists of strings of characters and "format characters". A format character is substituted with the value of an expression after invoking the formatter. As an example, in C, we use printf and the format character %d to substitute an integer into a format string. E.g., printf("%d", 5 + 10); outputs 15 to standard output. We can, of course, use other format characters for different data types, e.g., %s for strings, and so on. How can we add this functionality to our language?

First, let us decide on the syntax of invoking/displaying a format string. C uses percent signs, e.g., %, to denote that the next character is a format character. $\mathcal{L}_{\text{OUT}}$ will, instead, use the tilde ~. As an example, to output a number, we might invoke (printf "~d" (+ 5 10)). To output a string, we may write ~s. For s-values in general, we will use ~a, which is useful for outputting data structures, e.g., vectors, lists, or pairs. Escape characters, e.g., a new-line character \n, will instead be escaped via a tilde, e.g., ~n. Thus, to output a tilde in text, we escape a tilde via ~~.

Because printf is a built-in function, we will add it to apply.c.

Listing 8.33—Adding Built-in printf (apply.c)

```
1    void builtin_functions_init(struct environment *env) {
2      ...
3      environment_put(env, "printf", sval_builtin_create(apply_printf));
4    }
5
6    struct sval *apply_printf(struct sval **args, size_t num_args,
7                              struct environment *env) {
8      if (0 == num_args) {
9        EPF("printf requires at least one argument but got 0\n");
10       exit(EXIT_FAILURE);
11     }
12     ...
13     char *fstr = args[0]->data.string;
14     size_t len = strlen(fstr);
15     size_t arg_idx = 1;
16   }
```

We first extract the string argument from the array of arguments. It must, by definition, be a string. Now, we need to traverse through the string and replace any instances of "format characters" with their respective arguments, if any. For now, we can assume that any arguments provided are correct and the input string has exactly as many format characters as it does arguments (without the string argument itself).

Listing 8.34—Evaluating Format Specifiers (apply.c)

```
1   struct sval *apply_printf(struct sval **args, size_t num_args,
2                             struct environment *env) {
3     ...
4     // Traverse through the string to find any occurrence of '~'.
5     for (int i = 0; i < len; i++) {
6       char curr = fstr[i];
7       // If there is at least one more character available after a tilde, scan it.
8       if (i < len - 1) {
9         ...
10      }
11    }
12    ...
13  }
```

We do two things in this loop: first, we grab the current character. Then, if there is at least one more character afterward, we scan it as well. This is known as "lookahead"—we perform some action based on the current symbol and one character ahead. Let us add the functionality for the new-line character.

Listing 8.35—Adding New Line Format Specifier (apply.c)

```
1   struct sval *apply_printf(struct sval **args, size_t num_args,
2                             struct environment *env) {
3     ...
4     for (int i = 0; i < len; i++) {
5       ...
6       if (i < len - 1) {
7         char next = fstr[i + 1];
8         if ('~' == curr) {
9           switch (next) {
10            case 'n':
11              printf("\n");
12              break;
13          }
14        }
15      }
16      ...
17    }
18  }
19    ...
20  }
```

Whenever we encounter a new-line character, i.e., n, we output a new line to standard output. Let us handle the s-values next. Fortunately, we do not need to distinguish between different s-values because we have a function to do that already: sval_print. So, if we encounter ~a, we invoke sval_print on the current argument. The current argument starts at one because the argument at index zero is the format string. Finally, because we found a format character, we increment i. Notice that we only increment arg_idx if we output an argument using, e.g., ~a. This is to prevent from going out of the bounds of the argument array if we want to output something that is not raw data, such as a new line, tilde, or carriage return.

Listing 8.36—Array Indexing Depends On the Input (`apply.c`)

```
1    struct sval *apply_printf(struct sval **args, size_t num_args,
2                              struct environment *env) {
3      ...
4      if ('~' == curr) {
5        switch (next) {
6          ...
7          case 'a':
8            sval_print(args[arg_idx++]);
9            break;
10         default:
11           printf("printf: unknown format specifier %c\n", next);
12           exit(EXIT_FAILURE);
13         }
14       i++;
15     }
16   }
```

There is one extra case we must account for, which is the simplest of them all: if the current character is not a tilde, then we output said character.

Listing 8.37—Any Other Character Printing (`apply.c`)

```
1    struct sval *apply_printf(struct sval **args, size_t num_args,
2                              struct environment *env) {
3      ...
4      if (curr != '~') {
5        printf("%c", curr);
6      }
7      return NULL;
8    }
```

Tying this together to the "non-functional", printing values via `printf` has the side-effect of outputting data to the standard output stream, i.e., the console. Intuitively, this may not necessarily seem like a side-effect because data is not being directly altered, but remember that side-effects need not only be the altering of variables directly; anything that is not "substitutable" via referential transparency breaks the side-effect "promise", so to speak. Astute readers may, therefore, question why we chose not to affix an exclamation point to the end of `printf`, e.g., `printf!`. We made this decision because we use `printf` many times throughout the remainder of this textbook, and caring about the fact that `printf` has side-effects is not as necessary as are the conveniences it inherently provides.

Exercise 8.10. (⋆)
Add the following escape character sequences to the `printf` function:

Escape Character	Functionality
~r	Carriage return character
~~	Print tilde character
~"	Print double quote character
~'	Print single quote character

Exercise 8.11. (⋆⋆⋆)
Some programming languages offer the ability to format strings directly without printing them to an output via the format function. It receives the same arguments as printf and behaves almost identically with the exception that the string is returned from the function rather than printed to standard output. Implement format as part of $\mathcal{L}_{OUT}$.

8.4   Parameter Passing Styles

Pass-By-Value

All functions that we have written within our language are *pass-by-value*. When we introduced the C programming language, we discussed both pass-by-value and another style called pass-by-pointer. In this section, we will describe pass-by-value in greater detail about what exactly occurs.

When we pass values to a function by value, it means that the function receives a *copy* of that value and not the original. For example, suppose we create a variable x and assign it the value 10.

Listing 8.38

```
1   int main(void) {
2     int x = 10;
3     return 0;
4   }
```

Now, further suppose that we pass this value to a function and alter its value to, say, 20.

Listing 8.39

```
1   void alter(int val) {                                              10
2     val = 20;                                                        10
3   }
4
5   int main(void) {
6     int x = 10;
7     printf("x before calling alter is %d\n", x);
8     alter(x);
9     printf("x after calling alter is %d\n", x);
10  }
```

Despite what we might expect at first glance, we are not actually modifying the original x! We instead created a copy of x when we invoked `alter`. This copy is then passed, and is, thereby, the one whose value we update to 20. Therefore, the output of x both before and after calling `alter` remains 10. This also happens when we supply, for instance, structs—namely, the entire struct (and its fields) copied when passing by value. So, it is largely a disadvantage to pass structs by value. Arrays, on the other hand, may only be passed by value, at least in C, when wrapped in a struct. This is because arrays are treated as pointers in C and, therefore, are not passable by value. In the languages we have written thus far, all values are passed by value. As an example, when we supply a list, number, symbol, procedure, etc., to a function, we pass a copy of the list. To exemplify this, let us write an interpreter, in our language, that implements pass-by-value semantics.

Listing 8.40

```
(define reduce-symbol
 (λ (exp env)
  (let ([b (apply-env exp env)])
   (unbox b))))

(define reduce-begin2
 (λ (exp env)
  (let ([rand1 (value-of-pbv (second exp) env)]
        [rand2 (value-of-pbv (third exp) env)])
   (begin
    rand1
    rand2))))

(define reduce-set
 (λ (exp env)
  (let ([y (second exp)]
        [body (third exp)])
   (set-box! (apply-env y env) (value-of-pbv body env)))))

(define reduce-application
 (λ (exp env)
  (let ([rator (value-of-pbv (first exp) env)]
        [rand (value-of-pbv (second exp) env)])
   (rator (box rand)))))

(define value-of-pbv
 (λ (exp env)
  (cond
   [(number? exp) (reduce-number exp env)]
   [(symbol? exp) (reduce-symbol exp env)]
   [(add? exp) (reduce-add exp env)]
   [(begin2? exp) (reduce-begin2 exp env)]
   [(set? exp) (reduce-set exp env)]
   [(fib? exp) (reduce-fib exp env)]
   [(loop? exp) (reduce-loop exp env)]
   [(lambda? exp) (reduce-lambda exp env)]
   [(application? exp) (reduce-application exp env)]
   [else #f])))
```

This interpreter looks not so different from previous interpreters that we have written–the only distinction being that we add a few new forms that our evaluator recognizes: begin2, set!, fib, loop. Moreover, our environment stores values as *boxes*. Boxes store values, and we may change the box contents when we pass the box across functions. Consider the following example:

Listing 8.41

```
(define alter                          │
 (λ (b)                                 │
  (set-box! b 10)))                     │
                                        │
(define my-box (box 5))                 │
                                        │
> (unbox my-box)                        │ 5
> (alter my-box)                        │
> (unbox my-box)                        │ 10
```

We have the `alter`, which receives a box and replaces its stored value with 10. Below the definition of `alter` we define `my-box` to wrap the constant integer 5. To retrieve the value from within a box, we use the "unbox" function. So, as the output suggests, before we modify the value inside the box, its value is 5. After passing it to `my-box`, its contents are updated to 10. The question now is, why are boxes important for pass-by-value? We will soon understand why! As a brief aside from our discussion on parameter passing styles, we will implement boxes in $\mathcal{L}_{\text{SET!}}$ to show how they work under the hood.

Boxes are nothing more than fancy pairs whose *first* is the tag `'box` and whose *rest* is the item it encapsulates. So, if we want to create a box via a function appropriately named box, we return a `cons` pair with the aforementioned contents. The argument to this function is, hence, the value to wrap.

Listing 8.42

```
(define box
 (λ (val)
  (cons 'box val)))
```

If we want to test a value for "boxness", i.e., whether it is a box or not, we may write a predicate box?.

Listing 8.43

```
(define box?
 (λ (b)
  (and (cons? b)
       (eqv? (first b) 'box))))
```

This definition is a little generic in that it means that pair whose *first* is the symbol `'box`, but such a lax framework allows us to easily implement boxes. Next, we should write `set-box!` and `unbox` where the former receives a box and an expression to assign, and the latter receives a box and returns its stored expression.[1]

Listing 8.44

```
(define set-box!
 (λ (b exp)
  (set-rest! b exp)))

(define unbox
 (λ (b)
  (rest b)))
```

Let us test this implementation using the small example from before.

Listing 8.45

```
(define alter                          │
 (λ (b)                                 │
  (set-box! b 10)))                     │
                                        │
(define my-box (box 5))                 │
                                        │
> (unbox my-box)                        │ 5
> (alter my-box)                        │
> (unbox my-box)                        │ 10
```

---

[1]Unboxing a box is, according to our implementation, equivalent to invoking `rest` on the box.

With our discussion on boxes, we can return to our pass-by-value interpreter and see how it uses boxes. As we stated, environment symbols are wrapped in boxes. At the moment, this will be rather meaningless since this is a pass-by-value interpreter.

This interpreter contains several new forms, including fib and loop. These are two simple functions: fib implements the traditional doubly-recursive algorithm, whereas loop simply loops infinitely. Given the simplicity of these functions, we omit their inclusion. Though, some may wonder why we include them in the first place. Again, this motivation will be brought to life soon.

We also omit the environment "helper" functions as well as the irrelevant recognizers and reducers so as to not clutter our discussion. We know that with pass-by-value semantics, functions always evaluate their arguments before application. Trying out a few programs, we see that, even arguments that are never referenced in the body of a function, are still evaluated ahead of time. This is problematic if that argument is an infinite loop, which means that the function is never fully invoked!

Listing 8.46

```
> (value-of-pbv '((lambda (x)              5
                    ((lambda (y)
                      (begin2
                       (set! y 2)
                       x)) x)) 5)
                  (empty-env))
> (value-of-pbv '(((lambda (x)             3
                    (lambda (y) x))
                   3)
                  (fib 40))
                  (empty-env))

> (value-of-pbv '(((lambda (x)             ⊥
                    (lambda (y) x))
                   3)
                  (loop))
                  (empty-env))
```

Our first example shows that modifying the value of the argument y does not change its original value. In other words, we pass a copy of y to the lambda function and not a reference to y. The last two examples demonstrate the problems that emerge when pass-by-value is the only option. In the second example, we pass an invocation of (fib 40) to the function. Because we have to evaluate a function's arguments before its application, (fib 40) is evaluated, even though we never actually reference the variable it binds! y never occurs bound in the function, meaning its evaluation is superfluous. Our final example passes an invocation of loop to a function. Because loop never terminates, this program will run forever (or at least eventually crash). We use the up tack, '⊥' or falsum, to reference a program that never terminates. We will tackle this problem in the sections after next. For the time being, though, we want to address this issue of altering values passed to a function. In C, as we said, we call this notion pass-by-pointer, but because our language has no pointers, we will instead refer to it as *pass-by-reference*.

Pass-By-Reference

Passing values by reference allows us to change the data at the original reference of a variable. Note that passing constants, e.g., numbers and symbols, by reference is no different than the semantics present when passing by value. Let us see the changes we need to make to the interpreter to implement pass-by-reference semantics. Fortunately, we only need to add one recognizer and reducer (and change all instances of value-of-pbv to value-of-pbr)!

Listing 8.47

```
(define symbol-application?
 (λ (exp)
  (and (cons? exp)
       (= (length exp) 2)
       (symbol? (second exp)))))

(define reduce-symbol-application
 (λ (exp env)
  (let ([rator (value-of-pbr (first exp) env)]
        [rand (apply-env (second exp) env)])
   (rator rand))))

(define value-of-pbr
 (λ (exp env)
  (cond
   [...]
   [(symbol-application? exp) (reduce-symbol-application exp env)]
   [(application? exp) (reduce-application exp env)]
   [else #f])))
```

Here's the thing: what exactly *is* pass-by-reference? Well, we wrap all values within boxes, right? So, if the argument in a function application is a symbol, instead of passing the unboxed argument itself, we should pass the box! This way, we can change the contents of the argument box, and these mutations are reflected in the original. Other than this slight modification, everything is identical to the pass-by-value interpreter. If we try the first example from the previous section, we should receive 2 instead of 5 as our result.

The paradigm of passing values by reference does not solve the problem of arguments, that are not referenced, being superfluously evaluated; it is made evident if we decide to re-run either the fib or loop programs. So, how can we dispel this predicament? By being lazy, of course!

Exercise 8.12. (⋆⋆⋆⋆⋆)

The *Rust* programming language uses *references* and *borrowing* for objects [Klabnik and Nichols, 2018]. In essence, Rust contains a paradigm such that an object may only have one owner at a time. An object, in this case, is anything that encapsulates a value, e.g., boxes, lists, and so on. For example, if we create a box b with a value 10, and pass b by reference to a function f, we say that f borrows b for the lifetime of the function. Attempting to modify b inside f, at least in Rust, causes a compilation error. Our interpreters are not compiled, so we will have to settle for runtime errors. Implement function borrowing of lists (and by extension boxes), in which if a function attempts to call set-fst!, set-rst!, or set-box! on the borrowed reference, an error is displayed and the value is not altered. In addition to this, allow the programmer to define variables that act as references themselves, similar to pointers in C. This might be achieved via a tagged list:

Listing 8.48—Borrowed References in Nested Interpreter

```
> (value-of                                              err: attempted to
   '(let ([x (cons 1 (cons 2 (cons 3 (quote ()))))])      alter immutable
      (let ([y (cons (quote ref) (cons x (quote ())))])   object (1 2 3).
        (let ([f (lambda (ls)
                   (begin2
                    (set-first! ls 5)
                    ls))])
          (f y))))
   (empty-env))
```

Passing y to a function indicates that y is an immutable reference to x. Note that this is a multi-pronged exercise because it requires implementing cons, quote, set-fst!, and set-rst! into the nested interpreter; none of which are substantially more difficult than the other special forms.

Exercise 8.13. (⋆⋆⋆⋆⋆)

Rust also has mutable references, which allow the programmer to designate that a reference may be altered by a function [Klabnik and Nichols, 2018]. Add mutable references to the pass-by-reference interpreter via tagged lists, i.e., add the 'mut symbol as the *first* of the provided box or list. Finally, it is not possible to have both a mutable and immutable reference to the same variable in an environment. For instance, the following program should display a relevant error because we attempt to declare both mutable and immutable references to x:

Listing 8.49—Borrowed References in Nested Interpreter

```
> (value-of                                              err: cannot create
   '(let ([x (cons 1 (cons 2 (cons 3 (quote ()))))])      both mutable and
      (let ([y (cons (quote ref) (cons x (quote ())))])   immutable
        (let ([z (cons (quote mut)                        references to the
                   (cons (quote ref)                      same object
                     (cons x (quote ()))))])
          (+ (first x) (first y) (first z)))))
   (empty-env))
```

On the other hand, the following example should be perfectly fine and produce a result:

Listing 8.50—Borrowed References in Nested Interpreter

```
> (value-of                                              (5 2 3)
    '(let ([x (cons 1 (cons 2 (cons 3 (quote ()))))])
      (let ([z (cons (quote mut)
               (cons (quote ref)
               (cons x (quote ()))))])
    (begin2
     (set-first! z 5)
     z)))
  (empty-env))
```

To compensate for the increased difficulty, you do not need to consider lists that contain a 'mut tag without a 'ref tag.

Lazy Evaluation by Name

Deferred evaluation, or *lazy evaluation*, is a core concept in programming with particular significance in certain data structures. Sometimes, we do not always want to perform a computation immediately. We can defer evaluation of some expression, until it is referenced, via *thunks*. Before we properly define a thunk, let us look at a motivating example.

Listing 8.51

```
(define fib
 (λ (n)
  (cond
   [(<= n 1) 1]
   [else (+ (fib (- n 1))
           (fib (- n 2)))])))
```

The above code segment is a definition of the standard Fibonacci function, as we have repeatedly referenced. If we run this with any value of $n > 20$, this function will take a while to compute. Let us say that we define a variable f to hold the value of (fib 30).

Listing 8.52

```
(define f (fib 30))
```

Here's the catch: what if this is the last line in our program? Or even worse: what if we simply never reference f? Thus, we computed (fib 30) for absolutely no reason, wasting valuable time. So, what can we do to fix the problem? If we wrap the expression in a thunk, the issue disappears! *Thunks* are functions of no arguments, and a thunk's body is the code to lazily evaluate. Let us wrap f in a thunk to see what this changes.

Listing 8.53

```
(define f (λ () (fib 20)))
```

If we run this program now, it instantaneously finishes because we did not compute (fib 20)! f is now a thunk, and if we try to display the value of f, we will get <procedure>. And, more importantly, we only evaluate (fib 20) upon invoking f:

Listing 8.54

```
(define f (λ () (fib 20)))

> f                                            <function>
> (f)                                          10946
```

Aside from the fitting name of lazy-evaluation (compared to pass-by-value, which is sometimes referred to as eager-evaluation), this parameter passing paradigm is called *pass-by-name*.[1] Let us make the necessary changes to our interpreter to implement pass-by-name semantics.

Listing 8.55

```
(define reduce-symbol
 (λ (exp env)
  (let* ([b (apply-env exp env)]
         [th (unbox b)])
   (th))))

(define reduce-application
 (λ (exp env)
  (let ([rator (value-of-pbv (first exp) env)]
        [rand (second exp)])
   (rator (box
           (λ ()
            (value-of-pbname rand env)))))))

(define value-of-pbname
 (λ (exp env)
  (cond
   [...]
   [else #f])))
```

The only differences between this interpreter and the pass-by-value interpreter occur in the symbol and application reductions. The latter is more important; we create a thunk containing the code to evaluate later when invoked and then wrap this in a box. The former, when a symbol is found, retrieves the box and unwraps it, revealing a thunk. From there, it is as simple as invoking the thunk identical to how we invoke regular functions. Re-running the long-winded examples from before show us that neither fib nor loop are ever invoked: our desired outcome. The third example, however, does invoke fib because we reference y in the addition expression.

Listing 8.56

```
> (value-of-pbname '(((lambda (x)                    3
                       (lambda (y) x)) 3)
                     (fib 40))
                   (empty-env))
> (value-of-pbname '(((lambda (x)                    3
                       (lambda (y) x)) 3)
                     (loop))
                   (empty-env))
> (value-of-pbname '(((lambda (x)                    1346272
                       (lambda (y) (+ y x)))
                      3)
                     (fib 30))
                   (empty-env))
```

---

[1]ALGOL 60 was the language that pioneered pass-by-name semantics, which is also called *call-by-name* in the older literature [Backus et al., 1960].

One problem with this pass-by-name approach is that we have to constantly evaluate symbols each time they are encountered. Consider the following function:

Listing 8.57

```
(value-of-pbname '((lambda (x)
  (+ x (+ x (+ x (+ x (+ x (+ x (+ x (+ x (+ x
  (+ x (+ x (+ x (+ x (+ x (+ x (+ x (+ x (+ x
  (+ x (+ x (+ x (+ x (+ x (+ x (+ x (+ x (+ x
  x)))))))))))))))))))))))))))) (fib 30))
  (empty-env))
```

While this is indeed a very silly example, it demonstrates the issue with pass-by-name semantics. We want this code to evaluate (fib 30) exactly once since it does not change anything in between invocations. A way to solve this is to evaluate variable references once and only once. Then, store the result in the environment, and simply retrieve it when it is referenced in the body. *Pass-by-need* semantics solve this problem.[1]

Lazy Evaluation by Need

Some creative readers may be inclined to implement pass-by-need on their own by setting the box of a thunk to its evaluated value.

Listing 8.58

```
(define reduce-symbol
 (λ (exp env)
  (let* ([b (apply-env exp env)]
         [th (unbox b)]
         [res-th (th)])
   (begin
    (set-box! b res-th)
    res-th))))
```

Unfortunately, trying this out on the following simple example displays an error.

Listing 8.59

```
(value-of-pbneed '(((lambda (x) (lambda (y) (+ y y))) 3) (fib 5)) (empty-env))
```

The problem is that we are storing the result directly back into the box. Thus, when we reference the symbol again, it assumes that there is a thunk in place of the expression and, therefore, performs a function application. We can solve this by simply wrapping the evaluated expression in another thunk, as the cost of creating and evaluating thunks is effectively zero.

---

[1]Chris Wadsworth is credited with introducing pass-by-need, or *call-by-need*, semantics for the λ-calculus in his PhD dissertation [Wadsworth, 1971]. Though, both Henderson & Morris [Henderson and Morris, 1976] and Friedman & Wise [Friedman and Wise, 1976] independently introduced lazy evaluation in 1976.

Listing 8.60

```
(define reduce-symbol
 (λ (exp env)
  (let* ([b (apply-env exp env)]
         [th (unbox b)]
         [res-th (th)])
   (begin
    (set-box! b (λ () res-th))
    res-th))]))
```

Executing the wildly silly example from before returns the result very quickly since it only needs to compute (fib 30) once. The idea is to save the value of a computed expression after its evaluation to avoid unnecessary computations. Caching results in this manner is called *memoization* and provides extreme performance improvements in certain scenarios like we have presented.

8.5 $\mathcal{L}^*_{\text{EVAL}}$: A Metacircular Evaluator

At the beginning of the nested interpreters section of Chapter 7, we wrote an interpreter that evaluates simple expressions such as `let` bindings, one-argument `lambda` procedures, conditionals, booleans, symbols, and numbers. In this section, we will extend this idea into $\mathcal{L}^*_{\text{EVAL}}$: a nested interpreter that evaluates more complex expressions and controls the entire evaluation pipeline.

When we say "metacircular evaluator", we mean an evaluator that evaluates expressions written in that language. We have, technically, written several metacircular evaluators, but none to the extent that $\mathcal{L}^*_{\text{EVAL}}$ shall be. In particular, when we wrote $\mathcal{L}^*_{\text{PROC}}$, we only wrote `value-of` standing in for the evaluator. We relied on the host interpreter to perform function application for any arbitrary function. Furthermore, we also restricted the arity of some functions, e.g., addition, to only two arguments. Sure, we can combine additive expressions together to simulate multi-arity addition, but this is a bit too limiting. We want to be able to allow the programmer to write any arbitrary procedure of any number of arguments... how is this even possible?

First, we need to understand the "type" of expressions that our evaluator interprets. Our language allows for "self-evaluating" expressions, e.g., numbers and booleans that resolve to themselves. It also allows symbols that are looked up in the current environment. Quoted expressions are similarly supported via the `quote` function, e.g., `(quote 5)`. Additionally, `if`, `lambda`, and function application are all supported.

Fortunately, several functions/recognizers/reducers are identical to our previous implementations. Our environment helpers, i.e., `apply-env`, `extend-env`, and `empty-env`, are identical and use association lists as the backing representation.

Listing 8.61

```
(define quote?              (define eval-quote
  (λ (exp)                    (λ (exp env)
    (eqv? (first exp) 'quote)))   (second exp)))
```

Listing 8.62

```
(define if?                 (define eval-if
  (λ (exp)                    (λ (exp env)
    (eqv? (first exp) 'if)))    (if (eval (second exp) env)
                                    (eval (third exp) env)
                                    (eval (fourth exp) env))))
```

Listing 8.63

```
(define lambda?             (define eval-lambda
  (λ (exp)                    (λ (exp env)
    (eqv? (first exp) 'lambda)))  ...))
```

Listing 8.64

```
(define eval
 (λ (exp env)
  (cond
   [(number? exp) exp]
   [(symbol? exp) (apply-env exp env)]
   [(quote? exp) (eval-quote exp env)]
   [(if? exp) (eval-if exp env)]
   [(lambda? exp) (eval-lambda exp env)]
   [else #f])))
```

All of these definitions should be understandable by the reader. As a refresher, though, evaluating a quoted expression simply returns the expression that is quoted. if expressions evaluate the consequent if the predicate is true and the alternative otherwise. lambda expressions are more complicated and require careful explanation.

lambda expressions contain three components as a list: its *first* is the symbol lambda, its *second* is a list of symbols representing the formal parameters, and its *third* is the procedure body. As we have before, when we encounter a lambda, we want to return a procedure. The thing is, however, we do not know how many arguments the procedure will receive! Fortunately for us, we have variadic arguments to the rescue!

Listing 8.65

```
(define eval-lambda
 (λ (exp env)
  (λ-var (args)
   ...)))
```

By using variadic arguments, we say that the lambda procedure that is returned accepts any number of arguments. Inside the procedure definition, args is a list of received arguments. When we had only one argument, we invoked extend-env to bind the formal parameter of the lambda to the given argument. Because we may have more than one argument, however, we need to write a procedure that binds a list of formals to a list of arguments in an extended environment. We call this procedure bind-formals. Also, as a measure of simplification, we do not consider "malformed lists", i.e., when the number of formals does not match the number of arguments and vice-versa.

Listing 8.66

```
(define bind-formals
 (λ (formals args env)
  (cond
   [(or (null? formals) (null? args)) env]
   [else
    (extend-env (first formals)
                (first args)
                (bind-formals (rest formals) (rest args)))])))
```

From here, we can complete the definition of eval-lambda. That is, we extract the formal parameter list into a let* binding, invoke bind-formals, then evaluate the body of the lambda. All of this, of course, is encapsulated within a lambda to defer evaluation until its invocation.

Listing 8.67

```
(define eval-lambda
 (λ (exp env)
  (λ-var (arg-list)
   (let* ([formals (second exp)]
          [args (first arg-list)]
          [body (third exp)]
          [new-env (bind-formals formals args env)])
    (eval body new-env)))))
```

Last but not least, we need to handle function application. Recall how this is done at the interpreter level: each argument is evaluated, then applied by the function. Because function arity is unknown before runtime, we have to approach this issue slightly differently. Namely, we will write a function `apply` that receives a function and a list of arguments. `apply` is analogous (in fact almost identical in how it operates) to `eval_application` at the interpreter level.

Listing 8.68

```
(define apply
 (λ (rator rands)
  (rator rands)))
```

Furthermore, we do not permit `apply` to evaluate its operator and operand list, but rather it assumes that these are already pre-evaluated coming into the function definition. So, we must evaluate these in the body of eval—an easy task when coupled with `map`.

Listing 8.69

```
(define eval
 (λ (exp env)
  (cond
   [...]
   [else (apply (eval (first exp) env)
               (map (λ (a) (eval a env)) (rest exp)))])))
```

Sadly, there is a subtle issue with how `apply` works, or more specifically, how we deal with function application. A function such as + does not receive a list of arguments but rather any *number* of arguments! So, binding the symbol + to the *function* + in the empty environment will not work for our purposes. Instead, we need write a function, e.g., `apply-plus`, that receives a list of (evaluated) values and computes their sum. We can do this in one of two ways: naturally recursive or via `foldr`. For pedagogical reasons, we choose the former but note that apply-plus can be written more succinctly with `foldr`. Updating the environment is also mandatory, which we define as `base-env` so as to not constantly alter the implementation of `empty-env`.

Listing 8.70

```
(define base-env
 (λ ()
  (extend-env '+ apply-plus (empty-env))))

(define apply-plus
 (λ (rands)
  (cond
   [(null? rands) 0]
   [else (+ (first rands)
            (apply-plus (rest rands)))])))
```

At long last, we may write a few test cases to show that addition works as intended.

Listing 8.71

> (eval '(+ 2 2) (base-env))	4
> (eval '(+ 50 (+ 100 20) 90) (base-env))	260
> (eval '(+ (+ (+ 1 2) 3 4 5 6) 7 8 (+ 9 10))	55
(base-env))	

Excellent! Let us now write some lambda procedures; one test will receive only one argument, another will return a function of one argument, and one more will receive three arguments from the onset.

Listing 8.72

> (eval '((lambda (x) (+ x 5)) 10)	15
(base-env))	
> (eval '(((lambda (x) (lambda (y) (+ x y))) 2) 3)	5
(base-env))	
> (eval '((lambda (x y z)	120
(+ (+ x x) (+ y y) (+ z z)))	
10 20 30)	
(base-env))	

Suppose that we wanted to implement side-effects, i.e., assignment statements such as set!. How can we do that? The thing to note is that we have to modify our environment to keep references to items. Because our interpreter passes lists by *reference* and not by value, if we somehow store a reference to a *first* or *rest*, we modify the original list and not a copy. So, let us amend our environment implementation to store boxed expressions as the *rest* of an association. This requires updating all environment helper functions as well as the symbol? case of the evaluator to utilize boxed values.

With this, we may implement assignment statements which alter the value within a box.

Listing 8.73

```
(define eval-set
 (λ (exp env)
  (let* ([y (second exp)]
         [b (apply-env y env)])
   (set-box! b (eval (third exp) env)))))
```

Though, assignment statements are not very useful if our procedures are only allowed one expression in their bodies. So, we should add chained expressions via begin.

Implementing a "variadic" begin handler is not difficult—the idea, exactly how it is defined at the interpreter level, is to evaluate each expression sequentially and return the result of the last-evaluated expression. Therefore, we must assume that the list of expressions in a begin is non-empty. We define a local recursive procedure so we may invoke it with the list of expressions to evaluate, trimming the 'begin symbol at the front.

Listing 8.74

```
(define eval-begin
 (letrec ([helper
           (λ (exp env)
            (cond
             [(null? (rest exp)) (eval (first exp) env)]
             [else
              (begin
               (eval (first exp) env)
               (helper (rest exp) env))]))])
  (λ (exp env)
   (helper (rest exp) env))))
```

With this, we should certainly write a test or two that modifies/reassigns the argument(s) to a lambda. The second example requires adding a function to apply multiplication to a list of values.

Listing 8.75

```
> (eval '((lambda (x)                                  100
           (begin
            (set! x 100)
            x))
          50)
        (base-env))
> (eval                                                1320000
   '((lambda (x y z)
       (begin
        (set! x (+ x y z)) ; x=(+ 10 20 30) =60
        (set! y (+ x y z)) ; y=(+ 60 20 30) =110
        (set! z (+ x y z)) ; z=(+ 60 110 30) =200
        (* x y z))) ; =(* 60 110 200)=1320000
      10 20 30)
   (base-env))
```

How about we allow programmers to write define statements? Is this even possible? Of course it is! It requires a bit of work, but it is certainly manageable.

First, let us consider what happens when we invoke define. Rather than extend, we amend the environment to include a new binding. We will revisit this again in the next few sections, but the idea is as follows: we create a side-effect inducing environment-utility function amend-env! that updates the environment passed as an argument. Recall, though, that in order to modify a value by reference, it must be passed as a box. Therefore, we must update our environment representation to be pass-by-reference encapsulated in a box. This way, when we want to amend its contents with a new binding, we update the environment itself and not just a local copy passed to the function.

Again, because our environments use a representation-independent structure, any modifications made to them should not require altering the interpreter/evaluator, and this change is no exception.

Listing 8.76

```
(define apply-env
  (λ (y env)
    (let ([env (unbox env)])
      (cond
        [(null? env) #f]
        [else
          (let ([binding (first env)])
            (cond
              [(eqv? (first binding) y) (rest binding)]
              [else (apply-env y (box (rest env)))]))]))))

(define extend-env
  (λ (x arg env)
    (box (cons (cons x (box arg)) (unbox env)))))

(define empty-env
  (λ ()
    (box '())))
```

With these updates, apply-env now unboxes the environment and searches its content association list for a variable binding. If it does not exist, however, we recursively "re-box" the environment so that in the next recursive step, we may "re-unbox" the environment. extend-env unboxes the current environment, prepends the new binding to the front of the old association list, and finally "re-boxes" the environment. empty-env simply boxes the empty environment. Though, as we stated, we need to write amend-env!, which we will do now.

Listing 8.77

```
(define amend-env!
  (λ (x arg env)
    (set-box! env (unbox (extend-env x arg env)))))
```

As an example, if we invoke (amend-env! 'x 5 e), where e is defined as an environment containing (extend-env 'y 10 (extend-env 'z 20 (box '()))), we modify the box contents of e to be (extend-env 'x 5 (extend-env 'y 10 (extend-env 'z 20 (box '())))). This behavior is precisely what we are looking for with define. So, we can now write the recognizer and reducer combination.

Listing 8.78

```
(define define?                    (define eval-define
  (λ (exp)                           (λ (exp env)
    (eqv? (first exp) 'define)))       (let ([x (second exp)]
                                             [arg (eval (third exp) env)])
                                         (amend-env! x arg env))))
```

That is all it takes! Adding this clause to the cond inside eval is trivial, and we can now write a few tests. Note that to take full advantage of a define, we must enclose it with begin. Below is an example of defining add using natural recursion. Note that to implement this, one must first add a apply-minus function into the empty environment (this is harder than it may first appear!).

Listing 8.79

```
(eval '(begin
    (define add1
      (lambda (n) (+ n 1)))
    (define sub1
      (lambda (n) (- n 1)))
    (define add
      (lambda (n m)
        (if (= m 0)
            n
            (add (add1 n) (sub1 m)))))
    (add 5 7))
  (base-env))
```

Exercise 8.14. (⋆⋆)
Implement local `let` bindings into the metacircular evaluator. To make this simpler, you may start out by adding one-variable bindings and working your way up to any number of bindings.

Exercise 8.15. (⋆⋆)
Implement `let*` bindings into the metacircular evaluator. If you got the previous bindings to work, then this one should not be as difficult as all it requires is a bit of manipulating and extending environments.

Exercise 8.16. (⋆⋆)
Write an invocation of `eval` that defines (then calls) `factorial`. To do this, you will need to write three functions `apply-=`, `apply-minus`, and `apply-mult` (assuming you have not done so previously).

Exercise 8.17. (⋆⋆⋆⋆)
Write the `map*` function, which receives at least two arguments, namely a function *f* followed by lists of arguments to *f*. The function `map*` serves as a variadic variant of the `map` function; *f* should share an arity with the number of list arguments.

Listing 8.80

```
> (map* cons '(2 3) '(4 5))           ((2 . 4) (3 . 5))

> (map* (lambda (x y z)               (1121 234 173 36)
          (+ (* x x) (* y y) (* z z)))
        '(4 7 8 2)
        '(9 8 3 4)
        '(32 11 10 4))
```

8.6 $\mathcal{L}^*_{\text{ASM}}$: A Micro-Assembly Interpreter

In Chapter 5, we discussed compilation and the distinction between compiled and interpreted programs. In this section, we will write a nested interpreter $\mathcal{L}^*_{\text{ASM}}$ to interpret a small subset of an assembly-like programming language.

The assembly-esque language we will write contains only statements—a stark contrast from the nested interpreters we have experimented with previously. Recall that a statement is an expression that does not resolve to a value. For instance, the assignment statement $x = 5$ has a side-effect of setting the value of x to 5, but this line of code does not, itself, resolve to some value.

Our assembly code consists of registers and labels. The language contains primitive arithmetic operations, conditionals, and jump statements. There are four broad types of operators: register-to-register, immediate-to-register, comparison-based operations, and label-based operations.

A *register-to-register* operation uses only registers as its operands. An example is add r1 r2 r3, which adds the values in registers r2 and r3 and stores the sum in r1. An immediate-to-register operation performs on a register and an immediate value, i.e., a constant. For instance, subi r5 15 subtracts 15 from the contents in register r5.

A *comparison-based* operation is special in that it compares the values in two registers and sets a flag based on the result. For instance, (cmp r2 r3) will subtract r3 from r2, then store this result in the flag register.

Finally, we have *jump-based* operations, which act on labels. Recall that a *label* is an identifier placed in code to signify a destination. Namely, we can jump to a label with a jmp statement. The result of a comparison-based operation is accessible via, for example, jez (jump if equal to zero), which checks if the zero flag in the flags register is enabled and, if so, jumps to a given label. Our language also contains two "non-assembly" primitives: begin and disp, where the former receives a list of statements, and the latter outputs the contents of a register. These two will not be listed in the language grammar definition.

```
program            ::=   '( begin ' stmt+ ')'
stmt               ::=   reg-to-reg
                   |     imm-to-reg
                   |     cmp-operation
                   |     jmp-operation
reg-to-reg         ::=   '(' reg-to-reg-op reg reg reg ')'
imm-to-reg         ::=   '(' imm-to-reg-op reg imm ')'
cmp-operation      ::=   '(' cmp-operation-op reg reg ')'
jmp-operation      ::=   '(' jmp-operation-op lbl ')'
reg-to-reg-op      ::=   'add' | 'sub' | 'mul' | 'div'
imm-to-reg         ::=   'addi' | 'subi' | 'muli' | 'divi' | 'li'
cmp-operation-op   ::=   'cmp'
jmp-operation-op   ::=   'jmp' | 'jez' | ...
reg                ::=   'r'[1-9] | 'fl' | 'pc'
imm                ::=   number
lbl                ::=   [a-zA-Z][a-zA-Z0-9]*
```

Figure 8.5: BNF Grammar for $\mathcal{L}^{*}_{\text{ASM}}$

This grammar gives us some hints as to how we should design the language. First, though, we need to establish some environment contingencies. Our "root" environment will not be passed around to other functions since we need to modify it throughout program execution. By default, it contains all registers set to zero as association lists. We have two special registers: pc and fl. The former stores the current instruction number to execute next while the latter is a "flags" register, which is set by comparison-based operations and used by jump operations.

Listing 8.81

```
(define env `((r1 . 0) (r2 . 0) (r3 . 0) (r4 . 0) (r5 . 0) (pc . 0) (fl . 0)))
```

extend-env! updates env by prepending a cons pair that consists of an identifier and a value. Updating the environment with an identifier that already exists, therefore, shadows the original binding. This is somewhat akin to amend-env! from our metacircular evaluator; the difference here, though, is that there are no environments aside from the global root environment. Accordingly, we do not pass the environment as a parameter to any functions, so it is acceptable to call set! on the global environment object.

Listing 8.82

```
(define extend-env!
(λ (x arg)
  (set! env (cons (cons x arg) env))))
```

Finally, apply-env uses assv to find a binding and, if it exists, we return the value (i.e., the *rest* of the pair returned by assv).

Listing 8.83

```
(define apply-env
 (λ (v)
  (let ([res (assv v env)])
   (cond
    [(eqv? res #f) (printf "Value not found in env ~a~n" v)]
    [else (rest res)]))))
```

Now, we **need** our recognition functions for each of the four operation classes. We can distinguish between these by saying that a register-to-register operation contains three registers, an immediate-to-register operation contains one register and one immediate value, a comparison-based operation contains two registers, and a label operation contains one symbol. With these descriptions, we can easily design correct recognizers. Note that we also need to write recognizers for the two primitives begin and disp.

Listing 8.84

```
(define reg-to-reg?
 (λ (exp)
  (and (cons? exp)
       (= (length exp) 4)
       (symbol? (second exp))
       (symbol? (third exp))
       (symbol? (fourth exp)))))
```

Listing 8.85

```
(define imm-to-reg?
 (λ (exp)
  (and (cons? exp)
       (= (length exp) 3)
       (symbol? (second exp))
       (number? (third exp)))))
```

Listing 8.86

```
(define cmp-operation?
 (λ (exp)
  (and (cons? exp)
       (= (length exp) 3)
       (symbol? (second exp))
       (symbol? (third exp)))))
```

Listing 8.87

```
(define lbl-operation?
 (λ (exp)
  (and (cons? exp)
       (= (length exp) 2)
       (symbol? (second exp)))))
```

Listing 8.88

```
(define begin?
 (λ (exp)
  (and (cons? exp)
       (= (length exp) 2)
       (eqv? (first exp) 'begin)
       (cons? (second exp)))))
```

Listing 8.89

```
(define disp?
 (λ (exp)
  (and (cons? exp)
       (= (length exp) 2)
       (eqv? (first exp) 'disp))))
```

Now we write the evaluation functions. Conveniently enough, the four operation classes follow a very similar template. The latter two, however, are a bit more involved. Consequently, we show those first.

Listing 8.90

```
(define value-of-begin
 (λ (exp)
  (let ([los (second exp)])
   (letrec ([execute
             (λ ()
              (cond
               [(>= (apply-env 'pc) (length los)) 'PROGRAM-TERMINATED]
               [else
                (begin
                 (value-of (list-ref (apply-env 'pc) los))
                 (extend-env! 'pc (add1 (apply-env 'pc)))
                 (execute))])]])
    (execute)))))
```

Listing 8.91

```
(define value-of-disp
 (λ (exp)
  (let ([r (second exp)])
   (printf "~a~n" (apply-env r)))))
```

Now, let us write the templates for the four operation classes.

Listing 8.92

```
(define value-of-reg-to-reg
 (λ (exp)
  (let ([op (first exp)]
        [r1 (second exp)]
        [r2 (third exp)]
        [r3 (fourth exp)])
   (cond
    [(eqv? op 'add) ...]
    [(eqv? op 'sub) ...]
    [(eqv? op 'mul) ...]
    [(eqv? op 'div) ...]
    [else 'error-value-of-reg-to-reg]))))
```

Listing 8.93

```
(define value-of-imm-to-reg
 (λ (exp)
  (let ([op (first exp)]
        [r (second exp)]
        [i (third exp)])
   (cond
    [(eqv? op 'addi) ...]
    [(eqv? op 'subi) ...]
    [(eqv? op 'muli) ...]
    [(eqv? op 'divi) ...]
    [(eqv? op 'li) ...]
    [else 'error-value-of-imm-to-reg]))))
```

Listing 8.94

```
(define value-of-cmp-operation
 (λ (exp)
  (let ([op (first exp)]
        [r1 (second exp)]
        [r2 (third exp)])
   (cond
    [(eqv? op 'cmp) ...]
    [else 'error-value-of-cmp-operation])))))
```

Listing 8.95

```
(define value-of-lbl-operation
 (λ (exp)
  (let ([op (first exp)]
        [name (second exp)])
   (cond
    [(eqv? op 'lbl) ...]
    [(eqv? op 'jmp) ...]
    [else 'error-value-of-lbl-operation])))))
```

Due to how similar many of these operations are, we will only implement a subset and leave the rest as exercises to the reader.

First, let us implement the register-to-register operation add. As we said, it adds the contents of two registers and stores the result in another register. All we need to do is retrieve the contents of r2 and r3 with apply-env, then update the environment to contain the new binding to r1.

Listing 8.96

```
(define value-of-reg-to-reg
 (λ (exp)

  [(eqv? op 'add) (extend-env! r1 (+ (apply-env r2) (apply-env r3)))]
   ...))
```

Our registers, at the start, contain only zeroes, so adding any two registers together, at this point, makes little sense. We need a way of adding literal values into a register. As hinted, we can do this via addi.

Listing 8.97

```
(define value-of-imm-to-reg
 (λ (exp)

  [(eqv? op 'addi) (extend-env! r (+ (apply-env r) i))]
   ...))
```

We stated that the comparison operator subtracts the contents of its register arguments and stores the sign of the result in the fl register. Let us now add this behavior to the relevant function.

Listing 8.98

```
(define value-of-cmp-operation
 (λ (exp)

  [(eqv? op 'cmp) (extend-env! 'fl (- (apply-env r1)
                                      (apply-env r2)))]
   ...))
```

As part of the label operators, we will implement lbl and jnez. lbl declares a label and stores it in the environment. A label, in the environment, is stored as a pair where the *first* is the label name and the *rest* is the associated program counter value. jnez determines if the fl register is not zero and if so, we set the program counter to be the value associated with the label that we jump to.

Listing 8.99

```
(define value-of-lbl-operation
 (λ (exp)
   ...
   [(eqv? op 'lbl) (extend-env! name (apply-env 'pc))]
   [(eqv? op 'jnez) (if (not (zero? (apply-env 'fl)))
                        (extend-env! 'pc (apply-env name))
                        (extend-env! 'pc (+ (apply-env 'pc) 0)))]
   ...))
```

The only remaining piece is the value-of procedure.

Listing 8.100

```
(define value-of
 (λ (exp)
   (cond
    [(begin? exp) (value-of-begin exp)]
    [(disp? exp) (value-of-disp exp)]
    [(lbl-operation? exp) (value-of-lbl-operation exp)]
    [(cmp-operation? exp) (value-of-cmp-operation exp)]
    [(imm-to-reg? exp) (value-of-imm-to-reg exp)]
    [(reg-to-reg? exp) (value-of-reg-to-reg exp)]
    [else 'error])))
```

As a proof-of-concept, we will write a program to compute the factorial of an integer. Note that we also implemented the mul and subi operations to make this a possibility.

Listing 8.101

```
> (value-of                                  120
   '(begin
      ((li r1 1)
       (li r2 5)
       (li r3 0)
       (lbl loop)
       (mul r1 r1 r2)
       (subi r2 1)
       (cmp r2 r3)
       (jnez loop)
       (disp r1))))
```

We will explore a different dialect of the assembly programming language in much greater detail in our later chapter on compilation. For now, though, we hope that this brief exposure is enough to convince the readers that assembly, in general, is a *very* low-level language!

Exercise 8.18. (⋆⋆)
Finish the rest of the interpreter to add support for sub, mul, div, and the remaining immediate-to-register operations. The registers in a register-to-register operation may all be the same. Division between two registers stores the result in r1 and its remainder is discarded. Note the issue of dividing by zero!

8.7　$\mathcal{L}^*_{\text{IMPERATIVE}}$: Thinking Imperatively

In this section, we will take a big leap into the world of imperative language design via $\mathcal{L}^*_{\text{IMPERATIVE}}$: a language with imperative constructs.

Imperative languages often use statements to express ideas with side effects, as we have previously discussed. The most prominent of which is the assignment statement. For example, x := 5 binds the value 5 to the variable x. More examples include looping and decision statements, e.g., for, if, and while. In the C language, none of these resolve to a value themselves, but rather they may return a value as part of a function. $\mathcal{L}^*_{\text{IMPERATIVE}}$ will differ slightly from this idea in that certain constructs are still expressions and resolve to values accordingly. Let us look at an example of a program written in $\mathcal{L}^*_{\text{IMPERATIVE}}$.

Listing 8.102

```
((fn fact n := (if (n = 0)
                  1
                  (n * (fact (n - 1)))))
 (fn fib x := (if (x = 0)
                  0
                  (if (x = 1)
                      1
                      ((fib (x - 1)) + (fib (x - 2))))))
 (val1 := 5)
 (val2 := (val1 + val1))
 (z := (fact val1))
 (w := (fib val2))
 (z := (w * (fib (2 * (val2 - 5)))))))
```

This program has a lot of details and new constructs to explain! Firstly, we see that a program is a list of expressions or statements. Programs are evaluated from top-to-bottom. A programming language is, from a convenience perspective, rather incomplete without functions or procedures of some kind. So, we declare two functions: fact and fib, which compute the factorial of some number n and the xth Fibonacci number respectively. Next, we declare five variables and assign them values. Unlike previous languages, binary operators are infix rather than post-fix, i.e., instead of (+ 2 3), we write (2+3). Though, because such a notation introduces precedence and associativity issues, all binary operators must be enclosed by parentheses. Regarding the assignment statements, a variable can be reassigned throughout program execution. In other variants of our interpreter, we allow such modifications via set!, but as we know, this introduces the side-effect of altering the value of a variable.

So, how do we begin? We first must introduce the notion of an *environment stack* and how function invocation plays a role. Unlike our other interpreters, functions may be of more than one argument and are not saved between function invocations. Namely, once we invoke a function that declares a variable, say, z, the lifetime of z extends only to the end of the function. To simulate this, as well as variable modification, we need to keep track of environments on a stack. That is, each time a function is invoked, we push an extended environment to the stack and, whenever the function body is finished being evaluated, we pop this environment off the stack.

How do we go about building an environment stack? Firstly, we need to have some notion of empty and base environments. The base environment contains a few built-in function operators as an association list, which extends the empty environment.

Listing 8.103

```
(define empty-env
 (λ ()
  '()))

(define extend-env
 (λ (x arg env)
  (cons (cons x arg) env)))

(define base-env
 (λ ()
  (extend-env '+ +
   (extend-env '- -
    (extend-env '* *
     (extend-env '/ /
      (extend-env '= =)))))))
```

Now, we want to represent an environment stack. But before we construct it, we should understand that, because environments are dynamic and may be continuously updated (to contain a new variable or binding), we need to store environments in *boxes*. Recall that we used boxes when implementing *pass-by-reference* interpreters. This way, updating the environment alters the original copy between function invocations.

Listing 8.104

```
(define environment-stack (list (box (empty-env))))
```

From here, we want to be able to access the current environment. By design, the current environment, i.e., the environment in-use, is the environment on the top of the stack. Because the stack is a list of boxes, we can retrieve the first, or top-most value, via *first*.

Listing 8.105

```
(define current-env
 (λ ()
  (first environment-stack)))
```

Next, we need two procedures for adding an environment to the stack and removing the top-most environment. The latter is trivial, but the former is a bit more abstract. Because we want the new environment to hold the same values as the current environment, we first need to unbox the current, create a new environment box, and prepend it to the front of the environment stack.

Listing 8.106

```
(define push-env!
 (λ ()
  (let ([cenv (unbox (current-env))])
   (set! environment-stack (list (box cenv) environment-stack)))))

(define pop-env!
 (λ ()
  (set! environment-stack (rest environment-stack))))
```

Finally, we implement the environment extension and application functions. The former has a few modifications to account for the fact that we retrieve, then alter, the box of the current environment. On the other hand, the only change to the latter is a removed parameter and an unboxing step.

Listing 8.107

```
(define apply-env
  (λ (y)
    (let ([res (assv y (unbox (current-env)))])
      (cond
        [(eqv? res #f) 'error-unknown-symbol]
        [else (rest res)]))))

(define alter-env!
  (λ (x arg)
    (let* ([benv (current-env)]
           [cenv (unbox benv)])
      (set-box! benv (cons (cons x arg) cenv)))))
```

Now, we should design this language one step at a time, so let us think about how we want to feed a program to the evaluator. An efficient solution would be to write a `letrec` helper function that takes a list of statements/expressions representing a program written in $\mathcal{L}^*_{\text{IMPERATIVE}}$ and evaluates each one at a time in a similar pattern to our evaluator for $\mathcal{L}^*_{\text{ASM}}$.

Listing 8.108

```
(letrec ([value-of-helper
          (λ (lexp)
            (cond
              [(null? lexp) 'PROGRAM-TERMINATED]
              [else
               (let ([res (value-of (first lexp) (current-env))])
                 (begin
                   (printf "~a~n" res)
                   (value-of-helper (rest lexp))))]))])
  (value-of-helper '()))
```

None of this code should be all too perplexing, as it is, effectively, identical to the evaluation loop used in $\mathcal{L}^*_{\text{ASM}}$.

At this point, we should start writing the evaluator itself! Let us start by evaluating number, symbol, and boolean since they are simple and require minimal effort. Accordingly, we will not write separate recognizers and reducers.

Listing 8.109

```
(define value-of
  (λ (exp env)
    (cond
      [(number? exp) exp]
      [(symbol? exp) (apply-env exp)]
      [(boolean? exp) exp]
      [...])))
```

Next, we can address assignment statements. An assignment statement is a list where the *first* is a symbol representing the variable to use, the *second* is the symbol :=, and the *third* is an expression to assign as the value. The recognizer is, therefore, easy to write. Assignment evaluation is also straightforward since all we need is to extract the important components, i.e., the variable and expression, evaluate the latter, and invoke `alter-env!` to update the current environment. One important detail to make note of is the fact that an assignment is considered a statement and not an expression. Therefore, assignments do not return a value. Our interpreter does not understand expressions/statements that do not produce values. So, we should return a symbol, perhaps, `'ok` to designate that the operation was successful. Then, inside of `value-of-helper`, we can simply ignore, i.e., not print, the value of the expression if it returns `'ok`. Afterwards, we can amend the definition of `value-of`, and lastly, write some test cases!

Listing 8.110

```
(define assignment?                    (define value-of-assignment
 (λ (exp)                               (λ (exp env)
  (and (cons? exp)                       (let ([var (first exp)]
       (= (length exp) 3)                     [rhs (value-of (third exp)
       (symbol? (first exp))                                env)])
       (eqv? (second exp) ':=))))       (begin
                                         (alter-env! var rhs)
                                         'ok))))
```

Listing 8.111

```
(define value-of
 (cond
  ...
  [(assignment? exp) (value-of-assignment exp env)]))
```

Listing 8.112

```
(letrec ([value-of-helper
          (λ (lexp)
            (cond
             [(null? lexp) 'PROGRAM-TERMINATED]
             [else
              (let ([res (value-of (first lexp) (current-env))])
               (begin
                (if (eqv? res 'ok)
                    (printf "")
                    (printf "~a~n" res))
                (value-of-helper (rest lexp))))])])
 (value-of-helper '((x := 5)
                    x)))
```

Because our language is still extremely simple with no understanding of control flow structures or procedures, we can only create, then display, variables, numbers, and booleans.

Listing 8.113

```
> (value-of-helper '((x := 5)          |  5
                     x                  |  10
                     (y := 10)          |  5
                     y                  |  25
                     (y := x)           |  PROGRAM-TERMINATED
                     y                  |
                     (x := 25)          |
                     x))                |
```

The next interesting piece of this language is the introduction of infix binary operators. An infix operator expression list consists of two operands on either side as the *first* and *third* respectively, and the operator as the *second*. So, once again, the recognizer is familiar. Nicely enough, its evaluator is also a trivial matter. We need to evaluate all three pieces of the expression, as the operands resolve to expressions themselves, and the operator is a symbol retrieved from the environment. So, when we retrieve the operator, we use the built-in function application to apply said operator to the two operands.

Listing 8.114

```
(define binary-op?                 (define value-of-binary-op
  (λ (exp)                           (λ (exp env)
    (and (cons? exp)                   (let ([l (value-of (first exp) env)]
         (= (length exp) 3)                  [f (value-of (second exp) env)]
         (symbol? (second exp)))))))       [r (value-of (third exp) env)])
                                       (f l r))))
```

Now, just add it into `value-of`, and let us introduce some tests.

Listing 8.115

```
> (value-of-helper                 |  50
   '((x := (5 * 10))               |  425.0
     x                             |  183125.0
     (y := (x + (7.5 * x)))        |  -91537.5
     y                             |  PROGRAM-TERMINATED
     (y := ((x * x) + (y * y)))    |
     y                             |
     (x := ((x / 2) - (y / 2)))    |
     x))                           |
```

Conditionals are another fascinating part of programming, so let us add those next. Because any `if` construct may be built in terms of `if` itself, e.g., `else if`, `else`, or even `cond`, we will only implement `if`. An `if` expression, identical to the counterpart in past interpreters, contains three components (aside from the `if` symbol): a predicate as the *second*, the consequent case as the *third*, and the alternative case as the *fourth*. So, both the recognizer and evaluation functions are easy to write and understand. We first need to evaluate the predicate, and if it is true, evaluate the consequent expression, and otherwise evaluate the alternative expression.

Listing 8.116

```
(define if?                         (define value-of-if
 (λ (exp)                            (λ (exp env)
  (and (cons? exp)                    (let ([test (second exp)]
       (= (length exp) 4)                  [conseq (third exp)]
       (eqv? (first exp) 'if))))          [alt (fourth exp)])
                                      (if (value-of test env)
                                          (value-of conseq env)
                                          (value-of alt env)))))
```

Because we have booleans and not functions, we can only write simple if tests.

Listing 8.117

```
> (value-of-helper               10
  '((x := (if #t 10 20))         10
    x                            100
    (y := (if (3 = (1 + 2)) x (x + x)))   PROGRAM-TERMINATED
    y
    (z := (if (y = 20) (x * x) (y * y)))
    z))
```

All we need now, to deem this language complete, are procedures. Procedures are, by far, the hardest component of this process due to having to account for more than one argument. First, let us write the recognizer for a procedure definition. A procedure definition consists of the 'fn symbol as the *first* of a list, the function name as its *second*, as well as its formal parameters, if any exist, as the remaining components up until the ':= symbol. The last element of the "procedure list" is the function body. We need to extract each of these components. Let us begin by writing the recognizer.

Listing 8.118

```
(define function?
 (λ (exp)
  (and (cons? exp)
       (>= (length exp) 4)
       (eqv? (first exp) 'fn))))
```

Now, we need to write the evaluation function. When evaluating a function, we know it is of the form (fn foo ... := body) where ... consists of the formal parameters. Therefore, we need to, somehow, extract these into a list. We know that the formal parameters end when we encounter the ':= symbol. Thus, we can write a helper function get-formals to traverse over the function definition and continuously accumulate a list of formals until we encounter the := symbol.

Listing 8.119

```
(define get-formals
 (λ (lof)
  (cond
   [(eqv? (first lof) ':=) '()]
   [else (cons (first lof) (get-formals (rest lof)))])))
```

In addition to the formals, we need a way of recognizing the body of a function. The body occurs immediately after the ':=' symbol. Though, more generally, we can say that the body of a function is the last element of a list, and therefore, its *rest* is the empty list. So, we can iterate through the function definition and, if we run into the last element (meaning the *rest* of the current element is the empty list), extract its contents.

Listing 8.120

```
(define get-body
 (λ (exp)
  (cond
   [(null? (rest exp)) (first exp)]
   [else (get-body (rest exp))]))))
```

Now, we can evaluate a function definition. First, let us extract each component in a let block. We know that the *second* is the function name, and that the formal parameters exist until the ':=' symbol. The only noteworthy piece of this function is that we wrap the body in a list. We do this to account for how we store a procedure in the environment. Because a function definition consists of its formal parameters as well as its body, we need to wrap the body in a list. Otherwise, it will break each element of the body up into separate elements; an undesired result.

Listing 8.121

```
(define value-of-function
 (λ (exp env)
  (let ([name (second exp)]
        [formals (get-formals (rest (rest exp)))]
        [body (list (get-body exp))])
   ...)))
```

Conveniently enough, the body of this function is rather simple—the only thing we need to do is extend the environment to contain the function name as well as its formal parameters and body. So, as an association list, the function will be stored with its name as the *first*, and its *rest* is a pair where its *first* is the list of formal parameters, and its *rest* is the function body. Because function definitions do not inherently produce results, we need to wrap the body in a begin and return 'ok, similar to how we handle variable assignments.

Listing 8.122

```
(define value-of-function
 (λ (exp env)
  (let ([name (second exp)]
        [formals (get-formals (rest (rest exp)))]
        [body (list (get-body exp))])
   (begin
    (alter-env! name (cons formals body))
    'ok))))
```

With function definitions in the bag, we can move on to function application. Similar to our previous languages, a function application consists of a function name, i.e., a symbol, and its arguments, if any.

Listing 8.123

```
(define application
 (λ (exp)
  (and (cons? exp)
       (symbol? (first exp)))))
```

Evaluating a function is a bit more difficult than one may initially expect. We need to retrieve, then evaluate, each argument from the function call, map them to the formal parameters of the function, then finally invoke the function body. When we map the arguments to the formal parameters, we push a new environment to the environment stack that contains these (and only these) new bindings. This way, they (the bindings) only live in the scope of the function body. Immediately afterwards, we pop the environment off the stack, designating that those variables are no longer live and, therefore, cannot be used.

Listing 8.124

```
(define value-of-application
 (λ (exp env)
  (let* ([fn (apply-env (first exp))]
         [formals (first fn)]
         [args (map (λ (a) (value-of a env)) (rest exp))]
         [body (second fn)])
   (begin
    (push-env!)
    (map-formals-args formals args)
    (let ([res (value-of body (current-env))])
     (begin
      (pop-env!)
      res))))))
```

Notice that we use the convenient helper function map. map, as we recall from Chapter 7, receives a function and a list of values, and returns a list of values after applying the supplied function to each of the list elements. As we said, we need to evaluate each argument before binding its value to the formal parameters, and the map function allows us to achieve this concisely. After retrieving the necessary components, we push a new environment to the environment stack, map the arguments to the function formal parameters, evaluate the function body, pop the top of the environment stack, and return the expression resolved by the body.

After we implement function definitions and applications, we have enough to write the complicated program we described earlier.

Listing 8.125

```
> (value-of-helper                                    5
  '((fn fact n := (if (n = 0)                         10
                    1                                  120
                    (n * (fact (n - 1))))))           55
    (fn fib x := (if (x = 0)                          3025
                   0                                  PROGRAM-TERMINATED
                   (if (x = 1)
                     1
                     ((fib (x - 1)) +
                      (fib (x - 2))))))
    (val1 := 5)
    (val2 := (val1 + val1))
    (z := (fact val1))
    (w := (fib val2))
    val1
    val2
    z
    w
    (z := (w * (fib (2 * (val2 - 5)))))
    z))
```

Imperative languages often have a strict distinction between functions and variables. Namely, functions are not data and, therefore, cannot be passed around, i.e., returned from other functions or passed as arguments, as if they are a variable. Our interpreters need not distinguish between the two, leading to the notion of first-class functions as described in Chapters 6 and 7. Interestingly, because of how we designed $\mathcal{L}^*_{\text{IMPERATIVE}}$, functions are, by default, first class and can, therefore, be passed as arguments to other functions.

Listing 8.126

```
> (value-of-helper                               720
  '((fn fact n := (if (n = 0)
                    1
                    (n * (fact (n - 1))))))
    (fn another-function f n := (f n))
    (another-function fact 6)))
```

Exercise 8.19. (★★)

Write a function, product, in $\mathcal{L}^*_{\text{IMPERATIVE}}$ that receives two arguments: a starting natural number s, and an ending natural number n, that computes the product of s to n inclusive. As a hint, a recursive helper function is essential.

Exercise 8.20. (★★)

Add a while loop, similar to the while statement in C, to $\mathcal{L}^*_{\text{IMPERATIVE}}$. Such a loop should receive a boolean expression and, as long as that expression holds true, the loop body continues. Do not implement this as a function—rather, add it as a new language construct. Also, assume that while loops introduce a new variable scope; meaning you must modify the environment stack as necessary.

Exercise 8.21. (⋆⋆)
Add a for loop, similar to the for statement in C, to $\mathcal{L}^*_{\text{IMPERATIVE}}$. Such a loop
should receive three statements: an initialization counter, a conditional expression,
and a step statement. Only execute the body of the loop if its conditional expression
is true. After the body finishes its execution, evaluate the step expression. Do not
implement this as a function—rather, add it as a new language construct. Also,
because for loops introduce a new variable scope; meaning you must modify the
environment stack as necessary.

8.8   Object-Oriented Programming

In C, we have the notion of structures, which classify, or categorize, groups of variables to collectively represent a broad concept or object. As an example, a two-dimensional "Point" struct is comprised of two numbers x and y. Is it possible to represent structs, or *objects* in our language?

Objects contain properties and *methods*. Methods resemble functions but with the added exception that methods are associated with an object. Many computer scientists interchangeably use functions and methods, but there are important distinctions between the two in different programming contexts.

Anyways, let us discuss object representation. There are a couple of ways we can represent an object and its encapsulated state. The first is via tagged lists, and the second is via closures. We will work with tagged lists first.

A *tagged list*, as previously defined, is a standard list where the *first* is a header or identifier. For instance, we can represent a "point" and its values as a tagged list, e.g., `(point ,x ,y)` where x and y are arguments in a `make-point` function. So, we can represent this as follows:

Listing 8.127

```
(define make-point
 (λ (x y)
  `(point ,x ,y)))
```

Next, let us say that we want to access these values. We can access x by retrieving the *second* of the point. Likewise, we can retrieve y by retrieving the *third* of the point. Accordingly, we should wrap this behavior inside of functions.

Listing 8.128

```
(define point-x
 (λ (pt)
  (second pt)))

(define point-y
 (λ (pt)
  (third pt)))
```

What happens if we want to mutate the values in the point? Simple: we can use the setter functions, i.e., `set-first!`, that we recently investigated. So, to alter x, we need to retrieve the *rest* of the point, then invoke `set-first!` to update the value. Altering y requires only a slight change; we need to get the *rest of the rest* of the point, then invoke `set-first!`.

Listing 8.129

```
(define point-set-x!
 (λ (pt x)
  (set-first! (rest pt) x)))

(define point-set-y!
 (λ (pt y)
  (set-first! (rest (rest pt)) y)))
```

Let us test this with some points:

Listing 8.130

```
(define p1 (make-point 10 20))
(define p2 (make-point 17 25.5))

> (point-x p1)                                    10
> (point-y p1)                                    20
> (point-set-x! p1 30)
> (point-set-y! p1 50)
> (point-x p1)                                    30
> (point-y p1)                                    50

> (point-x p2)                                    17
> (point-y p2)                                    25.5
> (point-set-x! p2 77)
> (point-set-y! p2 190.25)
> (point-x p2)                                    77
> (point-y p2)                                    190.25
```

Something seems amiss with this representation. The problem that should be scaring the readers is that these functions are all in global scope. Thus, any arbitrary object or function can access these "point methods". We want to abstract these away somehow. The answer to this dilemma comes through closures. Recall closures from Chapter 6—a closure binds an environment and a function definition. Whenever a closure is invoked, it restores, then uses, the environment from its declaration. So, we can declare a closure, e.g., make-point which receives and keeps track of two values x and y. The question, though, is what do we do with these values? Well, we need to bind them somewhere in the environment, so why not create a let to hold their bindings?

Listing 8.131

```
(define make-point
  (λ (x y)
   (let ([point-x x]
         [point-y y])
    ...)))
```

Now, what exactly does this function return? One may be inclined to think that it returns a "point", but this is not necessarily the case. We want to be able to invoke methods on a "point", so what we could do is have some sort of command central, so to speak, that delegates commands. For example, if we define a point p, and we want to get the x coordinate, we can invoke a method, e.g., (p 'point-x). So, we know that make-point should return a function that receives one argument: a command. This command, depending on its symbol argument, determines the action to take.

Listing 8.132

```
(define make-point
  (λ (x y)
   (let ([point-x x]
         [point-y y])
    (λ (cmd)
     (cond
      [(eqv? cmd 'point-x) point-x]
      [(eqv? cmd 'point-y) point-y])))))
```

So, we can now create distinct "point" objects and only access the data from said points:

Listing 8.133

```
(define p1 (make-point 2 10))
(define p2 (make-point 5.25 9.50))

> (p1 'point-x)                              2
> (p1 'point-y)                              10
> (p2 'point-x)                              5.25
> (p2 'point-y)                              9.50
```

What about data mutation? If we want to change the value of a coordinate, we will need to **return** a function that receives an argument:

Listing 8.134

```
(define make-point
 (λ (x y)
  (let ([point-x x]
        [point-y y])
   (λ (cmd)
    (cond
     [(eqv? cmd 'point-x) point-x]
     [(eqv? cmd 'point-y) point-y]
     [(eqv? cmd 'point-set-x!) (λ (v) (set! point-x v))]
     [(eqv? cmd 'point-set-y!) (λ (v) (set! point-y v))]
     [else 'invalid-method])))))
```

Thus, invoking one of the setters returns a procedure:

Listing 8.135

```
(define p1 (make-point 2 10))

> (p1 'point-set-x!)                         <function>
```

We need to **supply** the setter with a value:

Listing 8.136

```
(define p1 (make-point 2 10))

> (p1 'point-x)                              <function>
> ((p1 'point-set-x!) 50)                    2
> (p1 'point-x)                              50
```

Class Design and Development

Objects, methods, and properties were defined in the previous section. We will continue to **make** use of these terms as well as a few new additions to the lineup, such as classes, inheritance, polymorphism, and encapsulation.

A *class* is the blueprint of an object, i.e., how an object is defined. We used a form of classes without the term when designing make-point and the dispatch commands. Let us create a class called, say, Point (similar to the one defined from the previous section) that stores two properties: an x-coordinate and a y-coordinate. Properties of a class are also called *instance variables*, because they belong to each created instance of a class. In addition, we will now take a slight detour to describe a fundamental property of object-oriented programming: encapsulation. In other programming languages, e.g., Java, when defining instance variables for a class, we make a design choice to either declare them as public or private instance variables. A public instance variable is directly-modifiable from an instance of the class. Consider the following Java example:

Listing 8.137—Java Implementation of Point Class

```
1   class Point {
2     int x-coordinate;
3     int y-coordinate;
4   }
```

Here we define a class called Point (as we will in our interpreter), with two instance variables. We can create a Point object by using its constructor, i.e., Point p = new Point(). The potential for trouble comes from our attempts to access the instance variables. We can use the dot operator to modify and access their values, e.g., p.x-coordinate = 5. Manipulation and accessibility in this fashion breaks our encapsulation principle because a class should only be able to directly modify its instance variables from inside the class. To fix this problem (in Java), we should instead declare the instance variables as private. In doing so, we prohibit access to the instance variables through an object. Though, what if we want to retrieve a particular coordinate? By blocking access to the variables, does that not completely restrict our access, and if so, why would we ever care about encapsulation? Indeed, it does restrict our access, but not entirely; we can write an accessor method to retrieve the property. Such a method, i.e., getX(), is callable from a constructed Point object, e.g., p. Mutability is also preserved through mutator methods.

Listing 8.138—X-Coordinate Accessor Method in Java

```
1    class Point {
2      private int xCoordinate;
3      private int yCoordinate;
4      Point(int x, int y) {
5        xCoordinate = x;
6        yCoordinate = y;
7      }
8      int getX() { return xCoordinate; }
9      void setX(int x) { xCoordinate = x; }
10   }
```

So, if we want to declare p to have an x-coordinate of 5, we can do so by invoking this method on the object, i.e., p.setX(5);. Again, newcomers to Java in particular often question the need for verbose syntax to do what is a seemingly innocuous task. It allows us to couple our class data with the class itself and separate the behavior we provide to clients of the class and the behavior given to the class implementer/designer. Circling back to our point class example in the interpreter, we could return boxes to directly modify instance variables from outside the class. Doing so, as we have repeatedly mentioned, breaks down encapsulation and hinders things even more because our language would need to unbox the value to retrieve it and set the box to update its contents. In our previous section, we somewhat introduced the idea of *accessor and mutator methods* via the dispatch function within the object closure without providing the context behind encapsulation as it was not entirely necessary. An additional difference between our language and many other object-oriented languages is that our interpreter returns callable methods whenever we want to set a value, whereas Java hides this from the programmer, invoking the method for them. Our accessor and mutator methods will be aptly named get-x/y and set-x/y! respectively.

Listing 8.139

```
(define class-point
 (λ (x y)
  (let ([property-x x]
        [property-y y])
   (λ (dispatch)
    (cond
     [(eqv? dispatch 'get-x) (λ () property-x)]
     [(eqv? dispatch 'get-y) (λ () property-y)]
     [(eqv? dispatch 'set-x!) (λ (new-x) (set! property-x new-x))]
     [(eqv? dispatch 'set-y!) (λ (new-y) (set! property-y new-y))]
     [else 'invalid-method])))))
```

We know that, to *construct* a point, we invoke class-point with the x and y we wish to store.

Listing 8.140

```
(define pt1 (class-point 10 20))

> ((pt1 'get-x))                            10
> ((pt1 'set-x!) 30)
> ((pt1 'get-x))                            30
```

Though, imagine that, in addition to an (x, y) pair, we want to store an associated color. With our current knowledge of objects, there are, effectively, two options. The first of which is to add a color property to class-point, whereas the second requires us to create a separate class that includes the (x,y) pair as well as the color. The disadvantage of the former should be apparent: we must modify our original implementation of the point class to add an additional property. The issue with this, however, is that we must alter all occurrences class-point invocation with a supplemental color. What if we do not want all points to contain a color? Changing the implementation of point in this manner means we have no choice.[1] A second option is to create a new class that has all three properties together. While this option is more flexible than the former and requires less overhaul to existing code, it means we have to rewrite existing code, namely the x and y properties. A third solution is to use object *inheritance*. One class that inherits from another is known as a *subclass*, and the class that is being inherited from is the *superclass*. Any properties or methods defined in the superclass, in our implementation at least, are accessible in the subclass. Therefore if we could somehow extend the point class into a color-point class, we would not need to re-define the properties and methods associated with the (x, y) pair. How is this even possible, though? We will demonstrate by example. Let us write the starting code to represent a color-point class. We know that, because we want color-point to be a subclass of point, it should receive the same arguments as a point, but with the addition of the color property.

Listing 8.141

```
(define class-color-point
 (λ (x y color)
  (let ([...]
        [property-color color])
   (λ (dispatch)
    (cond
     [...])))))
```

Though, how do we specify that this is a subclass and, therefore, use properties from the superclass? All we need to do is declare an instance of the superclass inside the let binding before we initialize the properties owned solely by class-color-point. When we declare the instance, we in essence invoke the constructor of the superclass, meaning we need to pass along, to it, the x and y arguments.

Listing 8.142

```
(define class-color-point
 (λ (x y color)
  (let ([super (class-point x y)]
        [property-color color])
   (λ (dispatch)
    (cond
     [...]))))))
```

---

[1]Python has support for *optional parameters*, which remove the need to change all constructor invocations when adding a parameter.

super is **an object** instance of the superclass. Now, if an instance of the subclass calls a method, we need to tell the dispatch function to look up the method name in the superclass **if it does** not exist in the subclass. We will also add the corresponding accessor and **mutator** methods for the color property.

Listing 8.143

```
(define class-color-point
 (λ (x y color)
  (let ([super (class-point x y)]
        [property-color color])
   (λ (dispatch)
    (cond
     [(eqv? dispatch 'get-color) (λ () property-color)]
     [else (super dispatch)]))))))
```

So, if we **declare** an instance of the subclass and attempt to invoke a method from its superclass, we see that it works perfectly.

Listing 8.144

```
(define pt1 (class-point 10 20))
(define cpt1 (class-color-point 30 50 "Blue"))

> ((pt1 'get-x))                                  10
> ((pt1 'get-color))                              invalid method
> ((cpt1 'get-color))                             "Blue"
> ((cpt1 'get-y))                                 50
```

Notice *how* **we** implement inheritance: we create an instance of the superclass directly, then **any** methods that do not exist in the subclass, we look up in the superclass. **Class inheritance** does not stop at one level, however, as we can create as many **subclasses** as our heart desires. Imagine that we have a class that describes the size of a color-point called sized-point. If we declare an instance of the superclass, **namely,** color-point, it will inherit all of its properties, which include those from point. In essence, the chain of inheritance may grow continuously.

We may **also** *override* a method's functionality from its superclass. Suppose that, in point, **there** is a method to_string that returns a string representation of the object. E.g., "(x=10, y=20)" may be a string representation of a point whose property-x **is** 10, and whose property-y is 20.

Listing 8.145

```
(define class-point
 (let ([property-x x]
       [property-y y])
  (λ (dispatch)
   (cond
    [...]
    [(eqv? dispatch 'to-string)
     (λ ()
      (string-append "(x="
                      (number->string property-x)
                      ", y="
                      (number->string property-y)
                      ")"))]))))
```

If we want to add this functionality to color-point, we need to override the method by redefining it in the subclass. Though, we may not want to re-type the information provided by the to-string method from the superclass. Thus, we may invoke the point to-string from within the subclass to-string method.

Listing 8.146

```
(define class-color-point
 (λ (x y color)
  (let ([super (class-point x y)]
        [property-color color])
   (λ (dispatch)
    (cond
     [ . ]
     [(eqv? dispatch 'to-string)
      (λ ()
       (string-append (super dispatch)
                       ",color="
                       color))]))))

(define pt1 (class-point 10 20))              "(x=10, y=20)"
(define cpt1 (class-color-point 5 3 "Blue"))  "(x=5, y=3),color=Blue"

> ((pt1 'to-string))
> ((cpt1 'to-string))
```

What if, however, we want to directly access a method from the superclass? That is, imagine we have an instance of a color-point, but decide that we would rather only see the coordinate information instead of said pair and the color? We could add a second parameter to the dispatch function, namely args, that provides extra information to the invocation of a method. That is, if we pass the symbol 'super when invoking a method, it means we want to access the superclass method rather than the class that the object is an instance of. The problem with this approach is that it requires us to modify the implementation of all other existing method calls. A solution to this predicament is to utilize variadic arguments. Therefore, because a variadic argument procedure receives a list of arguments, we can extract out both the method name and "method flags" if they exist. To help with this problem, we will write two helper functions that access the method name and flags.

Listing 8.147

```
(define method-name
 (λ (args)
  (first args)))

(define method-flags
 (λ (flags)
  (if (> (length flags) 1) (second flags) #f)))
```

Now, let us amend our implementation of both the superclass and subclass to use variadic arguments. In the subclass, if the "flags" argument is the 'super symbol, we immediately invoke the superclass with the specified method.

Listing 8.148

```
(define class-point
 (λ (x y)
  (let ([property-x x]
        [property-y y])
   (λ-var (dispatch)
    (let ([method (method-name dispatch)]
          [flags (method-flags dispatch)])
     (cond
      [...]))))))
```

Listing 8.149

```
(define class-color-point
 (λ (x y color)
  (let ([super (class-point x y)]
        [property-color color])
   (λ-var (dispatch)
    (let ([method (method-name dispatch)]
          [flags (method-flags dispatch)])
     (cond
      [(eqv? flags 'super) (super method)]
      [...]))))))
```

Finally, we can add an additional test that invokes the superclass to-string method from an instance of color-point.

Listing 8.150

```
(define cpt1 (class-color-point 5 3 "Blue"))

> ((cpt1 'to-string))                              "(x=5, y=3),color=Blue"
> ((cpt1 'to-string 'super))                       "(x=5, y=3)"
```

The power of object-oriented programming comes in many dimensions, but we will show a convenient example. Imagine we want to write a program that will compute the area of a given shape. To do so, we may write something of the following form:

Listing 8.151

```
;; area: [ListOf Any] -> Number
;; Computes the area of a given shape. The first
;; value in the list is the shape type as a symbol.
(define area
 (λ-var (args)
  (let ([shape (first args)])
   (cond
    [(eqv? shape 'circle) (circle-area (rest args))]
    [(eqv? shape 'rectangle) (rectangle-area (rest args))]
    [(eqv? shape 'triangle) (triangle-area (rest args))]
    [else #f]))))
```

Where we must also write accompanying shape-area computation functions. This not only clutters the area definition, but continuously increases its size and unwieldiness. Using objects allows us to write *polymorphic methods*, which is a way of composing the solution to multiple problems in a compact manner. Let us create a shape class that has an "area" method that, by default, returns zero.

Listing 8.152

```
(define class-shape
 (λ ()
  (λ-var (dispatch)
   (let ([method (method-name dispatch)]
         [flags (method-flags dispatch)])
    (cond
     [(eqv? method 'area) (λ () 0)]
     [(eqv? method 'to-string) (λ () "shape")]
     [else 'invalid-method])))))
```

Now, we can create three subclasses of shape: circle, rectangle, and triangle that all extend shape and have their own properties alongside and override the area method.

Listing 8.153

```
(define class-circle
 (λ (radius)
  (let ([super (class-shape)]
        [property-radius radius])
   (λ-var (dispatch)
    (let ([method (method-name dispatch)]
          [flags (method-flags dispatch)])
     (cond
      [...]
      [(eqv? method 'area)
       (λ ()
        (* property-radius property-radius pi))]
      [(eqv? method 'to-string)
       (λ ()
        (string-append "radius=" property-radius))]
      [else (super method)]))))))
```

Listing 8.154

```
(define class-rectangle
 (λ (l w)
  (let ([super (class-shape)]
        [property-length l]
        [property-width w])
   (λ-var (dispatch)
    (let ([method (method-name dispatch)]
          [flags (method-flags dispatch)])
     (cond
      [...]
      [(eqv? method 'area)
       (λ ()
        (* property-length property-width))]
      [(eqv? method 'to-string)
       (λ ()
        (string-append "length=" property-length ", width=" property-width))]
      [else (super method)]))))))
```

Listing 8.155

```
(define class-triangle
 (λ (b h)
  (let ([super (class-shape)]
        [property-base b]
        [property-height h])
   (λ-var (dispatch)
    (let ([method (method-name dispatch)]
          [flags (method-flags dispatch)])
     (cond
      [(eqv? method 'area)
       (λ ()
        (/ (* property-base property-height) 2))]
      [ ]
      [(eqv? method 'to-string)
       (λ ()
        (string-append "base=" property-base ", height=" property-height))]
      [else (super method)]))))))
```

What makes this interesting is if we want to, say, have a list of different shapes, then compute the area of every shape in the list!

Listing 8.156

```
(define los
 (list (class-triangle 2.25 10)
       (class-rectangle 10 20)
       (class-circle 45)
       (class-rectangle 47.75 15)
       (class-triangle 100 200)
       (class-circle 90)
       (class-circle 439)))

> (map (λ (s) ((s 'area))) los)          (11.25 200 6361.725 716.25 10000
                                          25446.900 605450.878)
```

Inheritance, Polymorphism, Encapsulation, and Automation

Creating classes manually is cumbersome. Plus, the burden lies on the programmer for having to worry about methods being returned from invoking a closure function such as a setter. What if we could write a system that abstracted these concepts away from the end user, but still allows for inheritance, encapsulation, polymorphism, and so on? That is what we will do! Our system will mimic that of Java, using several fundamental properties it defines of classes and objects.

As we said, classes are blueprints for objects, but they contain more than just instance variables and methods. Classes can, of course, extend another class and override existing methods. What we have not seen before are static variables and static methods. A member defined as static associates said member with the class and not to any particular instance of the class. We will go over this in greater detail once we get to a proper example.

In Java, every class has six properties: a name, its superclass, its instance variables and methods, and its static variables and methods. We will represent this structure as a list. Every class, if it does not extend any other class, implicitly extends `Object` (which does not extend itself). A class can be instantiated which makes a copy of the class as an object along with all instance variables, instance methods, static methods, and a reference to the static variables among the class. Our implementation will be different from Java in several ways, including:

- **No interfaces.** Interfaces are used to control behavior amongst a group of classes. Enforcement of the "behavioral hierarchy" is done as a compile-time check, meaning it makes little sense to replicate Java's interfaces in our system.

- **All instance and static variables are mutable and accessible only from mutator and accessor methods predefined by the class**. We have seen that classes can have methods such as `get-x` and `set-x`, but these had to be written directly by the programmer. Our class implementation will automatically create accessor functions that return the requested variable, as well as mutator functions that receive one argument and reassign the variable accordingly. In a sense, this indicates that all variables are public because we could directly access them from the class (list) structure, but preventing this would be almost an impossibility at runtime.

- **Method overloading is impossible.** Overloading a method means that the same method name exists, just with differing input parameters. For instance, in Java, we may declare a method `void foo(int x, int y)`, but also declare another method `void foo(String x, String y)`. The Java compiler checks the method invocation to see which function to call based on the types. Our system is dynamically typed, meaning we do not explicitly specify the types of our data. So, this is not possible. This includes different constructors for a class; a class can have at most one constructor.

Moreover, object-oriented programming languages frequently use compile-time checks to their advantage, a la method overloading, as well as inheritance method and variable usage. Since this language is not compiled, we forgo any benefits that come with such semantic program analysis tricks. Fortunately, we do get access to a neat system for designing and instantiating classes that does not restrict us to using closures as the object representation.

Representation Independence with Respect to Classes

As mentioned, our previous object system used closures for storing properties and methods of objects. Because we strive for representation independence whenever possible, we extend this approach to our new class design system. We will write several functions that build classes and add methods to those classes. Though, the programmer should not have to worry about how objects are represented by the system; whether it be via closures or data structures. Namely, a user of our system should need only functions that define classes and methods. Note the distinction between "define" and "build": defining a class is similar to what we do in Java; we use the class keyword, its identifier, and associated properties. What we do not see is how classes are represented "under the hood" by Java; it is unnecessary for most intents and purposes.

Let us begin writing `define-class`: a function that receives four arguments: a tag representing the class name, the class it extends, a list of instance variables, and a list of static variables. These variables are merely symbols at the end of the day, and cannot be extended past the point of class construction. While we cannot add or remove instance variables, their values may certainly change. As a corollary, what can be extended are the methods used by a class. Because of this, we will use boxes to store the lists of methods. For now, these boxes are empty, but we will return to them in due time. Note that CLASS is simply the symbol 'CLASS.

Listing 8.157

```
(define define-class
  (λ (id super loiv losv)
    (let ([loim-box (box '())]
          [losm-box (box '())])
      (list CLASS id super loiv losv loim-box losm-box))))
```

We now need a way of adding both static and instance methods to a class. Therefore, let us write `add-static-method` and `add-instance-method` which call `add-method`.[1] add-method is the true worker here: it receives a symbol denoting the method name, a function describing the method to add, as well as a function denoting the "type" of method to add (which is either `class-instance-methods` or `class-static-methods`). There is one caveat here, and that is the fact that every instance method must receive at least one argument called "self". The "self" argument is implicit and will be passed alongside the instance method, but it is required because if we want to access a particular object's properties, we need to know what object were invoking the method on. For instance, in Java, we may have a Point p, then call a method int getX() on it as follows: p.getX(). Although it seems as if this method receives no arguments, it implicitly receives a reference to "p" identified as this. Thus, inside the body of getX(), when we write "return x", it knows to refer to the particular x instance variable that belongs to p. Python explicitly requires that a "self" reference be passed to the method. Consider the following Python class:[2]

---

[1] As a corollary, what we are describing is a paradigm called *reflection*, in which we dynamically modify or access elements of some structure. In this case, we have the ability to view the names of class/instance variables, class/instance methods, and add new elements at runtime.

[2] The __init__ function acts as the class constructor in Python.

Listing 8.158

```
1   class Point {
2     def __init__(self, x, y):
3       self.x = x
4       self.y = y
5
6     def get_x(self): return self.x
7     def get_y(self): return self.y
8     def set_x(self, x): self.x = x
9     def set_y(self, y): self.y = y
10    }
```

Notice that each accessor and mutator method has a "self" parameter which works as previously described. Because it is easier to visualize the process behind Python's design choice, we will mimic it rather than Java. This means that, every instance method must receive a "self" as its first parameter.

Listing 8.159

```
;; add-method: Class Symbol Function Function -> Void
;; Adds a method of a given type to the given class definition.
(define add-method
  (λ (class id body tp)
    (set-box! (tp class) (cons (cons id body) (unbox (tp class))))))

;; add-instance-method-class : Class Symbol Function -> Void
;; Adds an instance method to a class definition.
(define add-instance-method
  (λ (class id body)
    (add-method class id body class-instance-methods)))

;; add-static-method-class : Class Symbol Function -> Void
;; Adds a static method to a class definition.
(define add-static-method
  (λ (class id body)
    (add-method class id body class-static-methods)))
```

All we do is update the class box based on the given method type tag by appending the method to the corresponding association list.

We can now add methods to a class! There is one immediate instance method to add: a constructor. The constructor will receive a list of arguments to initialize to an object's instance variables in the received order. It then returns a newly-created instance of the given class type with its instance variables initialized. How do we represent an instance of a class, though? By make-instance, of course! This function receives a class type and returns a new instance of the class with its instance variables uninitialized. An incredibly important bit of information to note is that this is *not* the class constructor; that is defined momentarily. What we are writing via make-instance is the value returned from a constructor invocation. make-instance returns the instance represented as a list whose *first* is the symbol 'INSTANCE. Another important distinction is the fact that every instance has a reference to an instance of its superclass defined. This is isomorphic to how we define the superclass in the closure representation of objects. The root class, namely object-class, cannot have a superclass, which is why we have a nested if expression.

Listing 8.160

```
; An Instance is a (make-instance Class).

;; make-instance : Class -> Instance
;; Creates an instance of a class. An instance is an object whose
;; instance variables are declared but initialized to '(). If a
;; superclass exists, an instance is generated inside the current instance.
(define make-instance
  (λ (cl)
    (let* ([iv (class-instance-vars cl)]
           [iv-ls (map (λ (x) (cons x (box '()))) iv)])
      (list INSTANCE (class-id cl) (class-super cl) iv-ls (class-static-vars cl)
            (class-instance-methods cl) (class-static-methods cl)
            (if (false? (class-super cl))
                #f
                (make-instance (class-super cl)))))))))
```

Let us now **write** the `make-constructor` function that allows the programmer to define a **constructor** for a class. Fortunately, this function is only one line long: we invoke `add-instance-method` with the symbol `'new` and the constructor body. A constructor **should receive** at least one argument: a `self` to which instance variables are assigned.

Listing 8.161

```
;; make-constructor : Class Function -> Void
;; Defines a constructor for a class. Constructors are
;; invoked using 'new and must receive at least one parameter.
(define make-constructor
  (λ (class fn)
    (add-instance-method class 'new fn)))
```

We have **repeatedly** mentioned static methods and variables, but what are they and what is **their** connection to objects?

Listing 8.162

```
(define build-class
  (λ (...)
    (let ([...]
          [sv-box (cons 'new (λ-var (args) (build-object args)))])
      ...)))
```

We are **going to** further complicate our `define-class` definition a bit by adding helper functions **which** add the accessor and mutator methods for the class instance variables. **Fortunately**, we can make repeated use of `add-instance-method`, but we need a **separate** function that appends symbols to other symbols. This is because we **want to** say that the accessor method names are prefixed by "get-", whereas **mutator** methods are prefixed by "set-". Note that this requires writing `symbol->string` **and** `string->symbol` or `symbol->append` at the interpreter level. Either **approach is** acceptable, and due to this, we leave it as an exercise to the reader.

Let us write two pairs of functions: add-accessor/accessor-id for retrieving instance variables, and add-mutator/mutator-id for mutating instance variables. The respective "add" functions retrieve the instance method box and update its contents accordingly to bind the generated method identifiers to lambda functions. Each method receives a self parameter denoting the object we wish to access or mutate. The setters, of course, receive an additional parameter denoting the new value to which the respective instance variable is assigned. The "id" functions simply generate a unique identifier which bind the accessor and mutator methods in the list of instance methods. All of these are local to a add-accessor-mutator-methods function, since their visibly should not pollute the global namespace. This function receives a list of the variables as well as a function describing which methods to retrieve. For the time being, we want to create accessor and mutator methods for all instance variables, but we can just as easily write accessor and mutator methods for all static variables, which we leave as an exercise to the reader.

Listing 8.163

```
;; create-accessor-mutator-methods : [ListOf Symbol] Function -> [ListOf Symbol]
;; Declares the accessor/mutator methods for the provided instance variables.
;; Each accessor/mutator is prefixed with get- or set-, respectively, followed
;; by the instance variable identifier.
(define create-accessor-mutator-methods
  (let ([accessor-id (λ (v) (symbol-append 'get- v))]
        [mutator-id (λ (v) (symbol-append 'set- v))]
        [add-accessor
         (λ (v vars-fn)
          (λ (self)
            (unbox (rest (assv v (vars-fn self))))))]
        [add-mutator
         (λ (v vars-fn)
          (λ (self nv)
            (set-box! (rest (assv v (vars-fn self))) nv)))])
   (λ (lov vars-fn))
    ...))
```

We want to create association pairs that bind accessor identifiers to their accessor function, and similarly, for mutator identifiers and their mutator functions. To do so, we will use foldr and return a list containing these newly-created methods. We do so because we want to add these methods at class-definition time.[1]

Listing 8.164

```
(define add-accessor-mutator-methods
  (let (...)
   (λ (lov vars-fn)
    (foldr
     (λ (v acc)
      (append (list (cons (accessor-id v) (add-accessor v vars-fn)))
              (list (cons (mutator-id v) (add-mutator v vars-fn)))
              acc))
     '()
     lov)))
```

Then, as we said, we update define-class to create accessor and mutator methods for all variables, both static and non-static. Again, these are stored as boxes because the programmer adds custom-defined methods after a class declaration.

---

[1] The astute reader will question why append receives three arguments rather than the standard two. We wrote a variadic append function; using two append invocations works just as well.

Listing 8.165

```
(define define-class
  (λ (id super loiv losv)
    (let ([loim-box (box (create-accessor-mutator-instance-methods loiv))]
          [losm-box (box (create-accessor-mutator-static-methods losv))])
      (list CLASS id super loiv losv loim-box losm-box))))
```

Lastly we **arrive at**, arguably, the most important function: our dispatcher. Our old object-oriented system used closures to wrap the dispatch function; this time, however, it is a top-level function that receives at least two arguments: a recipient of a command and the command to perform. The recipient can be either a class definition or an object instance. Passing a class definition is required to call or reference static variables and methods, whereas passing an instance is required to call or reference instance methods. *Commands* refer to any invokable method, including object instantiation. Any subsequent arguments are used as arguments to the command. Note that if the recipient is an object, we cons onto the list of arguments the recipient, serving as the implicit (first) argument to each instance method. We use the "apply" function to use function application on the arguments provided by the dispatcher. We have one special case to deal with, and that is object instantiation. We need to create an instance, using make-instance, and cons said instance onto the list of constructor arguments, serving as the self parameter to the constructor. To aid us, we will write local lookup functions to search class definitions for desired methods. Because these are relatively repetitive and simple to design, we omit their implementation for the time being.

Listing 8.166

```
;; send : Any Symbol ... -> Any
;; Dispatches a command to either an object or a class definition.
;; The function is variadic but must receive at least two arguments.
(define send
  (λ-var (args)
    (let ([recv (first args)] [cmd (second args)] [args (rest (rest args))])
      (cond
        [(eqv? 'new cmd)
         (let ([instance (make-instance recv)])
           (begin
             (apply (constructor-lookup recv) (cons instance args))
             instance))]
        [(instance? recv)
         (apply (instance-method-lookup recv cmd) (cons recv args))]
        [(class? recv)
         (apply (static-method-lookup recv cmd) args)]
        [else
         (printf "unknown command ~a~n" cmd)]))))
```

At long last, let us create a class! We first need to write the root "object-class" that extends nothing, implements nothing, and has no instance or static variables.

Listing 8.167

```
(define object-class
  (define-class 'object #f '() '()))
```

To freshen things up, we will design a different set of classes rather than sticking with the overused "point" examples. Let us implement a `robot-class` that has five properties: x/y-coordinates, a direction they are facing, an item count, and its residing world.

Listing 8.168—Definition and Constructor of Robot Class

```
(define robot-class
  (define-class 'robot object-class '(x y dir item-count world) '()))
(make-constructor robot-class
  (λ (self x y world)
   (begin
    (send self 'set-x x)
    (send self 'set-y y)
    (send self 'set-dir 0)
    (send self 'set-item-count 0)
    (send self 'set-world world))))
```

A `World` is a `world-class`; it stores a list of world positions as elements. Each world position has a number denoting the number of items on the position. Item s are arbitrary and tangible collectibles. When we create a `World`, we want to pass it a width and height, representing the two-dimensional grid of world positions. The backing world position list, however, is only a one-dimension list. This means that, whenever we access an element index or reference a world position, we need to convert from Cartesian coordinates to indices and vice versa. Namely, $i = x+y{\cdot}W$, where W is the specified world width. Going the other direction, $x = \mathsf{floor(i\ /\ W)}$ and $y = i$ mod W.[1] We want a robot to be able to place and collect items from world positions. So, let us add methods to the `World` class that do as such: when given an x, y position, we retrieve the respective world position and update its item count. For the time being, we will not worry about a "negative" count. To initialize the list of world positions to boxes, we can use `foldr` and a function that returns a list of `width · height` numbers to fold over.[2] The numbers, themselves, are insignificant; they merely provide a bound on the number of recursive folds we make. Rather, what is more interesting is how many items we store at each world position. At its core, this number does not matter as much as some other values in our program, and we could set it to whatever natural number our heart desires. We could also store a random number of items on each world position. To keep the discussion simple, every position starts with three items.

Listing 8.169—Definition and Constructor of World Class

```
(define world-class
  (define-class 'world object-class '(lop) '()))
(make-constructor world-class
  (λ (self width height)
   (send self 'set-lop (foldr (λ (x acc)
                                 (cons (box 3) acc))
                               '()
                               (iota 0 (* width height))))))
```

[1]In this coordinate system, like those in computer graphics, the origin (0,0) is in the top-left of the grid.

[2]In programming and formal language theory, this is called the Iota ι function, which returns a list of integers from the interval $[i, j)$, e.g., $\iota(8)$ produces [0, 1, 2, 3, 4, 5, 6, 7].

We know that a robot exists at some location in the world. A robot that cannot move without directly setting its coordinate values limits the potential of the robot. Let us add two instance methods to the robot class: the ability to turn left via turn-left as well as a movement forward (in whatever direction they are currently facing) command via move-forward. Turning left is only a matter of adding ninety degrees to the robot direction (angle) α, followed by α mod 360 to normalize the direction into the correct range.[1]

Listing 8.170—Turn Left Method for Robot Class

```
(add-instance-method
 robot-class
 'turn-left
 (λ (self)
  (let ([d (send self 'get-dir)])
   (send self 'set-dir (modulo (+ d 90) 360)))))
```

Moving the robot is no more complicated; rather just cumbersome to write. Depending on the robot's direction, we update the respective x or y coordinate.

Listing 8.171—Move Forward Method for Robot Class

```
(add-instance-method
 robot-class
 'move-forward
 (λ (self)
  (let ([d (send self 'get-dir)])
   (cond
    [(= d 0) (send self 'set-x (add1 (send self 'get-x)))]
    [(= d 90) (send self 'set-y (sub1 (send self 'get-y)))]
    [(= d 180) (send self 'set-x (sub1 (send self 'get-x)))]
    [(= d 270) (send self 'set-y (add1 (send self 'get-y)))]
    [else (printf "ERR: invalid direction~n")]))))
```

We also need methods for interacting with the items placed around the world. Now, the robot could directly modify the state of the world by altering the item count of a world position, but this introduces an unnecessary coupling of unrelated objects. A better solution is to write two World instance methods: collect-item and place-item, which remove and add items from a given x and y world position. Namely, collecting a item decrements the item count for its respective position whereas placing a item increments its item counter. To get the logical world position, we use the aforementioned offset formulas.

Listing 8.172—Collect Item Method for World Class

```
(add-instance-method
 world-class
 'collect-item
 (λ (self x y)
  (let* ([idx (+ x (* y (send self 'get-width)))]
         [world-posns (send self 'get-lop)]
         [item-box (list-ref world-posns idx)])
   (set-box! item-box (sub1 (unbox item-box))))))
```

---

[1] We *add* ninety degrees to α rather than subtracting because we are following the unit circle, wherein angles increase in a counter-clockwise motion, with zero degrees facing east.

Listing 8.173—Place Item Method for World *Class*

```
(add-instance-method
 world-class
 'place-item
 (λ (self x y)
  (let* ([idx (+ x (* y (send self 'get-width)))]
         [world-posns (send self 'get-lop)]
         [item-box (list-ref world-posns idx)])
   (set-box! item-box (add1 (unbox item-box))))))
```

Finally, we need to add two methods for the robot, designating how it interacts with the world. It too shall have a collect-item and place-item method which invokes the corresponding function from its world. The difference, however, is that a robot who places down a item decrements its bag size rather than incrementing it. Parallel reasoning explains the other case.

Listing 8.174—Collect Item Method for Robot *Class*

```
(add-instance-method
 robot-class
 'collect-item
 (λ (self)
  (let* ([rx (send self 'get-x)]
         [ry (send self 'get-y)]
         [rbc (send self 'get-item-count)]
         [w (send self 'get-world)])
   (begin
    (send self 'set-item-count (add1 rbc))
    (send w 'collect-item rx ry)))))
```

Listing 8.175—Place Item Method for Robot *Class*

```
(add-instance-method
 robot-class
 'place-item
 (λ (self)
  (let* ([rx (send self 'get-x)]
         [ry (send self 'get-y)]
         [rbc (send self 'get-item-count)]
         [w (send self 'get-world)])
   (begin
    (send self 'set-item-count (sub1 rbc))
    (send w 'place-item rx ry)))))
```

We can create an example world of size 10×10 and a robot, then test moving and turning the robot to observe its stopping position. Note that a robot, as per its constructor, has a starting direction α of zero. We will initialize its position to the world origin.

Listing 8.176

```
(define world (send world-class 'new 10 10))
(define r1 (send robot-class 'new 0 0 world))

> (send r1 'move-forward)
> (send r1 'move-forward)
> (send r1 'move-forward)
> (send r1 'turn-left)
> (send r1 'turn-left)
> (send r1 'turn-left)
> (send r1 'move-forward)
> (send r1 'move-forward)
> (printf "x=~a, y=~a, dir=~a~n"                    x=3, y=2, dir=270
          (send r1 'get-x)
          (send r1 'get-y)
          (send r1 'get-dir))
```

As we expect, after moving forward three spots, turning left (counter-clockwise) three times, then moving forward twice more, we end up in (3, 2), facing south ($\alpha = 270$).

Notice, though, that our robot had to turn left *three times* just to turn clockwise, i.e., to its right. Why not add a method to robot that provides the ability to turn right? Indeed, that is simple to do with our add-instance-method function!

Listing 8.177—Turn Right Method for Robot Class

```
(add-instance-method
 robot-class
 'turn-right
 (λ (self)
  (begin
   (send self 'turn-left)
   (send self 'turn-left)
   (send self 'turn-left))))
```

Now, let us suppose that we want to write a robot that overrides the functionality of a normal robot to move several squares at once when calling move-forward. We do not want to add such functionality to the robot-class so as to obey the black-box principle of object-oriented programming—extending object capabilities, rather than "unboxing", so to speak, a theoretically complete class, is an important design paradigm. We want robot-class to remain, as basic as it is, in what it represents. There is one problem that we see immediately after writing the class definition, and that is the fact that we need to access the superclass (of the subclass) inside the constructor to pass the x, y coordinates, as well as the world. Fortunately, there is an easy solution to this problem: we store an generated instance of the superclass when calling make-instance. The superclass instance is stored inside the instance representation. For our purposes, we can write a representation-independent function for retrieving the superclass instance such as instance-super. Our instance (list) representation indicates that we store the superclass instance at index nine, referenced by the *tenth*.

Listing 8.178—Definition and Constructor for Long Mover Robot *Class*

```
(define long-mover-robot-class
  (define-class 'long-mover-robot robot-class '() '()))
(make-constructor long-mover-robot-class
  (λ (self x y world)
    (send (instance-super self) 'set-x x)
    (send (instance-super self) 'set-y y)
    (send (instance-super self) 'set-dir 0)
    (send (instance-super self) 'set-item-count 0)
    (send (instance-super self) 'set-world world)
    self))
```

With this addition, we can override `move-forward` to move however many times we wish a Long Mover Robot to move.[1]

Listing 8.179—Overridden Move Forward Method for Long Mover Robot *Class*

```
(add-instance-method
 long-mover-robot-class
 'move-forward
 (λ (self)
  (begin
   (send (instance-super self) 'move-forward)
   (send (instance-super self) 'move-forward)
   (send (instance-super self) 'move-forward)
   (send (instance-super self) 'move-forward)
   (send (instance-super self) 'move-forward)))))
```

Following this addition, we can test a new `long-mover-robot` and call *its* `move-forward` to see it matches the position and direction of a `robot` instance that moves five times using *its* own `move-forward` method.

Listing 8.180

```
(define world (send world-class 'new 10 10))
(define long-mover-r
        (send long-mover-robot-class 'new 0 0 world))

> (send long-mover-r 'move-forward)
> (send long-mover-r 'turn-left)
> (printf "x=~a, y=~a, dir=~a~n"
          (send long-mover-r 'get-x)
          (send long-mover-r 'get-y)
          (send long-mover-r 'get-dir))
                                              x=3, y=2, dir=270
```

Let us continue by designing another robot, perhaps one that bounces around the world. The `bounce-robot` will move two spaces ahead of its current location. Additionally, because the robot is bouncing, it shakes uncontrollably, causing it to lose an item for every bounce. If it has no collected items, then it of course drops none. Because its constructor is identical (aside from the name) to that of `long-mover-robot`, we omit its implementation, opting to jump straight into overriding the `move-forward` method:

---

[1] What do you think would happen if we accidentally called `self` instead of `(instance-super self)`?

Listing 8.181—Overriding Move Forward Method in Bouncer Robot *Class*

```
(add-instance-method
 bouncer-robot-class
 'move-forward
 (λ (self)
  (let ([rbc (send self 'get-item-count)])
   (begin
    (send (instance-super self) 'move-forward)
    (send (instance-super self) 'move-forward)
    (cond
     [(zero? rbc) (void)]
     [else (send self 'place-item!))])))))
```

Let us instantiate a bounce-robot and test its implementation.

Listing 8.182

```
(define bouncing-r (send bouncer-robot-class 'new 0 0      x=2, y=0, num items=2
    world))                                                x=4, y=0, num items=1
                                                           x=6, y=0, num items=0
(send bouncing-r 'move-forward)                            x=8, y=0, num items=0
(printf "x=~a, y=~a, num items=~a\n" (send bouncing-r
    'get-x) (send bouncing-r 'get-y) (send bouncing-r
    'get-item-count))

(send bouncing-r 'move-forward)
(printf "x=~a, y=~a, num items=~a\n" (send bouncing-r
    'get-x) (send bouncing-r 'get-y) (send bouncing-r
    'get-item-count))

(send bouncing-r 'move-forward)
(printf "x=~a, y=~a, num items=~a\n" (send bouncing-r
    'get-x) (send bouncing-r 'get-y) (send bouncing-r
    'get-item-count))

(send bouncing-r 'move-forward)
(printf "x=~a, y=~a, num items=~a\n" (send bouncing-r
    'get-x) (send bouncing-r 'get-y) (send bouncing-r
    'get-item-count))
```

Exercise 8.22. (⋆⋆)

Design a class SquareRobot that receives a parameter n. When invoking its move-forward method, it moves in a square whose side length is n, picking up all items in the square. After picking up these items, the robot returns to its original position and direction.

8.9 $\mathcal{L}_{\text{VECTOR}}$: Static Data Structures

In Chapter 7, we introduced lists and pairs—two constructs for encapsulating multiple pieces of data. Lists and pairs are flexible in that the number of elements is not necessary to create a list. Contrast this behavior with static arrays from C, whose size must be known at compile-time. We can create the following analogy: linked lists in C are to lists, as arrays are to *vectors*. In this section, we will write $\mathcal{L}_{\text{VECTOR}}$: an extension to $\mathcal{L}_{\text{OUT}}$ that adds fixed-length vectors.

```
expr          ::=   application | ...
application   ::=   vector
              |     vector-set
              |     vector-get
              |     ...
vector        ::=   'make-vector' expr
vector-set    ::=   'vector-set!' id expr expr
vector-get    ::=   'vector-get' id expr
```

Figure 8.6: Extended BNF Grammar for $\mathcal{L}_{\text{VECTOR}}$

One advantage of vectors over lists/pairs is element access times. A vector can access an element in constant time, whereas a list must iterate from the start to the end to find a specific element. Furthermore, the size of a list is determinate, but not instantly; vectors are static, meaning their size is unchangeable. So, when a vector is constructed, the programmer must provide a size to the vector. Additionally, vectors are zero-indexed, identical to arrays in C.

Internally, a vector will be represented as an array of s-values. So, let us create the corresponding s-value, its constructor, and type enumeration. Because the vector should always keep track of its size internally, we need to wrap it (i.e., its elements and size) in a struct.

Listing 8.183—Adding Vector S-value (sval.h)

```
1   enum sval_type { ... , SVAL_VECTOR}
2
3   struct vector {
4     struct sval **elements;
5     size_t size;
6   };
7
8   struct sval {
9     ...
10    union data {
11      ...
12      struct vector vector;
13    } data;
14  };
15
16  struct sval *sval_vector_create(size_t vector_size);
```

Next, let us write the body of the constructor function. When we create a vector, we pass a size, *n*, representing the number of elements to store in the vector. So, we need to allocate an array of *n* s-values, hence the double pointer.

Listing 8.184—Vector S-value Creation Function (`sval.c`)

```
1   struct sval *sval_vector_create(size_t vector_size) {
2     struct sval *vector = sval_create(SVAL_VECTOR);
3     vector->data.vector.elements = malloc(vector_size * sizeof(struct sval *));
4     ASSERT_ALLOC(vector->data.vector.elements, "sval_vector_create");
5     vector->data.vector.size = vector_size;
6     return vector;
7   }
```

We now must consider the representation of vectors. That is, how do we want to visually depict a vector? The solution is that we will prefix vectors with a hash, i.e., #, followed by a list-like syntax. E.g., #(1 2 3) is a vector of the three elements 1, 2, and 3. Let us amend `sval_print` to include vectors. We will similarly update `sval_type` to return a string representation of the type enum for vectors.

Listing 8.185—Printing Vector S-value (`sval.c`)

```
1    void sval_print(struct sval *sv) {
2      ...
3      else if (SVAL_VECTOR == sv->type) {
4        printf("#(");
5        // Print all but the last element with spaces afterwards.
6        for (int i = 0; i < sv->data.vector.size - 1; i++) {
7          sval_print(sv->data.vector.elements[i]);
8          // Do not add a space after printing this element.
9          // If there are no elements then this is skipped over.
10         if (i < sv->data.vector.size - 1) {
11           printf(" ");
12         }
13       }
14       printf(")");
15     }
16     ...
17   }
18
19   const char *sval_type(const enum sval_type type) {
20     ...
21     case SVAL_VECTOR: return "vector";
22   }
```

Now, we need an internal, built-in procedure for initializing a vector of some size. We will call this procedure "`make-vector`" which receives one value denoting the size of the vector.

Listing 8.186—Built-in `make-vector` *Function* (`apply.c`)

```
1    void builtin_functions_init(struct environment *env) {
2      ...
3      environment_put(env, "make-vector", sval_builtin_create(apply_make_vector));
4    }
5
6    static struct sval *apply_make_vector(struct sval **args, size_t num_args,
7                                          struct environment *env) {
8      ASSERT_ARITY("make-vector", 1, num_args);
9      return sval_vector_create(args[0]->data.number);
10   }
```

With this, we can now create empty vectors. But we encounter a pretty significant problem: there are ten element slots in the vector, sure, but what happens if we try to print out the vector? Right now, our code simply attempts to print the data at an element even if nothing exists. The question marks ? are used to emphasize that we do not know what will be printed.

Listing 8.187

```
(define vec1 (make-vector 10))

> vec1                                    #(? ? ? ? ? ? ? ? ? ?)
```

The problem is the start of the sval_print function. We attempt to retrieve the type of an s-value that does not exist. So, if we find a NULL s-value, we should print something akin to NULL. Though, the values themselves are not necessarily null; they exist, just in a non-sensical state. So, we will represent a "null" s-value as the string "nil".

Listing 8.188—Printing Null S-value (sval.c)

```
1   void sval_print(struct sval *sv) {
2     if (NULL == sv) { printf("nil"); }
3   }
```

If we try to recompile the interpreter and rerun the test, we still get a segmentation fault.[1] What is going on? Executing the program through GDB shows that the segmentation fault occurs on the same line in sval_print. The problem is how we are initializing the array of values. We call malloc to initialize an array of s-values. The issue, as we saw in Chapter 5, is that malloc does not preinitialize values; its sole purpose is to find available memory and provide it for use. Printing out the pointer value of the passed s-value argument shows this in greater detail.

0x1000000000000000

This is certainly not NULL! A null value is exactly zero. So, reading from "uninitialized" memory before useful data is inserted often results in catastrophic and head-banging errors. The solution is to populate this array with NULL values. We should use the "calloc" function to specify that we want each array slot to be "zero-initialized".

Listing 8.189—Using calloc *to "Zero-Initialize" Vector Elements* (sval.c)

```
1   struct sval *sval_vector_create(size_t vector_size) {
2     struct sval *vector = sval_create(SVAL_VECTOR);
3     vector->data.vector.elements = calloc(vector_size, sizeof(struct sval *));
4     ASSERT_ALLOC(vector->data.vector.elements, "sval_vector_create");
5     vector->data.vector.size = vector_size;
6     return vector;
7   }
```

The only other noteworthy difference is that calloc receives one extra parameter: a count. This count designates how many slots we want to allocate. So, we want vector_size slots each of size sizeof(struct sval *). Now, the program should work wonderfully.

---

[1]If we run this program several times, we may encounter a trial where the program is successful. Memory layouts are likely to change upon program execution, so sometimes the allocator gets lucky and finds a spot of ten zeroes in a row.

Listing 8.190

`(define vec1 (make-vector 5))`	
`> vec1`	`#(nil nil nil nil nil)`

Let us add something useful: the ability to update and retrieve vector elements via `vector-set!` and `vector-get` respectively.

`vector-set!` receives three arguments: a vector to manipulate, an index, and the item to store at the index. `vector-get`, on the other hand, receives two arguments: a vector to access, and the index of the element to retrieve. Neither of these functions are overly complicated.

Listing 8.191—Built-in `vector-set!` & `vector-get` Functions (`apply.c`)

```
1   static struct sval *apply_vector_set(struct sval **args, size_t num_args,
2                                         struct environment *env) {
3     ASSERT_ARITY("vector-set!", 3, num_args);
4     struct sval *vector = args[0];
5     struct sval *index = args[1];
6     struct sval *element = args[2];
7     vector->data.vector.elements[(int) index->data.number] = element;
8     return NULL;
9   }
10
11  static struct sval *apply_vector_get(struct sval **args, size_t num_args,
12                                        struct environment *env) {
13    ASSERT_ARITY("vector-get", 2, num_args);
14    struct sval *vector = args[0];
15    struct sval *index = args[1];
16    return vector->data.vector.elements[(int) index->data.number];
17  }
```

Remember that, when working with indices, we must use integers. So, the passed index argument cannot be, for example, a floating-point number. So, trying this out with our previous example:

Listing 8.192

`(define vec1 (make-vector 5))`	
`> vec1`	`#(nil nil nil nil nil)`
`> (vector-set! vec1 3 250)`	
`> vec1`	`#(nil nil nil 250 nil)`

Great! We are on our way to a useful data structure. Though, it would be nice to have a function akin to "list"; one that creates a vector out of its arguments. E.g., `(vector 1 2 3 4)` => `#(1 2 3 4)`. So, let us write one! All we need to do is write a procedure that takes any number of arguments, creates a vector where its size is said number, then sets each element.

Listing 8.193

```
(define vector
 (letrec ([vector-helper
            (λ (v l idx)
              (cond
                [(null? l) v]
                [else
                 (begin
                   (vector-set! v idx (first l))
                   (vector-helper v (rest l) (+ idx 1)))]))])
   (λ-var (args)
     (let ([vec (make-vector (length args))])
       (vector-helper vec args 0)))))
```

Before vectors, we implemented boxes as tagged *cons* pairs whose *first* is `'box` and whose *rest* is the encapsulated value. Vectors provide a slightly easier method for designing boxes due to the `vector-set!` function. Let us rewrite our box implementation to use a one-element vector rather than a tagged list. Again, this implies that all one-element vectors are, by our standards, boxes. To do so, we must create a `vector?` (recognition) predicate, something we leave as a trivial exercise to the readers.

Listing 8.194

```
(define box
 (λ (v)
   (let ([vec (make-vector 1)])
     (begin
       (vector-set! vec 0 v)
       vec))))

(define box?
 (λ (v)
   (and (vector? v)
        (zero? (sub1 (vector-length v))))))

(define set-box!
 (λ (bx v)
   (vector-set! bx 0 v)))

(define unbox
 (λ (bx)
   (vector-get bx 0)))
```

Exercise 8.23. (★★★)

Vectors can be multidimensional and contain vectors as elements. Though, we can always represent an n-dimensional vector using a one-dimensional vector by using index and size offsets. For example, if we want to declare an $m \times n$ two-dimensional vector, we could, instead, create a one-dimensional vector of size mn. To correctly reference given indices x and y for a two-dimensional vector of size $m \times n$, we use the following calculation:

$$x+y{\cdot}m$$

Recall that we saw an identical transformation in our object-oriented programming discussion with worlds and robots; the only difference being that we used lists as opposed to vectors. Implement functions for creating a two-dimensional vector: (make-vector-2d m n), (vector-ref-2d v x y), and vector-set-2d! v x y e). Note that to write the latter two functions, you will also need to provide m. Perhaps an alternative solution is to wrap the two-dimensional vector in a closure or tagged list containing m and n.

$\mathcal{L}^*_{AL}$: An Array List Data Structure

It would be nice if there existed a data structure with the constant access times of vectors but with the flexibility of dynamically adding and removing elements that we get with traditional *cons*-style lists. Java has such a structure called an *array list*, named as such because it is a hybrid of constant access time vectors and resizable lists. In this section, we will write $\mathcal{L}^*_{AL}$: a language that implements a similar data structure.

We previously wrote $\mathcal{L}$VECTOR, which adds support for vectors: a non-resizable data structure with constant element access time. What is exciting about this is that we can create a data structure that uses vectors under the hood while providing the flexibility of adding and removing any number of elements we so desire.

Our array list implementation will use a closure to store its properties and a variadic dispatch function, identical to our object-oriented programming section. By default, we will say that an array list stores ten values with a logical size of zero. The logical size indicates how many meaningful elements exist in the list. Moreover, as we hinted at, the underlying data structure will be a vector thanks to its constant-access time operations.

Listing 8.195—Initial Array List Closure Definition

```
; How many elements can be stored initially?
(define INITIAL-CAPACITY 10)
; By what multiplicative factor will we resize the underlying vector?
(define RESIZE-FACTOR 2)
; Initially, we have zero elements in the list.
(define INITIAL-SIZE 0)

;; arraylist : Void -> [Symbol ... -> Any]
;; Creates a closure with the structure of an array list.
;;
;; An array list has an initial capacity of INITIAL-CAPACITY,
;; logical size of INITIAL-SIZE, and an elements vector. There
;; are several functions associated with an array list.
(define arraylist
  (λ ()
    (let* ([capacity INITIAL-CAPACITY]
           [size INITIAL-SIZE]
           [elements (make-vector capacity)])
      (λ-var (args)
        (let ([cmd (first args)]
              [rest (rest args)])
          ...)))))
```

The most important operation for such a data structure is add!, i.e., the ability to add an element to the end of the array list. When we invoke add! on the array list, the element to add is stored at the next-available index, which is referenced by size. Let us begin working on add-val: a local procedure to add an element to the array list. Upon adding a new value to the array list, we perform two side effects: first, we add the element to the backing vector, and second, we increment the size by one.

Listing 8.196—Add Element to Array List

```
(define arraylist
 (λ ()
  (let* (; Syntax: (lst add! val)
         [add-val
          (λ (val)
           (begin
            (vector-set! elements size val)
            (set! size (add1 size))))]
   (λ-var (args)
    (let ([cmd (first args)]
          [rest (rest args)])
     (cond
      [(eqv? cmd 'add!) (add-val (first rest))]
      [else #f]))))))))
```

Let us create an example array list and add some elements. We will make use of the (omitted) print! function that displays the backing vector of an array list.

Listing 8.197

```
(define al (arraylist))

> (al 'print!)                           #(nil nil nil nil nil
> (al 'add! 106)                            nil nil nil nil nil)
> (al 'add! 439)
> (al 'add! 521)
> (al 'add! 316)
> (al 'add! 17)
> (al 'print!)                           #(106 439 521 316 17
                                            nil nil nil nil nil)
```

Our current setup is not very interesting—the question now is what happens when we try to add an element to a "full" array list. As we know, a *cons* does not suffer from this problem, and vectors are unfortunately plagued with such a curse. The solution is to increase the size of the array list! Some may view this with skepticism since vectors are static data structures. This may be the case, but we can create a new vector with the old elements copied over and a new increased capacity. What is more is that the user of the array list needs not to know this happens. So, by what factor should the vector increase? We will choose a resizing factor (RESIZE_FACTOR) of two to double the vector capacity, i.e., the size goes from 10 to 20, then to 40, then 80, and so on.

Another question that inevitably presents itself is when to resize a vector. It is cumbersome to repeatedly check in the array list implementation. So, we will write c-resize!: a function that *conditionally resizes* a vector. It receives, of course, a vector, a logical size, and a current capacity. If the logical size is equal to the current capacity (i.e., the array list is full), we increase the vector capacity by creating a new vector and copying the old elements over. c-resize! returns its result as a *cons* pair whose *first* is the new capacity and whose *rest* is the new vector. On the other hand, if the logical size is less than the current capacity, we return the original capacity and vector as a *cons* pair. This way, the array list data structure does not concern itself with if a resize occurred. Rather, it presumes that a vector with enough space is always present.

To write c-resize!, we need a recursive helper function for copying elements from one vector to another. From here, the implementation is trivial.

Listing 8.198— "Resizing" a Vector

```
;; c-resize : {X} [VectorOf X] Number Number -> (cons Number [VectorOf X])
;; Conditionally resizes a vector from a given capacity to another.
;; If the capacity and given logical size are not equal (meaning a resize
;; is unnecessary), then the original is returned. A pair whose first is
;; the new capacity and whose rest is the new vector is returned.
(define c-resize!
  (letrec ([copy-vector
             (λ (e new-e sz)
               (cond
                 [(zero? sz) new-e]
                 [else
                  (begin
                    (vector-set! new-e (sub1 sz) (vector-ref e (sub1 sz)))
                    (copy-vector e new-e (sub1 sz)))])))])
    (λ (e size capacity)
      (cond
        [(= capacity size)
         (let* ([new-c (* capacity RESIZE-FACTOR)]
                [new-e (make-vector new-c)])
           (cons new-c (copy-vector e new-e size)))]
        [else (cons capacity e)]))))
```

We now use this function in our add-val implementation; the returned result is a *cons* pair, so we extract out each component. We then reassign the capacity and vector values using set!. Note that we still perform a (superfluous) assignment even if the vector and capacity do not change.

Listing 8.199

```
(define arraylist
  (λ ()
    (let* ([capacity INITIAL-CAPACITY]
           [size INITIAL-SIZE]
           [elements (make-vector capacity)]
           ; Syntax: (lst add! val)
           [add-val
             (λ (val)
               (let* ([res-pair (c-resize! elements size capacity)]
                      [new-c (first res-pair)]
                      [new-e (rest res-pair)])
                 (begin
                   (set! capacity new-c)
                   (set! elements new-e)
                   (vector-set! elements size val)
                   (set! size (add1 size)))))])
      ...)))
```

Assuming that we have the same array list from before, we can add a few more elements to demonstrate the vector resizing.

Listing 8.200

```
(define al (arraylist))
...
> (al 'add! 654)
> (al 'add! 505)
> (al 'add! 362)
> (al 'add! 250)
> (al 'add! 523)
> (al 'print!)              #(106 439 521 316 17 654 505
                               362 250 523)
> (al 'add! 543)
> (al 'print!)              #(106 439 521 316 17 654 505
                               362 250 523 543 nil nil nil
                               nil nil nil nil nil nil)
```

Adding elements is certainly one feature of array lists, but what about element removal? In fact, what exactly does it mean to "delete" an element of a vector, let alone an array list? Vectors have no inherent sense of element deletion because they are not resizable. Though, with our new approach, could we create a new vector that does not have a specific element? Sure, that is possible, but we present an even simpler solution: shift all elements in the array list down by one index. For example, consider the array list containing the values #(439 521 654 362 330 nil nil nil nil nil). If we want to remove the element 521, we can shift each element past 521 one index to the left, overwriting 521 with the corresponding data to its right. Finally, we decrement the array list logical size by one. Instead of a function to remove a specific value, we will instead write a function to remove the element at a particular index. Though, before we start, consider another operation that can cause a "shift". If we want to insert an element at some (valid) index, we need to shift all elements past the given index to the right. Inserting 656 at index 2 of the array list produces #(439 521 656 654 362 330 nil nil nil nil). We now have two operations, namely remove and insert, that rely on some shifting mechanic. So, let us write a function shift! that receives a vector, a logical size, an index to shift from, and a "shift direction". Because left shifting uses a different approach than right shifting, we define local recursive procedures which are invoked depending on the given direction symbol.

Listing 8.201—Recursive Vector Shifting Function

```
; A Shift is one of:
; - 'LEFT
; - 'RIGHT

;; shift!: {X} [VectorOf X] Number Number Shift -> Void
;; Shifts the values in a vector one unit either to the left or the right.
;;
;; "size" represents the logical number of elements in the vector, whereas
;; "idx" represents the index to start (left)/stop (right) shifting from.
(define shift!
 (letrec ([left
           (λ (e n idx)
            (cond
             [(zero? n) '()]
             [else
              (begin
               (vector-set! e idx (vector-ref e (add1 idx)))
               (left e (sub1 n) (add1 idx)))]))]
          [right
           (λ (e n idx)
            (cond
             [(= n idx) '()]
             [else
              (begin
               (vector-set! e n (vector-ref e (sub1 n)))
               (right e (sub1 n) idx))]))])
  (λ (e size idx direction)
   (cond
    [(eqv? direction 'LEFT) (left e size idx)]
    [else (right e size idx)]))))
```

One important property of shift! is that it assumes the input vector has enough room to shift its arguments (to the right). So, when we call shift! from within our array list closure, we should first invoke c-resize!.

At last, we can write remove! and insert!, which are respectively declared as the local functions remove-val and insert-val.

Listing 8.202

```
(define arraylist
 (let* (; Syntax: (lst remove! idx)
        [remove-val
         (λ (idx)
          (begin
           (shift! elements size idx 'LEFT)
           (set! size (sub1 size))))]
        ; Syntax: (lst insert! idx val)
        [insert-val
         (λ (idx val)
          (begin
           (shift! elements size idx 'RIGHT)
           (vector-set! elements idx val)
           (set! size (add1 size))))]
   ...)))
```

Testing this once more with the previous al definition yields predictable results.

Listing 8.203

```
(define al (arraylist))

> (al 'print!)                          #(106 439 521 316 17 nil nil nil nil nil)
> (al 'insert! 2 656)
> (al 'print!)                          #(106 439 656 521 316 17 nil nil nil nil)
> (al 'remove! 1)
> (al 'print!)                          #(106 656 521 316 17 nil nil nil nil nil)
> (al 'insert! 0 1000)
> (al 'print!)                          #(1000 106 656 521 316 17 nil nil nil nil)
```

Exercise 8.24. ($\star$)
Add the array list function get: $\{X\}$ Number $\to$ X, which receives an index i and returns the element at said index.

Exercise 8.25. ($\star$)
Add the array list function set!: $\{X\}$ Number X $\to$ X , which receives an index i and an element e; e is stored at index i, overwriting the current value.

Exercise 8.26. ($\star$)
Add the array list function contains?: $\{X\}$ X $\to$ Boolean , which receives an element e and returns true if it is in the array list and false otherwise.

Exercise 8.27. ($\star$)
Add the array list function index-of: $\{X\}$ X $\to$ Number, which receives an element e and returns the index of the first occurrence of e. If e is not present, return -1.

Exercise 8.28. ($\star$)
Add the array list function empty?: Void $\to$ Bool, which returns whether or not the array list has any elements.

Exercise 8.29. ($\star\star$)
Add the array list higher-order function map!: $\{X\}$ [X $\to$ Y] $\to$ Void, which applies a function to every element of the vector.

Exercise 8.30. ($\star\star$)
Add the array list variadic function add-all: $\{X\}$ X ... $\to$ Void, which receives any number of elements and adds them all to the array list, dynamically resizing as needed. Hint: use the map function.

Exercise 8.31. ($\star\star\star$)
Add the array list higher-order function filter!: $\{X\}$ [X $\to$ Bool] $\to$ Void, which removes all elements from the vector that do not satisfy the given predicate.

8.10 $\mathcal{L}_{\text{LIB}}$: External Libraries

There are a ton of helper functions that we could write that drastically improve the overall usability of our interpreter. In this section, we will write $\mathcal{L}_{\text{LIB}}$: an extension to $\mathcal{L}_{\text{VECTOR}}$ that adds support for loading other files with function definitions. Some may question, "Why not just designate these as built-in functions within apply?". The answer is that functions in apply are intended to be "implementer-level" functions, i.e., functions that cannot be implemented with the language itself. For instance, there is no possible way to re-implement first or rest using the constructs within $\mathcal{L}_{\text{VECTOR}}$. A library can provide convenience-functions that make a programmer's job easier and less "reinvent-the-wheel-y".

```
expr         ::=   application | ...
application  ::=   include | ...
include      ::=   'include' string
```

Figure 8.7: Extended BNF Grammar for $\mathcal{L}_{\text{LIB}}$

It may be tempting to simply write a function in apply that invokes the parser to read a new file, bringing in its definitions and storing them into the environment. While this is what we will eventually do, we first have to alter a few pieces of code. Recall that in eval_ast, we initialize the root/global environment as well as the special forms and built-in function table. We should move these to a function, i.e., eval_init which is invoked directly in the main function. This way, if we do need to load in a library or another file with definitions, it does not reinitialize any preexisting data.

Listing 8.204—Initializing a Global Environment (eval.c)

```
1   static struct environment *global_env = NULL;
2
3   void eval_init(void) {
4     global_env = environment_create(NULL);
5     builtin_functions_init(global_env);
6     special_forms_init();
7   }
```

Notice that we also moved the global environment declaration into global scope. This is acceptable because it is a static variable, meaning other files cannot modify or access its contents/state.

Now, let us think about what we want to happen when we bring in a file with new definitions. The idea is simple: parse a new file and store its definitions in the global environment. This sounds easy enough, and we can write a convenient function in apply to accomplish this task.

Listing 8.205—Built-in `include` *Function* (`apply.c`)

```
1   struct sval *apply_include(struct sval **args, size_t num_args,
2                                struct environment *env) {
3     if (1 != num_args) {
4       EPF("include expects one argument but got %zu\n", num_args);
5       exit(EXIT_FAILURE);
6     }
7     parser_parse(args[0]->data.string, PARSE_FILE);
8     return NULL;
9   }
```

We name the function "include" to designate that we are including other functions/definitions from an outside file. Now, here's the thing: we are destroying the abstract syntax tree and backing mpc abstract syntax tree immediately after invoking `eval_ast` in `parser.c`, so we need to remove these function calls. But, in doing this, we introduce a severe memory leak! What is the solution? We need to introduce a buffer.

Blocks of space that are reserved for data are *buffers*. Recall that we cannot free an mpc abstract syntax tree from anywhere other than the parser because other abstract syntax trees reference the children of the root. If we free the root, then any node that attempts to free its copy of the abstract syntax tree will receive a double free error. So, to remedy this, we can simply declare a "tree buffer" which keeps an array of all mpc abstract syntax trees in working memory. Then, at the end, when the parser is cleaning up, it traverses the buffer and deletes the trees via `mpc_ast_delete`.

Listing 8.206—Adding Buffer of Syntax Trees (`parser.c`)

```
1   #define MAX_TREES 10
2
3   /* Keeps track of all abstract available syntax trees. */
4   struct tree_buffer {
5     size_t tree_count;
6     mpc_ast_t *tree_buffer_array[MAX_TREES];
7   };
8
9   struct tree_buffer trees;
```

So, we create a syntax tree buffer struct that holds up to ten mpc abstract syntax trees. Ten is a reasonable limit for most intents and purposes. Now, let us modify the `read` and `cleanup` functions to add a new tree to the buffer and delete all existing trees respectively.

Listing 8.207—Deleting Buffer of Syntax Trees (`parser.c`)

```
1   void parser_cleanup(void) {
2     ...
3     for (int i = 0; i < trees.tree_count; i++) {
4       mpc_ast_delete(trees.tree_buffer_array[i]);
5     }
6   }
7
8   static void parser_read(const char *contents, int mode) {
9     ...
10    mpc_ast_t *mpc_ast = (mpc_ast_t *) result.output;
11    trees.tree_buffer_array[trees.tree_count++] = mpc_ast;
12    ast *my_ast = ast_create(mpc_ast, mpc_ast->tag,
13                             mpc_ast->children_num, mpc_ast->contents);
14    eval_ast(my_ast);
15    free(my_ast);
16  }
```

Now, let us create a library file: `library.lib`, and we can include it in a sample test. Suppose that `library.lib` contains a definition for `length`. We can then include this definition into another source file, which uses said definition.

Listing 8.208 (`library.lib`)

```
(define length
  (lambda (ls)
    (cond
      [(null? ls) 0]
      [else (add1 (length (rest ls)))])))
```

Listing 8.209 (`main.lib`)

```
(include "library.lib")

> (length '(1 2 3 a b c 4 5 6 d e f))        12
```

That is all there is to it! The buffer solution is not the most elegant, but it prevents absurd memory leaks, and also helps eradicate hard-to-debug errors, e.g,. use-after-free and double-free. We can write tons of helper functions to include (no pun intended!) in this file, e.g., `map`, `append`, `vector`, `list`, `fold`, `filter`, compositions of `first` and `rest`, and so on. Additionally, we can remove a couple of built-in functions, e.g., `not`, `modulo`, `remainder`.

Exercise 8.32. (⋆⋆⋆)

We have repeatedly seen the use of an association list to represent environments in nested interpreters. Association lists are a type of dictionary, i.e., a mapping of keys to values, and often come "preloaded" as a library in the language. Create the `dict.lib` file that serves as a library for association lists. You can assume that all keys are `eqv?`-comparable types. Inside, implement the following functions:

Listing 8.210 (`dict.lib`)

```
; A DictionaryLabel is 'DICTIONARY.

; A Dictionary is a [ListOf DictionaryLabel [PairOf X Y]]
; X and Y are generic types.

;; dict-create : (Void) -> Dictionary
;; Creates a dictionary with the aforesaid label.
(define dict-key ...)

;; dict? : Any -> Boolean
;; Determines whether the given object is a Dictionary.
(define dict? ...)

;; dict-contains-key? : {X} Dictionary X -> Boolean
;; Returns whether the given key exists in the dictionary.
(define dict-contains-key? ...)

;; dict-ref : {X} {Y} Dictionary X -> Y
;; Finds a value given a key in the given dictionary.
;; If X is not in the dictionary, we throw an (error).
(define dict-ref ...)

;; dict-set : {X} {Y} Dictionary X Y -> Dictionary
;; Inserts a key/value mapping into a dictionary,
;; returning a new dictionary in the process.
(define dict-set ...)

;; dict-empty? : Dictionary -> Boolean
;; Determines if a dictionary contains any pairs.
(define dict-empty? ...)

;; dict-keys : {X} Dictionary -> [ListOf X]
;; Returns a list of all the keys in the given dictionary.
(define dict-keys ...)
```

Exercise 8.33. (★★★★)

Our library implementation omits a pretty severe problem that C takes care of with include guards: circular inclusions. For instance, if we have two files `library1.lib` and `library2.lib`, where each include the other, what is the resolution? Implement a solution to this problem.

Exercise 8.34. (★★★★)

Similar to the previous exercise, what if a file includes two libraries that both implement the same function? Whose function definition is used? Implement a solution to this problem.

8.11 $\mathcal{L}^*_{\text{GRAPH}}$: Graph Library Implementation

In Chapter 3, we discussed the importance of the graph data structure. In this section, we will create a small implementation of a graph library.

Recall that a graph G has a set of vertices G_V and a set of edges G_E. An edge links two vertices together. We previously talked about two potential representations of graphs: adjacency lists and adjacency matrices. Our library will use the former representation. Namely, a graph is an association list whose elements are pairs where the *first* of each pair is a vertex and the *rest* is a list of adjacent vertices which, therein, denote edges. For instance, let us encode the following undirected graph:

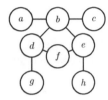

Figure 8.8: Pictorial Representation of the Graph G_1

We may encode the graph in Figure 8.8 as an association list, as follows. Note that, since it is an undirected graph, an edge between two vertices u and v implies that there is an edge from v to u, meaning that both $(u, v) \in G_E$ and $(v, u) \in G_E$.

Listing 8.211

```
(define g1
  '((a . (b)) (b . (a c d e)) (c . (b)) (d . (b f g))
    (e . (b f h)) (f . (d e)) (g . (d)) (h . (e))))
```

Suppose that we want to add/remove a vertex or an edge to this graph. We need to write functions, i.e., add/remove-vertex and add/remove-edge respectively. Note that, unlike the general theme of this chapter on "non-functionality", these functions do not alter the original graph, but rather create a new graph with the amendments. Let us begin by writing the vertex modification functions. All we need to do in the case of addition is prepend the vertex, as a list, to the graph (this means that we add a vertex with no edges to the graph). Removing a vertex is more complicated since we not only have to remove the vertex but also remove any connecting edges. A very helpful function to write (which may be stored in a separate library file) is list-remove: a function that removes a given element from a list. So, in effect, we remove the relevant vertex/edge pair from the graph and clear all remaining vertex/edge pairs of the now-removed vertex. It is important to understand that, in a graph that uses our design specification, the *first* references the first vertex/edge pair p, the *first* of p references the first vertex v, and the *rest* of p references v's edge list.

Listing 8.212

```
;; add-vertex : Graph Atom -> Graph
;; Adds a vertex to the start of a graph's
;; adjacency list. The added vertex has no edges.
;; Adding a preexisting vertex to G is undefined.
(define add-vertex
 (λ (G v)
  `((,v) . ,G)))
```

Listing 8.213

```
;; remove-vertex : Graph Atom -> Graph
;; Removes a vertex from a graph. This also
;; recursively removes edges from any other nodes.
(define remove-vertex
 (λ (G v)
  (cond
   [(null? G) '()]
   [else
    (let ([vtx-pair (first G)])
     (cond
      [(eqv? (first vtx-pair) v) (remove-vertex (rest G) v)]
      [else
       (let* ([edge-list (rest vtx-pair)]
              [filtered-list (list-remove edge-list v)])
        (cons (cons (first vtx-pair) filtered-list)
              (remove-vertex (rest G) v)))])])])))
```

Next, let us work on adding and removing edges. Adding an edge, from vertex u to vertex v, to a graph is a recursive function that searches for u in the adjacency list and adds v to the neighbors of u. Since we do not modify the original graph, we must handle all cases. Namely when the input graph is the empty list, when we have found u, and when we have not found u. Because this graph is generic, we want to write a procedure that adds both directed and undirected edges. An undirected edge is, as we previously mentioned, just a directed edge from u to v and v to u. Therefore, we may write a procedure add-undirected-edge in terms of add-directed-edge. Thankfully, removing a directed edge is simpler than removing vertices; all we need to do is search for the source vertex u and remove the destination vertex v from its list of neighbors.

Listing 8.214

```
;; add-directed-edge : Graph Atom Atom -> Graph
;; Adds a directed edge to a graph. Directed edge
;; simply means that the edge "flows" from one
;; vertex to another and only in that direction.
(define add-directed-edge
 (λ (G u v)
  (cond
   [(null? G) '()]
   [else
    (let ([vtx-pair (first G)])
     (cond
      [(eqv? (first vtx-pair) u) (cons (cons u (cons v (rest vtx-pair))) (rest G))]
      [else (cons (first G) (add-directed-edge (rest G) u v))]))])))

;; add-undirected-edge : Graph Atom Atom -> Graph
;; Adds a undirected edge to a graph. An undirected
;; edge is nothing but a directed edge that points both ways.
(define add-undirected-edge
 (λ (G u v)
  (add-directed-edge (add-directed-edge G u v) v u)))
```

Listing 8.215

```
;; remove-edge : Graph Atom Atom -> Graph
;; Removes an edge from the graph.
(define remove-edge
 (λ (G u v)
  (cond
   [(null? G) '()]
   [else
    (let ([vtx-pair (first G)])
     (cond
      [(eqv? (first vtx-pair) u) (cons (cons u (list-remove (rest vtx-pair) v))
                                       (remove-edge (rest G) u v))]
      [else (cons (first G) (remove-edge (rest G) u v))]))])))
```

Lastly, let us create two "convenience" procedures, namely one that receives an adjacency list to "create" the graph, and another that returns the neighbors of a vertex u (i.e., any vertices whose source is u).

Listing 8.216

```
; A Vertex is an Atom
;
; A Graph is
; - [ListOf (cons Vertex [ListOf Vertex])]
(define make-graph
 (λ (adj-list)
  adj-list))

;; get-neighbors : Graph Vertex -> [ListOf Vertex]
;; Returns the vertices adjacent to the given vertex u.
(define get-neighbors
 (λ (G u)
  (cond
   [(null? G) #f]
   [else
    (let ([vtx-pair (first G)])
     (cond
      [(eqv? (first vtx-pair) u) (rest vtx-pair)]
      [else (get-neighbors (rest G) u)]))])))
```

Let us test this implementation using the definition of g1 from above. Our output will show the result of the newly-defined graphs.

Listing 8.217

```
(define g2 (add-vertex g1 'j))         > g2    ((j) (a b) (b c d) (c b e)
(define g3                                     (d b e) (e c d f) (f e))
 (add-undirected-edge g2 'j 'a))       > g3    ((j a) (a j b) (b c d) (c b e)
(define g4                                     (d b e) (e c d f) (f e))
 (add-undirected-edge g3 'c 'f))       > g4    ((j a) (a j b) (b c d) (c f b e)
(define g5 (remove-vertex g4 'd))              (d b e) (c c d f) (f c e))
(define g6 (remove-edge g5 'e 'c))     > g5    ((j a) (a j b) (b c) (c f b e)
                                               (e c f) (f c e))
                                       > g6    ((j a) (a j b) (b c) (c f b e)
                                               (e f) (f c e))
```

Depth-First and Breadth-First Search Algorithms

There are two famous and classically-studied graph-traversal algorithms: depth-first search and breadth-first search.

Depth-first search on a graph receives a root node u and traverses the graph, as its name implies, depth-first. By depth, we mean to say that the traversal goes as far down a *path* as possible before backtracking to go down another branch. Consider our prior definition of g_1. If we perform a depth-first search traversal starting from node 'a', we travel down to the only neighbor of 'a', namely 'b', which has three neighbors: 'c', 'd', and 'e'. Picking the next node to visit is an arbitrary choice, so we will go in alphabetical order to 'c'. Because 'c' has no children, we backtrack to the next neighbor of 'b', namely 'd', which has three neighbors: 'b', 'f', and 'g'. Because 'b' has already been visited, it is not re-visited. So, we travel to 'f', which has two neighbors, 'd' and 'e'. We repeat the process until all nodes in the graph have been visited. Fortunately, the algorithm is inherently recursive, but almost all implementations use a *"for each"* construct when traversing over the neighbors N of a vertex u. Because we do not yet have equivalent iteration construct, we will write the recursive variant of depth-first search. To this end, we must pass around a store containing the visited vertices. This introduces the concept of *store-passing* style, which allows us to model state modification without directly modifying global or local variables after their initialization. If we could not use store-passing style variant, the visited vertex list must be wrapped in a box because the stack of visited nodes would not be persistent among recursive calls.

The store-passing style algorithm returns the list of visited vertices if we find that the given node is already a member of said list. Otherwise, we recursively fold the dfs-helper function over the neighbors of the current vertex u where we *end-cons* u onto the list of previously-seen vertices V, which acts as the store. You may be wondering: "What is *end-cons?*" This is the opposite of the typical cons function; instead of prepending a value u to the front of some pair P, we append u, as a list, to the end of P. For example, while (cons 5 '(1 2 3)) is '(5 1 2 3), (end-cons 5 '(1 2 3)) resolves to '(1 2 3 5). We can represent this using either natural recursion, or append and cons itself. We use end-cons because, otherwise, the DFS traversal would be reversed.

Listing 8.218—Depth-First Search Traversal Algorithm

```
;; dfs : Graph Vertex -> [ListOf Vertex]
;; Performs a depth-first search on the given graph starting at the vertex v.
(define (dfs G v)
  (letrec ([dfs-helper
            (λ (u visited)
              (cond
                [(member? u visited) visited]
                [else
                 (foldl dfs-helper (end-cons u visited) (get-neighbors G u))]))])
    (dfs-helper v '())))
```

Breadth-first search uses a different traversal approach: instead of heading down a path to its end, it gradually branches out one edge at a time at every step, keeping track of the next elements to visit. For example, suppose we have a graph G_2 as follows. We see that vertex 'a' has three neighbors: 'b', 'c', and 'd'. A depth-first search would enqueue 'b' as the next node to visit and begin heading down this branch. Breadth-first, on the other hand, enqueues all neighbors of 'a' and processes them piecemeal. That is, the neighbors of vertex 'b' are enqueued only after those neighbors of 'c' followed by 'd' are processed.

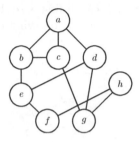

Figure 8.9: Pictorial Representation of the Graph G_2

The breadth-first search algorithm is similar to the depth-first search, with the exception that the neighbors of the current node u are added to the queue on the grounds that they have not already been visited in the traversal (hence the need for filter). Each pass through the traversal, we dequeue our to-visit vertex queue Q, enqueue its non-visited neighbors, and mark those non-visited neighbors as now-visited, since they are added to the to-visit vertex queue.

Listing 8.219—Breadth-First Search Traversal Algorithm

```
;; bfs : Graph Vertex -> [ListOf Vertex]
;; Performs a breadth-first search on the given graph starting at the vertex v.
(define bfs
  (letrec ([bfs-helper
            (λ (G Q V)
              (cond
                [(null? Q) visited]
                [else
                 (let* ([u (first Q)]
                        [nbrs (get-neighbors G u)]
                        [unvisited (filter (λ (n) (not (member? n V))) nbrs)])
                   (bfs-helper G
                               (append (rest queue) unvisited)
                               (append V unvisited)))])))]
    (λ (G v)
      (bfs-helper G (list v) (list v))))))
```

Let us encode G_2 into our nested interpreter representation and perform both depth-first and breadth-first searches starting from vertex 'a' to see the output traversals:

Listing 8.220

```
(define g2
  (make-graph
   '((a . (b c d)) (b . (a c e))
     (c . (a b g)) (d . (a e g))
     (e . (b d f)) (f . (e h))
     (g . (c d h)) (h . (f g)))))

> (dfs g2 'a)                          (a b c g d e f h)
> (bfs g2 'a)                          (a b c d e g f h)
```

An interesting application of breadth-first search is the ability to find paths between nodes. For example, consider the following moderately complex graph:

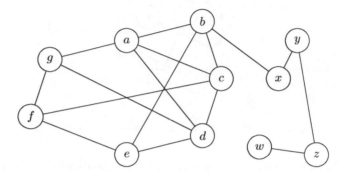

Figure 8.10: Pictorial Representation of Complex Graph

Suppose we want to find a shortest path between vertices 'f' and 'w'. Clearly, to us humans, we can quickly see that the path from $f \rightarrow c \rightarrow b \rightarrow x \rightarrow y \rightarrow z \rightarrow w$ is a shortest.[1] How can we use our new search algorithms to find this shortest path? In traditional imperative algorithms, the idea is to compute the path from each node to every other node, then once the target is found, return a shortest path found so far. If we want to apply this to a functional programming language without side-effects, we need to think creatively, because there do not exist "return" statements to quit a function early. Continuations provide the control flow we desire. That is, we write the algorithm using continuation-passing style semantics, and upon finding the destination, we mimic returning the path by invoking the continuation at that point.

We first need to write a function that "expands out" a path, where a path is a list containing the vertices along said path. Given a list of paths P seen so far, a current vertex u, and a list of unvisited vertices V, we want to append the vertices in V onto the path in P that ends in u. For example, if our paths seen so far include $P = ((f), (f\ c), (f\ e), (f\ g))$, $u =$'c', and $V = (a, b, d)$, then we retrieve the path '$(f\ c)$', and create new paths '$(f\ c\ a)$', '$(f\ c\ b)$', and '$(f\ c\ d)$'.

---

[1]We use the indefinite article 'a' to designate that our definition of "shortest" references the number of edges between two nodes. Because of this, there are potentially multiple shortest paths from one vertex to another.

Listing 8.221—Path-Expansion Algorithm

```
; A Path is a [ListOf [ListOf Vertex]]
;
;; expand-paths : Path Vertex [ListOf Vertex] -> Path
;; Creates new paths from the vertex u to every vertex in the second list.
(define expand-paths
  (λ (ls1 x ls2)
    (let ([flist (first (filter (λ (ls) (eqv? (last ls1) x)) ls))])
      (append ls1 (map (λ (x) (end-cons x flist)) ls2)))))
```

It is provable that there must always exist exactly one distinct path in the list that satisfies the filter predicate. In essence, if we breath-first search on some vertex u such that there is an edge from u to v, where v is unvisited, then $(u, v) \notin P$ prior to its insertion. Because each path is inserted exactly once, there cannot be two identical paths in P.

Now we come to the heart of the algorithm: bfs-search, which is a heavily-modified version of the bfs algorithm. There are two new locally-defined functions: unvisited-nbrs and find-smallest-path, the former of which is nothing more than a wrapper for a long filter invocation, whereas the latter finds all paths that start with a vertex u and end with a vertex v. Because the paths are inserted with respect to increasing size, the path at the front (which in fact satisfies this criteria) is a shortest path from u to v.

Listing 8.222—Breadth-First Shortest Path Helper Functions

```
(define bfs-search
  (letrec ([unvisited-nbrs
            (λ (nbrs visited)
              (filter (λ (n) (not (member? n visited))) nbrs))]
           [find-smallest-path
            (λ (paths u v)
              (first (filter (λ (and (eqv? (first p) u) (eqv? (last p) v)))
                             paths)))]
           [bfs-helper  ])
    ))
```

Aside from these changes, we now turn our attention to bfs-helper, whose signature has dramatically changed. It now receives a target vertex target, a list of paths paths, and a continuation k. If the queue is empty, then it means there is no path from u to v, meaning we invoke the continuation with false to designate that no path was found. The let identifiers are the same aside from our call to unvisited-nbrs. Where things change, though, is inside the cond clause; if the currently-visited vertex is equal to the target, then we want to return the paths seen so far, meaning we invoke the continuation with those paths. Otherwise, we tail-recursively call bfs-helper with the same first three arguments as the original bfs-helper. The target always stays the same, so it gets passed along. The continuation k also remains the same, so we can pass it along without modification as well. The paths must be expanded according to the current paths, u, and u's neighbors.

Listing 8.223—Breadth-First Shortest Path Algorithm

```
;; bfs-search : Graph Vertex Vertex Continuation -> [ListOf Vertex]
;; Performs a breadth-first search from u to v, returning a shortest path.
(define bfs-search
 (letrec ([bfs-helper
            (λ (G queue visited target paths k)
              (cond
               [(null? queue) (k #f)]
               [else
                (let* ([u (first queue)] [nbrs (get-neighbors G u)]
                       [unvisited (unvisited-nbrs nbrs visited)])
                  (cond
                   [(eqv? u target) (k paths)]
                   [else
                    (bfs-helper G (append (rest queue) unvisited)
                                (append visited unvisited) target
                                (expand-sublists paths u nbrs) k)]))])]))])
   (λ (G u v k)
     (find-smallest-path
      (bfs-helper G (list u) (list u) v (list (list u)) k) u v))))
```

The invocation of `bfs-helper` jump-starts the breadth-first search by passing the starting vertex u as a nested list to the paths, which indicates that all paths start at vertex u. Let us try our newly-designed search algorithm on G_3 with several starting and ending vertices:

Listing 8.224

```
> (bfs-search g3 'f 'w (λ (v) v))          (f c b x y z w)
> (bfs-search g3 'w 'f (λ (v) v))          (w z y x b c f)
> (bfs-search g3 'd 'w (λ (v) v))          (d a b x y z w)
> (bfs-search g3 'w 'e (λ (v) v))          (w z y x b e)
> (bfs-search g3 'b 'e (λ (v) v))          (b e)
```

Solving a real-world problem such as the shortest-path in a graph with continuations serves to tie everything together; continuations certainly have their theoretical potential, as do graphs. Demonstrating this potential separately often poses enough of a challenge.

Exercise 8.35. (⋆⋆)
Design the `contains-vertex?` function that, when given a graph G and a vertex v, returns true if v is a vertex of G and false otherwise.

Exercise 8.36. (⋆⋆)
Design the `get-vertices` function that, when given a graph G, returns the vertices of G. Hint: use map.

Exercise 8.37. (⋆⋆⋆)
Unweighted graphs, as shown in this section, are great to work with, but are limited in comparison to graphs with weights. Edge-weighted graphs are not only more commonplace in practice, e.g., GPS, but are also studied more rigorously. Design $\mathcal{L}^*_{\text{W-GRAPH}}$: a nested interpreter for edge-weighted graphs. The implementation details are up to your creative imagination, but perhaps a good starting point would be to use an edge data definition as containing a source, a destination, and a weight.

Exercise 8.38. (⋆⋆⋆)
Consider a college building in which rooms are locked behind digital keycard access. Figure 8.11 represents a building where each directed edge pointing vertex u to vertex v indicates that, to get to v, someone must have card access to u.

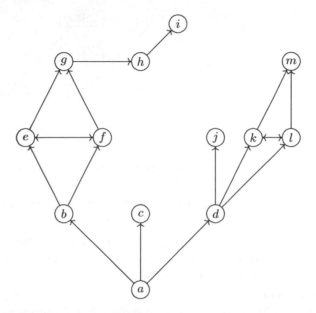

Figure 8.11: College Building Keycard Access Graph

We can, of course, model this as a directed graph in our $\mathcal{L}^*_{\text{GRAPH}}$ nested interpreter. Imagine that an undergraduate student gains access to a research lab inside this building. They are granted card access to that room, but in order to gain access to the lab after hours, they must have keycard access to every door in its path. Write a function that, when given a graph and a source and destination "door", returns the "doors" that the student should have added as keycard access.

Exercise 8.39. (⋆⋆⋆⋆)
Add functions to $\mathcal{L}^*_{\text{GRAPH}}$ that operate on a non-functional basis. That is, design add-vertex!, remove-vertex!, add-edge!, and remove-edge! functions that modify the contents of a graph rather than returning a new graph. While this exercise is not as hard as some of the other exercises, we pose it as a four-star problem due to its length/number of required functions.

Exercise 8.40. (⋆⋆⋆)
College courses, and their associated prerequisites, form a *directed acyclic graph*, which means that there are no cycles, i.e., loops, and all edges are directed. Vertices represent classes, whereas edges represent prerequisites. For instance, an edge $\langle A, B \rangle$ indicates that a student must take class A before taking class B. Consider the following prerequisite flowchart:

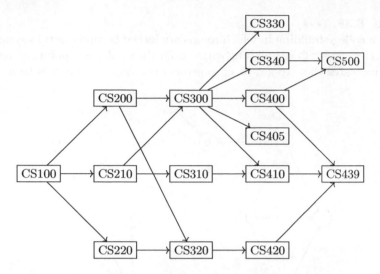

Figure 8.12: College Computer Science Course Prerequisites

Encode this as a directed graph in $\mathcal{L}^*_{\text{GRAPH}}$. Then write a function that, given a class A, returns a list of all the classes that succeed B. That is, the list returned should be all courses where A is a prerequisite.

Exercise 8.41. ($\star\star\star\star$)
Write the transpose function that, when given a graph G, returns a new graph G' where all edges from G are reversed. That is, if $\langle u, v \rangle \in G$, then $\langle v, u \rangle \in G'$. What do the edges in G' represent?

Exercise 8.42. ($\star\star\star\star$)
The *topological sort* algorithm, when performed on a directed acyclic graph, produces an ordering of the nodes L such that, for any edge $\langle u, v \rangle \in G$, u comes before v in L. Take the following graph as an example:

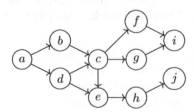

Figure 8.13: Directed Acyclic Graph Example

A valid topological ordering of the graph in Figure 8.13 is $\{a, b, d, c, f, g, i, e, h, j\}$. Though, another possible ordering is $\{a, d, b, c, e, h, i, g, f, i\}$. There are multiple possible topological orderings for this graph. Write the topological-sort function that, when given a graph G, performs a topological sort on G, returning one possible topological ordering. You will need to design a helper utility function. Hint: use map, the begin special form, and boxes. We provide skeleton code as follows:

Listing 8.225—Topological Sort Skeleton Code

```
;; topological-sort : Graph -> [ListOf Vertex]
;; Performs a topological sort on the given graph.
;; We use a utility search function that keeps track
;; of those vertices seen so far, as well as the output
;; stack of vertices.
(define topological-sort
  (letrec ([topological-sort-vertex
            (λ (G visited stack)
              (λ (v)
                ; If we haven't visited v before, call "util".
                (if ___ ___ #f)))]
           [topological-sort-util
            (λ (G visited stack)
              (λ (v)
                (begin
                  ; Add v to "visited" list box.
                  (set-box! ___ (cons ___ ___))
                  ; Add v to "stack" list box.
                  (set-box! ___ (cons ___ ___))
                  ; If we haven't visited v before, call "vertex".
                  (map ___ ___))))])
    (λ (G)
      (let ([visited (box '())]
            [stack (box '())])
        (begin
          (map ___ ___)
          (reverse ___))))))
```

Exercise 8.43. (⋆⋆⋆⋆⋆)

Edgar Dijkstra created *Dijkstra's algorithm* as an attempt to solve the shortest-path problem on edge-weighted graphs [Dijkstra, 1959]. Do some outside exploring, and try to come up with a shortest-path algorithm for weighted graphs. Then, if you feel up to the challenge, re-implement Dijkstra's algorithm in $\mathcal{L}^*_{\text{W-GRAPH}}$ from Exercise 8.33.

8.12 $\mathcal{L}_{\text{BIGNUM}}$: Arbitrarily-Precise Numbers

In this section, we will write $\mathcal{L}_{\text{BIGNUM}}$: an extension to $\mathcal{L}_{\text{LIB}}$ that adds support for arbitrarily-large (real) numbers and arithmetic.

Representation Independence with Respect to Numbers

GNU's *mpfr* library, which we will be using, is incredibly convenient and great to work with due to its performance and relative ease of use. Though, we should be thinking in terms of flexibility. What if, at some point, we wish to replace the library with something more powerful or faster? We once again reintroduce our old friend: representation independence. In this section, we will modify our implementation to be representation-independent with respect to arbitrarily-large (real) numbers.

Abstracting away from the innards of *mpfr* is good in the same way that abstraction hides *mpc* functions—we, as the programmer, should not have to care about the implementation of these libraries; only that they work. If, for instance, *mpfr* breaks, or we want to switch the library for something else, we would need to replace all occurrences of *mpfr* in the interpreter—a task that would frustrate even the most patient of programmers. Thus, we will create a module for creating, manipulating, and destroying big numbers, namely, `bignum`.

We will define a `bignum` typedef to prevent us from having to type out the `struct` keyword every time we wish to reference a `bignum`. In addition, we will create several function prototypes for `bignum` creation, alteration, and modification. Any function that performs arithmetic on a `bignum` modifies the given argument rather than returning it as a value. E.g., `bignum_floor` receives a `bignum` as a parameter, it computes the floor of said `bignum`, then stores the computation back into the parameter. This prevents us from having to return `bignum` pointers from any function except the creators.

Listing 8.226—Big Number Header File (`bignum.h`)

```
1    #ifndef BIGNUM_H
2    #define BIGNUM_H
3
4    #include <mpfr.h>
5    #include <gmp.h>
6
7    #define PREC 256
8
9    typedef struct bignum bignum;
10
11   bignum *bignum_create_str(const char *num_str);
12   bignum *bignum_create_num(const bignum *oth_num);
13   bignum *bignum_create_long(const long num_long);
14   void bignum_add(bignum *res, const bignum *rand);
15   bool bignum_equal(const bignum *rand1, const bignum *rand2);
16   int bignum_to_integer(const bignum *rand);
17   bool bignum_is_integer(const bignum *rand);
18   bool bignum_is_zero(const bignum *rand);
19   char *bignum_to_str(const bignum *rand);
20   void bignum_print(const bignum *rand);
21   void bignum_destroy(bignum *rand);
22   void bignum_cleanup(void);
23
24   #endif // BIGNUM_H
```

We have omitted the inclusion of several arithmetic functions and trigonometric operators. These, while useful, are important on a case-by-case basis, and can be implemented as exercises. More significant functions, e.g., comparing `bignums`, converting to C data-types, and printing to standard output are shown instead.

First, let us discuss how to create a `bignum`. There are multiple creation functions; the most prominent of which is `bignum_create_str`. Because `bignum` values may be arbitrarily large, they, of course, may not fit inside a C `int` or `double` or `long`. This function allocates space for a `bignum`, then invokes the appropriate *mpfr* functions for initializing the *mpfr* value within the `bignum` struct (note that we declare the struct itself within the source file—this is to prevent other files from accessing the number field). Though, what is `PREC`? We defined it in Listing 8.225, but what does it represent? Essentially, it designates how many bits of precision a value may use, if necessary. Because we defined it as 256, any `bignum` has access of up to 256 bits of floating-point precision.

Listing 8.227—Big Number Creation From String (`bignum.c`)

```
1   #include "bignum.h"
2
3   struct bignum { mpfr_t number; };
4
5   bignum *bignum_create_str(const char *num_str) {
6     bignum *operand = malloc(sizeof(bignum));
7     ASSERT_ALLOC(operand, "bignum_create_str");
8     mpfr_init2(operand->number, PREC);
9     mpfr_set_str(operand->number, num_str, 10, PREC);
10    return operand;
11  }
```

It is not always the case that our input is a string—depending on the arithmetic operator or circumstance, we may want to create a `bignum` out of a `long`. The *mpfr* library allows us to do this.

Listing 8.228—Creating Big Number from C `long` (`bignum.c`)

```
1   bignum *bignum_create_long(const long num_long) {
2     bignum *rand = malloc(sizeof(bignum));
3     ASSERT_ALLOC(rand, "bignum_create_long");
4     mpfr_init2(rand->number, PREC);
5     int flag = mpfr_set_si(rand->number, num_long, PREC);
6     assert(0 == flag);
7     return rand;
8   }
```

Let us now add the functionality to add two `bignum` values. `bignum_add` receives two arguments: a result variable `res` and a `const` operand `rand`. We will invoke the *mpfr* addition function which adds the values of `res` and `rand` and stores their sum back into `res`.

Listing 8.229—Adding Two Big Numbers (`bignum.c`)

```
1   void bignum_add(bignum *res, const bignum *rand) {
2     mpfr_add(res->number, res->number, rand->number, PREC);
3   }
```

Comparing numbers is relatively simple via the standard operators, e.g., $<$ and $>$, but we cannot use these on bignums. Instead, we rely on *mpfr* function invocations. Similar to how strcmp works, bignum_cmp returns -1 if rand1 is strictly less than rand2, 1 if rand1 is strictly greater than rand2, or 0 if they are equal.

Listing 8.230—Comparison of Big Numbers (bignum.c)

```
1  int bignum_cmp(const bignum *rand1, const bignum *rand2) {
2    return mpfr_cmp(rand1->number, rand2->number);
3  }
```

Converting a bignum to a C data-type is extremely important at times, e.g., in vector-access functions where the index must be an integer. We will write two functions: one for converting a bignum to a long double and another, more complicated, function for converting a bignum to an int. For the latter function, we will write a helper predicate bignum_is_integer to determine if the argument is a valid integer.

Listing 8.231—Converting a Big Number to a Primitive (bignum.c)

```
1  long double bignum_to_double(const bignum *rand) {
2    return mpfr_get_ld(rand->number, PREC);
3  }
```

Listing 8.232—Determining If a Big Number is an Integer (bignum.c)

```
1  bool bignum_is_integer(const bignum *rand) {
2    return mpfr_integer_p(rand->number);
3  }
```

Listing 8.233—Converting Big Number to Integer (bignum.c)

```
1   int bignum_to_integer(const bignum *rand) {
2     if (bignum_is_integer(rand)) {
3       int res;
4       mpz_t z_res;
5       mpz_init(z_res);
6       mpfr_get_z(z_res, rand->number, PREC);
7       res = mpz_get_si(z_res);
8       mpz_clear(z_res);
9       return res;
10    } else {
11      EPF("bignum_to_integer: rand is not an integer\n");
12      exit(EXIT_FAILURE);
13    }
14  }
```

When converting a bignum to an int, we create a short-lived mpz_t object that acts as a conversion between the floating-point mpfr library to the integer-only mpz library. From there, we retrieve the int component, if it exists and is valid.

Outputting a bignum to standard output is also quite important. In the case of a floating-point value, we invoke the *mpfr* format print function. When the argument is an integer, however, we need to be a bit more careful—printing trailing zeroes on an integer, i.e., 5.00000 is superfluous and unnecessary. Therefore, if we discover that the argument is an integer bignum, we should convert it to a mpz value and, instead, send that value to standard output.

Listing 8.234—Printing Big Number (`bignum.c`)

```
1   void bignum_print(const bignum *rand) {
2   if (bignum_is_integer(rand)) {
3     mpz_t int_rep;
4     mpz_init(int_rep);
5     mpfr_get_z(int_rep, rand->number, MPFR_RNDN);
6     mpz_out_str(stdout, 10, int_rep);
7     mpz_clear(int_rep);
8   } else {
9     mpfr_printf("%Rf", rand->number);
10   }
11   }
```

Finally, we should implement the destructor function, which receives a `bignum` argument and frees the associated memory. Namely, we need to invoke the appropriate *mpfr* clearing function and free the pointer allocated to the `bignum`.

Listing 8.235—Destructor Function for Big Numbers (`bignum.c`)

```
1   void bignum_destroy(bignum *operand) {
2   mpfr_clear(operand->number);
3   free(operand);
4   }
```

As a brief note: the *mpfr* library will often allocate memory and cache values to improve performance. Consequently, there is a function for de-allocating said memory via `mpfr_free_cache`. We invoke this function within `bignum_cleanup`, and invoke the cleanup function within `main.c`.

Listing 8.236—Freeing the mpfr Big Number Cache (`bignum.c`)

```
1   void bignum_cleanup(void) {
2   mpfr_free_cache();
3   }
```

Listing 8.237—Initializing Big Number Functions (`main.c`)

```
1   int main(int argc, char *argv[]) {
2     ...
3   ast_cleanup();
4   bignum_cleanup();
5   parser_cleanup();
6     ...
7   }
```

Exercise 8.44. (⋆)
Implement the remaining arithmetic functions, e.g., subtraction, multiplication, division, floor, ceiling, and so on.

Exercise 8.45. (⋆)
Write a function that determines if two `bignum` values are equivalent. Note that this should be a one-line function that invokes one of the functions that we implemented.

Exercise 8.46. (★★)
To simplify some of our future nested interpreters and code, we will not assume
a bignum implementation. Rather, we will resume with storing numeric values
as a long double type in the sval struct. As an exercise, though, go through
any arithmetic or number usage in our evaluator and function applier (eval.c and
apply.c respectively), and replace them with references to bignum values. Almost
all of these changes are purely mechanical, so do not overthink your design!

Exercise 8.47. (★★)
Write trigonometric functions that operate on bignum values, e.g., sine, cosine,
tangent, arcsine, arccosine, and arctangent.

8.13 $\mathcal{L}_{\text{IN}}$: Improved User Input

We revamped the output functionality in $\mathcal{L}_{\text{OUT}}$. In this section, we will write $\mathcal{L}_{\text{IN}}$: an extension to $\mathcal{L}_{\text{LIB}}$ that adds functions to read data from standard input.

Reading data or information from the user is an essential component of interactive programs. Our language will support two functions to start: one for reading strings and another for reading numbers.

A preliminary discussion of user input in the C programming language was had in Chapter 5. read_string reads a string from standard input using getline. Recall that the string s-value constructor for a string does not dynamically allocate memory, but getline does. Therefore, we do not need to allocate space ahead of time to store the string in the s-value. Additionally, pressing the return key signals, to the program, that we have finished entering our string and want to continue execution. An unintended consequence is that the buffer now contains a superfluous newline character. We want to trim this newline character from the end of the string. An easy and elegant solution is to set the last character of the string to be the NUL-character, i.e., \0.

Listing 8.238—Reading Strings from Standard Input (apply.c)

```
1   struct sval *apply_read_string(struct sval **args, size_t num_args,
2                                  struct environment *env) {
3     ASSERT_ARITY("read-string", 0, num_args);
4     char *str = NULL;
5     size_t n_chars;
6     if (-1 == getline(&str, &n_chars, stdin)) {
7       EPF("read-string: expected an input but received nothing.\n");
8       exit(EXIT_FAILURE);
9     }
10    str[strlen(str) - 1] = '\0';
11    return sval_string_create(str);
12  }
```

The read_number function reads a number from standard input using fgets and sscanf, as we did so in Chapter 5. If sscanf fails to interpret the value stored in the num buffer as a long double, we display an error and exit the program.

Listing 8.239—Reading Numbers from Standard Input (apply.c)

```
1   struct sval *apply_read_number(struct sval **args, size_t num_args,
2                                  struct environment *env) {
3     ASSERT_ARITY("read-number", 0, num_args);
4     char num[LINE_MAX];
5     if (NULL == fgets(num, LINE_MAX, stdin)) {
6       EPF("read-number: expected an input but received nothing.\n");
7       exit(EXIT_FAILURE);
8     }
9     long double val;
10    if (1 != sscanf(num, "%Lf", &val)) {
11      EPF("read-number: could not read number.\n");
12      exit(EXIT_FAILURE);
13    }
14    return sval_number_create(num);
15  }
```

8.14 $\mathcal{L}_{\text{FILE I/O}}$: **File Input and Output**

In the last section, we wrote $\mathcal{L}_{\text{IN}}$ to read data from standard input. For this section, we will extend $\mathcal{L}_{\text{IN}}$ to $\mathcal{L}_{\text{FILE I/O}}$: a language that supports reading and writing data to and from files.

This language supports eight new functions, which we describe below:

- `file-open!` receives two arguments: a string representing the file to open, and a string denoting the file "mode". File modes determine how the file is used, e.g., whether we read (`"r"`), write (`"w"`), or append (`"a"`) to said file. `file-open!` returns a s-value associated with a particular file. This s-value also contains a file "position", indicating where in the file data should be retrieved or inserted. By default, this position is placed at the beginning of the file.

- `file-close!` receives a file s-value and closes the file for writing and reading, meaning that it may no longer be worked with in subsequent expressions.

- `file-read-line!` receives a file s-value and returns a string s-value representing the next line of text read from said file. A line of text is terminated by the newline character.

- `file-read-integer!` receives a file s-value and interprets the next available data in the file as an integer. This integer is then returned in an s-value.

- `file-write-line!` receives a file s-value and a string, and writes said string to the current end of the file. It is terminated by a newline character.

- `file-write-integer!` receives a file s-value and an integer, and writes said integer to the current end of the file.

- `file-has-next?` receives a file s-value and returns a boolean s-value representing if the file has any data remaining to be read. Another way to view this predicate is, if the file pointer is at the EOF character (designated as end-of-file), we return #f; otherwise #t.

- `file-reset!` receives a file s-value and resets its file position to the beginning of the file. This is useful for re-reading files without having to repeatedly close and reopen said file.

First, let us begin by writing the corresponding s-value. A file s-value contains two fields: a FILE pointer and a boolean to keep track of whether or not the file is open for access. This requires including the `stdio.h` header since it defines FILE. We also use a new datatype, namely `off_t`, to store the current file position offset. In doing so we must include the `sys/types.h` header.

Listing 8.240—Adding File S-value (`sval.h`)

```
1   #include <stdio.h>
2   #include <sys/types.h>
3
4   enum sval_type { ..., SVAL_FILE };
5
6   struct file {
7    FILE *fp;
8    bool is_open;
9    off_t position;
10  };
11
12  struct sval {
13   ...
14   union data {
15    ...
16    struct file file;
17   } data;
18  };
19
20  struct sval *sval_file_create(char *filename, char *mode);
```

Writing the constructor function is simple and akin to how we operated on files in Chapter 5.

Listing 8.241—Constructor Function for S-values (`sval.c`)

```
1   struct sval *sval_file_create(char *filename, char *mode) {
2    struct sval *sv = sval_create(SVAL_FILE);
3    sv->data.file.fp = fopen(filename, mode);
4    if (NULL == sv->fp) {
5     EPF("could not open file %s with mode %s\n", filename, mode);
6     exit(EXIT_FAILURE);
7    }
8    sv->position = 0;
9    sv->data.file.is_open = true;
10   return sv;
11  }
```

Now, let us go through each function definition one-by-one. Remember that the ten functions we described above are at the application level, meaning they are defined in `apply.c`.

The respective `file-open!` and `file-close!` functions are trivial to write, as they involve invoking functions that operate on FILE pointers.

Listing 8.242—Built-in File Open and Close Procedure (`apply.c`)

```
1   static struct sval *apply_file_open(struct sval **args, size_t num_args,
2                                       struct environment *env) {
3    ASSERT_ARITY("file-open!", 2, num_args);
4    char *fname = args[0]->data.string;
5    char *fmode = args[1]->data.string;
6    return sval_file_create(fname, fmode);
7   }
8
9   static struct sval *apply_file_close(struct sval **args, size_t num_args,
10                                       struct environment *env) {
11   ASSERT_ARITY("file-close!", 1, num_args);
12   struct sval *f = args[0];
13   f->data.file.is_open = false;
14   fclose(f->data.file.fp);
15   return NULL;
16  }
```

file-read-line!, as we stated, reads a single line from a file. We can use the getline function since we only read in one line at a time. In addition to consuming the current line, we trim the newline character. There is, however, one exception to this function. If getline does not read any data, it returns −1. So, we must check nchars and return an empty s-value string if no characters are read. Otherwise, we risk writing data into a non-existent string.

Listing 8.243—Built-in Line Reading From File Function (apply.c)

```
1   static struct sval *apply_file_read_line(struct sval **args, size_t num_args,
2                                             struct environment *env) {
3     ASSERT_ARITY("file-read-line!", 1, num_args);
4     // Read the current line into a buffer. Also trim its newline char.
5     struct sval *fsv = args[0];
6     char *line = NULL;
7     size_t sz;
8     ssize_t nchars = getline(&line, &sz, fsv->data.file.fp);
9     if (0 > nchars) {
10      return sval_string_create("");
11    } else {
12      line[nchars - 1] = '\0';
13      return sval_string_create(line);
14    }
15  }
```

file-read-integer! consumes the next integer from a file. Because we are looking for an integer specifically, we may use the fscanf function. This is similar to how scanf works with the exception that it allows us to specify a FILE pointer.

Listing 8.244—Built-in Integer Reading From File Function (apply.c)

```
1   static struct sval *apply_file_read_integer(struct sval **args, size_t num_args,
2                                                struct environment *env) {
3     ASSERT_ARITY("file-read-integer!", 1, num_args);
4     // Scan the current item, assuming its an integer.
5     struct sval *fsv = args[0];
6     int n;
7     if (1 != fscanf(fsv->data.file.fp, "%d", &n)) {
8       EPF("file-read-integer!: failed to read integer.\n");
9       exit(EXIT_FAILURE);
10    }
11    return sval_number_create(n);
12  }
```

file-write-line! and file-write-integer! work similarly; they append data to the file using fprintf. The second argument is the data to write. Thankfully, writing to a file updates its FILE * accordingly. The former function is slightly different in that it appends a newline character to the end of the passed string.

Listing 8.245

```
1   static struct sval *apply_file_write_line(struct sval **args, size_t num_args,
2                                              struct environment *env) {
3     ASSERT_ARITY("file-write-line!", 2, num_args);
4     struct sval *fsv = args[0];
5     struct sval *line = args[1];
6     fprintf(fsv->data.file.fp, "%s\n", line->data.string);
7     return NULL;
8   }
9
10  static struct sval *apply_file_write_integer(struct sval **args, size_t num_args,
11                                               struct environment *env) {
12    ASSERT_ARITY("file-write-integer!", 2, num_args);
13    struct sval *fsv = args[0];
14    struct sval *n = args[1];
15    fprintf(fsv->data.file.fp, "%d", bignum_to_integer(n->data.number));
16    return NULL;
17  }
```

Finally we come to `file-has-next?` and `file-reset!`, where the former determines if the file is at the end (by using `feof`). The latter resets its file position to the start of the file (via `rewind`).

Listing 8.246—Built-in File Has Data Predicate and Reset Functions (`apply.c`)

```
1   static struct sval *apply_file_has_next_predicate(struct sval **args,
2                                                     size_t num_args,
3                                                     struct environment *env) {
4     ASSERT_ARITY("file-has-next?", 1, num_args);
5     struct sval *fsv = args[0];
6     return sval_boolean_create(!feof(fsv->data.file.fp));
7   }
8
9   static struct sval *apply_file_reset(struct sval **args, size_t num_args,
10                                        struct environment *env) {
11    ASSERT_ARITY("file-reset!", 1, num_args);
12    struct sval *fsv = args[0];
13    rewind(fsv->data.file.fp);
14    return NULL;
15  }
```

It makes little sense to write all of these functions without plenty of tests! So, let us do that. Create a file with the following contents and save it in the root of your project directory:

```
Hi! I am a line.
935
The previous num was 935.
Goodbye!
```

Listing 8.247

```
(define f1                              | First line: '"Hi! I am a new line."'
  (file-open! "test1.txt", "r"))        | Number: '935'
                                        | Is there more data? '\#t'
(printf "First line: '~a'~n"           | Next: '"The previous num was 935."'
  (file-read-line! f1))                 | Last: '"Goodbye!"'
(printf "Number: '~a'~n"               | Is there more data? '\#f'
  (file-read-integer! f1))
(printf "Is there more data? '~a'~n"
  (file-has-next? f1))
(printf "Next: '~a'~n"
  (file-read-line! f1))
(printf "Last: '~a'~n"
  (file-read-line! f1))
(printf "Is there more data? '~a'~n"
  (file-has-next? f1))
(file-close! f1)
```

Connecting this back to the motif of this chapter, we see that every function (except for file-has-next?) is suffixed with an exclamation point, indicating that they have side-effects. Of course, reading data from a file is, in and of itself, a side-effect; many variables and values are altered "under the hood" when working with files and I/O, e.g., file position pointers. It may make more sense to observe that the file-write produce side-effects because they output data to a file. What some may find a bit odd is that the file-read functions similarly induce side-effects for the aforementioned reasons.

Exercise 8.48. (⋆⋆)
Write a function in $\mathcal{L}_{\text{FILE I/O}}$ called file-read-lines! that, using file-read-line!, reads all lines from an input file and stores them in a list.

Exercise 8.49. (⋆⋆)
Write a function in $\mathcal{L}_{\text{FILE I/O}}$ called file-search! that opens a file, reads its contents as lines, and searches for occurrences of a given string k. To this end, write a lines-search function that performs the search logic rather than encapsulating it all within file-search!. lines-search receives a list of strings ls and a search string k; it returns a list of the lines containing k as a substring.

Exercise 8.50. (⋆⋆⋆)
Using file-read-integer!, write a program that reads a file containing numbers on each line and computes the average of those numbers. Hint: use map.

Exercise 8.51. (⋆⋆⋆)
Write a program that reads a file containing commands for a robot. These commands are strings representing four directions: UP, DOWN, LEFT, and RIGHT. After reading the commands from the file, continuously move the robot along quadrant one of the Cartesian coordinate plane. That is, assuming the robot starts at $(0, 0)$, when moving LEFT or RIGHT, decrement or increment the x-coordinate respectively. Similarly, when moving UP or DOWN, increment or decrement the y-coordinate respectively. Upon processing all commands, output the final robot position. As a bonus challenge, try to complete this without side-effects aside from the file input.

Exercise 8.52. (★★★)
Write a program that removes all comments from a given file containing a Scheme program. That is, given a file with Scheme code, remove all content following a semicolon on a line. As a bonus challenge, do not remove comments inside strings. For instance, `"Hello ;comment World!"` should output the same string. Multiline comments start with `#|` and end with `|#`. [1]

Exercise 8.53. (★★★★★)
Wordle is/was a popular game developed by Josh Wardle where the goal is to guess the letters to a randomly-selected word.[2]. For this exercise, you are tasked with recreating these game mechanics of a five-letter isogram-guessing puzzle. An *isogram* is a word in which no letter appears more than once, e.g., "plans".

1. Read in a list of five-letter isograms from a file. Design a function `is-isogram` to aid in the search, as well as `filter`.

2. Write a function `play-game`, which receives a secret word s and a word to guess g. The function should return a *cons* pair whose *first* represents the number of correctly-positioned characters and whose *rest* represents the number of correctly-identified characters. Note that a letter that is correctly-positioned should not also be marked as correctly-identified (even though this is tautologically the case).

3. Either allow the player to continue only if they have not yet exceeded a certain number of guesses, or let them play indefinitely until they find all correctly-positioned characters.

Listing 8.248

```
> (play-game "plans" "slant")        ¦ (3 . 1)
> (play-game "plans" "paint")        ¦ (2 . 1)
> (play-game "plans" "plans")        ¦ (5 . 0)
```

Data Serialization

In the previous section, we added the ability to read from and write to files. Though, we would be remiss if we neglected to discuss *data serialization*. When we serialize data, it means to convert it to a transmittable byte-oriented format. Normally, this consists of "stringifying" a data representation. For example, suppose we use a tagged list representation of personnel records in a program.

---

[1] This exercise is largely derived from the K&R C programming language book [Kernighan and Ritchie, 1988].

[2] Wordle was inspired by *Master Mind* [Knuth, 1977], which was inspired by the even older *Bulls and Cows* [$\aleph_0$ (Aleph-Null), 1971]

Listing 8.249

```
; A Person is a
; (make-person-record String
; Number String Number String).
(define make-person-record
 (λ (name age job salary country)
  `(person ,name ,age ,job ,salary ,country)))

> (make-person-record "Ada" 23                              (person "Ada" 23
  "Mathematician" 183800 "Eng")                              "Mathematician" 183800
                                                             "Eng")
```

Now, imagine we want to store this record from the program out to a file containing other records. We should not simply store the s-expression in the file as that is not always an effective way to store data. We can, instead, serialize the object into a string separated by a delimiter, e.g., commas.[1] Let us write the serialize-person-record function. It will receive a person tagged list and return a string with the corresponding five fields separated by commas. Because some fields are numbers, we will write a corresponding conversion function that receives any data and attempts to convert it to a string.

Listing 8.250

```
;; data->string : Any -> String
;; Attempts to convert the given datum to a string.
(define data->string
 (λ (d)
  (cond
   [(string? d) d]
   [(number? d) (number->string d)]
   [(char? d) (char->string d)]
   [else ""])))

;; serialize-person-record : Person -> String
;; Converts a Person to a string representation.
(define serialize-person-record
 (letrec ([spr-helper
           (λ (p)
            (foldr (λ (d acc)
                     (string-append
                      acc "," (data->string d)))
                   (data->string (first p))
                   (rest p)))])
  (λ (p)
   (spr (rest p)))))

(define p1 (make-person-record "Ada" 23
            "Mathematician" 183800 "Eng"))

> (serialize-person-record p1)                              "Ada,23,Mathematician,
                                                             183800,Eng"
```

---

[1]Serialization is not restricted to "stringification"; there are multiple ways to serialize data.

This string can then be written directly to a file. Though, suppose we have a file containing such a record and we want to load it into our program. Such a process is called *deserialization,* and it works in a similar manner to serialization, just with most of the logic reversed. Let us write a deserialize-person-record function that receives a string and parses it into a Person record. First, however, we will write a helper tokenize function that splits a string based on the given delimiter, returning a list of the substrings. To do this, we need to go up a step further and write take-string and drop-string: two recursive functions that return strings. The former receives a string and a delimiter and returns the substring up to the first occurrence of the delimiter. The latter returns the substring past the first occurrence of the delimiter.

Listing 8.251

```
;; take-string : String [1String] -> String
;; Returns the substring preceding the delimiter.
(define take-string
  (λ (s delim)
   (let ([idx (string-index s delim)])
    (cond
     [(zero? (add1 idx)) s]
     [else (substring s 0 idx)]))))

> (take-string "ada,23" ",")                    "ada"
> (take-string "ada" ",")                       "ada"
> (take-string "" ",")                          ""
> (take-string "ada,23,lovelace" ",")           "ada"
> (take-string "23,lovelace" ",")               "23"
> (take-string "lovelace" ",")                  "lovelace"
```

Listing 8.252

```
;; drop-string : String [1String] -> String
;; Returns the substring after the delimiter.
(define drop-string
  (λ (s delim)
   (let ([idx (string-index s delim)])
    (cond
     [(zero? (add1 idx)) ""]
     [else (substring s
                      (add1 idx)
                      (string-length s))]))))

> (drop-string "ada,23" ",")                    "23"
> (drop-string "ada" ",")                       ""
> (drop-string "" ",")                          ""
> (drop-string "ada,23,lovelace" ",")           "23,lovelace"
> (drop-string "23,lovelace" ",")               "lovelace"
> (drop-string "lovelace" ",")                  ""
```

This allow us to trivially define tokenize in terms of these functions.

Listing 8.253

```
;; tokenize : String [1String] -> [ListOf String]
;; Computes the strings separated by the [1String]
;; in the given first string.
(define tokenize
 (λ (line delim)
  (cond
   [(string-empty? line) '()]
   [else (cons (take-string line delim)
               (tokenize (drop-string line delim)
                         delim))])))
```

```
> (tokenize "haskell,28" ",")                          ("haskell" "28")
> (tokenize "haskell" ",")                             ("haskell")
> (tokenize "" ",")                                    ()
> (tokenize "haskell,28,cole" ",")                     ("haskell" "28" "cole")
> (tokenize "28,cole" ",")                             ("28" "cole")
> (tokenize "cole" ",")                                ("cole")
```

Now, we make use of `tokenize` parse out each sub-component of the person record.

Listing 8.254

```
;; deserialize-person-record : String -> Person
;; Converts a string, separated by commas, into
;; its corresponding person record.
(define deserialize-person-record
 (λ (s)
  (let* ([s (tokenize s ",")]
         [name (first s)]
         [age (string->number (second s))]
         [occupation (third s)]
         [salary (string->number (fourth s))]
         [country (fifth s)])
    (make-person-record name age occupation
                        salary country))))

(define p1 (make-person-record "Eve" 49
           "hacker" 5000 "USA"))
(define sp1 (serialize-person-record p1))
(define dsp1 (deserialize-person-record sp1))
```

```
> p1                                                   (person "Eve" 49
                                                        "hacker" 5000 "USA")

> sp1                                                  "Eve,49,hacker,5000,USA"

> dsp1                                                 (person "Eve" 49
                                                        "hacker" 5000 "USA")
```

As we can see, the original person record is identical to the serialized then deserialized record. Guaranteeing an equivalence is paramount to data serialization!

Let us ramp up the difficulty a bit by using data serialization for entire file types, e.g., CSV, or comma-separated value files. A CSV file consists of an optional row of headers delimited by commas.[1] Each subsequent row is populated with respective data. Taking the previous example, a file may contain the following data:

---

[1]Our implementation will assume the headers always exist.

Listing 8.255

```
name,age,occupation,salary,country
joshua,23,scientist,125000,usa
flannery,39,novelist,200000,usa
willard,92,logician,100000,usa
ada,36,mathematician,425000,england
stephen,76,physicist,300000,england
bjarne,72,computer scientist,500000,denmark
alonzo,92,computer scientist,250000,usa
katherine johnson,101,computer scientist,450000,usa
mary,53,novelist,300000,england
```

We can write serialization and deserialization functions for CSV files. Of course, we would like a way of serializing any type of data through some interface. Again, representation independence comes to the rescue. Let us design two higher-order functions: serialize and deserialize with the following signatures and definitions. The idea is that we pass a specific serialization function to these representation-independent functions. Using these passed serialization and deserialization functions, it creates either a byte-oriented string for transmission or converts a byte-oriented string into a respective data definition.

Listing 8.256

```
;; serialize : {X} X [X -> String] -> String
;; Applies a serialization function to a value.
(define serialize
  (λ (v f)
    (f v)))

;; deserialize : {X} String [String -> X] -> X
;; Applies a deserialization function to a string.
(define deserialize
  (λ (v f)
    (f v)))
```

These functions may seem cut and dry, and this is absolutely the case. For example, if we want to serialize a person record, we can invoke serialize with the data and its helper serialization function.

Listing 8.257

```
(define p1 (make-person-record "Quine" 48 "Logician" 195600 "USA"))
(define sp1 (serialize p1 serialize-person-record))
```

So, let us begin with writing a deserialize-csv function. Namely, we need to describe a data definition that aptly fits the criteria of a CSV file. CSV files have headers and elements, which aligns nicely with an association list. Namely, the *first* of each pair is the header and the *rest* is a list of values under that header. We denote that a Header is a String, and that each *rest* is a list encapsulated within a box. The box is necessary because we will update the list as we parse values from the CSV file. Therefore, we say that a CsvElement is also a String, but a CsvElementList is a (box (ListOf CsvElement)). Finally, a category is one column of a CSV file, matching one association pair in our list, indicating that a Category is a (cons Header CsvElementList). Combining all of these elements together produces the data definition for a CSV file.

Listing 8.258

```
; A Header is a String.
; A CsvElement is a String.
; A CsvElementList is a (box [ListOf CsvElement]).
; A Category is a (cons Header CsvElementList).
; A Csv is a [ListOf Category].

;; deserialize-csv : String -> Csv
;; Reads a CSV file and returns a list of the headers with their
;; respective values inside a box.
(define deserialize-csv
  (λ (lines)
    ...))
```

Reading in a CSV file is a recursive function, which begin by tokenizing the header strings and storing these into a *cons* cell whose *first* is the header and whose *rest* is a CSV element list.

Let us write a helper function that tokenizes the header string and returns the corresponding list.

Listing 8.259

```
(define deserialize-csv
  (letrec ([get-headers
             (λ (line)
               (map (λ (h)
                      (cons h (box '())))
                    (tokenize line ",")))])
    (λ (lines)
      (let* ([headers (get-headers (first lines))])
        ...))))
```

We now need a function that extracts the data from each line and adds it to the respective box category. First, though, let us write the function to extract the data out of one line, which we can then morph into another that handles all lines in a list. The idea is to use the header category (association list) to search for the desired box. Because we want to map over two lists sequentially, we need to invoke the map2 function. Accordingly, extract-data! has no return value because it modifies the existing contents of a list.[1] We also need a list of only the headers rather than categories for our map2 invocation.

Listing 8.260

```
(define deserialize-csv
  (letrec ([get-headers ...]
           [extract-data!
             (λ (line headers)
               (map2 (λ (e h)
                       (let* ([b (rest (assv h headers))]
                              [bv (unbox b)])
                         (set-box! b (cons e bv))))
                     (tokenize line ",")
                     (map fst headers)))])
    (λ (lines)
      (let* ([headers (get-headers (first lines))])
        ...))))
```

---

[1]It is more correct to say that extract-data has no *meaningful* return value, since it *does* return something, albeit a list of void statements.

At last, we will design the function that extracts the data from every row in the CSV file. Note the insignificance of the foldr return value—since we are modifying the headers argument, the value it returns is irrelevant. We further drive this point home by not using the accumulator argument to the passed binary function.

Listing 8.261

```
(define deserialize-csv
  (letrec ([get-headers ...]
           [extract-data! ...]
           [extract-all-data!
            (λ (lines headers)
              (foldr (λ (line acc)
                       (extract-data! line headers))
                     '()
                     lines))])
    (λ (lines)
      (let* ([headers (get-headers (first lines))])
        (begin
          (extract-all-data! lines headers)
          headers)))))
```

Running the aforementioned (abridged) CSV file of people and their basic information on the deserializer produces the following output:

Listing 8.262

```
(define f-csv
  (file-open! "people.csv", "r"))

(define lines (file-read-lines! f-csv))

> (deserialize lines)          '(("name" . #(("flannery" "joshua")))
                                 ("age" . #(("39" "23")))
                                 ("occupation" . #(("novelist"
                                                    "scientist")))
                                 ("salary" . #(("200000" "125000")))
                                 ("country" . #(("usa" "usa"))))
```

8.15 $\mathcal{L}_{\text{LOOP}}$: An Iterative Approach to Problem-Solving

In Chapter 7, we implemented a functional version of the do loop construct in $\mathcal{L}^*_{\text{IMPERATIVE}}$. In this section we will write $\mathcal{L}_{\text{LOOP}}$: an extension to $\mathcal{L}_{\text{BIGNUM}}$ that adds iteration-based control structures.

```
expr          ::=  application | ...
application   ::=  do | ...
do            ::=  'do ' expr expr
```

Figure 8.14: Extended BNF Grammar for $\mathcal{L}_{\text{LOOP}}$

C provides three methods of iteration: for loops, while loops, and do-while loops. We will implement a construct similar to do-while called do. do is a special form that has two components: a condition and a body. The body is evaluated as long as the condition is true. As an example, in the following code segment, we loop and execute the begin block while i is less than ten.

Listing 8.263

```
(let ([i 0])
 (do [< i 10]
  (begin
   (printf "~a~n" i)
   (set! i (+ i 1)))))
```

So, the intended and expected output is the integers from 0 to 9 inclusive. Let us add this form to our interpreter.[1]

Listing 8.264—Evaluation of do (eval.c)

```
1   static void special_forms_init(void) {
2     special_forms_create("do", eval_do);
3   }
4
5   static struct sval *eval_do(ast *doc, struct environment *env) { // TODO. }
```

Performing a similar analysis of the abstract syntax tree, we see that the third and fourth children (second and third indices) correspond to the condition and body respectively. We want to test the loop condition first, then evaluate the body. Additionally, a do expression should return the last evaluated expression before the condition evaluates to false.

---

[1]Similar to if, the name of our special form is a keyword in C, so we need to append a suffix, e.g., c, to the name of the abstract syntax tree parameter.

Listing 8.265—Finishing do Implementation (eval.c)

```
1   #define DO_CONDITION_IDX 2
2   #define DO_BODY_IDX 3
3   ...
4   static struct sval *eval_do(ast *doc, struct environment *env) {
5    struct sval *return_expr;
6    while (true) {
7     ast *condition = ast_child(doc, DO_CONDITION_IDX);
8     ast *body = ast_child(doc, DO_BODY_IDX);
9     struct sval *eval_condition = eval(condition, env);
10    if (!eval_condition->data.boolean) { return return_expr; }
11    else { return_expr = eval(body, env); }
12   }
13   return NULL;
14  }
```

Testing the previous program produces a correct result. We can write another program that computes the factorial of a natural number, and one more that computes the nth Fibonacci number. Both programs use the iterative paradigm.

Listing 8.266

```
> (let ([n 5] [i 1] [res 1])                    120
   (begin
    (do [<= i n]
     (begin
      (set! res (* res i))
      (set! i (+ i 1))))
    res))
```

Listing 8.267

```
> (let ([n 8] [a 0] [b 1] [res 1])              21
   (cond
    [(<= n 1) 1]
    [else
     (begin
      (do [> n 1]
       (begin
        (set! res (+ a b))
        (set! a b)
        (set! b res)
        (set! n (- n 1))))
      res)]))
```

What happens if we wrap the Fibonacci loop in a function?

Listing 8.268

```
(define fib-iter                                21
 (λ (v)                                          5
  (let ([n v] [a 0] [b 1] [res 1])              34
   (cond
    [(<= n 1) 1]
    [else
     (begin
      (do [> n 1]
       (begin
        (set! res (+ a b))
        (set! a b)
        (set! b res)
        (set! n (- n 1))))
       res)]))))

(printf "~a~n" (fib-iter 8))
(printf "~a~n" (fib-iter 5))
(printf "~a" (fib-iter 9))
```

We can write nested do loops similar to other languages, but we must be careful in doing so; it is easy to forget to reset the value of a variable in between loop statements. For instance, consider the following code segment, which does not "restart" the value of j. We observe that the inner do condition always remains true and, therefore, no further iterations of the nested loop body are performed.

Listing 8.269—Forgetting to Reset Nested Loop Variable y

```
> (let ([x 1] [y 1])                     1: 1 * 1 = 1
   (do [<= x 12]                         1: 1 * 2 = 2
    (begin                               1: 1 * 3 = 3
     (do [<= y 12]
      (begin
       (let ([res (* x y)])              1: 1 * 11 = 11
        (printf "~a * ~a = ~a~n"         1: 1 * 12 = 12
          x y res))
       (set! y (add1 y))))
     (set! x (add1 x)))))
```

The fix, as we stated, is to restart the value of j prior to entering the nested iteration loop. Another fix might be to declare separate let blocks altogether so as to always refresh its variable within the environment:

Listing 8.270—Explicit Reset to Nested Loop Variable y and Local Iteration y

```
> (let ([x 1] [y 1])          1: 1 * 1 = 1
    (do [<= x 12]             1: 1 * 2 = 2
      (begin                  1: 1 * 3 = 3
        (set! y 1)
        (do [<= y 12]
          (begin              1: 12 * 11 = 132
            (let ([res (* x y)])   1: 12 * 12 = 144
              (printf "1: ~a * ~a = ~a~n"
                    x y res))
            (set! y (add1 y))))
        (set! x (add1 x)))))

> (let ([x 1])                2: 1 * 1 = 1
    (do [<= x 12]             2: 1 * 2 = 2
      (begin                  2: 1 * 3 = 3
        (let ([y 1])
          (do [<= y 12]
            (begin            2: 12 * 11 = 132
              (let ([res (* x y)])   2: 12 * 12 = 144
                (printf "2: ~a * ~a = ~a~n"
                      x y res))
              (set! y (add1 y)))))
        (set! x (add1 x)))))
```

Exercise 8.54. (⋆⋆⋆)

In Chapter 7, we ventured down the rabbit hole that is tail-call optimization. We saw that any **function** call in tail position can be refactored into an iterative (loop) equivalent. **One way** of doing this in the language of the interpreter is via *trampolining*.[1] The idea is as follows: Write a function trampoline, which receives at least one argument: a function f. Any subsequent arguments to trampoline serve as arguments to f (meaning that trampoline is variadic). Invoke f. If the returned value is a **procedure**, continuously invoke f until it resolves to a non-procedure value.[2] The **trampoline** "bouncing" analogy refers to our repeated calling of f until we receive **something** that is not a procedure, in which we hop off the trampoline. Making a **function** compatible with a trampoline is trivial: we wrap all tail calls inside a thunk. **Because** the recursive stack is irrelevant with tail calls, once the thunk returns a non-**procedure**, we know that we reached the base case of the function.

Implement **the** trampoline function, using the "do" construct. We provide the skeleton for **implementing** said function. Run the following test to verify that it works.

---

[1] Trampolining **is used** in the following paper wherein the authors describe a translation pipeline for Scheme **programs to** C [Garcia et al., nd].

[2] Such a case **analysis requires** implementing a procedure? predicate at the interpreter level.

Listing 8.271 — Trampoline Implementation Skeleton Code

```
(define trampoline
 (λ-var args
  (let ([f (first args)]
        [f-args (rest args)])
   (let ([result (apply ___ ___)])
    (begin
     (do [___]
      (set! ___ ___)
      ___))))))

(define fact
 (letrec ([fact-tr
           (λ (n acc)
            (cond
             [(zero? n) acc]
             [else
              (λ ()
               (fact-tr
                (sub1 n)
                (* n acc)))]))])
  (λ (n)
   (trampoline fact-tr n 1))))

> (fact 15)                              │  1307674368000
```

Exercise 8.55. (⋆⋆⋆⋆)

Recall the *Levenshtein* distance exercise from Chapter 6. We made a note about the efficiency of the recursive algorithm, in that it is extremely slow. A better approach would be to take advantage of *dynamic programming*: an algorithmic technique that builds a solution from the bottom-up, constructing possibilities and eliminating previous answers. The key about what makes dynamic programming efficient is how it records prior computations by storing them in some data structure. Then, instead of having to recompute the answer, we simply look it up in our table. The thing is, though, dynamic programming algorithms often take advantage of two-dimensional arrays, state, and iteration, none of which are easily accessible in functional programming languages. Fortunately for us, we now have vectors and do loops.[1]

---

[1] This is not to say that loops and vectors are strictly necessary; we could achieve the same functionality with recursion and lists.

Algorithm 2 Levenshtein Distance Dynamic Programming Algorithm

---

procedure LEVENSHTEIN-DP(s, t)
    $m \leftarrow add1(|s|)$
    $n \leftarrow add1(|t|)$
    $d \leftarrow make\text{-}vector(m \times n)$
    loop $i \leftarrow 1$ **to** m
        $d[i][0] \leftarrow i$
    end loop
    loop $j \leftarrow 1$ **to** n
        $d[0][j] \leftarrow j$
    end loop
    loop $j \leftarrow 1$ **to** n
        loop $i \leftarrow 1$ **to** m
            $subCost \leftarrow 0$ **if** $s[sub1(i)] == t[sub1(j)]$ **else** 1

$$d[i][j] \leftarrow min \begin{cases} add1(d[sub1(i)][j]) \\ add1(d[i][sub1(j)]) \\ subCost + (d[sub1(i)][sub1(j)]) \end{cases}$$

        end loop
    end loop
    return $d[m][n]$
end procedure

In Algorithm 2 we list the pseudocode for a dynamic programming Levenshtein distance algorithm as presented by Robert Wagner and Michael Fischer [Wagner and Fischer, 1974].[1,2] Implement this into your interpreter as an exercise. We leave the task of translating the two-dimensional vector into a one-dimensional vector or using another solution up to you! Hint: if you completed the respective exercise from the section about vectors, this will make your life easier!

---

[1] All **loop intervals** are inclusive, i.e., **loop** $j \leftarrow 1$ **to** n means j increments by one up to and including n before the loop terminates.

[2] The initialization loops of populating the first row and column of our two-dimensional vector are not mandatory and can be computed via dynamic programming; we prepopulate these elements in particular because we already know their values; the distance from a string of m characters to a string of n characters is $m-n$, assuming they are identical. E.g., "s" to "ssss" requires 3 additional s characters, but this is inherently computed during the dynamic programming approach. So, initializing the values of the first row and column to 1 through 4 helps to reduce the number of necessary computations.

8.16 $\mathcal{L}_{\text{MACRO}}$: A Simple Macro System

Macros

We have previously seen examples of macros in the C programming language in Chapter 5. As a refresher, for all intents and purposes, in C, a *macro* is a textual substitution. So, if we define a macro to square two numbers and invoke it a follows:

Listing 8.272

```
1  #define SQUARE(x) x * x
2  int main(void) {
3    printf("The square of 5 is %d\n", SQUARE(5));
4  }
```

Before the program is compiled, the preprocessor replaces all instances of macro and preprocessor definitions with their respective bodies. To illustrate this idea, we will manually expand the SQUARE macro.

Listing 8.273

```
1  int main(void) {
2    printf("The square of 5 is %d\n", 5 * 5);
3  }
```

Macros in C, unfortunately, can cause problems due to type-checking and operator precedence. Let us pass an expression to this macro instead of a literal.

Listing 8.274

```
1  int main(void) {
2    printf("The square of 3 + 4 (7) is %d\n", SQUARE(3 + 4));
3  }
```

Now, in its expansion, we see that, instead of outputting the intended answer of 49, it outputs 5 as a result of direct substitution. Namely, the multiplication operation is applied before the two additions.

Listing 8.275

```
1  int main(void) {
2    printf("The square of 3 + 4 (7) is %d\n", 3 + 4 * 3 + 4);
3  }
```

A fix for this is to add parentheses around the macro body and any instances of its arguments:

Listing 8.276

```
1  #define SQUARE(x) ((x) * (x))
```

In this section, we will write $\mathcal{L}_{\text{MACRO}}$: an extension to $\mathcal{L}_{\text{LOOP}}$ that adds support for simple macros.

```
expr            ::=   application | ...
application     ::=   macro | ...
macro           ::=   'define-macro (' id id* ')' expr
```

Figure 8.15: Extended BNF Grammar for $\mathcal{L}$MACRO

First, we should explain the motivation behind the desire for macros. Suppose we want to add *promises* to a language, which are delayed, or deferred, expressions. That is, a promise defers evaluation of an expression until it is forced, or told, to evaluate. Recall from Chapter 7 the discussion of lazy evaluation via call-by-need and call-by-name. If we want to add lazy evaluation to our non-nested interpreter, we should add macros. Some curious thinkers out there may wonder why we cannot just define two functions, delay and force, where the former creates a thunk out of the passed expression, and force invokes the thunk. The latter function would certainly be acceptable. delay, on the other hand, is impossible with our system. Recall that, prior to applying a function, its arguments are evaluated. Therefore, if we want to pass an expression to delay with the intent of deferring its evaluation, we cannot design a function that immediately evaluates said argument. We can, instead, write a delay macro that wraps the supplied expression in a thunk without actually performing any evaluation.

Writing a macro system is somewhat challenging because it requires altering and manipulating the syntax tree directly. When we create a macro, we treat it similar to a procedure in that there are formals to bind and a macro body. Though, how do we wish to recognize a macro and differentiate it from, say, a variable or procedure? We can add a new special form to the language: define-macro. A define-macro will look similar to any other define with the exception that the macro name and formal parameters are wrapped in parentheses. The body is listed subsequently.

Listing 8.277

```
(define-macro (my-macro x y z)
  (+ x y z))
```

Now, let us create the accompanying s-value.

Listing 8.278—Macro S-value (sval.h)

```
1   enum sval_type { ..., SVAL_MACRO };
2
3   struct macro {
4    char **formals;
5    size_t num_formals;
6    ast *body;
7   };
8
9   struct sval {
10   ...
11   union data {
12    ...
13    struct macro *macro;
14   } data;
15  };
16
17  struct sval *sval_macro_create(char **formals, size_t num_formals, ast *body);
```

Next, we write the constructor function.

Listing 8.279—Macro S-value Constructor Function (sval.c)

```
1   struct sval *sval_macro_create(char **formals, size_t num_formals, ast *body) {
2    struct sval *sv = sval_create(SVAL_MACRO);
3    struct macro *macro = malloc(sizeof(struct macro));
4    ASSERT_ALLOC(macro, "sval_macro_create");
5    macro->num_formals = num_formals;
6    macro->formals = formals;
7    macro->body = body;
8    sv->data.macro = macro;
9    return sv;
10  }
```

Onto the evaluator—we need to write the recognizer. Conveniently enough, a
define-macro closely resembles the definition for a lambda.

Listing 8.280—Evaluation of Macro Declaration (eval.c)

```
1   static struct sval *eval_definition_macro(ast *defmacro,
2                                         struct environment *env) {
3    ast *formals_ast = ast_child(defmacro, MACRO_FORMALS_IDX);
4    size_t num_formals = ast_children_num(formals_ast) - MACRO_FORMALS_OFFSET;
5    char *macro_name = ast_contents(ast_child(formals_ast, MACRO_NAME_IDX));
6    char **formals = malloc(num_formals * sizeof(char *));
7    ASSERT_ALLOC(formals, "eval_definition_macro");
8
9    // Copy the formals over to the array.
10   for (int i = 0; i < num_formals; i++) {
11    char *f = ast_contents(ast_child(formals_ast, i + MACRO_CONTENTS_OFFSET));
12    formals[i] = strdup(f);
13   }
14
15   ast *body = ast_child(defmacro, 3);
16   struct sval *macro_sval = sval_macro_create(formals, num_formals, body);
17   environment_put(env, macro_name, macro_sval);
18   return NULL;
19  }
```

Now for the toughest piece: writing the macro evaluator. Before we begin, we
should add a clause to eval_application that hands over the abstract syntax tree
to another function if it is a macro (similar to the behavior of special forms).

Listing 8.281—Evaluating Macro Within Application Evaluation (eval.c)

```
1   static struct sval *eval_application(ast *application, struct environment *env) {
2     ...
3     else if (SVAL_MACRO == function->type) {
4       return eval_application_macro(application, env);
5     }
6   }
```

Macro evaluation is complicated because, as we said, we have to directly alter the abstract syntax tree. Not only this, but when we update the tree, we must be careful to not update the original macro body definition. In other words, we need to create a copy of the macro body abstract syntax tree so that subsequent macro evaluations are not afflicted or overwritten. Moreover, we must replace each occurrence of the formal parameter in the macro body with the correct substitution value. For example, using the following macro definition, when we evaluate (my-macro 10 30 20), we must traverse the tree to find the x, y, and z nodes, then replace them with the 10, 30, and 20 nodes respectively.

Listing 8.282

```
(define-macro (my-macro x y z)
  (+ x (* y (* z z) x) (- y x z)))
```

Therefore, in writing eval_application_macro, we need to write two new functions in our abstract syntax tree file: ast_copy, and ast_replace. The former creates a "deep copy" of the provided abstract syntax tree (i.e., all fields are copied), whereas the latter recursively traverses an abstract syntax tree to replace nodes with other nodes.

Listing 8.283—Macro Substitution (eval.c)

```
1   static struct sval *eval_application_macro(ast *appmacro,
2                                              struct environment *env) {
3     struct sval *defmacro = eval(ast_child(appmacro, APPLICATION_FUNCTION_IDX), env);
4     ast *body = ast_copy(defmacro->data.macro->body);
5
6     // Replace each instance of the symbol with the argument.
7     for (int i = 0; i < defmacro->data.macro->num_formals; i++) {
8       body = ast_replace(body, ast_child(appmacro, i + 2),
9                          defmacro->data.macro->formals[i]);
10    }
11
12    return eval(body, env);
13  }
```

When copying an abstract syntax tree, we must take some things into consideration. First, what do we copy, and second: how do we copy them? An abstract syntax tree consists of a tag, contents, and children. For the first two fields, because they are strings, we allocate and copy them over like any other abstract syntax tree. The latter, on the other hand, is even simpler—we recursively clone the children of the current AST.

Listing 8.284—Deep-copying an Abstract Syntax Tree (ast.c)

```
1   ast *ast_copy(const ast *old_tree) {
2     ast *tree = malloc(sizeof(ast));
3     ASSERT_ALLOC(tree, "ast_copy");
4     // Copy tag & contents over.
5     tree->tag = strdup(old_tree->tag);
6     tree->contents = strdup(old_tree->contents);
7
8     // Allocate children and flags.
9     tree->flags = 0;
10    tree->children_num = old_tree->children_num;
11    tree->children = malloc(tree->children_num * sizeof(ast *));
12    ASSERT_ALLOC(tree->children, "ast_copy");
13
14    // Copy the children.
15    for (int i = 0; i < tree->children_num; i++) {
16      tree->children[i] = ast_copy(old_tree->children[i]);
17    }
18
19    return tree;
20  }
```

Now, we need to write the ast_replace function, which is the essential component of a macro application. ast_replace will search for any nodes in tree whose
contents are equivalent to needle. If so, the tree node is replaced with replacement.
One exception to this is singleton nodes. Namely, if a macro body contains only a
single symbol or literal value, then we need not to traverse the rest of the definition
(because it does not exist!); we should simply return the replacement. Otherwise,
we recursively search the rest of the tree for any occurrences and replace them if so.

Listing 8.285—Root AST Replacement Function (ast.c)

```
1   ast *ast_replace(ast *tree, ast *replacement, const char *needle) {
2     if (NULL == tree) {
3       return NULL;
4     } else if (0 == tree->children_num && streq(ast_contents(tree), needle)) {
5       return replacement;
6     } else {
7       ast_replace_subtree(tree, replacement, needle);
8       return tree;
9     }
10  }
```

Notice that the second case corresponds to a singleton node whose contents
match the needle. We return replacement in this instance. If the tree is not a
singleton, then we invoke a separate helper function, ast_replace_subtree.

Listing 8.286—Recursive Subtree Replacement Function (ast.c)

```
1   static void ast_replace_subtree(ast *tree, ast *replacement, const char *needle) {
2     if (NULL == tree) { return; }
3     else {
4       for (int i = 0; i < tree->children_num; i++) {
5         // If we find a node whose contents are the needle, we replace it.
6         if (streq(ast_contents(ast_child(tree, i)), needle)) {
7           ast_set_child(tree, replacement, i);
8         }
9         ast_replace_subtree(ast_child(tree, i), replacement, needle);
10      }
11    }
12  }
```

Fortunately, **this** function is not too difficult to understand. Like copying, we traverse the **children** of a node, perform some operations, then recurse on the child. If we find a **child** node whose symbol matches the needle, we pass the parent, the replacement, **and** the child index to another function `ast_set_child`, which performs almost identically to the replacement of a singleton.

Listing 8.287—Altering a Child of an AST (`ast.c`)

```
1   void ast_set_child(ast *root, ast *new_tree, const size_t idx) {
2     root->children[idx] = ast_copy(new_tree);
3   }
```

That is it! Let us write, then run, the test example from before.

Listing 8.288

```
(define-macro (my-macro x y z)                │
  (+ x (* y (* z z) x) (- y x z)))            │
                                              │
> (my-macro 10 30 20)                         │   120010
> (my-macro (+ 20 30) (+ 40 50) 60)           │   16200030
```

So, we get **the correct** answers, but let us see how the macro expands these invocations.

Listing 8.289

```
(+ 10
   (* 30 (* 20 20) 10)
   (- 30 10 20))

(+ (+ 20 30)
   (* (+ 40 50) (* 60 60) (+ 20 30))
   (- (+ 40 50) (+ 20 30) 60))
```

With the **macro** implementation, we can finally add promises. Let us write a small test to **understand** how a promise works. First, though, we will write `delay` and `force`. **The former** creates a thunk out of the passed expression, whereas the latter invokes **the thunk**.

Listing 8.290

```
(define-macro (delay exp)
  (λ () exp))

(define-macro (force exp)
  (exp))
```

Therefore, **when** invoking `delay`, we replace the expression with a thunked version.

Listing 8.291

```
(define x 1)                  │  (define x 1)
                             │
(delay (begin (set! x 5) x))  │  (delay (λ () (begin (set! x 5) x)))
```

Now, for **the** example.

Listing 8.292

```
(define p 1)                                    1
(define q 2)                                     2
(define r 3)                                     3
(define v (delay (begin                         100
                   (set! p 100)                 200
                   (set! q 200)                 300
                   (set! r 300)))))

(printf "~a~n" p)
(printf "~a~n" q)
(printf "~a~n" r)
(force v)
(printf "~n")
(printf "~a~n" p)
(printf "~a~n" q)
(printf "~a" r)
```

Hygienic vs Unhygienic Macros

What is the output of the following macro replacement?

Listing 8.293

```
(define-macro (unhygienic-macro z)
  (let ([q 100])
    (set! z (+ q z))))

(let ([p 10]
      [q 20])
  (begin
    (unhygienic-macro p)
    (unhygienic-macro q)
    (+ p q)))
```

You might think of two possible answers: 130 and 230. With our current macro system, 130 is the returned result, but is that really the desired value? Notice that we declare a variable q in the scope of our macro. This q shadows the q declared within the let block outside the macro. As such, when we invoke (unhygienic-macro q), it "captures" q.

Listing 8.294

```
(let ([p 10]
      [q 20])
  (begin
    ...
    (let ([q 100])
      (set! q (+ q q))))
    (+ p q))
```

So, the outer-most q is never updated—only the q declared within the macro's local let environment. A macro that performs a variable capture like this is referred to as an *unhygienic macro*. It would be highly preferable to write a macro system that is *hygienic*, but how is that possible? One solution is to generate random symbols for every formal parameter and variable occurrence in the body of the macro. These random symbols would, ideally, be random enough to where a collision between a programmer-defined and a macro-defined symbol name has an irrefutably low probability.

When is it **appropriate** to rename symbols during a macro definition? Well, the only time a **macro** has the potential to become unhygienic is when it introduces a binding. **For example**, `let`, `let*`, `letrec`, and `lambda` all potentially introduce symbol bindings, **and** therefore, introduce the risk of creating an unhygienic macro. We said there **were** some ways to alleviate this bug, and we will discuss three. All possibilities **require** altering the abstract syntax tree of the macro definition. The first of these **fixes is** to generate random variable names in the context of a variable binding within **a macro**. For example, if we define a macro as follows:

Listing 8.295

```
(define-macro (unhygienic-macro z)
  (let ([q 100])
    (set! z (+ q z))))
```

We should **convert** "temp" into a string of random characters to reduce the likelihood of **a binding** collision. E.g.,

Listing 8.296

```
(define-macro (unhygienic-macro z)
  (let ([UwObQNZJMhzZBDyyNfCm 100])
    (set! z (+ UwObQNZJMhzZBDyyNfCm z))))
```

Though, **the issue** with this approach is that it does not truly remove the "unhygienic-**ness**" of the macro—it only obscures and reduces the probability of an unhygienic **macro usage**. What if we could remove that probability altogether? To do this, we **need some** way of marking certain symbols as "unmatchable". Namely, when we **declare a** symbol within a binding context, we should set a flag in the abstract syntax **tree** to denote that the symbol can never be equivalent to another, non-flagged **symbol**. A symbol with this property is called an *uninterned* symbol. Let us illustrate **this** with the previous example where we bind q to 100, which shadows the **previous** declaration of q. Due to the overall complexity of this approach, we will omit **its** inclusion in favor of a partially-hygienic macro system.

So, what **are we** after? We want to take a macro's abstract syntax tree, then obfuscate the **variable** bindings. The general approach will be to traverse the definition abstract **syntax** tree, look for `let` and `lambda` blocks, then append each bound symbol with **a random** string of characters. Then, as we traverse the tree, if we find a symbol **declared** elsewhere and it is one that was initialized in a binding, we append the **same random** string. Because this is a multi-step process, we will break it up.

First, let **us write** a function that receives an abstract syntax tree and invokes a recursive "unintern" helper function.

Listing 8.297—Uninterning Symbols of an AST (`ast.c`)

```
1   static void unintern_symbols_helper(ast *macro_ast, char ***us,
2                                        char ***obfs, size_t *nus);
3
4   static void unintern_symbols(ast *macro_ast) {
5     char **us = NULL;
6     char **obfuscations = NULL;
7     size_t nus = 0;
8     unintern_symbols_helper(macro_ast, &us, &obfuscations, &nus);
9     ...
10  }
```

First we had standard, single-pointers, then we introduced double-pointers, and now there are triple-pointers!? What gives? Well, recall that, intuitively, we can think of an array of strings as a char double pointer. Because we are modifying the contents of this array of strings in a function, we need to pass a pointer to this array of strings. Hence, the use of a triple-pointer! We declare two arrays of strings: one for the uninterned "raw" symbols, and another for the obfuscations. Essentially, when we find a binding, we want to store the identifier to search for later, as well as the random string to append.[1] We also need to keep track of how many elements are in these arrays. Because they should always be the same size, we can share one variable. Moreover, since we modify its value in between recursive calls, we pass the value as a pointer.

Now, onto the complex function. First, we should have a check to see if the input abstract syntax tree is NULL and, if so, just bail out from the function.

Listing 8.298—Recursive Uninterning Symbols Function (`ast.c`)

```
1   static void unintern_symbols_helper(ast *macro_ast, char ***us,
2                                        char ***obfs, size_t *nus) {
3     if (NULL == macro_ast) { return; }
4   }
```

Next, there is the case where the passed abstract syntax tree is an application. If this is the case, then there are two possible values of interest: let and lambda. We will investigate let first.

Listing 8.299—Recursive Uninterning Symbols Helper Function (`ast.c`)

```
1   static void unintern_symbols_helper(ast *macro_ast, char ***us,
2                                        char ***obfs, size_t *nus) {
3     if (NULL == macro_ast) { return; }
4     else if (ast_is_type(macro_ast, "application")) {
5       if (strstr(ast_contents(ast_child(macro_ast, 1)), "let") != NULL) { ... }
6     }
7     ...
8   }
```

What is nice about this function is that, similar to evaluating a let binding, we need to extract the symbols and perform some action on them. So, we can just reuse that code.

---

[1]Another term for arrays that correspond to one another is parallel arrays.

Listing 8.300—Uninterning a `let` *(ast.c)*

```
1  static void unintern_symbols_helper(ast *macro_ast, char ***us,
2                                      char ***obfs, size_t *nus) {
3      ...
4    if (strstr(ast_contents(ast_child(macro_ast, 1)), "let") != NULL) {
5      ast *let = macro_ast;
6      ast *bindings = ast_child(let, LET_ALL_BINDINGS_IDX);
7      int num_bindings = ast_children_num(bindings) - LET_BINDING_OFFSET_IDX;
8
9      for (int i = 0; i < num_bindings; i++) {
10       ast *curr_binding = ast_child(bindings, LET_BINDING_IDX + i);
11       ast *sym_tree = ast_child(curr_binding, LET_SYMBOL_IDX);
12       ...
13     }
14   }
15 }
```

In the following code blocks, we are going to make a lot of memory allocations. So, be wary!

First, we need to resize both of our arrays to account for a new variable binding. We also need to increment the passed array size variable.

Listing 8.301—Reallocation of Uninterned Symbol Storage Array (ast.c)

```
1  static void unintern_symbols_helper(ast *macro_ast, char ***us,
2                                      char ***obfs, size_t *nus) {
3      ...
4    (*nus)++; // Increment the size by one.
5    *us = realloc(*us, sizeof(char *) * (*nus));
6    *obfs = realloc(*obfs, sizeof(char *) * (*nus));
7  }
```

The above code resizes the two allocated arrays of strings to be one element larger than they were previously. Note that we took a similar approach to when we were replacing elements in the abstract syntax tree when implementing unhygienic macros.

Now, we need to allocate space for the string to copy. us requires enough space to store the original variable name, whereas `obfs` requires enough space to store the obfuscated variable name. One very important detail to take note of is that the dereference via the asterisk *must* happen *before* array indexing. According to the C programming language, however, array indexing has higher operator precedence than dereferencing a pointer. Thus, we wrap the dereference in parentheses to force its evaluation first.

Listing 8.302—Ordering of Dereferencing Matters! (ast.c)

```
1  static void unintern_symbols_helper(ast *macro_ast, char ***us,
2                                      char ***obfs, size_t *nus) {
3      ...
4    (*obfs)[(*nus) - 1] = gensym();
5
6    // Allocate the space for the new strings.
7    (*us)[(*nus) - 1] = malloc(strlen(ast_contents(sym_tree)) + 1);
8    ASSERT_ALLOC((*us)[(*nus) - 1], "uninterned_symbol_helper");
9  }
```

We have introduced a new function: gensym; what is that? The gensym function allocates and generates a new string of random characters. The implementation is not too difficult to understand, but assigning random *letters*, rather than integers, is a little funky for newcomers to the language. First, we use a C macro to declare a variable that keeps track of the length we want our to set our random strings. Then, because this is a string used across multiple functions, we of course must dynamically allocate the memory. Next, we traverse through the string and set each character to be a random upper-case letter using the rand function. Though, what is the deal with the modulus and addition operators? Well, rand is defined to return an integer from 0 inclusive to a preset constant RAND_MAX exclusive. For our purposes, we do not know nor care what this value is other than the fact that it is a sufficiently large number. Recall that we can use modulus to "truncate" a number to a specific range. Thus, no matter what number is generated between this range, it will always be an integer from 0 inclusive to 26 exclusive (note the exclusivity of 26, meaning our range of possible integers is 0 to 25). From there, we can treat character literals as numbers and perform arithmetic on them. As an example, 'A' + 5 = 'E'. This allows us to generate a random letter from 'A' to 'Z'. Finally, because sym is a string, we must NUL-terminate it.

Listing 8.303—Generating Pseudorandom Symbol Identifier (ast.c)

```
1   #define MAX_LENGTH 20
2
3   char *gensym(void) {
4     char *sym = malloc(MAX_LENGTH + 1);
5     ASSERT_ALLOC(sym, "gensym");
6     for (int i = 0; i < MAX_LENGTH; i++) {
7       sym[i] = 'A' + (rand() % 26);
8     }
9     sym[MAX_LENGTH] = '\0';
10    return sym;
11  }
```

Getting back on track, we must copy the symbol name into us, and amend the abstract syntax tree with the obfuscated name.

Listing 8.304—Using strcpy to Copy Generated Symbol (ast.c)

```
1   static void unintern_symbols_helper(ast *macro_ast, char ***us,
2                                       char ***obfs, size_t *nus) {
3
4     // Copy the contents over to the buffer.
5     strcpy((*us)[(*nus) - 1], ast_contents(sym_tree));
6     ast_strcat_contents(sym_tree, (*obfs)[(*nus) - 1]);
7   }
```

What is ast_strcat_contents? It is a new helper function we introduced; it receives an abstract syntax tree and a string, then concatenates, or appends, the passed string onto the contents of the tree. We need to re-size the contents to ensure we have enough space for both the old and the new contents. In addition, we resize, then amend, the contents of the underlying mpc abstract syntax tree.

Listing 8.305—Concatenating Contents of AST (ast.c)

```
1  void ast_strcat_contents(ast *ast, char *contents) {
2    size_t ast_len = strlen(ast->contents);
3    size_t con_len = strlen(contents);
4    ast->contents = realloc(ast->contents, ast_len + con_len + 1);
5    ASSERT_ALLOC(ast->contents, "ast_strcat_contents");
6    strcat(ast->contents, contents);
7  }
```

Okay! That is the hardest part out of the way. We will omit lambda declarations so we can test our let bindings and then fix any problems we encounter (this will be an exercise for the reader). We now need to add the clause for updating symbol occurrences in the abstract syntax tree. In essence, whenever we find a symbol, we search for its existence in us and, if there is a binding, it means that it was declared within a block inside the macro, meaning we need to append the obfuscated string onto the end.

Listing 8.306—Macro Substitution Implementation (ast.c)

```
1  static void unintern_symbols_helper(ast *macro_ast, char ***us,
2                                      char ***obfs, size_t *nus) {
3    ...
4    else if (ast_is_type(macro_ast, "symbol")) {
5      char *s = ast_contents(macro_ast);
6      for (int i = 0; i < *nus; i++) {
7        if (streq(s, *us[i])) {
8          ast_strcat_contents(macro_ast, (*obfs)[i]);
9          return;
10       }
11     }
12   }
13   ...
14 }
```

Last but not least, because this is a recursive function, we need to invoke this function on each child of the passed abstract syntax tree node.

Listing 8.307—Recursively Uninterning AST Children (ast.c)

```
1  static void unintern_symbols_helper(ast *macro_ast, char ***us,
2                                      char ***obfs, size_t *nus) {
3    ...
4    for (int i = 0; i < ast_children_num(macro_ast); i++) {
5      unintern_symbols_helper(ast_child(macro_ast, i), us, obfs, nus);
6    }
7  }
```

We also must update eval_definition_macro to include a call to unintern_symbols on the macro's body.

Listing 8.308—Uninterning Macro Definitions (eval.c)

```
1  static struct sval *eval_definition_macro(ast *defmacro,
2                                            struct environment *env) {
3    ...
4    for (int i = 0; i < num_formals; i++) { ... }
5    ast *body = ast_child(defmacro, MACRO_BODY_IDX);
6    unintern_symbols(body);
7    struct sval *macro_sval = sval_macro_create(formals, num_formals, body);
8    environment_put(env, macro_name, macro_sval);
9    return NULL;
10 }
```

Phew! That is a lot of programming to implement what is seemingly a simple feature! Let us re-run the macro definition from before examine both the output and AST.

Listing 8.309

```
(define-macro (hygienic-macro z)
  (let ([q 100])
    (set! z (+ q z))))

> (let ([p 10] [q 20])              230
    (begin
      (hygienic-macro p)
      (hygienic-macro q)
      (+ p q)))
```

```
expr|application|>
 char:1:1 '('
 expr|datum|symbol|regex:1:2 'define-macro'
 expr|application|>
  char:1:15 '('
  expr|datum|symbol|regex:1:16 'hygienic-macro'
  expr|datum|symbol|regex:1:33 'z'
  char:1:34 ')'
 expr|application|>
  char:2:3 '('
  expr|datum|symbol|regex:2:4 'let'
  expr|application|>
   char:2:8 '('
   expr|application|>
    char:2:9 '['
    expr|datum|symbol|regex:2:10 'qJHRJEUOPABPUMOTBAHLB'
    expr|datum|number|regex:2:12 '100'
    char:2:15 ']'
   char:2:16 ')'
  expr|application|>
   char:3:5 '('
   expr|datum|symbol|regex:3:6 'set!'
   expr|datum|symbol|regex:3:11 'z'
   expr|application|>
    char:3:13 '('
    expr|datum|symbol|regex:3:14 '+'
    expr|datum|symbol|regex:3:16 'qJHRJEUOPABPUMOTBAHLB'
    expr|datum|symbol|regex:3:18 'z'
    char:3:19 ')'
   char:3:20 ')'
  char:3:21 ')'
 char:3:22 ')'
```

From the abstract syntax tree, we see that only the variables bound by the macro let are obfuscated. Therefore, we see a "correct" output of 230 because q is no longer captured by the macro. What a relief!

As another example of the benefits of using macros, we can define or2 and and2. Recall that or and and are built-in operators in our language that do not strictly evaluate their arguments. Treating them as standard functions would, of course, not be correct because of their potential to short-circuit. Using macros, on the other hand, allows us to bypass this limitation. Let us implement or2: a macro that resolves to true if either of its arguments evaluate to true. If its first argument evaluates to true, the macro short-circuits and does not evaluate the second.

Listing 8.310

```
(define-macro (or2 exp1 exp2)
  (if exp1 #t (if exp2 #t) #f)))
```

Suppose we now substitute two expressions for exp1 and exp2 where the latter sets a variable. The macro guarantees that, if exp1 resolves to true, exp2 is never evaluated. Using the below example, we see that the macro outputs #\t and 10, because the second expression, of course, is never evaluated.

Listing 8.311

```
(define x 0)

> (or2 (begin                           #t
        (set! x 10)
        (> x 9))
       (begin
        (set! x 20)
        #f))
> x                                     10
```

Exercise 8.56. (⋆)
We wrote the or2 macro as an example. Implement and2 that returns true just in case each operand is true. If the first expression is false, the second is not evaluated.

Exercise 8.57. (⋆)
Write a macro ifm that, similar to our built-in if, receives three expressions: a predicate, a consequent, and an alternative. If the predicate is true, the consequent is evaluated. Otherwise, the alternative is evaluated.

Exercise 8.58. (⋆⋆)
The Python programming language (along with several others) allows programmers to write *list comprehensions*, which is a way of building lists from a filter. For example, in the first code listing below is a method of squaring all the odd numbers in a list of numbers from 1 to 10. In our language, we can do this via the map and filter as demonstrated in the second listing. Though, it would be interesting to see if we could implement the "Pythonic" method in our language using macros. Write a macro list-comp that has the signature from the third listing.

Listing 8.312

```
lst = [1..10]
[x * x for x in lst if x % 2 == 1]
```

Listing 8.313

```
(define lst '(1 2 3 4 5 6 7 8 9 10))
(map (λ (x) (* x x))
     (filter (λ (x) (odd? x)) lst))
```

Listing 8.314

```
(define-macro (list-comp map-expr for var in lst if filter-expr)
  ...)
```

for, in, and if are all constant "symbols" that are not evaluated since they are just copied as raw text into the macro (realistically we could put anything in these spots, but it is irrelevant since they are unused). We may invoke the macro as follows:

Listing 8.315

```
(define lst '(1 2 3 4 5 6 7 8 9 10))

> (list-comp (* x x) for x in lst if (odd? x))          (1 9 25 49 81)
```

Complete the definition of the `list-comp` macro. It should be only one (prettily indented) line.

Exercise 8.59. (⋆⋆)
The Racket programming language also has list comprehensions via *for/list*. The only difference is that this construct can receive any "iterable structure" as input. As an example, consider the following code segments:

Listing 8.316

```
> (for/list i '(1 2 3 4)                                (1 4 9 16)
    (* i i))

> (for/list j "abcdef"                                  (96 97 98 99 100 101)
    (char->number (string->char j)))

> (for/list k (vector 144 169 16 49 81)                 (12 13 4 7 9)
    (sqrt k))
```

For simplification purposes, we will consider only lists, vectors, and strings as "iterable structures". Write a macro `for/list` that behaves as we have described.

Exercise 8.60. (⋆⋆⋆)
The Racket programming language, in addition to `for/list`, has other iteration-based constructs. One of these includes `for/fold`, which accumulates results as they are generated. It receives an accumulator and its initial value, as well as an iteration variable and a corresponding "iterable structure" as we described in the preceding exercise. The expression resolves to the accumulator. As an example, consider the following code segments:

Listing 8.317

```
> (for/fold sum 0 i '(1 2 3 4)                          10
    (+ sum i))

> (for/fold str "" j '(#\H #\e #\l #\l #\o)             "Hello"
    (string-append j str))
```

Implement `for/fold` as a macro in $\mathcal{L}_{\text{MACRO}}$. Hint: this should be a one-line definition, and should use `foldl` or `foldr`. Which variant works with the given examples?

Exercise 8.61. (⋆⋆⋆⋆)
We can declare `lambda` functions inside a macro. For instance, consider the macro in the listing below. `foo` is a macro that, itself, reduces to a procedure of one argument: `z`. The problem is that this is an unhygienic macro that shadows any occurrences of `z` in its environment. Implement uninterning for formal parameters to `lambda` procedures.

Listing 8.318

```
(define-macro (foo x y)
  (let ([tmp-x x]
        [tmp-y y])
    (λ (z)
      (+ tmp-x tmp-y z))))

((foo 10 20) 30)
```

Exercise 8.62. (★★★★)

We do *not* intern symbols used both as "arguments" to a macro and as formal parameters to a lambda. An example is shown below. The reason is that these variable occurrences are substituted with the "arguments" to the macro and, therefore, do not need to be uninterned. Fix your implementation to only unintern formal parameters that are not "arguments" to the macro. Hint: eval_definition_macro creates an array of formals—passing this, along with its size, to unintern_symbols may prove to be helpful.

Listing 8.319

```
(define-macro (my-lambda x body)
  (λ (x) body))

((my-lambda y (+ y 5)) 10)
```

Streams

Designing macros into our language brings a lot of potential to the table. One such feature is the notion of *streams*, or "infinite" data. Consider a trivial function square that returns the square of a number. Now, suppose we want to return a list of squared natural numbers. The inherent question that arises is, "How many squares do we want to compute?". Streams allow us to get infinitely many squares without actually computing infinitely many squares. The problem there, of course, is that if we wanted to get the square of every natural number in a predefined list, that would be impossible since there are countably-infinite natural numbers.

Streams use lazy evaluation, which is now possible via macros. If we want to, say, compute a theoretical infinite number of squared natural numbers, we surely need to use cons. Unfortunately, this will not work, because cons always evaluates its two arguments before creating the *first* and *rest* pair. What we need, instead, is a macro cons$ that evaluates its *first*, but delays the evaluation of its *rest*. Recall that we cannot define a cons$ function because it would evaluate its arguments!

Listing 8.320

```
(define-macro (cons$ a b)
  (cons a (delay b)))
```

Now, we need two functions to access the pieces of a stream. fst$ is just first with a fancy name. rst$, on the contrary, forces the thunk provided by delay.

Listing 8.321

```
(define fst$ fst)

(define rst$ (λ (p) (force (rest p))))
```

Let us work our way up to creating a "squared natural number" stream. We will start by writing a stream that produces "infinite numbers". The idea is to use cons$ that delays a seemingly infinite recursive function.

Listing 8.322

```
(define nat-copy$
 (λ (n)
  (cons$ n (nat-copy$ n))))
```

nat-copy$ produces a stream whose *first* is the input *n* and whose *rest* is a promise that produces another copy of *n*.

Listing 8.323

```
(define num-3s$ (nat-copy$ 3))          │
                                        │
> num-3s$                               │ (3 . <function>)
> (fst$ num-3s$)                        │ 3
> (rst$ num-3s$)                        │ <function>
> (fst$ (rst$ num-3s$))                 │ 3
```

So, while nat-copy$ is capable of producing an infinite stream of numbers, having to painstakingly and manually invoke the helper fst$ and rst$ functions seemingly invalidates the convenience. Let us write take$: a function that generates *n* elements from a stream $ and stores them into a list.

Listing 8.324

```
(define take$
 (λ (n $)
  (cond
   [(zero? n) '()]
   [else
    (cons (fst$ $)
          (take$ (rst$ $)))]))))
```

With this function, we can retrieve *n* copies of 3 in a list.

Listing 8.325

```
(define ten-3s (take$ 10 num-3$))       │
                                        │
> ten-3s                                │ (3 3 3 3 3 3 3 3 3 3)
```

We can write streams to produce any kind of "infinite data" that we so desire. For instance, suppose we want to write a stream that produces the Fibonacci sequence. We first need a function that adds stream values together.

Listing 8.326

```
;; add$ : [StreamOf Number] [StreamOf Number] -> [StreamOf Number]
;; Adds the elements of two number streams.
(define add$
  (λ ($1 $2)
    (let ([e1 (fst$ $1)]
          [e2 (fst$ $2)])
      (cons$ (+ e1 e2)
             (add$ (rst$ $1) (rst$ $2))))))
```

From here, we write a `fib$` function that computes the respective sequence starting with the two base values of 0 and 1.

Listing 8.327

```
(define fib$
  (cons$ 0
         (cons$ 1
                (add$ fib$
                      (rst$ fib$)))))

> (take 10 fib$)                            (0 1 1 2 3 5 8 13 21 34)
```

Now let us write the stream of squared numbers. Fortunately, because this is a non-recursive procedure unlike the Fibonacci sequence, we need not to write a separate `multiply$`. Rather, we write `square-from$` that computes the square of integers starting from some given value n. We then write `square$` which invokes `square-from$` with a starting value of one. This allows us to nicely interweave our `take$` definition.

Listing 8.328

```
(define square-from$
  (λ (n)
    (cons$ (* n n)
           (square-from$ (add1 n)))))

(define square$ (square-from$ 1))

> (take$ 5 square$)                         (1 4 9 16 25)
```

Exercise 8.63. (⋆⋆)

Design a stream `random-ints$` that receives a number n returns a stream that produces random numbers in the interval $[0, n)$, where n is exclusive. To test your design, use the `take$` stream and poll ten numbers to see what you get!

$\mathcal{L}^*_{\text{SYNTAX}}$: **Syntactic Transformations**

Programs, and their accompanying syntax, may often be represented in several, semantically-equivalent, ways. For instance, as one of the exercises, we asked readers to implement the syntactic sugared version of function definitions, which abstract away the lambda. Though, either form is equivalent in functionality to the other, and interpreters will often rewrite syntactic sugar into its non-sugared counterparts. Using the previous example, a function of the form (define (foo ...)) may be converted into (define foo (lambda (...))). Doing so implies that the interpreter does not have to concern itself with ever seeing a syntactic sugar representation, which reduces code size and complexity. Such transformations are called semantic-preserving syntax transformations. In other words, a transformation from one piece of code into another may perhaps change its appearance, but its end behavior remains identical. A programming language that introduces such transformations must ensure that these guarantees are in-place so code does not induce unexpected behavior. Let us look at another syntactic sugar form, namely let. let is equivalently constructive via lambda abstraction and function application. That is, each binding has a identifier and a value, wherein the binding is a formal parameter to a lambda and the values are corresponding arguments applied to the lambda term.

Listing 8.329

```
(let ([x 5]
      [y 10]
      [z 100])
  (+ x y z))
```

The above let block can be represented as a lambda term whose formal parameters are the identifiers. Each formal parameter is bound by function application to the associated values from the bindings. The body of the let transfers nicely as the body of our new lambda. If we wish, we could also, equivalently, curry this function.

Listing 8.330

```
((λ (x y z)             ((((λ (x)
   (+ x y z))               (λ (y)
 5 10 100)                   (λ (z)
                              (+ x y z))))
                          5)
                         10)
                        100)
```

In this section, we will write $\mathcal{L}^*_{\text{SYNTAX}}$: a language for converting certain special forms into more "primitive" counterparts.

By having syntactical transformation equivalences of forms in a programming language, it reduces the overall complexity of the interpreter or compiler. Being able to convert a let to a lambda means we could outright remove separate let evaluation. Because of the complexities of C and modifying the abstract syntax trees, we will only implement syntax transformation equivalence functions in our interpreted language. We section this under our discussion of macros because macros *are* syntactic transformations of code. In a more powerful programming language, e.g., Racket, we could certainly write macros to implement language constructs such as let, let*, and more in terms of lambda, if we chose to do so.[1]

Our nested interpreter will perform desugaring, or unwrapping of syntactically-sugared special forms. We have, thus far, seen one such form: let. Let us write the recognizer and reducer for converting a let into a lambda. We need to extract all formal parameters and bindings into separate lists. We can use map and a few calls to list and append to get our desired result.

Before writing this recognizer/reducer pair, we should write the root reducer: desugar.

Listing 8.331

```
;; desugar : Expression -> Expression
;; Desugars an expression from its syntactic-sugar'd form
;; into its non-sugar'd counterpart.
(define desugar
  (λ (exp)
    (cond
      [(let? exp) (desugar-let exp)]
      [else exp])))
```

We use map to collect the identifiers and values, then construct a lambda with the identifiers as its formal parameters and the let body as its body. Finally, we wrap this term in a function application to the values.

Listing 8.332

```
(define let?                        (define desugar-let
  (λ (exp)                            (λ (exp)
    (and (cons? exp)                    (let* ([bindings (second exp)]
         (= (length exp) 3)                    [body (desugar (third exp))]
         (eqv? (first exp) 'let))))          [vars (map first bindings)]
                                             [values
                                               (map second bindings)])
                                        (append
                                         (list (list 'lambda vars body))
                                         values)))))
```

Now, let us test our implementation.

Listing 8.333

```
> (desugar                          ((lambda
   '(let ([x 5]                        (x y z)
         [y 10]                        (+ x y z))
         [z 100])                    5 10 100)
     (+ x y z)))
```

---

[1]This would be superfluous since the language performs built-in macro-expansion on special forms anyways, but it is a good exercise nonetheless.

With one special form out of the way, we should attempt to desugar let*. We know that let* allows for mutually-referencing bindings. Our implementation of let*, though, proved that it is nothing more than a sequence of nested let expressions. With that in mind, the desugar-let* reducer is more complex than its desugar-let counterpart since it uses a recursive definition, but its implementation is, nonetheless, straightforward. The idea is to recursively construct "singleton" let expressions, i.e., let expressions with exactly one identifier binding. The body of each let is either another singleton let or the body of the original let* expression as indicated by the recursive base case. Note that our definition does not use unquote and quasiquote for clarity purposes; the symbolic expression is built using list and local variable bindings.

Listing 8.334

```
(define let*?
  (λ (exp)
    (and (cons? exp)
         (= (length exp) 3)
         (eqv? (first exp) 'let*))))
```

```
(define desugar-let*
  (letrec
    ([dl*-helper
      (λ (vars vals body)
        (cond
          [(null? vars) body]
          [else
           (let ([curr-binding
                  (list
                   (list
                    (first vars)
                    (first vals)))]
                 [rest
                  (dl*-helper
                   (rest vars)
                   (rest vals)
                   body)])
             (list 'let
                   curr-binding
                   rest))])])])
    (λ (exp)
      (let*
        ([bindings (second exp)]
         [body (third exp)]
         [vars (map first bindings)]
         [values (map second bindings)])
        (dl*-helper vars values body)))))
```

After including this recognizer/reducer pair in our root reducer, we can run a test.

Listing 8.335

```
> (desugar
   '(let* ([x 5]
           [y 6]
           [z (+ x y)])
      (+ x y z)))
```

```
((lambda (x)
  ((lambda (y)
    ((lambda (z)
      (+ x y z))
     (+ x y)))
   6))
 5)
```

Let us take a detour from local variable desugaring and turn our attention to cond. A cond expression is nothing more than a sequence of if expressions. Going the other direction, an if expression is nothing more than a cond with only two clauses. So, we could desugar either into the other, just like we could with let, let*, and lambda, but we choose the former direction since it is more intuitive. cond expressions may be represented as lists whose *first* is the symbol cond and whose *rest* is a list of predicate/consequent pairings. We can extract these pairing out, which we denote as cases, then collect these into separate lists. Finally, we build symbolic if expressions, recursively, where the base case is the final clause in the cond designated by the else keyword.

Listing 8.336

```
(define cond?                    (define desugar-cond
  (λ (exp)                         (letrec
    (and (cons? exp)                 ([dc-helper
         (>= (length exp) 2)            (λ (lop loc)
         (eqv? (first exp) 'cond))))      (cond
                                           [(eqv? (first lop) 'else)
                                            (first loc)]
                                           [else
                                            (let ([rest
                                                   (dc-helper (rest lop)
                                                              (rest loc))])
                                              (list 'if
                                                    (first lop)
                                                    (first loc)
                                                    rest))])])])
                                       (λ (exp)
                                         (let* ([cases (rest exp)]
                                                [lop (map first cases)]
                                                [loc (map second cases)])
                                           (desugar-cond-helper lop loc)))))
```

Listing 8.337

```
> (desugar                       | (if (eqv? x 5)
    '(cond                       |     10
      [(eqv? x 5) 10]            |     (if (zero? y)
      [(zero? y) #f]             |         #f
      [else #t]))               |         #t))
```

There are a few other syntactic sugar forms that we could transform, and we present those as exercises.

Exercise 8.64. ($\star$)
In Chapter 6, we presented a form of function definitions that abstracts away the lambda and asked readers to implement it into the interpreter. Add this form to $\mathcal{L}^*_{\text{SYNTAX}}$. As a refresher, we provide an example, along with its desugared counterpart, below.

Listing 8.338

```
> (desugar                       | (define !
    '(define (! n)               |   (lambda (n)
      (cond                      |     (if (zero? n)
       [(zero? n) 1]             |         1
       [else (* n (! (sub1 n)))])))) |         (* n (! (sub1 n)))))))
```

Exercise 8.65. (★★)

and, as well as or, are specials form in our interpreter, but they can be equivalently formed as a sequence of chained if expressions. Implement and/or into $\mathcal{L}^*_{\text{SYNTAX}}$. We provide examples, along with their desugared counterparts, below.

Listing 8.339

``
> (desugar
    '(and (odd? 4)
         (even? 6)
         (odd? 12)))
``
	``
	(if (odd? 4) (if (even? 6)
	  (if (odd? 12) #t #f) #f) #f)
	``

``
> (desugar
    '(or (odd? 4)
        (even? 6)
        (odd? 12)))
``
	``
	(if (odd? 4) #t (if (even? 6) #t
	  (if (odd? 12) #t #f)))
	``

Exercise 8.66. (★★★)

Recall named let bindings from Chapter 6. A named let defines a locally-recursive function with variable bindings that act as the formal parameters. Interestingly, named let bindings can be desugared into letrec. Implement such a desugaring function. Hint, remember that the number of bindings is equal to the number of formal parameters that the defined procedure receives. The bound expressions act as the arguments to the function.

Listing 8.340

``
> (desugar
    '(let loop ([i 10])
    (cond
      [(zero? i) '()]
      [else
        (cons i (loop (sub1 i)))])))
``
	``
	(letrec
	  ([loop
	    (λ (i)
	      (cond
	        [(zero? i) '()]
	        [else
	          (cons i (loop (sub1 i)))])])
	  (loop 10))
	``

Exercise 8.67. (★★★)

We have seen that Racket and Scheme allow the programmer to define functions without an explicit lambda by wrapping the identifier in parentheses, e.g., (define (foo x) ...). It is possible to return multiple functions, which unwrap as semi or fully-curried functions. For instance, consider the following equivalence:

Listing 8.341

``
(define ((foo x) y) ...)
``
	``
	(define foo
	  (λ (x)
	    (λ (y)
	      ...)))
	``

Each layer of parentheses desugars into a lambda. Extend $\mathcal{L}^*_{\text{SYNTAX}}$ to support this form of desugaring. Note that desugaring a function written like this should still support a λ-defined function, for example:

Listing 8.342

```(define (((foo x y) z w) v)```
  ```(λ (u)```
    ```...))```
	```(define foo```
	  ```(λ (x y)```
	    ```(λ (z w)```
	      ```(λ (v)```
	        ```(λ (u)```
	          ```...)))))```

Exercise 8.68. (★★★)

We can auto-curry a function by desugaring its definition into a series of one-argument functions. Taking the following definition of foo, we can curry it into a long chain of λ expressions.

Listing 8.343

```(define foo```
  ```(λ (x y)```
    ```(λ (z w)```
      ```(λ (v)```
        ```(λ (u)```
          ```...)))))```
	```(define foo```
	  ```(λ (x)```
	    ```(λ (y)```
	      ```(λ (z)```
	        ```(λ (w)```
	          ```(λ (v)```
	            ```(λ (u)```
	              ```...)))))))```

Write a function that desugars a function, written with only lambda terms, into its curried counterpart.

Exercise 8.69. (★★★)

begin, strangely enough, is also transformable. Its desugared form is a little less obvious at first, but the idea is to evaluate each expression in the begin body sequentially, while only caring about the result of the final expression. We may represent this idea with chained function application, where we pass the return value of an expression to subsequent lambda definitions without using the value. Implement begin into $\mathcal{L}^*_{\text{SYNTAX}}$. We provide an example, along with its desugared counterpart, below.

Listing 8.344

```> (desugar```
  ```'(begin (set! x 10)```
       ```(+ 20 20)```
       ```(set! y 30)```
       ```(* 40 40)))```
	```((lambda ()```
	  ```((lambda (_)```
	    ```((lambda (_)```
	      ```((lambda (_)```
	        ```((lambda (_) _)```
	         ```(* 40 40)))```
	       ```(set! y 30)))```
	     ```(+ 20 20)))```
	  ```(set! x 10))))```

Exercise 8.70. (★★★★★)

`letrec` is the hardest form to reduce, but we know how because of the explanation from Chapter 6. Implement `letrec` into $\mathcal{L}^*_{\text{SYNTAX}}$. We provide two examples, along with their desugared counterparts, below. Our desugared counterparts are recursively desugared from `let` into `lambda`. Hint: you will need to generate new symbols for each recursive function definition. It may be a good idea to implement gensym as an interpreter-level function, callable from $\mathcal{L}^*_{\text{SYNTAX}}$, so as to get a seemingly hygienic transformation. Consequently, the generated symbols that we show will almost certainly be different from those from your interpreter. You will also have to write a `desugar-lambda` function in order to desugar lambda procedure bindings within the `letrec` construct. This should not be difficult, though, as it only requires a structural reconstruction of the lambda term, its formal parameters, and desugaring its body.

Listing 8.345

```
> (desugar                    ((lambda (fact)
   '(letrec ([fact              ((fact fact) 5))
            (lambda (n)        (lambda (g79037)
             (cond              (lambda (n)
              [(zero? n) 1]      (if (zero? n)
              [else              1
               (* n              (* n ((g79037 g79037)
                 (fact                (sub1 n)))))))))
                  (sub1 n)))])])
     (fact 5)))
> (desugar                    ((lambda (is-even?)
   '(letrec ([is-even?          ((lambda (is-odd?)
            (lambda (n)          ((is-odd? is-even? is-odd?) 11))
             (or (zero? n)      (lambda (g85495 g85496)
               (is-odd?          (lambda (n)
                 (sub1 n))))]     (and (not (zero? n))
            [is-odd?               ((g85495 g85495 g85496)
            (lambda (n)             (sub1 n)))))))
             (and (not (zero? n))  (lambda (g85495 g85496)
               (is-even?           (lambda (n)
                 (sub1 n))))])      (or (zero? n)
     (is-odd? 11)))                 ((g85496 g85496 g85496)
                                     (sub1 n)))))))
```

Exercise 8.71. (★★★★)

Some compilers optimize their instructions to use *administrative normal form*, or ANF [Sabry and Felleisen, 1992a]. Administrative normal form rewrites complex expressions, e.g., `(+ (* 23 45) (- 17))`, into ones that define temporary local variables for function calls.[1] The above example might be rewritten as follows:[2]

Listing 8.346

```
> (anf '(+ (* 23 45) (- 17))    (let ([t0 (* 23 45)])
   (empty-env)))                 (let ([t1 (- 17)])
                                   (+ t0 t1)))
```

We can syntactically transform `let` expressions as well. Note that we do not transform expressions that resolve to atomic/self-evaluating values, i.e., numbers, booleans, or symbols.

---

[1]This exercise is inspired by two compiler transformations from Siek's *Essentials of Compilation* [Siek, 2023].

[2]Our code is not exactly in ANF due to allowing `let` blocks as the right-hand side of an identifier binding.

Listing 8.347

```
> (anf                                    (let ([x
    '(let ([x (* (- (+ 25 y)))])             (let ([t0 (+ 25 y)])
       (let ([z (+ (- x) (- y))])              (- t0))])
         (+ (* x x) (+ (* y y) (* z z))))))   (let ([z
    (empty-env))                               (let ([t1 (- x)])
                                                  (let ([t2 (- y)])
                                                    (+ t1 t2)))])
                                              (let ([t3 (* x x)])
                                                (let ([t4
                                                  (let ([t5 (* y y)])
                                                    (let ([t6 (* z z)])
                                                      (+ t5 t6)))])
                                                  (+ t3 t4))))))
```

Within local blocks, bindings that ultimately reduce to atomic non-symbol values should reduce to themselves. For instance, (let ([y 10]) y) reduces to 10.[1] On the other hand, do not desugar (let ([y z]) y) into z. Write the anf root reducer function, which receives a quoted expression and returns its ANF equivalent. You only need to consider numbers, booleans, symbols, addition, subtraction, multiplication, unary negation, and let bindings.[2] Hint: write a function that generates a new unique symbol each time it is invoked using closures. In the next section, we will introduce gensym: a function at the interpreter-level that shares a similar role.

---

[1] If we were to desugar this let into a lambda, we would see that we perform an application on the identity function.

[2] What purpose does this seemingly verbose form serve, you might wonder? In transforming the program to ANF, we are presented with the explicit control flow of variables and expressions, which simplifies the writing of low-level instructions. Such rewriting is sometimes also referred to as static-single assignment, or three-address code [Aho et al., 2006].

8.17 $\mathcal{L}^*_{\text{MATCH}}$: A Pattern Matcher

Many programming languages offer the ability to pattern match expressions. That is, given an arbitrary expression exp, we can determine its structure and manipulate it accordingly. Here's an example of something we may be able to do in another language.

Listing 8.348

```
(match-pattern '(+ 2 3)
 [n (guard? (number? n)) (* n n)]
 [y (guard? (symbol? y)) y]
 [(+ a a) (+ a a a a)]
 [(+ a b) (+ a b)]
 [_ #f]) => 5
```

Here we have a fairly complex function. match-pattern is a function of two arguments: an expression to pattern match, and a list of patterns and qualifiers. Patterns are expressions to match against; if the given expression is "bindable" to the pattern, then it is deemed matchable. We can bind an expression to a pattern if and only if exactly one of the following properties holds true:

1. The expression and pattern are both numbers, strings, booleans, or characters and they are equal (according to eqv?), OR

2. The pattern is a symbol that has not been bound yet by the current context, OR

3. The expression and pattern are both keywords and they are equal (according to eqv?), OR

4. Both the expression and the pattern are lists each of whose elements are recursively matchable.

And the following property is true: If there is a (guard? gpred) inside the pattern and qualifier, then its predicate, namely gpred, is true under the current context.

We introduced a lot of things with these rules. What exactly do we mean by "bound" and "the current context"? Well, we can think of the context in terms of an environment—take the expression '(1 2 3) and the pattern (x y z). Because both are lists, we follow rule 3 and recursively try to match their elements. When matching on 1 and x, we follow rule 2. At the start of a pattern match, the current context is empty. Since this is the case at the start of the rule, x has no binding expression, meaning we can extend the context to include the binding of $x \mapsto 1$. Then, if we find another occurrence of x in the pattern, we check to make sure its corresponding expression is 1 and, if not, return a failed match.

A guard? is straightforward: in order for the match to succeed, the predicate specified by guard? must be true under the current context. Otherwise, the match fails.

This is a **fairly** complex nested interpreter and, in fact, requires us to use one of our other nested interpreters, namely $\mathcal{L}^*_{\text{CLOSURE}}$: our representation-independent (with respect to environments and closures) value-of nested interpreter. We will build $\mathcal{L}^*_{\text{PATTERN}}$: a nested interpreter that allows the programmer to define patterns like the one above.

In designing this function we will start very, very small. Our first match function will only recognize self-evaluating expressions, i.e., expressions defined by property 1. Recall that match receives two arguments: a quoted expression and a list of patterns.

We will start with find-match: a function that receives an Expr and a list of Patterns. It returns an Expr if the given Expr pattern matches a Pattern, and false otherwise. The returned Expr corresponds directly to the expression to evaluate if a pattern match is successful.

Listing 8.349

```
; A Pattern is an Expr.

;; find-pattern : Expr [ListOf Pattern] -> Expr
;; Returns the expression-to-evaluate in the case of a successful match.
(define find-match
 (λ (exp lpat)
  (let ([curr-pair (first lpat)]
        [curr-pat (first curr-pair)]
        [curr-exp (second curr-pair)])
   (cond
    [(null? patterns) #f]
    [(matches? exp curr-pat) curr-exp]
    [else (find-match exp (rest lpat))]))))
```

find-match **calls** matches? with a specific Pattern. Because matches? is the meat of the **algorithm**, so to speak, we will write it next.

matches? **receives** an Expr: namely, the expression to match, and a Pattern. Again, to **simplify** the starting matcher, we only match against self-evaluating expressions.

Listing 8.350

```
;; matches? : Expr Expr -> Boolean
;; Determines if a given expression matches the given pattern.
;; Note that "pat" is not a Pattern, but rather the fst of a pattern.
;;
;; Four matching conditions:
;; 1. exp is not a symbol and it is eqv to the pattern.
;; 2. Only pat is a symbol and it either does not contain
;; a binding of the symbol in its context or, if it does,
;; the expression is eqv? to the pattern's stored expr.
;; 3. If the two symbols are "keywords" and are eqv?.
;; 4. Both exp and pat are lists and each element returns
;; #t when invoked with matches?.
(define matches?
 (λ (exp pat)
  (cond
   [(and (not (symbol? exp)) (eqv? exp pat)) #t]
   [else #f])))
```

Lastly, we will write the "root" initialization function: `match-pattern`, which receives an `Expr` and a `ListOf Patterns` and calls `find-match`. We want to evaluate the expression returned by `find-match`. So, we hand it off to our `value-of` evaluator.

Listing 8.351

```
(define match-pattern
 (λ (exp patterns)
  (value-of (find-match exp patterns ctx) (empty-env))))
```

Calling `match-pattern` with a very simple expression yields predictable results (note that this requires amending the root `value-of` dispatch function to include strings as self-evaluating expressions).

Listing 8.352

```
> (match-pattern '3                         "It is three!"
   '([4 "It is four"]
     [5 "It is five"]
     [3 "It is three!"]
     [#t "It is true!"]))
```

Let us ramp up the complexity a bit by introducing symbols. To do so we must talk a bit more about contexts. *Contexts* are similar to environments; contexts map variable bindings to expressions. If the pattern matcher encounters a symbol inside a `Pattern`, we check to see if it already exists inside the context as a binding. If so, we verify that its expression is `eqv?` to the checking expression. On the other hand (i.e., if it is not bound), we append the symbol and the current "checking expression" to the context (by checking expression, we mean the expression to evaluate after a successful match). We need to update all our functions to now receive contexts as an argument (except for `match-pattern`). The reason we make an explicit distinction between contexts and environments is because we will soon use environments when evaluating certain pieces of patterns.

Listing 8.353

```
; A Context is a (Box [ListOf [PairOf Expr Pattern]])

;; matches? : Expr Expr Context -> Boolean
;; Determines if the expression matches the pattern with the context.
(define matches?
 (λ (exp pat ctx)
  ...))

;; find-pattern : Expr [ListOf Pattern] Context -> Expr
;; Recursively attempts to match the expression to each pattern.
;; If a match fails, the context is reset and we try the next pattern.
(define find-match
 (λ (exp patterns ctx)
  ...))
```

Because our context changes over time, we will need to store it in a box. We cannot return a context from functions since they already have values/results to return. Therefore, the initial call to find-match must wrap the empty context in a box. Moreover, inside the body of find-match, we need to reset the context to the empty context before attempting to match on the next available pattern. We do this so variables that are bound in a previous pattern are not bound in the new pattern.

Listing 8.354

```
(define find-match
 (λ (exp patterns ctx)
  (cond
   [(null? patterns) #f]
   [else
    (let* ([curr-pair (first patterns)]
           [curr-pat (first curr-pair)]
           [curr-exp (second curr-pair)])
     (cond
      [...]
      [else
       (begin
        (set-box! ctx '())
        (find-match exp (rest patterns) ctx))])])])))
```

When working with a context, we must apply the context to a symbol to determine its existence as a binding (note the connection to apply-env). apply-context?, a new function, performs two actions: first, it determines if a binding exists and returns true or false depending on the given checking expression. If the binding does not exist, it extends the context to include this new binding and automatically returns true because we implicitly state that the binding is successful, since there was no preexisting binding. In other words, it is analogous to saying, "we did not find a match, so we will create it ourselves".

Listing 8.355

```
;; apply-context? : Expr Expr Context -> Boolean
;; Searches for an expression (the Pattern fst) in the given context.
(define apply-context?
 (λ (exp pat ctx)
  (let ([res (assv pat (unbox ctx))])
   (cond
    [(eqv? res #f)
     (begin
      (set-box! ctx (cons (cons pat exp) (unbox ctx)))
      #t)]
    [else (eqv? (rest res) exp)]))))
```

Now we add cases to matches? that recognize symbols. If the pattern is a symbol, we call apply-context?. For the moment, it is difficult to understand why we write such a handler. In due time, however, the reasoning will become clear.

Listing 8.356

```
(define matches?
 (λ (exp pat ctx)
  (cond
   [...]
   [(symbol? pat) (apply-context? exp pat ctx)]
   [else #f])))
```

Adding a new test is always beneficial.

Listing 8.357

```
> (match-pattern 'x                           |  "n is returned"
  '([n "n is returned"]                        |
    [1 #t]                                      |
    [2 #f]                                      |
    [x (+ 100 200)]))                           |
```

The previous test may raise some eyebrows. This behavior, however, is to be expected—n is an arbitrary symbol that we want to bind to x. The empty context does not contain a binding of n, meaning it successfully binds and matches x.

We now turn our attention to guarded patterns. A guarded pattern is a pattern that has three elements, where the *second* is a guard? predicate. Let us write its recognizer.

Listing 8.358

```
;; guard-pattern? : Pattern -> Boolean
;; Determines if the given Pattern contains a (guard? ...) clause as its snd.
(define guard-pattern?
  (λ (pat)
    (and (cons? pat)
         (= (length pat) 3)
         (cons? (second pat))
         (eqv? (first (second pat)) 'guard?))))
```

Then, we update find-match to call match-guarded? if it encounters a guarded pattern. Note that, in order to resolve the expression bound to a guarded pattern, the pattern must, of course, be guarded, but it must also successfully match. We express this with and as well as not. Another necessary alteration is to remove the let* binding for curr-exp since the *second* of a Pattern is no longer guaranteed to be the resulting expression to resolve.

Listing 8.359

```
(define find-match
  (λ (exp patterns ctx)
    (cond
      [(null? patterns) #f]
      [else
       (let* ([curr-pair (first patterns)]
              [curr-pat (first curr-pair)])
         (cond
           [(and (guard-pattern? curr-pair) (matches-guard? exp curr-pair ctx))
            (third curr-pair)]
           [(and (not (guard-pattern? curr-pair)) (matches? exp curr-pat ctx))
            (second curr-pair)]
           [else ...]))])))
```

Finally, we write matches-guarded?, which evaluates the guard predicate and invokes matches?. Again, both must return true for matches-guarded? to return true. Though, this brings to attention the idea of a "merged context". We must evaluate gpred, i.e., the guarded predicate, to determine if the guard holds true. In doing this, we evaluate it using value-of, but we cannot just use the current context because we lose the bindings from the "base" or empty environment for the evaluator. So, we create a representation-independent merge-env function that receives two environments (where the latter may be a context) and conjoins the latter bindings onto the former. To demonstrate, we include its definition and a relevant test.[1]

Listing 8.360

```
(define merge-env
 (λ (new old)
  (cond
   [(null? new) old]
   [else (cons (first new)
               (merge-env (rest new) old))])))

(define env1 `((x . 5) (y . 6) (z . 7)))
(define env2 `((+ . ,+) (- . ,-)))

> (merge-env env1 env2)                          ((x . 5) (y . 6) (z . 7)
                                                  (+ . ,+) (- . ,-))
```

Listing 8.361

```
;; matches-guard? : Expr Pattern -> Boolean
;; Determines if the expression matches the given guarded Pattern.
(define matches-guard?
 (λ (exp pat ctx)
  (let ([p (first pat)]
        [gexpr (rest pat)]
        [logpred (first gexpr)]
        [gpred (first (rest logpred))])
   (and (matches? exp p ctx)
        (value-of gpred (merge-env (unbox ctx) (empty-env)))))))
```

Because a guard? receives an arbitrary expression, we must update the base evaluation environment to contain predicates we may use in a pattern matcher. We only include four primitive predicates, but we encourage the readers to add more should they see fit. Instead of using (and polluting) empty-env, we extend a "base" environment to include primitives. This results in empty-env remaining true to its name (note that we need to update apply-context? to include the base environment rather than empty).

Listing 8.362

```
(define base-env
 (λ ()
  (extend-env 'number? number?
   (extend-env 'symbol? symbol?
    (extend-env 'string? string?
     (extend-env 'boolean? boolean? (empty-env)))))))

(define empty-env
 (λ ()
  '()))
```

---

[1] Does this definition look suspiciously similar to another function, perhaps append? If so, then your intuition is correct; we could define merge-env as append and it achieves an identical functionality.

Another test is warranted:

Listing 8.363

```
> (match-pattern '5                                              10
  '([n (guard? (number? n)) (+ n n)]
    [y (guard? (symbol? y)) y]
    [s (guard? (string? s)) "It is a string!"]
    [b (guard? (boolean? b)) "It is a boolean!"]))
```

Next, we take care of matching against "keywords". Keywords are any operation defined at the meta-interpreter level. For instance, first, rest, and so on are all "keywords", in this sense. Therefore if we encounter a keyword, we should not attempt a rebinding. Instead, we need to check if it matches the symbol defined by the checking expression. We defined a list of keywords below and an accompanying recognition predicate. All that is necessary is an amendment to matches? that adds a case for handling keywords.

Listing 8.364

```
(define keywords '(first rst cons + - / * list? null? number? symbol? boolean?
                   string? char? lambda define))

(define keyword?
 (λ (exp keywords)
  (memv exp keywords)))

(define matches?
 (λ (exp pat ctx)
  (cond
   [(and (keyword? exp keywords) (keyword? pat keywords))
    (eqv? exp pat)]
   [...])))
```

Matching keywords by themselves, though, is somewhat meaningless. It would be much better if we could match, say, quoted applications! The last criterion, namely pattern matching lists, is perhaps one of the easiest since it has well-defined clauses.

We define matches-list? which receives a list (of expressions) lexp, a list of expressions defined as a pattern lpat, and a context. Our four clauses/cases are as follows:

1. If both lists are empty, then they match because the empty list matches the empty list.

2. If exactly one of the lists is non-empty, we return false, because an empty list does not match a non-empty list.

3. If the *first* of lexp matches the *first* of lpat, recursively match the rest of the list against the pattern.

4. Otherwise, return false.

Determining if exactly one of the lists is non-empty is easy but requires redundant code if we use the naive approach. We can, instead, use exclusive-or (xor) to test this property (note that, to use xor, you will need to define a $\mathcal{L}^*_{\text{MATCH}}$ function apply_xor).

Listing 8.365

```
;; matches-list? : [ListOf Expr] [ListOf Expr] -> Boolean
;; Recursively determines if each element of a list expression
;; match to each element of the pattern list. The second argument
;; is not a Pattern; just a list of expressions.
(define matches-list?
 (λ (lexp lpat ctx)
  (cond
   [(and (null? lexp) (null? lpat)) #t]
   [(xor (null? lexp) (null? lpat)) #f]
   [(matches? (first lexp) (first lpat) ctx)
    (matches-list? (rest lexp) (rest lpat) ctx)]
   [else #f])))
```

Now we add a clause for list matching inside `matches?` as follows:

Listing 8.366

```
(define matches?
 (λ (exp pat ctx)
  (cond
   [...]
   [(and (cons? exp) (cons? pat))
    (matches-list? exp pat ctx)]
   [else #f])))
```

At long last, we run the original provided test case and get 5 as the result.

Listing 8.367

```
> (match-pattern '(+ 2 3)                    | 5
   '([n (guard? (number? n)) (* n n)]        |
    [y (guard? (symbol? y)) y]               |
    [(+ a a) (+ a a a a)]                    |
    [(+ a b) (+ a b)]                        |
    [_ #f]))                                 |
```

Another detail about variable bindings is that the bindings, themselves, are significant only if they are reused in a `Pattern`. For example, consider the following invocation of `match-pattern`:

Listing 8.368

```
(match-pattern (+ 5 5 5 5)
 '([(+ x y z w) 1000]
   [(+ x x x x) 2000]
   [(+ x y x y) 3000]))
```

It may be tempting to say that the above match resolves to 2000, since the second case binds x to 5 and the only number that exists in the given expression is 5. Thinking this way, however, gets us in trouble since it suggests a misunderstanding of how bindings occur. Consider the first pattern to match: (+ x y z w). We bind x to 5, y to 5, z to 5, and w to 5. None of these variables are reused later in the pattern, meaning there are no conflicting usages and, therefore, this match succeeds, producing 1000. If we want to consider only the case where all variables are equal, we need to make one of two alterations: either move the (+ x x x x) pattern to the top, or add and and eqv? clauses to our evaluator (this is an exercise to the reader). Reordering the clauses as follows produces our desired result of 2000, but this, in actuality, does nothing to prevent, say, a "faulty match" of (+ x y z w), in which using a guard is mandatory.

Listing 8.369

```
(match-pattern (+ 5 5 5 5)
  '([(+ x x x x) 2000]
    [(+ x y z w) 1000]
    [(+ x y x y) 3000]))
```

On a related note, is often handy to have a "wild card" match, i.e., a match that always succeeds. In Listing 8.364, we denote the wild card match as the underscore '_' symbol. Choosing the underscore as the wild card symbol is a completely arbitrary selection, but we label it as such since it denotes that we care so little about the result so as to not explicitly name the bound variable. So, we can add a clause in matches? that returns true if we encounter the wild card symbol.

Listing 8.370

```
(define wildcard '_)

(define matches?
  (λ (exp pat ctx)
    (cond
      [(eqv? wildcard pat) #t]
      [...])))
```

We may use the wildcard in several ways. For instance, we might use it to indicate a failed match.

Listing 8.371

```
> (match-pattern '(cons (cons 10 20) (cons 20 10))      200
    '([(cons (cons x y) (cons x y)) (+ x y)]
      [(cons (cons y x) (cons x y)) (* x y)]
      [(cons (cons (cons x y) x) (cons x y)) 1000]
      [_ (print "Invalid match!")]))
```

This pattern matcher is not very elegant nor will it annihilate any "professional" pattern matcher, but it goes to show how much we can truly express in our languages!

Exercise 8.72. (⋆⋆)

Our pattern matcher does not recognize symbols as input. For instance, if we want to check that our input is a literal symbol, we would need to quote it. Unfortunately, "double-quoted" expressions are complicated to implement. Thus, the solution is to use the quote function as follows:

Listing 8.372

```
> (match-pattern 'x                                "The symbol is x!"
    '([y (guard? (eqv? y (quote x)))
      "The symbol is x!"]
      [y (guard? (eqv? y (quote z)))
      "The symbol is z!"]
      [_ "I do not know this symbol"]))
```

This exercise consists of two small parts: first, add quote to the evaluator. Then, implement eqv?. Both of these come with respective recognizer and reducer functions, neither of which should be complex. Notice that this also gives us the flexibility of guarding over eqv? data.

Exercise 8.73. (⋆⋆)

Add the empty list () to value-of. That is, write the recognizer empty? and the reducer value-of-empty. In doing so, we can write patterns that contain the empty list if we, for instance, want to construct a pattern that reverses a list of three distinct elements. Note that, in order to use the empty list, we must quote it via quote as we would otherwise with '.

Listing 8.373

```
> (match-pattern '(1 2 3)                              (3 2 1)
    '([(x y z) (cons z (cons y (cons x (quote ()))))]
      [_ #f]))
```

Exercise 8.74. (⋆⋆⋆⋆)

Using a nested evaluator, i.e., value-of, severely hinders the capabilities of our pattern matcher. A better solution would be to use eval, but it is a bit more difficult because eval does not use an environment to look up symbol mappings. What we need, instead, is to substitute the bound symbols in the environment for those matched inside a pattern. For example, consider matching the pattern containing a guard expression (x y) (guard? (< x y)) (* x y)) with the expression '(5 6). If we substitute x and y for 5 and 6 respectively in the result clause, we get (* 5 6), which can be evaluated using eval. Implement this feature into the pattern matcher. Hint: this exercise is particularly tricky and requires a careful understanding of how eval works. Any substitutions made must account for quoted symbols and applications. E.g., attempting to match the symbol 'z to the pattern x needs to bind x to an explicitly quoted z. There are two places where evaluation occurs: after a successful pattern match and when encountering a guard? clause following a successful pattern match. To get started, write a match-subst function that receives three arguments: an expression, a pattern, and an environment containing variable bindings. Assume that the expression indeed matches the pattern, so all that needs to happen is a substitution. We present some examples below to serve as a guide.

Listing 8.374

```
> (match-subst '(+ 2 3)                    (+ 2 3)
               'n
               '())
> (match-subst '(+ x y)                    (+ 2 3)
               '(+ x y)
               '((x . 2) (y . 3)))
> (match-subst '(cons x y)                 (cons 1 2)
               '(cons x y)
               '((x . 1) (y . 2)))
> (match-subst '3                          3
               '3
               '())
> (match-subst '(number? n)                (number? '(+ 2 3))
               '(number? n)
               '((n . (+ 2 3))))
> (match-subst '(eqv? y (quote x))         (eqv? (quote x)
               'y                                (quote x)))
               '((y . (quote x))))
```

Exercise 8.75. (★★★★)
Assuming that quoted expressions work (in the pattern matcher) without a hitch, this exercise should be a breeze! Implement a series of pattern matches to compute the sum of a sequence of numbers in a list. Your solution should be recursive and part of a function definition that uses match-pattern.

Listing 8.375

```
> (match-pattern              | 100
    '(cons 10                 |
      (cons 20                |
       (cons 30               |
        (cons 40              |
         '(quote ()))))))     |
    '([...]                   |
     [_ #f]))                 |
```

8.18 $\mathcal{L}^*_{\text{SCHELOG}}$: **Logic Programming**

Suppose we have a "fact" database that stores information in the following format:

Listing 8.376

```
(child joe bob) (child steve joe) (child stephanie pauline)
(child jonah alfred) (child john carlos) (child breanna megan)
(male joe) (male bob) (male steve)
(male jonah) (male alfred) (male john)
(male carlos) (female stephanie) (female pauline)
(female breanna) (female megan)
```

This database stores *facts* as predicates in prefix form. E.g., (child john carlos) indicates that john is a child of carlos. Similarly, (female breanna) indicates that breanna is female. What if we wanted to determine relationships about these individuals? For instance, we could write a *rule* to determine if someone is a mother of someone else as follows:

Listing 8.377

```
(mother X Y) ← (child Y X) (female X)
```

The above *rule* reads as X is the mother of Y if Y is the child of X and X is female. X and Y are variables that can be substituted for constants during evaluation. If we execute a *query* on the database, e.g., (mother X Y), we will receive a list of all solutions for X and Y that satisfy the mother rule. In the previous database of facts, we see that (X=pauline, Y=stephanie) and (X=megan, Y=breanna) are both solutions, so a list containing this tuple would be returned. Similarly, we can write queries that determine the truthfulness of a claim. For example, if we want to see whether pauline is a child of joe, we would run (child pauline joe). In this instance the query should return $\bot$ because this relation does not hold. Conversely, (male carlos) returns $\top$ because this relation does hold. In this section, we will explore logic programming and how to write a simple nested interpreter for a language that interprets this style of programming.

Logic programming is commonly used as a form of *declarative programming*. That is, instead of writing expressions that evaluate to a result, one presents a list of rules and facts that compose the way to design and derive *other* facts and information. In the previous paragraph, we described a logic programming language almost identical in style to Prolog: a historical favorite among the early artificial intelligence community. To design a language like Prolog is not very difficult as we will show.[1] We will write this nested language in a series of disjoint functions that, in the end, conjoin into our final product.

First, we need to discuss how we will encode and represent information within our system. Namely, we need to distinguish between constants and variables, as well as facts and rules. Since we are working with the schemata of our previous interpreters, let us say that variables are lists of the form (V X) where X is any symbol. Constants are anything else, e.g., child, samantha, and so on. Terms are any composition of variables and constants, e.g., (foo (V X) (bar (baz (V Y)))). Let us write the accompanying recognizers.

---

[1]Optimizing such a language, however, is a challenge!

Listing 8.378

```
(define const?
 (λ (tm)
  (or (symbol? tm)
      (null? tm))))

(define var?
 (λ (tm)
  (and (cons? tm)
       (eqv? (first tm) 'V))))
```

Next, we want a function that extracts all variables from a term. We will write a function `get-vars` to do so. `get-vars` makes use of the higher-order function `filter` to extract out all variables from a term. There is the added issue in that a term may be made up of sub terms, e.g., `(foo (bar (baz (V 3))))`. A potential solution is to flatten the list which removes any and all nested lists. Using `flatten` seems like a solid option until we realize that it also flattens variables! So, we need to amend the definition of flatten to account for variables and not recursively flatten them. From this, the definition of `get-vars` reveals itself.

Listing 8.379

```
(define flatten
 (λ (lst)
  (cond
   [(null? lst) '()]
   [(not (cons? lst)) (cons lst '())]
   [(and (cons? (first lst)) (eqv? (first (first lst)) 'V))
    (cons (first lst) (flatten (rest lst)))]
   [else (append (flatten (first lst))
                 (flatten (rest lst)))])))

;; get-vars : Term -> [ListOf Term]
;; Extracts all variables of the form (V ...) from a
;; term if any exist.
(define get-vars
 (λ (lst)
  (filter var? (flatten lst))))
```

Now, we turn to the fundamental piece of any logic programming system: `unify`. We wrote something similar to `unify` in our pattern matcher. This time, though, it will return an environment where its inputs u and v are successfully unified, or false if the unification failed. There are a few sub-parts to unification. First, if the environment is false, then we immediately return false. Second, if u is a variable, we attempt to match u with v, and the converse is true for v. If either u or v (or both) is a constant, then we return the existing environment if they are equal, designating that they are already unified and false otherwise. Lastly, we encounter the case when u and v are both lists which need to be unified recursively. Since the environment of a unification updates in between calls to `unify`, we pass it along to the recursive unification of the *rest* of u and v.

Listing 8.380

```
;; unify : Term Term Environment -> Environment
;; Returns an environment where a successful unification
;; occurred, or #f otherwise.
(define unify
  (λ (u v env)
    (cond
      [(false? env) #f]
      [(var? u) (match-var u v env)]
      [(var? v) (match-var v u env)]
      [(or (const? u) (const? v))
       (cond
         [(equal? u v) env]
         [else #f])]
      [else
       (let* ([env^ (unify (first u) (first v) env)]
              [env^^ (unify (rest u) (rest v) env^)])
         env^^)])))
```

Next we **write** `match-var`: a function that receives a variable v, a pattern to match against p, and an environment env; it returns an environment with the variable "matched against" the pattern. If v and p are equal, then it means that we do not need to amend the environment, meaning we simply return env. Otherwise, we retrieve the associated pattern with the given variable. If there is no association, it means we can try to unify the pattern with p. Otherwise, we return an environment where v and p are associated. Notice that `unify` and `match-var` are mutually recursive, i.e., they call each other. One additional note about this function, which is extremely subtle, is that we use `assv` for looking up a value in an association list. `assv` under the hood, as we know, uses `eqv?` for comparison. We need to write a new function `assoc` that uses `equal?`.

Listing 8.381

```
;; assoc : Any [ListOf [PairOf Any Any]] -> Boolean/[PairOf Any Any]
;; Finds an association of the input v in an association list
;; ls using equal? for comparison. Returns #f is no association is found.
(define assoc
  (λ (v ls)
    (cond
      [(null? ls) #f]
      [else
       (let ([pair (first ls)])
         (cond
           [(equal? (first pair) v) (first ls)]
           [else (assoc v (rest ls))]))])))

;; match-var : Term Term Environment -> Environment
;; Returns an environment where v and p are associated.
(define (match-var v p env)
  (cond
    [(equal? v p) env]
    [else
     (let ([binding (assv v env)])
       (cond
         [(not (false? binding)) (unify (second binding) p env)]
         [else (cons (list v p) env)]))]))
```

Notice one easy-to-overlook distinction from `assv`: we have this function 'equal?'; why not 'eqv?'? Here is the thing: eqv? checks only individual terms for equality, e.g., (eqv? v 50), (eqv? #f #t), and so on. We need a function that determines if lists are equivalent, i.e., have the same elements, including nested lists. It is time we introduce equal?: a function identical to eqv? with the added benefit of checking lists for equality.

Writing this function brings nothing new to the table; natural recursion is always to the rescue.

Listing 8.382

```
;; list-eqv*? : {X} {Y} [ListOf X] [ListOf Y] -> Boolean
;; Determines whether all elements of two lists are identical.
;; This function also works on recursive/nested lists.
(define list-eqv*?
 (λ (ls1 ls2)
  (cond
   [(and (null? ls1) (null? ls2)) #t]
   [(equal? (first ls1) (first ls2))
    (list-eqv*? (rest ls1) (rest ls2))]
   [else #f])))

;; equal? : {X} {Y} X Y -> Boolean
;; Determines if two "things" are equal. Two "things" are equal
;; iff they are either eqv? or they are equivalent lists.
(define equal?
 (λ (a b)
  (cond
   [(eqv? a b) #t]
   [(and (cons? a) (cons? b)) (list-eqv*? a b)]
   [else #f])))
```

Next, we write expand which receives a term and an environment. It returns a term with all variables substituted for the constants that are unified with the variables in the given environment. For instance, expanding (child (V Y) (V X)) with the environment '((X joe) (Y bob)) returns the term (child joe bob).

Listing 8.383

```
;; expand : Term Environment -> Term
;; Receives a term of two variables and an environment
;; with these variables unified and returns a term where the
;; variables are substituted with the constants.
(define expand
 (λ (tm env)
  (cond
   [(null? env) tm]
   [else
    (let* ([binding (first env)]
           [var (first binding)]
           [const (second binding)])
     (expand (subst var const tm) (rest env)))])))
```

expand makes use of a helper function: `subst`, which receives a variable, a constant, and its "parent" term. If the term is only a constant, we return the term itself. If the term is a variable, we return u if tm is equal? to v and tm otherwise. If neither of these are true, then tm is a more complex term that must be recursively substituted. So, we make clever use of map; each element of the term is substituted individually and reconstructed via map.

Listing 8.384

```
;; subst : Term Term Term -> Term
;; Attempts to substitute a variable v with a replacement
;; term u in some term tm. If the variable occurs, we return
;; u, and otherwise return tm.
(define subst
 (λ (v u tm)
  (cond
   [(const? tm) tm]
   [(var? tm)
    (cond
     [(equal? tm v) u]
     [else tm])]
   [else (map (λ (t) (subst v u t)) tm)])))
```

Now we will write four functions for cleaning up the output. The first two of these are expand-binding and extend-env. The former receives a binding and an environment and returns a *cons* pair whose *first* is the *first* of our binding, i.e., the variable, and whose *rest* is the expanded *rest* of binding. The latter receives a term and an environment and calls extend-binding on each element of the term.

Listing 8.385

```
(define extend-binding
 (λ (binding env)
  (cons (first binding) (expand (rest binding) env))))

(define extend-env
 (λ (e env)
  (map (λ (binding) (extend-binding binding env)) e)))
```

Up next is collapse-env, which performs a technique called environment reduction. That is, suppose we have two solutions to a query such as the following: (foo (V (V M) 2))) ((V (V M) 2) (foo x)). We see that (V (V M) 2) binds foo x, meaning we can substitute the "binder" into the first solution and omit the second altogether, thereby producing (foo (foo x)).

Listing 8.386

```
;; collapse-env : Environment -> Environment
;; Reduces all variable occurrences to their bound constants
;; in a term, if they exist.
(define (collapse-env env)
 (let* ([new-env (extend-env env env)])
  (cond
   [(equal? env new-env) new-env]
   [else (collapse-env new-env)])))
```

Lastly we have filter-vars which filters out any non-variables from an environment, e.g., variables unified with other variables, meaning our solutions specify variable bindings to constants and only constants.

Listing 8.387

```
;; filter-vars : Environment [ListOf Term] -> [ListOf Term]
;; Removes all non-variable bindings from a list of terms.
(define filter-vars
 (λ (env vars)
  (filter (λ (v) (member? (first v) vars)) env)))
```

Now come the functions that tie everything together: search and query. The former is much more complex, so we will explain it thoroughly. search receives a database of facts *db*, a list of goals *goals*, an environment *env*, and a "recursive depth" *d*. First we handle the base case: if there are no more goals to solve, we wrap the environment in a list.

Listing 8.388

```
;; search : [ListOf Term] [ListOf Term] Environment Number -> [ListOf Environment]
;; Recursively searches for solutions to the given goals.
(define search
 (λ (db goals env d)
  (cond
   [(null? goals) (list env)]
   [else ...])))
```

Next, we will use another higher-order function to collect results as they are found: foldl. The binary function provided will receive a clause and the accumulating value. We proceed by renaming the clause with a depth identifier to "uniquify" the variable. Then, we retrieve the head and body of the clause and attempt to unify the first goal with the head.

Listing 8.389

```
;; uniquify : Term Symbol -> Term
;; Renames all terms within a given term with a given value.
(define uniquify
 (λ (tm name)
  (cond
   [(const? tm) tm]
   [(var? tm) (list 'V v n)]
   [else (map (λ (t) (uniquify t name)) tm)])))

;; search : [ListOf Term] [ListOf Term] Environment Number -> [ListOf Environment]
;; Recursively searches for solutions to the given goals.
(define search
 (λ (db goals env d)
  (cond
   [(null? goals) (list env)]
   [else
    (foldl
     (λ (clause acc)
      (let* ([fresh (uniquify clause d)] [head (first fresh)]
             [body (rest fresh)] [unifier (unify (first goals) head env)])
       (cond
        [(not unifier) ...]
        [else ...])))]))))
```

If we succeed in unifying the head with the first goal, we need to expand out the results provided by unifier as well as the existing body. These two combined get us our new/next list of goals to satisfy. Because we recurse into search, we add one to *d* to designate one further depth into the search. If the unification failed, however, we can no longer proceed and must return. So, we return the accumulated value from foldl. As we know from foldr, foldl similarly receives three arguments: a binary function, a starting accumulator value, and the list to fold over. The starting value is, of course, the empty list, and the list to fold over is our database.

Listing 8.390

```
(define (search db goals env d)
 (λ (db goals env d)
  (cond
   [...]
   [else
    (foldl
     (λ (clause acc)
      (let* ([fresh (uniquify clause d)] [head (first fresh)]
             [body (rest fresh)] [unifier (unify (first goals) head env)])
       (cond
        [(not unifier)
         (let* ([exp-goals (map (λ (g) (expand g unifier)) (rest goals))]
                [exp-body (map (λ (t) (expand t unifier)) body)]
                [new-goals (append exp-body exp-goals)]
                [new-acc (append acc (search db new-goals unifier (add1 d)))])
           new-acc)]
        [else acc])))
     '()
     db)])))
```

Last but certainly not least, we write query: the driver function for our system.
It receives a database and a list of goals and returns a list of solutions, if any exist.
We kick-start the function with the initial call to search, which returns a list of
unifiers. We then call collapse-env on these unifiers to condense the solution
list. This is followed by a call to filter-vars, which retrieves only those solutions
bound by variables from the original list of goals.

Listing 8.391

```
;; query : [ListOf Term] [ListOf Term] -> [ListOf Term]
;; "Jump-starts" the query and collects the results. If the
;; input is a 'fact' and has no solutions, the empty list is returned.
;; Otherwise, either a solution is returned or '(()) which designates
;; that a fact was successfully derived.
(define query
 (λ (db goals)
  (let* ([unifiers (search db goals '() 1)]
         [solns (map collapse-env unifiers)])
   (map (λ (u) (filter-vars u (get-vars goals))) solns))))
```

That is all there is to it! Let us write a family tree to test the program.

Listing 8.392

```
(define database
 '(((female darlene)) ((female shannon)) ((female paula)) ((female madison))
   ((female abigail)) ((male mauricio)) ((male joshua)) ((male cameron))
   ((male dennis)) ((male travis)) ((male fred)) ((male clarence))
   ((parent darlene joshua)) ((parent mauricio joshua))
   ((parent shannon cameron)) ((parent paula madison))
   ((parent dennis madison)) ((parent mauricio abigail))
   ((parent paula abigail)) ((parent shannon darlene))
   ((parent clarence darlene)) ((parent fred clarence))
   ((parent travis clarence))))
```

We may also encode some rules into this database, e.g., X is the mother of Y if
X is female and X is the parent of Y. Another possibility is X is the ancestor of
Z if X is the parent of some Y and that Y is the parent of Z. Though, parents
are technically the ancestors to their children. So, we need two rules to govern the
ancestor relation.

Listing 8.393

```
(define database
  '(...
    ((mother (V X) (V Y)) (female (V X)) (parent (V X) (V Y)))
    ((ancestor (V X) (V Z)) (parent (V X) (V Y)) (parent (V Y) (V Z)))
    ((ancestor (V X) (V Y)) (parent (V X) (V Y)))))
```

Let us run the following queries:

Listing 8.394

```
; Is paula the mother of madison?
> (query database '((mother paula madison)))              (())

; Who is shannon the mother of?
> (query database '((mother shannon (V X))))              ((((V X) cameron))
                                                           (((V X) darlene)))

; Who is the mother of joshua?
> (query database '((mother (V X) joshua)))               ((((V X) darlene)))

; Is darlene the mother of fred?
> (query database '((mother darlene fred)))               ()

; Who all is clarence an ancestor of?
> (query database '((ancestor clarence (V X))))           ((((V X) joshua))
                                                           (((V X) darlene)))

; Who are the ancestors of darlene?
> (query database '((ancestor (V X) darlene)))            ((((V X) fred))
                                                           (((V X) travis))
                                                           (((V X) shannon))
                                                           (((V X) clarence)))
```

Excellent! We now have a pretty powerful logic programming language!

Exercise 8.76. (★★)

The logic programming language Prolog outputs results to queries in a more human-centric way. For instance, the above queries would output something similar to the following if we used Prolog:

```
true
-------------
Solution 1:
X = cameron
X = darlene
-------------
Solution 1:
X = darlene
-------------
false
-------------
Solution 1:
X = joshua
Solution 2:
X = darlene
-------------
Solution 1:
X = fred
Solution 2:
X = travis
Solution 3:
X = shannon
Solution 4:
X = clarence
-------------
```

Write a function `query-print` that receives the same parameters as `query` (and calls `query` itself) but outputs the solutions/results in this tabular format.

Exercise 8.77. (⋆⋆)

Prolog allows the programmer to define lists using a construct similar to that of cons using brackets. For example, if we have a list u and attempt to unify it with the variable defined as $[H \mid T]$, the head/*first* of u is unified with H, and T is unified with the tail/*rest* of u. We do not have access to this fancy notation, but we can certainly implement a cons logic predicate. A *cons* pair has an element as its *first* and either 'nil or another pair as its *rest*. A *cons* pair p whose *rest* is defined in terms of *cons* p' is a pair if p' is a valid *cons* pair. Implement cons into $\mathcal{L}^*_{\text{SCHELOG}}$. This consists of a cons base case, and a recursive definition.

Exercise 8.78. (⋆⋆)

Variables are lists that are prefixed with 'V. In Prolog, however, any sequence of characters that starts with an upper-case letter is considered a variable, e.g., the variable X versus the non-variable x. Implement Prolog-style variables into your interpreter. Assuming that you have designed them, you will need to take advantage of two interpreter-level functions: symbol->string and char-upper-case?.

Exercise 8.79. (⋆⋆)

We can do a surprising amount of arithmetic in $\mathcal{L}^*_{\text{SCHELOG}}$, despite not having built-in operators. We can inductively define a num with the base case and a succ predicate as follows:

Listing 8.395

```
(define num-db
  '(((num 0))
    ((num (succ (V N))) (num (V N))))))
```

The above database definitions state that 0 is a num, and that (succ N) is a num if N is a num. Using this, define the (add X Y Z) predicate that adds X and Y to produce Z.

Exercise 8.80. (⋆⋆)

Prolog is an optimistic logic programming language. Optimism, in this context, refers to its approach to unification. Take the unification of X and f(X), for instance. If we try to instantiate X to f(X), then this means the former f(X) becomes f(f(X)), repeat ad nauseam. A way to fix this is through an algorithm called the *occurs check*. When we attempt to match a variable with a term through match-var, we should check to make sure the variable v does not occur anywhere inside the term p. Write a recursive function occurs? that receives a variable v and a term p and returns true if v occurs in p and false otherwise. As a hint, if p is a constant, then v cannot occur in p. Similarly, if v is a variable and p is a variable, the only way v can occur in p is if they are equal.

Exercise 8.81. (⋆⋆⋆⋆)

We can use logic programming to determine solutions to list operations such as appending and even sorting. First, implement the cons predicate construct from exercise 2.43. Then, using the three numeric comparison predicates we provide, write the merge predicate, which merges the numbers in two sorted lists. We also provide its two base cases, namely for when either list is empty. You should implement the other two (non-base) cases.

Listing 8.396

```
(define db
  '(((num 0))
    ((num (succ (N))) (num (N)))
    ((eq 0 0))
    ((eq (succ (X)) (succ (Y))) (eq (X) (Y)))
    ((gt (succ (M)) 0))
    ((gt (succ (N)) (succ (M))) (gt (N) (M)))
    ((lt 0 (succ (M))))
    ((lt (succ (N)) (succ (M))) (lt (N) (M)))
    ((merge (L) nil (L)))
    ((merge nil (L) (L)))))
```

Exercise 8.82. ($\star\star\star\star\star$)

In Chapter 7, we wrote a small type inferencer as a nested interpreter. Interestingly, though, it is easier to build a type inferencer in logic programming languages. Consider the following small programming language grammar:

exp	::=	app | if | let | lam | var | num | bool
app	::=	' (' 'app' ' ' exp ' ' exp ')'
if	::=	' (' 'if' ' ' exp ' ' exp ' ' exp ')'
lam	::=	' (' 'lambda' '(' var ')' exp ')'
var	::=	' (' 'var' symbol ')'
num	::=	' (' 'num' number ')'
bool	::=	' (' 'bool' boolean ')'

Figure 8.16: Extended BNF Grammar for Simple Programming Language

In which symbol is a lower-case identifier, number is defined in terms of succ, and boolean is either true or false. We want to be able to infer types about expressions written in this language. To do so, we need to list the typing rules, or type judgments, of this language.

$$\tau\text{-VAR} \quad \frac{((\text{var } v) : \tau) \in \Gamma}{\Gamma \vdash v : \tau} \qquad \tau\text{-NUM} \quad \frac{(\text{num } n)}{\Gamma \vdash n : \text{NAT}} \qquad \tau\text{-BOOL} \quad \frac{(\text{bool } b)}{\Gamma \vdash b : \text{BOOL}}$$

$$\tau\text{-IF} \quad \frac{\Gamma \vdash b : \text{BOOL} \qquad \Gamma \vdash e_1, e_2 : \tau}{\Gamma \vdash (\text{if } b\, e_1\, e_2) : \tau} \qquad \tau\text{-LAM} \quad \frac{\Gamma :: ((\text{var } v) : \tau_1) \vdash e : \tau_2}{\Gamma \vdash (\text{lam } v\, e) : \tau_1 \to \tau_2}$$

$$\tau\text{-APP} \quad \frac{\Gamma \vdash f : \tau_1 \to \tau_2 \qquad \Gamma \vdash e : \tau_1}{\Gamma \vdash (\text{app } f\, e) : \tau_2}$$

Figure 8.17: Typing Rules for the Simple Programming Language

Figure 8.17 shows a series of inference rules. Gamma, Γ, is a type environment and τ is a type. Words written in typewriter refer to predicates defined by our (logic) language; words in SMALL CAPITAL LETTERS are the types of an expression. We read such inference rules from top-to-bottom, where the inference premises are above the line and its conclusion is below the line. For example, to read τ−IF, we say "if we know that b is of type BOOL and both expressions e_1 and e_2 are of type τ, then we conclude that the (conditional) expression (if b e_1 e_2) is of type τ". In the τ−LAM rule, we must extend Γ to include the type binding of the formal parameter v (where the double colon '::' is synonymous with *cons*), meaning that we read this rule as "If, by extending Γ to include v we can prove that e is of type τ_2, then we know (lam v e) is of type $\tau_1 \rightarrow \tau_2$".

Write the type predicate. It binds three arguments: a type environment G, an expression E, and the type T. Your program should be able to infer the type of some expression e given a type environment G. To get you started, we provide the type predicate to infer the type of booleans and numbers.

Listing 8.397

```
(define type-db
 '(((bool true)) ((bool false)) ((num zero))
   ((num (succ (V N))) (num (V N)))
   ((type (V G) (V N) nat) (num (V N)))
   ((type (V G) (V B) bool) (bool (V B)))))

(define exp1
 '(succ (zero)))
(define exp2
 '(fun (x) (fun (y) (fun (z)
   (if (var x)
       (add (var y)
            (var z)
            (succ (succ (succ zero))))
     zero)))))

> (query type-db `((type nil ,exp1 (V T))))          nat

> (query type-db `((type nil ,exp2 (V T))))          (bool ->
                                                       (nat ->
                                                        (nat -> nat)))
```

This exercise requires a lot of work, including a rewrite of the cons predicates to account for lists. As we mentioned, lam expressions must extend its environment to include the type of its parameter, so use a cons on the provided type environment. The system has three types: nat, bool, and arrow, the last of which has parameter and body types.

8.19 $\mathcal{L}_{\text{GRAPHIC}}$: **Turtles and Graphics Galore**

Many beginning programmers enjoy working with graphical interfaces and loathe the idea of staying confined to the world of a blinking cursor and text. In this section, we will write $\mathcal{L}_{\text{GRAPHIC}}$: an extension to $\mathcal{L}_{\text{MACRO}}$ that adds graphics and the ability to draw to a screen.

A Representation-Independent Graphics Library

A preface to this section: we will not be demonstrating the inner-workings of a complex graphical library in C, as they are mostly full of mysterious wonders. This ideology is similar to the approach we took with MPC—the only difference being that we wrote the code for this library. With this in mind, we provide a representation-independent graphics library in the form of gfx.h and gfx.c, which uses the SDL (Simple DirectMedia Layer) framework as a base. Appendix 11.3 describes how to install SDL, and Appendix 11.3 shows the implementation of gfx.h and gfx.c. There are several functions of interest to us:

gfx_init initializes the graphics context. This function should be called at the beginning of main.c regardless of if it is ever used or not.

gfx_open_window opens a graphical window of a given size, in pixels, and title. The background, by default, is painted black. The origin, i.e., (0, 0) is located at the top-left of the window. The maximum coordinate is (width−1, height−1), located in the bottom-right of the window.

gfx_clear paints the background of the window black. This is useful in loops where, say, an animation occurs.

gfx_draw_line draws a single line with a given color starting at (x_1, y_1) and ending at (x_2, y_2).

gfx_draw_rect draws a single rectangle with a given width, height, and color starting at (x, y).

gfx_delay tells the graphics context to halt execution for n milliseconds. During this time, the window still listens and responds to events, e.g., mouse clicks.

gfx_cleanup shuts down the graphics system and frees any associated memory.[1]

Our language will use these functions to write a "turtle API". Turtle is a frequently-used approach to teaching computer science via graphics. It largely emphasizes functions and iteration, but also creativity. $\mathcal{L}_{\text{GRAPHIC}}$ adds several functions for creating a turtle, moving it about the screen, and drawing objects such as lines.

---

[1]Note that SDL, alongside many other graphics APIs, e.g., OpenGL, Vulkan, and so on often leak memory. So, checking these programs with Valgrind will yield "false positive" memory leaks that the programmer is at no fault for.

Before we work with turtles, though, we should integrate the graphics library with our language. Namely, we should add a command that opens a window and leaves it open for some unit of time, say, five seconds. Let us call these two functions gfx-window and gfx-delay respectively. The former receives three arguments: a window title, a width in pixels, and a height in pixels. The latter receives one argument: the number of seconds to delay closing the window by. We can add this functionality in apply.c. Because these functions introduce side-effects, e.g., opening a window, they only return NULL.

Listing 8.398—Bult-in Graphics Functions (apply.c)

```
1   static struct sval *apply_gfx_open(struct sval **args, size_t num_args,
2                                      struct environment *env) {
3     ASSERT_ARITY("gfx-open", 3, num_args);
4     const char *title = args[0]->data.string;
5     const int width = args[1]->data.number;
6     const int height = args[2]->data.number;
7     gfx_open_window(title, width, height);
8     return NULL;
9   }
10
11  static struct sval *apply_gfx_delay(struct sval **args, size_t num_args,
12                                      struct environment *env) {
13    ASSERT_ARITY("gfx-delay", 1, num_args);
14    gfx_delay(args[0]->data.number);
15    return NULL;
16  }
```

A test program is as follows:

Listing 8.399

```
(gfx-open "GRAPHIC" 640 480)
(gfx-delay 5000)
```

Next, we need to write two functions for clearing the screen and updating the contents of the screen. gfx_clear and gfx_refresh are the two functions of interest. We will construct gfx-clear and gfx-refresh respectively. Both of these functions receive zero arguments. We use gfx-clear to wipe any existing graphics on the window. gfx-refresh, on the other hand, updates the window to account for any changes made. We will explore this in greater detail soon.

Listing 8.400—More Built-in Graphics Functions (apply.c)

```
1   static struct sval *apply_gfx_clear(struct sval **args, size_t num_args,
2                                       struct environment *env) {
3     ASSERT_ARITY("gfx-clear", 0, num_args);
4     gfx_clear();
5     return NULL;
6   }
7
8   static struct sval *apply_gfx_refresh(struct sval **args, size_t num_args,
9                                         struct environment *env) {
10    ASSERT_ARITY("gfx-refresh", 0, num_args);
11    gfx_refresh();
12    return NULL;
13  }
```

Finally, we need a way of drawing something to the screen. Lines are simple, so we will implement these before any other primitive shapes. Recall that gfx_-draw_line receives five arguments representing the starting and ending coordinates of the line as well as its color. The color is perhaps the strangest argument of all since it is received as a number.[1] Colors, in most digital contexts, use what is known as the RGB color spectrum. Namely, a color consists of three bytes, where each byte is a channel of "color". The first byte is the "amount of red" in the color, the second is the "amount of green", and the last byte is the "amount of blue". Because each channel is one byte in size, each channel is a natural number from 0 to 255, where 0 represents no color, and 255 represents maximum color. Thus, we can represent the color red via (255, 0, 0). Similarly, blue is (0, 0, 255). In our library, however, there is one more channel called the alpha channel, which represents how transparent, or visible, a color appears. For example, a fully-visible, i.e., opaque, green color is (0, 255, 0, 255). A half-visible yellow is (255, 255, 0, 127). From Chapter 5, we know that integers are 4 bytes long, meaning we can store all four bytes of a color into an integer. gfx.h provides a useful macro for retrieving this specific value: GET_COLOR(r, g, b, a). So, we can write a function that receives eight arguments which invokes the line-drawing function from gfx.c.

Listing 8.401—Built-in Line Drawing Function (apply.c)

```
1   static struct sval *apply_gfx_draw_line(struct sval **args, size_t num_args,
2                                           struct environment *env) {
3     ASSERT_ARITY("gfx-draw-line", 8, num_args);
4     const int x1 = args[0]->data.number;
5     const int y1 = args[1]->data.number;
6     const int x2 = args[2]->data.number;
7     const int y2 = args[3]->data.number;
8
9     int r = args[4]->data.number;
10    int g = args[5]->data.number;
11    int b = args[6]->data.number;
12    int a = args[7]->data.number;
13
14    gfx_draw_line(x1, y1, x2, y2,
15                  GET_COLOR(r, g, b, a));
16    return NULL;
17  }
```

Let us draw a red line to the screen. Note that we need to invoke gfx-clear and gfx-refresh to account for the newly-drawn line.

Listing 8.402

```
(gfx-open "GRAPHIC" 640 480)
(gfx-clear)
(gfx-line 300 300 300 400 255 0 0 255)
(gfx-refresh)
(gfx-delay 5000)
```

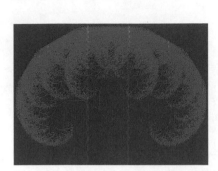

Figure 8.18: Fractal Tree and Colorful Spiral

Figure 8.19: Spiral Star and Yarn Ball

With just this gfx-line function, we can draw some spectacular images. Before we continue into the turtle language, we provide a few possibilities of drawable art in Figures 8.18 and 8.19.

We have everything we need to implement turtle graphics. Even though this chapter is dedicated to non-functional programming, we will write $\mathcal{L}^*_{\text{TURTLE}}$: an interpreter with turtle programming. Listing 8.405 demonstrates an example program written in $\mathcal{L}^*_{\text{TURTLE}}$, and Figure 8.20 shows the graphical output.

---

[1]We reiterate this topic due to its inclusion only as an exercise in Chapter 5.

Listing 8.403

```
(gfx-open "GRAPHIC*" 640 480)
(gfx-clear)
(value-of
 '(begin
    ((pen-color (255 0 0 255))
     (forward 90)
     (turn 45)
     (pen-color (0 255 0 255))
     (forward 60)
     (turn 90)
     (pen-color (0 0 255 255))
     (forward 30))))
(gfx-refresh)
(gfx-delay 10000)
```

So, as we can see, this language, for now, contains three commands of interest: pen-color, forward, and turn. pen-color changes the current line color. forward moves the turtle in the direction it faces by a certain number of pixels. Lastly, turn changes the angle that the turtle faces. Internally, we will work with radians, but when calling/invoking this function, we will use degrees.

As always, we need to write the recognition functions. Fortunately enough, these are not at all different from the style of previous recognition functions.

Listing 8.404

```
(define begin?
 (λ (exp)
  (and (cons? exp)
       (eqv? (first exp) 'begin)
       (= (length exp) 2)
       (cons? (second exp)))))

(define forward?
 (λ (exp)
  (and (cons? exp)
       (eqv? (first exp) 'forward)
       (= (length exp) 2)
       (number? (second exp)))))

(define turn?
 (λ (exp)
  (and (cons? exp)
       (eqv? (first exp) 'turn)
       (= (length exp) 2)
       (number? (second exp)))))

(define pen-color?
 (λ (exp)
  (and (cons? exp)
       (eqv? (first exp) 'pen-color)
       (= (length exp) 2)
       (cons? (second exp)))))
```

Before we go further and write the evaluation functions, we need to understand our environment structure. Unlike previous nested interpreters (and the root language interpreter we wrote in C), we will not pass the environment to functions alongside the expression. Instead, it will be manipulated globally. Initially, the environment will contain four values: the starting x and y coordinates of the turtle, its angle, and the default pen color. To make the structure easier to understand, we store these as an association list in the environment with tags. For example, we could use the following default environment to initialize the turtle to (100, 100), an angle of 0, and the default pen color to white.

Listing 8.405

```
(define root-env
 `((x . 100) (y . 100) (angle . 0) (color . (255 255 255 255))))
```

With this in mind, `apply-env` and `extend-env` will be slightly different than what we have previously written. The former will receive a tag to search and retrieve the corresponding *rest*, or value, of the pair. E.g., (apply-env 'y) returns 100. The latter modifies the environment to prepend a new value pairing, shadowing previous declarations. For instance, if we modify the turtle's position, we may invoke (extend-env 'x 300), (extend-env 'y 150). These, accordingly, shadow the original bindings. Thus, `root-env` is altered. With these descriptions, we can write `apply-env` and `extend-env`.

Listing 8.406

```
(define root-env
 `((x . 300) (y . 150) (x . 100) (y . 100)
   (angle . 0) (color . (255 255 255 255))))

(define apply-env
 (λ (tag)
  (rest (assv tag root-env))))

(define extend-env
 (λ (tag val)
  (set! root-env (cons (cons tag val) root-env))))
```

Now, we can dive into the evaluation functions. A `begin` invocation receives a list of commands to execute in sequential order. We can simulate this via a `letrec` binding.

Listing 8.407

```
(define value-of-begin
 (λ (exp)
  (let ([loc (second exp)])
   (letrec ([eval-cmd
             (λ (c)
              (cond
               [(null? c) #f]
               [else
                (begin
                 (value-of (first c))
                 (eval-cmd (rest c)))]))])
    (eval-cmd loc)))))
```

Next, forward moves the turtle by n units in the direction it faces. Thus, we will need to use a bit of trigonometry to figure out the correct position of the turtle. After this, we extend the environment to include the new positional bindings. Lastly, we invoke gfx-line to draw a line from the old turtle position to its new location. Additionally, because the color is stored as a list (where the red, green, blue, and alpha channels are the elements), we extract these via list-accessor procedures (e.g., *first*, *second*, *third*, and *fourth*).

Listing 8.408

```
(define value-of-forward
 (λ (exp)
  (let ([n (second exp)])
   (let* ([ox (apply-env 'x)]
          [oy (apply-env 'y)]
          [a (apply-env 'angle)]
          [c (apply-env 'color)]
          [nx (+ ox (* n (cos a)))]
          [ny (+ oy (* n (sin a)))])
    (begin
     (extend-env 'x nx)
     (extend-env 'y ny)
     (gfx-line ox oy nx ny (first c) (second c) (third c) (fourth c)))))))
```

Now that we can move, we certainly want the turtle to be able to turn! Turning is even simpler than moving, since all we do is extend the environment to bind the new angle.

Listing 8.409

```
(define value-of-turn
 (λ (exp)
  (let* ([a (second exp)])
         [oa (apply-env 'angle)]
         [na (+ oa (* a (/ pi 180)))])
   (extend-env 'angle na)))))
```

Finally, we have the easiest procedure of them all: pen-color extends the environment to bind a new color.

Listing 8.410

```
(define value-of-pen-color
 (λ (exp)
  (let ([c (second exp)])
   (begin
    (extend-env 'color c)))))
```

Nicely enough, value-of is, once again, almost identical to other nested interpreters; the only difference being the recognition and evaluation function names.

Listing 8.411

```
(define value-of
 (λ (exp)
  (cond
   [(begin? exp) (value-of-begin exp)]
   [(forward? exp) (value-of-forward exp)]
   [(turn? exp) (value-of-turn exp)]
   [(pen-color? exp) (value-of-pen-color exp)]
   [else 'error])))
```

Trying the program from Listing 8.400 produces the following output:

Figure 8.20: Turtle Listing 8.400 Graphical Output

If we want to complete this small spiral, we can write the following program:

Listing 8.412

```
(value-of
 '(begin
   ((pen-color (255 0 0 255)) (forward 90) (turn 45)
    (pen-color (0 255 0 255)) (forward 80) (turn 45)
    (pen-color (0 0 255 255)) (forward 70) (turn 45)
    (pen-color (255 0 0 255)) (forward 60) (turn 45)
    (pen-color (0 255 0 255)) (forward 50) (turn 45)
    (pen-color (0 0 255 255)) (forward 40) (turn 45)
    (pen-color (255 0 0 255)) (forward 30) (turn 45)
    (pen-color (0 255 0 255)) (forward 20) (turn 45)
    (pen-color (0 0 255 255)) (forward 10) (turn 45))))
```

The thing is, this is a bit cumbersome to write. What if we want to extend this to add a looping construct to repeat expressions multiple times? We, for instance, could add (loop n exp), which evaluates exp n times. Let us add this! We need to write the **recognizer** and reducer.

Listing 8.413

```
(define loop?                        (define value-of-loop
 (λ (exp)                             (λ (exp)
  (and (cons? exp)                     (let ([i 0]
       (eqv? (first exp) 'loop)             [n (second exp)]
       (= (length exp) 3)                   [e (third exp)])
       (number? (second exp)))))       (do [< i n]
                                         (begin
                                          (value-of e)
                                          (set! i (+ i 1)))))))))
```

As a simple test, we can write some code to draw an octagon.

Listing 8.414

```
(value-of
 '(begin
   ((pen-color (255 0 0 255))
    (loop 8
     (begin
      ((forward 45)
       (turn 45)))))))
```

What is intriguing about this interpreter is that we could add symbols, functions, and much more, similar to previous nested interpreters. Get creative!

8.20 $\mathcal{L}^*_{\text{COROUTINE}}$ **Coroutines and Continuations**

In Chapter 11, we will explore concurrent programming, i.e., completing more than one task simultaneously. In this section, however, we narrow our scope and potential of events a bit by discussing coroutines and how to implement them into our interpreter using continuations.

First, we provide a bit of background. A *coroutine* is, at a very high-level, a program that can be stopped and resumed over time. Such programs are great candidates for multi-tasking. So far, all of our programs are sequential and do exactly one thing after another, including the related sections on continuations and continuation-passing style. Writing coroutines and the ability to juggle different tasks simultaneously is an immensely powerful programming construct. The thing is, how exactly can we divert program control between a coroutine?

Let us consider the following scenario: we have some function producer that adds data, e.g., random numbers, to a buffer. We also have another function consumer that removes data from this buffer and prints it to standard output. Both of these functions run indefinitely. This scenario is currently not possible unless we write a separate function that bounces back and forth between calling one and the other. Indeed, this mindset is close to how coroutines work! A producer will add some data to the buffer, then yield its control over to the next task to complete, whether it is another producer or a consumer.[1] Using this, we can depict something akin to a thread, which oversees the execution of a specific action, regardless of its nature.[2]

To illustrate the concept of threads, we will create a program in $\mathcal{L}^*_{\text{COROUTINE}}$ that implements threads as well as the notion of a producer/consumer coroutine. One important detail to note is that we will take advantage of the existing $\mathcal{L}^*_{\text{CONTINUATION}}$ interpreter from Chapter 7 along with some extra additions to add support for identifier (re)assignment, let* bindings, and multi-argument function definitions.[3] The reason for reusing $\mathcal{L}^*_{\text{CONTINUATION}}$ is because we can model coroutines using continuations! Program control is directed between one thread and another (using as many as desired) to complete the coroutine. Swapping between threads, in this fashion, is a perfect practical example of continuations outside tail-call optimization.

---

[1] Nothing restricts us to using exactly one consumer and exactly one producer; if we add more producers, the buffer will fill faster than it can be consumed, and vice versa.

[2] For our purposes, a thread is something that executes a function. "Realistic" threads have limitations imposed by their respective operating system.

[3] letrec is, fortunately, not required in this nested interpreter, but adding the other features still means substantial changes to $\mathcal{L}^*_{\text{CONTINUATION}}$ that we will omit. We use global definitions via define, but it is possible to use a let* block, or even let, to write all shown definitions.

To start, we need to establish properties of a thread. Threads are created using the spawn command, which receives a function denoting the thread action. A thread action must contain a call to the yield function, relinquishing control from that thread to one awaiting in the thread queue (the thread queue is nothing more than a list of threads with associated functions for enqueueing and dequeueing elements). Before the coroutine starts, all threads that execute actions on it are spawned. How, exactly, do we "spawn" a thread? The thread queue contains, interestingly enough, not threads, but continuations! Namely, when we invoke spawn, we push a continuation to the thread queue, denoting a "point of initialization", so to speak. The continuation marks this point of initialization via call/cc. We will constantly refer to the current continuation as a point of reference above the majority of a function body and, because of this, we will write a thread-create-k function accordingly. When we initially invoke spawn, the continuation will be a procedure generated by call/cc, which is added to the rear of the thread queue. Threads/continuations that are awoken, however, receive the AWAKE symbol and, therefore, either begin or resume execution of the coroutine. In these instances, we want to invoke the thunk provided to spawn.

Listing 8.415—Thread Queue Manipulation Functions

```
;; threads-enqueue : Continuation -> Void
;; Pushes a thread (as a continuation) to the existing thread queue.
(define threads-enqueue
  (λ (th)
    (set! threads (append threads (list th)))))

;; threads-dequeue : Void -> Void
;; Removes a thread from the existing thread queue.
(define threads-dequeue
  (λ ()
    (set! threads (rest threads))))

;; threads-rotate : Continuation -> Void
;; Adds a thread (as a continuation) to the thread queue while removing
;; the head of the queue.
(define threads-rotate
  (λ (th)
    (set! threads (append (rest threads) (list th)))))
```

Listing 8.416

```
(define thread-awake?
 (λ (th)
  (eqv? th 'AWAKE)))

(define thread-procedure?
 (λ (th)
  (not (thread-awake? th))))

;; thread-create-k : Void -> Continuation
;; Creates a continuation for a thread.
(define thread-create-k
 (λ ()
  (call/cc (λ (k) (k k)))))

;; spawn : Function -> Void
;; Creates and enqueues a thread to execute the given function.
(define spawn
 (λ (th)
  (let ([cc (thread-create-k)])
   (cond
    [(thread-procedure?)
     (thread-enqueue (list cc))]
    [else (th)]))))
```

Now that we have a way of creating threads, we need a way of running each one sequentially, via run. run, itself, does not manage control over which thread is currently under execution, meaning that it will execute a thread until it relinquishes control to the system. We do, however, need to establish a form of program termination. We will generate a continuation, inside run, that after invoked, receives #t, indicating that the coroutine is complete. So, our "jump-start" condition within run is to check whether or not the generated continuation is true. In all but the most trivial scenario (which includes when the list of threads is empty), we want to retrieve the first thread from the queue and invoke it as if it were a continuation (because it *is* a continuation!). This, in turn, is where we pass 'AWAKE; the continuation created in spawn is, adequately named, awoken by the invocation and, because it receives the aforesaid symbol, runs the thunk, thereby executing a "piece" of the coroutine.

Listing 8.417

```
(define done #f)

;; run : Void -> Void
;; Runs all threads in the queue until the done flag is toggled.
(define run
 (λ ()
  (let ([cc (thread-create-k)])
   (begin
    (set! done (λ () (cc #t)))
    (cond
     [(or (null? threads) done) 'DONE]
     [else
      (let ([curr (first threads)])
       (begin
        (thread-dequeue)
        (curr 'AWAKE)))]))))))
```

We now need the crucial function that defines a coroutine: yield. As we stated, yield relinquishes control from one thread to the next in the thread queue. yield shares much similarity to run; the difference between the two is that we enqueue the newly-instantiated continuation into the queue while, as we said, awakening the next in line.

Listing 8.418

```
;; yield : Void -> Void
;; Returns control to the next thread in the queue.
(define yield
 (λ ()
  (let ([cc (thread-create-k)])
   (cond
    [(thread-procedure? cc)
     (let ([next (first threads)])
      (begin
       (thread-rotate (list cc))
       (next 'AWAKE)))]
    [else #f]))))
```

Lastly, we need to write a function that stops a thread, which we will name join. To join a thread, in this context, means to stop its execution, but allow other threads to continue. Eventually, all threads will invoke join themselves, and the coroutine is complete. When there are no remaining threads in the thread queue, we invoke the done continuation whose value is reset atop run.

Listing 8.419

```
;; join : Void -> Void
;; Polls each thread from the queue, stopping their execution.
(define join
 (λ ()
  (cond
   [(null? threads) (done)]
   [else
    (let ([next (first threads)])
     (begin
      (thread-dequeue)
      (next 'AWAKE)))])))
```

Suppose we want to recreate the producer/consumer pattern described at the start of this section. This would require two thunk coroutines, since a thread can do one or the other, i.e., be a producer or a consumer. We first need to define a buffer, which will be the empty list. We then need a limit to the buffer, defining how many numbers are insertable into the buffer before we reject further productions.

Listing 8.420

```
(define buffer '())
(define BUFFER-MAX 10)
```

The producer will continuously generate random numbers between 1 and 10 and append them to the rear of the buffer, so long as the buffer is not full.

Listing 8.421

```
(define producer
 (λ ()
  (begin
   (cond
    [(< (length buffer) BUFFER-MAX)
     (set! buffer (append buffer (list (random-int 1 10))))]
    [else (printf "producer: full buffer~n")])
   (yield)
   (producer))))
```

The consumer, on the other hand, retrieves and pops values from the buffer and prints them out to standard output, so long as the buffer contains an element.

Listing 8.422

```
(define consumer
 (λ ()
  (begin
   (cond
    [(> (length buffer) 0)
     (let ([next (first buffer)])
      (begin
       (set! buffer (rest buffer))
       (printf "~a~n" next)))]
    [else (printf "consumer: empty buffer~n")])
   (yield)
   (consumer))))
```

Let us create exactly one producer and one consumer to see the behavior. Note that the program never terminates, so we will show only a few lines of output.

Listing 8.423

```
> (spawn producer)          | 8
> (spawn consumer)          | 3
> (run)                     | 6
                            | 9
                            | 5
                            | 7
```

Of course, we get a sequence of random numbers as expected. What happens if we spawn more producers than consumers or vice versa? In the former case, the producer threads will add values to the buffer, the consumer will then remove one, and then the producers will try to add two values again, but receive a message saying the buffer is full. Interestingly, this means that the buffer will never be fully saturated of values. Conversely, when we have more consumers than producers, there will only ever exist one value inside the buffer.

Listing 8.424

```
> (spawn producer)          | 7
> (spawn producer)          | 3
> (spawn consumer)          | ...
> (run)                     | producer: full buffer
                            | 4
                            | producer: full buffer
                            | 3
```

Listing 8.425

```
> (spawn producer)                    8
> (spawn consumer)                    consumer: empty buffer
> (spawn consumer)                    1
> (run)                               consumer: empty buffer
                                      9
                                      consumer: empty buffer
                                      9
```

Modeling Preemption with Macros

Coroutines are not preemptive because they require manual invocation of `yield`. A thread/process/routine is *preemptive* if some process can automatically switch out the currently-executing thread in favor of the next in the queue. It is impossible to model this behavior with our current setup because any thread that does not call `yield` holds control over the routine forever. Even if we, say, created a "master thread" that somehow managed all threads, it would proceed by relinquishing control to the first thread which would then, itself, never relinquish control. It is possible, however, to model preemption with macros. That is, if we define a macro, e.g., `make-thread-thunk-macro`, that receives an identifier and a procedure body, we can have the macro create a `lambda` thunk that invokes itself using the given identifier, but also calls `yield`. Such a representation really only abstracts away the `yield` from the programmer/user of the coroutine, but it is an interesting thought experiment nonetheless. We demonstrate this with the following factorial example. It is important to realize, though, that implementing this into the nested interpreter would be extremely challenging because it would require evaluating a quoted macro expression, something we do not cover in this text.

Listing 8.426

```
(define-macro                          Thread=1, n=10, f=1
 (make-thread-thunk ID BODY)           Thread=2, n=9, f=10
  (begin                               Thread=3, n=8, f=90
   (letrec ([ID                        Thread=4, n=7, f=720
             (λ ()                     Thread=1, n=6, f=5040
              BODY                      Thread=2, n=5, f=30240
              (yield)                   Thread=3, n=4, f=151200
              (ID))])                   Thread=4, n=3, f=604800
     ID)))                              Thread=1, n=2, f=1814400
                                        Thread=2, n=1, f=3628800
(define make-factorial-thunk           'DONE
 (λ (id)
  (make-thread-thunk
   loop
   (begin
    (cond
     [(zero? n) (join)]
     [else #f])
     (printf "Thread=~a, n=~a, f=~a~n"
             id n f)
     (set! f (* n f))
     (set! n (sub1 n)))))))

> (spawn (make-factorial-thunk '1))
> (spawn (make-factorial-thunk '2))
> (spawn (make-factorial-thunk '3))
> (spawn (make-factorial-thunk '4))
> (run)
```

9 Compilation

"Trying to outsmart a compiler defeats much of the purpose of using one."
—Brian W. Kernighan and Phillip James (P. J.) Plauger

Compilers are, understandably, fabulously complex. A *compiler* is a piece of software that takes a program written in a high-level language, e.g., C, and translates it into a semantically-equivalent low-level language such as assembly. Compilers frequently generate machine-dependent assembly code, meaning compiled source code that runs on one machine may not work on another.

There are two popular approaches to compiler design: the traditional "large-pass" architecture, and the incremental "nano-pass" architecture made famous by Sarkar's 2004 paper [Sarkar et al., 2004]. Traditional compiler design consists of five phases: lexical analysis, syntax analysis, semantic analysis, intermediate representation generation, and finally code generation followed by optimization passes [Aho et al., 2006].

In this chapter, we will delve into the challenging endeavor of developing a compiler for subsets of the language utilized by our interpreter.

9.1   Code Generation

An Assembly Primer

Assembly is, effectively, one level above machine instructions written in binary. A compiler, as we stated, translates code written in a high-level language into low-level assembly. Assembly utilizes mnemonic instructions that move and alter values between registers. *Registers* contain values stored as "slots" in the CPU. For instance, if we want to move a value, e.g., 5, into register R0, we may use an instruction that resembles "movq 5, R0". If we want to add two registers together, e.g., R0 and R1, and store their sum in a third register R2, we may use an instruction similar to "add R0, R1, R2". We briefly saw this style of programming in Chapter 8. In this chapter, however, we will explore a specific dialect of assembly in greater detail, alongside how to write code that generates assembly from a high-level language. Refer to Appendix 11.3 for setting up and compiling assembly language source files.

Registers

First, we need to discuss a few preliminary details about the particular assembly dialect that we will use: x64 AT&T Assembly.[1] There are several flavors of assembly that we could work with, but x86 assembly is widely used in introductory computer organization courses, so the modern 64-bit counterpart is a great place to start. We will introduce pieces of this assembly dialect at a time to ease the transition. We have previously discussed what a register is, so it must be the case that assembly has a few named registers, and indeed it does! The four most common registers to work with are rax, rbx, rcx, and rdx. There are also a few more important registers to know of such as rsi, rdi, rsp, and rbp. Finally, there are eight more "general-purpose" registers labeled as r8 to r15. A register, as we recall, holds a value. x64 assembly is 64-bit, meaning each register holds a 64-bit, or eight-byte, value. These values are often referred to as "quad-words" due to the traditional nomenclature of denoting 16-bit values as words, and 32-bit values as double-words. Let us now introduce a few "need-to-know" instructions.

Moving Values

To move data between registers, we use "movq", which stands for "move quad-word value" We can move data or immediate values between registers. For instance, to move the immediate value 9 into register rbx, we prefix the immediate value with a dollar sign $, the register name with a percent sign %, and use the following syntax: movq <src>, <dest>, e.g., movq $9, %rbx. Let us create a test file, hello.s, to showcase what we know.

Listing 9.1—Move Constant into %rbx (hello.s)

```
.section .text
 .global main
main:
  movq $9, %rbx      # Move the constant 9 into rbx.
```

We see that, before our movq instruction, we added .section .text. This indicates that everything declared afterwards is code that should be either loaded or executed somehow. One note about the assembly language is that the use of short mnemonics makes reading the source code as a programmer quite laborious if there is no assembly manual nearby. Thus, we comment almost all instructions to provide humancentric context to their meaning.

---

[1]Brown University provides a nice cheat-sheet reference for several instructions and registers in x64 AT&T Assembly at https://cs.brown.edu/courses/cs033/docs/guides/x64_cheatsheet.pdf.

Text (.text) Segment

Recall that in C, every program must have a main function somewhere, and indeed this also holds true in x64 assembly! Defining functions in assembly, though, is a bit different than C. We need to first declare "main" using the "global" directive, which is effectively identical to how it is defined in a normal C program; other modules have access to this function during the link phase of the compiler and assembler. We then define main as a function by suffixing its name with a colon, and its body as subsequent instructions. Also, all functions must end with a ret statement whose return value is located in the rax register. Because our main function should return 0 upon success, we need to move 0 into rax before our retq instruction (note that void functions disregard whatever is stored in rax).

Listing 9.2—Move Constant into %rbx (hello.s)

```
.section .text
  .global main
main:
  movq $9, %rbx      # Move constant 9 into rax.
  movq $0, %rax      # Return 0 from main.
  retq
```

Is it possible to print the value stored in the rbx register, before we return, to see if our move instruction works as intended? Well, yes, we certainly can, but doing so requires a bit more knowledge than we care do explain at the moment. In due time, we will explain exactly how this printing works, but for the meantime, understand that we can use the following function to output the value currently loaded into the rax register.

Listing 9.3—Move Constant into %rbx (hello.s)

```
.section .data
  fmt: .asciz "%d\n"
.section .text
  .extern printf
  .global main
print_rbx:
  movq %rbx, %rsi         # Move value from rbx to 2nd parameter.
  leaq fmt(%rip), %rdi    # Load fmt variable into 1st parameter.
  movq $0, %rax           # Move 0 to rax for variadic args printf.
  callq printf
  retq
main:
  movq $9, %rbx           # Move 9 to rbx for print_rbx.
  callq print_rbx
  movq $0, %rax           # Return zero from main.
  retq
```

Data (.data) Segment

This slice of code introduces what is known as a directive: the .data directive allows us to define variables in memory as well as string literals. In C, string literals are not defined as variables as we may think; they are, in reality, stored in a separate section of memory called the "data" segment, hence the name. Oftentimes, when using printf, we pass a string literal as the first argument which specifies the format string. Accordingly, we need to store said format string, i.e., fmt used to print the value in the rbx register. fmt is declared as a string that is NUL-terminated using the .asciz directive, which stands for "ascii-zero".

We can compare this assembly source to a roughly-equivalent C source.[1] It is important to realize that we cannot access registers directly in C, so we will need to store our number in a variable to represent the rbx register.[2]

Listing 9.4

```
1    int main(void) {
2      const char *fmt = "%d";
3      int rbx = 9;
4      printf(fmt, rbx);
5      return 0;
6    }
```

We can use gcc to compile not only C, but also assemble programs written in this dialect of assembly as follows: gcc hello.s -o hello, which creates the executable hello. This is then runnable as we have seen before, to which we should receive the correct output of 9.

Suppose we want to declare a number as a local variable. As we will soon see in Chapter 10, local statically-allocated variables are declared on the *stack*. We can access the stack contents, from the return address, via %rbp, which stands for the register holding the "base pointer". Within a function, we must declare how much space is reserved for local variables in the event that they are necessary. If we want to declare space for two quad-words, we must subtract sixteen bytes, eight for each number, from the stack.[3] Before we return from the function, however, we need to re-add sixteen bytes to the stack to clear the space we designated for local variables. Though, one extra bit of information that must be clarified is that, at the beginning of every assembly function we must save the previous stack value by doing a push of %rbp to the stack and then saving %rsp in %rbp to set up the new base pointer. This allows us to easily locate not only local variables, but also parameters (if any exist) of functions on the stack (not to mention that, as we will soon explain, it preserves stack alignment). At the end of every function we restore the previous stack and base pointers by reversing these steps and moving %rsp back to %rsp, then popping the saved value of %rbp from the stack.

---

[1]We use the phrase "roughly-equivalent" because local variables are not *at all* the same as registers on the CPU, as we will show in due time.

[2]This is technically false as we could use *inlined assembly*, but that is beyond the scope of this book.

[3]Why subtraction instead of addition? The stack (memory model) grows downwards, with higher addresses towards the top and lower addresses at the bottom.

Listing 9.5

```
.section .data
  fmt: .asciz "\%d"
.section .text

print_rbx:
  ...

main:
  pushq %rbp
  movq %rsp, %rbp
  subq $16, %rsp        # Allocate 16 bytes for local vars.

  addq $16, %rsp        # Free 16 bytes for local vars.
  movq $0, %rax         # Return zero from main.
  movq %rbp, %rsp
  popq %rbp
  retq
```

Unfortunately, unlike high-level languages, we cannot reference local variables by symbolic name; rather, we must use offsets from the base pointer. These offsets are negatively-indexed. For instance, bytes $0-7$, offset downward from the base pointer, may be used for the first number. Similarly, bytes $8-15$ offset downward may be used for the second. To make our discussion less cumbersome, we denote the first value as x and the second as y. To access the value at an address stored in a register, we enclose the register with parentheses. Offsets are computed by affixing a constant to the front of a stack-access instruction, e.g., -8(%rsp). Local variables are always declared as negative offsets from the base pointer. Thus, to access x, we write -8(%rbp). To access y, write -16(%rbp). So, if we wish to declare two variables x and y with the values 20 and 35 respectively:

Listing 9.6

```
.section .data
  fmt: .asciz "%d\n"
.section .text
  .extern printf
  .global main
main:
  pushq %rbp
  movq %rsp, %rbp
  subq $16, %rsp           # Allocate 16 bytes for local vars.
  movq $20, -8(%rbp)       # Store 20 in "var 1".
  movq $35, -16(%rbp)      # Store 35 in "var 2".
  addq $16, %rsp           # Free 16 bytes for local vars.
  movq %rbp, %rsp
  popq %rbp
  movq $0, %rax            # Return zero from main.
  retq
```

What if we want to define a global numeric variable like fmt? All we need to do is use another directive for numeric quad-words, i.e., .quad. For instance, if we want to define a global variable, num1, with a value of 200:

Listing 9.7

```
.section .data
  num1: .quad 200
  fmt: .asciz "%d\n"
```

Conveniently enough, we can also use movq to move numeric literals between registers and memory.

Listing 9.8

```
.section .text
  .global main
main:
  ...
  movq num1(%rip), %rbx
  callq print_rbx
  ...
  retq
```

What if we want to do something slightly more useful than just playing with numbers and move operations, e.g., calling functions? Functions take a bit of work to mess around with in assembly, and we will exemplify this point with our definition of printf.

Calling Convention

First, note that there is a *calling convention* that must be obeyed by the caller and callee of functions. The main rule, when invoking a function, certain arguments should be stored in specific registers. E.g., argument 1 is stored in %rdi, argument 2 is stored in %rsi, argument 3 in %rdx, argument 4 in %rcx, argument 5 in %r8, and argument 6 in %r9 (see Figure 9.10). Any remaining arguments should be pushed to the stack. In our definition of print_rbx where we call printf, we know that everything after the first argument is the data to-be formatted via printf. Thus, when outputting the value in the rbx register, we move the value to the register designated for argument 2, namely %rsi. Argument 1, on the other hand, is a format string. Because strings are pointers, we need to load the address of the format string into %rdi. Hence, we use leaq, which stands for "load effective address (quadword)", and says that we will load the starting address of fmt into the rdi register. There is a special register that we use when referencing the address of global variables: %rip. If we wish to load the address of some variable declared in the .data segment, we need to load its address via leaq, offset from %rip, into a register (understanding the reasoning behind this logic is not essential to our primer on assembly and compilation). Finally, printf is special in that it is a variadic-argument function, which we have taken advantage of hundreds of times by now. Being that this is the case, x64 assembly has an oddly particular protocol for handling variadic-argument functions: %rax should hold the value of how many SSE registers will be used in the function. SSE registers are, effectively, 128-bit registers for storing floating-point values; we will investigate these in greater detail later in the chapter. Thus, any instance of invoking a variadic-argument procedure always results in storing 0 in %rax. Finally, we invoke the function via callq. The return value from a function must be stored in the rax register (if there is no return value, this register is, effectively, ignored). Because neither printf nor print_rbx return a value, we simply end off the function with a retq.

Memory Alignment

The x86/x64 assembly standard requires that all callers align the stack on sixteen-byte boundaries. Calling a function places its return address on the stack, thereby misaligning the stack. To compensate, we push the base pointer to the stack and restore it upon termination of the program. By pushing the eight-byte base pointer, our code intentionally realigns the stack. Therefore, the system, when calling main, pushes an eight-byte address to the stack, which warrants our choice to push and pop the base pointer at the beginning and end of the main function.

Using this logic, let us write a function that prints *any* value that is passed, as an argument. We can use print_rbx in our definition; namely, we move the value from %rdi into %rbx, then invoke print_rbx. We can then invoke print_number as follows:

Listing 9.9

```
.section .text
  .global main
  ...
print_number:
  pushq %rbp
  movq %rsp, %rbp
  movq %rdi, %rbx
  callq print_rbx
  movq %rbp, %rsp
  popq %rbp
  retq
main:
  ...
  movq $300, %rdi
  callq print_number
  ...
  retq
```

Let us tie in a few arithmetic instructions, as well as the use of scanf. scanf is an infamous and dangerous C function because of its lack of error-handling features and how easy it is to write code that induces security vulnerabilities, e.g., buffer-overflow attacks; hence why we heavily discouraged its use during our discussion on user input in Chapter 5 in favor of getline, fgets, and sscanf. Regardless, we will make use of it in our assembly programs. Let us write a small example of reading a number (and only a number!) from the user using scanf in C.

Listing 9.10

```
1  #include <stdio.h>
2
3  int main(void) {
4    int x;
5    scanf("%d", &x);
6    return 0;
7  }
```

scanf reads from standard input, expecting data formatted according to its first argument, i.e., a format string. The data that is received is stored in the variables passed as arguments. These variables must be addresses, however, since scanf wants to know *where* to store any received/scanned values. Now, we know enough to write a basic assembly program. Suppose we want to write a program that receives two numbers and computes the sum, difference, product, and quotient of the two values (assuming both are integers and a non-zero divisor). As we stated previously, these values shall be local to main, meaning we need to allocate space. Because we push eight bytes to the stack with the base pointer, we allocate (only) sixteen bytes for local variables, since the stack remains aligned.

Listing 9.11

```
.section .data
  infmt: .asciz "%d"
  sumoutfmt: .asciz "The sum is %d\n"
.section .text
  .extern scanf
  .extern printf
  .global main
main:
  pushq %rbp
  movq %rsp, %rbp
  subq $16, %rsp
  ...
  retq
```

Now, we know that scanf must receive a format string that reads a number, and its second argument is the address of some number. Since we store local variables on the stack, to get the address of a variable, we may use leaq. E.g., to get the address located at %rbp, we invoke leaq on the rbp register using parentheses. Recall that parentheses allow us to access the value at a memory location if we do not load the address. On the off chance that we do, we, of course, retrieve its address. We intend to store the two values we read in via scanf at memory addresses pointed to by %rbp offset by minus eight and minus sixteen bytes respectively. Then, like printf, scanf is a variadic-argument procedure, meaning we must modify the value in %rax (in this case, we store zero). Now, -8(%rbp) stores the first number scanned by scanf, and -16(%rbp), i.e., eight-bytes above the address pointed to by -16(%rbp), stores the second number. We can now perform basic arithmetic on these numbers! To compute their sum, we need to use an available register, e.g., rbx. Therefore, we move the first number into rbx, then add to it the second number. Lastly, to print the sum, using printf is a viable option.

Listing 9.12

```
.section .data
  infmt: .asciz "%d"
  sumoutfmt: .asciz "The sum is %d\n"
.section .text
  .extern scanf
  .extern printf
  .global main
main:
  pushq %rbp
  movq %rsp, %rbp
  subq $16, %rsp           # Allocate 16 bytes.
  ## Read first number from user. ##
  leaq -8(%rbp), %rsi      # Move the first address at rbp into rsi.
  leaq infmt(%rip), %rdi   # Load the input format string into rdi.
  movq $0, %rax            # Clear rax since it is a var-args procedure.
  callq scanf
  ## Read second number from user. ##
  leaq -16(%rbp), %rsi     # Move the second address at rbp into rsi.
  leaq infmt(%rip), %rdi   # Reload the input format.
  movq $0, %rax
  callq scanf
  ## Setup the output sum. ##
  movq -8(%rsp), %rbx           # Move first address into rbx.
  addq -16(%rsp), %rbx          # Compute sum of two values.
  movq %rbx, %rsi               # Move sum into second parameter.
  leaq sumoutfmt(%rip), %rdi    # Load output format into first parameter.
  movq $0, %rax
  callq printf
  addq $16, %rsp                # Free 24 bytes; 16 for vars, 8 for alignment.
  movq %rbp, %rsp
  popq %rbp
  retq
```

Arrays

Arrays, in this language, must have a predefined (constant) size. Therefore, it is illegal to create an array of some size n, where n is unknown at compile-time.[1] What is the process of compiling arrays? Well, it is very similar to how it is done in C: we declare enough space to store all elements in the array on the stack, just like variables. Each slot in the array will be eight bytes long since the only data type that we care about is eight-byte integers. We know from our discussion on arrays and pointers in Chapter 5 that we can access array indices using pointer arithmetic, and in fact, this is the only way to index array elements in x64 assembly! So, before we begin to define and compile our language, let us discuss the structure of arrays in assembly.

Suppose we wish to write a program that computes the average number of an array of five integers. Let us write this program in C first, then assembly.

---

[1]Just like it is possible to use C library functions in assembly, we can also invoke dynamic memory allocation functions such as malloc. Our comment assumes forgoing dynamically-allocated arrays.

Listing 9.13—Computing the Average of Five Integers Using Arrays

```
1   #include <stdio.h>
2
3   int main(void) {
4     long arr[5];
5     long sum = 0;
6     long average = 0;
7     long i = 0;
8     // Populate the array.
9     arr[0] = 100;
10    arr[1] = 91;
11    arr[2] = 62;
12    arr[3] = 77;
13    arr[4] = 84;
14    for (i = 0; i < 5; i++) {
15      sum += arr[i];
16    }
17    average = sum / 5;
18    printf("%ld\n", average)
19    return 0;
20  }
```

As we see, we declare four variables: a counter for the loop, a placeholder for the running sum and average, and an array of values.

Let us compute the number of bytes required to store these local variables. The long datatype is eight bytes in size, and we have an array of five long values. Therefore, the array uses 40 bytes. The other three (long) variables take up 24 bytes for a total of 64 bytes. Now, we know how much space to subtract and add from the stack pointer in the main prologue and epilogue.

Listing 9.14

```
main:
  pushq %rbp
  movq %rsp, %rbp
  subq $64, %rsp

  callq printf
  addq $64, %rsp
  movq %rbp, %rsp
  popq %rbp
  retq
```

Suppose we designate the array to be the first local value declared on the stack. Since array index memory addresses grow from the bottom-up, the lowest index, i.e., 0, will have the lowest memory address and, therefore, the highest (absolute) offset value from the base pointer. Given that the array is the first local variable declared, index $n-1$ is located at -8(%rbp), and index 0 is located at $-8 \times l$, where l is the length of the array.[1] Let us see this written out.

---

[1] Due to how clunky $-8 \cdot l$ appears, we instead opt to use the $\times$ symbol to denote multiplication.

Listing 9.15

```
main:
  pushq %rbp
  movq %rsp, %rbp
  subq $64, %rsp
  ...
  movq $84, -8(%rbp)      # arr[4] = 84
  movq $77, -16(%rbp)     # arr[3] = 77
  movq $62, -24(%rbp)     # arr[2] = 62
  movq $91, -32(%rbp)     # arr[1] = 91
  movq $100, -40(%rbp)    # arr[0] = 100
```

Array indexing is not quite as intuitive as one may think. The general formula for computing the offset is as follows. Let A be an array, and let $|A|$ denote the number of elements A may hold. Then, let i be the index to access, and h is the address of said index. Notice that we have to negate the calculation to produce a negative offset value.

$$h = -(|A|-i)$$

In our code example, we want to compute the sum of each element in the array. An ideal situation would be to use a loop to keep track of the current offset. We can load the address of an array index by using "scale offset indexing".[1] Consider the following line of x64 assembly: movq (%rbp, %r13, 8), %r13. This calculation says that we want to load the address pointed to by this offset calculation: using the address pointed to by %rbp, offset by 8 × %r13. Thus, to store the address of index 1 in %rax, we write the following:

Listing 9.16

```
main:
  ...
  movq $-4, %r13              # r13 = -(|A| (5) - i (1))
  movq (%rbp, %r13, $8), %r13 # r13 = rbp + 8 * r13, i.e., arr[1]
```

To store a value in the index pointed to by %r13, we use a form of the dereference operator. By enclosing the register in parentheses, we treat it as an address and not a value.

Listing 9.17

```
main:
  ...
  movq $84, (%r13)
```

Let us continue to write the "average" program. We certainly need a loop. Assume that -64(%rbp) is the address of i and contains the length of the array, i.e., 5.

---

[1]The term "scale" refers to the size of each element, and by multiplying the scale by the index, we produce an offset from the zeroth element of the array pointer.

Listing 9.18

```
main:
    ...
loop:
    movq -64(%rbp), %r13          # rax = i
    cmpq $0, %r13                 # is i = 0?
    jz done
    movq $5, %r13
    subq -64(%rbp), %r13          # r13 = 5 - r13
    negq %r13                     # r13 = -r13
    movq (%rbp, %r13, 8), %r13    # r13 = [(rbp + 8 * r13)]
    addq %r13, -48(%rbp)          # sum += r13
    subq $1, -64(%rbp)            # i -= 1
    jmp loop
done:
    ...
```

System Calls

Most introduction-to-assembly tutorial mediums begin by writing the stereotypical "Hello, world!" program. Writing said program using the external `printf` function is rather simple and straightforward. On the other hand, there exist functions that are not part of the C library and are, instead, system calls. A system call is a function that interacts directly with the operating system. `printf` is an abstraction over a system call that outputs data to standard output. What if, on the off chance, `printf` is unavailable? How can we output data to standard out? By using a system call, of course!

Outputting strings of text to standard output, using only system calls, involves usage of the `write` system call. `write` receives three arguments: a file descriptor `fd` where data is written, a buffer/sequence of bytes `buffer` to output to `fd`, and the number of bytes to output `n`. Suppose we wish to output the string, "Hello, world!\n" to standard output. We need three other pieces of information: the standard output file descriptor, the number of bytes that our string contains, and the system call identifier for `write`. We provide a reference chart for some frequently-used system calls below.

Id. No. (%rax)	System Call
0	sys_read
1	sys_write
2	sys_open
3	sys_close
4	sys_stat

Reading the chart says that the system call identifier is stored in %rax, and the relevant system call for `write` is 1. The file descriptor for standard output is also 1. Lastly, our message contains fifteen bytes because it holds fourteen characters plus one for the NUL-byte. We use the same process for passing arguments to functions for supplying the arguments for a system call: the first argument is stored in %rdi, second in %rsi, third in %rdx, and so on. The only differences are that we set the system call identifier in %rax, and invoke the system call via `syscall`. Let us see an example.

Listing 9.19

```
.section .data                              | Hello, world!
  msg: .asciz "Hello, world!\n"             |
  msglen: .quad 15                          |
.section .text                              |
  .global main                              |
main:                                       |
  pushq %rbp                                |
  movq %rsp, %rbp                           |
  movq $1, %rdi          # fd = %rdi (stdout: 1)   |
  leaq msg(%rip), %rsi   # buffer = %rsi (msg)     |
  movq msglen(%rip), %rdx # n = %rdx (msglen)      |
  movq $1, %rax          # syscall = 1      |
  syscallN the address                      |
  movq %rbp, %rsp                           |
  popq %rbp                                 |
  retq                                      |
```

There are several other system calls that we could use. One disadvantage of them is that they severely handicap the programmer—outputting, say, format strings, is excruciatingly difficult without `printf`. There is, however, a way that we can output raw bytes directly. Recall that the second argument to `write`: namely `buffer`, is a `const void *`, meaning it does not have to be a `const char *`, i.e., a string. If we wish to output a character stored in a local variable, we can easily do so. All we must do is convert a quadword integer into a quadword pointer. In C, we would do this by retrieving the address of a variable via the ampersand operator. We can mimic this result on a non-pointer variable by using `leaq`. So, imagine we wish to output the character 'A'. This corresponds to the ASCII value 65, meaning that if we store 65 in a char, i.e., a `.byte`, the program will output 'A' when invoked with a system call.

Listing 9.20

```
.section .data                                              The character to
  firststr: .asciz "The character to display is "           display is A.
  firststrlen: .quad 28
  secondstr: .asciz ".\n"
  secondstrlen: .quad 3
  val: .byte 65
.section .text
  .global main
main:
  pushq %rbp
  movq %rsp, %rbp

  # Output the first string.
  movq $1, %rdi
  leaq firststr(%rip), %rsi
  movq firststrlen(%rip), %rdx
  movq $1, %rax
  syscall

  # Output the byte. Treat as char pointer.
  movq $1, %rdi
  leaq val(%rip), %rsi
  movq $1, %rdx    # One byte value.
  movq $1, %rax
  syscall

  # Output the second string.
  movq $1, %rdi
  leaq secondstr(%rip), %rsi
  movq secondstrlen(%rip), %rdx
  movq $1, %rax
  syscall

  movq %rbp, %rsp
  popq %rbp
  retq
```

Suppose that we want to read an ASCII character from standard input, then output it to the user via standard output using only system calls.[1] Well, we first need to declare a section of memory reserved for an input buffer. We can use the .bss segment to declare storage for variables that by default can only be zero (0). In C, we may do something similar with `fgets` wherein we create a `char[]` buffer of some predetermined size. Because we plan to read only one character from standard input (plus the trailing newline character), we can declare a buffer of size 2 with the `.space` directive. In general, however, it is advised to declare a "more-than-necessary" amount of space. As is typically done in C, we might declare an input buffer to hold 1024 bytes.

Listing 9.21

```
.section .bss
  buffer: .space 2
.section .text
  .global main
main:
  ...
```

---

[1] This is commonly called an "echo" program.

Let us now **write** the corresponding code to read a character from standard input using system **calls**. As we know from the above table, the system call identifier for sys_read is 0. Otherwise, the arguments are identical to sys_write, with the only exception being that the supplied buffer is populated with whatever the user enters.

Listing 9.22

```
.section .bss
  buffer: .space 2
.section .text
  .global main
main:
  pushq %rbp
  movq %rsp, %rbp
  movq $0, %rdi              # Standard input file descriptor.
  leaq buffer(%rip), %rsi    # Buffer for data read.
  movq $2, %rdx              # Max num. chars to read is 2.
  movq $0, %rax              # sys_read identifier.
  syscall

  movq %rbp, %rsp
  popq %rbp
  retq
```

At this **point, we** can invoke the write system call similar to how it was done before.

Listing 9.23

```
main:
  ...
  movq $1, %rdi              # Standard output file descriptor.
  leaq buffer(%rip), %rsi    # Buffer for data to write from.
  movq $2, %rdx              # Max number of chars to display.
  movq $1, %rax              # sys_write identifier.
  syscall
  ...
  retq
```

Running the **program** allows us to type any key, and the program echos it back.

Exercise 9.1. (★★)

Write a **program** to output the number 127 using only system calls. Do not use .asciz to do **this.** Hint: use .byte with comma-separated values to designate an array, e.g., .byte 90, 80, 70. If you try to declare the array as .byte 1, 2, 7, it will not **work! Why?**

Exercise 9.2. (★★)

Write a **program that** reads an (eight-byte) integer from standard input and outputs said **integer to** standard output only using system calls. Hint: it is perfectly acceptable to **echo** the buffer read from standard input.

Exercise 9.3. (★★)

Write an x64 **assembly** function that computes the power of some base integer b raised to some **exponent** x. You can do this recursively or iteratively.

Exercise 9.4. ($\star\star$)

Write an x64 assembly function that converts the ASCII representation of an integer to its integer counterpart. Return this value from the function. For example, the number 5 has an ASCII value of 53. Assume that only ASCII values that represent the digits between 0 and 9 are possible arguments to the function.

Exercise 9.5. ($\star\star\star\star$)

Using the previous exercises as a basis, write a program that reads an integer from standard input, writes that integer to standard output using only system calls *and by storing the number in a quadword*. In other words, do not store the number as a string (aside from the input buffer). This is a rather challenging problem, and it may be helpful to attempt this in C or one of our interpreter's languages before trying it in assembly. Hint: sys_read stores the number of characters it read from standard input as a return value in %rax.[1] Use this value to mathematically store the ASCII numeric characters from a string as a quadword. Think about it this way: 521 is equivalent to $(10^2 \cdot 5) + (10^1 \cdot 2) + (10^0 + 1)$.

---

[1] It also returns the newline character in its length so be aware!

9.2   Compiling $\mathcal{L}^-_{\mathrm{PF1}}$ to $\mathcal{L}^-_{\mathrm{PF1}_{x64}}$

With our primitive knowledge of x64 assembly, we can finally begin to write a compiler that converts code written in the language of our interpreters into x64 assembly! Instead of attempting to write the compiler in C (which would prove to be a laborious undertaking), we will write all of our code in the interpreter (that is right—our interpreter is now powerful enough to parse and compile programs!). As with our incremental definitions and implementations of the interpreter and languages for the said interpreter, we will grow our compiler in stages, adding more features and complexities with each. This sub-journey begins similarly to how it started for the interpreter: with $\mathcal{L}_{\mathrm{PF1}}$, except it is not quite $\mathcal{L}_{\mathrm{PF1}}$; our first compiler will compile expressions that print integers. Therefore, since this is a largely stripped-down language, we will classify it as $\mathcal{L}^-_{\mathrm{PF1}}$. Therefore, our compiler will take source code written in $\mathcal{L}^-_{\mathrm{PF1}}$ and compile it to $\mathcal{L}^-_{\mathrm{PF1}_{x64}}$.

```
expr       ::=   '(call (print' ' ' constant '))'
constant   ::=   [0-9]+
pf1-       ::=   expr*
```

Figure 9.1: Extended BNF Grammar for $\mathcal{L}^-_{\mathrm{PF1}}$

There are several steps to take when writing a compiler for $\mathcal{L}^-_{\mathrm{PF1}}$. We need to generate the assembly preamble, i.e., data segment, compute the required local stack space for main, convert each instruction into an assembly counterpart, then generate the cleanup for main. Our compiler will be designed in several parts that, when combined, generate x64 assembly for a program written in a slightly-extended version $\mathcal{L}^-_{\mathrm{PF1}}$. We can write a procedure compile that receives a list of statements (which, themselves, are lists), and compiles those statements. Note that we will make modifications to compile as we design the compiler.

Listing 9.24

```
(define compile
 (λ (los)
  (begin
   ...)))
```

Let us now describe the variant of $\mathcal{L}^-_{\mathrm{PF1}}$ that we will compile: $\mathcal{L}^-_{\mathrm{PF1}_{x64}}$. It supports exactly one function invocation: printing of variables with a newline via print, and binary operators, e.g., (call print ...), where ... is any number. The reason for such an odd syntax will become apparent later on.

Assembly Preamble

Assembly programs that use global variables or string literals must have a data segment as we have previously seen with printf/scanf. Because $\mathcal{L}^-_{PF1_{x64}}$ contains a print procedure, we need a corresponding format string that outputs a number and a newline. Additionally, the preamble will declare the .text segment, printf as an .extern function, and define main as .global. It makes the most sense to write a function that outputs the data to standard output via printf. Afterward, we can add this as the first line to the begin clause of compile.

Listing 9.25

```
(define generate-preamble
 (λ (los)
  (begin
   (printf ".section .data~n")
   (printf " outnumfmt: .asciz ~"~a~n~"~n")
   (printf ".section .text~n")
   (printf " .extern printf~n")
   (printf " .global main~n")))))

(define compile
 (λ (los)
  (begin
   (generate-preamble los))))
```

Statement Reduction

Statement reduction is the heart of our compiler. That is, we take our statements written in the given input language and reduce them into assembly language counterparts. We can write a procedure similar to value-of from our interpreters. reduce, that receives a statement and converts it into its assembly counterpart.

Listing 9.26

```
(define reduce
 (λ (stmt)
  (cond
   [...])))
```

$\mathcal{L}^-_{PF1}$ recognizes only two types of statements: (numeric) constants and function calls. Realistically, though, $\mathcal{L}^-_{PF1}$ only directly reduces a call, since constants cannot be reduced on their own without some integrated context. Let us add these functions to reduce, then work on their implementation. Each recognizer and reducer will be invoked here.

Listing 9.27

```
(define reduce
 (λ (exp)
  (cond
   [(constant? exp) (reduce-constant exp)]
   [(call? exp) (reduce-call exp)]
   [else (printf "ERR: cannot reduce ~a~n" exp)])))
```

Now we can write the recognizer and reducer for a constant. Constants are simple in that they reduce to themselves. The recognizer is similarly trivial since it is effectively a wrapper around the number? predicate.

Listing 9.28

```(define constant? (λ (exp) (number? exp)))```	```(define reduce-constant (λ (exp) exp))```

On the other hand, a function call is a list where the *second* is the function name, and the *rest of the rest* is the list of arguments passed to the function. Of course, we know that our current language only supports `print` calls, but generalizing the approach is handy. Let us implement the recognizer first, as the corresponding reducer is more complex.

Listing 9.29

```
(define call?
 (λ (exp)
  (and (cons? exp)
       (>= (length exp) 2)
       (eqv? (first exp) 'call))))
```

The `call` reducer should extract a few components out into a `let*` block, namely the procedure name and its arguments.

Listing 9.30

```
(define reduce-call
 (λ (exp)
  (let* ([procname (second exp)]
         [procargs (rest (rest exp))])
   ...)))
```

Now, we perform a case analysis on the procedure name and, if we invoke `print`, we must output a series of instructions to invoke `printf` in assembly. We could certainly use our built-in `printf` function to output instructions directly, but this is a bit cumbersome and prone to errors. Why not write a procedure for outputting instructions?

There are three broad types of instructions, where each type corresponds to the number of arguments it receives. Namely, some instructions receive one argument, some receive two, and the majority receive three. We will implement two and three-argument printing functions for the time being.

When we output an instruction, there are a few considerations to make: whether an operand references a register or is a constant. Let us write two functions: `print-instruction2` and `print-instruction3`. The arguments to the former are the instruction to use and its operand. The arguments to the latter are the instruction to use and its two operands. We will extract the components out in `let*` blocks. In addition, we should invoke `reduce` on the operands as they may themselves need to be reduced (this is impossible in the current language, but again, future-proofing is important!).

Listing 9.31

```
(define print-instruction2
 (λ (stmt)
  (let* ([op (first stmt)]
         [rand1 (reduce (second stmt))])
   ...)))

(define print-instruction3
 (λ (stmt)
  (let* ([op (first stmt)]
         [rand1 (reduce (second stmt))]
         [rand2 (reduce (third stmt))])
   ...)))
```

print-instruction2, for the current language, needs to consider only two "types" of operands: constants and registers. If its operand is a constant, we affix a dollar sign, $, in front. Otherwise, we affix a percent sign %. We already have a recognizer for constants, so let us write one for registers. As we discussed, there are sixteen available registers. So, if we store these in a list, we can check to see if something is a list by determining if it is a member of said list.

Listing 9.32

```
(define registers '(rax rbx rcx rdx rsp rbp rsi rdi
                     r8 r9 r10 r11 r12 r13 r14 r15))

(define register?
 (λ (exp)
  (member exp registers)))
```

Listing 9.33

```
(define print-instruction2
 (λ (op rand)
  (let* ([res-rand (reduce rand)])
   (cond
    [(constant? res-rand) (printf " ~a $~a~n" op res-rand)]
    [(register? res-rand) (printf " ~a %~a~n" op res-rand)]
    [else #f]))))
```

print-instruction3 is slightly more involved. Since the destination must always be a register, instructions with a constant destination argument (constant-constant and register-constant) are impossible. The two other combinations with the destination as a register (register-register and register-constant) are valid and fair game.

Listing 9.34

```
(define print-instruction3
 (λ (op src dest)
  (let ([res-src (reduce src)]
        [res-dest (reduce dest)])
   (cond
    [(and (register? res-src) (register? res-dest))
     (printf " ~a %~a, %~a~n" op res-src res-dest)]
    [(and (constant? res-src) (register? res-dest))
     (printf " ~a $~a, %~a~n" op res-src res-dest)]
    [else #f]))))
```

These functions allow us to simply pass symbols that are conveniently format-ted into a printf, meaning we do not need to worry about outputting an incorrect symbol. With this, we can finish reduce-call's print handler: output three in-structions to move the argument into %rsi, load the output number format string into %rdi, zero out %rax (remember why we need to do this from the note in the assembly primer), then invoke printf. Notice, however, that we still must use a leaq to invoke printf. This is because outnumfmt is neither a register nor a con-stant, but a variable that resides in global memory. Our language, as of now, has no understanding of variables whatsoever, so the print-instruction functions will not work.

Listing 9.35

```
(define reduce-call
 (λ (exp)
  (let* ([procname (second exp)]
         [procargs (rest (rest exp))])
   (cond
    [(eqv? procname 'print)
     (let* ([arg (first procargs)])
      (begin
       (print-instruction3 ' movq arg 'rsi)
       (printf " leaq outnumfmt(%rip), %rdi~n")
       (print-instruction3 ' movq 0 'rax)
       (print-instruction2 ' callq 'printf)))]
    [else #f]))))
```

With reduce-call and reduce-constant out of the way, we can integrate reduce into a function that reduces a list of statements recursively. Then, we can invoke said function in compile after generating the preamble. Because our in-put is assumed to be a list of statements (represented as lists), we need a recursive helper function to reduce each statement one-by-one.

Listing 9.36

```
(define reduce-statements
 (λ (los)
  (cond
   [(null? los) (printf "")]
   [else
    (begin
     (reduce (first los))
     (reduce-statements (rest los)))])))

(define compile
 (λ (los)
  (begin
   (generate-preamble)
   (reduce-statements los))))
```

Function Prologue

All functions in assembly (and C and other languages) contain what is known as the prologue and an epilogue. Essentially, the prologue "sets up" the function, whereas the epilogue "tears it down". By setting up, we mean that it pushes callee-saved registers to the stack and allocates memory for local variables. Understanding what a "callee-saved" register is, at this point, is unnecessary. Similarly, we will explore local variables in the next section. For now, we just need to know that the `main` function has the following prologue. The general idea is as follows: we declare the existence of the main function. Then, push %rbp to the stack. Finally, we move %rsp into %rbp. Again, we will explore what these concepts mean in greater detail later on. Because all functions have a prologue and epilogue, it makes sense to generalize this function as much as possible by printing a symbol representing the current function being reduced.

Listing 9.37

```
(define generate-prologue
 (λ (los)
  (begin
   (printf "~a:~n" 'main)
   (print-instruction2 'pushq 'rbp)
   (print-instruction3 'movq 'rsp 'rbp))))
```

The `main` function prologue must come before reducing the statements in its body.

Listing 9.38

```
(define compile
 (λ (los)
  (begin
   (generate-preamble)
   (generate-prologue los)
   (reduce-statements los))))
```

Function Epilogue

Function epilogues are the mirror of function prologues; that is, we restore %rbp to %rsp, and pop the old value of %rbp off the stack and, therefore, back into the register.

Listing 9.39

```
(define generate-epilogue
 (λ (los)
  (begin
   (print-instruction3 'movq 'rbp 'rsp)
   (print-instruction2 'popq 'rbp)
   (printf "ret~n"))))
```

The `main` function epilogue must come after reducing the statements in its body.

Listing 9.40

```
(define compile
 (λ (los)
  (begin
   (generate-preamble)
   (generate-prologue los)
   (reduce-statements los)
   (generate-epilogue los))))
```

So, we can now compile very simple programs that print integers to standard output. Let us write one and examine its assembly output.

Listing 9.41

```
> (compile '((call print 5)))
```

```
.section .data
  outnumfmt: .asciz "%d\n"
.section .text
  .extern printf
  .global main
main:
  pushq %rbp
  movq %rsp, %rbp
  movq $5, %rsi
  leaq outnumfmt(%rip), %rdi
  movq $0, %rax
  callq printf
  movq %rbp, %rsp
  popq %rbp
  retq
```

We obey the rules of the prologue and epilogue and invoke `printf`, which outputs the integer 5 to standard out. Programs in $\mathcal{L}_{\mathrm{PF1}}^{-}$ are not restricted to one instruction, meaning we can output multiple numbers if so desired.

Listing 9.42

```
(compile '((call print 5)
           (call print 10)
           (call print 15)))
```

Compiling $\mathcal{L}_{\mathrm{PF1}}$ to $\mathcal{L}_{\mathrm{PF1}_{x64}}$

Compiling very simple print statements is exhilarating to see for the first time, but it rapidly loses its appeal after trying a few different integers. To spice up this adventure, let us compile $\mathcal{L}_{\mathrm{PF1}}$ to $\mathcal{L}_{\mathrm{PF1}_{x64}}$. The only noteworthy addition (no pun intended) from $\mathcal{L}_{\mathrm{PF1}}^{-}$ to $\mathcal{L}_{\mathrm{PF1}}$ is that we can inline arithmatic expressions into the print statement. That is, expressions of the form, e.g., (call print (+ 5 10)) are reducible.

```
expr       ::=   '(call (print' ' ' (constant | arithexpr) '))'
arithexpr  ::=   '(' binop ' ' constant ' ' constant ')'
binop      ::=   '+' | '-' | '*' | '/'
constant   ::=   [0-9]+
pf1        ::=   expr*
```

Figure 9.2: Extended BNF Grammar for $\mathcal{L}_{\mathrm{PF1}}$

Being that all four of the primitive arithmetic operators are implemented in similar manners, we will only implement addition, i.e., addq. Let us write a recognizer for an addition arithmatic expression.

Listing 9.43

```
(define add?
 (λ (exp)
  (and (cons? exp)
       (= (length exp) 3)
       (eqv? (first exp) '+))))
```

Its reducer is trivial—we reduce both operands, move the result of the first operand into %rbx, add the second operand into %rbx, and finally return the symbol 'rbx to designate that the result is stored in %rbx. Though, this introduces a slight problem with our reducer: registers do not currently reduce to anything. This is easily fixable by adding a reduce-register function that, identical to constants, reduces to itself. This allows us to fully implement reduce-add and amend our definition of reduce.

Listing 9.44

```
(define reduce-register
 (λ (exp)
  exp))

(define reduce-add
 (λ (exp)
  (let* ([rand1 (reduce (second exp))]
         [rand2 (reduce (third exp))])
   (begin
    (print-instruction3 'movq rand1 'rbx)
    (print-instruction3 'addq rand2 'rbx)
    'rbx))))
```

Listing 9.45

```
(define reduce
 (λ (exp)
  (cond
   [(constant? exp) (reduce-constant exp)]
   [(register? exp) (reduce-register exp)]
   [(variable? exp) (reduce-variable exp)]
   [(add? exp) (reduce-add exp)]
   [(var? exp) (reduce-var exp)]
   [(call? exp) (reduce-call exp)]
   [else (printf "ERR: cannot reduce ~a~n" exp)])))
```

Let us write a program that computes the sum of the constants 5 and 10, and look at the corresponding assembly instructions.

Listing 9.46

```
> (compile '((call print (+ 5 10))))

        ...
        movq $5, %rbx
        addq $10, %rbx
        movq %rbx, %rsi
        ...
```

As we see, we utilize the rbx register to store the sum of this computation. Namely, we move \$5 into %rbx, then add to it the second immediate value \$10. Because we immediately invoke a call to print, this result is transferred into %rsi. Interestingly, our compiler would certainly generate instructions to compute the sum of some arbitrary expression without a place to store it, i.e., as an argument to print. This would be meaningless, however, since the program would never re-use said computation.

One important point to take note of is that arithmatic expressions may only receive constants as arguments to the operator. This is because of how we apply an arithmetic operator to its arguments: the first operand is moved into %rbx and the second (operand) has the arithmetic operator applied to it and the value stored in %rbx. This inherently limits the power of our expressions for the time being. Once we introduce variables, though, we can circumvent this issue by assigning sub-expression results to temporary variables.

Exercise 9.6. ($\star$)
Add the remaining three binary operators for subtraction, multiplication, and division.

9.3 Compiling $\mathcal{L}_{PF2}$ to $\mathcal{L}_{PF2_{x64}}$

$\mathcal{L}_{PF1}$ compiles only very simple expressions: those that compute, then print, the result of some binary operator on two constants. What if we want to store values in variables? In this section, we will compile $\mathcal{L}_{PF2}$, which introduces local variables, down to $\mathcal{L}_{PF2_{x64}}$.

```
expr          ::=   call
              |     var
              |     arithexpr
              |     constant
              |     id
call          ::=   '(call (print' ' ' expr '))'
var           ::=   '(var ' id ' = ' expr')'
arithexpr     ::=   '(' binop binopval binopval ')'
binopval      ::=   {call | constant | id};
id            ::=   [a-zA-Z]+
pf2           ::=   expr*
```

Figure 9.3: Extended BNF Grammar for $\mathcal{L}_{PF2}$

Variable Homes

As we described in the assembly primer, each locally-declared variable has a "home" located somewhere on the stack as an offset from the base pointer. Therefore, we should use environments to create an association list that maps variables to their offset number. E.g., if we declare three variables x, y, and z, perhaps x has an offset of -8, y has an offset of -16, and z has an offset of -24. Unfortunately, it is not quite this simple.

Procedures, aside from main, make defining local variables a bit more difficult than it seems at first glance. We want to allow each function to have its own local variable environment. A solution to this is to keep a list of "function associations" in a root environment, e.g.,

Listing 9.47

```
(define env `((main . ())))
```

The problem with this approach is that we also need the function to know how many local variables are declared within its scope, so as to assign correct homes to variables. Therefore, we will say that a function, as an association, maps to a pair whose *first* is a box representing the number of variables declared within its scope, and whose *rest* is an association list of variables whose name is the *first* and whose *rest* is its offset "home". Let us rewrite the example from above that defines x, y, and z as an environment.

Listing 9.48

```
(define env `((main . (,(box 3) . ,(box '((z . -24) . (y . -16) . (x . -8)))))))
```

The default environment initializes the environment with `main` preloaded, in a sense. In future languages, we will remove this default definition to allow a user-defined `main` function.

Listing 9.49

```
(define env `((main . ,(cons (box 0) (box '())))))
```

Now, we want to write a function that extends the environment to contain a new variable with a unique offset value. The box denoting the length of the environment, i.e., the number of currently-stored variables, means we do not need to continuously query the environment each time a definition is encountered.

Listing 9.50

```
(define extend-env!
 (λ (var)
  (let* ([proc-pair (assv 'main env)]
         [offset-box (second proc-pair)]
         [offset (add1 (unbox offset-box))]
         [binding-box (rest (rest proc-pair))]
         [binding-list (unbox binding-box)])
   (begin
    (set-box! binding-box (cons (cons var offset) binding-list))
    (set-box! offset-box offset)))))
```

So, what all is taking place in this code segment? We retrieve the "procedure pair" from the environment, as well as the boxes containing the offset length and variable bindings. The first variable declared has an offset of -8, so we need to increment the offset by one before assigning said variable an offset. After updating the environment, we encapsulate the new offset back into its box for later query and modification. With this procedure, we can begin writing `assign-homes`. The general process is as follows: recursively iterate through the list of statements of a function and, if we find a variable declaration, assign it an offset in the environment. We could write a "global" definition recognizer since we may need it later, but localizing the assignment in a `letrec` is a good use of abstraction.

Listing 9.51

```
(define var?
 (λ (exp)
  (and (cons? exp)
       (= (length exp) 4)
       (eqv? (first exp) 'var))))
```

Listing 9.52

```
(define assign-homes
 (letrec ([rec
            (λ (los)
             (cond
              [(null? los) #f]
              [else
               (begin
                (assign (first los))
                (rec (rest los)))]))]
           [assign
            (λ (stmt)
             (cond
              [(var? stmt) (extend-env! (second stmt))]
              [else #f]))])
  rec))
```

Home assignment takes place during the prologue of a function since we need to know the size of the environment to allocate the required space on the stack for local variables.

Listing 9.53

```
(define generate-prologue
 (λ (los)
  (begin
   (printf "~a:~n" 'main)
   (assign-homes los)
   (print-instruction2 'pushq 'rbp)
   (print-instruction3 'movq 'rsp 'rbp))))
```

Another function to write, `compute-stack-space`, determines the required space to store the local variables on the stack for a function. If we have an odd number of variable declarations, we need to offset it by eight extra bytes to align the stack.

Listing 9.54

```
(define compute-stack-space
 (λ (los)
  (let ([size (length (unbox (rest (rest (assv 'main env)))))])
   (if (odd? size) (* 8 (add1 size)) (* 8 size)))))
```

From this, we amend our definitions of `generate-prologue` and `generate-epilogue` to include invocations of both `assign-homes` and `compute-stack-space`.

Listing 9.55

```
(define generate-prologue
 (λ (los)
  (begin
   (printf "~a:~n" 'main)
   (assign-homes los)
   (print-instruction2 'pushq 'rbp)
   (print-instruction3 'movq 'rsp 'rbp)
   (print-instruction3 'subq (compute-stack-space los) 'rsp))))

(define generate-epilogue
 (λ (los)
  (begin
   (print-instruction3 'addq (compute-stack-space los) 'rsp)
   (print-instruction3 'movq 'rbp 'rsp)
   (print-instruction2 'popq 'rbp)
   (printf " retq~n"))))
```

We also need to update our print-instruction3 function to account for three new statement types: register-to-memory, constant-to-memory, and memory-to-register. To compute the offset of a given variable in memory, we look up its value in the environment association list and multiply it by -8. Because we utilize this result multiple times over in print-instruction3, we will write a function, local-var-offset, to do the heavy lifting for us.

Listing 9.56

```
(define local-var-offset
 (λ (var)
  (let* ([proc-pair (assv current-proc env)]
         [bindings (unbox (rest (rest proc-pair)))])
   (* -8 (rest (assv var bindings))))))
```

Listing 9.57

```
(define print-instruction3
 (λ (op src dest)
  (let ([res-src (reduce src)]
        [res-dest (reduce dest)])
   (cond
    ...
    ; Register to memory.
    [(and (register? res-src) (variable? res-dest))
     (printf " ~a %~a, ~a(%rbp)~n" op res-src (local-var-offset res-dest))]
    ; Memory to register.
    [(and (variable? res-src) (register? res-dest))
     (printf " ~a ~a(%rbp), %~a~n" op (local-var-offset res-src) res-dest)]
    ; Constant to memory.
    [(and (constant? res-src) (variable? res-dest))
     (printf " ~a $~a, ~a(%rbp)~n" op res-src (local-var-offset res-dest))]
    [else
     (printf "ERR print-instruction:
       cannot reduce 'op=~a, res-src=~a, res-dest=~a'~n" op res-src res-dest)]))))
```

All that is left is to implement the recognizer and reducer for variables and variable declarations according to our language grammar.

Variables are neither constants nor registers; they are instead symbols that resolve to themselves.

Listing 9.58

```
(define variable?               (define reduce-variable
 (λ (exp)                        (λ (exp)
  (and (not (constant? exp))      exp))
       (not (register? exp))
       (symbol? exp))))
```

Variable declaration reductions require only one assembly instruction. Recognizing a variable declaration is just as simple as always.

Listing 9.59

```
(define var?                    (define reduce-var
 (λ (exp)                        (λ (exp)
  (and (cons? exp)                (let* ([v (second exp)]
       (= (length exp) 4)                [res (reduce (fourth exp))])
       (eqv? (first exp) 'var)     (print-instruction3 'movq res v))))
       (variable? (second exp)))))
```

Each recognizer and reducer are added to our current definition of reduce.

Listing 9.60

```
(define reduce
 (λ (stmt)
  (cond
   [(constant? stmt) (reduce-constant stmt)]
   [(variable? stmt) (reduce-variable stmt)]
   [(add? stmt) (reduce-add stmt)]
   [(var? stmt) (reduce-var stmt)]
   [(call? stmt) (reduce-call stmt)]
   [else #f])))
```

Let us write a test program and investigate the compiled output.

Listing 9.61

```
> (compile              .section .data
   '((var x = 20)         outnumfmt: .asciz "%d\n"
     (var y = 35)       .section .text
     (var z = (+ x        .extern printf
            y))           .global main
     (call             main:
      print              pushq %rbp               # Save value of %rbp.
      z)))               movq %rsp, %rbp          # Move %rsp into %rbp.
                         subq $16, %rsp           # Alloc 16 bytes to x,y.
                         movq $20, -8(%rbp)       # Move constant 20 into "x".
                         movq $35, -16(%rbp)      # Move constant 35 into "y".
                         movq -8(%rbp), %rax      # Move "x" into %rax.
                         addq -16(%rbp), %rax     # Add "y" into %rax.
                         movq %rax, %rsi          # Mv %rax into 2nd arg. reg.
                         leaq outnumfmt(%rip), %rdi # Mv fstr into 1st arg. reg.
                         movq $0, %rax            # Clear rax reg for printf.
                         callq printf             # Invoke C "printf" function.
                         addq $16, %rsp           # De-allocate 16 bytes.
                         movq %rbp, %rsp          # Restore %rsp val.
                         popq %rbp                # Rst %rbp val from stack.
                         retq
```

We can slightly optimize our implementation of local variables by amending the prologue and epilogue to exclude adding and subtracting bytes from the stack if no local variable declarations exist in the function.

Exercise 9.7. ($\star$)
Implement set!, which receives a previously-defined variable and assigns it a new value, e.g., (set! x 10), or (set! y (+ 20 x)). The right-hand side of the set! can be no more complex than those in var declaration statements.

Exercise 9.8. ($\star\star$)
Write an extension to $\mathcal{L}_{\mathrm{PF2}_{x64}}$ namely $\mathcal{L}_{\mathrm{IN}_{x64}}$, which adds a function read-integer that uses scanf to read a number from standard input.

Exercise 9.9. ($\star\star$)
Add support for a function print-string that allows outputting of a string literal to standard output. Note that this requires "pre-processing" of the input instructions to scan for string literals since they must be stored in the .data segment. It is acceptable (and a good idea, in fact) to generate random identifiers for strings.

Exercise 9.10. ($\star\star$)
Right now, the basic arithmetic operations only support two constant operands. Rewrite +, -, and * to support any number of variables and constants. This, however, means that you will need to change the register used for arithmatic operations. Use, and return, %r13. Follow the grammar given in Figure 9.4.

```
expr       ::=   call | var | aexpr | const | id
call       ::=   '(call (print' ' ' expr '))'
var        ::=   '(var ' id ' = ' expr')'
aexpr      ::=   '(' binop binopval+ ')'
binopval   ::=   {call | const | id};
id         ::=   [a-zA-Z]+
pf2        ::=   expr*
```

Figure 9.4: Extended BNF Grammar for Arithmetic Operators

9.4   Compiling $\mathcal{L}_{COND}^{-}$ to $\mathcal{L}_{COND_{x64}}^{-}$

Every use of a conditional, whether it be through if, else if, else, or cond, has been at a high level with said constructs that abstract what is truly going on with a conditional. Assembly removes such abstractions and requires us to work with conditional statements "directly". So, before we compile $\mathcal{L}_{COND}$, let us discuss how conditionals and jump statements work in assembly, namely by compiling a subset of $\mathcal{L}_{COND}$: $\mathcal{L}_{COND}^{-}$ to assembly.

```
expr       ::=   cmp-expr | ...
cmp-expr   ::=   '(' cmp-op ' ' expr ' ' expr ')'
cmp-op     ::=   '?=' | '!=' | '<' | '<=' | '>' | '>='
cond-      ::=   expr*
```

Figure 9.5: Extended BNF Grammar for $\mathcal{L}_{COND}^{-}$

Suppose we want to check whether two integers are equivalent. We, traditionally, use =, e.g., (= x y), which returns #t if x is numerically equal to y, and #f otherwise. How can we determine if two values are equivalent without a numeric comparison like this? Well, we can subtract y from x and see if the result is zero. Assembly allows us to do this very operation via cmp. cmp takes two registers, subtracts them, and sets flags dependent on the result. For instance, assuming %r10 stores $5 and %r11 stores $3, the instruction cmpq %r10, %r11 takes two registers, subtracts their values, and because the result is $2, $2 is obviously not zero, so while some flags are set, the zero flag is not set. Let us write this in x64 assembly.

Listing 9.62

```
main:
    ...
    movq $5, %r10     # Move 5 into rand1.
    movq $3, %r11     # Move 3 into rand2.
    cmpq %r10, %r11   # Compare 5 and 3.
```

Doing this comparison, on its own, is rather useless. We may want to do something *with* the fact that $2 is not equal to zero. If we write code such as, e.g., (define x (= 5 3)), we are stating that we want x to hold "true" if 5 is numerically equal to 3, and "false" otherwise. Our assembly language has no understanding of "true" and "false", so we must encode these choices as "1" and "0" respectively. So, x in this example holds 0. But how can we represent this in x64 assembly? We will use jump statements to illustrate. A *jump statement* allows us to change program flow. For instance, if we want to set %r12 to one only when the zero flag is set (indicating $5 and $3 are numerically equal), we may write a *label* that jumps to an instruction that moves $1 into %r12. If the zero flag is not set, then the jump statement is ignored.

Listing 9.63

```
main:
    ...
    movq $5, %r10    # Move 5 into rand1.
    movq $3, %r11    # Move 3 into rand2.
    cmpq %r10, %r11  # Compare 5 and 3.
    je L1            # If 5==3, jump to L1.
    movq $0, %r12    # Otherwise, move 'false' into bool reg.
    jmp L2           # Alt. jump to L2.
L1: movq $1, %r12    # Move 'true' into bool reg.
    ...
L2: retq
```

Notice how the alternative case is written first, which jumps to a label *after* the consequent case is written.[1] So, going back through this, we first compare the r10 and r11 register values. If they are equal, we jump to label L1. If they are not equal, we move "false", i.e., 0, into %r12 and jump to label L2. This jump is pertinent to avoiding the "true" case. We then write the consequent case which moves "true", i.e., 1 into %r12. Finally, we define a label L2 where code execution continues after the conditional. A general template is as follows:

```
Compare V1, V2
If T is True, Jump to L1, otherwise, continue.
Code That Executes Only When T is False
Jump to L2
L1: Code That Executes Only When T is True
L2: ...
```

There are several other instructions for arithmatic comparisons: jne for jump if not equal, js for jump if negative, jg for jump if greater than, jge for jump if greater than or equal to, jl for jump if less than, and jle for jump if less than or equal to. Full x64 assembly supports several more, but we omit their inclusion for simplicity.

Let us begin the process of compiling $\mathcal{L}^-_{\text{COND}}$ to $\mathcal{L}^-_{\text{COND}_{x64}}$ by allowing comparison expressions, e.g., (= 10 20). There are a few ways that we can implement this, but we want a way that allows us to add as many comparison operators, and hence be as flexible, as we see fit. Thus, let us write reduce-cmp. A comparison operator reduces to an x64 cmp instruction, two jump labels, and code for the consequent and alternative cases. We can extract out each of these values as follows:

Listing 9.64

```
(define reduce-cmp
  (λ (exp)
    (let ([op (first exp)]
          [x (second exp)]
          [y (third exp)]
          [l1 (gen-label)]
          [l2 (gen-label)])
      (begin
        ...))))
```

---

[1]This is a completely arbitrary design choice; we could use a jne instruction to reverse the logic.

We prematurely introduced l1 and l2 through a gen-label function; what is that? Its implementation bears resemblance to how we previously used closures to increment, e.g., a counter, each time it is invoked. In essence, we create a "current label" counter, and each time we invoke gen-label, we increment the counter by one and return its new value. It may seem tempting to return the label as a string with 'L' prepended, but this is superfluous, as the only thing we need to generate a label is its unique identifier, namely its "value". In printf statements, we can prepend 'L' as we see fit.

Listing 9.65

```
(define gen-label
  (let ([curr-label 0])
    (λ ()
      (begin
        (set! curr-label (add1 curr-label))
        curr-label))))
```

Now, let us add the line that outputs cmp. We first must move x and y into the r10 and r11 registers respectively. Fortunately, we already have a well-built print-instruction function, so we may as well use that!

Listing 9.66

```
(define reduce-cmp
  (λ (exp)
    (let ([op (first exp)]
          [x (second exp)]
          [y (third exp)]
          [l1 (gen-label)]
          [l2 (gen-label)])
      (begin
        (print-instruction3 'cmpq x y)
        ...))))
```

We need to grab the appropriate x64 assembly comparison operator depending on what we want to compile. For instance, we say that ?= corresponds directly to je, and so on.[1] We can write a predicate comparison? and an association list cmp-ops which maps each high-level operator with its assembly counterpart. To simplify our language so as to not need a separate negation function, we will add != to the grammar to represent "numeric not equal to".

Listing 9.67

```
(define cmp-ops
  '((?= . je) (!= . jne) (< . jl) (<= . jle) (> . jg) (>= . jeq)))

(define cmp?
  (λ (exp)
    (not (false? (assv exp cmp-ops)))))
```

At this point, we can extract the assembly operator via assv and pass that to printf alongside l1.

---

[1]The suffix '?' is to help in distinguishing the comparison operator from the assignment operator.

Listing 9.68

```
(define reduce-cmp
 (λ (exp)
  (let ([...])
   (begin
    (print-instruction3 'movq x 'r10)
    (print-instruction3 'movq y 'r11)
    (print-instruction3 'cmpq 'r10 'r11)
    (printf "~a L~a~n" (rest (assv op cmp-ops)) l1)
    ...))))
```

Recall from the template: after the comparison result-dependent jump to l1, we write the alternate case code which, in this case, sets %r12 to "false", i.e., 0. We then jump directly to l2.

Listing 9.69

```
(define reduce-cmp
 (λ (exp)
  (let ([...])
   (begin
    (print-instruction3 'movq x 'r10)
    (print-instruction3 'movq y 'r11)
    (print-instruction3 'cmpq 'r10 'r11)
    (printf "~a L~a~n" (rest (assv op cmp-ops)) l1)
    (print-instruction3 'movq 0 'r12)
    (printf " jmp L~a~n" l2)
    ...))))
```

Now we generate the consequent case with its l1 label as well as the "continue" label l2. Finally, the register with the "boolean" value, namely %r12, is returned as a symbol.

Listing 9.70

```
(define reduce-cmp
 (λ (exp)
  (let ([...])
   (begin
    (print-instruction3 'movq x 'r10)
    (print-instruction3 'movq y 'r11)
    (print-instruction3 'cmpq 'r10 'r11)
    (printf " ~a L~a~n" (rest (assv op cmp-ops)) l1)
    (print-instruction3 'movq 0 'r12)
    (printf " jmp L~a~n" l2)
    (printf "L~a:~n" l1)
    (print-instruction3 'movq 1 'r12)
    (printf "L~a:~n" l2)
    'r12))))
```

We can now add reduce-cmp to reduce. The recognizer, cmp?, uses comparison?, but we have omitted its implementation.

Listing 9.71

```
(define reduce
 (λ (stmt)
  (cond
   [...]
   [(cmp? stmt) (reduce-cmp stmt)]
   [else #f])))
```

Testing the following simple program, we can examine the output and labels.

Listing 9.72

```
> (compile                .section .data
   '((call print             outnumfmt: .asciz "%d\n"
      (?= 2 3))))          .section .text
                             .extern printf
                             .global main
                           main:
                             pushq %rbp                    # Save rbp.
                             movq %rsp, %rbp               # Move sp into bp.
                             movq $2, %r10                 # Move 2 into rand1.
                             movq $3, %r11                 # Move 3 into rand2.
                             cmpq %r10, %r11               # Compare 2 and 3.
                             je L1                         # If 2==3 jump to L1.
                             movq $0, %r12                 # Move false into bool reg.
                             jmp L2                        # Alt. jump to L2.
                           L1:
                             movq $1, %r12                 # Move 'true' to bool reg
                           L2:
                             movq %r12, %rsi              # Mv bool reg to 2nd param
                             leaq outnumfmt(%rip), %rdi # Load fmt str to 1st param
                             movq $0, %rax
                             callq printf
                             movq %rbp, %rsp
                             popq %rbp
                             retq
```

This, of course, outputs 0, because $5 is not equal to $3. Let us determine if two "boolean" values are equivalent.

Listing 9.73

```
> (compile
   '((var x = (?= 5 5))
     (var y = (?= 6 5))
     (var z = (?= x y))
     (call print z)))
```

Boolean expressions like this allow us to directly implement conditional statements such as if.

Compiling $\mathcal{L}_{\text{COND}}$ to $\mathcal{L}_{\text{COND}_{x64}}$

Suppose we wish to compile the following program:

Listing 9.74

```
> (compile
   '((var x = 10)
     (if (?= 10 x)
         (call print 10)
         (call print 20))))
```

How can we reduce if statements? $\mathcal{L}_{\text{COND}}^{-}$ allows us to write comparison expressions using logical operators, but these are not very powerful compared to statements that alter program control. The if statement receives three expressions: a predicate, a consequent, and an alternative. Additionally, both the consequent and alternative receive destination labels. If the given predicate resolves to true, then program control should jump to the consequent label and otherwise to the alternative label. Our implementation of the if statement will reflect this by using the designated boolean register. In particular, we evaluate the predicate and, if it is true, jump to a label L_t, followed by moving "true" into the boolean register. When the predicate is false, we fall through to the consequent clause by not jumping to L_t, moving "false" into the boolean register, and *then* jumping to a label L_f. Immediately following L_f is a boolean flag check: if the boolean register is true, we jump to another label $L_{t'}$, which begins the assembly code for the consequent. Otherwise, we jump to a label $L_{f'}$, which begins the assembly code for the consequent. So, in essence, we have four generated jump statements for every if statement: two that govern the location of the predicate result, and two that control program flow for evaluating either the consequent or the alternative.

```
expr  ::=  if | ...
if    ::=  '(if ' expr expr expr ')'
cond  ::=  expr*
```

Figure 9.6: Extended BNF Grammar for $\mathcal{L}_{\text{COND}}$

The if recognizer is straightforward as usual. Its reducer requires us to recursively reduce each expression and place the labels in the appropriate locations. We first produce the cmp instruction to receive the boolean result in %r12, output the jump instruction to $L_{t'}$, reduce the alternative case, jump to after the consequent case, output $L_{t'}$. We then reduce the consequent, followed immediately by $L_{f'}$. Note that we handle the labels L_t and L_f via reducing a comparison instruction through the predicate.

Listing 9.75

```
(define if?                                (define reduce-if
 (λ (exp)                                   (λ (exp)
  (and (cons? exp)                           (let* ([test (second exp)]
       (= (length exp) 4)                           [conseq (third exp)]
       (eqv? (first exp) 'if))))                    [alt (fourth exp)]
                                                    [lt (gen-label)]
                                                    [lf (gen-label)])
                                             (begin
                                              (print-instruction3
                                               'cmp 1 (reduce test))
                                              (printf " jz L~a~n" lt)
                                              (reduce alt)
                                              (printf " jmp L~a~n" lf)
                                              (printf "L~a:~n" lt)
                                              (reduce conseq)
                                              (printf "L~a:~n" lf)))))
```

Let us see the x64 assembly output of our previous example.

Listing 9.76

```
.section .data
  outnumfmt: .asciz "%d\n"
.section .text
  .extern printf
  .global main
main:
  pushq %rbp                       # Save rbp.
  movq %rsp, %rbp                  # Move sp into bp.
  subq $16, %rsp                   # Allocate 16 bytes for 'n' and align.
  movq $10, -8(%rbp)               # Move 10 into 'n'.
  movq -8(%rbp), %r10              # Move n into rand1.
  movq $10, %r11                   # Move 10 into rand1.
  cmpq %r10, %r11                  # Compare 'n' and 10.
  jz L3                            # If 'n'==10, jump to L3.
  movq $0, %r12                    # Otherwise move 'false' into bool reg.
  jmp L4                           # Alt. jump to L4.
L3:
  movq $1, %r12                    # Move 'true' into bool reg.
L4:
  cmpq $1, %r12                    # Determine if the 'if' condition is true.
  jz L1                            # If so, jump to L1.
  movq $20, %rsi                   # Move 20 into 2nd param.
  leaq outnumfmt(%rip), %rdi       # Load format str into 1st param.
  movq $0, %rax
  callq printf
  jmp L2
L1:
  movq $10, %rsi                   # Move 10 into 2nd param.
  leaq outnumfmt(%rip), %rdi       # Load format str into 1st param.
  movq $0, %rax
  callq printf
L2:
  addq $16, %rsp                   # Free 16 bytes.
  movq %rbp, %rsp
  popq %rbp
  retq
```

Exercise 9.11. (★★★)

Extend $\mathcal{L}_{\text{COND}_{x64}}$ by adding support for (begin e_1 e_2 ... e_n), which reduces statements e_1, e_2, ..., e_n in sequential order. Note that variables cannot be declared within a begin block.

9.5 Compiling $\mathcal{L}_{\text{COND}}^{+}$ to $\mathcal{L}_{\text{COND}_{x64}}^{+}$

Part of what makes a language feel more complete is the ability to perform actions multiple times. In this section, we will extend our compiled $\mathcal{L}_{\text{COND}}$ language to $\mathcal{L}_{\text{COND}}^{+}$, which adds a while loop construct.

```
expr       ::=   while | ...
while      ::=   '(while ' expr ' ' expr ')'
condplus   ::=   expr*
```

Figure 9.7: Extended BNF Grammar for $\mathcal{L}_{\text{COND}}^{+}$

Adding a while loop to our language is no harder than adding conditionals because while loops, at their core, are nothing more than conditional jump statements. If the condition, i.e., the predicate, is false, we jump to the bottom of the loop code. We generate a label before the predicate that serves as the loop continuation label.

Listing 9.77

```
(define while?                    (define reduce-while
  (λ (exp)                          (λ (exp)
    (and (cons? exp)                  (let* ([test (second exp)]
         (= (length exp) 3)                  [body (third exp)]
         (eqv? (first exp) 'while))))        [lt (gen-label)]
                                             [lf (gen-label)])
                                      (begin
                                        (printf "L~a:~n" lt)
                                        (print-instruction3
                                         'cmp 1 (reduce test))
                                        (printf " jne L~a~n" lf)
                                        (reduce body)
                                        (printf " jmp L~a~n" lt)
                                        (printf "L~a:~n" lf)))))
```

To demonstrate this new addition, let us write a loop that computes the factorial of five:

Listing 9.78

```
> (compile                              .section .data
  '((var n = 5)                           outnumfmt: .asciz "%d\n"
    (var fact = 1)                      .section .text
    (while (!= n 1)                       .extern printf
     (begin                               .global main
      (set! fact (* fact n))            main:
      (set! n (- n 1))))                  pushq %rbp
    (call print fact)))                   movq %rsp, %rbp
                                          subq $16, %rsp
                                          movq $5, -8(%rbp)
                                          movq $1, -16(%rbp)
                                        L2:
                                          movq -8(%rbp), %r10
                                          movq $1, %r11
                                          cmpq %r10, %r11
                                          jne L3
                                          movq $0, %r12
                                          jmp L4
                                        L3:
                                          movq $1, %r12
                                        L4:
                                          cmpq $1, %r12
                                          jne L1
                                          movq -16(%rbp), %rbx
                                          imulq -8(%rbp), %rbx
                                          movq %rbx, -16(%rbp)
                                          movq -8(%rbp), %rbx
                                          subq $1, %rbx
                                          movq %rbx, -8(%rbp)
                                          jmp L2
                                        L1:
                                          movq -16(%rbp), %rsi
                                          leaq outnumfmt(%rip), %rdi
                                          movq $0, %rax
                                          callq printf
                                          addq $16, %rsp
                                          movq %rbp, %rsp
                                          popq %rbp
                                          retq
```

Exercise 9.12. (⋆⋆)
Write a program that computes the nth Fibonacci number using a while loop.

9.6   Compiling $\mathcal{L}_{\text{PROC}}^-$ to $\mathcal{L}_{\text{PROC}_{x64}}^-$

In this section, we will further extend our compiler to generate assembly code for simple procedures. Note that such a journey requires a bit of refactoring, so buckle up!

```
expr   ::=   proc | ...
proc   ::=   '(proc ' id ' ' '(' id* ')' lstmt ')'
lstmt  ::=   expr lstmt | expr
id     ::=   [a-zA-Z]+
proc-  ::=   expr*
```

Figure 9.8: Extended BNF Grammar for $\mathcal{L}_{\text{PROC}}^-$

We denote our input language as $\mathcal{L}_{\text{PROC}}^-$ because we are compiling only simple procedures. A *simple procedure* is a procedure that does not receive any arguments and is not recursive. This may seem like a staggering limitation, which it certainly is, but there is a lot of work to go before compiling even these.

Suppose we want to compile the following program, where fact5 computes 5!:

Listing 9.79

```
> (compile
  '((proc fact5 ()
    ((var n = 5)
    (var prod = 1)
    (while (!= n 1)
     (begin
      (set! prod (* n prod))
      (set! n (- n 1))))
     (return prod)))
   (proc main ()
    ((var y = (call fact5))
    (call print y)))))
```

We need to modify a couple of pieces to our puzzle regarding procedures. Up until now, we currently assumed that the only function that existed was main. Now, though, we must differentiate between the scopes of functions. We can achieve this goal by requiring that every procedure, including main, must be declared. According to our grammar, a procedure declaration is a list containing the call symbol, the procedure name, and a list of its arguments (if any exist), and a list of statements designating its body.[1] We must compute a unique prologue and epilogue for every procedure. Thus, instead of generating those in reduce-statements, it would be wise to invoke these functions from a procedure-reduction function, i.e., reduce-proc.

---

[1] Note that we acknowledge the existence of procedure arguments even though we do not use them in $\mathcal{L}_{\text{PROC}}^-$ in an attempt to future-proof our compiler.

Let us write the accompanying recognizer and reducer. `reduce-proc` stores the newly-defined procedure in the environment, assigns variable homes, generates its prologue, reduces its statements, and finally generates its epilogue. To make things slightly more convenient, we use a global variable to keep track of what procedure we are currently defining for stack size and variable home assignment purposes. This change means that we need to update our definition of `compute-stack-space` to use `current-proc` rather than a fixed `'main`.

Listing 9.80

```
(define proc?                        (define reduce-proc
 (λ (exp)                             (λ (proc)
  (and (cons? exp)                     (let* ([procname (second proc)]
        (= (length exp) 4)                    [procargs (third proc)]
        (eqv? (first exp) 'proc)             [procbody (fourth proc)])
        (symbol? (second exp))        (begin
        (cons? (third exp))           (set! env
        (cons? (fourth exp)))))              `((,procname . (,(box 0) .
                                                   ,(box '())) . ,env))
                                      (set! current-proc procname)
                                      (assign-homes procbody)
                                      (generate-prologue procbody)
                                      (reduce-statements procbody)
                                      (generate-epilogue procbody)))))
```

With these changes, `compile` shrinks to only two lines in its body, because `main` is now treated as any other user-defined procedure.

Listing 9.81

```
(define compile
 (λ (los)
  (begin
   (generate-preamble)
   (reduce-statements los))))
```

Now, we need to alter `reduce-call` to account for user-defined procedures. Fortunately, all we need to do is add an `else` clause that calls the given procedure name and returns %rax, as a symbol, since return values are always stored in the rax register.

Listing 9.82

```
(define reduce-call
 (λ (exp)
  (let* ([procname (second exp)]
         [procargs (rest (rest exp))])
   (cond
    [(eqv? procname 'print)
     (let* ([arg (first procargs)])
      (begin
       (print-instruction3 'movq arg 'rsi)
       (printf " leaq outnumfmt(%rip), %rdi~n")
       (print-instruction3 'movq 0 'rax)
       (print-instruction2 'callq 'printf)))]
    [else
     (print-instruction2 'callq procname)]))))
```

Speaking of return values, let us handle statements of the form (return exp). All we need to do is recognize and reduce the return expression by moving its result into %rax.

Listing 9.83

```
(define reduce-return
 (λ (exp)
  (let* ([retexp (reduce (second exp))])
   (reduce-value 'movq retexp 'rax))))
```

Let us see the generated x64 assembly for fact5 as defined in Listing 9.80.

Listing 9.84

```
fact5:
  pushq %rbp
  movq %rsp, %rbp
  subq $16, %rsp
  movq $5, -8(%rbp)
  movq $1, -16(%rbp)
L2:
  movq -8(%rbp), %r10
  movq $1, %r11
  cmpq %r10, %r11
  jne L3
  movq $0, %r12
  jmp L4
L3:
  movq $1, %r12
L4:
  cmpq $1, %r12
  jne L1
  movq -8(%rbp), %rbx
  imulq -16(%rbp), %rbx
  movq %rbx, -16(%rbp)
  movq -8(%rbp), %rbx
  subq $1, %rbx
  movq %rbx, -8(%rbp)
  jmp L2
L1:
  movq -16(%rbp), %rax
  addq $16, %rsp
  movq %rbp, %rsp
  popq %rbp
  retq
```

9.7 Compiling $\mathcal{L}_{\text{PROC}}$ to $\mathcal{L}_{\text{PROC}_{x64}}$

Our gentle introduction to compiling simple procedures is over—we will now take a deep dive into compiling complex procedures. A complex procedure is one that may receive parameters.

```
expr      ::=  call | proc
call      ::=  '(call ' id '(' expr* '))'
procdecl  ::=  '(proc ' id '(' id* ')' expr* ')'
proc      ::=  expr+
```

Figure 9.9: Extended BNF Grammar for $\mathcal{L}_{\text{PROC}}$

All of our additions will reside in two functions: reduce-call and reduce-proc. First, when we invoke a function, we evaluate its arguments via reduce. Then, we move them into specific registers depending on their argument position. Passing arguments in registers poses a problem: what happens if we pass more arguments than we have assigned registers? $\mathcal{L}_{\text{PROC}}$ does not solve this problem, but the x64 assembly solution is to push those arguments to the stack in reverse order.

Argument Position	Register
1	%rdi
2	%rsi
3	%rdx
4	%rcx
5	%r8
6	%r9
≥ 7	*stack*
# of SSE Registers	%rax

Figure 9.10: Mapping of Argument Positions to Registers

We need a few local procedures to help us map evaluated arguments into registers. But first, let us discuss a subtle predicament that introduces itself only after testing this language. What happens when we evaluate a procedure with multiple calls as its arguments? Consider the following sequence of function calls:

Listing 9.85

```
(call foo (call bar 10 20) (call baz 30 40))
```

A well-defined order of argument evaluation must be set in stone before we continue. foo's arguments should be evaluated as follows: we must reduce each argument before moving its value into a register. In other words, if a procedure has arguments a, b, and c, we must reduce a, b, and c, before moving any into an argument register. The reasoning is because a, b, and c are all arguments that represent some expression; these expressions may, themselves, be function calls. So, if we were to, for instance, reduce argument a, then move it into %rdi, this results in a possible argument-register interference. If argument b contains a call to a function of at least one argument, it needs access to a free %rdi register. Overwriting the value in %rdi erases the previous argument stored. A possible solution is to push all argument register values to the stack and pop them before and after evaluating an argument, but this is too cumbersome and only serves to hide the problem at hand rather than solve it. Instead, we should, as we previously explained, reduce all arguments to a call, then and only then, move the reduced arguments into registers.

Let us create a function that reduces every argument. Function arguments have a property of guaranteed resolution, i.e., it is impossible for the argument to a function to resolve to something that cannot be passed. Therefore, we can write a local procedure, namely reduce-args, which invokes reduce on each argument.

Listing 9.86

```
(define reduce-call
 (λ (exp)
  (letrec ([...]
          [reduce-args
           (λ (args)
            (cond
             [(null? args) '()]
             [else
              (cons (reduce (first args)) (reduce-args (rest args)))]))])
   ...)))
```

Because map returns another list, we know by the property of guaranteed resolution that this list contains a reduced value for each function argument. So, all we must do is move these reduced values, one by one, into the appropriate argument registers. We can use a function map-args to do this process.

Listing 9.87

```
(define reduce-call
 (λ (exp)
  (letrec ([...]
          [map-args
           (λ (redargs i)
            (cond
             [(null? redargs) (print-empty)]
             [else
              (begin
               (print-instruction3
                'movq (first redargs) (list-ref arg-registers i))
               (map-args (rest redargs) (add1 I)))]))])
   ...)))
```

Finally, we compositionally invoke these procedures by feeding the output of reduce-args into map-args: (map-args (reduce-args procargs)).

Listing 9.88

```
(define reduce-call
 (λ (exp)
  (letrec ([...])
   (cond
    [...]
    [else
     (begin
      (map-args (reduce-args procargs) 0)
      (print-instruction2 'callq procname)
      'rax)])))))
```

Each argument is evaluated before being stored in an argument register. Now we need to begin the process of unwrapping the registers and storing parameters on the stack as local variables. To do this, we can write a local procedure reduce-params inside reduce-proc that moves each value in the argument registers, as a parameter, into a stack-declared variable. The idea is that we allocate enough space for not only locally-declared variables but also parameters. This way, we do not need to worry about where and which register an arbitrary argument is contained.

Listing 9.89

```
(define reduce-proc
 (λ (proc)
  (let* ([...]
         [reduce-params
          (λ (lop)
           (map
            (λ (a)
             (print-instruction3
              'movq
              (list-ref arg-registers (index-of lop a))
              a))
            lop))])
   ...)))
```

Though, this introduces a problem: we now need a way to designate that parameters should be treated as local variables. A simple solution is to write another local procedure: assign-param-homes that invokes extend-env! on each parameter.

Listing 9.90

```
(define reduce-proc
 (λ (proc)
  (let* ([...]
         [assign-param-homes
          (λ (lop)
           (map extend-env! lop))])
   ...)))
```

Lastly, we must assign parameter homes before their reduction.

Listing 9.91

```
(define reduce-proc
 (λ (proc)
  (let* (...)
   (begin
    (set! env `((,procname . (,(box 0) . ,(box '()))) . ,env))
    (set! current-proc procname)
    (assign-param-homes procparams)
    (assign-homes procbody)
    (generate-prologue procbody)
    (reduce-params procparams)
    (reduce-statements procbody)
    (generate-epilogue procbody)))))
```

We can now analyze the code generated for reducing parameters into local variable homes.

Listing 9.92

```
sum_of_args:
  movq %rdi, -8(%rbp)
  movq %rsi, -16(%rbp)
  movq %rdx, -24(%rbp)
  movq %rcx, -32(%rbp)
```

All of this preparation allows us to write functions that contain up to (and including) six arguments. These functions may be recursive, so let us define addition over natural recursion as an example. Assume that we also have add1, sub1, and is_zero defined.

Listing 9.93

```
> (compile                          add:
   '((proc add (n m)                  pushq %rbp
     ((if (call is_zero n)            movq %rsp, %rbp
          (return m)                  subq $16, %rsp
          (return                     movq %rdi, -8(%rbp)
           (call add1                 movq %rsi, -16(%rbp)
            (call add                 movq -8(%rbp), %rdi
             (call sub1 n)            callq is_zero
             m)))))))                 cmpq $1, %rax
                                      jz L3
                                      movq -8(%rbp), %rdi
                                      callq sub1
                                      movq %rax, %rdi
                                      movq -16(%rbp), %rsi
                                      callq add
                                      movq %rax, %rdi
                                      callq add1
                                      movq %rax, %rax
                                      jmp L4
                                    L3:
                                      movq -16(%rbp), %rax
                                    L4:
                                      addq $16, %rsp
                                      movq %rbp, %rsp
                                      popq %rbp
                                      retq
```

Compiling $\mathcal{L}^+_{\mathrm{PROC}}$ to $\mathcal{L}^+_{\mathrm{PROC}_{x64}}$

Here's the deal: $\mathcal{L}_{\mathrm{PROC}}$ compiles most procedures down to x64 assembly correctly. There is a bit of an issue, however, when there are multiple arithmetic expressions within the arguments of a function call. Consider the following tail recursive Fibonacci code:

Listing 9.94

```
> (compile
  '((proc fib_iter (a b n)
    ((if (?= n 0)
        (return b)
        (return (call fib_iter (+ a b) a (- n 1))))))
    (proc fib (n)
      ((return (call fib_iter 1 0 n))))
    (proc main ()
      ((call print (call fib 8)))))))
```

Pay careful attention to the recursive call to fib_iter. Namely, we pass to it three arguments: an expression representing the sum of a and b, b, and an expression representing the difference between n and 1. Now, let us investigate the relevant x64 assembly output.

Listing 9.95

```
fib_iter:
    ...
    movq -8(%rbp), %rax   # Move a into rax.
    addq -16(%rbp), %rax  # Subtract b from a.
    movq -24(%rbp), %rax  # Move n into rax (collision!)
    subq $1, %rax         # Subtract 1 from n.
    movq %rax, %rdi       # Move (n-1) into arg 1.
    movq -8(%rbp), %rsi   # Move a into arg. 2.
    movq %rax, %rdx       # Move (n-1) into arg 3.
    callq fib_iter
```

Notice that we have a race for who gets access to the rax register for arithmetic. The problem is that we delay setting argument registers until after all arguments are evaluated. It seems that we are back where we started—in a dilemma about when we should move argument evaluations into argument-registers. We could create a complex register-allocation algorithm, but that is not necessary; we have a stack for a reason, right? Why not do the following: evaluate the arguments to a function *in reverse*, push the result to the stack via pushq. Then, once all arguments have been evaluated, pop the results off the stack into the appropriate argument-registers via popq. The following is an example using the fib procedure from before.

Listing 9.96

```
fib_iter:
  movq -24(%rbp), %rax   # Move n into rax.
  subq $1, %rax          # Subtract n-1 from rax.
  movq %rax, %rax
  pushq %rax             # Push n-1 to stack.
  movq -8(%rbp), %rax    # Move a into rax.
  pushq %rax             # Push a to stack.
  movq -8(%rbp), %rax    # Move a into rax.
  addq -16(%rbp), %rax   # Add b to rax.
  movq %rax, %rax
  pushq %rax             # Push (a+b) to stack.
  popq %rdi              # Pop (a+b) into rdi.
  popq %rsi              # Pop a into rsi.
  popq %rdx              # Pop (n-1) into rdx.
  callq fib_iter
```

There are a few superfluous instructions, e.g,. movq %rax, %rax, but otherwise, this code is relatively straightforward. We push each evaluated argument to the stack in reverse order (i.e., we evaluate the nth argument first, down to the first). Then, we pop each evaluated argument off the stack into the respective registers. Since the first argument is the last one pushed, we can pop the values in the order specified by arg-registers. Note that the following two functions, push-args and pop-args, replace reduce-args and map-args respectively.

Listing 9.97

```
(define reduce-call
 (λ (exp)
  (letrec ([...]
          [pop-args
           (λ (args i)
            (cond
             [(null? args) (print-empty)]
             [else
              (begin
               (print-instruction2 'popq (list-ref arg-registers i))
               (pop-args (rest redargs) (add1 i)))])])
    ...)))
```

Therefore, we invoke these helper functions as follows. From there, if we re-compile the Fibonacci example from before, we get a pleasant surprise: a correct result!

Listing 9.98

```
(define reduce-call
 (λ (exp)
  (letrec (...)
   (cond
    [...]
    [else
     (begin
      (push-args (reverse procargs))
      (pop-args procargs 0)
      (print-instruction2 'callq procname)
      'rax)]))))
```

One thing that we neglected to do, though, is conform to the requirement that, across function calls, certain registers are to be preserved by the callee. In AT&T x64 assembly, the following registers, should they be used in a function definition, must store their current values onto the stack: %r12, %r13, %r14, %r15, %rsp, %rbp, %rbx. We already preserve the base pointer register since we modify its value upon making a function call. It is certainly rather brazen to push all seven callee-saved registers to the stack even if they are not used in the function body, but out of simplicity, we will add the relevant pushq and popq instructions to our generate-prologue and generate-epilogue functions. Note that, in saving these registers to the stack, we considerably increase our code size due to the lack of optimization, but it is tolerated for the purposes of demonstration.

Listing 9.99

```
(define generate-prologue
 (λ (los)
  (begin
   ...
   (print-instruction2 'pushq 'rbp)
   (print-instruction2 'pushq 'rbx)
   (print-instruction2 'pushq 'rsp)
   (print-instruction2 'pushq 'r12)
   (print-instruction2 'pushq 'r13)
   (print-instruction2 'pushq 'r14)
   (print-instruction2 'pushq 'r15)
   ...)))

(define generate-epilogue
 (λ (los)
  (begin
   ...
   (print-instruction2 'popq 'r15)
   (print-instruction2 'popq 'r14)
   (print-instruction2 'popq 'r13)
   (print-instruction2 'popq 'r12)
   (print-instruction2 'popq 'rsp)
   (print-instruction2 'popq 'rbx)
   (print-instruction2 'popq 'rbp)
   ...)))
```

Exercise 9.13. (★★★★)
If a function has more than six parameters, according to the System V AMD64 ABI, they are to be pushed to the stack. Implement this feature into $\mathcal{L}_{\text{PROC}}^{+}$. This means that parameters past the sixth will need to have assigned homes relative to the stack frame pointer.

9.8 Compiling $\mathcal{L}_{\text{ARRAY}}$ to $\mathcal{L}_{\text{ARRAY}_{x64}}$

In this section, we will compile $\mathcal{L}_{\text{ARRAY}}$ to $\mathcal{L}_{\text{ARRAY}_{x64}}$: a language that allows for locally-declared arrays.

expr	::=	getindex | setindex | ...
decl	::=	arraydecl | ...
arraydecl	::=	'(array ' number ')'
getindex	::=	'(get-index ' id ' ' expr ')'
setindex	::=	'(set-index ' id ' ' expr ' ' expr ')'
array	::=	decl* expr*

Figure 9.11: Extended BNF Grammar for $\mathcal{L}_{\text{ARRAY}}$

Let us begin by writing a recognizer for array "declarations" as per the grammar. Later on, we will see that its respective reducer is not necessary.

Listing 9.100

```
(define array?
 (λ (stmt)
  (and (cons? stmt)
       (= (length stmt) 2)
       (eqv? (first stmt) 'array))))
```

If we want to implement locally-declared arrays in our language, we have a long way to go. Fortunately, many of the changes are not all that difficult—rather, they can be pretty tedious since it involves editing existing code.

Our environments recognize only one datatype: quad-word integers. A local variable, of this type, needs only to know its offset from the base pointer. Arrays, on the other hand, need to keep track of a few bits of information: the size of the datatype stored, its length, and the offset from the base pointer. We also need the environment to recognize that a variable *is* an array and not just a standard quad-word integer. Let us think about how to represent different data types in a uniform fashion.

As we stated, each variable in the association list corresponds to its local variable offset from the base pointer. We can modify this correspondence pair to have the *rest* be a list where its *first* is a tag denoting the type of the variable, its *second* denoting its offset, its *third* representing its size, and for arrays only, its *fourth* representing the number of elements it contains. When we say "size", we mean how many bytes are used when storing the variable. Arrays *are* pointers, which we know from our discussion in Chapter 5, so these should store eight bytes each. We need to amend `extend-env!`. There are three instances in which `extend-env!` is invoked:

1. Formal parameter extension.

2. Home assignment for local array variables in the function prologue.

3. Home assignment for local non-array variables in the function prologue.

So, our definition should be updated to account for these three types.

Listing 9.101

```
(define extend-env!
  (λ (stmt)
    (let* (...)
      (cond
        [(variable? stmt) ...]
        [(and (var? stmt) (array? (third stmt))) ...]
        [(var? stmt) ...]
        [else (printf "ERR: invalid argument to extend-env!: ~a~n" stmt)]))))
```

The second clause is perhaps the most confusing—all we are checking is to see if our statement is a variable declaration and if the expression-to-assign is an array. The last clause (outside the error case) catches all non-array-based local variable declarations.

Let us analyze these cases one by one. First, if our statement is a variable and only a variable, e.g., y, we extend the environment to include it as we have before. The only modification is that the *rest* of the association pair mapping for the variable is now a list containing four elements as we described previously.

Listing 9.102

```
(define extend-env!
  (λ (stmt)
    (let* (...)
      (cond
        [(variable? stmt)
         (begin
           (set-box!
            binding-box
            (cons (cons stmt (list 'var offset 8 0)) binding-list))
           (set-box! offset-box offset))]
        [...]))))
```

Local array declarations are up next. The only difference is that the array size should be added to the list instead of 0, as well as the change in the tag. Lastly, the offset calculation accounts for the size of the array. We also include a let* block to extract out the array declaration and variable identifier.

Listing 9.103

```
(define extend-env!
  (λ (stmt)
    (let* (...)
      (cond
        [...]
        [(and (var? stmt) (array? (fourth stmt)))
         (let* ([id (second stmt)]
                [arr (fourth stmt)]
                [size (second arr)])
           (begin
             (set-box!
              binding-box
              (cons (cons id (list 'array offset 8 size)) binding-list))
             (set-box! offset-box (+ offset size))))]
        [...]))))
```

Conveniently, the last case is simpler than the array but slightly more complex than formal parameter extension. We extract out the variable identifier from the declaration and add it to the environment.

Listing 9.104

```
(define extend-env!
 (λ (stmt)
  (let* (...)
   (cond
    [...]
    [(var? stmt)
     (let* ([v (second stmt)])
      (begin
       (set-box!
        binding-box
        (cons (cons v (list 'var offset 8 0)) binding-list))
       (set-box! offset-box offset)))]
    [...]))))
```

These changes to `extend-env!` mean that we also must modify `local-var-offset` to account for arrays.

Listing 9.105

```
(define local-var-offset
 (λ (var)
  (let* ([proc-pair (assv current-proc env)]
         [bindings (unbox (rest (rest proc-pair)))]
         [val (rest (assv var bindings))]
         [tag (first val)])
   (cond
    [(eqv? tag 'var) ...]
    [(eqv? tag 'array) ...]
    [else (printf "ERR: local-var-offset invalid var ~a~n" var)]))))
```

With the `'var` tag, we simply need to retrieve the offset and multiply it by −8.

Listing 9.106

```
(define local-var-offset
 (λ (var)
  (let* (...)
   (cond
    [(eqv? tag 'var) (* -8 (second val))]
    [(eqv? tag 'array) ...]
    [else (printf "ERR: local-var-offset invalid var ~a~n" var)]))))
```

Arrays are a bit more complicated. We first need to use the offset to compute the position of the top, or end, of the array on the stack. This is just another multiplication by −8. We then offset this value by adding on the length of the array, multiplied by −8, to get the index of the first element.

Listing 9.107

```
(define local-var-offset
 (λ (var)
  (let* (...)
   (cond
    [...]
    [(eqv? tag 'array) (+ (* -8 (fourth val))
                          (* -8 (second val)))]
    [else (printf "ERR: local-var-offset invalid var ~a~n" var)]))))
```

The environments now recognize array declarations. Thus, we should write the reducer... right? Wrong! There is never a case where an array will need to be reduced and, therefore, should not be added to `reduce` as part of the case analysis.

Let us write a few test programs to see if it correctly allocates memory with the right offsets.

Listing 9.108

```
> (compile '((proc main ()
             ((var arr1 = (array 5))))))
> (compile '((proc main ()
             ((var x = 2000)
              (var arr1 = (array 8))))))
> (compile '((proc main ()
             ((var arr1 = (array 2))
              (var y = 2000)))))
> (compile '((proc main ()
             ((var x = 1000)
              (var arr1 = (array 3))
              (var y = 2000)))))
```

We should expect the code to produce the following local variable offset amounts. The columns indicate the test number, the number of non-array local variables, the number of elements in the declared array, the starting index offset value, the ending index offset value, and the number of bytes to dedicate to local variables.

Test	# NALV	$|A|$	SAO	EAO	B
1	0	5	-48	-8	48
2	1	8	-72	-16	80
3	1	2	-16	-8	32
4	2	3	-32	-16	48

The calculations are as follows: test 1 requires 40 bytes to store the array, but the function must be aligned on a 16-byte boundary, so we round it up to the next multiple of 16, which is 48. Test 2 requires 64 bytes to store the array and 8 bytes to store the non-array local variable. This amounts to 72 bytes, but the function must be aligned, so we round up to 80. Test 3 requires 16 bytes to store the array and 8 bytes to store the non-array local variable. This amounts to 24 bytes, but the function must be aligned, so we round up to 32. Test 4 requires 24 bytes to store the array and 16 bytes to store the two local variables. This amounts to 40 bytes, but the function must be aligned, so we round up to 48. The table also shows the starting and ending offsets for the array bounds. We show these numbers to emphasize the importance of ensuring the bounds are correct so as to not clobber any other variables on the stack. Though, how can we test these programs to make sure that they are correct? In other words, if we want to verify that we are not clobbering the stack or otherwise overwriting preexisting data at another memory location, what can we do? We should certainly write two functions to alter and retrieve the values at an array: set-index and get-index respectively.

The recognizers for these functions are simple and more or less a carbon copy of previous recognizers.

Listing 9.109

```
(define get-index?
  (λ (stmt)
   (and (cons? stmt)
        (= (length stmt) 3)
        (eqv? (first stmt) 'get-index))))

(define set-index?
  (λ (stmt)
   (and (cons? stmt)
        (= (length stmt) 4)
        (eqv? (first stmt) 'set-index))))
```

Let us write `set-index` first because it is not only more difficult but also more interesting. Retrieving the data at an index is worthless if no meaningful (i.e., non-garbage) data exists there! An example of a `set-index` comes through this small program that sets the values of an array equal to its index squared.

Listing 9.110

```
> (compile
   '((proc main ()
     ((var arr = (array 10))
      (var i = 0)
      (while (!= i 10)
       (begin
        (set-index arr i (* i i))
        (set! i (+ i 1)))))))))
```

As we see, `set-index` receives three arguments: an identifier corresponding to an array, an expression representing the index to modify, and an expression to assign at that index.

First, we need to extract out the components of the `set-index` expression, i.e., the array identifier, the association pair that binds the identifier in the environment, its offset, size/length, the index to assign, and the value to assign.

Listing 9.111

```
(define reduce-set-index
  (λ (stmt)
   (let* ([array (second stmt)]
          [addr (assv array (unbox (rest (rest (assv current-proc env)))))]
          [offset (third addr)]
          [size (fourth addr)]
          [idx (reduce (third stmt))]
          [val (fourth stmt)])
     ...)))
```

`idx` may not be a constant; it could be an expression that resolves to a register. So, we need to use this value and subtract it *from* the length of the array using the equation we derived earlier. These are all assembly instructions that must be emitted. This value must also be negated.

Listing 9.112

```
(define reduce-set-index
 (λ (stmt)
  (let* (...)
   (begin
    (print-instruction3 'movq idx 'r13)
    (print-instruction3 'subq size 'r13)
    (print-instruction2 'negq 'r13)))))
```

We load the address of the index we wish to modify via `leaq` using the given offset into %r13. We also want to move the value to assign at the index into %rbx, and finally, store this at the address designated by %r13.

Listing 9.113

```
(define reduce-set-index
 (λ (stmt)
  (let* (...)
   (begin

    (printf " leaq ~a(%rbp, %r13, 8), %r13~n" (* -8 (sub1 offset)))
    (print-instruction3 'movq val 'rbx)
    (printf " movq %rbx, (%r13)~n")))))
```

Let us write a very small test program to see the generated assembly.

Listing 9.114

```
> (compile              main:
  '((proc                  ...
     main ()               subq $88, %rsp                    # Allocate 88 bytes (8x10+8)
    ((var arr =            movq $4, %r13                     # Move 4 into array idx reg.
     (array               subq $8, %r13                     # Sub 8 from array idx reg
      10))                negq %r13                         # Negate array idx val.
    (set-index            leaq 0(%rbp, %r13, 8), %r13       # Ld add. idx %r13 to %r13.
     arr                  movq $120, %rbx                   # Move 120 value into rbx.
     4                    movq %rbx, (%r13)                 # Move 120 in idx ref. %r13.
     120)))))             addq $88, %rsp                    # Deallocate 80 + 8 bytes.
                             ...
```

9.9   Compiling $\mathcal{L}_{\text{FLOAT}}$ to $\mathcal{L}_{\text{FLOAT}_{x64}}$

Interpretation of different values is simple. Their compilation, on the other hand, introduces a whole host of new issues. In this section, we will compile $\mathcal{L}_{\text{FLOAT}}$ to $\mathcal{L}_{\text{FLOAT}_{x64}}$: a language that allows for floating-point variables.

Unfortunately, adding floating-point value support to our programming language and compiler is not as simple as changing a few operands and some recognizers. We have to heavily restrict and modify our language subset to support both floating-point and integer values. If we cannot even store a floating-point value in a standard register, i.e., %rax, what do we do? The answer is to use the SSE (Streaming SIMD Extensions) instruction set, which contains sixteen floating-point "registers": %xmm0 to %xmm15.

For example, let us write two programs: one that loads a global float variable into a floating-point register, and another that computes the average of three integers.

Listing 9.115

```
.section .data
  num1: .double 123.456
.section .text
  .global main
main:
  movsd num1(%rip), %xmm0      # Load 123.456 into %xmm0.
  retq
```

Listing 9.116

```
.section .data
  avg: .double 0
  sum: .quad 0
  n: .quad 3
.section .text
  .global main
main:
  pushq %rbp
  movq %rsp, %rbp
  subq $32, %rsp                # Allocate 32 bytes for 3 quadwords + 8 alignment.
  movq $71, -8(%rbp)
  movq $93, -16(%rbp)
  movq $84, -24(%rbp)
  movq -8(%rbp), %rbx
  addq -16(%rbp), %rbx
  addq -24(%rbp), %rbx
  movq %rbx, sum(%rip)          # Store %rbx in sum memory.
  cvtsi2sd sum(%rip), %xmm0     # Load sum into %xmm0
  cvtsi2sd n(%rip), %xmm1       # Load n into %xmm1
  divsd %xmm1, %xmm0            # Divide %xmm0 by %xmm1, store quotient in %xmm0
  movsd %xmm0, avg(%rip)        # Store quotient in avg memory.
  subq $32, %rsp
  movq %rbp, %rsp
  popq %rbp
  retq
```

The first few lines of main, where we compute the sum of three locally-declared integers should be nothing new. What is new, however, is the cvtsi2sd instruction. The long-winded cvtsi2sd (i.e., "ConVerT Signed Integer to Signed Double") allows us to take an integer from a register or direct memory and convert it into a floating-point value. This value is then stored in a destination register. In our case, we load the integer sum from direct memory, convert it into a floating-point value, and store it in xmm0. Similarly, we load the integer n (representing how many numbers we want to compute the average of) from direct memory and convert it into a floating-point value to store in %xmm1. Subsequently, we invoke divsd: an instruction to divide the destination register by the source register, storing the quotient in the destination register. Finally, use movsd to store the floating-point quotient from %xmm0 out to memory in avg.

Because working with floating-point values is such a chore, we will restrict our input language $\mathcal{L}_{\text{FLOAT}}$. Namely, it contains no user-defined procedures other than main, no immediate values, and all variables are declared in global scope. Primitive operators, e.g., addition, receive exactly two operands. As an example, if we want to define, store, then print the sum of two floating-point values, we use the following program:

Listing 9.117

```
> (compile
   '((var a = 5.25)
     (var b = 10.1275)
     (var sum = 0)
     (proc main ()
       ((sum = (+ a b))
        (call print-float sum)))))
```

expr	::=	arithexpr | setexpr | callexpr
callexpr	::=	'(call ' id id* ')'
proc	::=	'(proc main ()' '(' expr+ '))'
constant	::=	number
float	::=	vardecl* proc

Figure 9.12: Extended BNF Grammar for $\mathcal{L}_{\text{FLOAT}}$

Because $\mathcal{L}_{\text{FLOAT}}$ has no local variables, there is no need to use extend-env!, reset-env!, current-proc, or keep track of environments at all. A big change, however, is the addition of a function compute-global-floats. As we stated (and as the grammar illustrates), all variable declarations are global and appear before the main function. So, this means we need to generate appropriate declarations. That is, whenever we encounter a variable declaration, output a line containing its identifier, a colon, the .double directive, and its value. This is eerily similar to how we assign homes to local variables; the only difference is that instead of invoking extend-env!, we output the variable to the .data segment.

Listing 9.118

```
(define compute-global-floats
 (letrec ([bind-float
            (λ (stmt)
             (let ([id (second stmt)]
                   [value (fourth stmt)])
               (printf " ~a: .double ~a\n" id value)))]
           [rec
            (λ (los)
             (cond
              [(null? los) (print-empty)]
              [(var? (first los))
               (begin
                (bind-float (first los))
                (rec (rest los)))]
              [else (rec (rest los))]))])
   rec))
```

Then, to **update** generate-preamble. Note that we modified the output format string to, instead, output a double rather than a 64-bit integer.

Listing 9.119

```
(define generate-preamble
 (λ (los)
  (printf ".section .data~n")
  (printf " outfloatfmt: .asciz ~"%lf~"~n")
  (compute-global-floats los)
  (printf ".section .text~n")
  (printf " .extern printf~n")
  (printf " .global main~n")))
```

Now, let us modify the addition (and other arithmatic operators) to work with floating-point values. We will use %xmm1 and %xmm2 to hold the result of a computation such as addition. We load the first operand, e.g., a, from memory into %xmm1, then load the second operand, e.g., b, from memory into %xmm2. At last, we perform the corresponding arithmetic operation on those registers where %xmm1 is the destination register and %xmm2 is the source register. To move a floating-point value between registers and memory, we use movsd.

Listing 9.120

```
(define reduce-add
 (λ (exp)
  (let* ([r1 (second exp)]
         [r2 (third exp)])
   (begin
    (printf " movsd ~a(%rip), %xmm1~n" r1)
    (printf " movsd ~a(%rip), %xmm2~n" r2)
    (printf " addsd %xmm2, %xmm1~n")
    'xmm1))))
```

Let us also modify the reduction for setting variables to use movsd instead of movq.

Listing 9.121

```
(define reduce-set
 (λ (exp)
  (let* ([var (first exp)]
         [res (reduce (third exp))])
   (begin
    (printf " movsd %~a, ~a(%rip)~n" res var)))))
```

Finally, we need to write a version of print that receives floats and not integers. We will call it print-float. Namely, its argument is an identifier that is loaded into %xmm0. As we stated, %xmm0 is the first floating-point argument register. We load the format string the same way as we did previously. Finally, since printf is a variadic procedure, %rax must contain the number of floating-point arguments (i.e., xmm registers) printf uses. In this case, we only use %xmm0, so the value in %rax is 1.

Listing 9.122

```
(define reduce-call
 (λ (exp)
  (letrec ( )
   (cond
    [ ]
    [(eqv? procname 'print-float)
     (let* ([arg (first procargs)])
      (begin
       (printf " movsd ~a(%rip), %xmm0~n" arg)
       (printf " leaq outfloatfmt(%rip), %rdi~n")
       (printf " movq $1, %rax~n")
       (printf " callq printf~n")))])))))
```

We may amend our definitions of generate-prologue and generate-epilogue to exclude any mention of the stack or environments. We should also make the necessary changes to reduce to only recognize expressions and statements defined by FLOAT. Making these changes allows us to compile the aforementioned program which produces the following assembly output (we added comments to help with understanding):

Listing 9.123

```
.section .data
  outfloatfmt: .asciz "%lf\n"
  a: .double 5.25
  b: .double 10.1275
  sum: .double 0
.section .text
  .extern printf
  .global main
main:
  pushq %rbp

  movq %rsp, %rbp
  movsd a(%rip), %xmm1        # Load 'a' into xmm1.
  movsd b(%rip), %xmm2        # Load 'b' into xmm2.
  addsd %xmm2, %xmm1          # Add xmm2 into xmm1.
  movsd %xmm1, sum(%rip)      # Store value in xmm1 out to 'sum'.
  movsd sum(%rip), %xmm0      # Load 'sum' into xmm0 (f.p. arg. #1).
  leaq outfloatfmt(%rip), %rdi  # Load format string into 1st arg.
  movq $1, %rax              # rax stores var. args., # of xmm regs used.
  callq printf
  movq %rbp, %rsp

  popq %rbp
  retq
```

Compiling the assembly outputs 15.377500. Let us write another program that computes the square root of a sum of the squares of three floating-point numbers. We run into a small roadblock: how do we get the square root of some arbitrary value? There is an instruction designed specifically for this! Namely, sqrtsd is exactly what we need. In other words, we want to compute $\sqrt{a^2 + b^2 + c^2}$ where a, b, and c are floating-point numbers. sqrtsd works differently than the way we will implement it, however. It receives a source, computes the square root of said source, and stores the result in a destination. Therefore, sqrtsd receives two arguments. Our implementation will only provide one argument to the function and assume that it *returns* the square root of the input argument in a register. This can be used in other computations, e.g., storing out into a variable in memory.

Listing 9.124

```
(define reduce-call
 (λ (exp)
  (letrec (...)
   (cond
    [...]
    [(eqv? procname 'sqrt)
     (let* ([arg (first procargs)])
      (begin
       (printf " movsd ~a(%rip), %xmm1~n" arg)
       (printf " sqrtsd %xmm1, %xmm1~n")
       'xmm1))]))))
```

Showing the abridged output of main produces the following results:

Listing 9.125

```
.section .data
  outfloatfmt: .asciz "%lf\n"
  a: .double 6.125
  b: .double 7.875
  c: .double 13.5
  aa: .double 0
  bb: .double 0
  cc: .double 0
  aapbb: .double 0
  sos: .double 0
  sossqrt: .double 0
.section .text
  .extern printf
  .global main
main:
  pushq %rbp
  movq %rsp, %rbp
  movsd a(%rip), %xmm1        # Load 'a' into xmm1.
  movsd a(%rip), %xmm2        # Load 'a' into xmm2.
  mulsd %xmm2, %xmm1          # Square 'a' and store the result in xmm1.
  movsd %xmm1, aa(%rip)       # Store val in xmm1 out to 'aa'.
  movsd b(%rip), %xmm1        # Load 'b' into xmm1.
  movsd b(%rip), %xmm2        # Load 'b' into xmm2.
  mulsd %xmm2, %xmm1          # Square 'b' and store the result in xmm1.
  movsd %xmm1, bb(%rip)       # Store val in xmm1 out to 'bb'.
  movsd c(%rip), %xmm1        # Load 'c' into xmm1.
  movsd c(%rip), %xmm2        # Load 'c' into xmm2.
  mulsd %xmm2, %xmm1          # Square 'c' and store the result in xmm1.
  movsd %xmm1, cc(%rip)       # Store val in xmm1 out to 'cc'.
  movsd aa(%rip), %xmm1       # Load 'aa' into xmm1.
  movsd bb(%rip), %xmm2       # Load 'bb' into xmm2.
  addsd %xmm2, %xmm1          # Add 'bb' to 'aa'.
  movsd %xmm1, aapbb(%rip)    # Store sum out to 'aapbb'.
  movsd aapbb(%rip), %xmm1    # Load 'aapbb' into xmm1.
  movsd cc(%rip), %xmm2       # Load 'cc' into xmm2.
  addsd %xmm2, %xmm1          # Add 'cc' to 'aapbb'.
  movsd %xmm1, sos(%rip)      # Store sum out to 'sos'.
  movsd sos(%rip), %xmm1      # Load 'sos' into xmm1.
  sqrtsd %xmm1, %xmm1         # Sqrt value in xmm1, store res. in xmm1.
  movsd %xmm1, sossqrt(%rip)  # Store sqrt out to 'sossqrt'.
  movsd sossqrt(%rip), %xmm0
  leaq outfloatfmt(%rip), %rdi
  movq $1, %rax
  callq printf
  movq %rbp, %rsp
  popq %rbp
  retq
```

If we try to implement certain functions, e.g., sine and cosine, we will see that SSE actually does not provide any functions to do so. This is where the x87 floating-point unit comes into play. x87 is an extension to x86/64 assembly that includes support for certain floating-point instructions. A prime difference between SSE and x87 is the fact that x87 does not use "registers" in the sense that x64 and SSE use them. Namely, x87 has eight floating-point registers: %st(0) to %st(7). These pseudo-registers act as a floating-point stack of values. Consequently, many x87 instructions only work off values pushed to this stack. For example, if we want to compute the sine of some arbitrary value, we use the fsin instruction.[1] Though, we cannot just pass it a value, as it does not receive any arguments! Instead, we load a value into the st(0) "register", and invoking fsin computes the sine of the value in %st(0), and stores it back into this "register". So, we load a variable into %st(0) via fldl. Invoke fsin, and store the newly-generated result of %st(0) back into %xmm1. There is a catch, though! As we stated, fsin computes its result from %st(0) and stores it *into* %st(0). We, unfortunately, cannot save the result to a temporary register and then assign it to a target destination variable. As such, we need to write the result out to a temporary variable, tmp, then load that into an xmm register, and finally store it back out to the desired variable in memory via movsd. Before our compilation step, let us hand-write the respective assembly code. Suppose that we wish to compute the sine of 2.0944 radians.

Listing 9.126

```
.section .data
  outfloatfmt: .asciz "%lf\n"
  val: .double 2.0944
  tmp: .double 0
  sinres: .double 0
.section .text
  .extern printf
  .global main
main:
  pushq %rbp
  movq %rsp, %rbp
  fldl val(%rip)                 # Load value into st(0)
  fsin                           # Compute sine of st(0), store res. in st(0).
  fstl tmp(%rip)                 # Store quadword sine in temp var 'tmp'.
  movsd tmp(%rip), %xmm1         # Load 'tmp' into xmm1.
  movsd %xmm1, sinres(%rip)      # Store xmm1 out to 'sinres' value.
  movsd sinres(%rip), %xmm0
  leaq outfloatfmt(%rip), %rdi
  movq $1, %rax
  callq printf
  movq %rbp, %rsp
  popq %rbp
  retq
```

---

[1] A rule of thumb is that all x87 instructions are prefixed with 'f'.

Now, let us up the ante by converting this result into degrees. $\sin(2.0944\text{rad}) \approx$ 49.62°. To convert radians into degrees, we multiply the input radians by 180°, then divide this result by π (approximately 3.1415). Now, we *could* define a constant pi in the .data segment, but this is not as accurate as using the fldpi instruction, which loads a predefined constant pi onto the top of the stack. So, to convert a value from radians to degrees, we need to use the relevant x87 instructions to push the sine (radians) result to the FPU stack, push a variable holding the constant 180, multiply these and store the result in %st(0), push π, then divide. There is a small catch to this, and that is the division operation. We all know that division and subtraction are not commutative operations. That is, $a-b \neq b-a$ and $a/b \neq b/a$ for every a and b such that $a \neq b$. Therefore, we need to swap the values in %st(0) (containing π) and %st(1) (containing $\sin(120\text{rad})\cdot180$). We can do this with fxch. Let us write *only* the relevant code.

Listing 9.127

```
.section .data
  RAD2DEG: .double 180

.section .text
  ...
main:
  ...
  ffree %st(0)          # Remove value from %st(0).
  fldl sinres(%rip)     # Push 'sinres' to the FP stack.
  fldl RAD2DEG(%rip)    # Push 'RAD2DEG' to the FP stack.
  fmulp %st(0), %st(1)  # Multiply st(0) by st(1), store result in %st(0) and pop.
  fldpi                 # Push PI to FP stack.
  fxch                  # Swap res and PI values so res is in st(0).
  fdivp                 # Divide res by PI. Store res in %st(0).
  fstl sinres(%rip)     # Store st(0) in 'sinres'.
  ...
```

Let us walk through this since it is rather abstract. Because we load a value into %st0 via an earlier invocation of fldl, we need to pop that value off the stack, and we can do so with ffree. Then, we load sinres and RAD2DEG to the stack such that sinres is in %st(1) and RAD2DEG is in %st(0). We then multiply these two values together, store the result in %st(1), and pop %st(0) off the stack because RAD2DEG is no longer an important value. Then, we push π to the stack via fldpi, storing it in %st(0). We swap the values in %st(0) and %st(1) to designate the result as the dividend and π as the divisor. fdivp divides %st(0) by %st(1) and stores the result in %st(0). At long last, we store this result out to sinres in memory.

Here's the thing: we could avoid all of this complicated logic by doing something similar to what we did with printf: namely, use an external function to do the work for us! One of those handy-dandy functions is sin. Let us declare this as an extern function.

Listing 9.128

```
.section .data
  outfloatfmt: .asciz "%lf\n"
  val: .double 2.0944
  sinres: .double 0
.section .text
  .extern sin
  .extern printf
  .global main
main:
  ...
  movsd val(%rip), %xmm0      # Load value into first arg.
  callq sin                   # Call sin procedure with 'val' in radians.
  movsd %xmm0, sinres(%rip)   # Store sine result out to 'sinres'.
```

As we can see, this is significantly easier to understand! Though this requires dipping further into C libraries, the benefits largely outweigh the disadvantages. One disadvantage, albeit incredibly minuscule, is the need to link the math library when compiling via -lm. Below is a full program that computes the sine of val, converts it from radians to degrees, and prints it to standard output.

Listing 9.129

```
.section .data
  outfloatfmt: .asciz "%lf\n"
  val: .double 2.0944
  sinres: .double 0
  PI: .double 3.14159265359
  RAD2DEG: .double 180
.section .text
  .global main
main:
  pushq %rbp
  movq %rsp, %rbp
  movsd val(%rip), %xmm0      # Load value into first arg.
  callq sin                   # Call sin procedure with 'val' in radians.
  movsd %xmm0, sinres(%rip)   # Store sine result out to 'sinres'.
  movsd sinres(%rip), %xmm1   # Load 'sinres' into xmm1.
  mulsd RAD2DEG(%rip), %xmm1  # Multiply 'sinres' by RAD2DEG.
  divsd PI(%rip), %xmm1       # Divide above result by PI.
  movsd %xmm1, sinres(%rip)   # Store xmm1 out to 'sinres'.
  movsd sinres(%rip), %xmm0   # Load 'sinres' into memory.
  leaq outfloatfmt(%rip), %rdi
  movq $1, %rax
  callq printf
  movq %rbp, %rsp
  popq %rbp
  retq
```

Let us write the compiler code that adds support for the sin function. These changes are apparent in reduce-call (albeit we need to modify the preamble to declare sin as an extern function). We add a clause to reduce sin function calls. Much like sqrt, our sin function receives an argument and returns a result that may be stored. E.g., (y = (call sin x)) where x is a previously-declared angle in radians. Unlike sqrt, however, we return %xmm0 instead of %xmm1 because this sin a C library function and, therefore, stores its return value in %xmm0.

Listing 9.130

```
(define reduce-call
 (λ (exp)
  (letrec ([...])
   (cond
    [...]
    [(eqv? procname 'sin)
     (let* ([arg (first procargs)])
      (begin
       (printf " movsd ~a(%rip), %xmm0~n" arg)
       (printf " callq sin~n")
       'xmm0))]
    [...]))))
```

Exercise 9.14. ($\star$)

Add code to support the other two "main" trigonometric functions, i.e., cos and tan.

Exercise 9.15. ($\star\star$)

Define an x64 assembly procedure rad2deg that receives a floating-point radian value as an argument in %xmm0, converts it to degrees, and returns the result in %xmm0. Use global variables, as we have before, for π and the conversion factor 180°. You may also use fldpi as we did before.

Exercise 9.16. ($\star\star$)

Add support for calling the rad2deg function in your compiler. That is, it should support a function call, e.g., (var deg = (call rad2deg rad)), where rad is defined as some floating-point value.

9.10   Optimizing Generating Assembly

The code that our compiler generates is certainly correct, but it can be improved by
a substantial amount. In this section, we will explore a few optimization techniques
used in real compilers.

Redundant Instruction Elimination

There are certain instances of instruction emitting that can be eliminated while
preserving the semantic behavior of our program. As an example, instructions
that move a value from a register into the same register are wasteful. Similarly,
arithmatic operations performed on identity elements are also superfluous, e.g.,
$x+0$, $y-0$, $z\cdot1$. All we need to do is add, to the respective reducers, code that
checks for these conditions and, if they are true, does not emit code.

First, we will remove unnecessary instructions that are tautological, i.e., they
move a value into themselves, e.g., movq %rax, %rax. Hopefully the caveat of
this optimization is clear in that we can only remove instructions that do not
change the value of the destination register. We add the optimization directly
into print-instruction3 because it is the last "point of contact", so to speak,
with the instruction before it is emitted. We can consider the print-empty function as one that invokes printf with the empty string. One important property of
compiler optimization, however, is to only remove operations that do not have side-
effects. Namely, if some operation sets the flag register, it should not be optimized
prematurely. For example, consider the statement orq %rax, %rax. Even though
this *appears* to be tautological, since performing a bitwise-OR on the same number
does nothing to the resulting register, it does affect the flags. So, if a program relies
on this instruction to perform a comparison, optimizing out the statement breaks
semantic equivalence.

Listing 9.131

```
(define print-instruction3
 (λ (op src dest)
  (let ([res-src (reduce src)]
        [res-dest (reduce dest)])
   (cond
    [(and (eqv? res-src res-dest) (eqv? op 'movq)) (print-empty)]
    [... ])))))
```

To optimize our addition functions, we should rework reduce-add to only add
non-zero values into a register.

Listing 9.132

```
(define reduce-add
 (λ (exp)
  (letrec ([rec
            (λ (lon)
             (cond
              [(null? lon) (print-empty)]
              [else
               (let ([val (reduce (first lon))])
                (cond
                 [(zero? val) (rec (rest lon))]
                 [else
                  (begin
                   (print-instruction3 'addq val 'rbx)
                   (rec (rest lon)))])])])])
   ...)))
```

Listing 9.133

```
> (compile                         main:
   '((proc main ()                   ...
      ((var y - 5)                   movq $5, -8(%rbp)
       (var x = (+ y 0))             movq -8(%rbp), %rbx
       (call print x)))))           addq $0, %rbx
                                     movq %rbx, -16(%rbp)
                                     movq -16(%rbp), %rsi
                                     leaq outnumfmt(%rip), %rdi
                                     movq $0, %rax
                                     callq printf
                                     ...
                                     retq
```

Exercise 9.17. (★★★★)

As we mentioned, some instructions cannot be prematurely optimized due to their potential to cause side-effects on the flags register. This includes comparison, bitwise, and even arithmetic operations. For example, if we overflow a register when performing an addition, the overflow flag is toggled. Perform some analysis with your compiler and see if you can write code that only optimizes instructions that preserve program semantic behavior.

Exercise 9.18. (★★★★★)

Dataflow analysis is the study of where and how data moves through a program. Part of such analysis is determining variable propagation, i.e., where and when variables are live/accessible. Pushing every callee-saved registers to the stack, even if they are not used, is overly ambitious and wasteful. Add an optimization pass to the compiler that determines whether a function body uses any callee-saved registers and, if so, pushes only those to the stack.

Constant Folding

Consider the following expression; to what instructions does it compile?

Listing 9.134

> (var x = (+ 5 10 15 20 25 30 35 40))	movq $5, %rax
	addq $10, %rax
	addq $15, %rax
	addq $20, %rax
	addq $25, %rax
	addq $30, %rax
	addq $35, %rax
	addq $40, %rax
	movq %rax, -8(%rbp)

There are **nine** instructions for one simple arithmetic and store operation! Would it not be simpler to just move the sum of these values into %rax, then into the memory location?[1]

Listing 9.135

```
movq $180, %rax
movq %rax, -8(%rbp)
```

What we are aiming for is an optimization technique called *constant folding*. That is, instead of wasting time on simple arithmatic operations at the assembly level, we can fold the constants into numbers and store them directly. Let us write a function `fold-constants` that receives an arbitrary statement and returns said statement with the operations, if any exist, reduced to a single number.

Now, it may be tempting to use a "fold" operation to sum the values in an addition operation, but this will not always work; if we have, say, an inlined expression within the summation, we must account for it upon folding the overall expression. So, this looks like a good opportunity to write a small interpreter that receives an s-expression written in the input language and outputs another s-expression with the necessary optimizations, should they exist. Note the the constant-folding pass of our compiler occurs before we even see the assembly language; consider it a pre-processing step. We will implement only `fold-add` and a few other special forms, leaving the rest as exercises.

Listing 9.136

```
(define fold-constants
 (λ (stmt)
  (cond
   [(number? stmt) stmt]
   [(symbol? stmt) stmt]
   [(var? stmt) (fold-var stmt)]
   [(add? stmt) (fold-add stmt)]
   [(cmp? stmt) (fold-cmp stmt)]
   [(if? stmt) (fold-if stmt)]
   [(return? stmt) (fold-return stmt)]
   [(proc? stmt) (fold-proc stmt)]
   [else stmt])))
```

We know that numbers and symbols resolve to themselves. So, the first reducer to concern ourselves with is `fold-var`, which recursively folds its expression, recreating the form of a `var` s-expression:

---

[1]In actuality, a smart compiler would remove the use of %rax if it were unnecessary.

Listing 9.137

```
(define fold-var
 (λ (stmt)
  (let ([id (second stmt)]
        [expr (fourth stmt)])
   `(var ,id = ,(fold-constants expr)))))
```

Up next, we will fold addition expressions. The idea is to apply the `foldr` operation to the addition s-expression after mapping `fold-constants` over the expression itself. This way, we fold constants in all sub-expressions.

Listing 9.138

```
(define fold-add
 (λ (stmt)
  (let ([expr (rest (rest stmt))])
   (foldr + 0 (map fold-constants stmt)))))
```

To test our implementation, we should write a function for processing several sequential statements using `foldr`, perhaps `fold-statements`:

Listing 9.139

```
(define fold-statements
 (λ (los)
  (foldr (λ (s acc)
          (cons (fold-constants s)
                acc))
         '()
         los)))
```

```
> (fold-statements                          ((var x = 90))
   '((var x = (+ 20 30 40))))
> (fold-statements                          ((var y = 180)
   '((var y = (+ (+ 20 20)                    (var z = 270))
               (+ 30 30)
               (+ 40 40)))
     (var z = (+ 100 (+ 70 100))))))
```

Let us search for possible constant folds within `if` statements as well; we must search the predicate, consequent, and alternative. Within each clause rests an easy call to `fold-constants`.

Listing 9.140

```
(define fold-if
 (λ (stmt)
  (let ([p (second stmt)]
        [c (third stmt)]
        [a (fourth stmt)])
   (list 'if (fold-constants p) (fold-constants c) (fold-constants a)))))
```

Before we test `fold-if`, we need to fold constants found within expressions that return booleans; fortunately we have a `cmp?` recognizer, which we will recycle. All this requires is a fold over the two operands of a comparison operator:

Listing 9.141

```
(define fold-cmp
 (λ (stmt)
  (let ([op (first stmt)]
       [fst (second stmt)]
       [snd (third stmt)])
   (list op (fold-constants fst) (fold-constants snd)))))
```

Now, let us go ahead and implement constant folding for procedure definitions. What is different about procedures is that their bodies consist of statement lists, meaning we must use `fold-statements` rather than mapping `fold-constants` over the statements. In doing this, we also have to account for `return` statements, which we will omit due to redundancy.

Listing 9.142

```
(define fold-proc
 (λ (stmt)
  (let ([id (second stmt)]
       [formals (third stmt)]
       [body (fourth stmt)])
   (list 'proc id formals (fold-statements body)))))
```

Let us put these two together in a couple of test cases.

Listing 9.143

```
> (fold-statements                    ((proc foo (x y)
   '((proc foo (x y)                    (if (?= x y)
     (if (?= x y)                        (return 150)
        (return (+ 10 20 30 40 50))      (return 1000))))
        (return (+ 100
                  (+ 400 500)))))))

> (fold-statements                    ((proc bar ()
   '((proc bar ()                       (if (?= 200 400)
     (if (?= (+ 100 100) (+ 200 200))    (return 150)
        (return (+ 10 20 30 40 50))      (return 1000))))
        (return (+ 100
                  (+ 400 500)))))))
```

Exercise 9.19. (⋆)
Add constant folding for expressions containing subtraction operations. As an example, (var x = (- 10 20 30)), which becomes (var x = -60).

Exercise 9.20. (⋆)
Add constant folding for multiplicative expressions. As an example, (var x = (* 10 20 30)), which becomes (var x = 6000).

Exercise 9.21. (⋆⋆⋆⋆)
Our implementation of the `fold-add` optimization falls apart if we throw a variable into the mix, e.g., (var x = (+ 10 20 30 y 50)) . A smart compiler could optimize this into (var x = (+ 110 y)), where y is some value to be utilized in the assembly code. Implement this form of constant folding into your compiler.

10   Memory Management

One of the main causes of the fall of the Roman Empire was that, lacking zero,
they had no way to indicate successful termination of their C programs.

—Robert Firth

10.1   Memory Allocation

Our interpreters, so far, have relied on the fact that our programs are relatively small and do not use copious amounts of memory. Though, what if we, once again, write a program to compute the Fibonacci sequence of a double-digit number?

Listing 10.1

```
(define fib
 (λ (n)
  (cond
   [(<= n 1) 1]
   [else (+ (fib (- n 1))
            (fib (- n 2)))])))

> (fib 15)                                    610
```

If we check the output of Valgrind, we observe that our interpreter leaks approximately two megabytes of memory. Recall that, in the primer on C and memory allocation, we said that it is a desire to free memory whenever it is previously allocated. In this section, we will explain this desire in further detail.

Let us try computing the twentieth Fibonacci number. In doing so, we see that Valgrind leaks around twenty-four megabytes of memory. This is starting to leave the realm of insignificant memory losses, and we need to properly clean up what we allocate. The big issue is that if we attempt to free, say, an s-value at any point, we do not know when it will be referenced again. If we immediately free a lambda procedure, then we no longer have access for function invocation. We need to introduce a *proper* memory allocation system. Though, in order to do this, we need to understand the fundamental differences between the two types of memory: stack-allocated memory, and heap-allocated memory.

Stack-Based Memory

When we declare variables within a function, they are stored on the stack. The stack is the location of all locally-defined variables as well as function calls. That is, each call to a function stores an *activation record* on the stack. We can visualize the stack as a sequence of memory addresses. As we stated, any local variables that are not dynamically allocated via, e.g., `malloc`, `calloc`, or `realloc`, are stored on the stack.[1] When a function terminates, any variables declared within the function are clobbered/destroyed from the stack.

One important distinction between stack-based variables and heap-allocated memory comes through pointers. Suppose we declare a pointer as follows.

Listing 10.2

```
1   int main(void) {
2     char *foo = NULL;
3     return 0;
4   }
```

The pointer, namely `foo`, is stored on the stack. If we explicitly allocate memory to `foo` via, e.g., `malloc`, that allocated memory is stored on the heap.

Function calls make prolific use of the stack through activation records. As we discussed in Chapter 9, when we call a function, we push the address-to-return, and certain arguments onto the stack. Once we jump to the first instruction of the function in memory, if the function requires space for local variables, we make room for these on the stack by subtracting from the stack pointer. Additionally, some registers are "callee-saved", meaning the function must push their contents to the stack. Before returning from a function, we "de-allocate" the local variable/alignment space by simply moving the stack pointer back up to its prior location. We end off by popping the callee-saved registers and return address from the stack.[2] Due to the fact that registers and stack space are reclaimed or popped off the stack only upon reaching the end of a function, it becomes apparent how non-tail recursive functions can be susceptible to segmentation faults. Consider a never-terminating non-tail recursive factorial function:

Listing 10.3—Faulty Non-Tail-Recursive Function (`main.c`)

```
1   int fact(int n) {
2     if (n == 0) { return 1; }
3     else { return n * fact(n - 1); }
4   }
5
6   int main(void) {
7     fact(-1);
8     return 0;
9   }
```

---

[1] Recall from Chapter 9 that variables declared in the `.data` or `.bss` segments are not located on the stack in our sense of the term.

[2] These definitions and explanations are applicable to AT&T x64 assembly and do not strictly apply to all variants of assembly and architectures. For example, some architectures and standards require different callee-saved registers.

By calling fact with -1, we never reach a base case, meaning we continuously push more and more return addresses, arguments, and callee-saved registers to the stack without ever unwinding any recursive calls. Eventually, the stack runs out of its limited space, resulting in a segmentation fault. In other programming languages with better-detailed error messages, this is known as a *stack overflow* error/exception.

Heap-Based Memory

Dynamically-allocated memory is an incredibly important and sometimes frustrating concept not only in C, but also in all of computer science. Generally, we use dynamically-allocated memory or variables when there is an indeterminate number of allocations to be made. The *heap*, in and of itself, is a pool of memory that a program may access/utilize/alter at runtime. Heap-allocated variables are also accessible across functions. Recall from the previous section that all stack-based variables are clobbered once a function terminates. Consider the following code segment:

Listing 10.4

```
1   char *foo(void) {
2     char *str = malloc(1024);
3     return NULL;
4   }
5
6   int main(void) {
7     char *bar = foo();
8     return 0;
9   }
```

Once foo finishes execution, the pointer str is clobbered from the stack and we lose the foo activation record. The difference, though, is that the memory pointed to by str is not lost and still exists in the heap. What is unfortunate is that upon losing reference to that memory by, e.g., not returning a valid pointer, we can no longer access said memory, thus introducing a memory leak.

Garbage Collection

Garbage collection is a feature in many modern programming languages. A *garbage collector* is a form of automatically managing dynamic memory allocation. In C, when we allocate memory via `malloc` (or a similar function), there must be an accompanying call to `free`. Until this point, we have been rather liberal in our use of `free` or associated destructor functions (often opting to not use them at all) because a premature de-allocation in an interpreter can cause troublesome segmentation faults and bugs that are tricky to trace.

Writing a Lazy Garbage Collector

In contrast to the more powerful garbage collection algorithms that are available, we will start by implementing a lazy garbage collector. A lazy garbage collector will only automatically free allocated memory at the end of the program. Though, the issue with this approach is a lazy garbage collector is only marginally better than not freeing dynamically-allocated memory at all. So, there will still be times when we want to free certain dynamic memory allocations, i.e., the garbage collector should not intervene and free these pointers. These types of allocations are called *uncontrolled allocations*, in contrast to *controlled allocations*, which are allocations managed solely by the garbage collector. We will implement our lazy garbage collector outside the interpreter first, then replace our dynamic allocation function calls with ones suited for a garbage collector.

As a motivating example, let us write some C code to allocate some arrays of integers, but forget to free some of the resources.

Listing 10.5

```
1   int main(int argc, char *argv[]) {
2     int *arr1 = malloc(1000 * sizeof(int));
3     int *arr2 = malloc(2000 * sizeof(int));
4     int *arr3 = malloc(3000 * sizeof(int));
5
6     free(arr2);
7     return 0;
8   }
```

Running this through Valgrind, we get a memory leak of 16,000 bytes, which is expected, as we allocate a total of 6,000 integers, each using four bytes, for a total of 24,000 bytes. Because we only free `arr2`, we only free 8,000 bytes. So, what happens if we forget to do this on a much larger and harder-to-trace scale, i.e., our interpreters? What we are after is a garbage collector. So, let us write one! We first need an interface for tracking allocated and freed dynamic memory. Then, we need a way of storing each tracker. Let us construct the former struct first. As an aside, we abbreviate the garbage collector as `mgc` to stand in for, "Mini Garbage Collector".

Listing 10.6—Mini Garbage Collector Allocation Chunk (mgc.h)

```
1   #ifndef MGC_H
2   #define MGC_H
3
4   #include <stdbool.h>
5
6   struct mgc_allocation {
7     void *ptr;
8     struct mgc_allocation *next;
9     void (*dfree)(void *);
10    bool is_free;
11  };
12
13  #endif // MGC_H
```

Our garbage collector needs four pieces of information to manage a block of dynamically-allocated memory: the pointer to the heap-allocated memory, the next allocation in the linked list chain, a "method" of freeing the allocated chunk, and a flag to keep track of the state of the allocation. If we, for instance, prematurely free a chunk of memory, we want the garbage collector to know that it should not be freed twice. Moreover, referencing a pointer that has been previously freed results in a *use-after-free* vulnerability.

To keep track of allocations, we will introduce a type definition for the garbage collector that stores the head and the tail of the linked list allocations.

Listing 10.7—Garbage Collector Linked List Definition (mgc.h)

```
1   struct mgc {
2     struct mgc_allocation *head;
3     struct mgc_allocation *tail;
4   };
```

Then in the corresponding source file, we should initialize a static mgc variable (static is used to ensure that only mgc.c is aware of its existence). We initialize the garbage collector by setting the head and tail pointers to NULL.

Listing 10.8—Initialization of Garbage Collection Linked List (mgc.c)

```
1   #include <stddef.h>
2
3   #include "mgc.h"
4
5   static struct mgc gc;
6
7   void mgc_init(void) {
8     gc.head = gc.tail = NULL;
9   }
```

We previously mentioned the idea of controlled versus uncontrolled allocations. Controlled allocations are those that the garbage collector responds to. Namely, when we create a controlled allocation, the garbage collector is informed of the allocation's existence. Therefore we need to write a function that creates a controlled allocation.

Listing 10.9—Controlled Allocation Function Header (mgc.c)

```
1   void *mgc_alloc(size_t sz, void (*dfree)(void *)) {    }
```

This function looks eerily similar to `malloc` with one added exception: the function pointer `dfree`. Because we want our garbage collector to be as flexible as possible, we need to tell it how to free certain objects. Consider the following code example:

Listing 10.10

```
1   #include <stdlib.h>
2   #include <string.h>
3
4   struct student {
5     char *name;
6     double gpa;
7   };
8
9   void student_init(struct student *s, char *name, double gpa) {
10    s->name = strdup(name);
11    s->gpa = gpa;
12  }
13
14  void student_destroy(void *ptr) {
15    struct student *s = (struct student *) ptr;
16    free(s->name);
17    free(s);
18  }
19
20  int main(void) {
21    struct student *s = malloc(sizeof(struct student));
22    ASSERT_ALLOC(s, "main");
23    student_init(s, "Albert", 4.0);
24    ...
25    free(s);
26    ...
27    return 0;
28  }
```

We create a `struct student` with a dynamically-allocated field within, namely the `char *` through a call to `strdup`. If we were to inform the garbage collector of this allocation and told it that, in order to free a `struct student`, it is to invoke `free`, then it would not be a correct deallocation because the memory allocated by `strdup` to hold the name would no longer be reachable by the programmer. We, instead, should pass `student_destroy` as a function pointer.

Listing 10.11

```
1   #include "mgc.h"
2
3   void student_create(struct student *s, char *name, double gpa) {
4     s->name = strdup(name);
5     s->gpa = gpa;
6     return s;
7   }
8
9   int main(void) {
10    struct student *s = mgc_alloc(sizeof(struct student), student_destroy);
11    ...
12    return 0;
13  }
```

But we still have the problem of the name field. We could, theoretically, tell the garbage collector that it too is a controlled allocation. If we do this, though, we would need to change student_destroy to not free name, because that is the job of the garbage collector. Therefore, we introduce the notion of an uncontrolled allocation, which is just a normal allocation and free with a fancy name. That is, it is the programmer's responsibility to handle the memory and not the garbage collector. So, when the garbage collector attempts to destroy a struct student, it not only frees said struct, but invokes an uncontrolled de-allocation. The only reason it is uncontrolled is because we explicitly call free. Assuming we have a function mgc_ualloc to create an uncontrolled allocation, we may modify our code to not use strdup as follows:

Listing 10.12

```
1   #include "mgc.h"
2
3   void student_create(struct student *s, char *name, double gpa) {
4     s->name = mgc_ualloc(strlen(name) + 1);
5     strcpy(s->name, name);
6     s->gpa = gpa;
7     return s;
8   }
```

Of course, our garbage collector could also contain a function, e.g., mgc_strdup, which allocates memory for the duplicated string in the garbage collector.[1] In doing so we relinquish responsibility of freeing the memory from the programmer, but they then consequently lose control over when and where the de-allocation occurs.

With this simple example out of the way, we take a deep dive into the implementation of controlled allocations.

First, we must allocate a block of memory of some specified size. Then, we should allocate a node to store inside the garbage collector. What is returned from this function is ultimately a pointer to the allocated chunk of memory, so we may as well add that in now to prevent confusion down the road.[2]

Listing 10.13—Chunk Allocation Node Creation (mgc.c)

```
1   void *mgc_alloc(size_t sz, void (*dfree)(void *)) {
2     void *ptr = calloc(1, sz);
3     ASSERT_ALLOC(ptr, "mgc_alloc");
4     struct mgc_allocation *alloc = calloc(1, sizeof(struct mgc_allocation));
5     ASSERT_ALLOC(ptr, "mgc_alloc");
6     ...
7     // TODO.
8     ...
9     return ptr;
10  }
```

So, because we have a node, we can directly access and mutate its fields ptr, is_free, and dfree.

---

[1] Moreover, the garbage collector might have many functions from the C standard library that by default allocate memory for the programmer such as asprintf.

[2] As an aside, we use calloc rather than malloc to ensure that the memory allocated by our garbage collector is zeroed before its utilization. Using malloc provides no guarantees on what exists in a memory chunk; only that it is free to be read from or written to.

Listing 10.14—Assigning Chunk Allocation Node Fields (mgc.c)

```
1   void *mgc_alloc(size_t sz, void (*dfree)(void *)) {
2     ...
3     alloc->ptr = ptr;
4     alloc->is_free = false;
5     alloc->dfree = dfree;
6
7     return ptr;
8   }
```

Finally, we need to append the allocation to the tail of the garbage collector linked list.

Listing 10.15—Add Allocation Chunk to Linked List (mgc.c)

```
1    void *mgc_alloc(size_t sz, void (*dfree)(void *)) {
2      ...
3      // If there's nothing in the garbage collector list, then add it as the head.
4      if (NULL == gc.head) {
5        gc.head = gc.tail = alloc;
6      } else {
7        gc.tail->next = alloc;
8        gc.tail = alloc;
9      }
10     return ptr;
11   }
```

That is all there is to controlled allocations! An uncontrolled allocation, on the other hand, is absolutely trivial.

Listing 10.16—Uncontrolled Allocation Creation (mgc.c)

```
1   void *mgc_ualloc(size_t sz) {
2     void *ptr = calloc(1, sz);
3     ASSERT_ALLOC(ptr, "mgc_ualloc");
4     return ptr;
5   }
```

At this point, because we have controlled allocations, we certainly need a way for the garbage collector to free data inside its linked list. Accordingly, we will now design mgc_free which receives a pointer to a memory block to de-allocate. Then, we traverse through the garbage collector and, if we find the memory chunk, we only free it if it has not been previously freed.[1]

---

[1]Our implementation includes a check that validates the existence of the "free" function pointer for safety purposes.

Listing 10.17—De-allocation of Controlled Allocation (mgc.c)

```
1   void mgc_free(void *ptr) {
2    for (struct mgc_allocation *curr = gc.head; curr != NULL; curr = curr->next) {
3     if (curr->ptr == ptr && curr->dfree) {
4      if (!curr->dfree) {
5       EPF("mgc_free: Address at %p does not have a destructor function\n", ptr);
6       exit(EXIT_FAILURE);
7      } else if (curr->is_free) {
8       EPF("mgc_free: Attempted to free a pointer that is already freed\n");
9       exit(EXIT_FAILURE);
10     }
11     curr->dfree(curr->ptr);
12     curr->is_free = true;
13     return;
14    }
15   }
16  }
```

So, if we **ever invoke** mgc_free manually, i.e., without the intervention of the garbage collector, it will not accidentally free the memory again thanks to the flag. Conveniently, **just like** mgc_ualloc, the accompanying mgc_ufree is as simple as they come.

Listing 10.18—Deallocation of Uncontrolled Allocation (mgc.c)

```
1   void mgc_ufree(void *ptr) {
2    if (ptr != NULL) { free(ptr); }
3   }
```

So, we have access to allocation functions which store memory that the garbage collector oversees. What about when we want to *run* the garbage collector? Since this is a lazy garbage collector, it will only run once the program terminates (or, to be more precise, immediately before execution finishes). Thus, we will write mgc_cleanup that frees all memory inside the garbage collector using the stored function pointers. We also free the mgc_allocation nodes.

Listing 10.19—Destruction of All Mini Garbage Collector Chunks (mgc.c)

```
1   void mgc_cleanup(void) {
2    struct mgc_allocation *tmp = gc.head;
3    while (NULL != gc.head) {
4     tmp = gc.head;
5     gc.head = gc.head->next;
6     if (!tmp->is_free) {
7      tmp->dfree(tmp->ptr);
8      tmp->is_free = true;
9     }
10    free(tmp);
11   }
12  }
```

Lastly, **inside our** main function, we invoke the garbage collector initializer and clean up functions. It is important that we activate the garbage collector only after all other allocations are destroyed so as to not accidentally double-free variables and pointers.

Listing 10.20—Adding Mini Garbage Collector to Interpreter (`main.c`)

```
1   int main(int argc, char *argv[]) {
2     srand(time(NULL));
3     mgc_init();
4     eval_init();
5     parser_init();
6
7     parser_parse(argv[1], PARSE_FILE);
8
9     ast_cleanup();
10    parser_cleanup();
11    mgc_cleanup();
12    return 0;
13  }
```

Though, before we go through the trouble of changing all dynamic allocations to those that use the garbage collector, let us revisit our integer array allocation example. We will modify the implementation to instead use mgc.

Listing 10.21

```
1   #include "mgc.h"
2
3   int main(int argc, char *argv[]) {
4     mgc_init();
5     int *arr1 = mgc_alloc(1000 * sizeof(int), free);
6     int *arr2 = mgc_alloc(2000 * sizeof(int), free);
7     int *arr3 = mgc_alloc(3000 * sizeof(int), free);
8     mgc_cleanup();
9     return 0;
10  }
```

Running this code through Valgrind shows that all memory was freed. The nice thing about our lazy garbage collector implementation is that, if we manually free the allocated memory (by calling `mgc_free`), the garbage collector notices that the allocations were freed and, therefore, skips over freeing that memory.

Listing 10.22

```
1   #include "mgc.h"
2
3   int main(int argc, char *argv[]) {
4     mgc_init();
5     int *arr1 = mgc_alloc(1000 * sizeof(int), free);
6     int *arr2 = mgc_alloc(2000 * sizeof(int), free);
7     int *arr3 = mgc_alloc(3000 * sizeof(int), free);
8
9     mgc_free(arr1);
10    mgc_free(arr2);
11    mgc_free(arr3);
12    mgc_cleanup();
13    return 0;
14  }
```

All that is left is to go and replace any calls to `malloc` and `free` to `mgc_alloc` and `mgc_free`. Though, it is important to recall the problem with the `student` struct example—if there exists a controlled allocation that has associated memory, those variables should use uncontrolled allocations. When replacing each allocation, be sure to incrementally test the interpreter, one piece at a time, to ensure everything works in between modifications. We also reiterate that this garbage collector is a lazy garbage collector and is only a step above not freeing memory at the end of a program. `mgc` only keeps track of what memory is allocated; not what points to it or if it is valid (or ever becomes invalid).

Exercise 10.1. (⋆)

Write two functions `mgc_calloc` and `mgc_realloc` that work similar to their non-mgc counterparts.

Exercise 10.2. (⋆)

Write a function `mgc_urealloc` that serves as an uncontrolled reallocation function.

10.2   Reference-Counted Garbage Collection

As we stated, our previous implementation is a very lazy garbage collector, and is the one we will continue to use throughout the rest of our journey of computer science due to its ease of implementation. As a brief aside, we will explore and implement a more powerful garbage collection algorithm, which utilizes reference counting.

A *reference*, at least in C, is often synonymous and used interchangeably with "pointer". We can declare a "reference" to some arbitrary pointer as follows:

Listing 10.23

```
1   int main(void) {
2     int *ptr = malloc(  );
3     int *ref = ptr;
4     return 0;
5   }
```

Now, `ref` refers to the same pointer as `ptr`. So, if we were to alter the data pointed to by `ptr` in some way, `ref` would see these changes. Consider the following example:

Listing 10.24

```
1    #include <stdio.h>                          100
2    #include <stdlib.h>                         100
3
4    int main(void) {
5      int *ptr = malloc(10 * sizeof(int));
6      int *ref = ptr;
7      ptr[3] = 100;
8      printf("ptr[3]=%d\n", ptr[3]);
9      printf("ref[3]=%d\n", ref[3]);
10     free(ptr);
11     return 0;
12   }
```

Both `printf` invocations output the same data. If we `free` the data pointed to by `ptr`, the `ref` pointer still points to that freed data in memory, which when accessed may result in a segmentation fault, but at the very least is an example of a use-after-free vulnerability. How does this relate to garbage collection? A *reference-counting* garbage collector stores a counter alongside each allocation. This counter represents how many pointers reference the data. So, if we reassign references down the road, we lose the ability to de-allocate that heap-allocated memory! A reference-counting garbage collector alleviates this problem by de-allocating any memory that is pointed to by exactly zero references. Let us create a garbage collector that follows this approach: rcgc, i.e., "Reference-Counting Garbage Collector".

The underlying data structure of rcgc is a linked list, much like mgc. We will keep track of two structs: `rcgc`, and `rcgc_allocation`. The former functions identically to mgc, and the latter to `mgc_allocation`.

Listing 10.25—Reference-Counting Garbage Collector Header (`rcgc.h`)

```
1    #ifndef RCGC_H
2    #define RCGC_H
3
4    struct rcgc_allocation {
5      void *data;
6      struct rcgc_allocation *next;
7      size_t counter;
8      bool is_free;
9    };
10
11   struct rcgc {
12     struct rcgc_allocation *head;
13     struct rcgc_allocation *tail;
14   };
15
16   #endif // RCGC_H
```

We now need to make a decision as to how we will allocate and assign references to pointers. We need a way of informing the garbage collector that we wish to allocate some memory and store it in the garbage collector. This is a trivial matter and similar to that of the mgc allocator. What is not as trivial is how references are swapped around. Normally, if we want to change a pointer's value, we use the assignment operator. We cannot do this with a reference-counting garbage collector, because reassigning the pointer directly does not update the reference counter of some allocated memory chunk. Thus, we will write a function `rcgc_assign` that receives a `void **` argument `dest` and a `void *` argument `src`, with the intent of assigning `dest` to point to the data pointed to by `src`. There are, therefore, two cases to consider: first, if `dest` points to NULL, then `dest` does not point to memory located within the garbage collector. On the contrary, if `dest` is non-NULL, then whatever it points to **must** already exist in the garbage collector and that data needs to have its reference count decremented, since `dest` will no longer point to it. In either case the reference count of `src` must be incremented since `dest` now refers to it.

With the explanations out of the way, let us begin by writing `rcgc_alloc`: a function that allocates memory into the garbage collector and returns a pointer to said allocated memory, much like the functionality of `mgc_alloc`. Since the implementation is rather redundant, we omit the code that adds the `rcgc_allocation` node to the linked list.

Listing 10.26—Reference-Counting Garbage Collector Chunk Allocation (`rcgc.c`)

```
1   void *rcgc_alloc(size_t sz) {
2     // Allocate the node in the tree.
3     struct rcgc_allocation *node = malloc(sizeof(struct rcgc_allocation));
4
5     // Add to linked list.
6     ...
7
8     // Now assign the ptr data.
9     void *ptr = calloc(1, sz);
10    ASSERT_ALLOC(ptr, "rcgc_alloc");
11    node->data = ptr;
12    node->counter = 1;
13    return ptr;
14  }
```

Next, we write the function that, effectively, manages references: `rcgc_assign`. This function takes the place of, e.g., `ref = ptr` in the previous code segment. That is, whenever we want to change what a pointer points to, we use this function. As we stated, if `dest` is `NULL`, then it currently does not exist in the garbage collector. Otherwise, we need to find its reference and decrement the counter by one. `src`, on the contrary, must always exist in the garbage collector. Otherwise, it would be an invalid reference.

Listing 10.27—Reference/Pointer Assignment (`rcgc.c`)

```
1   void rcgc_assign(void **dest, void *src) {
2     // If "dest" is already in the tree, find it and decrement its ref ctr.
3     if (NULL != dest) {
4       struct rcgc_allocation *dest_alloc = rcgc_search(*dest);
5       if (NULL != dest_alloc) {
6         dest_alloc->counter--;
7       }
8     }
9
10    // If we cannot find the source, then it does not exist.
11    struct rcgc_allocation *src_alloc = rcgc_search(src);
12    if (NULL == src_alloc) {
13      EPF("rgrc_assign: Could not find memory address %p\n", src);
14      exit(EXIT_FAILURE);
15    }
16    src_alloc->counter++;
17    *dest = src;
18  }
```

We said that `src` must always be in the garbage collector, but what if we want to assign a pointer to be `NULL`, i.e., clear its reference? We can write another function, `rcgc_release`! Note that, it is similarly non-sensical to assign a pointer that is already `NULL` to `NULL`, so we add the case to check.

Listing 10.28—Releasing an Acquired Reference (`rcgc.c`)

```
1   void rcgc_release(void **dest) {
2     if (NULL != dest) {
3       struct rcgc_allocation *dest_alloc = rcgc_search(*dest);
4       if (NULL != dest_alloc) {
5         dest_alloc->counter--;
6       }
7       *dest = NULL;
8     }
9   }
```

Searching through the linked list/garbage collector via `rcgc_search` is simple:

Listing 10.29—Chunk Allocation Search Procedure (`rcgc.c`)

```
1   static struct rcgc_allocation *rcgc_search(void *ptr) {
2     for (struct rcgc_allocation *curr = gc.head; curr != NULL; curr = curr->next) {
3       if (ptr == curr->data) {
4         return curr;
5       }
6     }
7     return NULL;
8   }
```

We now need two more functions: one to activate the garbage collector, and another to clean up everything within the garbage collector at the end of the program. Let us write the former first. All we must do is traverse through the list, find all references with a zero counter, and free the data (if it has not been previously freed).

Listing 10.30—Activation of Garbage Collector (`rcgc.c`)

```
1   void rcgc_activate(void) {
2     for (struct rcgc_allocation *curr = gc.head; curr != NULL; curr = curr->next) {
3       if (0 == curr->counter && !curr->is_free) {
4         free(curr->data);
5         curr->data = NULL;
6         curr->is_free = true;
7       }
8     }
9   }
```

Lastly, we need to write a function that deletes all allocated memory from the garbage collector. Being that it is identical to mgc's underlying structure, we will copy its `cleanup` function, only modifying it to work with `rcgc_allocation` structs rather than `mgc_allocation`.

Listing 10.31—Destruction of Reference-Counting Chunk Allocations (`rcgc.c`)

```
1    void rcgc_cleanup(void) {
2      struct rcgc_allocation *tmp = gc.head;
3      while (gc.head != NULL) {
4        tmp = gc.head;
5        gc.head = gc.head->next;
6        if (!tmp->is_free) {
7          free(tmp->data);
8          tmp->is_free = true;
9        }
10       free(tmp);
11     }
12   }
```

That is all there is to it! Let us write some tests:

Listing 10.32

```
1   intmain(void) {
2     rcgc_init();
3     int *arr1 = rcgc_alloc(sizeof(int) * 10);
4     int *arr2 = NULL;
5     int *arr3 = rcgc_alloc(sizeof(int) * 100);
6     rcgc_assign(( void ** ) &arr2, ( void * ) &arr1); // arr2 = arr1
7     rcgc_assign(( void ** ) &arr3, ( void * ) &arr2); // arr3 = arr2
8     rcgc_assign(( void ** ) &arr1, ( void * ) &arr2); // arr1 = arr2
9     rcgc_activate();
10    rcgc_cleanup();
11    return 0;
12  }
```

Upon running this code, we see that the memory pointed to by arr3 is lost once we assign the pointer arr2 to arr3. So, after activating the garbage collector, it determines that arr3 has zero references and, therefore, is eliminated.

There are some problems with our current reference-counting algorithm. Suppose we are within a loop that repeatedly allocates memory that is pointed to by the same pointer.

Listing 10.33

```
1   for (int i = 0; i < n; i++) {
2     int *arr = rcgc_alloc( );
3   }
```

We now have a new problem to deal with: pointers that are prematurely reassigned no longer point to the data they were originally assigned, but rather whatever was the last allocation in the loop. A reasonable solution is to pass the pointer, as a reference, alongside our call to allocate memory. Therefore, the garbage collector can check to see if that pointer already points to memory and, if so, decrement its respective counter prior to reassigning the pointer.

Unfortunately, this does not solve the problem of pointers that go out of scope. Consider the following code:

Listing 10.34

```
1   void foo() {
2     int *x = malloc(1024);
3   }
```

A smart compiler may see this line of code and optimize it out of execution since it (the allocated memory) is never referenced or mutated outside the scope of foo. This type of analysis, however, is beyond the scope of our chapter on memory management. Though, rest assured that the memory is always freed at the end of the program by the garbage collector, similar to how our implementation of mgc works.

Garbage collection is not a feature of C, but is imperative to languages such as Scheme, Lisp, and so forth. Think about how many allocations are necessary for things such as *cons* pairs or lists. Any time that we return/create a new data structure whose value results from a preexisting structure, we potentially lose a reference. For instance, consider the following code segment:

Listing 10.35

```
(define ls '(1 2 3))
(set! ls '(a b c))
```

The list '(1 2 3) is no longer pointed to by any existing and reachable variables, so keeping its content in memory is wasteful. Now, scale this idea up to hundreds of function calls and variable declarations, and we quickly understand the significance of garbage collection in such functional (and non-functional) languages.

Exercise 10.3. (⋆⋆)
When de-allocating a block of memory due to a zeroed reference counter, we only de-allocate the data itself and not the node, reserving the node cleanup for later. Modify the current implementation to completely remove the node from the linked list (hint: keep track of the previous node, then re-assign the links).

Exercise 10.4. (⋆⋆)
In the third-to-last paragraph, we described a solution to allocations made within a block of code whose scope ends, such as a loop. In particular, we want to pass in an allocation, i.e., a void *, then check to see if it exists in the garbage collector. If so, decrement its reference counter by one and return a pointer to the new allocation. Write a function void *rcgc_owalloc(void *dest, size_t sz), standing for "overwrite allocation", that implements this idea.

Exercise 10.5. (⋆⋆)
Explicitly casting the input to rcgc_assign to type void ** is incredibly cumbersome. A way around this is to use macros. Define a macro RCGC_ASSIGN(dest, src) that calls rcgc_assign and casts its macro arguments. If you finished the previous exercise, write RCGC_OWALLOC(dest, sz) that calls rcgc_owalloc and casts its first argument to a void *.

11   Event-Driven Programming

*For over a decade prophets have voiced the contention that the organization of a
single computer has reached its limits and that truly significant advances can
be made only by interconnection of a multiplicity of computers in such a
manner as to permit co-operative solutions.*

—Gene Amdahl

11.1   Concurrent Programming

Our programs so far have been loaded in via files. What if we want to run a
program and make changes on the fly? This is where a REPL, or read-evaluate-
print-loop, comes into play. In essence, we use an infinite loop to read content from
the terminal, evaluate said content, print it out, and repeat. Implementing such a
system seems intuitive at first, and it largely is, with a few caveats. First, each line
must be parsed and sent to the evaluator. Second, all initialization functions must
occur before the REPL starts, and all cleanup functions can only occur at the end
(usually denoted by some sentinel character).

What does this have to do with concurrent programming? Our system must
be constantly listening for input, ready for action when the user presses a key. If
we write a program that forever listens, i.e., using an infinite loop, then we cannot
spend any time on interpretation. By using *concurrency*, we can both listen/read
input and run our interpreter simultaneously.

We will implement our REPL in the `main` function as a `while` loop that runs
forever. If the user specifies an argument when executing the program, we will
assume that they want to run a file through the interpreter.

Listing 11.1 (main.c)

```
 1   int main(int argc, char *argv[]) {
 2     ...
 3     if (2 == argc) {
 4       parser_parse(argv[1], PARSE_FILE);
 5     } else {
 6       while (true) { ... }
 7     }
 8     ...
 9     return 0;
10   }
```

There are a couple of ways that we can read input directly from standard input, i.e., the terminal. One of those is through fgets and the other is getline. The former uses a preallocated buffer to store input, whereas the latter may dynamically allocate memory to store whatever is entered. Because getline allocates a large-enough buffer (when receiving a NULL pointer), we will take advantage of it over fgets. So, let us create a pointer inside the while loop and free it at the end.

Listing 11.2 (main.c)

```
1   int main(int argc, char *argv[]) {
2     ...
3     else {
4       while (true) {
5         char *input = NULL;
6         ...
7         free(input);
8       }
9     }
10    ...
11    return 0;
12  }
```

We will provide a prompt that informs the user that they can type something into the interpreter. If they do not type anything and only press "Enter", we designate that key press as the end of the interpreter and break from the loop. Typing nothing and pressing the return key is equivalent to only a newline character being present in the input buffer, which we can check.

Listing 11.3 (main.c)

```
1   int main(int argc, char *argv[]) {
2     ...
3     else {
4       while (true) {
5         char *input = NULL;
6         size_t len;
7         ssize_t nread = -1;
8         memset(input, 0, sizeof(input));
9         printf("\n>>> ");
10        if ((nread = getline(&input, &len, stdin)) != -1) {
11          if ('\n' == input[0]) { break; }
12          parser_parse(input, PARSE_STRING);
13        }
14        free(input);
15      }
16    }
17    ...
18    return 0;
19  }
```

All that is left, at this stage at least, is to remove the line of code that frees the current abstract syntax tree in parser_read: mgc_free(my_ast);. Running the program now allows us to enter one expression at a time.

```
>>> (define x 10)
>>> x
10
>>> (include "stdlib.scm")
>>> (define fact (lambda (n) (if (zero? n) 1 (* n (fact (sub1 n))))))
>>> (fact 5)
120
```

Event-Driven Programming

Input Events

When typing commands in a shell, it quickly becomes excruciating to type the same command repeatedly. Thus, almost every (worthwhile) shell implements a feature where, when the up or down arrows are pressed, the previous commands are visible and displayed. Implementing such a feature from scratch involves several features that we have not yet discussed, so before we dive into the deep end, we will implement previous command viewing via the GNU readline library (see Appendix 11.3 on installing and linking the library).

Using this library is extremely easy, as it only requires understanding a couple of functions to make use of its most powerful features: read_line and add_history.

read_line functions similarly to getline in that it dynamically-allocates memory to store the contents of a line, but different in that it also allows the programmer to pass a prompt that is displayed before reading the input. Whenever we read a line from standard input via read_line, to make further use of it, we must add it to the history, i.e., previously-typed expressions, via add_history. To start, we must include two new header files, and then we modify the REPL to use the readline library functions:

Listing 11.4—Adding readline Library Functions (main.c)

```
1    #include <readline/readline.h>
2    #include <readline/history.h>
3
4    int main(int argc, char *argv[]) {
5      ...
6      else {
7        while (true) {
8          char *line = readline(">>> ");
9          add_history(line);
10         parser_parse(line, PARSE_STRING);
11         free(line);
12         printf("\n");
13       }
14     }
15     ...
16     return 0;
17   }
```

Now, upon running the interpreter, if we enter a few definitions, then press the up arrow, we see what we typed previously. Such a convenient feature to have, for sure!

Exercise 11.1. (⋆⋆⋆)
Tab-completion is a command auto-completion function that allows the user to enter part of a command, press the Tab key, and the shell attempts to find the closest match to what has been typed thus far. Investigate the readline documentation and try to implement this on your own!

Reinventing The Readline Wheel

Using GNU's readline library is extraordinarily convenient, but perhaps mystifying to those curious about its innards. Consequently, in this section, we will implement the core functionality of GNU's readline library on our own. Before we can begin, though, there are a few concepts to thoroughly understand, e.g., the difference between blocked versus non-blocked input and output, file descriptors, pipes, and system calls.

Blocking versus Non-Blocking IO

Both `fgets` and `getline` are referred to as "blocked" input functions. That is, main program execution halts entirely until something, i.e., data, is received by these functions.[1] While this is a rather loose description of blocking input, it helps us understand the distinction. Why is this discussion necessary? Think about how the `readline` library "scrolls" through history. The user presses the 'Up' and 'Down' arrow keys respectively but does not need to press "Enter" for the program to parse and recognize these characters. If we want to mimic this functionality, we will need to switch from blocking input to non-blocking. By default, `read` is a blocking system call and to disable this behavior, we must make use of the `fcntl`, or file control, function. In summary, we must change the state of the standard input file descriptor to be non-blocking via the `O_NONBLOCK` flag.

Listing 11.5

```
1   #include <fcntl.h>
2   #include <unistd.h>
3
4   int main(void) {
5     ...
6     int flags = fcntl(STDIN_FILENO, F_GETFL, 0);
7     fcntl(STDIN_FILENO, F_SETFL, flags | O_NONBLOCK);
8     ...
9     return 0;
10  }
```

File Descriptors. When interacting with files in C, we use the `FILE *` wrapper structure alongside a few helpful functions. At a lower level there exist *file descriptors*, which are identifiers for input and output resources. System calls make use of file descriptors via, for example, the read and write functions, which we saw in our compilation chapter in assembly. Though, file descriptors are more general than just for writing and reading to and from standard output and input respectively. The operating system creates a table of every open resource, thereby providing each (resource) a unique file descriptor that a program may access. We very often make use of the `FILE *` struct as a means of abstracting from the low-level representation of file descriptors. Indeed, to retrieve the corresponding file descriptor of a `FILE *`, invoke the `int fileno(FILE *fp)` function:

---

[1]We use this term "main program execution" to distinguish between what the programmer writes versus the underlying implementation of `fgets` and `getline`.

Listing 11.6—Retrieve File Descriptor of FILE * (main.c)

```
1   #include <stdio.h>                                          fp file descriptor=3
2
3   int main(void) {
4     FILE *fp = fopen("test.txt", "r");
5     printf("fp file descriptor=%d\n", fileno(fp));
6     fclose(fp);
7     return 0;
8   }
```

We see that fp has a file descriptor of '3'. This is because stdin, stdout, and stderr use the first three file descriptors 0, 1, and 2 respectively. Because there are no other open resources, the next-available file descriptor is the one identified by our test.txt file.

Like we stated, we can use file descriptors for more than reading and writing to what we traditionally call "files"; any available resource, including networking data, can be read/written to given the correct permissions.[1] More importantly, we can use *pipes* to pass information across processes.

Pipes and Multiprocessing. *Pipes*, as their name implies, are unidirectional paths of information flow between processes, or independent programs, often mentioned as a means of discussing inter-process communication. A pipe has a "read-end", and a "write-end", meaning that one process reads data from the pipe while another writes data into the pipe. Demonstrating an example of pipes without multiprocessing is hard to visualize, so let us briefly describe how to create a process.

C programs, in and of themselves, *are processes*, but sometimes we wish to have another process to perform some task or computation. To create a child process from a parent process, we use the fork function, which returns an integer representing the process identifier of the created child process, i.e., a pid_t . Once we fork a process, there are, in essence, two chains of program execution; the parent process resumes after the fork, wherein its fork() return value is its own process identifier. On the other hand, upon forking a child, the return value of fork is zero to designate that it is a child process. Child processes are born during a call to fork from the parent and exist thereafter. To distinguish between paths that the parent and child take in the program, we use, of course, a case analysis on the fork return value. Let us create a pipe using the pipe() system call; it receives an array of two integers, where index zero refers to the "read-end" of the pipe and index one refers to the "write-end" of the pipe. Our program will have the parent process write a series of bytes to the pipe, and the child process will read bytes from the pipe until it is exhausted. Note that in addition to the checks for child/parent processes, we make sure to check whether or not the fork failed, as we do with the pipe:

---

[1]Operating systems often keep track of file descriptors on a per-process and a system-wide basis; those allocated by the process are visible to only that process. Similarly, system-wide file descriptors are accessible by other processes. Accordingly, the same identifiers can be used in each process for per-process file descriptors.

Listing 11.7—Using Pipes Across Processes (main.c)

```
1   #include <stdio.h>
2   #include <stdlib.h>
3   #include <string.h>
4   #include <unistd.h>
5
6   #define BUFFER_SIZE 64
7
8   int main(void) {
9     int fd[2];
10    // Pipe error check.
11    if (pipe(fd) < 0) {
12      EPF("main: pipe failed\n");
13      exit(EXIT_FAILURE);
14    } else {
15      pid_t pid = fork();
16      // Fork error check.
17      if (-1 == pid) {
18        EPF("main: fork failed\n");
19        exit(EXIT_FAILURE);
20      } else if (0 == pid) {
21        // Child process; reads from pipe.
22        char in_buffer[BUFFER_SIZE];
23        memset(in_buffer, 0, BUFFER_SIZE);
24        read(fd[0], in_buffer, BUFFER_SIZE);
25        printf("printf (%u): read from the buffer:
26              %s\n", pid, in_buffer);
27      } else {
28        // Parent process.
29        char out_buffer[BUFFER_SIZE];
30        memset(out_buffer, 0, BUFFER_SIZE);
31        sprintf(out_buffer, "data from process %u",
32              pid);
33        size_t len = strlen(out_buffer);
34        write(fd[1], out_buffer, len);
35        printf("printf (%u): wrote data\n", pid);
36      }
37    }
38    return 0;
39  }
```

```
printf (637308):
  wrote data
printf (0):
  read from the
  buffer: data from
  process 637308
```

Child processes can, of course, have their own child processes, which reflects similarly to how the original parent process spawns its own child(ren). Namely, the child has its own specific process identifier returned by the fork, and in its child process fork will return zero. To obtain a child's own process identifier from within that child (or any other process), use the getpid function. Moreover, when a parent process terminates, this does not mean that the child processes are finished. So, running the following program will almost certainly produce output from the child/grandchild processes, which is not desired.[1]

---

[1]By "not desired", we mean that, a parent process that finishes its execution before its children is somewhat confusing. A child can live on after its parent (process) terminates, thereby denoting it as an *orphan*. Moreover, the exact behavior and output differs depending on the operating system process scheduler; the parent process might terminate before it can even spawn a child process!

Listing 11.8—Child and Grandchild Processes (main.c)

```
1   #include <stdio.h>
2   #include <sys/wait.h>
3   #include <sys/time.h>
4   #include <unistd.h>
5
6   int main(void) {
7     pid_t pid = fork();
8     if (-1 == pid) { ... }
9     else if (0 == pid) {
10      pid_t gpid = fork();
11      if (-1 == gpid) { ... }
12      else if (0 == gpid) { printf("grandchild(%u)\n", getpid()); }
13      else { printf("child(%u)\n", getpid()); }
14    } else {
15      printf("parent(%u)\n", getpid());
16    }
17    printf("process %u finished\n", getpid());
18    return 0;
19  }
```

The solution to this problem is to introduce the wait(NULL) function; wait(NULL) halts the parent process until one of its children is finished. What remains an issue is that, if a parent process forks multiple children, as soon as one child terminates, the parent terminates.[1] To continuously poll for terminating children, we wrap wait(NULL) inside a while loop, which returns the process identifier of the terminated child, and -1 otherwise. In the output, notice that the child process has a process identifier one greater than its parent, and likewise for the grandchild. These numbers will certainly vary depending on how many active and inactive processes there are on your individual computer.

Listing 11.9—Child and Grandchild Processes (main.c)

```
1   ...                                 | parent(722)
2   int main(void) {                    | child(723)
3     pid_t pid = fork();               | grandchild(724)
4     ...                               | process 724 finished
5     while (wait(NULL) > 0);           | process 723 finished
6     printf("process %u finished\n",   | process 722 finished
7             getpid());                |
8     return 0;                         |
9   }                                   |
```

Why do we care this much about processes and pipes? Our prior discussion preludes much of our topics on *multi-threading* and serves as motivation for concurrent programming. As shown in Chapter 5, we used pipes to communicate between two programs: the evaluation tester and the evaluator itself. We excluded fork and pipe in favor of popen, which opens a pipe, spawns a child process, and invokes a command all-in-one.

---

[1] It is possible, however, that all child processes terminate before the parent terminates, depending on the process scheduler.

Termios. `termios.h` is C header file; termios is a set of functions that allows us to modify certain properties of our terminal, including how it reads and processes characters. The default behavior of the terminal is to read input while blocking. Therefore we need to modify this behavior to use non-blocking input. First, we need to write two functions: `set_terminal_mode` and `reset_terminal_mode`. The former alters and changes the input properties to use non-blocking input, whereas the latter resets this change to its default behavior when the program exits. We need to define an instance of a `termios` struct to keep track of the "old" terminal properties; it is declared, as static, outside of `set_terminal_mode` to remain persistent and usable by our reset function. Inside `set_terminal_mode`, we declare a new termios struct that contains the properties of the "old" struct, but we also initialize the "old" struct via `tcgetattr`.

Listing 11.10—Saving Old Terminal Properties (repl.c)

```
1   #include <termios.h>
2
3   static struct termios old_termios;
4
5   void reset_terminal_mode(void) { // TODO. }
6
7   void set_terminal_mode(void) {
8    // Save properties of old terminal into old_termios.
9    tcgetattr(STDIN_FILENO, &old_termios);
10
11   // Copy over properties from old to new.
12   struct termios new_termios;
13   memcpy(&new_termios, &old_termios, sizeof(new_termios));
14  }
```

Now, we need to define the new termios mode to use raw, or unblocked, input. We do this via `cfmakeraw`. Additionally, we should set an attribute that tells termios to immediately change the terminal properties, rather than waiting for, say, an empty file descriptor. We also want to tell the program that, upon exiting the program, we should invoke the `reset_terminal_mode` function. This is done via the `TCSANOW` flag in the respective `tcsetattr` call. Again, `reset_terminal_-mode` changes the terminal attributes back into those previously-defined.

Listing 11.11—Changing Terminal Behavior to Raw Mode (repl.c)

```
1   void set_terminal_mode(void) {
2    ...
3    cfmakeraw(&new_termios);
4    tcsetattr(STDIN_FILENO, TCSANOW, &new_termios);
5    atexit(reset_terminal_mode);
6   }
```

Listing 11.12—Reset Terminal Mode Function (repl.c)

```
1   void reset_terminal_mode(void) {
2    tcsetattr(STDIN_FILENO, TCSANOW, &old_termios);
3   }
```

Up next we write the most important additional function: `getch`. `getch` reads in a character from the input file descriptor and, depending on what said character is, performs an action. Because we only care about ASCII keys, the returned result is an unsigned character.

First, we use the `read` system call to read a single character from standard input. If this fails, we return the error code, and otherwise continue onto evaluation of said input character.

Listing 11.13—Using the `read` *System Call* (`repl.c`)

```
1   static unsigned char getch(void) {
2     int ret_code;
3     unsigned char ch;
4     if ((ret_code = read(STDIN_FILENO, &ch, sizeof(ch))) < 0) {
5       return ret_code;
6     } else {
7       // Do something...
8     }
9   }
```

To start off simply, let us just write code that writes back, to standard output, whatever the user enters. Again, we use the system call `write`. Finally, `getch` should return the character that it read.

Listing 11.14—Character Echoing (`repl.c`)

```
1    static unsigned char getch(void) {
2      int ret_code;
3      unsigned char ch;
4      if ((ret_code = read(STDIN_FILENO, &ch, sizeof(ch))) < 0) {
5        return ret_code;
6      } else {
7        write(1, &ch, sizeof(ch));
8        return ch;
9      }
10   }
```

Let us test this function! Inside `main`, we must call `set_termios_mode` at the start and `reset_termios_mode` at the end (before `return`). In between, we have an infinite loop that continuously reads characters. As a sanity test, if the user enters 'q', the loop ends, simply because not having an easy way to break out of an infinite loop is a recipe for disaster.

Listing 11.15

```
1   int main(void) {
2     set_terminal_mode();
3     unsigned char key = 0;
4     while (true) {
5       if ((key = getch()) == 'q') { break; }
6     }
7     return 0;
8   }
```

Compiling and running the program shows that we can enter any character with a few exceptions. Pressing 'Enter' behaves differently than one may expect: instead of returning to the next line, it simply shifts the cursor to the start of the line. This notion is called a *carriage return*. This behavior is desired, but we also want to output a new line character \n to standard output. So, we may add a conditional to check and see if the input character is "Enter", i.e., \r and, if so, write both a carriage return and a new line character to standard output.

Listing 11.16—Parsing "Enter" Key Events (repl.c)

```
1   static unsigned char getch(void) {
2     int ret_code;
3     unsigned char ch;
4     if ((ret_code = read(STDIN_FILENO, &ch, sizeof(ch))) < 0) {
5       return ret_code;
6     } else {
7       // Handle 'Enter' key presses--adds \r and \n.
8       if ('\r' == ch) {
9         write(STDOUT_FILENO, "\r\n", 2);
10      } else {
11        write(STDOUT_FILENO, &ch, sizeof(ch));
12      }
13      return ch;
14    }
15  }
```

That is one special character handled. Though, what if we want to process lines of text and store them in a "history" like the library? There are a couple of things we need to take care of before we begin our discussion on "history". First and foremost, recall that when reading blocked input, we use fgets or getline to read one line at a time. We will use a similar methodology; the only difference being we populate the "line" manually. So, we declare a local buffer of a large size, say, 2048 bytes. Then, whenever we read a character, we copy said character into the next slot of the buffer. So, we will keep track of a global static "buffer_idx" which records the location of the next character (should be inserted) in the buffer. Moreover, when we hit "Enter", we clear the buffer.

Listing 11.17—Clearing Input Buffer After Pressing Enter (repl.c)

```
1   static int buffer_idx = 0;
2   ...
3   static unsigned char getch(void) {
4     char buffer[2048];
5   ...
6     else {
7       // If Enter is pressed.
8       if ('\r' == ch) {
9         buffer_idx = 0;
10        write(STDOUT_FILENO, "\r\n", 2);
11        memset(buffer, 0, sizeof(buffer));
12      }
13    }
14  }
```

What about deleting characters? Backspace does not seem to work as intended! Indeed, since we are in raw mode, no special characters are processed, meaning we must handle the backspace character ourselves. Upon pressing Backspace, read returns a character whose ASCII code is 127, which corresponds with "Delete". We may, therefore, naively assume that all we need to do is NUL-terminate the buffer at the previously-entered character index and subtract one. This line of thought, however, forgets that we must also update the text that already exists in standard output. An interesting and highly necessary bit of information about backspace is that it does not actually delete a character by default—it merely moves the "cursor", or terminal position, backward by one. It is up to us, as the programmer, to implement the typical backspace behavior. So, let us ask the question, what actually happens when we press Backspace? The cursor moves back one spot, a "blank" character, i.e., a space, is written, then the cursor moves backward again. We mimic this behavior with a single call to write:

Listing 11.18—Parsing Backspace Character Input (repl.c)

```
1   #define ENTER 127
2
3   static unsigned char getch(void) {
4     ...
5     else {
6       // If Backspace is pressed.
7       if (ENTER == ch) {
8         if (0 == buffer_idx) {
9           return ch;
10        } else {
11          // Remove one character from the buffer.
12          buffer[--buffer_idx] = '\0';
13          write(STDOUT_FILENO, "\b \b", 3);
14        }
15      }
16      ...
17    }
18  }
```

With these preliminaries out of the way, we can finally begin our discussion on how to implement a true command "history". To do so, we need a data structure that lets us quickly access the most recently entered information. This sounds like a job for the stack data structure! Implementing such a structure is trivial and mimics a linked list. The nodes inside the stack store a string, namely the last-entered command.

Listing 11.19—Command Stack and Command Node Definitions (repl.c)

```
1   struct node {
2     char *value;
3     struct node *next;
4   };
5
6   struct stack {
7     struct node *top;
8   };
```

With this, let us write two convenience functions: stack_push_last_command, and stack_write_command. The former pushes the existing contents of the buffer to the stack and clears the buffer, whereas the latter writes the contents of the currently "focused item" to standard output; more on this later.

Listing 11.20—Pushing Buffer to Command Stack (repl.c)

```
1   static void stack_push_last_command(char[] buffer) {
2    struct node *n = calloc(1, sizeof(struct node));
3    n->value = strdup(buffer);
4    if (NULL == stk.top) {
5     stk.top = n;
6    } else {
7     n->next = stk.top;
8     stk.top = n;
9    }
10   no_items++;
11  }
12
13  static void stack_write_command(void) {
14   // Traverse to the item idx.
15   struct node *curr = stk.top;
16   for (int i = 0; i < stack_idx; i++) {
17    curr = curr->next;
18   }
19   write(STDOUT_FILENO, curr->value, strlen(curr->value));
20  }
```

At this point we need to update the Enter clause. If we press "Enter", we push the current buffer to our history stack, clear the buffer, and reset the string position.

Listing 11.21—Pushing Last Command After Pressing "Enter" (repl.c)

```
1   static unsigned char getch(void) {
2    ...
3    else {
4     // If Enter is pressed.
5     if ('\r' == ch) {
6      // Push item to the stack and clear buffer.
7      stack_push_last_command(buffer);
8      memset(buffer, 0, sizeof(buffer));
9      buffer_idx = 0;
10     write(STDOUT_FILENO, "\r\n", 2);
11    }
12    ...
13   }
14  }
```

Now comes the fun part: handling "Up" and "Down" key presses. Interestingly, pressing these keys is not as simple as reading an "Up" or "Down" key code. Instead, when an arrow key is pressed, three characters are sent to standard input: Escape, "[", and either A, B, C, or D, representing "Up", "Down", "Left", or "Right" respectively. So, if "Up" is pressed, we enable a flag "scroll", consume '[', and process the corresponding direction. After processing, we disable the scroll flag. We use flags so we can type '[' without always assuming it is part of an arrow direction key press.

Listing 11.22—Write Command Upon Pressing Arrow Keys (repl.c)

```
1   #define ESC 27
2
3   static void stack_write_command(void) {
4     // If the stack is empty, we cannot write anything.
5     if (0 == no_items) { return; }
6
7     // Otherwise, traverse to the item idx.
8     struct node *curr = stk.top;
9     for (int i = 0; i < stack_idx; i++) {
10      curr = curr->next;
11    }
12    write(1, curr->value, strlen(curr->value));
13    scroll = false;
14  }
15
16  static unsigned char getch(void) {
17    ...
18    else {
19      // If ESC is pressed.
20      if (ESC == ch) {
21        scroll = true;
22      }
23      // If we are actively "scrolling", consume '['.
24      else if (scroll && '[' == ch) {
25        return ch;
26      }
27      ...
28    }
29  }
```

So, what **action** do we perform after pressing "Up" or "Down"? Well, we update the stack index variable accordingly and write the corresponding string to standard output along with the carriage return and newline characters. Modifying the stack index variable means to change the "focused item". That is, when pressing the "Up" key, we travel down the history stack for older commands hence increasing the stack index, and pressing "Down" decreases the stack index to view newer commands. If the stack is empty, we simply bail out. Though, it is not enough to write the data to standard output; Rather, we also update the buffer contents.

Listing 11.23—Update Buffer Index After Scroll Command (repl.c)

```
1   static void stack_write_command(void) {
2     scroll = false;
3     // If the stack is empty, we cannot write anything.
4     if (0 == no_items) { return; }
5
6     // Otherwise, traverse to the item idx.
7     struct node *curr = stk.top;
8     for (int i = 0; i < stack_idx; i++) {
9       curr = curr->next;
10    }
11
12    // Write both the value and a CR+NL.
13    write(STDOUT_FILENO, curr->value, strlen(curr->value));
14    write(STDOUT_FILENO, "\r\n", 2);
15
16    // Copy text into buffer and update buffer idx.
17    strncpy(buffer, curr->value, sizeof(buffer));
18    buffer_idx += strlen(curr->value);
19  }
```

Trying this out allows us to enter text and see previously-entered text!

All of this motivation allows us to integrate our command history implementation into our interpreter. First, though, we should refactor some identifiers and functions to resemble a library rather than a single file test example. We will move the stack implementation to `cmd_stack` and rewrite the history module into `cmd_history`.

When we read input from the user, it is stored in a buffer. We "send" the buffer to the parser after pressing "Enter". Therefore, we need a flag that is enabled upon pressing "Enter" that denotes the end of character reading. To use a familiar approach, we will write `cmd_history_readline` which receives a string denoting a "prompt". It then continuously receives characters and stores them in the static string buffer. Upon pressing "Enter", send is set to `true`, thereby creating a duplicate of the string, deactivating the send flag, and returning the input.

Listing 11.24—Continuously Loop Until Time to Send (`repl.c`)

```
1    void cmd_history_init(void) {
2      ...
3      send = false;
4      ...
5    }
6
7    char *cmd_history_readline(void) {
8      memset(buffer, 0, sizeof(buffer));
9      while (!send) { cmd_history_getch(); }
10
11     // Create a duplicate of the current buffer. Turn off "sending".
12     send = false;
13     return strdup(buffer);
14   }
15
16   static unsigned char getch(void) {
17     ...
18     else {
19       ...
20       // If Enter is pressed.
21       else if (ENTER == ch) {
22         ...
23         send = true;
24       }
25       ...
26     }
27   }
```

Because we add the possibility of a prompt, we need to offset the buffer index, meaning `write` sees characters written to a different index than they are stored in the buffer itself. We compute this offset via the length of the prompt, which we store in a variable for bookkeeping across functions. Note where we make these modifications.

Listing 11.25—A Flexible "Read line" Function With Prompts (repl.c)

```
1   char *cmd_history_readline(char *prompt) {
2     // Clear the buffer, write the prompt, and offset buffer idx.
3     memset(buffer, 0, sizeof(buffer));
4     prompt_len = strlen(prompt);
5     write(STDOUT_FILENO, prompt, prompt_len);
6     buffer_idx = prompt_len;
7     ...
8   }
9
10  static unsigned char cmd_history_getch(void) {
11    ...
12    else {
13      ...
14      else {
15        buffer[(buffer_idx++) - prompt_len] = ch;
16        write(STDOUT_FILENO, &ch, sizeof(ch));
17      }
18    }
19  }
20
21  static void handle_backspace(void) {
22    if (0 == buffer_idx) { return; }
23    else {
24      // Remove one character from the buffer.
25      buffer[(--buffer_idx) - prompt_len] = '\0';
26      write(STDOUT_FILENO, "\b \b", 3);
27    }
28  }
```

In place of stack_write_command, we now use cmd_history_write to do, effectively, the same task. The only noteworthy modification is that we offset the buffer index from not just the command length, but also the prompt length.

Listing 11.26—Offset From Prompt Length and History Size (repl.c)

```
1   static void cmd_history_write(void) {
2     // Clear existing buffer.
3     memset(buffer, 0, sizeof(buffer));
4
5     // Now, output history and write it to the buffer.
6     char *cmd = cmd_stack_get(&stk, stack_idx);
7     size_t cmd_len = strlen(cmd) + 1;
8     write(STDOUT_FILENO, cmd, cmd_len);
9     buffer_idx = prompt_len + cmd_len;
10    strncpy(buffer, cmd, cmd_len);
11  }
```

We clear the buffer inside of cmd_history_write than delegate it to the "Up" and "Down" key handlers. Their responsibility only consists of modifying the stack index value and invoking cmd_history_write.

Listing 11.27

```
1   static void handle_up(void) {
2     int no_items = cmd_stack_get_num_elements(&stk);
3     stack_idx = stack_idx >= no_items - 1 ? no_items - 1 : stack_idx + 1;
4     cmd_history_write();
5   }
6
7   static void handle_down(void) {
8     stack_idx = stack_idx > 0 ? stack_idx - 1 : 0;
9     cmd_history_write();
10  }
```

Everything else remains the same. We will omit showing cmd_history_getch since it is almost identical to the previous implementation, except that keys now have dedicated function handlers.

Lastly, we need a way of swapping to and from non-canonical mode. When we input data, we want to use non-canonical mode so we may read the arrow characters accordingly. After sending the data to the parser and interpreter, however, we should re-enable canonical mode so the internal printing mechanisms used by the interpreter are not adversely affected. The most straightforward approach is to store two termios structs: one for canonical mode and another for non-canonical mode. These two structs are populated in a helper function cmd_history_set_-terminal_mode. From here, before and after we begin reading characters, we invoke cmd_history_swap_terminal_mode.

Listing 11.28

```
1   void cmd_history_init(void) {
2     memset(buffer, 0, sizeof(buffer));
3     send = false;
4     scroll = false;
5     raw = false;
6     cmd_stack_init(&stk);
7     cmd_history_set_terminal_mode();
8   }
9
10  char *cmd_history_readline(char *prompt) {
11    ...
12    // Swap the terminal mode to raw for input.
13    cmd_history_swap_terminal_mode();
14    while (!send) { cmd_history_getch(); }
15    cmd_history_swap_terminal_mode();
16    ...
17  }
18
19  static void cmd_history_swap_terminal_mode(void) {
20    // If currently raw, we swap to normal and vice-versa. We also account for fcntl.
21    int flags = fcntl(STDIN_FILENO, F_GETFL, 0);
22    if (raw) {
23      tcsetattr(0, TCSANOW, &old_termios);
24      flags &= ~O_NONBLOCK;
25    } else {
26      tcsetattr(0, TCSANOW, &new_termios);
27      flags |= O_NONBLOCK;
28    }
29    fcntl(STDIN_FILENO, F_SETFL, flags | O_NONBLOCK);
30    raw = !raw;
31  }
32
33  static void cmd_history_set_terminal_mode(void) {
34    tcgetattr(0, &old_termios);
35    memcpy(&new_termios, &old_termios, sizeof(new_termios));
36    cfmakeraw(&new_termios);
37  }
```

Exercise 11.2. (★★)

As we saw with the readline library, when we scroll through our command history, we do not simply output the previous command on a new line. Instead, we clear the current line of text in standard out and replace it with the new text. Implement this behavior in our new input system. As a hint: you should do this all inside cmd_history_write. No new variables are necessary. Our solution incorporates only one loop and one call to write.

Exercise 11.3. (★★★)
In almost all terminals, pressing the "Left" or "Right" keys move the cursor either left or right respectively. This allows the user to correct typos they may have made when typing a command. Implement this feature in our new input system.

Exercise 11.4. (★★★★★)
The *shell* is, as we know, the interface between a user and the (operating) system; it allows the user to execute commands, scroll, change directories, and much more. A basic project in some system programming/operating system courses is to design a shell from scratch. At its core, a shell reads and parses commands from standard input and creates sub-processes for executing commands. For instance, in a basic Linux shell, if we execute the "list" command, i.e., `ls`, a new process is forked, which executes `ls`, then once it finishes, the process finishes. While the child process is executing, the parent (shell) process waits. Commands are executed from a process using variants of the `exec` function. Do some research on these functions and implement a very basic shell in C. Start small by adding the ability to execute basic commands, without arguments, such as `ls`. Then, work your way up by adding the ability to specify arguments to commands. Building a shell opens a portal for effectively endless customization, so go crazy! Hint: changing directories via `cd` cannot be done in a child process and must be parsed/handled separately from other commands, using the `chdir` C function.

Multithreaded Approach

Our readline/command history implementation works well enough. Though, it suffers from one subtle problem: the use of busy looping. With non-blocking I/O, there is very little that we can do to prevent a constant loop that, in effect, listens for standard input events. What we can do, however, is spin up a *thread* to listen for these events. Threads manage separated sequence of actions for the current program to execute. Multi-threaded programming allows us to write programs and software that may take a while using only one thread, but are much faster with multiple threads. Of course, this is certainly not a hard and fast rule, but we will see how using a second thread helps us in our circumstances.[1] We will make use of the pthread library on Unix/Linux. Before diving deep into integrating a separate thread for our interpreter, let us discuss the basics.

Pthreads. To create a *pthread*, we use `pthread_create`. It receives four arguments: a pointer to the `pthread_t` to initialize, pthread attributes, a function pointer that the thread controls, and arguments for said function pointer.

---

[1]Certain situations benefit from multi-threading, but performance gains are not guaranteed and, depending on thread and process scheduling, a program may see a net performance loss due to multi-threading.

Mutexes and Condition Variables. Imagine this: two threads A and B attempt to update a variable x by incrementing it by one. Suppose thread A increments x, but before it finishes setting the variable, thread B comes into the picture and also increments x where both threads use its (x's) old value. The order is irrelevant; if B performs the increment rather than A and A swoops in after, the end result is the same; x contains an incorrect value. This is known as a *race condition*, i.e., a problem where a program state is dependent on timing rather than preset conditions. We, instead, want thread A to fully increment x, then B to fully increment x, or vice-versa. The second thread should see the change made by the first and act on it accordingly. As a larger motivating example, suppose each thread iterates from 1 to a large number, say, one million, wherein x is incremented by one each iteration. If we have no mechanism for preventing one thread from altering data that another accesses, the end result of x is non-deterministic. Namely, the value of x depends on several factors, including the scheduling of the threads, the speed of the processor, and other external factors. These factors introduce unpredictability and make it difficult to determine the final value of x with certainty. Consequently, running the following program produced seemingly arbitrary numbers, highlighting the need for synchronization mechanisms to ensure the correct execution of concurrent programs.

Listing 11.29

```
1   #include <pthread.h>                                           1000164
2                                                                  1037486
3   #define ITERATIONS 1000000                                     1000020
4                                                                  1000000
5   static int x = 0;                                              1000297
6
7   static void * thread_handler(void *arg) {
8     for (int i = 0; i < ITERATIONS; i++) { x++; }
9     return NULL;
10  }
11
12  int main(void) {
13    // Initialize the threads.
14    pthread_t a;
15    pthread_t b;
16    pthread_create(&a, NULL, thread_handler, NULL);
17    pthread_create(&b, NULL, thread_handler, NULL);
18
19    // Now wait for them to finish.
20    pthread_join(a, NULL);
21    pthread_join(b, NULL);
22    printf("%d\n", x);
23    return 0;
24  }
```

Mutexes are the fix to this problem. A *mutex*, or a lock is, in effect, a guard to a *critical section*, which is an area of code shared by multiple threads. Only one thread may acquire a mutex at a time. If another thread attempts to enter a critical section that does not have the lock, it "goes to sleep" until the lock is released. It is desired to minimize the critical section size because, the longer a thread holds onto a lock, the longer other threads take to complete their task that requires holding the lock. With the alterations below, we should now, deterministically, see 2000000.

Listing 11.30

```
1    static pthread_mutex_t mutex = PTHREAD_MUTEX_INITIALIZER;        2000000
2
3    static int x = 0;
4
5    static void *thread_handler(void *args) {
6      for (int i = 0; i < ITERATIONS; i++) {
7        pthread_mutex_lock(&mutex);
8        x++;
9        pthread_mutex_unlock(&mutex);
10     }
11     return NULL;
12   }
13
14   int main(void) {
15     // Initialize the threads.
16     pthread_t a;
17     pthread_t b;
18     pthread_create(&a, NULL, thread_handler, NULL);
19     pthread_create(&b, NULL, thread_handler, NULL);
20
21     // Now wait for them to finish.
22     pthread_join(a, NULL);
23     pthread_join(b, NULL);
24     printf("%d\n", ITERATIONS * 2);
25     return 0;
26   }
```

Let us build something more complex to demonstrate the power of multi-threaded programming. Suppose we are writing a "task handler". A task, in this context, is a segment of code that a thread should execute.[1] For instance, we may have a thread to compute the nth Fibonacci number, or some other time-consuming task. Running said code segments on the main thread is wasteful since we could spin up another thread to handle said task and let the main thread continue to prompt the user for another task. In essence, we want a program that provides a list of options, or tasks, to the user. Upon selection, a separate thread is spun up to complete the task. While said thread works on that task, the user may ask to complete different tasks *concurrently*. We may also want to query the system for the result of any previously-requested task. The part of this mini-project that is interesting is "a separate thread is spun up to complete the task" because we need to introduce *condition variables*.

A *condition variable* is, at a very high level, a mechanism that blocks or alerts a thread based on some condition. For our "task handler", we want a pool of threads to listen for tasks. While no tasks are available, all of them, in a sense, "go to sleep". This is called a *conditional wait*. When a task become available, a thread "wakes up" and evaluates the respective task. We refer to the awakening action as the *thread signal*. As a somewhat odd analogy, it is akin to an alarm clock in that people go to sleep, and when they need to wake up, the alarm goes off. The alarm clock in this scenario is the thread signal, the act of "sleeping" is the conditional wait, and "starting one's day" is the task.

---

[1]Some contexts describe multi-threading as multi-tasking, and hence use the term "task" in place of thread. We use it as a general unit of work to execute/perform.

Let us begin this mini-project: First, we need a thread-safe queue. When we say thread-safe, we mean that it is safe for concurrent access/modification. Fortunately, all we need to do to make a normal queue implementation thread-safe is to add mutexes wherever data or queue "state" is accessed/modified. Said queue will store pending tasks for threads to execute. So, before we start implementing the queue, we must define a task. Suppose that a task has a name, a function pointer, and an argument. The name is for task identification purposes, whereas the function pointer and argument are the "segments of code" to execute. Our data definition for the task structure is as follows:

Listing 11.31— "Event" Task Data Definition (task.h)

```
1   #ifndef TASK_H
2   #define TASK_H
3
4   /**
5    * A 'struct task' contains:
6    * - name: Identifier of task.
7    * - fn: Function of one argument to execute.
8    * - args: Argument to fn.
9    */
10  typedef struct task {
11    char *name;
12    void *(*fn)(void *args);
13    void *args;
14  } task;
15
16  #endif // TASK_H
```

A task should not care about its function definition or its arguments. In other words, it knows that they exist, but how they work is irrelevant to the task. Therefore, we pass a function of one void * argument and return a void * result. More importantly, this is the signature desired by pthread_create. This way, we may pass and return any desired datatypes.

Though, how do we know what type of task to construct? This is up to us to decide. Suppose that we have a enum task_type that defines the segment of code for a task to execute. For the time being, we will say that the only possible enum task_type is FIB, which computes the nth Fibonacci number. task_create receives a enum task_type and initializes the appropriate task. Its accompanying destructor function, task_destroy, frees the associated memory of a task.

Listing 11.32—Task Enumeration and Prototypes (task.h)

```
1   enum task_type { FIB };
2
3   task *task_create(enum task_type tid, char *name, void *arg);
4   void task_destroy(task *tsk);
```

We will come back to the source file for task. For the time being, let us shift gears and implement a non-thread-safe queue using a linked list as a template. Afterwards, we will extend it to use mutexes for thread-safety. Each node in the queue has two fields: a pointer to a task, and a next pointer. The accompanying source file should be familiar.

Listing 11.33—Task Queue Header Definition (taskqueue.h)

```
1   #ifndef TASKQUEUE_H
2   #define TASKQUEUE_H
3
4   #include "task.h"
5
6   struct taskqueue_node {
7     struct task *tsk;
8     struct taskqueue_node *next;
9   };
10
11  typedef struct taskqueue {
12    struct taskqueue_node *head;
13    struct taskqueue_node *tail;
14    int no_elements;
15  } taskqueue;
16
17  void taskqueue_init(taskqueue *tq);
18  void taskqueue_enqueue(taskqueue *tq, struct task *tsk);
19  void taskqueue_destroy(taskqueue *tq);
20
21  #endif // TASKQUEUE_H
```

Listing 11.34—Task Queue Source Implementation (taskqueue.c)

```
1   #include "taskqueue.h"
2
3   void taskqueue_init(taskqueue *tq) {
4     tq->head = tq->tail = NULL;
5     tq->no_elements = 0;
6   }
7
8   void taskqueue_enqueue(taskqueue *tq, struct task *tsk) {
9     struct taskqueue_node *node = calloc(1, sizeof(struct taskqueue_node));
10    ASSERT_ALLOC(node, "taskqueue_enqueue");
11    node->tsk = tsk;
12    if (0 == tq->no_elements) { tq->head = tq->tail = node; }
13    else {
14      tq->tail->next = node;
15      tq->tail = node;
16    }
17    tq->no_elements++;
18  }
19
20  void taskqueue_destroy(taskqueue *tq) {
21    for (int i = 0; i < tq->no_elements; i++) {
22      struct taskqueue_node *curr = tq->head->next;
23      task_destroy(curr->tsk);
24      free(tq->head);
25      tq->head = curr;
26    }
27  }
```

Notice that we do not have a function for removing an element from the queue. We will circle back to this fact. Let us add mutexes to make this a thread-safe queue. In particular, a taskqueue now stores a pthread_mutex_t and, whenever a function accesses or modifies a queue field, we lock the mutex and unlock after we no longer access/modify the queue.

Listing 11.35—Adding Mutex to Task Queue (taskqueue.h)

```
1   typedef struct taskqueue {
2     ...
3     pthread_mutex_t tq_mutex;
4   } taskqueue;
```

Starting with `taskqueue_init`, we need to initialize the mutex via `pthread_-mutex_init`. Before, we used `PTHREAD_MUTEX_INITIALIZER`, but this only works if we create the mutex directly; we cannot do this if the mutex is stored inside a struct or initialized after its declaration.[1]

Listing 11.36—Initializing the Queue Mutex (`taskqueue.c`)

```
1   void taskqueue_init(taskqueue *tq) {
2     tq->head = tq->tail = NULL;
3     tq->no_elements = 0;
4     pthread_mutex_init(&(tq->tq_mutex), NULL);
5   }
```

Inside `taskqueue_enqueue`, we lock before we enter the conditional since it accesses the `no_elements` field. After updating, we unlock the mutex.

Listing 11.37—Acquiring and Releasing the Mutex in Queue Enqueue (`taskqueue.c`)

```
1    void taskqueue_enqueue(taskqueue *tq, struct task *tsk) {
2      ...
3      node->tsk = tsk;
4      pthread_mutex_lock(&(tq->tq_mutex));
5      if (0 == tq->no_elements) {
6        tq->head = tq->tail = node;
7      } else {
8        tq->tail->next = node;
9        tq->tail = node;
10     }
11     tq->no_elements++;
12     pthread_mutex_unlock(&(tq->tq_mutex));
13   }
```

In the destructor function, we lock before clearing the elements and unlock afterwards.

Listing 11.38—Acquiring and Releasing the Mutex in Queue Destruction (`taskqueue.c`)

```
1    void taskqueue_destroy(taskqueue *tq) {
2      pthread_mutex_lock(&(tq->tq_mutex));
3      for (int i = 0; i < tq->no_elements; i++) {
4        ...
5      }
6      pthread_mutex_unlock(&(tq->tq_mutex));
7    }
```

Now we can think about what it means to *be* a task. As we stated, a task contains a name, a function to execute, and an argument to said function. We initialize the function to execute depending on the provided enumeration. Namely, if our passed enumeration is FIB, we assign, to the task `fn` field, the static function `fib`.

---

[1]The second argument to `pthread_mutex_init` being NULL tells the library to use the default mutex attributes.

Listing 11.39—Creation and Destruction of an Arbitrary Task (task.c)

```
1   #include "task.h"
2
3   task *task_create(enum task_type tid, char *id, void *arg) {
4     task *tsk = calloc(1, sizeof(task));
5     tsk->id = strdup(id);
6     tsk->args = arg;
7     switch (tid) {
8       case FIB: {
9         tsk->fn = fib;
10        break;
11      }
12      default: {
13        printf("task_create: invalid id %d\n", tid);
14        exit(EXIT_FAILURE);
15      }
16    }
17    return tsk;
18  }
19
20  void task_destroy(task *tsk) {
21    free(tsk->id);
22    free(tsk);
23  }
```

But wait a minute, what even is fib? Based on the function pointer, it must be of type (void *) → (void *), so we can at least write the signature.

Listing 11.40—Describing the Fibonacci Task (task.c)

```
1   task *task_create(enum task_id tid, char *id, void *arg) { ... }
2   void task_destroy(task *tsk) { ... }
3   static void *fib(void *args) { return NULL; }
```

So, what is next? Surely we want this function to mimic a recursive Fibonacci procedure. Indeed, this is true, but we need to do a bit of casting beforehand. Recall that because this function receives a void *, we must cast its argument to a number. One may be tempted to immediately cast to an int, but the C compiler will warn that this is not a good idea because pointers are eight bytes (on 64-bit machines) and integers are typically four bytes long. The type intptr_t from stdlib.h has us covered! If we cast all inputs to fib to void * and any returned values to intptr_t, we achieve the same effect as a normal recursive Fibonacci function.[1]

Listing 11.41—Fibonacci Task Type Definition (task.c)

```
1   static void *fib(void *args) {
2     intptr_t n = (intptr_t) args;
3     if (n <= 1) { return (void *) 1; }
4     else {
5       intptr_t f1 = (intptr_t) fib((void *) (n - 1));
6       intptr_t f2 = (intptr_t) fib((void *) (n - 2));
7       return (void *) (f1 + f2);
8     }
9   }
```

---

[1]Having to intertwine our logic with integers and integer pointers is cumbersome, but it helps to ensure our variables remain the same size across function calls.

Two more pieces to this puzzle; we will solve the simpler of the two first: user input. We want to have a continuous loop that prompts the user for tasks to do (with the caveat that, for now, we only have one task, i.e., fib). All that is necessary is an infinite loop inside the main function. We read in the "task to do" referred to by its task enumeration identifier, name, and argument.

Listing 11.42—Helpful String Reading and Extraction Functions

```
1    #include <stdio.h>
2    #include <stdlib.h>
3
4    /**
5     * Reads a line from standard input; dynamically allocated.
6     *
7     * @return char * line from standard input.
8     */
9    char *read_line(void) {
10     char *line = NULL;
11     size_t sz = 0;
12     ssize_t nread = -1;
13     if ((nread = getline(&line, &sz, stdin)) == -1) {
14       fprintf(stderr, "read_line: failed to read line from stdin\n");
15       free(line);
16       exit(EXIT_FAILURE);
17     } else {
18       return line;
19     }
20   }
21
22   /**
23    * Converts a string into an integer.
24    *
25    * @param char * pointer to string.
26    *
27    * @return integer
28    */
29   int string_to_number(char *s) {
30     int n = 0;
31     if (0 == sscanf(s, "%d", &n)) {
32       fprintf(stderr, "string_to_number: failed to scan number\n");
33       exit(EXIT_FAILURE);
34     } else {
35       return n;
36     }
37   }
```

Listing 11.43—Testing the Task Queue

```
1   #include "taskqueue.h"
2
3   struct taskqueue tq;
4
5   int main(int argc, char *argv[]) {
6     taskqueue_init(&tq);
7     while (true) {
8       // Enter task enumeration identifier.
9       printf("Enter something to do:\n");
10      printf("1. Fibonacci\n");
11      char *line = read_line();
12      intptr_t tid = (intptr_t) string_to_number(line);
13      free(line);
14
15      // Argument for the task.
16      printf("Okay, enter an argument:\n");
17      line = read_line();
18      intptr_t arg = (intptr_t) string_to_number(line);
19      free(line);
20
21      // String task identifier. If it fails to read, bail out.
22      printf("And finally a name for the task:\n");
23      char *id = read_line();
24
25      // Enqueue task into queue.
26      taskqueue_enqueue(&tq, task_create((enum task_type) (tid - 1), "", (void *) arg));
27      free(id);
28    }
29    taskqueue_destroy(&tq);
30  }
```

Last but not least, we come to the multi-threading part of this project. We
want to have a "pool" of several (say, four) threads, that constantly listen for a
task. If a task is not available, the thread goes to sleep. How do we know if a
task is available? Simple: if the queue size is at least one, then there is a task for
a thread to perform. We define a "pool of threads" to be an array of N threads,
declared in the taskqueue struct:

Listing 11.44—Thread Pool Creation in Task Queue (taskqueue.h)

```
1   #define NO_THREADS 4
2   ...
3   typedef struct taskqueue {
4     ...
5     pthread_t thread_pool[NO_THREADS];
6     ...
7   } taskqueue;
```

It is the responsibility of the taskqueue to initialize these threads. Each thread,
as we know, calls a provided function. We name this function taskqueue_execute_-
handler. In addition, we pass it a reference to the taskqueue (which must be casted
as void * since the signature of taskqueue_execute_handler is (void *) →
(void *).

Listing 11.45—Thread Pool Initialization in Task Queue (taskqueue.c)

```
1   static void *taskqueue_execute_handler(void *arg);
2
3   void taskqueue_init(taskqueue *tq) {
4    tq->head = tq->tail = NULL;
5    tq->no_elements = 0;
6    pthread_mutex_init(&(tq->tq_mutex), NULL);
7
8    // Initialize the task thread pool.
9    for (int i = 0; i < NO_THREADS; i++) {
10     if (pthread_create(&(tq->thread_pool[i]), NULL,
11                        taskqueue_execute_handler, (void *) tq) < 0) {
12      EPF("taskqueue_init: could not initialize thread pool\n");
13      exit(EXIT_FAILURE);
14     }
15    }
16   }
17
18   static void *taskqueue_execute_handler(void *arg) { return NULL; }
```

Each task, as we stated, loops indefinitely, listening for tasks as they become available.

Listing 11.46—Thread Handler Function Stub (taskqueue.c)

```
1   static void *taskqueue_execute_handler(void *arg) {
2    taskqueue *tq = (taskqueue *) arg;
3    while (true) { // TODO.}
4    return NULL;
5   }
```

Though, what exactly should we do while a task is *not* available? The naive solution is to simply loop until the queue size is at least one, using a mutex where mandatory. Then, we access the task by removing the head of the queue and invoking the function pointer with its respective argument.

Listing 11.47—Thread Handler to Poll for Tasks (taskqueue.c)

```
1   static void *taskqueue_execute_handler(void *arg) {
2    taskqueue *tq = (taskqueue *) arg;
3    while (true) {
4     pthread_mutex_lock(&(tq->tq_mutex));
5     while (tq->no_elements < 1);
6
7     // Poll the head from the queue and update its pointers.
8     struct task *tsk = tq->head->tsk;
9     struct taskqueue_node *next = tq->head->next;
10    tq->head = next;
11    tq->no_elements--;
12    free(tq->head);
13    pthread_mutex_unlock(&(tq->tq_mutex));
14
15    // Execute the task, display its returned result, then destroy.
16    intptr_t result = (intptr_t) tsk->fn(tsk->args);
17    printf("Task %s produced %ld\n", tsk->id, result);
18    task_destroy(tsk);
19    }
20    return NULL;
21   }
```

This thread has a glaring problem: the busy loop. We do not want a thread to constantly loop over and over, wasting CPU time, when it is entirely unnecessary. Furthermore, we acquire the lock before checking the loop condition, meaning no other thread can begin listening since they do not have the lock! Hence, the need for some other solution: condition variables.[1] We can conditionally wait inside the loop and, when we invoke enqueue, we issue a thread signal, waking up a sleeping thread. So, we must declare a pthread_cond_t field inside taskqueue:

Listing 11.48—Declaring Condition Variable in Task Queue Struct (taskqueue.h)

```
1   typedef struct taskqueue {
2     ...
3     pthread_cond_t tq_cond;
4   } taskqueue;
```

As with the mutex, we initialize the condition variable inside taskqueue_init.

Listing 11.49—Initialization of Condition Variable in Queue (taskqueue.c)

```
1   void taskqueue_init(taskqueue *tq) {
2     ...
3     pthread_cond_init(&(tq->tq_cond), NULL);
4   }
```

We now update taskqueue_enqueue to issue the thread signal via pthread_-cond_signal and taskqueue_execute_handler to conditionally wait via pthread_-cond_wait. Everything else remains the same. As a very important but supplemental note: in order to issue a thread signal or conditionally wait, a thread must hold the specific lock associated with the condition variable. As reinforcement, pthread_cond_wait receives both a reference to the condition variable and the accompanying mutex. A conditional wait implicitly releases the lock by a thread (since it "goes to sleep" it does not need the lock anymore!), whereas a thread signal, in a sense, causes the thread to "reacquire" the lock (which is why we still unlock the corresponding mutex after the conditional wait).

---

[1]If threads were created "on-demand", so to speak, then we would not have this issue.

Listing 11.50—Conditional Wait in Task Queue (taskqueue.c)

```
1   void taskqueue_enqueue(taskqueue *tq, struct task *tsk) {
2     struct taskqueue_node *node = calloc(1, sizeof(struct taskqueue_node));
3     if (NULL == node) { ... }
4     node->tsk = tsk;
5     pthread_mutex_lock(&(tq->tq_mutex));
6     if (0 == tq->no_elements) { tq->head = tq->tail = node; }
7     else {
8       tq->tail->next = node;
9       tq->tail = node;
10    }
11    tq->no_elements++;
12    pthread_cond_signal(&(tq->tq_cond));
13    pthread_mutex_unlock(&(tq->tq_mutex));
14  }
15
16  static void *taskqueue_execute_handler(void *arg) {
17    taskqueue *tq = (taskqueue *) arg;
18    while (true) {
19      pthread_mutex_lock(&(tq->tq_mutex));
20      while (tq->no_elements < 1) {
21        pthread_cond_wait(&(tq->tq_cond), &(tq->tq_mutex));
22      }
23
24      // Poll the head from the queue and update its pointers.
25      struct task *tsk = tq->head->tsk;
26      struct taskqueue_node *next = tq->head->next;
27      tq->head = next;
28      tq->no_elements--;
29      free(tq->head);
30      pthread_mutex_unlock(&(tq->tq_mutex));
31
32      // Execute the task, display its returned result, then destroy.
33      intptr_t result = (intptr_t) tsk->fn(tsk->arg);
34      printf("Task %s produced %ld\n", tsk->id, result);
35      task_destroy(tsk);
36    }
37    return NULL;
38  }
```

At long last, let us run the program. Dispatching a few 'large' Fibonacci tasks will return their results in different times.

Listing 11.51

```
Enter something to do:
1. Fibonacci
1
Okay, enter an argument:
45
And finally a name for the task:
Fib45
Enter something to do:
1. Fibonacci
1
Okay, enter an argument:
42
And finally a name for the task:
Fib42
Enter something to do:
1. Fibonacci
1
Okay, enter an argument:
Task Fib42 produced 433494437
Task Fib45 produced 1836311903
35
And finally a name for the task:
Fib35
Enter something to do:
1. Fibonacci
Task Fib35 produced 14930352
^C
```

We see that the tasks are dispatched to different threads accordingly. Moreover, we further see that response messages are intertwined with the user input. It would be nice to not have them interrupt when the user is typing, i.e., stored in a "message alert" system of sorts. We leave this as an exercise to the reader.

Let us detach from this mini-project and return to the initial reason for this aside: condition variables for the REPL thread and why they are necessary. We have a separate thread that constantly listens for input, reading characters as they are typed. While this thread listens for individual character input, the main thread waits until a full line is entered, thereby signaled by pressing the "Enter" key. We want the main thread to sleep while waiting for a line of input, hence the need for a condition variable. First, we need a separate function to process "Enter" key presses. Our previous solution inlined the logic within cmd_history_getch, but we now delegate it to another function:

Listing 11.52—Separating Logic for "Enter" Key Presses (repl.c)

```
1   static unsigned char cmd_history_getch(void) {
2     ...
3     else if ('\r' == ch) {
4       handle_enter();
5     }
6     ...
7   }
8
9   static void handle_enter(void) {
10    send = true;
11    write(STDOUT_FILENO, "\r\n", 2);
12    buffer_idx = 0;
13    stack_idx = 0;
14  }
```

Up next we must modify `cmd_history_readline` to conditionally wait, while holding the mutex, until the user presses the "Enter" key, designating a new line. Once the send flag is set, the thread in control of the `cmd_history_handler`, i.e., the individual character thread, issues a signal to awaken the read-line thread. With this approach, the read-line thread does not need to use a busy loop and waste CPU time while, effectively, doing nothing meaningful. Let us declare the mutex and condition variable as global static variables. Fortunately, for the time being, there are only critical sections: upon reading a line, inside the character read-loop, and when modifying the send flag by pressing the "Enter" key.

Listing 11.53—Adding Mutex and Condition Variables to Command History (`repl.c`)

```
1    static pthread_mutex_t mutex = PTHREAD_MUTEX_INITIALIZER;
2    static pthread_cond_t cond = PTHREAD_COND_INITIALIZER;
3    ...
4    char *cmd_history_readline(char *prompt) {
5     // Swap the terminal mode to raw for input.
6     cmd_history_swap_terminal_mode();
7     // Block the current thread until we get data from the "reader thread".
8     pthread_mutex_lock(&mutex);
9     while (!send) { pthread_cond_wait(&cond, &mutex); }
10    send = false;
11    pthread_mutex_unlock(&mutex);
12    cmd_history_swap_terminal_mode();
13    ...
14   }
15
16   static void *cmd_history_handler(void *args) {
17    while (true) {
18     pthread_mutex_lock(&mutex);
19     cmd_history_getch();
20     if (send) { pthread_cond_signal(&cond); }
21     pthread_mutex_unlock(&mutex);
22    }
23    return NULL;
24   }
25
26   static void handle_enter(void) {
27    ...
28    pthread_mutex_lock(&mutex);
29    send = true;
30    pthread_mutex_unlock(&mutex);
31    ...
32   }
```

All that is left is to create the thread that listens for single character input. We designate `cmd_thread` as this thread and initialize it appropriately. Its delegation function, of course, is `cmd_history_handler` because it conveniently aligns with the required function pointer signature for pthread initialization.

Listing 11.54—Creating Command Character Processor Thread (`repl.c`)

```
1    static pthread_t cmd_thread;
2    ...
3    void cmd_history_init(void) {
4     ...
5     // Create the thread and send it the command handler.
6     pthread_create(&cmd_thread, NULL, cmd_history_handler, NULL);
7    }
```

Everything else is already established, so all we need now is a destructor function for the command history. We first acquire the lock and issue a *broadcast command* to awake any asleep threads that are blocked on a condition variable. In doing so we follow this with a pthread_join, which blocks the issuing thread until its given thread terminates. We want to block the main thread from continuing until cmd_thread finishes. Closing the program also resets the terminal mode from non-blocking to blocking. Of course, this raises the question of how the command thread knows when to quit the program. Indeed, we need a second flag, which keeps track of when to shut down said thread. The only point of its modification comes through cmd_history_destroy, which acquires the lock beforehand. Consequently we must change the loop condition from an infinite loop to only looping while this flag is false. Note the superfluity of toggling or untoggling send; the broadcast signal serves as the remedy.[1]

Listing 11.55—Destructor Function for Command History (repl.c)

```
1    static bool done = false;
2    ...
3    static void *cmd_history_handler(void *args) {
4      while (!done) {
5        cmd_history_getch();
6        pthread_mutex_lock(&mutex);
7        if (send) { pthread_cond_signal(&cond); }
8        pthread_mutex_unlock(&mutex);
9      }
10     return NULL;
11   }
12
13   void cmd_history_destroy(void) {
14     pthread_mutex_lock(&mutex);
15     done = true;
16     pthread_cond_broadcast(&cond);
17     pthread_mutex_unlock(&mutex);
18     if (pthread_join(cmd_thread, NULL) < 0) {
19       fprintf(stderr, "cmd_history_destroy: failed to terminate cmd_thread\n");
20       exit(EXIT_FAILURE);
21     }
22     cmd_stack_destroy(&stk);
23     cmd_history_reset_terminal_mode();
24   }
```

---

[1] The stack destructor called by cmd_stack_destroy is akin to destroying a linked list, so we leave it as an exercise to the reader to implement.

11.2   Multi-threading and Garbage Collection

In Chapter 10, we discussed two very simple garbage collection approaches. The latter of these two was a reference-counting garbage collector that we activate at the end of the program. It would be nice, however, if we could periodically enable the garbage collector to clean up any lost references while the program runs. Doing this from the main thread causes problems because it means the main thread has to halt its current job to tend to the garbage collector. What if we had a second thread that manages the garbage collector and runs it periodically? In this section, we will implement such a feature.

We can implement two methods to periodically "collect" memory that is no longer accessible. The first method involves using a timer to constantly activate the garbage collector after a period of allotted time. The second method involves activating the garbage collector when a certain predetermined condition is met, such as after a number of allocations are created.

Let us first implement the "timer" solution. We know that we can block a thread using a condition variable, but there is another way to block a thread that involves a timer: `pthread_cond_timedwait`. Similar to its non-timed counterpart, it receives a reference to the condition variable and mutex, but it also receives a `timespec` struct. The `timespec` struct is a way of denoting units of time. Specifically, we need to specify that a segment of code should be executed by the waiting thread every three seconds. Let us see how we can use `timespec` in conjunction with `pthread_cond_timedwait`. The following code listing contains some starter code:

Listing 11.56

```
1   #include <time.h> // For struct timespec.
2
3   pthread_mutex_t mutex = PTHREAD_MUTEX_INITIALIZER;
4   pthread_cond_t cond = PTHREAD_COND_INITIALIZER;
5
6   void *execute(void *arg) { return NULL; }
7
8   int main(void) {
9     pthread_t thread;
10    if (pthread_create(&thread, NULL, execute, NULL) < 0) {
11      EPF("main: failed to create pthread\n");
12      exit(EXIT_FAILURE);
13    }
14
15    if (pthread_join(thread, NULL) < 0) {
16      EPF("main: failed to join pthread\n");
17      exit(EXIT_FAILURE);
18    }
19    return 0;
20  }
```

Now, let us integrate an infinite loop into our thread handler function `execute`. In this loop, we will perform a conditional wait for a given unit of time. How we do this is unclear at the moment:

Listing 11.57

```
1   void *execute(void *arg) {
2     while (true) {
3       pthread_mutex_lock(&mutex);
4       // Wait on the condition variable.
5       pthread_mutex_unlock(&mutex);
6     }
7     return NULL;
8   }
```

We need to do two things: acquire the current time and offset it by a preset value, say, three seconds. To get the current time, we first create a timespec struct and pass it to the clock_gettime function as the second argument. The first argument, on the other hand, is a clock identifier, i.e., what source to "poll" time from. In our case, we will use CLOCK_REALTIME.

Listing 11.58

```
1    void *execute(void *arg) {
2      while (true) {
3        struct timespec current_time;
4        clock_gettime(CLOCK_REALTIME, &current_time);
5
6        pthread_mutex_lock(&mutex);
7        // Wait on the condition variable.
8        pthread_mutex_unlock(&mutex);
9      }
10     return NULL;
11   }
```

Let us now advance the current retrieved time by three seconds to indicate that, from the time that the mutex acquires the lock, we want to wait on the condition variable for three seconds. We do this by adding three to the tv_sec field of the timespec struct. To perform a timed wait on the condition variable, we pass a reference to the current_time variable.

Listing 11.59

```
1    #define PAUSE_TIME 3
2    ...
3    void *execute(void *arg) {
4      while (true) {
5        printf("This executes once every three seconds.\n");
6        struct timespec current_time;
7        clock_gettime(CLOCK_REALTIME, &current_time);
8        current_time.tv_sec += PAUSE_TIME;
9        pthread_mutex_lock(&mutex);
10       pthread_cond_timedwait(&mutex, &cond, &current_time);
11       pthread_mutex_unlock(&mutex);
12     }
13     return NULL;
14   }
```

If we run this program, a second thread is created that executes printf every three seconds.

Before we invoke rcgc_activate in our child thread, we must amend our reference-counting garbage collector to use a mutex. Namely, whenever we allocate memory or run the garbage collector, we need to lock a mutex to prevent any race conditions between the two threads. So, let us add a mutex to the rcgc struct:

Listing 11.60—Adding Lock to Reference-Counting Garbage Collector (`rcgc.h`)

```
1   struct rcgc {
2     struct rcgc_allocation *head;
3     struct rcgc_allocation *tail;
4     pthread_mutex_t mutex;
5   };
```

Now, like we did with the task queue, we initialize the mutex inside the relevant `rcgc_init` function, and lock/unlock inside any function that multiple threads access.

Listing 11.61—Making Garbage Collector Thread-Safe (`rcgc.c`)

```
1   #include "rcgc.h"
2
3   void rcgc_init(void) {
4     pthread_mutex_init(&(gc.mutex), NULL);
5     gc.head = gc.tail = NULL;
6   }
7
8   void *rcgc_alloc(size_t sz) {
9     // Allocate the node in the tree.
10    struct rcgc_allocation *node = calloc(1, sizeof(struct rcgc_allocation));
11    ASSERT_ALLOC(node, "rcgc_alloc");
12    pthread_mutex_lock(&(gc.mutex));
13    // Add to linked list.
14      ...
15
16    // Now assign the ptr data.
17      ...
18
19    pthread_mutex_unlock(&(gc.mutex));
20    return ptr;
21  }
22
23  void rcgc_assign(void **dest, void **src) {
24    pthread_mutex_lock(&(gc.mutex));
25      ...
26    pthread_mutex_unlock(&(gc.mutex));
27  }
28
29  void rcgc_release(void **dest) {
30    pthread_mutex_lock(&(gc.mutex));
31    if (dest != NULL) { ... }
32    pthread_mutex_unlock(&(gc.mutex));
33  }
34
35  void rcgc_activate(void) {
36    pthread_mutex_lock(&(gc.mutex));
37    for (struct rcgc_allocation *curr = gc.head; curr != NULL; curr = curr->next) {
38
39      ...
40    }
41    pthread_mutex_unlock(&(gc.mutex));
42  }
43
44  void rcgc_cleanup(void) {
45    pthread_mutex_lock(&(gc.mutex));
46    struct rcgc_allocation *tmp = gc.head;
47    while (gc.head != NULL) { ... }
48    pthread_mutex_unlock(&(gc.mutex));
49  }
50
51  static struct rcgc_allocation *rcgc_search(void *ptr) {
52    for (struct rcgc_allocation *curr = gc.head; curr != NULL; curr = curr->next) {
53      if (ptr == curr->data) { return curr; }
54    }
55    return NULL;
56  }
```

Notice that we do not lock and unlock the mutex inside `rcgc_search`. This is because the only way for this function to be called is by a thread that already has the lock acquired, i.e., from another function inside this source file. Thus, if we tried to acquire the lock again, this would result in a deadlock since the thread would wait until the lock that it is holding is available (threads are not quite as smart or sentient as they may seem). Moreover, we do not lock and unlock in `rcgc_-activate` because, the only thread that has access to this function is the thread handler which, by definition, must already acquire the lock.

Now, let us write some code in our main testing file to call the garbage collector every three seconds. In addition, we will use a loop to continuously reallocate and assign pointers to show that the garbage collector works as intended.

Listing 11.62—Allocations Inside a Loop (`main_rcgc.c`)

```
1   #define PAUSE_TIME 3
2
3   static bool done = false;
4   static pthread_mutex_t rcgc_handler_mutex = PTHREAD_MUTEX_INITIALIZER;
5   static pthread_cond_t rcgc_handler_cond = PTHREAD_COND_INITIALIZER;
6
7   void *rcgc_thread_handler(void *arg) {
8     while (!done) {
9       // Get the current time and increment.
10      ...
11
12      // Wait for n seconds.
13      pthread_mutex_lock(&rcgc_handler_mutex);
14      pthread_cond_timedwait(&rcgc_handler_cond, &rcgc_handler_mutex, &ts);
15      rcgc_activate();
16      pthread_mutex_unlock(&rcgc_handler_mutex);
17    }
18    return NULL;
19  }
20
21  int main(void) {
22    rcgc_init();
23    // Create the gc thread handler.
24    pthread_t pid;
25    if (pthread_create(&pid, NULL, rcgc_thread_handler, NULL) < 0) {
26      EPF("main: failed to create rcgc thread handler\n");
27      exit(EXIT_FAILURE);
28    }
29
30    // Create a few arbitrary allocations and assignments.
31    int *arr1 = rcgc_alloc(sizeof(int) * 10);
32    int *arr2 = NULL;
33
34    // Do something for a while...
35    double val = 0;
36    while (val < 0) {
37      val += 0.0001;
38      arr1 = rcgc_realloc((void **) &arr1, sizeof(int));
39      rcgc_assign(( void ** ) &arr2, ( void ** ) &arr1);
40    }
41    done = true;
42    if (pthread_join(pid, NULL) < 0) {
43      EPF("main: failed to join rcgc thread handler\n");
44      exit(EXIT_FAILURE);
45    }
46    rcgc_cleanup();
47    return 0;
48  }
```

On our system, we kept track of how many allocations the garbage collector freed on each invocation. For the above test, we received the following output:

```
Activating the garbage collector, freed 6993 chunks.
Activating the garbage collector, freed 2895 chunks.
Activating the garbage collector, freed 113 chunks.
```

Because the final invocation of the garbage collector had so few chunks to free, it is safe to assume that, soon after the second invocation, the "counting task" finished.

Now, let us switch gears from a time-based garbage collection alert system to one that alerts it based on the number of allocated chunks. Making this alteration is not as trivial as using a timer; we need an additional mutex/condition variable pair to let the allocator know that the garbage collector is running. Additionally, let us move the thread handler mutex/condition variable pair into the type definition. We also need a boolean flag for the condition variable to depend on, and a number chunks currently allocated.

Listing 11.63—Modifying the Garbage Collector (rcgc.h)

```
1   struct rcgc {
2     struct rcgc_allocation *head;
3     struct rcgc_allocation *tail;
4
5     int num_chunks;
6     bool collect;
7
8     pthread_mutex_t mutex;
9     pthread_mutex_t chunk_mutex;
10    pthread_cond_t cond;
11    pthread_cond_t chunk_cond;
12  };
```

Initialization of these fields follows suit:

Listing 11.64

```
1   void rcgc_init(void) {
2     pthread_mutex_init(&(gc.mutex), NULL);
3     pthread_mutex_init(&(gc.chunk_mutex), NULL);
4     pthread_cond_init(&(gc.cond), NULL);
5     pthread_cond_init(&(gc.chunk_cond), NULL);
6     gc.head = gc.tail = NULL;
7     gc.num_chunks = 0;
8     gc.collect = false;
9   }
```

Here's our end-goal: our garbage collector thread handler activates whenever there are n allocations inside the garbage collector, where n is some predefined constant. Upon activating, we block the main thread (or any other thread, for that matter) from accessing or mutating the garbage collector using the chunk_-mutex and chunk_cond pair. Accordingly, let us write a static function rcgc_wait that locks the mutex and waits until the garbage collector is finished clearing old allocations using the gc.collect flag. If, on the other hand, the garbage collector is not running, gc.collect is false, meaning we do not block on the condition variable.

Listing 11.65—Block Until Garbage Collection Finishes (rcgc.c)

```
1  static void rcgc_wait(void) {
2    pthread_mutex_lock(&(gc.chunk_mutex));
3    while (gc.collect) {
4      pthread_cond_wait(&(gc.chunk_cond), &(gc.chunk_mutex));
5    }
6    pthread_mutex_unlock(&(gc.chunk_mutex));
7  }
```

We must **invoke** rcgc_wait in every function that other threads (aside from the thread handler) access.

Listing 11.66—Block Accessing/Mutating Garbage Collector If It Is "Active" (rcgc.c)

```
1  void *rcgc_alloc(size_t sz) {
2    rcgc_wait();
3    pthread_mutex_lock(&(gc.mutex));
4    ...
5    pthread_mutex_unlock(&(gc.mutex));
6    return ptr;
7  }
8
9  void *rcgc_owalloc(void *dest, size_t sz) {
10   rcgc_wait();
11   pthread_mutex_lock(&(gc.mutex));
12   if (NULL == dest) { ... }
13   else {
14     ...
15     pthread_mutex_unlock(&(gc.mutex));
16     return rcgc_alloc(sz);
17   }
18 }
19
20 void rcgc_assign(void **dest, void *src) {
21   rcgc_wait();
22   pthread_mutex_lock(&(gc.mutex));
23   ...
24   pthread_mutex_unlock(&(gc.mutex));
25 }
26
27 void rcgc_release(void **dest) {
28   rcgc_wait();
29   pthread_mutex_lock(&(gc.mutex));
30   ...
31   pthread_mutex_unlock(&(gc.mutex));
32 }
```

We now **update** rcgc_alloc and rcgc_activate to take advantage of our new approach. The former increments the number of chunks and, if it is greater than our limit, send a signal to the thread handler's condition variable and enable gc.collect.

Listing 11.67—Invoking the Garbage Collector When Limit is Reached (rcgc.c)

```
1   void *rcgc_alloc(size_t sz) {
2     rcgc_wait();
3     pthread_mutex_lock(&(gc.mutex));
4     // Try to find a free node.
5     ...
6     // If we allocate more than enough chunks, send the signal.
7     gc.num_chunks++;
8     if (gc.num_chunks > MAX_CHUNKS) {
9       gc.collect = true;
10      pthread_cond_signal(&(gc.cond));
11    }
12    ...
13    pthread_mutex_unlock(&(gc.mutex));
14    return ptr;
15  }
```

On the other hand, the latter simply decrements the number of chunks in the collector if we free an allocation. Additionally, we disable the gc.collect flag and signal the chunk_cond condition variable which, as we previously stated, blocks concurrent modification while the collector is active.

Listing 11.68—Modifying Garbage Collector Activation (rcgc.c)

```
1   void rcgc_activate(void) {
2     for (struct rcgc_allocation *curr = gc.head; curr != NULL; curr = curr->next) {
3       if (0 == curr->counter && !curr->is_free) {
4         free(curr->data);
5         curr->data = NULL;
6         curr->is_free = true;
7         gc.num_chunks--;
8       }
9     }
10    gc.collect = false;
11    pthread_cond_signal(&(gc.chunk_cond));
12  }
```

Placing an upper-bound on the number of chunks to allocate before invoking the garbage collector can be a bad idea. Consider a situation in which we allocate MAX_-CHUNKS blocks of memory, then proceed to allocate one more chunk. The garbage collector then attempts to free some memory and finds one unreachable reference, thereby freeing its associated memory. So, the collector now has MAX_CHUNKS allocated again, and if we allocate one more chunk again, the garbage collector reruns after only one allocation. Invoking the garbage collector this often typically induces a hit to performance. Some solutions might be to only run the garbage collector after some unit of time after the previous iteration passes, or only after some number of chunks have been allocated since the previous iteration, and so forth.

11.3   A Powerful Garbage Collector

Writing a fully-featured and working garbage collector is, to put it bluntly, difficult. Other languages such as Java, Racket, and more have built-in garbage collectors. C, because it is designed to be a fast and small language, does not have one. Fortunately, other people have designed libraries that we may take advantage of, such as "*gc*" by Marc Kirchner (see Appendix 11.3).[1]

Like *mpc*, we can simply add the gc.c and gc.h files (alongside their logging source files) into our working directory and compile them alongside our code. So, let us rework *mgc* to hook into *gc*, which will be a breeze thanks to representation independence! We no longer need to worry about uncontrolled and controlled allocations, since both are deferred to the garbage collector. Therefore we should remove the code inside ufree and only invoke the pertinent garbage collector functions as specified by the library.

Listing 11.69—Updating mgc to Use gc (mgc.c)

```
1   #include "mgc.h"
2   #include "gc.h"
3
4   void mgc_init(void) {}
5
6   void *mgc_alloc(size_t sz, void (*dfree)(void *)) {
7    return gc_calloc_ext(&gc, 1, sz, dfree);
8   }
9
10  void mgc_free(void *ptr) {
11   gc_free(&gc, ptr);
12  }
13
14  void *mgc_ualloc(size_t sz) {
15   return gc_calloc(&gc, 1, sz);
16  }
17
18  void *mgc_urealloc(void *ptr, size_t sz) {
19   return gc_realloc(&gc, ptr, sz);
20  }
21
22  void mgc_ufree(void *ptr) {}
23
24  void mgc_cleanup(void) {}
```

After changing *mgc*, we must start and stop the garbage collector inside our main function. Garbage collectors in C require access to the bottom of the stack so it can detect variables across the stack that point to live allocations in the heap.

Listing 11.70—Starting and Stopping Garbage Collector (main.c)

```
1   #include "gc.h"
2
3   int main(int argc, char *argv[]) {
4    gc_start(&gc, &argc);
5    ...
6    gc_stop(&gc);
7    return 0;
8   }
```

---

[1]These alterations were made on the minified interpreter language from our section on tail-call optimization in Chapter 7.

At long last, our language is fully able to run forever when given an infinitely recursive function due to the garbage collector. We also now have definitive proof that tail recursion, after implementing tail-call optimization, is much, *much* faster than standard recursion. Moreover, our program no longer segmentation faults because it runs out of memory.

Function Call	Execution Time (seconds)
(! 1000)	8.14
(! 60000)	> 500
(!-tr 1000)	0.029
(!-tr 60000)	1.31

Figure 11.1: Factorial Function Performance on 2021 MacBook Pro

Epilogue

Congratulations on reaching this point! You have taken a significant step towards a future in computer science. Reaching the end of this book, however, does not mark the end of your journey; it only provides a glimpse into the vast world of computer science with intertwined theory and practice. This book covers a small fraction of computer science; omitting topics such as cryptography, software engineering practices, (advanced) algorithm analysis and data structures, machine learning, data science, and many other seemingly infinite areas of knowledge. If our brief exploration has sparked your motivation, we strongly encourage you to continue forward. Some may find the theoretical side of computer science to be tedious and opt for careers in software development, whereas others may be captivated by the mathematical and so-called "academic" perspectives. Regardless of the path you choose, as long as it excites you, it fulfills its purpose. Practice, hard work, and endurance go far in this field: a ubiquitous mindset across all specializations and domains.

Environment and Code Setup

Welcome to the back of the book; we hope this is not after you have finished the book but rather before you have even started the main content! In this appendix, we describe how to setup your programming environment across different operating systems.

Environment Setup

Whatever your programming environment may be, make sure to choose a text editor that can display code with syntax highlighting. We recommend either VSCode or Sublime Text. Other options exist, e.g., Vim, Emacs, but these are, in general, geared towards (hardcore) users with programming experience. Do not use a program such as Microsoft Word, Pages by Apple, or LibreOffice Writer, as these save other information inside of the file as opposed to raw text, which is what we want. It is best to have a program that allows you to save documents with custom extensions.

Using the Online `replit` Sandbox

Using the online `replit` (sandbox) environment is ideal for someone who does not want to download a ton of files to their own system. All of the libraries are installed and ready to use.

Make a free account on https://replit.com. Then, go to the template provided at https://replit.com/@Joshua_Crotts/POCS?v=1. Click the button labeled, "Use Template". Afterwards, you will have a sandbox to write code. The right-hand panel is the code output window and shell. Click in this window and type "make". There should be no errors. Then type ./myprogram, which should output the following text:

```
Principles of Computer Science
MPFR version: 4.1.0
If your program output got to here
without crashing, the environment worked!
```

MacOS

To install certain programs on MacOS, we will take advantage of the brew package manager. In short, this is a command-line application that lets users quickly download applications without an absurdly large installation interface. To install brew, follow the steps on the https://brew.sh/ website. From here, we must install the C compiler gcc. Type 'brew install gcc', then allow the installation to proceed. Verify that gcc is installed by checking its version with the gcc --version command.

Linux

We assume that Linux users, for the most part, know what they're doing. Regardless, we will demonstrate installing the C compiler on both Debian-based Linux distributions, e.g,. Ubuntu and Mint, as well as Arch-based Linux distributions, e.g., Arch and Manjaro. In Linux, it is always important to ensure that packages are up-to-date, so perform the necessary update commands to refresh the package repositories.

Debian-Based Distributions

Use the apt package manager to download and install gcc along with other useful project build utilities: 'sudo apt install build-essential'. Verify that gcc is installed by checking its version with the gcc --version command. Additionally, install the package configuration command pkg-config with 'sudo apt install pkg-config'.

Arch-Based Distributions

Use the pacman package manager to download and install gcc: 'sudo pacman -S gcc'. Verify that gcc is installed by checking its version with the gcc --version command. Additionally, install the package configuration command pkg-config with 'sudo pacman -S pkg-config'.

Using the C Compiler and Linker

Normal C Programs

To compile a .c file, we invoke gcc in the terminal via 'gcc file.c'. After compiling the program, any errors or warnings will appear if they exist. Errors prevent the compilation process from finishing successfully. Warnings, on the other hand, allow the program to compile, but may result in unpredictable program behavior. To this end, we always favor a program that compiles without any warnings at all. We can compile multiple C source files by supplementing them as gcc arguments, e.g., 'gcc main.c list.c utils.c'. A successful compilation produces an executable file a.out, executable (runnable) via './a.out'. The file name a is not very descriptive; we can customize the output file name with the -o flag, e.g., 'gcc main.c list.c utils.c -o program.out'.

The gcc compiler can be supplemented with *flags*, which give the compiler more information about how to treat the resulting output file. For instance, we may enable an option -Werror that treats all warnings as errors. -Wall generates (almost) all C warning messages that the program could generate (by default, the compiler omits warnings that it, perhaps, deems unnecessary to warn the programmer of). Enabling both of these flags is a good idea in every C program one writes. There are several others that we will utilize, and we present an example configuration.

Listing .71—Example Compilation Command

```
1   gcc -g -Wall -Werror -Wno-unused-function
2       -Wno-unused-command-line-argument -Wno-unused-variable
3       -Wno-unused-but-set-variable
4       -Wformat-security -fPIE <src-files>
5       -o <output-file>
```

Linking Libraries

Sometimes external libraries and header files need to be directly linked to the compiler. We present the steps and commands necessary to get up and running below. Note that some of these may not make sense at the start of your adventure with this text, so come back as they appear in your reading.

Using MPC

Daniel Holden's Micro Parser Combinators (*mpc*) library is easy to bundle into our project. First, go to the GitHub repository where the source and header files are located https://github.com/orangeduck/mpc, download mpc.c and mpc.h, then drag these two into your project directory. Compiling these files is identical to how we compile our own C programs; there is no linking process with *mpc*.

Using GC

Marc Kirchner's garbage collection (*gc*) library is, similar to *mpc*, easy to bundle into our project. First, go to the GitHub repository where the source and header files are located https://github.com/mkirchner/gc, download gc.c, gc.h, log.c, and log.h, then drag these two into your project directory. Compiling these files is identical to how we compile our own C programs; there is no linking process with *gc*.

Using GNU GMP and MPFR

We present three ways to install and link the GNU Multi-Precision Arithmetic and the GNU Multi-Precision Floating Point libraries, whose approaches vary based on your operating system. In the event that you are using the `replit` environment, these two libraries are already installed.

GMP & MPFR on MacOS. Using `brew`, install `gmp` and `mpfr` via 'brew install gmp' and 'brew install mpfr'. To include the header files, execute the following commands in your terminal and copy the results.

```
pkg-config --variable=includedir gmp
pkg-config --variable=includedir mpfr
```

Then, when invoking `gcc`, type the received results preceding by `-I`. E.g.,

```
gcc main.c -I/opt/homebrew/include -o program
```

We also need to link the libraries with the compiler. To do so, we need the location of the (prebuilt) libraries on our system. Execute the following commands in your terminal and copy the results.

```
pkg-config --libs gmp
pkg-config --libs mpfr
```

Then, when invoking `gcc`, type the received results preceding by `-l`. E.g.,

```
gcc main.c -I/.../ -lmpfr -lgmp -o program
```

GMP & MPFR on Debian-Based Distributions. Using `apt`, install `gmp` and `mpfr` via 'sudo apt install libgmp-dev' and 'sudo apt install libmpfr-dev'. To include the header files, execute the following commands in your terminal and copy the results.

```
pkg-config --variable=includedir gmp
pkg-config --variable=includedir mpfr
```

Then, when invoking `gcc`, type the received results preceding by `-I`. E.g.,

```
gcc main.c -I/usr/include -o program
```

We also need to link the libraries with the compiler. To do so, we need the location of the (prebuilt) libraries on our system. Execute the following commands in your terminal and copy the results.

```
pkg-config --libs gmp
pkg-config --libs mpfr
```

Then, when invoking `gcc`, type the received results preceding by `-l`. E.g.,

```
gcc main.c -I/.../ -lmpfr -lgmp -o program
```

GMP & MPFR on Arch-Based Distributions. Using pacman, install gmp and mpfr via 'sudo pacman -S gmp' and 'sudo pacman -S mpfr'. To include the header files, execute the following commands in your terminal and copy the results.

```
pkg-config --variable=includedir gmp
pkg-config --variable=includedir mpfr
```

Then, when **invoking** gcc, type the received results preceding by -I. E.g.,

```
gcc main.c -I/usr/include -o program
```

We also need to **link** the libraries with the compiler. To do so, we need the location of the (prebuilt) libraries on our system. Execute the following commands in your terminal and **copy** the results.

```
pkg-config --libs gmp
pkg-config --libs mpfr
```

Then, when **invoking** gcc, type the received results preceding by -l. E.g.,

```
gcc main.c -I/.../ -lmpfr -lgmp -o program
```

Using SDL2

We present three ways to install and link the Simple DirectMedia Layer (version 2) library, whose approach varies based on your operating system. In the event that you are using the `replit` environment, SDL2 is already installed.

SDL2 on MacOS. Using `brew`, install SDL2 via the command 'brew install sdl2'. To include the header file(s), execute the following command in your terminal and copy its result.

```
sdl2-config --cflags
```

Then, when invoking gcc, type the received results (which should already come with a prefixed -I):

```
gcc main.c -I/opt/homebrew/include/SDL2 -D_THREAD_SAFE
```

We also need to link the libraries with the compiler. To do so, we need the location of the (prebuilt) libraries on our system. Execute the following commands in your terminal and copy the results.

```
sdl2-config --libs
```

Then, when invoking gcc, type the received results (which should come with a prefixed -L).[1] E.g.,

```
gcc main.c -I/.../ -L/opt/homebrew/lib -lSDL2 -o program
```

SDL2 on Debian-Based Distributions. Using apt, install SDL2 via the command 'sudo apt install libsdl2-dev'. To include the header file(s), execute the following command in your terminal and copy its result.

```
sdl2-config --cflags
```

Then, when invoking gcc, type the received results (which should already come with a prefixed -I):

```
gcc main.c -I/usr/include/SDL2 -D_REENTRANT
```

We also need to link the libraries with the compiler. To do so, we need the location of the (prebuilt) libraries on our system. Execute the following commands in your terminal and copy the results.

```
sdl2-config --libs
```

Then, when invoking gcc, type the received results (which should come with a prefixed -l), E.g.,

```
gcc main.c -I/.../ -lSDL2 -o program
```

---

[1]There *is* a difference between the upper-cased -L and lower-cased -l linker flags; the former references a directory of libraries whereas the latter references a specific library.

SDL2 on Arch-Based Distributions. Using `pacman`, install SDL2 via the command 'sudo pacman -S sdl2'. To include the header file(s), execute the following command in your terminal and copy its result.

```
sdl2-config --cflags
```

Then, when invoking `gcc`, type the received results (which should already come with a prefixed -I):

```
gcc main.c -I/usr/include/SDL2 -D_REENTRANT
```

We also need to link the libraries with the compiler. To do so, we need the location of the (prebuilt) libraries on our system. Execute the following commands in your terminal and copy the results.

```
sdl2-config --libs
```

Then, when invoking `gcc`, type the received results (which should come with a prefixed -l), E.g.,

```
gcc main.c -I/.../ -lSDL2 -o program
```

Using GNU Readline

We present three ways to install the GNU Multi-Precision Arithmetic and the GNU Multi-Precision Floating Point libraries, whose approach varies based on your operating system. In the event that you are using the `replit` environment, the library is already installed.

GNU Readline on MacOS. Using `brew`, install `readline` via 'brew install readline'. To include the header file(s), execute the following command in your terminal and copy its result.

```
pkg-config --variable=includedir readline
```

Then, when invoking `gcc`, type the received results preceding by -I. E.g.,

```
gcc main.c -I/opt/homebrew/include -o program
```

We also need to link the libraries with the compiler. To do so, we need the location of the (prebuilt) libraries on our system. Execute the following commands in your terminal and copy the results.

```
pkg-config --libs readline
```

Then, when invoking `gcc`, type the received results preceding by -l. E.g.,

```
gcc main.c -I/.../ -l?????? -o program
```

GNU Readline on Debian-Based Distributions. Using apt, install readline via 'sudo apt install libreadline-dev'. To include the header file(s), execute the following command in your terminal and copy the results.

    pkg-config --variable=includedir libreadline-dev

Then, when invoking gcc, type the received results preceding by -I. E.g.,

    gcc main.c -I/usr/include -o program

We also need to link the libraries with the compiler. To do so, we need the location of the (prebuilt) libraries on our system. Execute the following commands in your terminal and copy the results.

    pkg-config --libs libreadline-dev

Then, when invoking gcc, type the received results preceding by -l. E.g.,

    gcc main.c -I/.../ -lreadline -o program

GNU Readline on Arch-Based Distributions. On Arch, the readline package is generally pre-installed as a prerequisite/dependency of Bash. In case not, though, use pacman to install it via 'sudo pacman -S readline'. To include the header files, execute the following command in your terminal and copy its result.

    pkg-config --variable=includedir readline

Then, when invoking gcc, type the received results preceding by -I. E.g.,

    gcc main.c -I/usr/include -o program

We also need to link the libraries with the compiler. To do so, we need the location of the (prebuilt) libraries on our system. Execute the following commands in your terminal and copy the results.

    pkg-config --libs readline

Then, when invoking gcc, type the received results preceding by -l. E.g.,

    gcc main.c -I/.../ -lreadline -o program

Makefiles

Having to remember flags and compilation commands is cumbersome. In particular, if we have to rewrite a compile command every time we want to test a program, then we also have to ensure we do not forget, say, a new file addition. Makefiles are a popular tool in software development for automating the compilation and building of projects. They provide a convenient way to define dependencies between files and specify the commands needed to build an executable or other targets. Makefiles consist of rules that define how to create targets from prerequisites.

Installing make on MacOS

Install make with brew via 'brew install make'.

Installing make on Debian-Based Distributions

The make build system comes with build-essential, so there is no need to install a separate package.

Installing make on Arch-Based Distributions

Install make with pacman via 'sudo pacman -S make'.

Designing a (Simple) Custom Makefile

Let us design a very simple yet highly effective makefile for our project(s).

```
CC = gcc
```

First, we need a rule to specify the compiler of choice, in this case that is gcc.[1] The left-hand side of a rule is its name, otherwise called the target. The right-hand side is the expression that is substituted whenever we reference CC later on.

```
CFLAGS = ...
```

We can add and remove compilation flags as necessary with the CFLAGS target.

```
LDFLAGS = ...
```

When linking against external libraries, we need to add those under the LDFLAGS target.

```
IFLAGS = ...
```

Any header files that we intend to use outside the C standard library and our own source code must have a file path reference and linked under IFLAGS.

---

[1]It seems a bit superfluous to do this when we know for a fact that our compiler is gcc. For us, such a belief is true, but there are more compilers than just gcc, and being flexible is a huge part of programming and design!

```
SRC = $(wildcard src/*.c)
OBJS = $(SRCS:.c=.o)
```

When compiling a source file, we know that the resulting file is an object file. We need to list these as targets in the make file to collectively reference them in subsequent rules. All source files have a .c extension and all object files have a .o extension. We also say that all source files are located in the src/ directory. The OBJS expression looks a little strange, but all it says is that the object files share the same name as their source counterparts, just with a different file extension.

```
TARGET = program
all = $(TARGET)
```

We must specify an output executable name that is the result of the compilation. In this instance we refer to it as "program" in a target TARGET. Additionally, the "all" target is implicitly referenced when we type "make" in the terminal. It is certainly possible to create different targets to compile separate source files, but for our purposes, we just say that compiling everything is equivalent to compiling our program.

```
$(TARGET) = $(OBJS)
        $(CC) $(LDFLAGS) $^ -o $@
```

Now we describe how the target program is built. The rule states that it uses our compiler with the linker flags to build the target OBJS, producing an output described by the target. The funny-looking symbols $ând $@ respectively represent the dependencies necessary for the command to execute, and the rule target. So, the rule requires the object files to be present when compiling, meaning $^ references $(OBJS), whereas $@ refers to the rule target, which in our case is $(TARGET). These short-hand forms allow us to change the names of TARGET and OBJS, should we so choose, without having to change their names in several different places.

```
%.o: %.c
        $(CC) $(CFLAGS) $(IFLAGS) -c $< -o $@
```

We now come to the most important rule in which the source files are compiled to object files. We once again reference the C compiler of choice, then the compiler and include flags, followed by the C source files using a shortcut command $<, and finally succeeded by the output object file. In theory, we could write a separate target for every object and source file pair, but there is absolutely no need to do so in our case.

```
.PHONY clean:
        rm -f $(OBJS) $(TARGET)
```

The last rule for "cleaning up"; it clears all object and build files from the directory. This is helpful for deleting failed or previous compilation objects, or in the event that we simply want to clean up our directory of output files.

Putting everything together gets us the following makefile example (note that you need to include the appropriate headers and link libraries accordingly):

Listing .72—Makefile Example

```
# Compiler of choice.
CC = gcc

# Compiler flags.
CFLAGS = -g3 -Wall -Werror -Wno-unused-function -Wno-unused-command-line-argument
         -Wno-unused-variable Wno-unused-but-set-variable -Wformat-security -fPIE

# Linker flags.
LDFLAGS = ''

# Include flags.
IFLAGS = ''

# Source files.
SRCS = $(wildcard src/*.c)

# Object files.
OBJS = $(SRCS:.c=.o)

# Output executable.
TARGET = myprogram

# Default target.
all: $(TARGET)

# Rule to build the executable.
$(TARGET): $(OBJS)
        $(CC) $(LDFLAGS) $^ -o $@

# Rule to compile source files.
%.o: %.c
    $(CC) $(CFLAGS) $(INCFLAGS) -c $< -o $@

# Clean target.
.PHONY clean:
    rm -f $(OBJS) $(TARGET)
```

Graphics Library Source Code

In the latter half of Chapter 8, we introduce a representation-independent graphics library via $\mathcal{L}_{\text{GRAPHIC}}$ without concern for the library internals. This appendix provides, in text, the code for our library. You can safely use it with little-to-no regard for how it works.

GFX Header

Listing .73—Graphics Library Header (gfx.h)

```
1   #ifndef GFX_H
2   #define GFX_H
3
4   #include "SDL.h"
5
6   void gfx_init(void);
7   void gfx_open_window(const char *title, const size_t width, const size_t height);
8   void gfx_poll_events(void);
9   void gfx_draw_rect(double x, double y,
10                     double width, double height, unsigned int color);
11  void gfx_draw_circle(double cx, double cy, double radius, unsigned int color);
12  void gfx_draw_line(double x1, double y1,
13                     double x2, double y2, unsigned int color);
14  void gfx_clear(void);
15  void gfx_refresh(void);
16  void gfx_delay(size_t ms);
17  long gfx_time_ns(void);
18  void gfx_cleanup(void);
19
20  #endif // GFX_H
```

GFX Source

Listing .74—Graphics Library "Include" Directives (gfx.c)

```
1   #include <math.h>
2   #include <stdbool.h>
3   #include <stdio.h>
4   #include <stdlib.h>
5
6   #include "SDL.h"
7
8   #include "gfx.h"
```

Listing .75—Graphics Library Preprocessor Definitions (gfx.c)

```
1   #define MAX_NUM_EVENTS 256
2   #define MAX_SHAPES 2048
3   #define GET_COLOR(r, g, b, a) (((r) << 24) | ((g) << 16) | ((b) << 8) | (a))
4   #define RED(rgba) (((rgba) >> 24) & (0xff))
5   #define GREEN(rgba) (((rgba) >> 16) & (0xff))
6   #define BLUE(rgba) (((rgba) >> 8) & (0xff))
7   #define ALPHA(rgba) ((rgba) & (0xff))
8   #define TORADIANS(degree) ((degree) * (M_PI / 180.0))
```

Listing .76—Graphics Library Enumerations and Type Definitions (gfx.c)

```
1    enum ShapeType { FRECT, FLINE, FOVAL };
2
3    typedef struct shape_data {
4      void *data;
5      unsigned int color;
6      enum ShapeType TYPE;
7    } shape_data;
8
9    typedef struct gfx_context {
10     size_t width;
11     size_t height;
12
13     bool opened;
14
15     SDL_Window *window;
16     SDL_Renderer *renderer;
17   } gfx_context;
```

Listing .77—Graphics Library Static Variables and Prototypes (gfx.c)

```
1    static void gfx_draw_circle_helper(double cx, double cy, double radius);
2    static struct gfx_context ctx;
```

Listing .78—Graphics Library Functions (gfx.c)

```
1   /**
2    * Initializes the SDL graphics context.
3    */
4   void gfx_init(void) {
5     // Check error code.
6     if (SDL_Init(SDL_INIT_VIDEO | SDL_INIT_EVENTS) < 0) {
7       SDL_Log("SDL could not be initialized! SDL_Error: %s\n", SDL_GetError());
8       exit(EXIT_FAILURE);
9     }
10  }
11
12  /**
13   * Opens the SDL graphics window with the given size and title.
14   * Events are also polled.
15   *
16   * @param const char * - title of window.
17   * @param const size_t - width of window.
18   * @param const size_t - height of window.
19   */
20  void gfx_open_window(const char *title, const size_t width, const size_t height) {
21    ctx.window = NULL;
22    ctx.renderer = NULL;
23    if (SDL_CreateWindowAndRenderer(width, height,
24                                    SDL_WINDOW_RESIZABLE, &ctx.window,
25                                    &ctx.renderer) < 0) {
26      SDL_Log("SDL could not initialize window and renderer. SDL_Error: %s\n",
27              SDL_GetError());
28      exit(EXIT_FAILURE);
29    }
30    SDL_SetWindowTitle(ctx.window, title);
31    ctx.opened = true;
32    gfx_clear();
33    gfx_poll_events();
34    gfx_refresh();
35  }
36
37  /**
38   * Draws a filled-in rectangle starting from the top-left (x, y)
39   * coordinates of a given size and color.
40   *
41   * @param double - top-left x coordinate.
42   * @param double - top-left y coordinate.
43   * @param double - width of rectangle.
44   * @param double - height of rectangle.
45   * @param unsigned int - 32bit color (ARGB).
46   */
47  void gfx_draw_rect(double x, double y, double width,
48                     double height, unsigned int color) {
49    SDL_FRect fr = {x, y, width, height};
50    SDL_SetRenderDrawColor(ctx.renderer, RED(color), GREEN(color),
51                                         BLUE(color), ALPHA(color));
52    SDL_RenderFillRectF(ctx.renderer, &fr);
53  }
54
55  /**
56   * Draws a filled-in circle starting from the center (x, y)
57   * coordinates of a given radius and color.
58   *
59   * @param double - center x coordinate.
60   * @param double - center y coordinate.
61   * @param double - radius of circle.
62   * @param unsigned int - 32bit color (ARGB).
63   */
64  void gfx_draw_circle(double cx, double cy,
65                       double radius, unsigned int color) {
66    SDL_SetRenderDrawColor(ctx.renderer, RED(color), GREEN(color),
67                                         BLUE(color), ALPHA(color));
68    gfx_draw_circle_helper(cx, cy, radius);
69  }
70
```

```
71   /**
72    * Draws a line from (x1, y1) to (x2, y2) of a given color.
73    *
74    * @param double - x coordinate of point 1.
75    * @param double - y coordinate of point 1.
76    * @param double - x coordinate of point 2.
77    * @param double - y coordinate of point 2.
78    * @param unsigned int - 32bit color (ARGB).
79    */
80   void gfx_draw_line(double x1, double y1,
81                      double x2, double y2, unsigned int color) {
82     SDL_SetRenderDrawColor(ctx.renderer, RED(color), GREEN(color),
83                                          BLUE(color), ALPHA(color));
84     SDL_RenderDrawLineF(ctx.renderer, x1, y1, x2, y2);
85   }
86
87   /**
88    * Retrieves any queued events received by SDL and executes them.
89    * The only one of interest is the SDL_QUIT event.
90    */
91   void gfx_poll_events(void) {
92     if (ctx.opened) {
93       SDL_PumpEvents();
94       SDL_Event e[MAX_NUM_EVENTS];
95       int c = SDL_PeepEvents(e, MAX_NUM_EVENTS, SDL_GETEVENT,
96                              SDL_FIRSTEVENT, SDL_LASTEVENT);
97       for (int i = 0; i < c; i++) {
98         SDL_Event ce = e[i];
99         switch (ce.type) {
100          case SDL_QUIT:
101            gfx_cleanup();
102            return;
103        }
104      }
105    }
106  }
107
108  /**
109   * Delays the SDL event poll by some time.
110   *
111   * @param size_t - number of milliseconds to delay.
112   */
113  void gfx_delay(size_t ms) {
114    long now = gfx_time_ns() / 1000;
115    long wait = now + ms;
116    while (now <= wait) {
117      gfx_poll_events();
118      now = gfx_time_ns();
119    }
120  }
121
122  /**
123   * Returns the number of ticks in nanoseconds.
124   *
125   * @return long - ticks in ns.
126   */
127  long gfx_time_ns(void) {
128    return SDL_GetTicks();
129  }
130
131  /**
132   * Clears the renderer with a black screen.
133   */
134  void gfx_clear(void) {
135    SDL_SetRenderDrawColor(ctx.renderer, 0, 0, 0, 0xff);
136    SDL_RenderClear(ctx.renderer);
137  }
138
139  /**
140   * Refreshes the current renderer context.
141   */
142  void gfx_refresh(void) {
```

```
143    SDL_RenderPresent(ctx.renderer);
144  }
145
146  /**
147   * Frees all SDL memory and components.
148   */
149  void gfx_cleanup(void) {
150    if (ctx.opened) {
151      ctx.opened = false;
152      SDL_DestroyRenderer(ctx.renderer);
153      SDL_DestroyWindow(ctx.window);
154      SDL_Quit();
155    }
156  }
157
158  /**
159   * Draws a circle by drawing points representing octants of the circle.
160   *
161   * @param double - center x coordinate of circle.
162   * @param double - center y coordinate of circle.
163   * @param double - radius of circle.
164   */
165  static void gfx_draw_circle_helper(double cx, double cy, double radius) {
166    const float diameter = (radius * 2);
167    float x = (radius - 1);
168    float y = 0;
169    float tx = 1;
170    float ty = 1;
171    float error = (tx - diameter);
172    while (x >= y) {
173      // Each of the following renders an octant of the circle
174      SDL_RenderDrawPointF(ctx.renderer, cx + x, cy - y);
175      SDL_RenderDrawPointF(ctx.renderer, cx + x, cy + y);
176      SDL_RenderDrawPointF(ctx.renderer, cx - x, cy - y);
177      SDL_RenderDrawPointF(ctx.renderer, cx - x, cy + y);
178      SDL_RenderDrawPointF(ctx.renderer, cx + y, cy - x);
179      SDL_RenderDrawPointF(ctx.renderer, cx + y, cy + x);
180      SDL_RenderDrawPointF(ctx.renderer, cx - y, cy - x);
181      SDL_RenderDrawPointF(ctx.renderer, cx - y, cy + x);
182
183      if (error <= 0) {
184        ++y;
185        error += ty;
186        ty += 2;
187      }
188
189      if (error > 0) {
190        --x;
191        tx += 2;
192        error += (tx - diameter);
193      }
194    }
195  }
```

Assembly Environment Setup

By this point, you should be well-versed in functional and imperative programming. We now turn our attention to setting up the assembly language programming environment. Because the setup is the same across all systems thanks to our choice of C compiler, our instructions are environment-agnostic.

Assembly Files

Our assembly dialect is AT&T x64 assembly, which uses the .s file extension. Create a file hello.s, and add the following contents without worrying what they mean at the moment:

Listing .79—Assembly Test File (hello.s)

```
.section .data
  out_str: .asciz "Hello, world!\n"
.section .text
  .global main
main:
  movq $1, %rax           # Set sys_write syscall.
  movq $1, %rdi           # Stdout file descriptor.
  leaq out_str(%rip), %rsi # Load data string into argument register.
  movq $15, %rdx          # Load string length into second arg. register.
  syscall
  retq
```

gcc can compile assembly code just as it does standard C code. Invoke the compiler as normal, and pass hello.s to gcc.

```
gcc -g -fPIE hello.s -o hello.o
```

No error should appear, and this being the case, we run the program as ./hello.o to see a Hello, world! output.

Bibliography

[Abelson et al., 1996] Abelson, H., Sussman, G. J., and with Julie Sussman (1996). *Structure and Interpretation of Computer Programs*. MIT Press/McGraw-Hill, Cambridge, 2nd editon edition.

[Aho et al., 2006] Aho, A. V., Lam, M. S., Sethi, R., and Ullman, J. D. (2006). *Compilers: Principles, Techniques, and Tools (2nd Edition)*. Addison-Wesley Longman Publishing Co., Inc., USA.

[$\aleph_0$ (Aleph-Null), 1971] $\aleph_0$ (Aleph-Null) (1971). Computer recreations. *Software: Practice and Experience*, 1(2):201–204.

[Backus et al., 1960] Backus, J. W., Bauer, F. L., Green, J., Katz, C., McCarthy, J., Perlis, A. J., Rutishauser, H., Samelson, K., Vauquois, B., Wegstein, J. H., van Wijngaarden, A., Woodger, M., and Naur, P. (1960). Report on the algorithmic language algol 60. *Commun. ACM*, 3(5):299–314.

[Bergin et al., 2013] Bergin, J., Stehlik, M., Roberts, J., and Pattis, R. (2013). *Karel J Robot: A Gentle Introduction to the Art of Object-Oriented Programming in Java*. John Wiley & Sons.

[Braithwaite, 1613] Braithwaite, R. (1613). *The Yong Mans Gleanings*.

[Bratko, 1990] Bratko, I. (1990). *Prolog Programming for Artificial Intelligence*. Addison-Wesley Longman Publishing Co., Inc., USA, 2nd edition.

[Brooks and Matelski, 1981] Brooks, R. and Matelski, J. P. (1981). *The Dynamics of 2-Generator Subgroups of PSL(2, $\mathbb{C}$)*, pages 65–72. Princeton University Press, Princeton.

[Bryant and O'Hallaron, 2010] Bryant, R. E. and O'Hallaron, D. R. (2010). *Computer Systems: A Programmer's Perspective*. Addison-Wesley Publishing Company, USA, 2nd edition.

[Butterick, 2016] Butterick, M. (2016). *Beautiful Racket*. 1.6 edition.

[Chomsky, 1957] Chomsky, N. (1957). *Syntactic Structures*. Mouton and Co., The Hague.

[Church, 1941] Church, A. (1941). *The Calculi of Lambda Conversion. (AM-6)*. Princeton University Press.

[Clarke, 1984] Clarke, A. (1984). *Profiles of the Future: An Inquiry Into the Limits of the Possible*. Holt, Rinehart, and Winston.

[Cohen, 1981] Cohen, D. (1981). On holy wars and a plea for peace. *Computer*, 14(10):48–54.

[Cook, 1971] Cook, S. A. (1971). The Complexity of Theorem-Proving Procedures. In *Proceedings of the Third Annual ACM Symposium on Theory of Computing*, STOC '71, pages 151–158, New York, NY, USA. Association for Computing Machinery.

[Cormen et al., 2009] Cormen, T. H., Leiserson, C. E., Rivest, R. L., and Stein, C. (2009). *Introduction to Algorithms*. The MIT Press, 3rd edition.

[Dijkstra, 1959] Dijkstra, E. W. (1959). A note on two problems in connexion with graphs. *Numer. Math.*, 1(1):269–271.

[Dybvig, 2009] Dybvig, R. K. (2009). *The Scheme Programming Language, 4th Edition*. The MIT Press, 4th edition.

[Felleisen et al., 2018] Felleisen, M., Findler, R. B., Flatt, M., and Krishnamurthi, S. (2018). *How to Design Programs: An Introduction to Programming and Computing*. The MIT Press.

[Friedman et al., 2018] Friedman, D. P., Byrd, W. E., Kiselyov, O., and Hemann, J. (2018). *The Reasoned Schemer*. The MIT Press, 2nd edition.

[Friedman and Felleisen, 1986] Friedman, D. P. and Felleisen, M. (1986). *The Little Schemer*. The MIT Press, 4th edition.

[Friedman and Wand, 2008] Friedman, D. P. and Wand, M. (2008). *Essentials of Programming Languages*. The MIT Press. MIT Press, London, England, 3 edition.

[Friedman and Wise, 1976] Friedman, D. P. and Wise, D. S. (1976). Cons should not evaluate its arguments. In *International Colloquium on Automata, Languages and Programming*.

[Garcia et al., nd] Garcia, R., Siek, J. G., Akavipat, R., Byrd, W., Chun, S., Mack, D. W., Platte, A., Eoinestad, H., Blocher, K., Near, J. P., and et al. (n.d.). Using parenthec to transform scheme programs to c or how to write interesting recursive programs in a spartan host (program counter). *Indiana University*.

[Harris et al., 2018] Harris, R. A., Marco, C. D., Ruan, S., and O'Reilly, C. (2018). An annotation scheme for rhetorical figures. *Argument and Computation*, 9(2):155–175.

[Hein, 2002] Hein, J. L. (2002). *Discrete Structures, Logic, and Computability*. Jones and Bartlett Publishers, Inc., USA, 2nd edition.

[Hein, 2009] Hein, J. L. (2009). *Prolog Experiments in Discrete Mathematics, Logic, and Computability*. Portland State University.

[Henderson, 2019] Henderson, B. (2019). Netpbm history.

[Henderson and Morris, 1976] Henderson, P. and Morris, J. H. (1976). A lazy evaluator. In *Proceedings of the 3rd ACM SIGACT-SIGPLAN Symposium on Principles on Programming Languages*, POPL '76, page 95–103, New York, NY, USA. Association for Computing Machinery.

[Holden, 2014] Holden, D. (2014). *Build Your Own LISP*. Createspace Independent Publishing Platform, North Charleston, SC.

[ISO, 1999] ISO (1999). Iso c standard 1999. Technical report. ISO/IEC 9899:1999 draft.

[Kernighan and Plauger, 1982] Kernighan, B. W. and Plauger, P. J. (1982). *The Elements of Programming Style*. McGraw-Hill, Inc., USA, 2nd edition.

[Kernighan and Ritchie, 1988] Kernighan, B. W. and Ritchie, D. M. (1988). *The C Programming Language*. Prentice Hall Professional Technical Reference, 2nd edition.

[King, 2008] King, K. N. (2008). *C Programming: A Modern Approach, Second Edition*. W.W. Norton & Company.

[Klabnik and Nichols, 2018] Klabnik, S. and Nichols, C. (2018). *The Rust Programming Language*. No Starch Press, USA.

[Knuth, 1977] Knuth, D. E. (1977). The computer as master mind. *Journal of Recreational Mathematics*, 9:1–6.

[Kochan, 2004] Kochan, S. G. (2004). *Programming in C*. Sams Publishing, Indianapolis, IN, 3 edition.

[Lagarias, 1985] Lagarias, J. C. (1985). The 3x + 1 problem and its generalizations. *The American Mathematical Monthly*, 92(1):3–23.

[Levenshtein, 1966] Levenshtein, V. I. (1966). Binary codes capable of correcting deletions, insertions and reversals. *Soviet Physics Doklady*, 10(8):707–710. Doklady Akademii Nauk SSSR, V163 No4 845-848 1965.

[Mandelbrot, 1980] Mandelbrot, B. B. (1980). Fractal aspects of the iteration of $z \to \lambda z(1-z)$ for complex λ and z. *Annals of the New York Academy of Sciences*, 357(1):249–259.

[Matz et al., 2012] Matz, M., Hubicka, J., Jaeger, A., and Mitchell, M. (2012). *System V Application Binary Interface AMD64 Architecture Processor Supplement*. N/A, 0.99.6 edition.

[McCarthy, 1962] McCarthy, J. (1962). *LISP 1.5 Programmer's Manual*. The MIT Press.

[McCarthy, 1978] McCarthy, J. (1978). *History of LISP*, page 173–185. Association for Computing Machinery, New York, NY, USA.

[Mitchell, 1986] Mitchell, J. C. (1986). Representation independence and data abstraction. In *Proceedings of the 13th ACM SIGACT-SIGPLAN Symposium on Principles of Programming Languages*, POPL '86, page 263–276, New York, NY, USA. Association for Computing Machinery.

[Nystrom, 2021] Nystrom, R. (2021). *Crafting Interpreters*. Genever Benning.

[Okasaki, 1998] Okasaki, C. (1998). *Purely Functional Data Structures*. Cambridge University Press, USA.

[Okasaki, 1999] Okasaki, C. (1999). Red-black trees in a functional setting. *J. Funct. Program.*, 9(4):471–477.

[Parnas, 1972] Parnas, D. L. (1972). On the criteria to be used in decomposing systems into modules. *Commun. ACM*, 15(12):1053–1058.

[Pattis, 1995] Pattis, R. E. (1995). *Karel The Robot: A Gentle Introduction to the Art of Programming*. John Wiley & Sons.

[Pierce et al., 2021] Pierce, B. C., de Amorim, A. A., Casinghino, C., Gaboardi, M., Greenberg, M., Hriţcu, C., Sjöberg, V., Tolmach, A., and Yorgey, B. (2021). *Programming Language Foundations*, volume 2 of *Software Foundations*. Electronic textbook.

[Reynolds, 1972] Reynolds, J. C. (1972). Definitional interpreters for higher-order programming languages. In *Proceedings of the ACM Annual Conference - Volume 2*, ACM '72, page 717–740, New York, NY, USA. Association for Computing Machinery.

[Russell and Norvig, 2009] Russell, S. and Norvig, P. (2009). *Artificial Intelligence: A Modern Approach*. Prentice Hall Press, USA, 3rd edition.

[Sabry and Felleisen, 1992a] Sabry, A. and Felleisen, M. (1992a). Reasoning about programs in continuation-passing style. *SIGPLAN Lisp Pointers*, V(1):288–298.

[Sabry and Felleisen, 1992b] Sabry, A. and Felleisen, M. (1992b). Reasoning about programs in continuation-passing style. In *Proceedings of the 1992 ACM Conference on LISP and Functional Programming*, LFP '92, page 288–298, New York, NY, USA. Association for Computing Machinery.

[Sarkar et al., 2004] Sarkar, D., Waddell, O., and Dybvig, R. K. (2004). A nanopass infrastructure for compiler education. In *Proceedings of the Ninth ACM SIGPLAN International Conference on Functional Programming*, ICFP '04, page 201–212, New York, NY, USA. Association for Computing Machinery.

[Siek, 2023] Siek, J. G. (2023). *Essentials of Compilation*. MIT Press, London, England.

[Singhal, 2001] Singhal, A. (2001). Modern information retrieval: A brief overview. *IEEE Data Eng. Bull.*, 24:35–43.

[Sipser, 2013] Sipser, M. (2013). *Introduction to the Theory of Computation*. Course Technology, Boston, MA, third edition.

[Smith, 2013] Smith, E. E. (2013). Recognizing a collective inheritance through the history of women in computing. *CLCWeb: Comparative Literature and Culture*, 15(1).

[Springer and Friedman, 1989] Springer, G. and Friedman, D. P. (1989). *Scheme and the Art of Programming*. MIT Press, Cambridge, MA, USA.

[Sterling and Shapiro, 1994] Sterling, L. and Shapiro, E. (1994). *The Art of Prolog (2nd Ed.): Advanced Programming Techniques*. MIT Press, Cambridge, MA, USA.

[van der Linden, 1994] van der Linden, P. (1994). *Expert C Programming: Deep C Secrets*. Prentice-Hall, Inc., USA.

[van Orman Quine, 1950] van Orman Quine, W. (1950). *Methods of Logic*. Harvard University Press.

[Wadsworth, 1971] Wadsworth, C. P. (1971). *Semantics and Pragmatics of the Lambda-calculus*. University of Oxford.

[Wagner and Fischer, 1974] Wagner, R. A. and Fischer, M. J. (1974). The string-to-string correction problem. *J. ACM*, 21(1):168–173.

[Weiss, 1998] Weiss, M. A. (1998). Data structures and problem solving using java. *SIGACT News*, 29(2):42–49.

[Whitehead and Russell, 1927] Whitehead, A. N. and Russell, B. A. W. (1927). *Principia mathematica; 2nd ed.* Cambridge Univ. Press, Cambridge.

Index